Contextualizing Indian Experiences of COVID-19

This volume captures the social, political, psychological, administrative, and policy dimensions of the COVID-19 pandemic in the Indian context. The book is divided into four parts. Part I highlights social narratives from underprivileged workers, ASHA workers, the LGBTIQ+ community, and sanitary workers. It documents their struggles to develop mitigation, adaptation, and resilience strategies. Part II includes case studies and stories of self-management, the mental health of students from rural and urban Maharashtra, and of caregivers. It unveils the path of transformation of self to deal with the issues of anxiety and emotional turmoil caused during and due to the COVID-19 pandemic. Part III consists of resilience, philosophical hope, and solidarity, which reflect the contribution of seva by the Sikh community. It also highlights the contribution of government organizations like Indian Railways, Air India, and the Employee Provident Fund Organization to provide relief to both the people of India and Indians residing abroad to bring people back to the country during the unprecedented times. Part IV discusses the responses of various states of India to the COVID-19 pandemic and the implementation of policies by the government of India during those times.

Based on empirical research work, this book will be useful for students, teachers, researchers, behavioral scientists, and practitioners of psychology, sociology, human geography, mental health, political science, public health, and public policy. This book will also be of interest to policymakers and the general public to understand the intricacies involved and the essential propositions with regard to pandemics.

Rajesh Kharat is Professor and former Chairperson of the Centre for South Asian Studies, School of International Studies, JNU, and former Chief Advisor of EOO, JNU, New Delhi. He also served as Dean of Humanities at the University of Mumbai from 2019 to 2022 (on Deputation); he has an MA in Political Science from the University of Pune and an M.Phil. and Ph.D. from the Centre for South Asian Studies, SIS, JNU, New Delhi and LLB from University of Mumbai. He began teaching at the Department of Civics and Politics, University of Mumbai, in 1991, and has continued at JNU, New Delhi, since 2008. He is the recipient of the Latin American Council for Social Sciences, Argentina, and spent two months in Cuba in

2005. He has authored, edited, and co-edited 15 books and over 30 research papers. He has completed five major research projects in India and abroad on themes related to contemporary South Asia. As a Dean, he established the School of International Relations and Strategic Studies (SIRSS) at the University of Mumbai in 2021 and became the first Director of the SIRSS. He has also initiated three research online journals at the University of Mumbai and was Honorary Editor of *Sambhāṣaṇ*, an interdisciplinary humanities online journal of the University of Mumbai. He was also a visitor's representative at the Executive Council of Mahatma Gandhi Central University, Bihar.

Satishchandra Kumar is Professor and Head at the Department of Applied Psychology & Counselling Centre, University of Mumbai. He is also the former Coordinator of the Mahatma Gandhi Peace Centre. He received a Summer Fellowship from the Albert Ellis Institute in New York. He has also received a scholarship to undergo supervised training in the Enneagram Professional Training Programme from Helen Palmer Model San Francisco, USA. He was also awarded Research Fellowship by the Indian Council of Social Science Research (ICSSR), New Delhi. He has published in international peer-reviewed journals like the *Journal of Personality and Social Psychology, Psychological Science,* and *British Journal of Guidance and Counselling.* He has contributed to Sage's volume *Eminent Indian Psychologists: 100 Years of Psychology in India.* He has published over 50 research papers in national and internationally renowned journals. Apart from research publications, some edited books include *Beyond the Ordinary: Stories that Inspire and Challenge and Some Outstanding Women of India.* His research interest is industrial/organizational psychology, which provides for positive psychology, engagement at the workplace, and stress and coping. He is a reviewer in various international journals. He is also editor of *Sambhāṣaṇ,* an interdisciplinary humanities online journal of the University of Mumbai.

Kanchana Mahadevan is Professor at the Department of Philosophy, University of Mumbai. She has held visiting professorships at LUISS University, Rome (2016, 2019), and Leopold Franzens University, Innsbruck (2023). She has also been a senior fellow at the Justicia Amplificata, Goethe University Frankfurt and Bad Homburg (2018) and the Moore Institute, National University of Ireland, Galway (2019). She teaches and researches feminist philosophy, continental thought, critical theory, and political philosophy. She also works in the interdisciplinary areas of aesthetics and film. Her book *Between Femininity and Feminism: Colonial and Postcolonial Perspectives on Care* (DK Printworld and ICPR, 2014) examines the relevance of Western feminist philosophy in the Indian context while bringing Western feminism into dialogue with its Indian counterpart. Her publications on Ambedkar explore his re-articulation of democracy from the Indian perspective. In her recently published research papers on care ethics, she has explored its critical potential in relation to health work and the cosmopolitan character of care. She is the former editor of *Sambhāṣaṇ,* an interdisciplinary humanities online journal of the University of Mumbai.

Meher Bhoot is a Professor at the Department of German, University of Mumbai. Her areas of specialisation are German Literature with a focus on Literature of German Minorities, Postcolonial Studies, and Culture Studies, and her areas of interest are European cultural history and European history of art. She is an active member of the German Institutes Partnership with the Universities of Göttingen and Freiburg in Germany. Under the aegis of this partnership, she was Guest Professor at the Department of Intercultural German Studies, University of Göttingen, Germany, in 2017. She has been a DAAD Fellow since 2004 and received the Rotary Cultural and Ambassadorial Scholarship (1997–98). Apart from her published articles, some co-edited volumes include *Revisiting Günter Grass, Voices from India and Germany, Interkulturelle Momente, Einfach menschlich.* She has also co-edited textbooks for short courses on teaching Marathi to non-native speakers, including *Communicative Marathi for Nurses, Communicative Marathi for Rickshaw and Taxi Drivers, Communicative Marathi for Government Officials*, and *Communicative Marathi for Bank Employees.* She has recently authored a book in German entitled *Nicht Herkunft, sondern Dasein: Kulturelle Identität im Werke Rafik Schamis / Not Origin, but Existence: Cultural Identity in the Works of Rafik Schami* (Würzburg: Könighausen & Neumann, 2023). She is the former co-editor of *Sambhāṣaṇ*, an interdisciplinary humanities online journal of the University of Mumbai.

Contextualizing Indian Experiences of COVID-19

People, Pandemic, and Policies

Edited by Rajesh Kharat, Satishchandra Kumar, Kanchana Mahadevan, and Meher Bhoot

Routledge
Taylor & Francis Group
LONDON AND NEW YORK

First published 2024
by Routledge
4 Park Square, Milton Park, Abingdon, Oxon OX14 4RN

and by Routledge
605 Third Avenue, New York, NY 10158

Routledge is an imprint of the Taylor & Francis Group, an informa business

British Library Cataloguing-in-Publication Data
A catalogue record for this book is available from the British Library

ISBN: 978-1-032-29185-7 (hbk)
ISBN: 978-1-032-30328-4 (pbk)
ISBN: 978-1-003-30451-7 (ebk)

DOI: 10.4324/9781003304517

Typeset in Times New Roman
by Deanta Global Publishing Services, Chennai, India

To Accredited Social Health Activists (ASHA Workers)

Contents

Figures

Tables

Contributors

Jehanzeb Baldiwala has aligned herself with narrative ways of working for over twenty years and is a voracious reader who believes in dreams and magic. She is a therapist, supervisor, trainer, and co-founder of Narrative Practices India. Her work includes consulting with persons, families, and children in responding to a range of issues that include anxiety, depression, and school related issues, in addition to training and supervising mental health work.

Omkar Bhatkar is a sociologist with a doctoral thesis dealing in proxemics and social ecology. He is a visiting professor at St. Andrew's College and S.K. Somaiya College. His academic interest comprises cultural studies, phenomenology, film theory, and aesthetics, along with visual communication, gender studies, existentialism and inter-religious studies. He has contributed research papers/chapters for several national and international journals and book publications.

Braj Bhushan is Shri Deva Raj Chair Professor of Psychology at the Department of Humanities and Social Sciences, Indian Institute of Technology, Kanpur. Currently he is Head of the Department. He works in the area of cognitive neuropsychology with special focus on affective processes and assessment. He has authored four books and has more than one hundred journal papers, conference proceedings, and conference papers to his credit.

Chunku Bhutia is from Gangtok Sikkim. She completed her higher education and reached MA level at Delhi University, and pursued M.Phil: and Ph.D: at Jawaharlal Nehru University. She was a recipient of the Maulana Azad National Fellowship and is at present working with the Government of Sikkim in the Education Department.

Shailesh Bhutka is a passionate community worker and a keen learner. He has a double master's in law and in social work from reputed institutes in India and also has a bachelor's in commerce. His master's thesis focused on the "Role of Support Group among Gays Living with HIV/AIDS", for which he was awarded an INDAL (Social Science) Junior Research Fellowship from the Asiatic Society of Mumbai.

Kajal Boraste has been working as a gender activist, freelance writer, and program coordinator in civil society spaces and has in-depth experience working with women and marginalized groups in Maharashtra. Her main interests are grassroots journalism, women's empowerment, and community development.

Sagar Chahar is a doctor who became a civil servant. He works as an Indian Railway Traffic Service (IRTS) Officer for the Government of India. His All-India Rank was 437 in the Union Public Service Commission 2017.

Ravinder Kaur Cheema is Head of the Department of History at Guru Nanak Khalsa College of Arts, Science and Commerce (Autonomous), Mumbai. She is Curator of the Sikh Heritage Museum set up under CPR grants. She is the author of "Genesis and Growth of Guru Nanak Khalsa College, Bombay (1937–1962)" and author of the monograph *Henry John Carter* published by the Asiatic Society of Mumbai.

Abhijeet Chore is Program Head and Assistant Professor at the Department of Psychology, Faculty of Liberal Arts at MIT World Peace University, Pune. Abhijeet has completed his Masters in Clinical Psychology and he has cleared his National Eligibility Test exam. He is currently pursuing his Ph.D. in the field of Endurance Sports Psychology from the Department of Psychology, Savitribai Phule Pune University.

Aishe Debnath is a Ph.D. scholar and is currently Assistant Professor at the Department of Applied Psychology, University of Mumbai. She received her bachelor's degree in psychology and anthropology from St. Xavier's College, Mumbai and a master's degree in psychology with a specialization in industrial-organizational psychology. She completed a course on the science of well-being at Yale University and is also trained and certified in appreciative inquiry.

Juhi Deshmukh is Assistant Professor at the Department of Psychology, Savitribai Phule Pune University, Pune. She started her career as Assistant Professor at Department of Psychology, International College for Girls (ICG) Jaipur, Rajasthan in 2007. In 2015 she joined as Assistant Professor at Department of Psychology, Savitribai Phule Pune University and since then has been a part of the Department of Psychology, Savitribai Phule Pune University.

Sunil Gangwane is a trained development professional, With his more than twelve years of experience working with youth in the NGO and education sector, he brings expertise as a facilitator and participatory action researcher. He worked as a youth coordinator, program director in Mumbai, and core team member of the Training for Transformation program in South Africa.

Nikhil Gawai is a Ph.D. research scholar at Department of Geography, University of Mumbai. He has been deeply involved in the research on the geography of exclusion and marginalization. He is also involved in biodiversity conservation. He developed expertise and specializations in geo-informatics after receiving training in the Indian Institute of Remote Sensing, Dehradun.

Rashmi Lee George is Assistant Professor of English and Head of the Department of English at St. Xavier's College (Autonomous), Mumbai. Alongside teaching, she is currently Director of Council for International Programs at St. Xavier's. She was Coordinator of Special Courses: Environmental Studies and Giving Voice to Values, offered to students in their first year.

Mridula Ghai is Additional Central Provident Fund Commissioner Headquarters in Employees' Provident Fund Organization, Ministry of Labour and Employment. She is a Vice-Chairperson of the Technical Commission on Social Security Association, and an International Labour Organization affiliate for the last six years. She also has a keen interest in writing poetry, especially on women's issues and on the underprivileged.

Anjali Joshi is a practicing counselling psychologist. She holds a master's degree in counselling psychology, an M.Phil in geriatric counselling, and a Ph.D. in REBT psychotherapy. Presently, she is Associate Dean and Professor of Human Resources, at Welingkar Institute of Management Development and Research, Mumbai. She has spent extensive tenure working in the field of education. She provides services as a "Consulting Psychologist" to many organizations.

Ghazala Ali Khan is Regional Provident Fund Commissioner I, of the Employees Provident Fund Organization (EPFO) and Honorary Vice Chairperson, International Social Security Association (ISSA), ILO, Technical Commission for Family Benefits. She has over twenty-two years' experience in social security administration and is presently posted at PDNASS, a national level academy imparting training to group A officers in social security.

Ajay Kumar is currently Regional Provident Fund Commissioner and Course Director at the Pandit Deendayal Upadhyay National Academy of Social Security (PDNASS), the apex training academy of EPFO, which is the eighth largest sovereign social security fund with a corpus of over 16.5 lakh crores. Before his current assignment, he was actively engaged in managing the investments of funds while being posted at the headquarters, New Delhi.

Satishchandra Kumar is Professor and former Head of University Department of Applied Psychology & Counselling Center, University of Mumbai. He is Member of the Academic Council, Chairperson of Board of Studies in Psychology, University of Mumbai. He is the recipient of the Summer Fellowship from the Albert Ellis Institute, New York. He also received a scholarship to undergo supervised training in Enneagram Training from Helen Palmer Model, San Francisco.

Chaphiak Lowang is Assistant Professor in the department of Political Science at Jomin Tayeng Government Model Degree College, Roing, which is affiliated to Rajiv Gandhi University, Arunachal Pradesh. She completed her M.Phil. and Ph.D. from the Centre for South Asian Studies, School of International Studies, Jawaharlal Nehru University.

Biraj Mehta Rathi is Assistant Professor, Department of Philosophy, Wilson College, Mumbai. Former visiting faculty, Department of Philosophy, Sophia College for Women. She was also a resource person at various courses and workshops, Indian

Aesthetics course, University of Mumbai, Art Criticism and Theory course, Indian Aesthetics course at Jnanapravaha, Existentialism, Readings of Greek Tragedies conducted by St Andrews Centre for Philosophy and Performing Arts (SAPP) and Readings on Time conducted at TARQ to name a few.

Nilendu Mishra currently holds the post of Regional Provident Fund Commissioner – I in the Employees Provident Fund Organisation (EPFO). He holds a Master's degree in zoology from Utkal University, Bhubaneswar. He is also a CSIR scholar and was selected by IIT Roorkee to do research in the area of enzyme technology. He has more than eighteen years of experience in EPFO handling field postings in Chennai and Bengaluru.

Aparna Phadke is Assistant Professor in the Department of Geography, University of Mumbai. She has been engaged closely in innovative methods of learning for Jilla Parishad School children. She is also engaged in wetland protection movement in the capacity of expert. Currently she is working on a research project sponsored by the Indian Council of Social Science Research (ICSSR), New Delhi, IMPRESS on "Urban Liveability".

Suman Pujari has a Bachelor of Arts in Psychology. Since 1993, she has been working for women's empowerment and has contributed to various struggles of Asha workers in Maharashtra. She is currently working for ASHA (Accredited Social Health Activist) and Block Facilitators rights against unfair practices. She is General Secretary of ASHA Gat Pravartak Arogya Karmachari Sanghatana, Maharashtra.

Amit Ranjan is a research fellow at the Institute of South Asian Studies, National University of Singapore. He has authored *India–Bangladesh Border Disputes: History and Post-LBA Dynamics*. He edited three books, namely, *Partition of India: Post-colonial legacies*; *India in South Asia: Challenges and Management*; and *Water Issues in Himalayan South Asia: Internal Challenges, Disputes and Transboundary Tensions*.

Seema Rawat is a faculty in the Department of Human Resources and Behavioural Sciences at the School of Business Management, Narsee Moonjee Institute of Management Studies, Mumbai. Her research interests are within the wider field of organizations with a focus on employee behaviour and organizational critical studies in the global south. In her research, Rawat explores mobile work, labour relations, gender at work, and aviation through a qualitative approach.

Shweta Sahasrabuddhe is Assistant Professor at different institutes across Pune for their undergraduate and postgraduate programs. She is a Ph.D. Research Scholar at Mumbai University. She also works as a trainer for different organizations. The topics covered in the training include anxiety management, stress management, and emotional well-being.

Jill Sanghvi is a counsellor and trainer at Ummeed Child Development Center since 2009. She has a Master's in Psychology from Mumbai University and a

Masters in Mental Health Counselling from Pace University, New York. She engages in therapeutic conversations with young people and families experiencing disability using narrative ideas and practices. She is a part of the team that runs the family support group at Ummeed.

Arushi Sharma is Assistant Professor in the Department of English, University of Mumbai. She is a guest faculty member in the department of English, Institute of Distance and Open Learning (IDOL), University of Mumbai. She is a trainer for functional proficiency and professional proficiency conducted by the Department of English, University of Mumbai. She completed her Ph.D. at the Department of English, University of Mumbai.

Bhaskar R. Shejwal is Professor Emeritus in the Department of Psychology, Savitribai Phule, Pune University. He served the university for more than thirty years. He has published several research papers in national and international journals. He has guided twenty Ph.D. students. He specializes in industrial psychology and has provided consultancy to several public and private sector organizations, including Mahindra and Mahindra Nashik, and the Reserve Bank of India.

Praveen Singh is Additional Secretary, Central Vigilance Commission. She has around twenty-seven years of rich cross-functional administrative experience in the government and is the unique combination of being a career bureaucrat, an academician, and a scientist. She has vital experience in many core areas of governance in many sectors and functional expertise in specialized areas like artificial intelligence, Quality Assurance Group (QAG), manpower planning, and human resource development.

Dave Sookhoo is Senior Lecturer in the School of Health Sports & Bioscience, University of East London. Dr Sookhoo has wide ranging experiences over decades of teaching and researching in higher education in the fields of psychology, health sciences, and nursing. He has published systematic reviews and proposals and is currently collaborating with researchers on funded projects.

Vasundhra Singh works in the field of public policy. She graduated from the University of Delhi with a Bachelor's degree in political science, and then from Tata Institute of Social Sciences, Mumbai, with a Master's degree in regulatory governance. She is currently pursuing a Ph.D. in public policy from the National Law School of India University, Bangalore.

Shakoor Ahmad Wani is an independent researcher. He has a Ph.D from the Centre for South Asian Studies, School of International Studies, Jawaharlal Nehru University, New Delhi.

Preface

The book is an edited volume that captures reflections on COVID-19 from an Indian viewpoint using an interdisciplinary and multidisciplinary approach. The book is organized into four parts as follows: I. Narratives from Social Peripheries; II. Mental Health and the COVID-19 Pandemic; III. The COVID-19 Pandemic: Resilience and Setbacks; and IV. Indian States' Responses to the COVID-19 pandemic. It allows the reader to navigate through various dimensions of the COVID-19 pandemic and associated issues, perceptions, and responses. Part I deals with the experiences from the social periphery, which highlights the experiences of marginalized sections of society and the challenges of frontline workers that have been documented in this pandemic period. This marginalized section has struggled for its own survival and has also shown the spirit of collectiveness to others. Part II is categorically dedicated to the mental health of people in pandemic times. It details various case studies, narratives, and survey techniques to capture the effects and reactions of students, caregivers, and the general population. The chapters in this part unveil the path of transformation of self to deal with anxieties, emotional turmoil, etc.

Part III allows the reader to study the various transformations that occurred during this time. It offers a spectrum of responses through visual arts, public utility services like Employee Provident Fund Organization, Air India, participation of communities through Sewa, OxygenLangers, and the community reaching out to everyone and service orientation for all sections of society.

Part IV focuses on Indian states' responses to COVID-19, and the states included are Kashmir, Bihar, Haryana, Arunachal Pradesh, Sikkim, and Kerala. The chapters in this portion articulate how policymakers and non-governmental organizations have responded to COVID-19 and have struggled together to emerge with mitigation, adaptation, and resilience strategies.

This edited volume also discusses the union government policies and the way forward from COVID-19.

Introduction

Rajesh Kharat and Satishchandra Kumar

> *Turning and turning in the widening gyre*
> *The falcon cannot hear the falconer;*
> *Things fall apart; the center cannot hold*
> *Mere anarchy is loosed upon the world.*
>
> *"The Second Coming"* by W.B. Yeats (1994)

These lines appeared in W.B. Yeats' poem, "The Second Coming", which reflects the chaos and instability after World War I, appropriately throws light on the helplessness of human beings in some situations like wars or pandemics as in the "unprecedented times" of COVID-19 when order was not in anyone's control. In fact, speculations about this virus as a bioweapon in a bio war, which was first seen in China to distraught the whole world, situate human beings in a perplexed state in contemporary times.

December 2019 marked the beginning of a new, dark chapter in the history of the world. The world starts falling apart with a virus, invisible to the naked eye, bringing the ever-moving world to a sudden halt. COVID-19 has become a synonym for fear and anxiety, which brought about havoc, disruption, deterioration, death, severity, illness, collapse, and tremendous devastation among the human race. It has come to represent the negative aspects and sheer helplessness of human society. A small virus has affected individuals, groups, organizations, nations, and societies across the globe. The English dictionary describes COVID-19 as an acute respiratory illness in humans caused by a coronavirus, capable of producing severe symptoms and in some cases even death. It was originally identified in Wuhan, China in 2019 and has since affected almost the entire globe. On March 11, 2020, Dr. Tedros Adhanom, The World Health Organization Director-General, declared the COVID-19 outbreak a pandemic. COVID-19 cases started being reported from across the globe, be it in advanced countries, less advanced countries, or underdeveloped countries. It is one of the biggest challenges of the 21st century that the world has witnessed. Just as people were barely coping with one wave, we were hit by a new wave.

The COVID-19 outbreak was termed the "worst pandemic" witnessed by the world since the Spanish Flu that occurred in 1918 by the WHO (Banerjee & Meena, 2021). Lewis (2020) in his article, "Scientific American", argues that, besides

DOI: 10.4324/9781003304517-1

battling coronavirus, the world is also fighting a different sort of epidemic and that is misinformation. Misinformation is harmful because it downplays the severity of the disease and ignores public health advice. Lewis (2020) further argues that nine COVID-19 myths that still persist are that the novel coronavirus was engineered in a laboratory in China, wealthy elites intentionally spread the virus to win power and profit, COVID-19 is no worse than the flu, there is no need to wear a mask, that hydroxychloroquine is an effective treatment, that "Black Lives Matter" protests led to increased transmission of the virus, spikes in cases are because of increased testing, we can achieve herd immunity by letting the virus spread through the population, and that any vaccine will be unsafe and a bigger risk than getting COVID-19.

While scientists were looking for possible vaccines and drugs to tackle the "novel" coronavirus, governments across the globe tried to deal with this unprecedented situation with country-wide lockdowns, mass testing, and contact tracing. Countries and their states sealed their borders, travel restrictions were issued regarding international and domestic air travel and domestic road transport. Perhaps for the first time in 100 years, the roads that usually saw bustling crowds were suddenly deserted, in every city across the globe. (Morton, 2020)

The pandemic, while causing massive devastation, shed light on the fallibility of the public healthcare systems across the world. However, some countries, like India, managed to keep the death count low, despite the initial spike in active COVID-19 cases. India's earliest response to the outbreak included thermal screening of passengers arriving from China—the alleged epicenter of the current pandemic—as well as from other countries. As the number of cases increased, travel and entry restrictions were issued along with guidelines to maintain social distancing (Singh Bains, 2021). The government relied upon mass media to generate awareness among the public regarding the dos and don'ts during the pandemic, including a caller-tune that advised people to stay at home, wear masks, and practice social distancing (Pandey, 2020).

March 2020 witnessed the imposition of a nationwide lockdown, which allowed only essential services to function. Beginning with a Janata Curfew on March 22, 2020, followed by a 3-week lockdown which was extended twice, India was under lockdown until May 31, 2020. The lockdown allowed the administration enough time to set up testing facilities, isolation centers, and prepare the nation's healthcare system to deal with the outbreak (Ray & Subramanian, 2020).

During the lockdown, most of the daily activities switched to an online mode. Offices, classrooms, prayer meets, and get-togethers all adopted a virtual setting (Ray & Subramanian, 2020). However, this sudden change also exposed the digital divide that is prevalent among various classes of society. The scenario was far from ideal in most developing and developed nations. Those residing in rural areas, and also those belonging to low-income sections of society struggled to gain access to the Internet, which became the lifeline, providing all services from education to medical advice during the lockdown (Lai & Widmar, 2020).

While the lockdowns helped flatten the curve on the graph of Covid-19 cases, they left a massive impact on the economic and social conditions of society. Around 100 million migrant workers were badly hit by the lockdown restrictions.

The period following the lockdown saw a reverse migration of lakhs of workers, traveling thousands of kilometers, using any available mode of transport, including walking their way back. Apart from increased responsibilities at home and at work, women also suffered from an increase in domestic abuse, as they were locked down at home with their abusers. A surge was also seen in cases of child abuse, further worsening the situation.

The nationwide lockdowns imposed globally also added to the worries of those Indians who were stranded abroad. An evacuation, under the name "Vande Bharat Mission" was carried out, which has been hailed as one of the largest evacuation of civilians by any nation (Nandula, 2020).

Another government organization, Indian Railways, the lifeline of the country, came forward by helping in India's fight against the pandemic. In the first phase, when a three-week lockdown was announced by the Government of India, Indian Railways started special trains for Shramiks to help them relocate and avert transportation challenges due to the lockdown. In the second wave, Indian Railways played a very important role by running oxygen special trains, Kisan Rail, and Doodh Duronto to assist farmers in sending their produce to far-flung areas. Indian Railways was at the forefront in the fight against COVID-19. They deployed COVID-19 isolation coaches, met the demands of medical equipment, and medicine movements, and their skilled medical professionals provided timely medical help to large numbers of COVID-19 patients.

Apart from Indian Railways, the Sikh community through *gurdwaras* offered *Sewa* (Service) and started *langar* (free food and water). They also came up with the novel concept of oxygen *langar* (free distribution of oxygen cylinders) during the second phase of the pandemic, when medical facilities were in a shortage and privately acquiring oxygen would cost an exorbitant amount of money. Indulging in their community spirit even further, they opened the doors of the *gurdwaras* for migrant workers and others who were walking back home. They not only provided accommodation but also gave free food and water. This was one true example of service to humanity irrespective of caste, religion, and race.

Another government body, the Employee Provident Fund Organization (EPFO), provided succor to its affected beneficiaries. EPFO's digital journey provided service to its subscribers during the pandemic through its 138 field offices. The transformation of EPFO to e-EPFO through unique and unconventional initiatives and achieving full paperless claims settlement ensured saving of man-hours, cutting out procedural ineffectiveness, and ensuring not only ease of doing business with the organization but also disaster-proofing the organization going forward. Along with governmental bodies, education also moved online, which proved to be challenging for both teachers and students. Yet at the same time, the grit shown both by teachers and students to overcome these challenges was astounding.

While the pandemic took over the world, an "infodemic" of misleading information and rumors took over the digital world. The constant bombardment of detailed information regarding the coronavirus, the daily tally of the number of cases and deaths coming in from multiple sources, exacerbated the severity of the pandemic. To add to the woes, several rumors and conspiracy theories were circulated on social media on a daily basis, leading to panic and distress among the consumers of such information (Banerjee & Meena, 2021).

As the world adapted to the "new normal" conditions brought about by the pandemic, the virus also mutated, becoming more fatal for its victims. The result was a second wave of Covid-19, fiercer and more debilitating than the first one. The sudden spike in the number of cases and the rising need for hospitalization among patients put an immense amount of strain on the healthcare systems of all nations. The worst-hit regions in India during this wave were the national capital and the economic capital—Delhi and Mumbai, respectively. Shortage of liquid medical oxygen (LMO) and limited availability of the drug "remdesivir" led to lapses in treatment and created an environment conducive to black marketing. The "Delta" variant, attributed as the leading cause of infection during the second wave, also led to an increase in mortality rates (Madaan, 2021).

The vaccination program in India was divided into phases. Phase 1, which began in January 2021, was aimed at administering vaccines to the frontline workers, who were at the forefront of India's battle against COVID-19. In Phase 2, which began on March 1, 2021, an online portal, Cowin, allowed citizens above 45 years of age to register to be vaccinated. In April 2020, India set up a Vaccine Task Force and began preparing for a nationwide inoculation drive. By October 2021, India reached the milestone of administering 1 billion vaccine doses for Covid-19 (Kumar, 2021). At present, India has authorized nine vaccines for emergency use, of which only three are currently in use, namely Covishield, Covaxin, and Sputnik V. Covishield accounts for 85% of all administered vaccine doses (BBC News, 2022).

In India, the third wave of the pandemic, fueled by the "Omicron" variant of the SARS-Cov-2 virus, led to a huge rise in the number of cases during January 2022. However, the majority of these new cases were asymptomatic or mildly symptomatic, with lower hospitalization rates. The decrease in the severity of symptoms and quicker recovery was attributed to the effectiveness of the vaccines, which led to a lesser need for hospitalization, thereby reducing the strain on the healthcare facilities (Lahariya, 2022). The Indian Council of Medical Research (ICMR) had predicted that the third wave of COVID-19 was likely to ebb by the end of February to March 2022 (Nambiar, 2022).

As of February 23, 2022, the total number of active COVID-19 cases amounts to 164,522, with a total of 515,622 deaths attributed to COVID-19 (Ministry of Health and Family Welfare, 2022). While there are still newer cases being reported every day, there has been only a marginal increase in the number of cases. Several states like Maharashtra have considered relaxing the COVID-19 restrictions, in light of the dip in the number of active cases (Nambiar, 2022).

The pandemic, apart from the disease itself, had several ripple effects of quarantine and nationwide lockdowns. It induced acute panic, anxiety, obsessive behaviors, paranoia, and depression, and in many cases, we might observe post-traumatic stress disorder (PTSD) in the long run. All of this, coupled with uncertainty, losing loved ones, losing ones source of livelihood, and other factors, led to an increase in suicidal ideation and suicidal behaviors. COVID-19 also saw a marked increase in the use of technology in our day-to-day lives which over the course of two years has led to an increase in internet addiction or being addicted to some form of technology or the other. Severe internet addiction is also strongly predictive of depression, anxiety, and mental health distress.

The book, *Contextualizing Indian Experiences on COVID-19: People, Pandemic, and Policies* is divided into 4 sections with 5 chapters in sections I, III, and IV and 4 chapters in Section II. In all, the book consists of nineteen chapters along with an Introduction and a concluding write-up on the way forward in terms of policies and action steps. The 4 sections are as follows:

Section I: "Narratives from Social Peripheries" consists of 5 chapters dealing with underprivileged workers, ASHA workers, voices from the LGBTIQ+ community, sanitary workers, and theatre performers. The chapter "Underprivileged Migrant Workers in India at the Time of COVID-19" examines the effects of the pandemic on their precarious conditions even after the infection rate had declined. The second chapter, "Forgotten Warriors ASHA Workers in the COVID-19 Pandemic" exposed the already skewed health infrastructure in India and the role of frontline ASHA workers in the pandemic. The third chapter, "Voices from the Margins, Pandemic Experiences of the LGBTIQ+ Community in Mumbai", deals with the discrimination and challenges they faced as well as community-based initiatives to combat stigma and prejudice. Chapter 4 studies one of the frontline sanitary workers in the management and administration of the sanitation process and safe disposal. It reveals their everyday life situations through an ethnographic analysis. The last chapter in this section, "Epistemological Crisis of Performing Theater in Times of COVID-19 presents a picture of the epistemological crisis of theater, the dilemma of artists, and their existential crisis without the arts in COVID-19.

Section II: "Mental Health and the COVID-19 Pandemic" consists of 4 chapters. The first chapter in this section, "Rational Self-Management in the COVID-19 Pandemic", deals with how therapists help individuals deal with and manage their mental health during the pandemic. The next chapter in this section "The COVID-19 Pandemic and Rumour", consists of the Indian story of rumor during the pandemic. It analyses the experiences of human beings with rumor, how it builds anxieties and unwanted fears in them. The third chapter in this section, "Creative Responses to the COVID-19 Pandemic", consists of creative stories of how caregivers managed their mental health during this period and also how they supported and reached others in need. The last chapter in this section, "Mental Health of Students of Higher Education in Maharashtra During the COVID-19 Pandemic", deals with how higher education students in Maharashtra used grit to manage their mental health during the pandemic.

Section III: "COVID 19 Pandemic: Resilience and Setback" consist of 5 chapters. The first chapter in this section "Tears, Resilience and a Pandemic: A Visual (Semiological) Journey" deals with visual art that has existed from time immemorial to depict various epidemics, pandemics, and their aftermath including the intersection between the present and the past of visual art. This chapter is a visual journey of bouncing back during the pandemic. The second chapter, "Air

India's Response to the COVID-19 Pandemic", is a narrative of the national carrier response to the COVID-19 pandemic. It highlights Air India's sense of duty and responsibility to reach out to its citizens who were stuck in different countries during the pandemic. The third chapter, is "Finding Hope and Solidarity Through Camus and Derrida During COVID-19". In times of crisis, such as the COVID-19 pandemic, it exposes the helplessness of human existence with the backdrop of Greek narratives. It also deals with the absurdity of human existence and their desperation to seek hope and meaning in this disordered world. The fourth chapter is "EPFO to e-EPFO: Transformational Journey of a Service". It is a success story of an organization reaching out to its beneficiaries with technological initiatives in the process of digitizing Indian services. The next chapter in this section is "The Concept of *Seva* in Sikhism and Its Relevance in the COVID-19 Pandemic". *Seva* includes both *langar Seva*, oxygen *Seva* and other forms of *Seva* to fellow human beings by the Sikh community. This chapter reflects the Sikh community's virtues to serve the entirety of humanity without any discrimination. The last chapter in the section, "The Role of Indian Railways During COVID-19: An Appraisal", explores the role played by Indian Railways during the pandemic. Indian Railways not only helped in transporting migrant workers but also by running Oxygen Specials and other special trains to help farmers send their produce to distant regions in the country, and also assisted in dealing with the pandemic by providing COVID-19 isolation coaches in remote areas.

Section IV: "Indian States' Responses to the COVID-19 Pandemic", includes 5 chapters. The first chapter in this section, "COVID 19 and the Politics of Lockdowns in Kashmir", discusses the exceptional circumstances in the Kashmir region due to the pandemic and innovative strategies to deal with this. It also studies the response to political as well as health situations in Kashmir during the pandemic in relation to the national security framework. The second chapter in this section, "Conducting Bihar Assembly Election 2020 at during the COVID-19 Pandemic", discusses the various challenges faced in the process of conducting elections in the third-highest Indian populated state Bihar and also examines the preparation and management during this time. The third chapter deals with "Public Education in Times of COVID-19". It discusses the transition from the traditional classroom teaching-learning process and tracks down the success rate of digital education adopted during COVID-19. The fourth chapter, "The Response to COVID-19 in Arunachal Pradesh: An Overview", attempts to study the various factors in the healthcare system and economic and technological sectors responsible for lower infection rate in Arunachal Pradesh as well as their strategies to deal with the pandemic. The fifth chapter, "Sikkim's Response To Covid-19: The Fight Continues", explains how Sikkim responded to the coronavirus pandemic by analyzing the actions and decisions taken by the State Government in order to combat the crisis situation in the state. The sixth chapter in this section is "Understanding Kerala's Social Model of COVID-9 Containment: Perspectives from Below".

The last chapter of the book highlights some of the policies drafted by the Government of India to face the challenges that India encountered in the education, economic, and health sectors due to COVID-19. This chapter analyzes the policies framed by the Government of India during COVID-19 and its implication in these three sectors.

While wreaking havoc across the globe, the pandemic also exposed diverse shades of humanity, and the strive to cope with uncertain, hostile socioeconomic circumstances. It also brought to light the huge digital divide among countries and within countries and states based on their socioeconomic status. While the ripple effects of the pandemic are to be felt for a long time to come, what draws our immediate attention is the stark divide between the "haves" and the "have nots". Not only is this divide immensely huge but it is increasing at an alarming rate, especially with regard to access, availability, and affordability of resources like education, health facilities, and economic opportunities.

References

Banerjee, D., & Meena, K. S. (2021). COVID-19 as an "Infodemic" in public health: Critical role of social media. *Frontiers in Public Health, 9.* https://doi.org/10.3389/fpubh.2021.610623

British Broadcasting Corporation News. (2022, February 7). *Sputnik Light: What we know about the new Covid vaccine in India.* https://www.bbc.com/news/world-asia-india-55748124

Ellis, R. (2021, November 19). *Wuhan Market Vendor likely first case of COVID, scientist says.* WebMD. https://www.webmd.com/lung/news/20211119/wuhan-market-vendor-first-case-covid

Kumar, A. (2021, October 21). *India achieves 1 billion Jabs Feat, PM Says "History Scripted": 10 Points.* NDTV.Com. https://www.ndtv.com/india-news/india-reaches-1-billion-vaccinations-milestone-2582650

Lahariya, C. (2022, January 24). *Third wave of the COVID-19 pandemic in India: What lies ahead?* ORF. https://www.orfonline.org/expert-speak/third-wave-of-the-covid-19-pandemic-in-india-what-lies-ahead/

Lai, J., & Widmar, N. O. (2020). Revisiting the digital divide in the COVID-19 era. *Applied Economic Perspectives and Policy, 43*(1), 458–464. https://doi.org/10.1002/aepp.13104

Madaan, N. (2021, December 15). Delta main cause for Covid in Indian kids in second wave, says study. *The Times of India.* Retrieved February 23, 2022, from https://timesofindia.indiatimes.com/city/pune/delta-main-cause-for-covid-in-indian-kids-in-2nd-wave-study/articleshow/88286168.cms

Ministry of Health and Family Welfare. (2022, February 23). Ministry of Health and Family Welfare, Government of India. Retrieved February 23, 2022, from https://www.mohfw.gov.in/

Morton, C. (2020, April 1). *Coronavirus quarantine: A look at empty streets, highways and bridges from Paris to Florida.* CondÃ© Nast Traveler. https://www.cntraveler.com/gallery/coronavirus-quarantine-a-look-at-empty-streets-highways-and-bridges-from-paris-to-florida

Nambiar, N. (2022, February 5). Third wave to ebb in India by March: ICMR ADG. *The Times of India.* https://timesofindia.indiatimes.com/india/third-wave-to-ebb-by-march-icmr-adg/articleshow/89356406.cms

Nandula, R. (2020, October 28). Vande Bharat Mission: Numbers behind the largest civilian evacuation in history. *The Hindu BusinessLine.* https://www.thehindubusinessline.com/news/vande-bharat-mission-numbers-behind-the-largest-civilian-evacuation-in-history/article32965828.ece

Pandey, B. G. (2020, June 16). *Covid-19: The woman who has become India's "corona voice."* BBC News. Retrieved February 23, 2022, from https://www.bbc.com/news/world-asia-india-53047296

Ray, D., & Subramanian, S. (2020). India's lockdown: An interim report. *Indian Economic Review, 55*(S1), 31–79. https://doi.org/10.1007/s41775-020-00094-2

Singh Bains, I. (2021, August 27). *Covid 19: India's response and best practices adopted.* Invest India. Retrieved February 23, 2022, from https://www.investindia.gov.in/team-india-blogs/covid-19-indias-response-and-best-practices-adopted

Yeats, W. B., In Parkinson, T. F., & In Brannen, A. (1994). *Michael Robartes and the dancer: Manuscript materials*. Ithaca: Cornell University Press.

Part I
Narratives From Social Peripheries

1 The Unprivileged Migrant Workers in India at the Time of COVID-19

Amit Ranjan

Introduction

As of November 1, 2021, India had witnessed 34,285,814 positive coronavirus cases with 458,470 officially recorded deaths (Worldometer 2021). India recorded the first positive coronavirus case in January 2020 and, from then, saw a rise in the number of cases and deaths. The country faced a severe COVID-19 related health crisis between March and July 2021 when hospitals reported a scarcity of oxygen.

Earlier, to deal with the coronavirus, soon after its outbreak, Indian Prime Minister Narendra Modi announced 21 days of lockdown from the intervening night of March 24–25, 2020. The extended lockdown had halted regular activities of people, which had a negative psychological impact on many individuals. Job loss, lack of money, inability to obtain items that some people considered "essential" such as alcohol, and fear of being detected as a positive coronavirus case, among various other reasons, caused the deaths of many people in India. According to a dataset prepared by Thejesh GN, Kanika Sharma, Krushna, and Aman, which was last updated on July 30, 2020, between March 19 and July 30, 991 people died due to non-virus reasons (GN 2020). The non-virus reasons considered by Thejesh et al. includes 40 due to exhaustion (walking, standing in a queue), 224 due to starvation and financial distress, 12 due to state violence, 80 due to lack of medical care or required attention, 18 due to crime committed during the lockdown, 209 due to walking or going back home, 49 due to alcohol withdrawal, and 142 due to suicide, and 96 died on trains, 49 died in quarantine centers, and there were 65 deaths with unclassified reasons (GN 2020).

Among all, the unprivileged migrant workers suffered the most. They faced the double blow of infection from the virus and the loss of livelihood. This chapter looks at the precarity of unprivileged migrant workers. It examines the government of India's scheme to support them. Finally, it analyzes the impact of policy-related decisions by the Indian government. While doing so, this chapter chiefly attempts to answer two questions. *First*, which among the two—virus or job loss—affected the unprivileged workers most? *Second*, how much did the government's policies help the unprivileged migrant workers to face the challenges brought about by the pandemics? The unprivileged workers in India defined here are those with no permanent or well paid contractual job. Their job heavily depends on performance, health, and a relationship with the middleman or contractor. This category

DOI: 10.4324/9781003304517-3

of workers also includes daily wage workers, low salaried contractual workers, hawkers, rickshaw pullers, autorickshaw drivers, and those who work as helpers in shops, etc. They do not have a social security network and have little savings to depend on in a time of crisis. Moderately and highly paid skilled contractual workers also faced problems, but they were relatively less severe than those of marginalized workers.

Epidemics and Pandemics in India: A Brief History

An endemic disease is restricted to a particular region or population, while an epidemic is an outbreak in a specific area and affects a large number of people. The epidemic may remain present in the region without an outbreak every year. An epidemic turns into a pandemic when it spreads to a large part of the world and affects a vast section of the global population (World Health Organisation, n.d.a). Historically, both epidemics and pandemics have taken many lives. According to an estimate, between 1817 and 1920, over 70 million people worldwide died from pandemics, which occurred mainly in the form of three diseases—cholera, the plague, and influenza. In India, the number of deaths because of the mentioned pandemics was more than 40 million (Tumbe 2020, 4). Pandemics and epidemics occurred even in ancient India, but they received less attention than war, famines, and natural disasters, which killed many people (Tumbe 2020, 9).

One of the worst pandemics in history is the plague, whose cause, bacterium *Yersinia pestis,* was discovered in 1894 by Alexandre Yersin (Tumbe 2020, 10). The first recorded plague pandemic occurred in the 6th century during the reign of Emperor Justinian I of the Byzantine Empire and was also knowns as the "Justinianic" plague. The second plague pandemic occurred between 1346 and 1353 and ravaged Europe, West Asia, and North Africa. By the 19th century, the plague had moved out of Europe, and the last European outbreak occurred in Russia from 1877 to 1889, near the city of Astrakhan, north of the Caspian Sea (Orent 2004, 175). The third plague pandemic occurred in the 19th century and affected Asia more than other regions (Tumbe 2020). It started in the Yunnan province of China.

The 19th-century bubonic plague in India killed millions of Indians. An early case of plague in India was detected by a physician named A.G. Viegas in September 1896 in the dockland area near Masjid bridge in Mandvi in then Bombay Presidency, now in Kutch Gujarat. The bubonic plague was carried to British India from Hong Kong by ship merchants and sailors. The plague then spread to Calcutta (now Kolkata) and other parts of India within the next five years (Mahammadh 2020). In many parts of India, it was also known as "Marwadi Sickness" because it spread more by the traveling business community (See Arnold 1993; Mahammadh 2020). Between 1896 and 1914, the bubonic plague killed over 8 million people (Chandavarkar 1992, 2011, 203). By 1918, the number of deaths in India increased to around 10 million (Fernando 2020). The plague mortality rates between 1896 and 1920 in some of the significant Indian provinces was 1.87 million in Bombay Province, 100,000 in Madras, 2.64

million in Punjab, 2.35 million in the United Provinces, and 1 million in Bengal (Mahammadh 2020, 328).

The colonial state made strong interventions to prevent the spread of the plague. It introduced laws to regulate people's movement, surveil them, and manage their health. The Indians resisted such interventions, surveillance, and regulations. For example, in Poona (now Pune), Commissioner Walter Charles Rand prepared a containment plan that mandated house-to-house searches for infected patients and suspects (Rashid 2020). A significant section of the population was against such policies and resisted the house-to-house inspections by search parties. More than any other community, the Brahmins of Poona tried to obstruct such searches (Rashid 2020). There were instances where the search parties took away even "perfectly healthy" persons to the state-administered segregation camps. There were also some cases, as reported then, of violation of women's privacy (Rashid 2020). In protest, the Indians attacked the British officials and ordinary Europeans in some places (Chandavarkar 2011). Commissioner Rand was assassinated by the Chapekar brothers—Damodar Hari Chapekar and Balkrishna Hari Chapekar—in June 1897. The assassination of Rand was detrimental to the British measures to contain the plague (Rashid 2020). In fact, due to the resistance, the 1896 plague turned out to be the biggest crisis the British colonial state had faced since the rebellion in 1857 (Kidambi 2007).

In 1897, the Epidemic Disease Act was introduced. It gave the colonial state enormous power to control the colonized people through medicines (Foucault 2004). In Bombay, health camps were opened to isolate healthy residents from infected ones and monitor new arrivals. At those camps, "surveillance passes" were issued, daily-wage workers were given day passes, temperatures were noted on tickets, and some people were photographed as an added measure. On alternate days, they would be inspected and compared to the photograph (Fernando 2020). The bubonic plague also entrenched "social distancing" based on caste and communities. Many Indians were opposed to searches and check-ups by health professionals of other castes and communities. Hence, private hospitals were established in Bombay along caste and community lines (Fernando 2020). It is estimated that thirty-six such private hospitals had been established by 1898. Some of them were the Cutchi Memon Plague Hospital, Bhatia Plague Hospital, Parel Road Jain Hospital, and Dharavi Hospital for tannery owners, and Telugu Hospital in Kamathipura. (Fernando 2020).

A Ukrainian microbiologist, Waldemar Mordecai Haffkine, developed an anti-plague vaccine in 1897–98, which sparked many rumors concerning its nature, purpose, and effects (Arnold 1987,72). Haffkine tested the anti-plague vaccine on himself first and then tried on volunteered inmates from the Byculla prison in Bombay (Malhotra 2020). Although doctors and administrators tried to persuade people to take up immunization vaccines voluntarily, many were not interested in it (Arnold 1987, 83). Convincing efforts by the colonial state bore the fruit when the inoculation received support and cooperation from a section of the middle-class (Arnold 1987: 90). Due to such support, by 1902–03, one million people were inoculated in India. However, deaths could not be entirely controlled as the peak of mortality passed in 1907, with over 1.3 million deaths in a single year across India (Malhotra 2020). In the 1900s, the plague cases exceeded the late 1890s twelve times and proved far more lethal in Punjab (Chandavarkar 1992, 2011, 204). However, Punjab's plague policy (See Tandon 2014; Malhotra 2020) acquired less political prominence than it had achieved in Bombay (Chandavarkar 1992, 2011, 204).

During the plague, workers were discouraged from moving. The prevailing idea behind such discouragement was that they would carry the epidemic virus as railway passengers (Mahammadh 2020). Despite such discouragement, several migrant workers left their jobs and fled the major industrial towns. It is believed that in October 1896, 20,000 people left Bombay city. Then in November and December, 171,500 more migrants fled. By the end of January 1897, roughly 400,000 people had left Bombay (Sarkar 2014).

In addition to many other reasons, epidemic and endemic diseases that occurred inadvertently in colonial India were consequences of social and environmental material projects (Klein 2000) undertaken by the British to secure their commercial and security interests. For instance, the impact of the bubonic plague was more severe in areas where economic growth was in full swing, such as Bombay and Punjab, where the colonial government set up irrigation networks. After its independence in 1947, India witnessed several other epidemics and pandemics, such as smallpox in 1974, plague in 1994, and the swine flu pandemic in 2009. These epidemics and pandemics were for a shorter duration than the bubonic plague and killed fewer people. The COVID-19 virus, which originated in Wuhan, China, in 2019 and became a pandemic in 2020, has killed many people in India. A little over 120 years after the outbreak of bubonic plague, the COVID-19 pandemic hit the world. Like the bubonic plague, COVID-19 has also re-defined the relationship between state and medicine/health and affected migrant workers and the economy. The following section discusses the lockdown and related problems.

Necessity of Lockdown

As the virus began to spread, the government of India decided to lockdown the movements and economic activities across India without giving sufficient time to people to move or collect essential items for daily use. It was earlier thought that the lockdown was a matter of a few days, but, as the severity of the coronavirus became more apparent, the lockdown period got extended every month. Before clamping the lockdown, the Union Government of India invoked the 1897 Epidemic Diseases Act and Disaster Management Act, 2005, in the country to prevent the spread of the virus (Awasthi 2020). The Union Government advised the States and the Union Territories to invoke section 2 of the 1897 Epidemic Act (Awasthi 2020), further amended in September 2020 by the Indian Parliament. The section says (The Epidemic Diseases Act 1897, 3):

> When at any time the [State Government] is satisfied that [the State] or any part thereof is visited by, or threatened with, an outbreak of any dangerous

epidemic disease, the [State Government], if [it] thinks that the ordinary provisions of the law for the time being in force are insufficient for the purpose, may take, or require or empower any person to take, such measures and, by public notice, prescribe such temporary regulations to be observed by the public or by any person or class of persons as [it] shall deem necessary to prevent the outbreak of such disease or the spread thereof, and may determine in what manner and by whom any expenses incurred (including compensation if any) shall be defrayed.

The amended Act further says (The Epidemic Diseases Act, 1897, 3):

When the Central Government is satisfied that India or any part thereof is visited by, or threatened with, an outbreak of any dangerous epidemic disease and that the ordinary provisions of the law for the time being in force are insufficient to prevent the outbreak of such disease or the spread thereof, [the Central Government may take such measures, as it deems fit and prescribe regulations for the inspection of any bus or train or goods vehicle or ship or vessel or aircraft leaving or arriving at any land port or aerodrome, as the case may be, in the territories to which this Act extends and for such detention thereof, or of any person intending to travel therein, or arriving thereby, as may be necessary].

The Epidemic Act prohibits indulgence of any form of violence against healthcare service personnel or causing any damage or loss to any property during an epidemic. Anyone indulged in such activities shall be punished (The Epidemic Diseases Act 1897). The State governments gave power to the police to control the movement of people and prevent them from gathering in public or private in numbers more than prescribed by the government.

It was earlier estimated that each person with the virus can infect around 2.5 people, who would further infect another 2.5 people, and form an infection chain (Gavi: The Vaccine Alliance 2020). COVID-19 is regarded as more infectious than other coronaviruses such as SARS or MERS-CoV, but it is less deadly than them (Gavi: The Vaccine Alliance 2020). Social distancing and isolation are considered effective ways to break the infection chain. Both could be possible by imposing a lockdown, allowing people to leave their homes for limited activities such as buying foods, medicines and other essential goods (Gavi: The Vaccine Alliance 2020). People engaged in carrying out essential services were allowed to leave their homes.

Like all governments around the world, the Indian Government had options either to save people's lives or their sources of livelihood. The Modi government, like others, opted to protect people's lives. The lockdown prevented the movement of workers from cities to their villages. The Union and State governments feared that such moves could spread the virus in villages and other small towns of India. Even in the Supreme Court of India, the Union Government argued that almost one-third of migrant workers could be infected with coronavirus; therefore, to control the spread of the virus in villages and other small towns, they had to stay where they were (Bindra & Sharma 2020). Some of the employers were also against the workers going back to their villages. They anticipated that it would affect their factories' production process, which they predicted would start anytime soon after an ease in the lockdown.

In late 2020, as the number of COVID-19 cases declined, the Government of India made many relaxations. People came out of their homes, and markets opened during the Dussehra and Diwali festivals. At that time, people moved unfettered without paying much attention to take preventive and precautionary measures to protect themselves from the virus. Soon after the festivals, assembly elections were held to Bihar, Assam, West Bengal, Tamil Nadu, Kerala, and Puducherry. Even though the Election Commission of India made efforts to follow all COVID-19 safety measures during campaigns, voting, and counting, they were disregarded by the voters and contestants. Immediately after the assembly elections, India saw a rise in COVID-19 cases. The second wave of COVID-19 emerged in the middle of March 2021. Among the five states—Assam, Kerala, Tamil Nadu, and West Bengal—and the Union Territory of Puducherry saw a massive surge in the COVID-19 cases by the end of April 2021. By the end of March 2021, the non-electoral regions of India were reporting more than 2.5 times as many new infections than those that went on polls (52 new cases per million against 21 for the week ending March 31) (Mullick 2021). However, the statistics changed by the end of April 2021. Areas where elections were held reported more cases than the other parts of India—280 new infections per day per million against 273 in other parts (Mullick 2021).

The second wave of COVID-19 claimed several lives due to an unprecedented shortage of oxygen in Indian hospitals, mainly in April and May 2021. By July 2021, India witnessed 418,000 COVID-19 related deaths, half of those happened after April 16, when cases surged sharply (BBC 2021). Despite such an increase in cases, Modi clarified that the country would not go under nationwide lockdown and called on the states to think of total lockdown as the last option (Chamas 2021). Some of the States, such as Maharashtra, which saw around 150,000 cases per day in April 2021, imposed night curfews and closed down malls, eateries, bars and places of worship (Agarwal 2021). From August–September 2021, the COVID-19 situation began subsiding in India, which has made the Central and State governments announce more relaxations. Some individuals from New Delhi, Mumbai, Patna, and Kolkata to whom this author talked expressed fear that too much relaxation and casual attitude of people towards the virus may lead to a third wave and another severe surge in the number of COVID-19 cases. But, alternatively, they agreed that the government has to look at the economy and livelihood related concerns of the vulnerable section of India's population.

Workers on the Move

Despite the lockdown announced in March 2020, precarious economic conditions, panic, lack of social security net, job loss, and an uncertain future forced several unprivileged workers to move from cities to their villages. As the train and bus

services were closed, many started moving on foot or made whatever arrangements they could to go to their hometown. The jam-packed buses and trucks were
charging big money to transport people from one place to another (Rashid, Anand,
and Mahale 2020). The movement of people created heart-wrenching scenes on
the Indian roads. Some of them were reported by national and international media,
compelling the Government of India to make changes in its earlier position. At
the end of March 2020, on the status report on the exodus from cities to rural
areas sought by the Supreme Court of India, the government said that all migrants
had been taken to the nearest available shelter. It said that over 88 thousand persons, migrants, and daily-wage workers had been provided food and kept in shelter
homes (Mathur 2020).

In the middle of April, the Union Government permitted intra-state movement
of migrant workers. Subsequently, special trains were started to carry inter-state
workers to their villages and hometowns. Major migrant-receiving states sketched
a plan to send them back to their home. For example, after a go-ahead from the
Union Government, the Maharashtra cabinet cleared a plan to evacuate more than
about 1.3 lakhs of intra-state migrant workers, mainly sugar cane cutters who are
primarily from the Marathwada region of the State (Hindustan Times 2020). Later,
the Maharashtra Government coordinated with the Uttar Pradesh (UP) Government
to send migrant workers home (NDTV 2020).

Although the Government of India claimed that it bore 85% percent of migrant
workers' travel costs while the states paid for 15% there is no official communication about it or the breakup of costs (Dhingra 2020). Even then, Solicitor General
of India, Tushar Mehta, refused to divulge the details of train fares in the Supreme
Court, as he was not given "instructions" from the government (The Wire 2020).

As the workers were returning to their villages, in May 2020, the Government
of India allotted about Rs. 101,500 crore to the Mahatma Gandhi National Rural
Employment Guarantee Scheme (MGNREGS) in the fiscal year 2020–21 to boost
employment opportunities in villages. Under the scheme, in May 2020, an average
of 2.51 crore people per day were given jobs, which was 73% higher than the work
offered in May 2019 (Press Information Bureau 2020).

Then in June 2020, Modi launched the Rs. 50,000 crore Garib Kalyan Rojgar
Abhiyaan (GKRA), which aimed to address the issues of returnee migrant workers and similarly affected population from rural areas by the COVID-19 pandemic. GKRA focused on 25 works in 116 selected districts across 6 states: Bihar,
Jharkhand, Madhya Pradesh (MP), UP, Odisha, and Rajasthan (Ministry of Rural
Development, Government of India 2020). However, these Government of India
schemes and relief announced by the respective states could not engage many
returnee migrant workers. Also, many of them struggled to get timely wages which
forced them to return to the cities by the end of 2020 (Parth 2020).

Even the employers wanted the migrant workers to return to their work. They
wanted migrant workers because they are easy to fire, do not bring the local political connection to the workplace, and are relatively cheaper (Ranjan 2020). Some of
the workers told the author that their travel cost was taken care of by the employer.
However, the second wave of COVID-19 at the end of March 2021 made them

smell trouble again. Despite the state government's effort to quell the fears, anticipating another lockdown and related difficulties, many migrant workers, mainly
from Mumbai, Delhi, etc., began moving back to their villages (Agarwal 2021).
After the second wave of COVID-19 emerged in India in 2021, in its study, the volunteer researchers at the Stranded Workers Action Network (SWAN) indicated that
the vulnerabilities experienced by migrant workers during the nationwide lockdown
in 2020 had resurfaced. In its June 2021 report, SWAN said, "91% of the workers
we spoke to reported that work (daily and contractual) has stopped due to locally
declared lockdowns. The number of days since work has stopped has also steadily
risen in the later weeks of May" (SWAN 2021, 27). Then about 43% of workers (for
whom SWAN had information) had not received their full wages or had been paid
only partial wages for the previous month. Only 8% had received any money from
their employer since the work had stopped (SWAN 2021, 29). On April 20, 2021,
the Ministry of Labour and Employment, Government of India, announced that 20
control rooms, set up during the 2020 lockdown and used by "lakhs of workers",
were being relaunched. However, the control rooms were of no help. They turned
it into a "worker-unfriendly system for submitting complaints", there is no tracking
method, no assistance to address hunger, and no assistance to protect migrant workers from eviction and harassment by landlords (SWAN 2021, 31–32).

Workers' situation turned worse because of the fall in employment rate during
the COVID-19 crisis period when many industries saw the closure of economic
activities. The employment rate in India was 39.2% in the quarter ended in March
2020, which fell to 31.5% during the pandemic quarter of June 2020 and recovered
in a V-shape in July–September 2020 to 37.7% (Vyas 2021). It then stalled and
could not complete its recovery and remained around that level until the second
COVID wave hit India in March–April 2021 (Vyas 2021).

To take account of how much the fate of unprivileged workers has changed in
the post-second wave of COVID-19, I conducted fieldwork in Mumbai where I
talked to people who were affected during the two waves of COVID-19 related
lockdown. The city was chosen because it suffered a lot during the two phases of
COVID-19 and has witnessed a large number of workers returning to their villages.
I also talked to a few workers from outside Mumbai via mobile phone to know their
predicament. During my trip from Goregaon West to Goregaon East on December
16, 2021, by autorickshaw, I talked to the driver whose name was Rajkumar. He
was from Lucknow district in Uttar Pradesh. Rajkumar went to his village after the
outbreak of COVID-19 and the imposition of lockdown in India in early 2020. At
his hometown, Rajkumar tried to set up small businesses such as a grocery shop,
fruit and vegetable stall but could not get success. Hence, he returned to Mumbai.
On December 17, 2021, I talked to Ashok Kumar Yadav (name changed) who
drives his own autorickshaw in Mumbai. He was from Varanasi in Eastern Uttar
Pradesh. Ashok lives with his wife in Mumbai. He did not go to his village during
the COVID-19 outbreak but lost all his savings. Ashok said that he has to start
everything from the beginning.

Rachna Singh, who lives in Ganesh Nagar slum area in Oshiwara, talked to
me on December 18, 2021. She told me that many of the workers in her locality

who went to their villages during the outbreak of COVID-19 have returned. They have got jobs but are not receiving the salaries which they used to get in pre-COVID days. She told me that she knows a number of people, some related to her, who are getting almost half the salary of what they used to receive before the outbreak of COVID-19 in India. She told me that now most of the workers are paid on a daily basis instead of having a monthly fixed salary. They are also asked to report on alternate days. She lamented the Uttar Pradesh Government who made big announcements to stop the migration of the workers from the state but has done nothing on the ground.

Sheikh, an autorickshaw driver, who hails from Solapur in Maharashtra, told me on December 19, 2021 that his financial situation turned worse at the outbreak of COVID-19 in 2020. However, he did not leave Mumbai because he owns a house in the slum area of Goregaon. He was fearful due to the prospect of a new COVID variant striking Mumbai. On the same day, I met Bharat (name changed), an autorickshaw driver from Lakhisarai, Bihar. He owns an autorickshaw for which he paid the monthly loan even during the COVID-19 times. Due to a lockdown in 2020, Bharat went to his hometown. He parked his autorickshaw at a parking place for which he had to pay Rs. 12,000 as fees. Uday Singh, an autorickshaw driver from Gonda in Uttar Pradesh, told me that he paid 14,000 as parking fees for parking his autorickshaw for more than a year. He went to his village on 31 April 2020 and returned to Mumbai in October 2021. I met him on December 27, 2021. Some of Uday's friends have not yet returned to Mumbai because they lost their jobs. A few of them, Uday told me, do not want to return because of medical and economic uncertainties due toCOVID-19.

On December 19, 2021, I went to a construction site of Lodha builders in Mira Road. I met a security guard and three workers. They told me that now more than five to six hundred workers are working on the units and multi-storey parking slots that the Lodha builders are building in Mira Road. During the first phase of COVID-19, many workers went to their home towns as the construction work was closed due to the lockdown. Many returned after the lockdown was lifted and work at the construction site started. The breakdown of the second wave of COVID-19 halted the work again. However, unlike the first phase, the construction work continued soon after, bringing relief to the workers.

On December 22, 2021, I talked to Navin Rai on mobile. He works in a local jeans making company in Shakurpur in New Delhi. He said that the number of workers in December 2021 remains the same as it was before March 2020. No worker had been fired from the work due to COVID-19. However, the salary has remained the same for the last three years. Unlike him, Navin's brother Harendra had been fired by his employer. Harendra used to work in a shop in Tank Road, New Delhi. The shop owner said that he could not afford many helpers so removed seven of them including Harendra. All of them were given full salaries. Now, Harendra lives with his family in his village in Bihar and is trying to find a job in Delhi through his network. Another individual, Manu Ram from Bihar talked to me on December 26, 2021. He used to work as a helper in a small steel utensil manufacturing factory in Azadpur Mandi, New Delhi. In April 2021, along with four other helpers, was fired from the job. Manu returned to his village. He is now a daily-wage labourer doing whatever work he gets such as that in agriculture fields, brick kiln etc. Due to lack of work in his village, Manu does not get regular work. He said it is tough to earn money unlike in Delhi where he had a fixed monthly salary. When I asked about various policies launched by the Indian Government to help poor people who were badly affected due to the pandemics, he said that he has not received any benefits from all such policies. Manu does not want to go back to Delhi because he has no job there and, even if he manages to get a job, and COVID-19 spreads brutally then once again he would have to run back to the village, so better to live in a village, Manu said.

Vignesh Mule, who works as a housekeeping cleaner in a housing society in Mumbai, is from Ratnagiri in Maharashtra. I talked to him on December 27, 2021. During the COVID-19 period he has done various odd jobs like selling vegetables and driving an autorickshaw. Vignesh was not affected by the lockdown but his father, brother, and sister lost their jobs. They did not get a salary for 5 months. Vignesh's family has eight small houses in a slum in Kandivali east. Of the eight, five arerented out, two are on the *pagdi* system (tenants are part owners in the property), and Vignesh's family lives in one house. He told me that he did not pay rent for five months of the lockdown period.

Assistance and Reforms

Initially, to deal with the pandemic crisis in March 2020, the Union Government released a relief package of 1.7 lakh crore for the vulnerable section of the population (Iyer 2020). Subsequently, besides a few mentioned above, the Union Government announced relief measures and programs to help the people. Even the states announced measures to address the stranded migrant workers' plight. For example, the Maharashtra cabinet decided to expand the affordable meal scheme "Shiv Bhojan" to the taluka (sub-district) level. This meal was available at Rs. 5 at the centers opened across the State from April to June. This helped many stranded workers, daily wagers, and the poor who lost their jobs during the lockdown (Tare 2020). In December 2021, I saw one of the "Shiv Bhojan" centers at Goregaon West. The billboard put on the center said it is run by the Parvatibai ShankarRao Chavhan Trust. It had pictures of the Maharashtra Chief Minister Uddhav Thackeray, Deputy Chief Minister Ajit Pawar, Food Minister Chhagan Bhujbal, Water Resource Minister Jayant Patil, and Minister of State for Food and Urban Affairs, Vishwjit Kadam. It was written "garib ani garju nagriksanthi aahar (food for poor and needy citizens)".

Paradoxically, what looked like a punitive step, in May 2020 circular and advisory to cut salaries and initiate disciplinary action against the workers who failed to report back at their work stations within a stipulated period soon after the lockdown was relaxed (Sharma 2020a) were considered by some of the State governments. For instance, labor department officials from Gujarat, Madhya Pradesh (MP), Karnataka, and UP told *Economic Times* that such an advisory is under serious consideration of the top government officials (Sharma 2020a). On May 8, some employers' associations also met then Union Labor Minister Santosh Kumar Gangwar and urged the government to issue an advisory so that workers could return to work (Katju 2020). Such acts of compelling the workers to come back to work violate Article 23 of the Indian Constitution, which protects the citizens against exploitation (Katju 2020).

Further, as many sectors of the Indian economy faced hardships, several companies asked their workers to look for other jobs (The Times of India 2020). Such suggestions and firings affected the workers more in the informal than formal sectors. Even the relief measures announced for the workers were chiefly for those in the formal sectors and registered. According to an estimate, 450 million workers in India are employed in the informal sector. They constitute nearly 90 percent of India's workforce with no minimum wages or any kind of social security (Sharma 2020b).

To add to the woes, many state governments used the pandemic as an opportunity to carry out reforms in the labor laws through the ordinance. For example, Odisha government had tweaked the 1948 Factories Act to extend the work shift to 12 hours per day from 8 hours per day (The Hindu 2020). UP and MP governments have made drastic reforms in their labor laws. The UP Government approved the Uttar Pradesh Temporary Exemption from Certain Labor Laws Ordinance, 2020 (Jha 2020a). Under that ordinance, the State government had exempted all establishments, factories, and businesses from the purview of all but four labor laws for three years (Jha 2020a). The laws which remain effective are the Building and Other Construction Workers Act, 1996; Workmen Compensation Act, 1923; Bonded Labour System (Abolition) Act, 1976; and Section 5 of the Payment of Wages Act, 1936 (the right to receive timely wages). Provisions related to children and women in the labor laws continue (Jha 2020a).

In MP, according to a notification issued on May 5, 2020, as many as 11 categories of industries were exempted from the Madhya Pradesh Industrial Relations Act of 1961 (Jha 2020b). The factories include: textile, leather, cement, iron and steel, electrical goods, sugar, electricity, public motor transport, and engineering including the manufacture of motor vehicles, among others. New industrial relations terms in MP include no mechanism for raising industrial disputes and no need to seek permission to lay off. However, a permission is required for retrenchment or closure of firms and to give retrenchment compensation. The law is validated for existing firms not to recognize the trade unions and employer bodies for collective bargaining (Jha 2020b).

Punjab, Himachal Pradesh, and Gujarat had amended their factories act. Rajasthan had amended the Industrial Disputes Act to increase the threshold for lay-offs and retrenchment (Sharma 2020). It was changed to 300 from 100 workers earlier. The Act has also increased the recognized trade union's membership threshold from 15 percent to 30 percent of total workers (Sharma 2020 c). Under various labor laws, the Maharashtra Government asked all the shops and factories to submit consolidated annual returns instead of multiple returns. Kerala agreed to speed up the new industrial license facilitation process (Sharma 2020 c).

Looking at the reforms, particularly the big one by UP and MP, Professor K.R. Shyam Sundar from Xavier Labour Relations Institute—Xavier Institute of

Management, Jamshedpur observed "even industries would not have imagined getting these 'holidays from labour laws'" (Quoted in Jha 2020c). Most business groups already circumvented the labor laws to make profit and control workers (Mehta 2020). In his opinion piece in *The Indian Express*, Pratap Bhanu Mehta termed these ordinances to change labor laws a "travesty" (Mehta 2020).

All such labor reforms were termed "temporary" and mainly carried out to seize an opportunity to attract the multinational companies that were planning to shift from China after the COVID-19 pandemic. Many of the global manufacturers were in talks with Indian firms about such investments (Ghosh & Mukherji 2020). In April 2020, it was reported that about 1,000 foreign companies engaged in discussions at various levels with the Indian authorities, and at least 300 of them were actively pursuing production plans in sectors such as mobiles, electronics, medical devices, textiles, and synthetic fabric (Kumar 2020). It is not clear how many companies located or relocated their units in India, although India recorded a 13 percent jump in Foreign Direct Investment (FDI) in 2020 compared to 2019. The spike in FDI was recorded mainly in August 2020 after the subsidiary of Reliance Industries—Jio—run by Mukesh Ambani snagged US $ 5.7 billion (Rs. 424.5 billion) and US $ 4.5 billion (Rs. 336.95 billion) investment from Google and other US-based firms (Elegant 2021).

Conclusion

As mentioned in this paper, the COVID-19 pandemic health emergency situation exposed the dark underbelly of the Indian economy and apathy of the State towards its unprivileged migrant workers. Many of them took the train or bus, those who could not afford it, walked back to their villages, and some of those who can neither pay nor walk remained in the cities with a hope that they do not get infected (Hatekar & Belhekar 2020). Expectedly, several young and unmarried male workers returned to the cities as they could not find satisfactory jobs in their villages (Ranjan 2020). Many of them returned to a new job environment where the number of jobs is less, and reforms made in existing labor laws added to their difficulties (See Gopalakrishnan 2020).

Amidst the COVID-19 crisis, Modi, in an opinion piece for *The Indian Express* wrote

[A]s we were moving ahead at fast pace in the fulfilment of hopes and aspirations of our countrymen, coronavirus global pandemic engulfed our country as well...Our labourers, migrant workers, artisans and craftsmen in small-scale industries, hawkers and such fellow countrymen have undergone tremendous suffering...Due to the global pandemic this is certainly a time of crisis, but for us Indians this is also a time for a firm resolve.

(Modi 2020)

Modi accepted the suffering and talked about the resolve to fight back against the pandemic. However, such resolve could not prove themselves stronger than election-related calculation. As mentioned in this chapter, election-related events increased

COVID-19 cases in the states that went on assembly polls. Some days after assembly elections, India witnessed a fatal second wave that killed several people. Obviously, holding elections at the regular interval of time is the utmost democratic exercise in any democracy. Hence, taking all safety-related measures, many countries such as Singapore, Sri Lanka etc. conducted elections even during the pandemic. However, given the severity of the situation and people's attitude towards the coronavirus, assembly elections in the Indian states could have been postponed. Some of the political parties, such as Rashtriya Janata Party and Lok Janshakti Party in Bihar were in favor of deferring the assembly elections while the Bhartiya Janata Party and Janata Dal (United) were for having the elections on time. Legally, the Election Commission of India can defer elections in extraordinary cases. For instance, in 1991, due to the assassination of the then-Prime Minister and leader of the Congress Party, Rajiv Gandhi in Tamil Nadu, then ongoing parliamentary elections were postponed for three weeks (Chopra 2020). In normal circumstances, the elections to the assembly or parliament have to be held within the six months of their dissolution.

As discussed in this chapter, the government's relief measures helped some but could not prove adequate to address many problems of the migrant workers who decided to return to their villages from the cities. Consequently, as COVID-19 subsided by the end of 2020, many of the migrant workers returned to the cities. The second wave made some of them go back again to their villages. COVID-19 affected the informal sectors more where most migrant workers work; several of them remain unemployed. The schemes announced by the Central and the State governments have not absorbed all returned migrant workers. Some of those who are engaged in work have a complaint of being not paid on time or inadequately paid or find the work unsatisfactory.

The COVID-19 situation has come under control after the introduction of vaccines. As one of the biggest producers of vaccines, India began exporting them to other countries. However, the outbreak of the second wave paused the export. The Government of India re-started vaccine export in October 2021 after keeping stock to meet domestic demands. By early November, about 107.7 crore doses of vaccines had been administered. Many Indians have received two doses, while some are waiting to receive their second dose. After vaccination, the COVID-19 situation has drastically improved. Yet, the plight of the unprivileged migrant workers have not changed a lot. Many of them are still underpaid or underemployed, while some have not found a job.

References

Agarwal, Vibhuti (2021, April 14). "India's migrants flee to their villages as covid-19 prompts new lockdown". *Mint.* https://www.livemint.com/news/world/indias-migrants -flee-to-their-villages-as-covid-19-prompts-new-lockdown-11618404161569.html. Accessed on June 19 2021.

Arnold, D. (1993). *Colonising the Body: State Medicine and Epidemic Disease in Nineteenth Century India.* Berkeley, CA: University of California Press.

Arnold, D. (1987). "Touching the body: Perspectives on the Indian Plague, 1896–1900". In R. Guha (Ed.) *Subaltern Studies, V* (pp. 55–90). Delhi: Oxford University Press.

Awasthi, Prashasti (2020, March 12). "Centre invokes "Epidemic Act" and "Disaster Management Act" to prevent spread of coronavirus". *The Hindu Business Line.* https://www.thehindubusinessline.com/news/national/centre-invokes-epidemic-act -and-disaster-management-act-to-prevent-spread-of-coronavirus/article31049161.ece. Accessed on August 18 2021.

BBC. (2021, July 21). "Covid-19: India outrage over 'no oxygen shortage death data' claim". https://www.bbc.com/news/world-asia-india-57911638. Accessed on October 18 2021.

Bindra, Japnam & Sharma, Neetu Chandra (2020). "Coronavirus: Govt tells SC one-third of migrant workers could be infected". *The Mint.* April 1, 2020. https://www.livemint.com /news/india/covid-19-govt-tells-sc-one-third-of-migrant-workers-could-be-infected -11585643185390.html. Accessed on July 19 2021.

Chamas, Zena (2021, May 8). "Why is India not announcing a nationwide lockdown amid its deadly COVID second wave?". *Abc.net.* https://www.abc.net.au/news/2021-05-08/ why-is-india-not-announcing-a-lockdown-covid-second-wave/100124692. Accessed on October 12 2021.

Chandavarkar, R. (1992 and 2011). "Plague panic and epidemic politics in India, 1896– 1914". In Terence Ranger & Paul Slack (Eds.), *Epidemics and Ideas: Essays on Historical Perception of Pestilence* (pp. 203–240). Cambridge: Cambridge University Press.

Chopra, Ritika (2020, July 12). "Explained: Is EC empowered to delay Bihar elections due to Covid-19?". *The Indian Express.* https://indianexpress.com/article/explained /explained-is-ec-empowered-to-delay-bihar-elections-due-to-covid-19-6501317/. Accessed on July 15 2020.

Dhingra, Sanya (2020, May 5). "Modi govt claims it's paying 85% of migrants trains' cost but has no "ticket" to prove it". *The Print.* https://theprint.in/india/governance/modi-govt -claims-its-paying-85-of-migrants-trains-cost-but-has-no-ticket-to-prove-it/414349/. Accessed on May 19 2021.

Elegant, Naomi XU (2021, January 27). "Foreign investment cratered in 2020. India was a surprise bright spot". *Fortune.* https://fortune.com/2021/01/27/india-fdi-foreign -investment-2020/. Accessed on October 18 2021.

Fernando, B. (2020, May 31). "How the 1896 plague epidemic shaped Mumbai". *The Indian Express.* Accessed May 31 2020. https://indianexpress.com/article/express-sunday- eye/ how-the-1896-plague-epidemic-shaped-mumbai-6434766/. Accessed on June 5 2020.

Foucault, Michael (2004, December). "The Crisis of Medicine or the Crisis of Antimedicine?" *Foucault Studies,* 1, 5–19. https://rauli.cbs.dk/index.php/foucault-studies/article/view /562/607

Gavi: The Vaccine Alliance. (2020, March 25). "Why is coronavirus lockdown necessary?". https://www.gavi.org/vaccineswork/why-coronavirus-lockdown-necessary. Accessed on July 25 2021.

Ghosh, Malyaban & Mukherji, Biman (2020, April 22). "Global firms look to shift from China to India". *Live Mint.* https://www.livemint.com/industry/manufacturing/global -firms-look-to-shift-from-china-to-india-11587494725838.html. Accessed on May 19 2020.

GN, Thejesh (2020). "Non virus deaths". https://thejeshgn.com/projects/covid19-india/non -virus-deaths/. Accessed on May 19 2021.

Gopalkrishnan, Rampriya (2020, May 20). "Changes in labour laws will turn the clock back by over a century". *The Wire.* https://thewire.in/labour/labour-laws-changes-turning -clock-back. Accessed on July 28 2021.

Hatekar, Neeraj & Belhekar, Pallavi (2020). Why it makes sense to leave and stay gone: Understanding the mass exodus from Mumbai. Unpublished paper under consideration in a reputed journal. Received the paper through e-mail from Professor Neeraj Hatekar. I am thankful to him.

Hindustan Times. (2020, April 18). "State clears plan for evacuation of over 1.3L intrastate labourers". https://www.hindustantimes.com/mumbai-news/state-clears-plan-for-evacuation-of-over-1-3l-intrastate-labourers/story-ao78eIPxq4uK4v7y2Avpff.html . Accessed on May 21 2021.

Iyer, P. Vaidyanathan (2020, March 27). "Rs 1.7 lakh crore Covid-19 package: Many who have been hit still left out, relief too little". *The Indian Express.* https://indianexpress.com/article/explained/coronavirus-relief-package-nirmala-sitharaman-left-out-6333639/. Accessed on October 18 2021.

Jha, Somesh (2020a, May 9). "Covid-19 crisis: UP exempts biz from all but 4 labour laws for 3 years". *Business Standard.* https://www.business-standard.com/article/economy-policy/up-govt-to-exempt-businesses-from-all-but-three-labour-laws-for-3-years-120050701531_1.html. Accessed on July 25 2021.

Jha, Somesh (2020b, May 10). MP labour law changes: Relaxed licence norms for contract workers". *Business Standard.* https://www.business-standard.com/article/economy-policy/mp-labour-law-changes-relaxed-licence-norms-for-contract-workers-120051000529_1.html. Accessed on July 25 2021.

Jha, Somesh (2020c, May 7). "Adityanath Govt in UP to suspend key labour laws, workers' rights for three years". *The Wire.* https://thewire.in/labour/adityanath-govt-in-up-to-suspend-key-labour-laws-workers-rights-for-three-years. Accessed on July 25 2021.

Katju, Arundhati (2020, May 19). "Changes proposed to labour laws are unconstitutional". *The Indian Express.* https://indianexpress.com/article/opinion/columns/migrant-crisis-relaxation-in-labour-laws-india-trade-union-coronavirus-arundhati-katju-6416305/. Accessed on July 25 2021.

Kidambi, Prashant (2007). *The Making of an Indian Metropolis: Colonial Governance and Public Culture in Bombay, 1890–1920.* London: Routledge.

Klein, Ira (2000). "Materialism, Mutiny and Modernization in British India". *Modern Asian Studies*, 34(3), 545–580.

Kumar, Nirbhay (2020, April 20). "1,000 foreign firms mull production in India, 300 actively pursue plan as 'Exit China' mantra grows". *Business Today.* https://www.businesstoday.in/latest/economy-politics/story/1000-foreign-firms-mull-production-in-india-300-actively-pursue-plan-as-exit-china-mantra-grows-256000-2020-04-20. Accessed on October 21 2021.

Mahammadh, Vempalli Raj (2020). "Plague mortality and control policies in colonial South India, 1900–1947". *South Asia Research*, 40(3), 323–343.

Malhotra, Aanchal (2020, April 26). "When the 1897 bubonic plague ravaged India". *Livemint.* https://www.livemint.com/mint-lounge/features/when-the-1897-bubonic-plague-ravaged-india-11587876174403.html. Accessed on May 18 2020.

Mathur, Aneesha (2020, March 31). "Coronavirus lockdown: No migrant worker on road now, govt tells Supreme Court". *India Today.* https://www.indiatoday.in/india/story/coronavirus-lockdown-no-migrant-worker-on-road-now-govt-tells-supreme-court-1661723-2020-03-31. Accessed on April 13 2021.

Mehta, Pratap Bhanu (2020, May 12). "Ordinances by states to change labour laws are a travesty". *The Indian Express.* https://indianexpress.com/article/opinion/columns/industrial-relations-code-india-labour-law-amendment-pratap-bhanu-mehta-6405265/. Accessed on May 13 2020.

Ministry of Rural Development, Government of India. (2020, September 15). "Garib Kalyan Rojgar Yojna" https://rural.nic.in/press-release/garib-kalyan-rojgar-abhiyan. Accessed on October 19 2021.

Modi, Narendra (2020, May 30). "PM Modi writes: A letter to the nation in the midst of a crisis that calls for firm resolve". *The Indian Express.* https://indianexpress.com/article/opinion/columns/narendra-modi-prime-minister-bjp-government-6433655/. Accessed on May 31 2020.

Mullick, Jamie (2021, May 3). "Polls and Covid-19: 5 regions, 5 big spikes". *Hindustan Times*. https://www.hindustantimes.com/elections/polls-and-covid-19-5-regions-5-big -spikes-101619989743716.html. Accessed on October 19 2021.

NDTV. (2020, May 5). "Coronavirus lockdown: Over 1,000 migrant workers reach Lucknow from Maharashtra in special train". *NDTV*. https://www.ndtv.com/india-news /coronavirus-india-over-1-000-migrant-workers-reach-lucknow-from-maharashtra-in -special-train-2223876. Accessed on May 8 2020.

Orent, Wendy (2004). *Plague: The Mysterious Past and Terrifying Future of the World's Most Dangerous Disease*. New York: Free Press.

Outlook. (2020, May 3). "Suicide leading cause for over 300 lockdown deaths in India: Study". https://www.outlookindia.com/newsscroll/suicide-leading-cause-for-over-300 -lockdown-deaths-in-india-study/1822560. Accessed on July 20 2021.

Parth, M.N. (2020, October 19). "No jobs in villages, Bihar's migrants are returning to cities". *India Spend*. https://www.indiaspend.com/no-jobs-in-villages-bihars-migrants -are-returning-to-cities/. Accessed on November 1 2021.

Press Information Bureau, Ministry of Rural Development, Government of India. (2020, June 8) "Press release". https://pib.gov.in/PressReleasePage.aspx?PRID=1630332. Accessed on November 1 2021.

Ranjan, Amit (2020). "Slums, migrant workers, and COVID-19 in Mumbai". *Journal of Migration Affairs*, 3(I), 1–15.

Rashid, A. (2020, June 9). "How oppressive containment measures during Poona plague led to assassination of British officer". *The Indian Express*. Accessed June 9 2020. https:// indianexpress.com/article/research/how-oppressive-containment-measures-during- poona-plague-led-to-assassination-of-british-officer-6450775/. Accessed on June 18 2020.

Rashid, Omar, Anand, Jatin & Mahale, Ajeet (2020, April 4). "India coronavirus lockdown: Migrant workers and their long march to uncertainty". *The Hindu*. https://www.thehindu .com/news/national/india-coronavirus-lockdown-migrant-workers-and-their-long -march-to-uncertainty/article31251952.ece . Accessed on October 30 2021.

Sarkar, A. (2014). "The tie that snapped: Bubonic plague and mill labour in Bombay, 1896–1898". *International Social History*, 59(2), 181–214. https://www.cambridge .org/core/ journals/international-review-of-social-history/article/tie-that-snapped-bu bonic-plague-and- mill-labour-in-bombay-18961898/9100ECEA177113541FE8DE26 E48FD9C3.

Sharma, Yogima (2020a, May 11). "Workers refusing to rejoin factories post lockdown may face pay cuts, disciplinary action". *Economic Times*. https://economictimes.indiatimes .com/news/politics-and-nation/workers-refusing-to-rejoin-factories-may-face-action/ articleshow/75665970.cms?from=mdr. Accessed on November 1 2021.

Sharma, Yogima Seth (2020b, January 19). "National database of workers in informal sector in the work". *The Economic Times*. https://economictimes.indiatimes.com/news /economy/indicators/national-database-of-workers-in-informal-sector-in-the-works/ articleshow/73394732.cms Accessed on October 18 2021.

Sharma, Samrat (2020c, May 8). "India moves big labour law changes to limit coronavirus impact; UP, MP, Punjab, others make these changes". *Financial Express*. https://www .financialexpress.com/economy/labour-reforms-laws-rules-change-uttar-pradesh-up -madhya-pradesh-rajasthan-himachal-pradesh-punjab-kerala-coronavirus-reforms /1952023/. Accessed on July 28 2020.

SWAN. (2021, June 16). "The COVID-19 second wave, local lockdowns and migrant workers distress in India". http://strandedworkers.in/mdocuments-library/. Accessed on November 4 2021.

Tandon, Sasha (2014). *Social History of Epidemics in the Colonial Punjab*. Singapore: Partridge Publications.

The Epidemic Diseases Act. (1897). https://www.indiacode.nic.in/bitstream/123456789 /15942/1/epidemic_diseases_act%2C1897.pdf . Accessed on November 1 2021.

Tumbe, Chinmay (2020). *Age of Pandemics (1817–1920): How they shaped India and the World*. Noida: Harper Collins.

Tare, Kiran (2020, April 7). "Decision of extending Covid-19 lockdown only after April 14: Maharashtra CM Uddhav Thackeray". *India Today*. https://www.indiatoday.in/india /story/decision-of-extending-covid-19-lockdown-only-after-april-14-maharashtra-cm -uddhav-thackeray-1664433-2020-04-07. Accessed on May 18 2021.

The Hindu. (2020, May 9). "Coronavirus Lockdown: Odisha extends work shifts to 12 hours". https://www.thehindu.com/news/national/other-states/coronavirus-lockdown -odisha-extends-work-shift-to-12-hours/article31540556.ece. Accessed on July 18 2020.

The Times of India. (2020, May 18). "Swiggy to fire 1,100 employees: Read CEO's email on job cuts". https://timesofindia.indiatimes.com/gadgets-news/swiggy-to-fire-1100 -employees-read-ceos-email-on-job-cuts/articleshow/75803130.cms. Accessed on July 19 2021.

The Wire. (2020, May 8). "SC: Centre refuses to disclose details of train fares charged from migrant workers". https://thewire.in/law/suprem-court-petition-migrant-workers-train -travel. Accessed on May 9 2020. Accessed on July 19 2021.

Vyas, Mahesh (2021, July 26). "Employment recovery expected in July". *Centre For Monitoring Indian Economy Pvt Ltd*. https://www.cmie.com/kommon/bin/sr.php?kall =warticle&dt=20210726180747&msec=616. Accessed on July 31 2021.

Vyas, Sharad (2020, April 18). "Maharashtra announces financial assistance for 12 lakhs construction workers". *The Hindu*. https://www.thehindu.com/news/national/other -states/maharashtra-announces-financial-assistance-package-for-12-lakh-construction -workers/article31374711.ece. Accessed on July 19 2021.

World Health Organization. https://www.who.int/home/cms-decommissioning

Worldometer. (2021). "India". https://www.worldometers.info/coronavirus/country/india/. Accessed on November 1 2021.

2 The Forgotten Warriors

ASHA Workers in the COVID-19 Pandemic

*Aparna Phadke, Satishchandra Kumar, and
Suman Pujari*

Introduction

Public health has been a complicated arena in India. The access to public health infrastructure is shaped by various factors at individual and societal levels like individual economic status (income, purchasing power and priority for spending money), socio-political positions (political influences and social positions that govern access to government/ free/ subsidized medical facilities), and geographical location (urban, rural and semiurban), structure of governance (neoliberal governance that prefers private and paid infrastructureover government funded subsidized health infrastructure). The very socialist nature of the Indian state in the early decades of independence allowed the public health systems to expand and offer subsidized services to the masses. In 1947, public health care provided most of patient care, which was around 90–95% (Sengupta & Nundy, 2005). Interestingly, to build faith amongst the masses about the modern (based on allopathy) health system and treatment, it took almost four decades to accommodate the most polarized social class like Scheduled Tribes. The involvement of various stakeholders of society, including medical officers, health workers, primary teachers, auxiliary nurse midwives (ANMs) and *Anganwadi* (Rural Child Care Center) workers, extended their collective efforts to reach the targets set by the then state and central governments in improving the healthcare of children, pregnant women, and so on. The role of the government in achieving better safety nets for children to control infant mortality and malnourishment has been quite proactive and commendable. Conducting vaccination drives against illnesses such as polio and measles by Anganwadi workers strengthened the public health system to at least reach basic health facilities. The entire effort of developing public health infrastructure was carried out for at least four decades. In spite of deficiencies in the structure, family planning schemes, Janani Suraksha Yojana (Safe Motherhood Intervention), and many such schemes were achieved and implemented quite successfully. The efforts were aborted half-heartedly in the 1980s in the wake of privatization and neoliberal governance. The quality of government/public healthcare facilities was seen to be continuously deteriorating with shrinking support of the government by downsizing the investments in hiring the healthcare staff needed to run the public health systems in permanent tenures, curtailing on the provisions of medicines, equipment necessary for various

DOI: 10.4324/9781003304517-4

kinds of tests, and so on. Under the influence of new economic policy 1991 (glo-balisation, liberalisation, and privatisation), the investments on public healthcare system were discouraged to pave way towards developemt and growth of private healthcare options. As a result, public spending on healthcare in India dropped to one of the lowest in the world and remains around 0.9% to 1.2% of gross domestic product (GDP) from the year 1995 onward (Sengupta & Nundy, 2005). India has been among the bottom ten countries to spend the lowest amount on public health. Interestingly, this proportion has remained near to 1% since independence, even though the amount spent on public health has been increasing. The overall increase in actual amount spent on public health services is due to the general increase in the budget amount every year. There has been a consistent stagnancy or decrease in GDP since 1991 as a result of neoliberal economic reforms (Sengupta & Nundy, 2005). In 2005, the share of private health services increased to more than 70%. In spite of the efforts to develop the wider networks of public/government health facilities in the post-independent era, the share of the private health service sector consistently increased in the following decades. However, the private sector was in the form of small clinics and hospitals. Metrocities like Mumbai, Kolkata, and Delhi had hospitals that were mostly run by charitable trusts, cooperative indus-tries, and the like.

Following this, there have been stark incidences of socio-economic stratification and polarization associated with shaping the socio-spatial structures of inequality and inaccessibility. The prime factor in shaping the structures of inaccessibility has been the economics and costing of service provision. Nonetheless, availability of trained staff, medical expertise and specializations, and physical set-ups including surgical wards and intensive care units (ICUs) are some of the many factors that shape the structures of inaccessibility. The already existing unequal distribution of health facilities and services has been further affected recently with the prolifera-tion of private and corporate healthcare services in the form of super specialty, multi-specialty hospitals, and clinics that are largely urban in origin. The stark spa-tio-social divide in the availability and accessibility of health services has resulted in patterning the incidences of exclusion that range from individuals to larger com-munities on the basis of their spatio-social identities. The limited or lack of support to rejuvenate the public health infrastructure by providing adequate funding has paved way to a mushrooming of private health clinics and hospitals that are neces-sarily technocentric and laboratory-testing oriented (Sengupta & Nundy, 2005). The inaccessibility of proper health facilities had been expressed in terms of higher maternal mortality rate, infant mortality rate, less life expectancy, and so on. After privatization, India's performance remained poor as many rural hospitals and pri-mary health centers closed.

With this backdrop, the challenges posed by the COVID-19 pandemic need to be analyzed. The pandemic exposed the lacunas. The decision to go into lockdown was rooted in the fear of the spread of COVID-19 and inability of the Government of India to tackle the concomitant health emergency due to inadequate health infra-structure. The period of lockdown was a breathing period that allowed the Central Government and state governments to reengineer the existing health infrastructure with the new COVID-19 facilities. In rural areas, the moribund health infrastructure was brought back with the help of AMN, AWW, and Accredited Social Health Activist (ASHA) structures. This complete reengineering emerged to be successful in handling the COVID-19 pandemic due to the community connection of ASHAs in rural areas. The tracking and treating of coronavirus patients became easier. In the process of COVID-19 management, the need to strengthen the public health infrastructure was highlighted. In fact, COVID-19 pushed governments to modernize many of the rural public health facilities. In the state of Maharashtra, the state government showed a positive attitude towards bringing such transformation. ASHAs, being the backbone of rural community health programs, need to be investigated for their contribution, as they have been the forgotten warriors.

Context

In the year 2000, the United Nations (UN) emerged with a framework of Millennium Development Goals (MDGs) to offer a vision through 8 international goals (UN, 2022) that were mainly focusing on reduction of absolute poverty i.e., extreme forms of poverty (Development Management Institute, 2019). Goal four was about reducing child mortality wherein goal five was about improving maternal health (UN, 2022). India had not been just a signatory to MDGs but it had effectively ratified them in the month of September 2000 at the General Assembly of the United Nations (UNDP, 2022). Following the same, India emerged with an indicator framework for achieving the MDGs.

The maternal mortality rate (MMR) and child mortality rate in the year 2000 were much higher than anticipated. For the year 2000, the MMR was 327 per 100,000 births whereas the Infant Mortality Rate was 68 deaths per thousand births at all India level (UNDP, 2022). The rural spaces showed a greater number of deaths compared to the urban spaces. The greater number of deaths in rural areas was associated with the collapse of the public health system and inaccessibility of the private sector due to the cost factor. The public/government health services often remained understaffed. Many departments under health services were merged to curtail the staff following the announcement of zero salary budget by the World Bank in the post-globalization era. For years, the recruitments in the public/government sector remained suspended. The later recruitment drives mostly offered contract basis appointments leading to yearly tenure that too restricted for 11 months to extended based on the performance of the candidate and/ or as per the requirements. These developments made the lower income groups and poorer sections of the society most vulnerable as their socio-economic spaces started shrinking substantially, leaving hardly any room for their inclusion in any of the upcoming developments. The food basket of rural India, Low Income Group and Economic Weaker Section showed a major deterioration in terms of nutrition and the diversity of food items (Patnaik, 2008).

As India ratified MDGs in 2001, it became obligatory for the Government of India to emerge with an effective policy framework to extend the public health services to the majority of society. Nevertheless, there were larger intentions to improve the maternal mortality and infant mortality rate. Firstly, as the Indian economy was integrating with the world economy, there was a need to improve India's image internationally in terms of its approach towards penetration of private capital. Secondly, Human Development Indicator and other global frameworks consider public health as a major criteria to calculate global rankings. Thirdly, India had poor performance compared to other South Asian countries such as Sri Lanka and even Bangladesh (Zodpey & Negandhi, 2018).

The efforts to achieve to improve maternal health and reduce infant mortality culminated into a policy effort named the National health Mission in the year 2013. Under the National Health Mission, the ASHA scheme was introduced specifically for the vulnerable populations of rural areas (NHM, 2022). The need to develop closer contact with the community was felt to improve rural public health. It was also found that the then existing public/government health network in the form of Primary Health Centers and sub centers was not enough as it was expected to cater to 5000 plus people. The AMNs (Auxiliary Midwife Nurse) and the AWWs (Anganwadi Workers) were identified as overburdened. To supplement the existing rural health network, the ASHA scheme was offered initially in select areas and specifically to cater the Scheduled Tribe population. After reviewing its success, the scheme was extended to rural areas with the expectation that ASHA workers will be the agent of change (NHM, Accessed on 05/01/2022). The concept of ASHA workers was partially based on the concept of barefoot doctors that was established and implemented by Search Foundation in Gadchiroli, Maharashtra (DMI, 2019) (Pradnya, 2017). Doctor Abhay Bang and Doctor Rani Bang devoted their expertise to the health services meant for the tribal and poorer sections of society in Gadchiroli, Maharashtra. To make the people more knowledgeable about health and to provide them with primary aid, village women were trained to perform basic monitoring of health, specifically of pregnant women and to children. They were also trained to offer first aid for common health issues prevailing in the rural and tribal society of Gadchiroli District. These were the women who were traditional nurses known as *Dai*. These women were specially trained for providing help in the delivery of a child in a scientific manner. At present, the total number of ASHA workers countrywide are almost near to around 1,000,000. Looking at the success, the scheme of ASHA workers restricted to rural health has been extended to urban areas under National Urban Health Mission.

The responsibilities of ASHA were primarily towards connecting the vulnerable socio-economic groups with the government / public health systems. ASHAs were considered as health activists (NHM, Accessed on 05/01/2022) and catalyst in mobilizing the community towards having greater access to local health infrastructural facilities. It was also expected that the ASHAs would provide information and spread awareness about health and hygienic living practices to villagers (NHM, Accessed on 05/01/2022). The major emphasis on offering counselling to women regarding family planning and other necessary gynaecological information to women. The mobilization of villagers to take advantage of the government health care system was a major task given to the ASHA workers where they were expected to connect all the villagers to AMN, AWW, sub-centers and rural hospitals. Distribution of medicines, kits, and condoms were some of the other responsibilities (MoHFW, 2020).

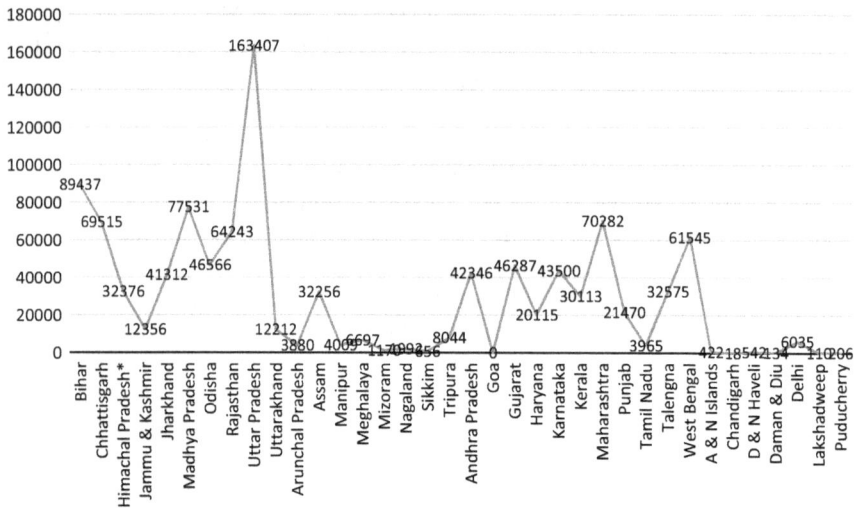

Figure 2.1 States and Union Territories: Distribution of ASHA Workers, 2020.

Source: NHM-MIS Rfeport as o Sept 2019

ASHA Workers: Struggle, Commitments and Impact

In 2005, the ASHA worker's scheme was launched. Ironically for the first few years, the workers had hardly any training. This resulted in lower performances, lack of self-confidence, and limited success in bridging the villagers to the public health services. From 2005 to 2009, there was a substantial increase in the number of ASHA workers in the state of Maharashtra. In the year 2009, the ASHA workers' union was formed. The unionization helped them to respond collectively and voice their concerns in front of the government authorities. The first demand made by the union was about arranging proper training sessions for the ASHA workers. The training sessions boosted their confidence and allowed them to work with the villagers more confidently. In the initial years, they were the topic of mockery and criticism due to lack of proper understanding about their responsibilities. Gradually, they emerged confident with training and experiential learning to understand the mentality of villagers and accordingly plan the dialogue with them and also offer counseling to them. The commitment and hard work of ASHA workers resulted in linking the vulnerable sections of rural societies with the government health systems. They also emerged as a major helping hand to AMN and AWW workers by providing them with vital information on various important elements of rural society that needed special attention like pregnant women and children.

Because of ASHA workers, the rural societies were drawn back to government health centers and hospitals. People became aware of the existence of such a system. The inflow of patients encouraged the reopening of the primary health centers (PHCs) and civil hospitals that were otherwise closed down or in a poor situation. As they started providing the knowledge about various government schemes and their benefits, the rural societies started connecting with the public health systems,

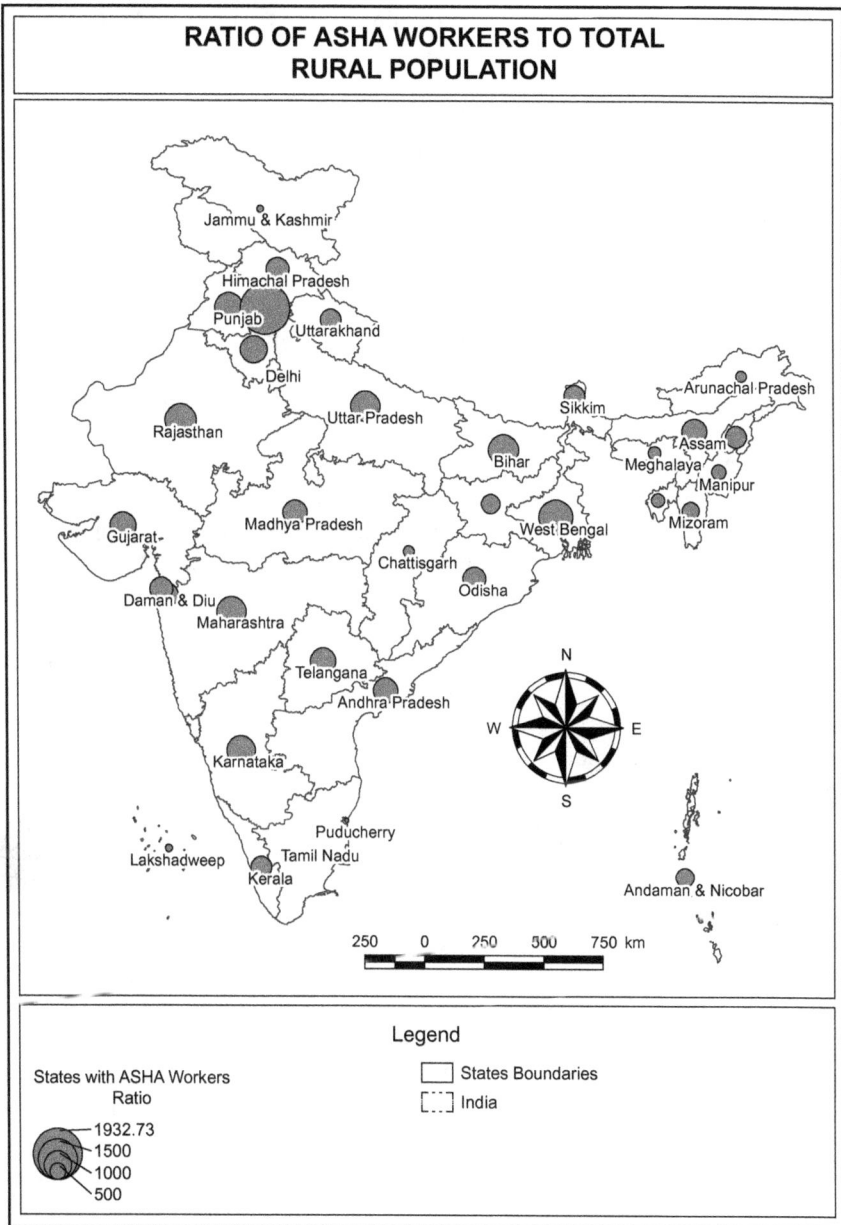

Figure 2.2 State wise ratio of ASHA workers.

Source: NHM-MIS report as of Sept 2019

for example, the pregnant women could be linked with the rural hospitals and doctors for her wellbeing. The success of ASHA is reflected in the substantial decrease in the maternal mortality rate (MMR) and also in infant mortality rate. The credit of course, needs to be shared with AMN and AWW workers as well. Table 2.1 represents the impact of strengthening the rural public health sector on mortality rates. However, in spite of collective efforts, targets set by Millenium Development Goals of bringing down the Infant Mortality rate to 28, the mortality rate of children under the age of 5 to 42, and maternal mortality rate to 109 were not achieved for various other reasons. Nonetheless, India could achieve a substantial improvement in maternal care and child mortality. Maharashtra has been one of the states to achieve the targets set under MDGs in 2015 by reducing the MMR to 55 (Ministry of Health and Family Welfare, 2021) from 130 in the year 2004–05 (RGI, 2011). The collective effort of AMN, AWW, and ASHA gave a major boost towards the rejuvenation of rural health systems. Table 2.1 reflects the achievements at all-India levels. A substantial decrease can be seen in the states that have been identified by the health ministry as the Empowered Action Group (EAG). Assam and the EAGs together showed substantial reduction in MMR, from 375 (RGI, 2011) in 2004–05 to 175 (Ministry of Health and Family Welfare, 2021) in the year 2015–16.

It is ironic to note that the major improvement in rural public health is at the stake of ASHA workers. As the name itself suggests, ASHA is considered a health activist group. The nomenclature indicates that ASHA work is more of a social work and necessarily comes with low expectations in terms of earning. The honorarium of ASHAs has been through case-based commissions and incentives offered by the government. Table 2.2 represents the monetary incentives offered by the government to ASHA workers.

Though the table appears to be assuring in terms of financial gains to ASHAs, the maximum schemes are in the incentive class of Rs. 51 to Rs. 300 per case including identification, referral of the case, follow up, and cure. For 27 schemes, the incentives are between Rs. 101 to Rs. 300. The closer observation reveals that the schemes that offer higher incentives have comparatively lower patient or case ratio. In Maharashtra, there have been no fixed monthly payment to ASHAs; their income was directly related with the incentives.

The reality is strikingly different. On an average, the monthly income of ASHAs in Maharashtra is near about Rs. 2,500. The lowest is Rs. 1,500 and the highest is Rs. 5,000 per month. They work at least 6 to 7 hours per day when they are expected to work 4 hours a day (Ambast, 2021). They do not have financial security. The central government claims that to secure them financially they have been made beneficiaries of life insurance, accidental insurance, and pension provided the beneficiaries are contributing to these schemes from 30% to 50%(MoHFW, 2020). The schemes are Pradhan Mantri Jeevan Jyoti Beema Yojana, Pradhan Mantri Suraksha Beema Yojana, and Pradhan Mantri Shram Yogi Maan Dhan (MoHFW, 2020). Ironically, the workers having such a meager amount of earning at the end of the month that they cannot think of such expenditures. Most of the ASHAs are from poorer backgrounds and accept the social health "activism" to support their families (Ambast, 2021). There is no consideration of minimum wages for them when such a law is already

Table 2.1 The Achievements by India at the Closure of MDGs—Year 2015

Millennium Development Goals	Title of the Goal	Indicator Selected	Targets by 2015	Unit of Measurement	Achievements – Actual figure in the year 2015
4	Reduce Child Mortality	Infant Mortality Rate (IMR)	28	Number of infants (< 1 year) deaths per 1,000 live births	36 (PIB data) (38 as per World Bank data)
		Under 5 Mortality Rate	42	number of children (0–4 years) who died before reaching their 5th birthday per 1,000 live births	43
5	Improve Maternal Health	Maternal Mortality Ratio (MMR)	108	women aged 15–49 years dying due to maternal causes per 100,000 live births	122 (PIB data) (176 as per World Bank Data)

Source: Macrotrends https://www.macrotrends.net/countries/IND/india/infant-mortality-rate;
Ministry of Health and Family Welfare, Government of India, Press Information Bureau

https://www.pib.gov.in/PressReleasePage.aspx?PRID=1697441;
World Bank http://www.data.worldbank.org/indicator/SH.STA.MMRT

Table 2.2 Monetary Incentives to ASHA Workers: Classification of Schemes as per the Incentives

Sr. No.	Name of the scheme		Incentives in INR						
	Head	Exact Activity	1 to 5	6 to 50	51 to 100	101 to 300	301 to 500	501 to 1000	1001 and Above
1	Maternal Health	JSY financial package	1	3	4	3			
2	Child Health			1	3	3			
3	Immunization								
4	Family Planning	Mission ParivarVikas—In 146 selected districts in 6states (57 in UP, 37 in Bihar, 14 RJS, 9 in Jharkhand, 2 in Chhattisgarh, and 2 in Assam)	2		3	8	3	1	
5	Adolescent Health		1			1			
6	Incentive for Routine Recurrent Activities		1			3			1
7	Participatory Learning and Action—In 10 selected states that have low RMNCH+A indicators (Assam, Bihar, Chhattisgarh, Jharkhand, MP, Meghalaya, Odisha, Rajasthan, Uttarakhand, and UP)				1				
8	Revised National Tuberculosis Control Programme	Honorarium and counselling charges for being a DOTS provider			1			1	2
9	National Leprosy Eradication Programme					2	1		

Sr. No.	Name of the scheme		Incentives in INR						
	Head	Exact Activity	1 to 5	6 to 50	51 to 100	101 to 300	301 to 500	501 to 1000	1001 and Above
10	National Vector Borne Disease Control Programme	Malaria	1		1				
		Lymphatic Filariasis		1	3				
		Acute Encephalitis Syndrome/ Japanese Encephalitis			1				
		Kala Azar elimination					1		
		Dengue and Chikungunya		1					
		National Iodine Deficiency Disorders Control Programme	1						
11	Incentives under Comprehensive Primary Health Care (CPHC) and Universal NCDs Screening		1	2				1	
12	Drinking Water and Sanitation				2				
	Total		**6**	**9**	**17**	**27**	**5**	**3**	**3**
	Percentage		**8.57**	**12.86**	**24.29**	**38.57**	**7.14**	**4.29**	**4.29**

Source: Ministry of Health and Family Welfare, Government of India, Press Information Bureau https://pib.gov.in/Pressreleaseshare.aspx?PRID=1606212

in place (Ambast, 2021) (PLOS, 2021). The status of workers has been vulnerable across the states in terms of receiving a basic fixed salary as they are considered activists. In some states like West Bengal, they are offered a fixed salary of Rs. 3,000. But most of the states do not offer them such fixed amounts, leaving them vulnerable to the fluctuating incentive-based incomes. Depending on the spatio-social profile of the area, which schemes can be prominently offered to people emerges to be the key question. The schemes, when implemented, have contradictory impacts. For example, distributing condoms would definitely bring down the number of unwanted pregnancies. Following the same, there would be limited cases for ANC (Antenatal procedures). Distribution of condoms would allow workers to earn R. 1for 3 condoms while one case of ANC would allow her to earn Rs. 150 (MoHFW, 2020). The population of 1,000 allotted to her may possess specific socio-cultural attributes and they may be interfering in the work of ASHAs. Ironically, all the schemes are with differential incentives and the gap between the incentives is too wide. The most paid schemes include Janani Suraksha Yojana, antenatal care, family planning, and immunization (Ambast, 2021). Apart from financial vulnerability, they have to also face cynicism (PLOS, 2021) by family members, the public, and authorities. The payment for ASHAs comes from the state government and, at village level, it has to be released by *Gramsevak*. There is an inexplicable delay in releasing the payment for ASHAs and sometimes it is as long as six months.

In spite of all these conditions, ASHAs continue to work relentlessly in the hope of better economic and income opportunities. It is interesting to observe how the state propagates feminization of work in a vital sector like health in the name of female empowerment. Feminization of work exposed the workers to deliberate patterns of exploitation. To understand the status of ASHA workers in Maharashtra, a detailed discussion with the union leaders, supervisors and ASHA workers have been done. Twenty-five ASHA workers representing different parts of Maharashtra were interviewed virtually on December 12, 2021. A telephonic conversation through conference call was planned for the collection of information through a questionnaire. On November 6, the union leaders including Mrs. Suman Pujari, who is a co-author, were interviewed.

Narrating the COVID-19 Experiences of ASHAs

The COVID-19 pandemic challenged the neoliberal economic reforms in most of the countries by exposing the fallacies of the private healthcare systems. It was, in a way, an eye-opening experience for most of the neoliberal states which were busy promoting reckless privatization of the healthcare system and infrastructure in the last two decades while deliberately discouraging the public sector utilities. It also exposed the major lacunae of the public health system and infrastructure that had completely collapsed. In Maharashtra, being the most and worst affected state in terms of transmission, mortality, and spatial spread, the entire public and private healthcare systems were at stake. The rural areas also displayed a major number of COVID-19 infections resulting in tremendous pressure being put on the already inadequate and inefficient rural health infrastructure and rural healthcare workers. The second wave of COVID-19 brought a major challenge with the escalated requirement of oxygen concentrators and ventilators as more people affected by the Delta variant required hospitalization. The strategy used successfully in the Mumbai model of tracing, testing, and tracking of patients and their contacts was applied in rural areas. The entire medical and paramedical staff was immensely pressurized with the flow of patients, remaining occupied in treating them 24/7. The inverse ratio of the number of patients and healthcare facilities created a health emergency in most of the metro areas of Maharashtra, as the equipped healthcare systems were largely concentrated in metro areas. These areas receive patients from different corners of Maharashtra. In rural areas, the backbone of the COVID-19 Mumbai Model were the ASHAs. In Maharashtra, ASHAs were given various types of responsibilities. These responsibilities included the following tasks: 1) Pamphlet distribution for creating awareness about the disease and the guidelines to be followed related with masks, sanitizers, and general precaution. They were not just expected to discuss but stick the pamphlets on the door of each house; 2) They were supposed to track the patients with symptoms and provide the information to the local health and administrative authorities (Niyati & Mandela, 2020); 3) They were also expected to prepare a list of people who were in close contact with the identified patient. The list consisted of contacts at high risk and low risk. The list was expected to be prepared within 24 hours after the identification of infected patients; 4) They were also expected to provide medicine to the patient if he or she is home quarantined, regardless of whether they were of the high risk and low risk category; 5) They were given the task of monitoring the population (1,000 people) by keeping the records of pulse and oxygen levels; 6) They were also deployed at various levels for COVID duty—Village survey of COVID positive patients and their relatives, Primary Health Centres (PHC), health subcentres, and rural hospital; 7) The survey of various areas also became part of their duty (Patil, 2021). There were multiple consequences of involvement of ASHAs in COVID-19 related works in terms of their personal, social, and professional lives.

Personal Loss

The ASHA workers risked their lives by offering their services at grassroot levels. Ironically, they were not provided with any kind of protective gear and on such a small income, they, in the initial phase, arranged masks and sanitizers for themselves (Niyati & Mandela, 2020). When they were provided with masks, they were told to reuse the same masks after washing. This needs to be seen against the situation of frontline workers who were then provided with personal protective equipment kits. The ASHA workers, in spite of no protective gear for themselves, are devoted to COVID-19 work. In the process, many ASHA workers were infected. Their families too have been infected. At least, 45 ASHA workers lost their lives due to coronavirus in Maharashtra in the second wave (Pujari, 2021). Many of the ASHAs have lost their family members, however, in this case, the authentic relevant data is not available (Pujari, 2021).

The deterioration of the health of ASHA workers has been another consequence of their involvement in COVID-19 related work. Some of the ASHA workers have been suffering with several side effects of the COVID-19 infection.

There have been major setbacks to ASHA in relation to their family lives. Many ASHAs had been outcasted by their families. They were not allowed to enter the house and were forced to stay in the front yard or backyard in even harsher conditions. They were also abandoned by their families in case they were infected with COVID-19. Suvarna, an ASHA from the Satara tehsil got infected while working. She was abandoned by her family and was told to stay away. From her maternal family too, she received a similar response. Finally, the Union interfered and sought the help of the collector of the district to make arrangements for her. For the next 15 days, she was provided with shelter in a government provided quarantine center. Suvarna is not alone in her suffering. Many workers have gone through similar experiences. Suvarna describes it as one of the most dreadful experiences of life, in which her own family members disowned her.

Financial Loss

Urmila, one of the ASHA workers, narrated her experience while saying that ASHAs are voluntary workers,

We have not been identified as government health workers. So, on what basis were we forced for the COVID-19 related tasks? We were supposed to work voluntarily and pick the tasks of our own choice when it comes to rural health. How does the government impose such a life-risking job without providing basic safety and financial support?

Asha workers were given the responsibilities related to COVID-19 in the year 2019. Until the month of April, 2021, not even a single rupee was assured to them for such life risking work. After the union took a strong stand to get proper honorarium, the state government declared Rs. 1000 per month with another Rs. 1000 from the central government as COVID-19 allowances. The state government recently offered an increment of Rs. 500 to workers and Rs. 700 to the supervisors. Due to COVID-19 related responsibilities, other activities for which the government had offered dedicated incentives were totally in a state of suspension leading to very limited or no income in the first and second waves. The honorarium offered was just Rs. 33 per day against Rs. 300 to Rs. 500 given daily to class I to class IV regular government employees as a COVID--19 allowance. It should be seen at the backdrop that other permanent staff members already have handsome salaries. They were offered a COVID-19 allowance that was almost 10 times more than ASHA workers. The honorarium given to ASHA workers by the state comes through Gramsevak. The state share that comes through Gram Panchayat and Gramsevak is responsible for the payment of ASHA workers.

COVID-19 as a Social Stigma

ASHAs were the important agents in the tracing, tracking, and treating model implemented as a part of the resilience policy. The list of positive and negative cases, and the quarantined and migrants was supposed to be prepared by ASHA workers. As ASHAs were expected to prepare the list of COVID infected patients and potential spreaders, they had to face the resistance from the local villagers leading to arguments and conflicts. They had been threatened, harassed and at times beaten by the locally affluent people for including their names for quarantine At least 25 ASHA workers have been beaten and tortured (Pujari, 2021). In Manmad, Nasik, Vidarbha, and Marathwada regions, ASHAs were attacked with choppers, axes, etc. Two workers were brutally beaten to death (Pujari, 2021). Rekha while narrating the experience, said,

It was a tough time. In a village, she had close community contacts and everybody else was known and related to each other in some or the other way. To make people aware about the consequences of transmission and convince them to understand the importance of quarantine was a herculean task for them. Most of the time, people would turn extremely stubborn and would argue with them. To save themselves from people's fury, ASHAs had to call the police in many cases. Her friend was brutally assassinated for including the name of the accused in the high-risk category. The workers had no support and they were the ones who faced the brunt and bruise.

Work and Stress

In the past two years, ASHA workers have been working for at least 10 to 16 hours a day when there actual contracted hours of work have been hardly 4 to 6 hours a day. (Ambast, 2021). The long working hours are without any kind of financial or monetary support. Most of the ASHA workers used to get engaged in some other work that would bring them some more income for survival. As the government health departments have many vacant seats. as they have not been filled since decades following the ban on recruitments, ASHA workers were compelled to work extra. Vijaya while sharing her experience opined that,

we are health volunteers and activists. The understaffed government health system was made efficient, functional and accessible by us. In COVID times, they were taken for granted. Her friend who survived through COVID, was told by the AMN to quit the job if she was not able to handle the work pressure. Her friend was already into a financial crisis. COVID weakened her to a great degree. When she was told to quit, she could not bear the pressure and died of heart attack. There were many such cases where the death is not due to COVID but because of tremendous work pressure. No one had counted these deaths and their families will also not get any compensation as their deaths are not due to COVID.

All the ASHA workers who were interviewed raised common concerns about their present and future status. They questioned their very categorization as frontline workers and associated benefits which they never received. The questions were raised on the insensitivity of the government that offered just the honorarium of 2000 INR per month, that too after continuously following the matter with the government through union. The worries about future were expressed and an anxiety over their identity as social health activists too emerged with the fear that the workers would never get any financial and economic benefits.

Answering these questions would probably lead us to constructive paradigm on public health and welfare of all the workers who are involved in the making of public health systems.

Conclusion

The COVID-19 pandemic is an eye opener for everyone—at personal and social levels. There have been several revelations at individual, socia,l and governance levels. A critical evaluation of neoliberal policies and privatization agendas is an urgent need of the hour. The pandemic has already pushed some millions of people into extreme poverty. How the government and public institutions and infrastructures can be reengineered and rejuvenated to mainstream more and more of these excluded people is the real question. ASHA workers too belong to the same class as the excluded. The pandemic demonstrated how ASHA workers, the "marginalised frontliners" can strengthen the rural health system and help the vulnerable groups even during COVID-19. A model of healthcare that is community-centric needs to be strengthened. The same can be achieved by

1. Keeping the ASHA. AMN (Auxiliary Nursing Midwifery), and AWW (Anganwadi Workers) at its core in promoting and publicizing various health schemes and benefits available to the rural and urban vulnerable population.
2. The ASHA and *Anganwadi* workers can be retained permanently by offering them fixed salaries and various other benefits including health insurance benefits.
3. Training and learning the skills of identifying the diseases, knowledge and basic knowledge about physical inspection, information about medicine, health monitoring, and basic surgical skills can be offered to workers to promote them as barefoot doctors. Similarly, training about conducting basic laboratory and clinical testing can also be availed at sub-centers. In the peak period of COVID-19, all testing was done in major metropolitan cities like Mumbai, Pune, Nasik, and Nagpur etc. This resulted in tremendous pressureon these laboratories and extraordinary delays in diagnosis and treatment.
4. ASHAs have emerged as a major link between the villagers and public health care systems. They as a community connect can also be trained as mental health workers. They can be also be barefoot counselors for the population they serve.
5. Finally, political will power is necessary to emerge with concrete policy interventions to improve the rural health infrastructure. The state has already witnessed such strong political will power where, at district level, the oxygen production plants have been granted to avoid a supply crunch. The rural hospitals have been well equipped to deal with the serious patients. The training has been provided to the health workers to deal with the pandemic situation.

As the name suggests, ASHAs can be the ray of hope for rural communities in terms of mental and physical health.

References

Ambast, S. (2021). *Why Do Asha Wokers in India Earn So Little*. Retrieved from https://www.cbgaindia.org: https://www.cbgaindia.org/blog/why-do-asha-workers-in-india-earn-so-little/, June 29, 2021.

Development Management Institute. (2019). *https://dmi.ac.in/photo/upload/2019/1576244544_6224.pdf*. PubMed Central. National Centre for Biotechnology Information. Retrieved from https://dmi.ac.in: https://dmi.ac.in/photo/upload/2019/1576244544_6224.pdf

Fox, L. (Director). (2007). *The Story of Stuff* [Motion Picture].

Ministry of Health and Family Welfare. (2021). *Maternal Mortality Rate*. Retrieved from https://www.pib.gov.in: https://www.pib.gov.in/PressReleasePage.aspx?PRID=1697441, February 12, 2021.

MoHFW, G. o. (2020). *Press Information Bureau, Government of India, Ministry of Health and Family Welfare*. Retrieved from https://pib.gov.in: https://pib.gov.in/Pressreleaseshare.aspx?PRID=1606212, March 13, 2020.

NHM. (2022). *Guidelines on Accredited Social Health Activists*. National Health Mission. Retrieved from https://nhm.gov.in: https://nhm.gov.in/images/pdf/communitisation/task-group-reports/guidelines-on-asha.pdf, January 5, 2022.

Niyati, S., & Mandela, S. (2020). Impact of the Pandemic on Accredited Social Health Activists (ASHA) in India. *Review of Agrarian Studies*, *10*(*1*), 204–212.

Patil, U. (2021). Role of Asha Workers in COVID - 19 Pandemic (A. Phadke, Interviewer), interviewed on December 12, 2021.

Patnaik, U. (2008). *Theorising Poverty and Food Security in the Era of Economic Reforms*. Retrieved from http://bibliotecavirtual.clacso.org.ar: http://bibliotecavirtual.clacso.org.ar/ar/libros/sursur/lech/12patna.pdf.

PLOS, J. H. (2021). *Harbingers of Hope: Giving ASHA Workers Their Due to Build a Resilient Maternal and Child Health System in Post-COVID-19 India*. Retrieved from https://yoursay.plos.org: https://yoursay.plos.org/2021/06/harbingers-of-hope-giving-asha-workers-their-due-to-build-a-resilient-maternal-and-child-health-system-in-post-covid-19-india/, June 6, 2021.

Pradnya, K. (2017). Editorial: A Tribute to Dr. Abhay Bang. *Journal of Dental Research and Review*, *4*(3), 57. Retrieved from GALE ONEFILE https://link.gale.com/apps/doc/A523651430/HRCA?u=anon~d133474c&sid=googleScholar&xid=fb3da492.

Pujari, S. (2021). Role of Union of ASHA Workers in Maharashtra in COVID Times (A. Phadke, Interviewer), November 6, 2021.

RGI, O. o. (2011). *Maternal & Child Mortality and Fertility Rates Sample Registration System*. Retrieved from https://censusindia.gov.in: https://censusindia.gov.in/vital_statistics/srs_bulletins/MMr_release_070711.pdf

Sengupta, A., & Nundy, S. (2005). PubMed Central. National Centre for Biotechnology Information. Retrieved from NCBI: https://www.ncbi.nlm.nih.gov/pmc/articles/PMC1285083/, November 19, 2005.

UN. (2022). *Millennium Development Goals and Beyond 2015*. United Nations. Retrieved from https://www.un.org: https://www.un.org/millenniumgoals, January 1, 2022.

UN. (2022). *Millennium Development Goals*. Retrieved from https://www.un.org: https://www.un.org/millenniumgoals, January 1, 2022.

UNDP. (2022). *United Nations Development Programme India*. Retrieved from https://www.in.undp.org: https://www.in.undp.org/content/india/en/home/post-2015/mdgoverview.html#:~:text=India%20and%20the%20MDGs&text=India%20is%20a%20signatory%20to,towards%20the%20eight%20development%20goals, January 1, 2022.

Zodpey, S., & Negandhi, P. (2018). Tracking India's Progress in Health Sector after 70 Years of Independence. *Indian Journal of Public Health*, *62*, 1–3.

3 Voices from the Margins

Pandemic Experiences of the LGBTIQ Community in Mumbai

Shailesh Bhutka, Kajal Boraste, and Sunil Gangavane

Introduction

For almost six months…there was nothing, there were no people at the signals. Where do we even beg then? Even if we do sex work who will even come as a customer? Everyone was in a deep economic crisis. Our community depends on them for survival. People from transgender community are already seen as dirty, and are labelled as unclean. People who beg at the signal and dance, who will take care of them? (People think) we are dirty, our clothes are untidy, we don't wear masks. What if we spread the disease? Kiran,[1] a 36-year-old transgender woman,[2] underlines the community's dependency and consequent powerlessness while sharing her life struggles. She also reminds us that it is inappropriate to generalize the impact of a pandemic, in fact doing that will be negating the experiences of the marginalized. The pandemic had a serious impact on disadvantaged people that are marginalized for their caste, class, gender, sexual orientation, and a number of other characteristics. One such marginalized group is the Lesbian, Gay, Bisexual, Transgender, Intersex, and Queer (LGBTIQ) community. The term LGBTIQ covers both sexual orientation and gender identity. However, it is frequently used as an umbrella word for anyone who does not identify as straight (heterosexual) or cisgender. The LGBTIQ, which is already neglected group as a result of the covid pandemic, has been severely impacted in every aspect of their development. What was it like for the LGBTIQ community to be subjected to repression and lockdown? What were their challenges? What kind of assistance was available? It's critical to research and document the ways, resources, and coping methods used to recover from this era when the dominant voices are rapidly erasing all forms and experiences of deprivation. By generalizing personal experiences, one may be led to believe that we have all encountered similar experiences. While doing this, not only are some privileges ignored while other people's experiences are appropriated, but the experiences of those on the margins are also conveniently erased. People are led to believe that there is no such thing as a privilege ladder that can be used to determine the distance between the center and the periphery. In such circumstances, it is even

DOI: 10.4324/9781003304517-5

more significant to document their evidences of deprivation before it goes unrecognised forever. It is necessary to listen to various narratives, connect the dots, and see if there is a way out for today and for tomorrow. With this intention, we spoke to persons from the LGBTIQ community and community leaders who are living in *bastis* of Mumbai, to capture the lived experiences of the LGBTIQ community. It is important to inform the readers that, despite several attempts, we were unable to communicate with anyone who identifies as intersex, lesbian, or a trans man. This also exemplifies the structural marginalization of specific identities. We spoke with a total of ten individuals, some over the phone and some in person. This article outlines insights, analysis, and recommendations based on these interactions, readings, and reflections.

Mumbai, Home, and Survival

The COVID pandemic has wreaked havoc on the LGBTIQ community in India (Newman et al., 2021, Rosario, 2020). The survival, poverty, income, and the other challenges related to identity were exacerbated in this period. These resulted in increased cases of anxiety, desperation, self-harm, and suicides (Das & Nair, 2020).

Like many others, some of the LGBTIQ members had also migrated from elsewhere in India to Mumbai (Shaikh, 2016) in search of a job and new life. Those who severed all ties with their families had no choice but to stay where they were. Many LGBTIQ people who had left their abusive and violent homes for the city to assert their "self-identity" were forced by the pandemic to return to the same homes. During the first wave of the pandemic, many LGBTIQ students returned to their homes and exploitative settings, hoping that whatever happens would happen in their "home". Some hid their "discovered true" identities, while others were willing to put up with whatever happened to them when they returned home. People were forced to the village, leaving behind their hard-won businesses, jobs, friends, and support systems. Rebuilding all these was difficult when they returned following the lifting of the lockdown restrictions.

Even though when the family was supportive, adding burden to their woes was a challenge and stress for many.

Khushboo, a 26-year-old transgender woman who is now living with her family in a predominantly Muslim-Dalit neighborhood on the outskirts of Mumbai, shares,

> It didn't matter how much I had saved; it was all gone. "What should I do now that my savings have been exhausted?" was my next thought. So one month went by, two months went by, but the problems just got worse! What would I have done if the problem had grown worse over time? So, I called home and said I don't have anything with me, so my mother said come back home. My family is so nice that they called me … there was no problem at home, I was eating well. However, I found it terrible to merely sit at home and eat. Because I lived alone when I was earning, but when I had nothing left, I joined the family. As a result, this struck me as odd.

Khushboo had to put her pride aside to ask her family for help. However, because of this uncertainty and adding to the number of people who needed to be fed in a house, a sense of shame and guilt developed.

Although the city provides livelihood and tentative shelters for the 'outsiders', it fails to provide structural support, especially in times of disaster. During the pandemic and subsequent lockdown of the economies, the city was at a halt, businesses were shuttered, and public spaces were closed. People lost income, food, and shelter pushing them further to the margins. This resulted in increased vulnerability not only to COVID infection but also to health and other survival challenges.

Health Risk and Missing Data

Bowleg's expression of why "we are all not in this together" are so prominent

> the ubiquitous phrase "We're all in this together" … reflects an intersectional color and class blinding those functions to obscure the structural inequities that befall Black and other marginalized groups, who bear the harshest and most disproportionate brunt of anything negative or calamitous: HIV/AIDS, hypertension, poverty, diabetes, climate change disasters, unemployment, mass incarceration, and, now, COVID-19.
>
> (Bowleg, 2020)

The LGBTIQ community is already stigmatized because of sexuality, socially excluded, vulnerable, and hence was at higher risk. The health implications of the pandemic were severe. Banerjee and Nair (2020) explain the sexual stigma and social discriminations which prevent or restricts communities' access to health care. In our interactions, many members reported that it became harder for them to acquire regular health check-ups, testing, and treatments due to the increased burden on the health system during the first and second waves. Medicines were difficult to access for people who were already on medication. For instance, those undergoing gender-affirming procedures (sex change/reassignment) have faced numerous challenges throughout the process and therapy. Despite the fact that these treatments were featured on the World Health Organization's (WHO) essential list.

The LGBTIQ community also became more vulnerable to HIV, STIs, or all such infections. Chakrapani et al., in their research (2021) further describe how the pandemic deprived the transwomen in India during this period. The Hijra[3] community who were engaged in sex work found it difficult to get access to safe sex precautions. This increased the risk of HIV infection along with COVID. The research also sheds light on how difficult it was to access HIV-related health services.

In the United States, Heslin and Hall (2021) discuss how same-sex couples are more susceptible to COVID infection and its detrimental repercussions. They cite Centers for Disease Control and Prevention (CDC) data showing that smoking gays and bisexuals are more likely than non-smoking non-homosexuals to have asthma, cancer, heart disease, chronic obstructive pulmonary disease, hypertension, renal disease, and obesity. It was more frequent among poor, ethnic, and sexual minorities. Deprivation, violence, and discrimination are among the challenges that the community faces. To acquire full information and plan and implement effective initiatives, they demand that sexual orientation data be documented. One of the transgender rights activists and political leaders in Maharashtra, Priya Patil, also highlights the need for accurate data for transgender persons in Maharashtra state.

> We don't have data for the sexual minorities community in the country. We have requested the Maharashtra government to start the survey to get the TG/ Hijra population data. But it's in the initial phase of approval. We don't have accurate data from the central governmentt or bodies either.

In the Aadhar card and vaccination registration, the government has offered individuals an option of enrolling themselves under the category of "other". Giving transgender people the choice of "other" makes "othering" common practice, this has been criticized by many community leaders too. UNAIDS estimates that HIV prevalence in India is 0.31 percent, and 8.2 percent among transgender people (Transgender People, HIV and AIDS, 2015). Many transgender people living with HIV are aware of their situation, implying that they are already fearful and stressed. Further there is a stark inequity noted in vaccination accessibility. Chakrapani (Alliance, 2021) have underlined the challenges of the transgender community in accessing vaccines, government schemes, benefits, vaccinations and medical treatment.

No Job, No Food

When a crisis strikes, the minority and vulnerable groups suffer the most. During economic downturns, for instance, women and daily workers are more likely to lose their jobs. The majority of marginalized LGBTIQ members who work in informal and unstable working conditions (Pandya and Redcay, 2021) were affected the most in the COVID pandemic.

As Kiran says above, the Hijra community's traditional means of survival are begging, blessing, or sex work. The very basic nature of these jobs is dependent on the "formal", "dominant", and "mainstream" groups. Trains, buses, markets, and public places were closed, and the sources of income for transgender people were blocked due to restrictions on crowds. Due to a ban on festivals, the *doli-badhai*[4] program and the money earned from it suddenly stopped, due to the rules of physical distancing and wearing masks, people grew conscious of touching each other's bodies. The number of people coming to the community for sex work decreased and gradually stopped. The source of income through sex work too slowed down. The closure of all these routes had a major impact on the livelihoods of transgender, kothi, and non-binary individuals.

Massage, hairdresser, fabric designer, cook, and dancer, all of which require physical contact, were among the most affected non-traditional employment for transgender, kothi, and gay people. Some educated sex workers turned to the internet to make money via sexting and phone sex (Chakrapani et al., 2021). To some extent, it succeeded, but because not everyone was technologically literate, it was also a restricted means to earn money. Many people were frustrated by consumers who refused to pay or blocked them after utilizing their services digitally. Worst of all, they couldn't even complain about it anywhere. Furthermore, people who have a steady employment and have openly recognized their sexual orientation and workplace choices have been regarded with scorn, shamed, and have been subjected to othering, which they have encountered even before the pandemic.

Khushboo says that at the time of the third wave, when her friends went out to ask for money, the shopkeepers too did not have any money, so what would they give? In many cases, people in the transgender community, especially in newer places, have been driven away by fear and by being labeled as dirty and carriers of infection. Many neighborhoods and buildings had barred entry in their premises. They were seen as potential spreaders. But people living in middle-class and upper-class societies, at other times, hate and fear the hijras, but in their happy life events like marriage or the birth of a child, they are also eager to receive the blessings from transgenders. At such times, they would be asked to dance at the entrance gate of the building, and blessings would be taken from a distance from the window. Moreover, the money received from such events has been very less.

On the other hand, Vijay (25, gay), was working as a ward-boy in the control room; he was happy to get this job. Even though he worked on a contractual basis and demonstrated how skilled he is with an aspiration to get more stable or permanent employment opportunities. He worked for almost a year and a half by putting his life at risk for this hope. But like many other people, he too was fired. Vijay has been at home for the last four months worrying about what to do next. Vijay says,

> (I have) fear of the future … What's next? Unemployment is already high, and it will only increase in covid. Many offices were firing people. I used to cry a lot … why I am not stable yet?

Kiran's words help to elaborate Vijay's worries even more. She says, "When we run out of rations at home, we know what the real problem is. When there is a problem with bhakri, the need for work becomes clearer". She goes on to say that during the pandemic period, the transgender community had a lot of problems with food.

This seems to be a universal trend. In the United States where LGBTIQ groups have legal recognition and more support, research reveals that 30% of people in the LGBTIQ community lost their working hours, and 19% lost their jobs (Moreau, 2020). These numbers are not so irrelevant to the Indian context too, in the consideration of the interrelationships between sexuality and caste, class, education, and ethnicity, it is often visible that the transgenders are the most vulnerable and oppressed groups. The pandemic added to the existing burden by snatching their livelihood options.

As a result, LGBTIQ individuals and their families started using their savings after their earnings stopped. The savings that Shankar (32, gay) saved for his sister's wedding, or the allowance that Vijay got at work, was spent on treatment, medicine, and other essentials. Pinky (27, transwoman) sold off jewelry, which she had bought with hard-earned money, to run the house and to support with food and medicines for her *guru bhai*.[5] Within the first 5 to 6 months, all the savings that were saved for the "difficult times in life" were exhausted, which forced them to take out a loan. When, due to lack of assets and no guarantee of repayment, the banks and other financial institutions refused to lend money, then the loans were taken from relatives, neighbors, or informal structures at high interest rates. With no bank account and no opportunity to save money, most transgender individuals spend their earnings as they earn them.

Making of the Invisibles

For many years in India, the LGBTIQ groups were criminalized under Article 377. They were looked at through the lens of morality, and were considered unnatural and sinful. The Supreme Court's decision in decriminalization of homosexuality is historical but the social acceptance is still a long journey for the community. In the 2011 census, for the first time, the "other" category was added for third gender, in addition to the female and male categories. In this census, only 4.88 lakhs (0.04%) transgenders were recorded in the "other" category (many have argued about the accuracy of the numbers too). Out of these 4.88 lakhs, only 2,500 people had the required identity documents (Thakur, 2020).

In the information age, when data is the new currency, it is important to have a record of one's identity in the formal system. Without these government recognized documents, asserting presence in the policy and schemes is impossible. System's collective apathy is visible in all their actions or inactions. It is far more convenient to profess ignorance than to bear the load of responsibility that will accompany the documentation of this data and this is precisely the system's strategy operates. Thus, sexual minorities are erased from documents/policies/provisions/and decisions.

Community leader from Mumbai Neeta Keni says,

> We don't even have a ration card. The government does not provide any facilities. No ration card, no voting card. Aadhar card is also of the old identity with which we do not identify with anymore. Why even use this as an identity card?

Along with administrative inefficiency, there seems to be a lack of political will to help the transgender community with documentation. The community has been fighting for their existence in government policies and records. When het-eronormativity is seen as the only way of life, and in a culture that exclusively celebrates and supports it, a group with "alternative" sexual identities and sex-ual preferences is quickly labeled as "strange", "outcaste", "invalid", and hence deserving of neglect.

Prior to the pandemic, the existence of the LGBTIQ community was visible in a variety of settings, including NGO programmes, pride events, community meet-ings, public transportation, railway stations, and traffic signals. Accessing these locations meant that members were at least seen in the heteronormative mainstream culture. In the pandemic, whatever limited places that were available were closed down, and even the streets were empty. People were confined at home, caging their identities and existence behind walls.

For many LGBTIQ individuals, disclosing one's sexuality, known as "com-ing out", is not an easy process. Individuals feel insecure to "come out" due to abhorrence, disrespect, shame, harm, and other negative consequences. With larger social acceptance, sensitization, and allyship, the safe spaces can be established.

Many people think it is unnecessary to be "loud" about one's sexuality. Their assertiveness can often seem bold, exaggerated or unnecessary by the majority or heterosexual community. It is ironic that, while the society legitimizes and celebrates "heteronormative" culture through various channels and processes, the sheer actions of identity assertions of LGBTIQ individuals are deemed super-fluous. The contempt that Dalits suffer when they declare their identities by put-ting blue flags on their cars is identical to the contempt that the community faces when they assert their sexual choices and identities with pride during the pride march. "What's the point of heading to the streets to show all of this?" is a question that is frequently voiced privately. In both cases, the identity assertion processes are similar.

However, whereas heteronormative standards are enforced subtly, the minor-ity community must make a concerted effort to stress its place in society in order to affirm its identity. The process of depriving a community of its necessities and rights begins with indifference, concealment, and disregard. Even when a person chooses to accept their identity, it is still labeled as something to be ashamed of. The question of why being so "bold" must be understood in connection to how brave it is. Instead of using the same old, unidimensional, and safer criteria pro-vided to decipher the bold stamp on someone's expression; there should be an anal-ysis of social, economic, and sexual factors which fostered them to attempt these articulations. During the pandemic, where only bodies were the identities when all other identities were hidden, the ways/places to assert one's identity were closed.

Stigma, Discrimination, and Dependency

During colonialism and the imposition of British morality, the Hijra communities in India were stigmatized and criminalised. As a result, fear and hatred towards the community started growing in society. Post-independence, even after several attempts at "mainstreaming", they have remained marginalized and socially unaccepted. The stigma and transphobia are widespread in Indian society.

Homophobia is still prevalent in many countries. In fact, at the beginning of the HIV epidemic, in many countries, the gays were blamed for the spread of HIV, for example, many newspapers carried stories describing HIV as a "gay plague" (Homophobia and HIV, 2015). Similarly to how rumors and disinformation about the Tablighi Jamaat were spread throughout the country in instilling fear and hatred in people (Zaffar & Abdulla, 2021), covert attempts to instill fear and hatred in the LGBTIQ community have persisted for many years.

Much research has revealed that human rights declarations are frequently violated in India's LGBTIQ population. According to a study on human rights violations against transgender people (PUCL 2004), prejudice and homophobia have manifested themselves in violence in public spaces, police stations, and homes. Discrimination also extends to denial of educational and employment opportunities, further weakening their social, economic, and political power and participation.

During the pandemic, many people were confined in their houses with their abusive partners resulting in a rise in violence. The feeling of being shunned by society was further reinforced. All spaces that could offer support were no longer were accessible or were closed.

LGBTIQ communities' experiences of discrimination and segregation are diverse. These experiences are also influenced by socioeconomic, political, and geographic factors. The pandemic added additional discriminatory factors resulting in increased direct and indirect discriminations. While registering for the covid vaccine, or even on the certificate, there was a "other" option instead of the word "transgender", for many community leaders this was an attempt to make this distinction of "other" even clearer. However, even within the existing system, there has been no attempt to comprehend and accommodate the demands of sexual minorities.

Many shared the discrimination in the COVID care centers; experiences of disrespect, shame, fear, and violations of confidentiality were frequently observed across our interactions. For instance, Kunal, a 43-year-old PLHIV gay man, shares his experience at the vaccination center.

the medical or vaccination centre required me to fill out and sign a consent form during the second dose of immunisation. On the consent form, I mentioned my pre-medical condition of being PLHIV. My consent document was verified by a medical executive at the vaccination clinic, and they denied a second vaccination due to my pre-medical health issues. They required that I produce the doctor's medical certificate. Because of my HIV condition, they denied the second immunization dose. I went to express my worry to the senior official. They refused to reimburse our payment too. After many arguments and fighting, we finally received the second immunization dosage.

It was frustrating. It is clearly mentioned in the government instructions that people with pre-medical health conditions should get vaccinations first. But in our instance, we had to observe a variety of norms and policies. The behavior of the health personnel made me feel helpless, discriminated against, and hurt during the vaccination process.

Due to such experiences, many community members are hesitant to participate in testing, vaccination, and take full treatment resulting in a low adherence rate. To make COVID treatment safe and inclusive, some activists demand a separate LGBTIQ isolation ward and care unit (Parveen, 2020).

Despite the fact that the virus might infect anyone, poor slum dwellers, religious minorities, and LGBTIQ communities were suspected as possible virus spreaders (Mumbai: At Dharavi, a Drop in Cases but Rise in Social Stigma, 2020; Posters Crop up in Hyderabad Inciting Violence against Transgenders, Blame Them for Spreading Coronavirus, 2020; Tablighi Jamaat: The Group Blamed for New Covid-19 Outbreak in India – BBC News, 2020)

The aspects of perceived cleanliness and hygiene play a role in one's identity and how community experience marginalization. Whether it's poor people living in rich localities, the Dalits in the "upper caste" community, or individuals living in rural areas who are constantly rejected by the city, they don't fit into the city's image of cleanliness. Hijras, kothis, and transgender people perhaps do not conform to the concept of standards of hygiene and cleanliness and are hence regarded as dirty, disgusting, and unfit. During the pandemic, the focus was on maintaining cleanliness. The LGBTIQ community members were considered as infection spreaders.

Mental Health Is an Unreachable Privilege

Research studies revealed that many LGBTIQ individuals encounter actual, perceived, and internalized stigma. They experience a lack of family acceptance, peer, family, and partner violence, institutional violence and harassment in schools and workplaces, and discrimination in employment, housing, and health care services (Ganju & Saggurti, 2017, Mal, 2018). However, very few individuals have access to mental health care. Some transgender people prefer self-medication or private health care over public health care. They delay getting mental health treatment due to stigma, fear of unwelcome medical procedures and prior negative experiences. Perpetual violence faced by LGBTIQ persons, purposeful discrimination against them, and lack of knowledge and sensitivity by health care providers may all be contributory health care concerns (Wandrekar, & Nigudkar, 2020). Individuals in the LGBTQI community frequently experience additional types of stigmas, including stigma associated with being HIV positive, stigma associated with sex work, and stigma associated with mental health disorders.

The pandemic, subsequent lockdowns, and isolations added more psychological burden to the people. The experience of non-acceptance, stress, fear, helplessness, insecurity, all has adverse effects on mental health. Many LGBTIQ members reported feelings of anger, irritability, humiliation, and dejection. Stigma of sexuality is often internalized in LGBTIQ society as a result of society's persistent rejection and stigmatization. It further leads to several mental distress and self-harm (Heslin & Hall, 2021, Ganju & Saggurti, 2017).

Individuals in the LGBTIQ community are fighting many battles on the mental health front. Bhushan (37 years, non-binary) says,

> My family knows about my sexuality but still they insist on getting me married. I live alone in Mumbai but I decided to not even think of going home in the pandemic. Because the family would have again pestered me to marry and I would have had a lot of stress on my mind.

This stress can result in feelings of loneliness, worry, insecurity, and even some severe mental disorders. Addiction, self-harm, and poor eating and sleeping habits are all linked to anxiety, sadness, and suicidal ideation. For the LGBTIQ community, places to get mental health support are less. Few NGOs provide such help in cities, but accessing them becomes difficult for closeted individuals. On the other hand, such spaces are rare to find in rural parts. There was a fear of getting infected with COVID, but at the same time, there was a lot of stress due to a lack of food, safety, unemployment, and other survival challenges.

Khushboo (26 years, transgender) puts this fear and insecurity into words. She says,

> I was wondering how will the days go by or when will the treatment be done, will it be cured or not, it is only one year now, and how many years will go on?" How will one live? Rich people will live their life anyways. Poor people who earn daily and eat daily, how will they live? How can those who are even poorer live after that? Even those who are distributing now, will share for one time, they will share two times, if they exhaust their supplies, where will they share from?

During the pandemic, even the NGO-run counseling centers were closed. Many online helplines sprung up. However, because it was easier and familiar to contact the center for direct assistance, these helplines were not widely accepted at first. However, in the second wave, both the need for and acceptability of these helplines grew. Pradip (28 years, bisexual man) says,

> Before, I didn't talk to anyone in the neighbourhood. I connected with them due to the lockdown. Then I started mingling more with them. Then people started making fun of my gestures, behaviour and speech.

Pradip knew about the discriminations because many started ridiculing him. But many other community members do not even realize that they are being discriminated against. At home, in school-college, at work, in public places, even in digital spaces, the discrimination is constant. Most of the time it is ignored or not noticed. Teasing in someone's name, verbal abuse, violence, and sexual violence are all considered minor. Due to lack of awareness and open discussion, many don't even don't feel the need for reporting it.

The deeply rooted homophobia and transphobia further enable this discrimination. The effect on the mental health of the community cannot be seen in isolation. It is the outcome of a variety of other injustices, in addition to the COVID pandemic. Therefore, temporary and short-run intervention is ineffective for addressing mental health conditions of the community. In addition, it is essential to broaden the psychological lens from a narrow pathological to a more comprehensive psychosocial lens. Understanding the collective influence of a person's caste, religion, class, age, ability, and gender lagging on their mental health is critical for the creation of effective policies and interventions.

Online Solace

"After the dinner, while my wife was working in the kitchen, I used to go to the bedroom and make video calls to my friend. Although we couldn't see each other, we chatted a lot on video calls, sang songs. I used to dance too." Said Sujit, 40, is not "out" to his family. He had to go to the office every day even during the COVID pandemic but could not meet his friends and partner. Sujit says that he felt lonely and needed someone's support.

During the pandemic, people could not meet in person so all the relations moved online. Work-from-home started with the closure of the workplace and with it came the habit of using online software. Learning this new medium was difficult but necessary for everyone. However, the number of those who could not read or write was higher in the transgender community. But as Sujit says, many began to get acquainted with the online world.

Prateek, a 30-year-old resident of Mumbai who describes himself as a gay sex-worker, says,

I used to do sex work. But suddenly COVID stopped everything. I was able to use mobile, and speak basic English. So I started my business online. The difficulties that come with doing real business are the same. People did not pay for the services, they abused too when they were asked for money.

The incidences of cyberbullying, rejection, and fraud were common on digital spaces too. People who used WhatsApp only for voice notes started experimenting with other social media applications like Instagram, Facebook, Zoom, and Google Meet. Many of them were comfortable using video calls too. We observed that in this period, people were forced to learn digital skills and use technology as a matter of necessity or inevitability, and that this led to an increase in familiarity with the digital world.

Home is seen as a claustrophobic environment by many. At home, it's difficult to freely express one's identity; however, one can experience freedom and a sense of belonging by being in an LGBTIQ group. But all of these outside areas were closed, and the online medium became the focal point of all desires and aspirations.

It is important to note that rising digital literacy is the result of inevitability rather than government, educational, or purposeful initiatives.

Because of illiteracy, poverty, different priorities, and lack of digital skills and gadgets, the voices of those on the periphery remain unheard also in digital spheres. It is great that, now at least, the voices of the poor, sexual minorities, and the underprivileged are beginning to be heard, but it also raises an issue of privacy and safety. The internet space may be dangerous for a group that has kept their sexual identity and interests largely private. (Abreu & Kenny, 2017, Anti-Cyber Bullying Campaign for the LGBTQIA+ Community, 2019).

The use of dating apps has also increased as it is not possible to meet in person. But this caused a greater risk to privacy. Mahesh, 39, a gay man says, "I didn't use the dating app because there were a lot of people from the neighborhood who were on it. It was too risky for me to use the app because they would find out about my sexual orientation". Although Mahesh made this decision, many decided to continue using it as they could not bear the loneliness.

In addition, various types of helplines, support groups, and community engagement sites were moved online. Learning digital skills was important to access that.

Ajit, 40 says, "I could survive because I had mobile with me. Mobile has become a companion when living alone or with family. With a mobile phone, I could always pick up the phone and talk to anyone. This helped a lot to reduce the stress on the mind".

Although marginalized groups' presence has risen in the digital realm, how significant their voice ius in this wide environment needs to be analysed carefully. The ensuing digital violence might unpack the new layers of digital marginalization.

Role of Community-Based Organizations

We only received assistance from non-governmental organizations such as the Humsafar Trust and United Way Mumbai. No political leader or official came forward to help us. The Rs. 1500 announced by the government has never been delivered. On the contrary, we assisted one another. Through our organization, we could assist other small transgender groups,

Leader of the transgender community in
Mumbai

During the pandemic, community-based organizations (CBOs) and non-governmental organizations (NGOs) were the first to respond to the hardships of LGBTIQ people. They worked tirelessly on everything from ration distribution to the provision of buses for migrants, public awareness, helplines, anti-violence assistance-guidance, and the organizing of vaccination camps.

Few government and state plans were provided during the pandemic period, especially for transgenders. These include the Pradhan Mantri Garib Yojana, which provides transgenders with three months of free rations and a one-time direct financial transfer of a thousand rupees, COVID-19 special economic package, and Atmanirbhar Bharat Yojana. The State governments of Odisha and Jammu & Kashmir have also made general initiatives available to transgender individuals. Aside from this, there were also particular schemes made accessible for transgenders, such as the NISD,[6] which provided a one-time cash award of 1,500 rupees, and states such as Tamil Nadu and Kerala provided food, lodging, and cash payment support to transgender individuals (TGs) (Chakrapani et al., 2021).

The majority of these programs and assistance services require transgender people to have valid legal identification documents. In 2020, only 5,711 transgender individuals received a bank transfer of 1,500 rupees and 1,229 received ration supplies (Raman, 2021). This is because many of the individuals do not have the required identity documents. Despite all such complications, NGOs supported the community with all their limited support. There were a few schemes and support was provided by Central and State governments, but most were limited to the cities and excluded rural populations or people who had migrated back to their villages.

To alleviate vaccination apprehension, the Humsafar Trust in Mumbai launched the "*Samaj*" (understanding) poster series. The posters were released in regional languages via WhatsApp and other social media platforms. Furthermore, under the title of "Vaccinated with Pride", special vaccination programs for transgender people were established. Similar camps were arranged in Delhi and other cities by social organizations and government authorities.

The number of transgenders who have been vaccinated as of the 3 February 2022 (CoWIN Dashboard, n.d.) is 3,98,098—up dramatically from 20,269 on 17 May 2021. This growth depicts collaborative partners' efforts and lobbying initiatives to improve vaccine access.

During the stricter lockdown, community people in the neighborhoods seemed to be prepared to deal with such adverse situations. They showed solidarity and came forward for support. Some actively participated in relief efforts, sometimes donating food by mortgaging their own valuables. Support was generated for medicines and treatment costs. One of the members shared with us,

> I assisted my friend in delivering ART drugs to the LGBTQ community members. Some of the community required immediate assistance, such as food rations and money assistance. I spent my day delivering life-saving medications to the community members. It allowed me to go out of the house and work for the community.

One transgender person also narrated how she was provided with food by neighbors and was also offered their mobile phone to be used for a full week. Such incidents of solidarity bring hope. Aayesha, (27 years, Hijra" said,

> [The] pandemic affected everyone. I started begging on the street but no one could give anything because they too had lost income. I thought everyone was in a similar situation, fearful and helpless. It was painful to see around

but I kept doing what I could. With the help of other friends we organised grains and food for the poor, the stock was insufficient. But I saw people sharing their grains with others. And that was the moment I felt so happy.

These various narratives underscore the grassroots solidarity and support which is frequently seen in many disastrous situations in history. How we can understand them better and build on them is a significant question.

Way Out for Tomorrow

These observations are illuminating, but far from complete. Our participants, which consisted primarily of gay, bi-sexual, non-binary, and transgender people living in urban settings, do not reflect the experiences of lesbians, intersex, and other queer persons. Those voices would have added more aspects to these discussions. Given this, the following are a few recommendations that emerged out of the interactions.

Members mentioned, exclusion and discrimination will be controlled, and community members' safety will be maintained if police, healthcare professionals, administrative, and judicial staff are sensitized. At the same time, it's essential to ensure that everyone in the community has equal access to all services, vaccines, mental health support, and schemes. Recognizing the unique needs of vulnerable groups within the LGBTIQ community, such as the homeless, elderly, people living with HIV, and those with disabilities, and making housing, geriatric care, and therapy-medicine assistance easily and safely accessible is necessary. Providing social security benefits is another way to safeguard the groups. To address mental health concerns, members urgently demand free, secure, and confidential mental health support systems staffed by sensitive and skilled professionals. The existence of an ecosystem for LGBTIQ individuals is critical for emotional well-being. Supportive family and friends, co-workers, therapists, and social allies all contribute significantly to community members' self-acceptance and self-esteem.

Many highlighted that the community-based organizations (CBOs) and non-governmental organizations (NGOs) played a significant role in relief response. With their deep community connections and ability to develop appropriate community interventions, they proved to be strong partners and hence more collaborative programs and research work should be initiated. Such partnerships can provide safety, confidentiality, and trust in the awareness, vaccination, and advocacy campaigns along with helping in assisting in necessary documents and connecting individuals with schemes and other benefits.

To empower community members by generating authentic data and advocating for their human rights based on evidence, policy papers must contain an analysis of marginalized communities; collaborative work in this area would also be beneficial. Even the judiciary and legislature must collaborate to provide equitable access to education, employment, social security, and other services for LGBTIQ persons. Collaborative, community-driven, and equity-based approaches and interventions are critical for ensuring LGBTIQ persons' human rights protection.

Conclusion

The LGBTIQ community has been disproportionately affected by the COVID-19 Pandemic. It has had an influence on their physical and mental health, and their social-economic situation. The individuals were already living in insecure conditions, with limited access to education, health care, employment, and legal protection. The virus and ensuing economic lockdowns have exacerbated the communities' predicament by raising health hazards, unemployment, poverty, economic issues, and violence. Transgenders, kothi, hijra, and the PLHIV are the most marginalized within the LGBTIQ community; the pandemic has rendered them even more vulnerable. Unemployment, discriminations, violence, lack of support groups, and inequity in immunization and relief support have all left a negative mark on the community. It is an urgent need for collaborative and progressive support in ensuring equity in support. The rights-based, inclusive, and community-driven future strategies need to be put in place for protecting them from further harm.

Notes

1 Names of all the participants are changed. All the interviews were done in Mumbai, some in-person and some over the phone.
2 The term transgender refers to people whose gender identity and expression are different from social expectations of their biological sex at birth.
3 In the Indian subcontinent, "Hijra" or "Kinnar" are transgender, intersex, or eunuch people who live in communities that follow a kinship system. They are officially recognized as "third gender".
4 "Doli Badhai" is a Hindi word for a task which is performed by a few hijra groups to celebrate and give blessings to families on special occasions like marriage or the birth of a newborn.
5 Guru bhai/behen is a peer member of the hijra family who is also a disciple of the same guru (mother) and hence called a brother or sister.
6 National Institute of Social Defence.

References

Abreu, R. L., & Kenny, M. C. (2017). Cyberbullying and LGBTQ Youth: A Systematic Literature Review and Recommendations for Prevention and Intervention. *Journal of Child & Adolescent Trauma*, 11(1), 81–97. Retrieved February 15, 2022, from https://doi.org/10.1007/s40653-017-0175-7

Anti-cyber Bullying Campaign for the LGBTQIA+ Community. (2019, July 10). *The Times of India*. Retrieved February 15, 2022, from https://timesofindia.indiatimes.com/city/chennai/anti-cyber-bullying-campaign-for-the-lgbtqia-community/articleshow/70159543.cms

Alliance, I. (2021, July 30). Discussion on Improving Vaccine Equity in India. *YouTube*. Retrieved February 15, 2022, from https://www.youtube.com/watch?v=mMDkFpZMF5U

Banerjee, D., & Nair, V. S. (2020). "The Untold Side of COVID-19": Struggle and Perspectives of the Sexual Minorities. *Journal of Psychosexual Health*, 2, 113–120. https://doi.org/10.1177/2631831820939017

Bowleg L. (2020). We're Not All in This Together: On COVID-19, Intersectionality, and Structural Inequality. *American Journal of Public Health*, 110, 917. Retrieved February 15, 2022, from https://ajph.aphapublications.org/doi/10.2105/AJPH.2020.305766

Chakrapani, V., Newman, P. A., Sebastian, A., Rawat, S., Shunmugam, M., & Sellamuthu, P. (2021). The Impact of COVID-19 on Economic Well-Being and Health Outcomes Among Transgender Women in India. *Transgender Health*. Retrieved February 19, 2022 from https://doi.org/10.1089/trgh.2020.0131

CoWIN Dashboard. (n.d.). CoWIN Dashboard. Retrieved February 7, 2022, Retrieved February 19, 2022 from https://dashboard.cowin.gov.in/

Das, M., & Nair, S. (2020, May 25). Transgenders in Mumbai Left with No Straws to Clutch at | Mumbai News - Times of India. Retrieved February 19, 2022, from https://timesofindia.indiatimes.com/city/mumbai/transgenders-in-mumbai-left-with-no-straws-to-clutch-at/articleshow/75961323.cms

Ganju, D., & Saggurti, N. (2017). Stigma, Violence and HIV Vulnerability Among Transgender Persons in Sex Work in Maharashtra, India. *Culture, Health & Sexuality*, 8, 903–917. Retrieved February 15, 2022, from https://doi.org/10.1080/13691058.2016.1271141

Heslin, K. C., & Hall, J. E. (2021). Sexual Orientation Disparities in Risk Factors for Adverse COVID-19–Related Outcomes, by Race/Ethnicity — Behavioral Risk Factor Surveillance System, United States, 2017–2019. *MMWR. Morbidity and Mortality Weekly Report*, 5, 149–154. https://doi.org/10.15585/mmwr.mm7005a1

Homophobia and HIV | Avert. (2015, July 20). Avert. Retrieved February 15, 2022, from https://www.avert.org/professionals/hiv-social-issues/homophobia

Mal, S. (2018). The Hijras of India: A Marginal Community with Paradox Sexual Identity. *Indian Journal of Social Psychiatry*, 1, 79. Retrieved February 15, 2022, from https://doi.org/10.4103/ijsp.ijsp_21_17

Moreau, J. (2020, May 12). LGBTQ People Face Higher Unemployment Amid Coronavirus Pandemic, Survey Finds. *NBC News*. Retrieved February 15, 2022, from https://www.nbcnews.com/feature/nbc-out/lgbtq-people-face-higher-unemployment-amid-coronavirus-pandemic-survey-finds-n1205296

Newman, P. A., Chakrapani, V., Williams, C., Massaquoi, N., Tepjan, S., Roungprakhon, S., Akkakanjanasupar, P., Logie, C., & Rawat, S. (2021). An eHealth Intervention for Promoting COVID-19 Knowledge and Protective Behaviors and Reducing Pandemic Distress Among Sexual and Gender Minorities: Protocol for a Randomized Controlled Trial (#SafeHandsSafeHearts). *JMIR Research Protocols*, 12, e34381. Retrieved February 15, 2022, from https://doi.org/10.2196/34381

Pandya, A., & Redcay, A. (2021). Impact of COVID-19 on Transgender Women and Hijra: Insights from Gujarat, India. *Journal of Human Rights and Social Work*. Retrieved February 15, 2022, https://doi.org/10.1007/s41134-021-00184-y

Parveen, S. (2020, March 17). Coronavirus: LGBT Community Demands Separate Isolation Wards. *ANI News; ANI*. Retrieved February 15, 2022, from https://www.aninews.in/news/national/general-news/coronavirus-lgbt-community-demands-separate-isloation-wards20200318040746/

Peoples' Union for Civil Liberties-Karnataka. (2004). Human Rights Violation Against Transgender Communities. Retrieved February 15, 2022, from http://ai.eecs.umich.edu/people/conway/TS/PUCL/PUCL%20Report.html

Raman, S. (2021, June 11). Transgenders Can't Get State Benefits as Most Official Data Ignores "other." Business Standard News; Business-Standard. Retrieved February 15, 2022, from https://www.business-standard.com/article/economy-policy/denied-visibility-in-official-data-transgenders-can-t-access-benefits-121061100148_1.html

Rosario, K. (2020, April 6). COVID-19 Lockdown: Transgender Community Pushed Further to the Margin. *The Hindu*. Retrieved February 15, 2022, from https://www.thehindu.com

/news/cities/mumbai/covid-19-lockdown-transgender-community-pushed-further-to-the
-margin/article31265535.ece

Shaikh, Z. (2016, September 13). Mumbai Paperclip: 'Most Transgenders in City Are
Migrants' | Cities News, The Indian Express. *The Indian Express*. Retrieved February
15, 2022, from https://indianexpress.com/article/cities/mumbai/mumbai-paperclip-most
-transgenders-in-city-are-migrants-3028194/

Tablighi Jamaat: The Group Blamed for New Covid-19 Outbreak in India - BBC News.
(2020, April 2). *BBC News*. Retrieved February 15, 2022, from https://www.bbc.com/
news/world-asia-india-52131338

Thakur, J. (2020, April 6). Coronavirus Has Compounded the Ostracisation of LGBTQ
Community. *The Wire*. Retrieved February 13, 2022, from https://thewire.in/lgbtqia/
coronavirus-lgbtq-rights

Wandrekar, J. R., & Nigudkar, A. S. (2020). What Do We Know About LGBTQIA+ Mental
Health in India? A Review of Research From 2009 to 2019. *Journal of Psychosexual
Health*, 2(1), 26–36. Retrieved February 15, 2022, from https://doi.org/10.1177
/2631831820918129

Zaffar, H., & Abdulla, S. (2021, March 25). *Tablighi Jamaat Men India Held for 'Spreading
COVID' Share Ordeal | News | Al Jazeera*. Breaking News, World News and Video
from Al Jazeera; Al Jazeera. Retrieved February 11, 2022, from https://www.aljazeera
.com/news/2021/3/25/tablighi-jamaat-members-held-for-spreading-covid-stuck-in-india

4 Sanitary Workers in Mumbai Metropolitan Region During the COVID-19 Pandemic

Nikhil Vilas Gawai and Aparna Ashok Phadke

Introduction

In the COVID-19 pandemic, it was probably "sanitisation" that emerged as the only feasible solution to save oneself from contacting the COVID-19 infection. It was a peculiar turn in everyday life where everything and anything needed to be sanitized—publics spaces, public transport, office spaces, residential spaces and so on. In a region like Mumbai Metropolitan Region (MMR), where the density of the population is 4764 persons per square kilometres (Census, 2011, Sharma, 2019, Bose, 2020) the urban local bodies had anticipated a community spread of COVID-19 infections. Sanitation emerged to be the preventive measure to control the spread in public spaces and personal residences. These were the sanitary workers who were put to the work of sanitation of public spaces. In a major proportions these were the temporarily hired sanitary workers who were mostly engaged without much of the safety precautions. They faced an immense pressure to keep the public and personal spaces cleaned and sanitized. The voluminous work exposed the workers to tremendous physical labor, mental stress, and exertion. The health emergency compelled the workers to be on their toes and always available to deal with any public emergency. The health workers too risked their lives and still continued to work in highly dangerous conditions.

In spite of their major contribution in pandemic management, the sanitary workers remained highly neglected and had to struggle to even get basic minimum facilities. Their hard work and dedication went unnoticed when their counterparts were appreciated and incentivised.

The structured ignorance towards sanitary workers has been long built. It has a context of caste and dignity of labor. Sanitation is not considered a white collar job. Rather it is considered one of the low and indecent employments. Historically, specific communities were imposed with the work of sanitation. So the analysis of sanitary workers in the present reference of COVID-19 cannot be completed without understanding the historical background of development in terms of socio-economic and cultural context. It needs to be noted that there has always been a caste angle to the work of sanitation. Specific sub-communities of Scheduled Caste (SC) have been involved in the work of public sanitation for centuries as part and parcel of occupation-based caste hierarchy (Ketkar, 1990, Karade, 2008). Cleaning and

DOI: 10.4324/9781003304517-6

sanitation were one of the key services expected to be offered by them to the rest of society (Ambedkar, 1946, Ghurye, 1961, Ganth, 2007, Iswalkar, 2017). They are "destined" to remain sanitary workers and "untouchables" for the impurity in their blood that was by birth (Ganth, 2007). It would be interesting to note that the occupational fixity of SCs as sanitary workers continued post-independence and the post-globalization period as well. The reservations in government recruitments meant for mainstreaming the downtrodden and backward classes, appeared to be the Class IV category for the SC community. In the Class IV category too, most of the SCs were absorbed as sanitary workers. The condition of sanitary workers worsened in the post-globalization period as the social (occupational) fixity got associated with contractual basis appointments of the younger SC population as sanitary workers in public utilities and sectors. Similar pattern could be drawn from the private and corporate sector establishments where about 70% of the staff in housekeeping and sanitation belong to the SC community.

According to the report of the Working Group on the Empowering of Scheduled Castes, over 113,450 job opportunities were lost by the SCs in the Central Government during the period 1992–97 (Thimmaiah, 2005). Similar conditions have been observed in all State Government. The New Economic Policy restructured the conditions of economic slavery and increased dependence of the SC community, leading them to vulnerable life situations with reference to livelihood and economic status in general, and sanitary workers in particular. The correlation of caste and sanitation work is evident across all states in India (Department of Social Justice and Empowerment, 2021). For example, in Coal India Limited and its subsidiaries, in group D (ESK), the percentage of SC without *Safai Kamgar* (SK) (Sanitary Workers) is 19.71%. After inclusion of *Safai Kamgar* (SK) the same percentage touches 99.36% which is almost 100%. The data clearly indicates how there has been 100% reservation of SCs in public sanitation jobs.

The working and living conditions of sanitary workers have been pathetic as they have to deal with various kinds of waste and disposal of waste. They have always been exposed to unhygienic environments. Low salary/daily wages/contract-based income, no or limited safety gear, lack of facilities in work places, health risks and hazards, and manual scavenging are some of the many problems that sanitary workers face daily. At a personal level, lower income, lack of access to various public and government facilities, social stigma, lower levels of education, lack of banking and financial facilities, and lower quality of facilities and social infrastructure are some of the stark issues they face. The situation of sanitary workers is unchanged or, in fact, deteriorating but challenges and complexities at work are getting much more complicated with increasing amounts of waste generation. In the post-globalization era, the amount of waste generated in urban India has been accelerating with the rise in consumerism and a tendency towards purchasing packaged goods. The estimated total waste generated in India has increased at a rate of 1.3% per annum which is 147,613 metric tonnes of solid waste generated per day (Swachh Bharat Urban, 2020).

The COVID-19 pandemic added a huge amount of biomedical and other types of wastes to already existing garbage. Sanitation workers were also termed as "front-liners" during the COVID-19 pandemic in which they had to handle not only all kinds of wastes like masks, PPE kits but also performing the final rites to the dead bodies of COVID positive patients. All the sanitary workers have worked relentlessly in the pandemic situation (Marpakwar, 2021).

Context: Sanitary Workers in Urban India

In the post-globalisation era, there has been a recentralisation of the urbanization process in megacities and their regions. It has become one of the most pertinent issues in contemporary times in India, as the metro and megacities and their regions are expected to experience exponential growth in terms of population. By 2025, 46% of the Indian population is expected to live in million cities, i.e., cities with more than 1 million people. Urbanization is necessarily linked with more generation of solid and other types of waste as urban spaces are spaces of more consumption. The newer forms of consumption accessible in the post-globalization period are responsible for adding to already existing wasts. For example, the packaging waste has emerged as one of the key wastes that contributes to urban solid waste. E-waste is another such category that adds to solid waste (MPCB, 2020).

The recent years have been marked with branding India at a global (politico-economic image building) level. The same includes proposition of one of the schemes like *"Swachcha Bharat"* (Clean India) campaign. The role and responsibilities of sanitary workers have been further highlighted in implementing this policy at various spatial scales with an additional responsibility of waste segregation. The workers were encouraged with a new nomenclature like *"Kachara* (waste) soldiers, warriers",* etc. but without any incentives and benefits.

Mumbai Metropolitan Region (MMR) is not only one of the most populated metropolitan regions in the world but also records the highest density of population in some of its sub-spaces like Dharavi. As per the 2011 census, the population of MMR is 20,998,395 making it one of the top 10 most populated urban agglomerations in the world. Mumbai Metropolitan Region extends over an area of 4355 sq. km. and comprises municipal corporations of Greater Mumbai, Thane, Kalyan, and New Mumbai incorporating 16 municipal towns, 7 non-municipal urban centers, and 995 villages. Recently, the metropolitan region has been expanded further to include more areas from Raigad and Thane districts. As per the 2020 resolution, Mumbai Metropolitan Region has been expanded to cover 6328 sq. km. with a staggering population of 23.6 million in the year 2020 (MMRDA, 2021). With the rapid expansion of MMR, the generation of solid and other types of waste is also on the rise. Table 4.1 shows the generation of solid waste in select cities in MMR for the year 2011. Table 4.1

It can be revealed from the table that there is a 50% rise in solid waste from 2001 to 2011 except Navi Mumbai. Interestingly, there is a simultaneous decrease in the number of sanitary workers in the last three decades in the case of MCGM (Municipal Corporation of Greater Mumbai) from 144,000 permanent sanitary workers to 97,000 permanent sanitary workers. The gap has been partially filled by temporary and contract basis workers. The tremendous pressure on sanitary workers in MMR can be understood from the ratio displayed in the map for select cities. Figure 4.1 indicates the same. Figure 4.1

Table 4.1 Waste Generation in Select Urban Centres in MMR

Year	2001				2011				Percentage increase (2001–11)
City	Population	Per capita waste generation (kg/day)	MSW TPD		Population	Per capita waste generation (kg/day)	MSW TPD		
Greater Mumbai	16,434,386	0.45	7,395.4737		21,660,521	0.51354	11,123.54382		50.41016
Navi Mumbai	81,855	0.474	289		107,884.9	0.540929	58.35804409		–79.8069
Thane	1,261,517	0.390006635	492		1,662,679	0.445076	740.0179872		50.41016
Kalyan-Dombivali	1,193,266	0.358	427		1,572,725	0.408	642		50.41016
Bhiwandi	621,427	0.500	311		819,041	0.571	467		50.41016
Ulhasnagar	472,943	0.357	169		623,339	0.408	254		50.41016

Source: Sustainable Solid Waste Management in India by Ranjith Kharvel Annepu & Nickolas J. Themelis Stanley-Thompson, School of Engineering and Applied Science Columbia University in the City of New York January 10, 2012.

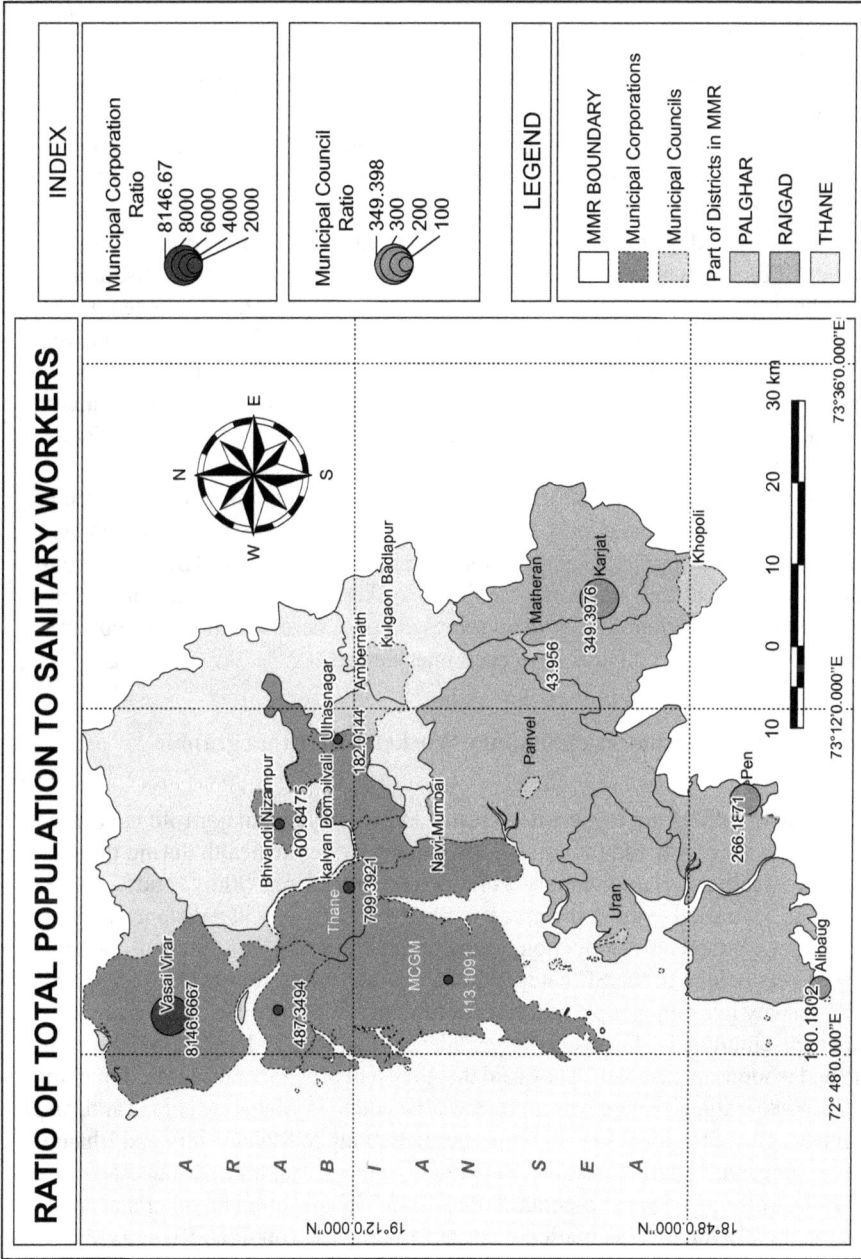

Figure 4.1 Ratio of Sanitary Workers to Total Population. Source: Authors

MCGM being the oldest of all municipal corporations has little better ratio with 1 sanitary worker for 113 people but peripheral corporations show skewed ratios. Vasai-Virar has a ratio of 1:8147. Matheran council has a ratio of 1:44, which is the lowest, and Karjat municipal council has a ratio of 1:349. Annually, 4,616,666 tonnes of municipal waste is generated in MMR (MPCB, 2020). Forty-five percent waste is biodegradable and the remaining waste is non-biodegradable and needs to be disposed either by recycling or through treatment.

The COVID-19 pandemic lead to major amounts of additional biomedical waste. Pre-COVID, the biomedical waste per day used to be around 10 to 12 tonnes in Mumbai. In the second wave, i.e., during March 2021 to July 2021, it increased to 36 tonnes per day in Mumbai (Marpakwar, 2021). This figure expresses the quantity of biomedical waste generated in hospitals. Apart from hospitals, in individual households and quarantine centers, biomedical waste has also been generated in individual centers. The hospital waste contained PPE kits, masks, gloves, various equipment, and dead bodies. Household waste too had masks, gloves, sanitizers bottles, other infected materials like cloths and utensils used by the patients in home quarantine. The same has resulted in affecting the workers physically, socially, and psychologically.

To understand the situation of sanitary workers in general, and in particular during the COVID-19 pandemic, a questionnaire was developed and a survey was conducted in select municipal corporations and councils in MMR. The target group includes permanent and temporary sanitary workers, union leaders, contractors, and office superintendents. Around 50 representatives across 6 municipal corporations and 4 municipal councils have been interviewed.

Narrating the Experiences of Sanitary Workers: An Ethnographic Analysis

The sanitary workers are those who "clean'"and so played a major role in keeping the public spaces sanitized to maintain the quality of public health during the pandemic. Ironically, the same sanitary workers were considered "filthy" and "impure" and hence out casted even in the modern urban systems, kept at a distance by their neighbors with the fear of infection. In the select cities of MMR, most of the sanitary workers belong to the SC category. When asked a question to all the respondents as to why it is only people of the SC community in the work of sanitation, most of them just hummed. The answers were silences and then sighs of despair, age old pain and wounds of casteism. They said that they had probably been been doing this work for generations. There was no foreseeable end to it. Mahar, Mehra, Taral, and Dhegu Megu are the local sub-communities belonging to Maharashtra and Bhangi, Mehtar, Olgana, Rukhi, Malkana, Halalkhor, Lalbegi, Balmiki, Korar, Zadmalli, and Hela are some of the sub-communities from Maharashtra and other states like Gujarat, mostly found in sanitation work in Mumbai Metropolitan Region (MMR) (Department of Social Justice and Empowerment, Ministry of Social Justice and Empowerment, Government of India). A documentary film directed by Mr. Atul Pethe titled as '*Kacharavyuh*' (Garbage Trap) features the condition of sanitary workers in Pune Municipal Corporation. Poet Mr. Dhurandar Mithbaonkar who was a former drainage worker recites his poem in the documentary while expressing the plight of sanitary workers (Pethe, 2007), "With no inkling of the beginning and the end/The living dead me was given birth.../And so I was born.../Had organs just like humans/And so identified as human being/But human just for the sake of recognizing..." (Pethe, 2007).

Most of the sanitary workers were not able to complete their service due to unhealthy and hazardous working conditions. Such vulnerabilities vis-à-vis sanitary workers prevailed in the city like Mumbai which is the financial capital of the state of Maharashtra and records highest revenues. Mr. Prabhu was formerly a sanitation worker and then promoted to a clerical post. He said that more than 70% of "sweepers" or sanitation jobs still belong to the SCs. He said that,

> no other communities were ready to take up the municipal jobs of sanitary workers. In the early 90s who joined as sanitary workers were mainly from SCs community as it was easy to get job security by being permanent in the public sector utility and access to all kinds of government concessions and facilities including residential quarters.

He himself, in spite of having better educational facilities, joined his workplace as a sanitary worker and then got promoted to clerk (Table 4.2, Table 4.3).

When investigated further, it was found that the sanitary workers in MCGM have never been superannuated naturally as they don't live to the age of retirement. Due to their job profile, they get exposed to unhygienic health conditions and various kinds of diseases. The average age of a sanitary worker is 50 and the age of superannuation is 60. They never reach the age of 60. So as a matter of compensation the job goes to the immediate family member only in this department. Ironically, the sanitation department is exclusively reserved for SC candidates. As they die before completing their job tenure, their children are again pushed into similar work even if they are educated and desire to take up other occupations and as a pity case (Lad & Page Committee). Mr. Prabhu was a commerce graduate when he became a sanitation worker and later he got promoted in MCGM as per his education qualification, but such cases are few and every one cannot enjoy such benefits.

Prabhu, while sharing his experience, says that they work in filth, dirt, and absolutely unhygienic and unhealthy conditions. Drainages, gutters, markets, hospitals, public latrines and toilets, slaughter houses, mortuaries, construction debris, heavy metals, radioactive waste, human organs, dead bodies of street animals, domestic wastes, storm water drainage and many more are managed by them. They narrate their experience as they are the living dead who deal with waste every day. Pethe (2007) continues and asks the questions to the mainstream population, "You mashed my whole life/in your filth, your shit.../Scrub me... it will only in filth just filth/Trash, worming and the breath of stink".

The workers said in spite of their contribution towards society, they were considered as social waste by the mainstream society. There has been a social stigma about the sanitation work and workers. Probably, in COVID times, people must

Table 4.2 Distribution of Sanitary Workers as per the Social Category in Select Cities in MMR

Sr.No.	Municipal Corporation	Total Sanitary Workers (Permanent & Contractual)	No. of Sanitary Workers				% of Community Involved		
			Permanent	Salary/Month	Contractual	Salary/Month	SC	OBC	Others
1	Greater Mumbai	110,000	97,000	28,000	13,000	20,000	80	2	18
2	Thane	2,303	2,303	25,000			80	5	15
3	Ulhasnagar	2,780	2,700	23,000	80	12,000	55	30	15
4	Mira-Bhayandar	1,660	60	23,000	1,600	18,000	65	5	30
5	Bhiwandi Nizampur	1,180	1,180	23,000	NA	NA			
6	Vasai-Virar	150	NA	NA	150	8,000	50	20	40

Source: Authors

Table 4.3 Distribution of Sanitary Workers as per the Social Category in Select Cities in MMR

Sr.No.	Municipal Councils	Total Sanitary Workers	Population: Sanitary Worker Ratio	No. of Sanitary Workers				% of Community Involved		
		Permanent & Contractual		*Permanent*	*Salary/ Month*	*Contractual*	*Salary/ Month*	*SC*	*OBC*	*Others*
3	Alibag	111	0.0056	36	19,000	75	10,000	75	5	10
4	Karjat	83	0.0029	23	20,000	60	12,000	90	0	10
6	Matheran	91	0.0228	31	20,000	60	12,000	70	0	30
8	Pen	139	0.0038	47	23,000	92	10,000	85	2	13

Source: Authors

have understood their pain as many of them had to go through the experience of social distancing and isolation that they and their families had been experiencing throughout life. The unorganized workers lead a further difficult and derogatory life due to very less payment and their being dependent entirely on the mercy of contractors. The contractor in Alibaug revealed that the temporary workers don't even have a simple shelter. Homelessness is very common among temporary sanitary workers across MMR. The workers are also not provided with any safety gears. Gloves, gumboots, and other necessary implements are provided once a year. The workers often fail to use these as they are not provided as per their size. Without using the safety gear, they continue to work and get exposed to various kinds of skin, respiratory diseases, and dangerous diseases such as various kinds of cancers. Due to COVID, the situation has temporarily improved and ordinary masks, gloves, and sanitizers were provided to them but they are unsure about similar provisions in the post-COVID period. The health situation of sanitary workers can be revealed through the words of Mithbaonkar. He continues to unveil the distress in the following words, "Look at my lungs, look at my heart, look at my eyes/ search for the complete human body with all its organs/ then you will see how you sucked life out of me" (Pethe, 2007).

The social stigma is too deep and segregates the workers from the rest of the society. The sub-communities of the SC involved in sanitation work are looked down on by not only the mainstream communities but also other sub-communities within SCs. The benefits of reservation in upper income groups are also enjoyed more by the other sub-communities belonging to SCs rather than the ones who are involved in sanitary work. Mithbaonkar questions the conscience of everyone and recalls the principles of humanity to treat the workers as human beings. "How you looked down on me/ just to keep you cleaned/ you forced this work on me/ that put humanity to shame and ruined me.../ Oh people! I suffocate in this living hell/ Living through this death throws/ I died life... I died life.... I died life" (Pethe, 2007).

Sanitary workers, being a part of essential services, were compelled to remain present for the work in COVID-19 pandemic. The workers suffered tremendously as the biomedical waste and other wastes almost tripled in the second wave that emerged as a massive outbreak with 400,000 positive cases every day. These were municipal workers who finally had to deal with all kinds of waste as they were at the tailor end of the collection chain. The workers were affected not only in terms of physical stress but also mental stress. The challenges faced by workers are discussed throughout this chapter.

Nature of Responsibilities and Work Pressure

As informed by all 50 respondents, the new responsibilities were added to the existing work profile of the workers. Collection and disposal of biomedical wastes generated in hospitals, quarantine centers, and home quarantines became a major task for the workers. In addition, the last rites on dead bodies of COVID positive patients were also performed by the municipal workers. In Alibaug municipal council, Mr. Tambe, the contractor, informed that for performing the last rites Rs. 1000 per dead body were given to them as an incentive (interview through google meet on January 15, 2022). But the amount was meager as that would get distributed between the drivers, porters, and other workers who were involved in transporting the dead bodies to the crematory. Those workers who were in direct contact with COVID patients were given PPE kits, N95 masks, gloves, and other necessary items. Most of the workers said that initially, in the first wave, they were not provided with the necessary supplements but due to the interference of and consistent follow up by the union, provision of necessary supplements was arranged for them. In the second wave, sanitary workers were better equipped. The waste collectors, sweepers, and cleaners were provided with ordinary masks when the guidelines released by the Central Government clearly instructed the municipalities to provide N95 masks. The work of sanitisation in the buildings, flats, premises, public spaces, and areas where COVID positive patients were found was also assigned to them. For sanitisation the workers were given some petty amount like Rs. 100. When asked, they were unsure about the source of that money. Thirty percent of workers said that the amount was given by the contractor. Around 25% of workers said that the amount was given by the particular residential society or the family of the patient. The amount was again distributed in the team. For sanitisation work, PPE kits were provided by the contractors to the worker who would spray the infected surface. The rest of the workers would be only be supplied with ordinary masks.

The seperate collection of waste of COVID positive patients and its proper disposal were additional major tasks. Though it was instructed by all the municipalities for people to store the waste of COVID positive patients separately, at least 10% of the population behaved irresponsibly and mixed the garbage. This led to conflicts between the people and workers. In Karjat municipal council, Mr. Gaikwad (interview through telephonic conversation on January 22, 2022), the union leader, said that contractors were good enough and instructed sanitation workers not to collect the garbage of COVID positive patents if not given separately. But all workers were not lucky to have such staunch contractors. Such variation could be seen even ward wise within individual municipalities.

Safety and Security

Mr. Vane, the union leader from MCGM said in an interview (through google meet on January 23, 2022) that the workers were really brave to face the precarious situations, especially in slums. Slums in Mankhurd, Govandi, and Dharavi were the real challenges. The workers had to face people's stubbornness, fury, and what not. In terms of safety from COVID transmissions, the workers were provided ordinary mask when they had the highest risk of getting exposed. Out of the surveyed municipalities, Only MCGM offered a COVID allowance of Rs. 300 per day to all the employees including workers. The allowance was specifically intended for travel and food as they had no options for traveling with the closure of all modes of transportation. MCGM also provided accommodation and food for workers who were staying very far and were not able to commute every day. It was the only corporation that was very prompt on providing the facilities to its workers. Ironically, the same corporation suspended workers for not reporting to their duties in spite of providing facilities. For providing the benefit of health insurance with specific reference to COVID-19, the union pursued the corporation to cover all the employees apart from health workers as beneficiaries of the Pradhan Mantri Garib Kalyan Package insurance scheme (PMGKP) (MoHFW, 2020). MCGM, after continuous persuasion, made its class I to IV employees beneficiaries of the same scheme but did not agree to extend it to sanitary workers. Later on, with the incremental pressure, the same scheme was extended to sanitary workers who were permanent. The temporary workers, however, were excluded. In other corporations, promises have been made to extend this scheme to sanitary workers but not yet implemented. Nonetheless, implementation of the PMGKP insurance scheme has not been very effective. In councils of Alibaug, Karjat, and Pen, such benefits were not offered. In Ulhasnagar municipal corporation, the reason for death of one workers was shown to be other than COVID, though the worker died due to post-COVID complications. The COVID allowance was also not given to the workers, it was just promised. The workers from other corporations remained underprivileged as compared to MCGM. Other than the insurance scheme, no other scheme or welfare policy has been offered to them. The plight of temporary workers is much deeper where they are at the mercy of the contractors. These workers are unaware of what has been provided by the municipalities/urban local bodies or State government to contractors. In spite of the tremendous workload, there was no increase in the salary of the sanitary workers. The casual and medical leaves were suspended for the peak periods in the first, second, and third wave.

Fight and Flight

It was surprising to note that very few sanitary workers suffered from the COVID-19 infection in the second wave. The reports on deaths suggest similar findings. The deaths have been reported in Ulhasnagar, MCGM, Alibaug, and Karjat municipalities but the average death rate has been less than 1%. The highest rate of COVID-19 infections among workers has been reported in Ulhasnagar. In Vasai-Virar, Pen municipalities, the COVID-positivite rate amongst the workers was zero. The families of sanitary workers too suffered due to the transmission of infections. Deaths of family members of sanitary workers due to COVID-19 are again reported to be very few. The reason behind this could be their constant exposure to viral and bacterial infections might have made their immune system strong. Secondly, the testing rate could be very less. Thirdly, the workers were continued to have similar symptoms even in the pre-COVID-19 period. Having such symptoms was quite common in them so most of the time the symptoms were neglected. In Bhiwandi, one women worker died due to black fungus infection.

When asked, like common people, were they not terrified and did they fear the COVID-19 virus, Mr. Gaikwad from Karjat said that for them it was just like a day-to-day job. They are already exposed to more fatal situations and hence have a strong psyche for dealing with such situations. He further added that in normal situations we work because it's our bread and butter. How can we deny work in a medical emergency situation? It is our social responsibility to serve people. We cannot deny work when it is most needed. We have to be loyal to our work and towards society. Similar feelings were expressed by almost all the stakeholders who were interviewed.

The temporary workers who didn't even have proper housing facilities and continue to have temporary shelters in Alibaug, MCGM, Pen, and Thane municipal corporations, expressed their helplessness as the job was the only hope for them during the COVID-19 pandemic. In fact, in many municipalities, more sanitary workers were recruited on a temporary basis. For many unemployed youths, sanitation work emerged as the only source of income in the conditions of total lockdown.

The firm sense of responsibility shown by sanitary workers in COVID-19 times is amazing. In spite of pathetic and discouraging working conditions, they courageously countered all odds.

Psychological and Mental Stress

Mr. Vane, the union leader, shared that the workers had to go through major psychological distress and trauma. During the COVID-19 pandemic, they have witnessed probably some of the worst life experiences that are against humanitarian principles. The fear of COVID-19 transmission and death among the general people and family members of the sanitary workers affected even their filial and family relations. As the sanitary workers also had to cremate the dead bodies of the COVID positive patients, the workers, many times, were told by their parents, wife and other family members to not come back to their own houses as they were considered as 'spreaders'. Such stigmas were faced by the workers every day. In the second wave, the death toll was quite high and the facilities fell short. The same affected the psyche of workers. Many workers were in need of psychological counselling. MCGM, on paper, had offered arrangement of workshops and counselling sessions for workers and employees but in reality nothing could happen. These were the union leaders and members who supported the workers morally and mentally in their own way. Test rest of the urban local bodies never had such planning for sanitary workers.

In the complete lockdown situation, all means and modes of transport were suspended completely in MMR. Many sanitary workers commuted every day to their work places. The suspension of public transport entirely prevented the entire movement of the workers. In the absence of the same, workers were reported to have walked 25 to 40 kilometers a day to reach their workplaces. The temporary workers suffered the most as they could not afford any private mode and means of transport due to their meager salary. With this backdrop, time management became a major issue for them. The late arrival of the workers became a major cause of conflicts between contractor and workers. The conflicts often brought severe consequences like drug abuse, discontinuation of service, depression, and anxiety. One of the sanitary workers committed suicide due to mental torture by the contractor. Another worker committed suicide as his salary for two years was not released by MCGM (Raj, 2021). The workers were discouraged and saddened due to the negligence of the urban local bodies as well as contractors.

The already existing social stigma about sanitation and associated practices of "untouchability" were refaced by the sanitary workers. Their relatives and neighbors continued to outcaste and avoid them because they were involved in COVID-19 related sanitation work. The workers expressed that this was one of the most difficulttime periods to live outcaste. The same adversely impacted people's morals. The family members too faced similar consequences.

The workers also suffered from fear and phobia of the COVID-19 infection as well as vaccines. Mr. Gaikwad from Karjat municipality said that the workers did not want to receive vaccines as there were rumors about the creditability of the COVID-19 vaccines. One of the rumors was about the death of those who are vaccinated within two years of receiving the vaccine. So initially, the workers refrained from getting the vaccine.

Hope and Expectations

All stakeholders expressed that they did their best. What they expect is just words of appreciation. The health workers were appreciated and felicitated publicly by all the authorities – municipality, state, center, non-governmental organizaitons, public forums, and all. According to them, they are always excluded when they are the ones who worked hard at grassroot levels. The entire planning of COVID-19 management was successfully implemented because of their strong support. Is it because the work they do is considered to have no social dignity?

They had to fight to have access all the facilities. Unions were their real hope. Due to the continuous persuasion by the unions, the stakeholders were able to generate pressure on the municipalities and State government to offer them the safety gears, health insurance, and so on.

The workers working on a contract basis from 2005 still have hopes that someday they will be made permanent and all benefits will be offered to them. Unlik, the permanent workers, they don't have any benefits like medical insurance, paid leave, uniforms, and payment slips.

Conclusion

Since the 17th century, the significance of cleanliness has not been understood, not just in terms of the public sanitation and health, but also in terms of personal health and hygiene. In Indian philosophy, there have been various connotations to sanitation, for example, Mahatma Gandhi offers a spiritual and moral dimension to sanitation by emphasizing the cleanliness of mind and soul (Singh, 2022). Buddhist philosophy proposes to apply mindfulness to sanitation by turning it to an opportunity for raising spiritual awareness (Jackie, 2019). Sanitation, hence, as a concept has many philosophical and social shades and those have been attained under different political and cultural regimes. Ironically, the specific sub-castes have been forced into sanitation work for hundreds of years and simultaneously, they are considered as the only polluters in a society that does not clean its own filth and dirt. Mr. Kamble from Thane Municipal Corporation explained that the major cause of SC communities being in the, so called, traditional job of sanitation in spite of having schemes for uplifting them from this, there are no or limited alternatives available for them due to their educational and socio-economic backgrounds. The solution could be on two fronts. First, there is a compulsion on a personal level for the young SC members to fight back against the circumstances that create hurdles in their path to progress, and second is the political will power to implement the schemes and policies effectively to reach the excluded sanitary workers. The social support to sanitary workers and their families can be constructed by involving individuals, trade unions, and non-governmental organizations to offer them trainings and development of modern skills to avoid this traditional employment.

At national level, the Central Government has established the National Safai Karmachari Finance and Development Corporation in the year 1997, offering 8 schemes for providing financial assistance to the sanitary workers who wish to initiate an alternate occupation for themselves (Department of Social Justice and Empowerment, 2021). The loan is offered through a mediating agency at 6% per year where 3% of interest will be given to the mediating agency. The Ministry of Social Justice and Empowerment offers three schemes like pre-metric scholarships to the siblings of sanitary workers, but these schemes are offered to all the reserved categories. There are no specific schemes for the siblings of sanitary workers. There is hardly any update available on the number of beneficiaries specifically with reference to sanitary workers. Besides two schemes, the rest of the schemes are interest-based loan facilities. Interest rate is between 2% to 6% and hence becomes inaccessible to most of the sanitary workers as, after 2005, all the recruitments have been done on a contractual basis. There are hardly any permanent positions filled.

In spite of the schemes and policies, the plight of sanitary workers continues. Political will power, strong community support, involvement of various stakeholders in offering the modern skill sets and education to the siblings, health and family insurance, and permanent positions are some of the key initiatives and urgent interventions that need to be taken up by the municipalities and State governments. The law of minimum wage needs to be effectively implemented for all workers to ensure financial security. Their contribution to society needs to be recognized by offering them more incentives, for example, to achieve the goal of sustainable cities and communities, the sanitary workers can be trained and offered additional incentives for contributing towards city sustainability. Rag pickers can also be networked with sanitary workers. The same will reduce the burden on workers and also offer better earnings to rag pickers. Finally, the trade unions can be involved in the welfare of the workers in a major way by making them as the mediating agencies to reach the benefits of various schemes and policies to the workers.

References

Ambedkar, B. R. (1946). *Who Were the Sudra?* Bombay: Bombay Thacker and Company Limited.

Bose, M. (2020, May 3). *coronavirus-mumbai-metropolitan-region-continues-to-be-concern-area-832966.html*. Retrieved from www.deccanherald.com: https://www.deccanherald.com/national/west/coronavirus-mumbai-metropolitan-region-continues-to-be-concern-area-832966.html

Census of India. (2011). *Census of India.* Census of India.

Department of Social Justice and Empowerment, M. (2021). *socialjustice.nic.in/UserView/index?mid=76750*. Retrieved from socialjustice.nic.in: https://socialjustice.nic.in/UserView/index?mid=76750/ (accessed in December 2021).

Ganth, S. (2007, October 31). *Manu_Smriti_Sanskrit_Text_With_English_Translation*. Retrieved from www.academia.edu: https://www.academia.edu/31478379/Manu_Smriti_Sanskrit_Text_With_English_Translation

Ghurye, G. S. (1961). *Caste, Class and Occupation*. Bombay-7: Popular Book Depot.

Iswalkar, D. (2017, September 27). Social Status of Scheduled Caste Population (N. V. Gawai, Interviewer).

Jackie, J. W. (2019, October 24). *Buddha's Teaching Regarding Cleanliness in Home*. Retrieved from https://shambhalatimes.org: https://shambhalatimes.org/2019/10/24/buddhas-teachings-regarding-cleanliness-in-the-home/

Karade, J. (2008). *Development of Scheduled Castes and Scheduled Tribes in India*. Newcastle: Cambridge Scholars Publishing 15 Angerton Gardens, Newcastle, NE5 2JA, UK British Library Cataloguing in Publication Data A Catalogue Record for This Book Is Available from the British Library.

Ketkar, S. V. (1990). *The History of Castes in India*. Delhi: Low Price Publications.

Marpakwar, C. (2021, August 7). *mumbai/mumbai-daily-bio-waste-halves-to-18-ton-from-may–june-20-covid-peak/articleshow/85116703.cms*. Retrieved from https://timesofindia.indiatimes.com/city/mumbai: https://timesofindia.indiatimes.com/city/mumbai/mumbai-daily-bio-waste-halves-to-18-ton-from-may-june-20-covid-peak/articleshow/85116703.cms

MMRDA. (2021, July 29). *MMRDA*. Retrieved from https://mmrda.maharashtra.gov.in/about-mmr

MoHFW. (2020, June 26). *PMGKP Insurance Extension Letter*. Retrieved from https://www.mohfw.gov.in: https://www.mohfw.gov.in/pdf/PMGKPnsuranceextensionletter.pdf

MPCB. (2020, September 1). *Championing Smart and Sustainable Solid Waste Management in MMR*. Retrieved from https://mpcb.gov.in: https://mpcb.gov.in/wastes-management/municipal-solid-waste

Pethe, A. (Director). (2007). *The Garbage Trap* [Motion Picture].

Raj, S. (2021, December 24). *Mumbai: BMC Worker Dies by Suicide After Not Receiving Pay for 2 Years, BJP Members Protest*. Retrieved from https://www.freepressjournal.in: https://www.freepressjournal.in/mumbai/mumbai-bmc-worker-dies-by-suicide-after-not-receiving-pay-for-2-years-bjp-members-protest

Sharma, S. (2019, February 17). *The Economic Times*. Retrieved from https://economictimes.indiatimes.com/news/politics-and-nation/delhi-could-be-the-worlds-most-populous-city-by-2028-but-is-it-really-prepared/articleshow/68027790.cms?from=mdr

Singh, S. (2022). *Cleanliness Is Next to Godliness −M. K. Gandhi*. Retrieved from https://www.mkgandhi.org: https://www.mkgandhi.org/articles/cleanliness-next-to-godliness.html#:~:text=Gandhi,-%2D%20by%20Dr%20Savita,/ (accessed in 2022).

Swachh Bharat Urban. (2020, Januray). *swachhbharaturban.gov.in/Auth/dsdocumentsfile .aspx?DOCTYPE=922&DOCID=679*. Retrieved from swachhbharaturban.gov.in: http://swachhbharaturban.gov.in/Auth/dsdocumentsfile.aspx?DOCTYPE=922&DOCID =679

Thimmaiah, G. (2005, February 19). *perspectives/implications-reservations-private-sector .html#*. Retrieved from www.epw.in: https://www.epw.in/journal/2005/08/perspectives/ implications-reservations-private-sector.html#

Appendix – I

Questionnaire

Sanitation Workers in the Globalising Metropolitan Region of Mumbai

I: Personal Information

1) Form number & name: _____
2) Geo-location _____
3) Date & time _____
4) Municipal Council / Municipal Corporation / Village
5) Name of the area _____
6) Ward/Name of the area _____
   1) Local name of your area _____
   2) How others address your area _____
   3) What do you write on your postal address?_____
7) What is your name? _____
8) By which name is your community referred _____
9) Family status: single / nuclear / joint family
   1) Single: Individual (Orphan) / Individual (Divorced) / Individual (Widow) / Employment / Education / Run away from home / Other
   2) Nuclear:
   3) Joint family:
   4) Other:
10) No. of members in the family: Below 4 / 5–8 / 9–12 / above 12

II. Access to Social and Physical Infrastructure

11) Give scaling to following facilities as per their availability and accessibility (5 = worst 4 = average 3 = moderate 2 = good 1 = best)

Sr. No.	Name of the facility	Scale for availability (in situ 500 meters)	Scale for accessibility (affordability, reachability)	Scale for livability (quality, quantity)
1	Water			
2	Electricity			
3	Housing			
4	Sanitation			
5	Medical facilities			
6	Nutritious food			
7	Education			
8	Transport			

12) Educational status of the family members: (total no. per category should be written)

Total Number	Uneducated	Up to 4th std.	5th to 7th	8th and 9th	SSC	HSC	Degree		Profess.	Vocational course
							Gradu.	Post Gradu.		
Men										
Women										

13) What are your ancestors / generational occupation?
14) How did you get in to this occupation?
   a. On your own
   b. Traditional
   c. Financial problem
   d. No other opportunity
   e. Petty case
   f. Compensation
   g. Other
   #. If petty case, please explain
   #. If compensation, please explain
15) Is there any difference in your ancestor's occupational social status to your occupational social status? (Y/N)
16) Is it a permanent job or contract? (Y/N)
17) How long has it taken for you to become a permanent employee?
18) What facilities are being provided to you, if you are permanent? (put yes or no beside each item)
   a) Hand gloves
   b) Equipment
   c) Sanitizers and soaps
   d) Medical facilities and subsidies
   e) Health insurance
   f) Any other
19) If you are a contractual employee (put yes or no beside ach item)
   a) Monthly income fluctuations as per the number of days attended duty
   b) Basic safety gears like hand gloves, equipment, etc.
   c) Sanitizers and soaps
   d) Medical facilities
   e) Health insurance
   f) Any other
20) What are the challenges faced by you in your job?
21) Since when the yearly or monthly tenure basis appointment have started?
22) Is the salary enough for you?

23) Are you working additionally to your current sanitation job on a wage or part time basis?
24) Is there any job security? (Y/N)
    1.   if yes, type of security?
    2.   if no, what kind of security you demand from the institution?
25) Largely, who are the people who join as sanitation workers?
26) What is the life expectancy of a sanitation worker?
27) What are the new challenges that you are facing after globalization in terms of
    Types of waste generated
    The practices of waste handling
    Amount of waste generated
    Waste segregation
    Cleaning and sanitation facilities
    Attitudes of common people
    Attitudes of municipal corporations/councils/panchayats
    Any other
28) Do you support the scheme of the government to appoint a son or daughter as a death compensation? (Y/ N)
29) Would you like your children to continue in a similar job profile?
30) When the new recruitments are taking place, what is the caste identity of the applicants?
31) Which applicants are finally recruited, especially in terms of caste?

III Social Status and Position

32) Are there any social welfare programs organised for you? (Y/N)
    If yes, what are those?

33) Are there any citizen's groups working for your welfare (Y/N)?
    If yes, what are those?

34) Are there any NGOs working for your welfare (Y/N)?
    If yes, what are those?

35) Does the government offer any special welfare schemes? (Y/N)
    If yes, what are those?

36) I sthere any union in your institution? (Y/N)
    If yes, what kind of rights have been ensured by the union to you?

    What are the issues the union is fighting for?

IV COVID 19 Pandemic and Status of Sanitary Workers

37) What kind of hazards do you face frequently?
    1.   Natural (eg.) _____
    2.   Accidental (eg.) _____
    3.   Man-made (eg.) _____

38) During hazardous conditions are you called for work? (Y/N)
    1. if yes what kind of job it would you be to perform? _____
39) Immediately after the hazard are you called for work? (Y/N)
    1. if yes, is it planned work or unplanned?
40) How many extra hours do you work during hazards?
41) Are the authorities going to pay extra money for your work? (Y/N)
    1. if yes, how much extra money would they pay to you?
    2. If not, how have these extra hours have been reflected in your career?
42) State what kind of difference you could observe vis-à-vis your work pressure in terms of?

	Pre-COVID-19 pandemic situation	During COVID-19 pandemic situation
Work hours		
Type of wastes		
Responsibilities		
Monetary compensation for extra work		
Health issues		
Attitudes of people		
Attitudes of authorities		
Family reaction		
Any other		

43) During the COVID-19 pandemic, were you provided with all the facilities to perform your daily work with COVID-19 precautions?
44) Can you tell us what was the work scenario during COVID-19?
45) What were the challenges you faced while working during the COVID-19 pandemic?
46) Can you tell us why you are called COVID-19 warriors?
47) When you went for door-to-door cleaning or waste collecting during the pandemic and tracing the COVID-19 patients at the collection locations, what were the difficulties you experienced? Can you narrate some experiences which were positive and some which were negative?
48) We heard that during the pandemic you lost many of your co-workers/colleagues? Can you tell us something about that?
49) What are your demands from the government to improve your conditions?
50) Can you tell us how one can apply to become a sanitary worker? How does the selection happen?
51) During the COVID-19 pandemic, how did urban local bodies perceive your job as a sanitary worker?
52) What kind of training did you get as a sanitary worker in general and during the pandemic? Can you tell us something about it?
53) How do your family members perceive the job of a sanitary worker? Did they worry about the risk involved in it during the COVID-19 pandemic?
54) As the government said that all health workers will get first preference in vaccination, did you and other sanitary workers that you know of get vaccinated?

5 Epistemological Crisis of Performing Theater in Times of COVID-19

Omkar Bhatkar

How hard is it, when everything encourages us to sleep, though we may look about us with conscious, clinging eyes, to wake and yet look about us as in a dream, with eyes that no longer know their function and whose gaze is turned inward.

- Antonin Artaud, 1958

In February 2019, the world was gloomily struck by the pandemic called COVID-19. The only way to live with this pandemic was through social distancing or physical distancing. The world was facing several crises, be it medical, agrarian, migration, or financial deficit. Crushed under the weight of this essential crisis was the epistemological crisis of theater. Theater has been the sole purpose of existence for many, who, during this pandemic, were struggling with existential crisis and staring into a foggy future.[1] The world of theater forced shut its doors to its artists, keeping the governmental norms in mind. A dark cloud of fear and uncertainty threatened the existence of the theater community. Theater, being a highly individually artistic effort, is a cluster of both unorganised and organized theater groups. From amateur to highly professional ones, from ticketed to free sponsored shows, be it at the rural or urban level; were standing on a continuously shifting precipice. This chapter attempts to look at the epistemological crisis of theater to thrive in the rapidly "digitizing world" and the herculean efforts to adapt to the new form of "virtual world". The chapter in the first section, Osmosis of Theater, looks at the shifting grounds of theater in times of lockdown during COVID-19 and examines the "shared experience" of theater. In the second section, Theater and Being, the chapter explores the dilemma of the artists and their existential crisis without the art of theater-making and the attempts of creating digital theater. In the third section, Visual and the Visceral, the chapter sheds light upon the visual and experiential elements of the theater audience that are transcending the role of written theater.

Osmosis of Theater

The message from the industry is clear. If grassroots theatre *dies, what else dies with it?*

(Lewis, 2020)

DOI: 10.4324/9781003304517-7

"Theatre is about being together, being in community together, experiencing stories together", Simon Godwin, the artistic director at the Shakespeare Theatre Company in Washington, DC told ABC News (Parks, 2020). The only remedy prescribed to fight this virus so far has been an end to socializing. This raises the question of the existence of theater, artists, and the innumerable people associated with this art form. With COVID-19 declared as a pandemic and social distancing being thrust upon the citizens by every country, the theaters have shut down with no economic package to combat this merciless decision. In India, no recognition is given to the art form that is serving people even in the current lockdown situation. It is merely considered a means to pas the time or an entertaining mechanism over digital platforms. Although, in Germany, a press release shared by the Ministry of Culture reports in Frankfurter Allgemeine,[2] a staggering Rs 38,000 crores in backing will be provided specifically to small businesses and freelancers, including those from the cultural, creative, and media sectors. Grütters emphasized that many artists have shown particular creative power in the crisis, which reached the audience with the help of digital technology—"We couldn't have stimulated these many new ideas on the net with the cleverest of programs". She had the impression that "very many have now directly understood the importance of culture". Culture is not a location factor and not a luxury that you can only afford in good times: "Culture is an expression of humanity". (Farnkfurter Allgemeine, March 24, 2020) If this has seeped in German minds, we are far away from any such thought. The Ministry of Culture has been silent with regards to performing arts as if it is the last thing to think about. In India, efforts have been made by independent organizations[3] and they are doing whatever they can in their capacity, to support the theater artists. (Sahani, 2021) However, the industry is way too large in India and, the "new normal" for performing arts is distant, almost invisible.

While imagining the new normal concerning the performing arts, the question remains—Will the theater ever open? If yes, when? Would there be hundreds of us sitting in an auditorium in the dark, sharing the experience of a collective reality, an imaginary world as real as outside? When will it be that we will spend time together, rehearsing and creating performance pieces? Or, are we imagining an auditorium where the audience passes through thermal scanning and are allowed only with masks and gloves? Will we be able to have the same experience of theater as we did then, with the audience wearing masks? Some of these questions were answered by February 2021 and October 2021 when some of the states like Delhi, Maharashtra finally let drama and cultural spaces open up with COVID-19 SOPs in place only to be shut again.[4]

Theater is an emotional exercise where stories are shared, that compel people to laugh, to cry, to reflect on life, and provoke their status quo. This emotional exercise is possible when the audience reacts through silence, coughs, eyes, gestures, facial expressions, and bodily reactions. These minute reactions of the audience in the dark silent room echo to the performers performing the piece. The performer decodes them like osmosis of sensual experiences and paces, heightens, accelerates, pauses, and adjusts the performance to suit that particular audience as if it's a language of theater—only understood by those present there.

Theater is not static, nor is every day the same show. Theater rediscovers itself every day, in a way unlike yesterday with its making and unmaking of language, style, and form to touch the audience like never before. Will it be the same to run a performance with the audience wearing masks or will it look like a dystopian theater of the crony capitalist era? Also, who will risk running a show and who will come to watch it? Who will dictate the terms to run performances and most importantly, when? And until then, whenever that happens, exists the "now". Is there a "now" for theater workers?

Theater was possible because people could come together, a group of people telling stories to another one, usually, the audience listening to it, watching them. Theater is an art form that brings people together to celebrate, think, shed collective tears, laugh infectiously, and challenge and provoke their ideologies. Needless to say, that theater is an immemorial art or, probably it could be dated back to the Greeks, 6th century BC In the late 14th century BC theatre[5] was defined as an "open-air place in ancient times for viewing spectacles and plays", from Old French *theatre* (12c., Modern French *théâtre,*) and directly from Latin *theatrum* "play-house, theatre; stage; spectators in a theatre" (source also of Spanish, Italian *teatro*), from Greek *theatron* "theatre; the people in the theatre; a show, a spectacle", literally "place for viewing", from *theasthai* "to behold" (related to *thea* "a view, a seeing; a seat in the theatre", *theates* "spectator") + *-tron*, suffix denoting place". Theater is seeing in a specific space—a space that is ritualized and has its norms. Theater brought people together. It was the only place where the higher and lower caste, upper and lower class, boundaries were blurred and all were equal in this space. "Theatre is the place people come to see the truth about life and the social situation. The theatre is a spiritual and social X-ray of its time. The theatre was created to tell people the truth about life and the social situation" (Adler 2001).

The ritual of coming together is an integral part of the theater. Theater is not possible without an audience. The artist creating a theater piece finds its meaning only in the presence of the audience. Theater is ephemeral, there is nothing that remains the same. The act is momentary, unique, and limited; it's there for a moment and vanishes in the other. Nothing is repetitive and every performance is different. If theater is so organic and so ritualistic, how is it possible to replicate it to any other form but live performance?

Theater is a shared reality, whatever happens in the auditorium is as much personal, as social. The audience member finds the experiences of the actors to be subjective and sheds tears for the tragedy of the protagonist. The tragedy of the protagonist and the agony of the individual are no more personal as theater transcends the personal and underneath the subjectivity of the expression, there lies objectivity of cohesion in the audience. The lines of performance are blurred, no sooner does the audience finds themselves entangled in the web of the story, forgetting their identity and where they belong to.

Theater provides escapism from our everyday reality into another world where one reflects and contemplates. Theater provides alternate perspectives, meanings, and the deconstruction of lived reality. It provides to the artist experiences of the unlived lives through the characters they play. Theater becomes a vibrational space, where the audience and actor feed on each other's energy and precisely the reason why this won't be possible in any other medium but live performance. Theater is *live*, and that's very important. Is it possible to create this live experience through digital platforms? Theater is amongst the oldest art forms that have survived until now, though it was predicted to die with the beginning of the television era, the waves in cinema, the rise of the internet, and finally the digital platforms growing at an unprecedented rate. Despite all this, theater persisted. The world over, it's more than a hundred days since the theaters have shut, the question is distressing— what about these theater artists and the art? The question only leaves us staring into a void.[6]

> A writer writes—he does not have to be present when his writing is being read. So, it is with the painter and the sculptor. In cinema, the film artists do not have to be present when the film is being projected. But in the theatre, the performers have to be present when the communication takes place. This is a fundamental difference. Theatre is a live show, cinema is not.
>
> (Sircar, 2009, p. 44)

The years 2020 and 2021 saw the rise of thespians and young theater-makers trying out online mediums like Zoom, Instalive, and YouTube to take their plays to the audience. These shows are often pre-recorded and, in some cases, live, but actors were talking to the camera to reach their audiences and that raises a new question about the essential quality of theater which is ritualistic and live and defined by the immediacy and a sensual encounter of human beings. Does digital theater invoke the immediacy and the live feeling of watching a play or is it an entirely new medium that has picked from theater but not theater, possibly closer to the cinema or somewhere in between both?

Theater and "Being"

Since human beings started to live in communities, they felt an innate desire to communicate, to share their stories and things that they understood. Therefore, stories, myths, and legends were passed through oral literature and hero stones. Nomadic life moved to settled agriculturalists and finally urban spaces were built. The passion to tell stories, to share experiences, survived and was eventually taken to the stage. From the need to communicate, to share concerns of the state, was born the Greek theater. Stories came to the stage and all that remained throughout was the act of "ritual".

Theater is a form not only limited to self-expression but is an act of purga-tion of the soul. The artist and the audience are both parts of a cathartic process of living an experience that is equally sublime and thought-provoking. Through living that experience, the artist can liberate himself in such a space. The stage of theater is the only space that makes it possible to live such an experience, for the artist and the audience. In the shared space of the theater, the rules and regula-tions are unlike the real world; it's a place where dreams, memories, fantasies, incomplete thoughts, actions unimagined, and thoughts uncensored manifest to a live audience by providing everyone present with the opportunity to live an "unlived life".

Real-life deprives us of the possibility of rehearsals and the opportunity to tread upon paths, to experiment with life freely without the angst of consequences involved, behind every choice that we make. Theater becomes this safe playground to trust co-workers and the audience, to go on such a journey of experimentation, living different lives otherwise unimaginable, and tofill the void of real life. In such a way, theater becomes a space of emotional healing for the artist and the audience, as it makes them feel liberated from the burden of unlived lives, at least momentarily, if not forever. Theater makes existence bearable.

"When I live, I do not feel myself live. But when I act, it is then that I feel myself exist" (Artaud in Sontang [1976] 1988, p. 275). "Artaud felt that his true self had been stolen at birth due to the eternally changing and unfolding nature of time, yet, he felt that theatre could provide a totality and unity to life that has been otherwise lost" (Johnston 2006). Theater to Artaud and the theater artists today is a space to feel alive and liberated. Life becomes monotonous, dictated, repetitive, and largely meaningless without this space. The world of randomness and absurdity found its expression in theatre. Theatre is largely a project of meaning-making from the absurdity we call real. It is the world of theatre that instead of telling us "how to be", lets us embrace the quality of "being as we are", with the "possibility of knowing the being".

"Being", which was misunderstood for a long time as a static thing separated from the world and consciousness, came under phenomenological gaze in the early 20th century and has been reinterpreted by Husserl, Garfinkel, Stumpf, Schutz, and Heidegger. With the renewed understanding of consciousness in Phenomenology and questioning of "Realism" in theater by the 20th-century theater makers such as Artaud, Vesovold, Maiakovskii, Leman, Ionesco, and many others, the theater was becoming more visual and less textual, more absurd and less real, with more dreamlike and less life-like characters. Theater was becoming a space for liberating the "Self" which was becoming sluggish, mechanical, and inhuman in the age of capitalism. Artaud wanted to return a sense of "Being" through the potency and force of theater. Becket embraced the absurd, toned down the language, and was more interested in talking about the "Self" in his plays.

"Heidegger's compound term 'Being-in-the-world' (*In-der-Welt-sein*), which is an indispensable characteristic of *Dasein*, emphasizes the fundamental unity between what is called the self, the world and time" (Johnston 2006). Heidegger's "Being-in-the-world" comes closer to explaining the sociability of theater where the "live" is necessary. Without the stage/theater, the artist can't exist. It is only within the performing space that the artists exist. Without theater, no artist can experience the existence of the performer/character. Without the artist, the art ceases to exist and becomes a nostalgia of the past (like it is now when the theater is non-existent). "Heidegger wanted to uncover Being—the experience of *Dasein* as intimately entwined with the world. In this sense, one might interpret Artaud's vision for the theater as a practical investigation of 'Being'" (Johnston 2006).

The real world is absurd, plagued by instability, irrationality, and the insane logic of science. Everything in this real world is beyond our control and we are merely creatures of limited free will, meant to suffer and participate in the random logic of this world. A theater is a place where we can release those forces to alter life itself. "The theatre is the unique moment of expression felt, not by the intellect in clear and rational thought, rather it is experienced in a bodily and sensuously immanent way in the theatre space itself" (Artaud in Sontang [1976] 1988, p. 283 The theater space is crucial for the transformation of the person into the performer and, of the clerk or a sales executive sitting in the audience, into a participative spectator to experience the synesthetic of "Being-there-in-the-moment". These theatrical spaces are meticulously designed to make such an experience possible. The designation and creation of such places is a highly charged matter.

> Greek tragedy originated in religious sites, around the altars to the God Dionysus. Japanese Kabuki theatre, by contrast, originated in the dry riverbeds of Kyoto, a place of disrepute. In London, the Globe Theatre, along with most other theatres, was forced to take residence outside the City of London on the South Side of the Thames.
>
> (Puchner 2014, p. 65)

In Mumbai, traditional theaters were often located in proximity to the railway station, so that they were easily accessible to the working-class patrons. Theater is this embodied space, which transported the performer and the patron into a world of memories, dreams, distant past, and even future. "Physical presence is part of the essence of theatre; so is occupying a common space", (Hughes 2020). All experiences lived in the theater qualify as "being there" from an embodied perspective, and replication of this experience of embodiment of space isn't possible outside the "theater space". The theater is precisely a place for making meaning from experiences whilst giving value, pleasure, insight, and potential transformation to our everyday lives. In such a process, we (humans) come to see ourselves not as "things", but as beings with unique qualities of "Being" and existence. The virtual medium isn't the world of theater,[7] it's another world and therefore the theater artists are unable to fit themselves as "being-in-the-virtual-theater". Further, accepting no difference between art and existence, Antonin Artaud stated that "If I am a poet or an actor, it's not so I can write or recite poetry, it's so I can live it" (Read 2017, p. 5). Theater, therefore, is existence and when it ceases to exist, it slides down into a black hole, putting the lives of all those who participate in this art at stake, into a void of non-existence, wiping their dreams, memories thoughts; in short "their life".

The Visual and the Visceral

If the 20th century started grappling with "Being-in-the–theater-world" in the approaches of Phenomenology, performance studies, and pedagogical changes in theater, it also witnessed the rise of visual language in theater while the power of the written word was becoming obscure. Along with Meyerhold, other directors developed approaches that advanced visual imagery, the dominance of non-verbal over word and descriptiveness, the use of decorative design as a way of expressing the emotional state of the characters and the atmosphere. "The naturalistic theatre has conducted a never-ending search for the fourth wall which has led it into a whole series of absurdities. The theatre fell into the hands of fabricants who tried to make everything 'just like real life', and turned the stage into some sort of antique shop" (Meyerhold 1969, p. 30). If Meyerhold found the stage to be some sort of antique shop filled with properties and set design belonging to an ossified period, then Ionesco found language as limiting the experience of the viewer.

> As our knowledge becomes separated from life, our culture no longer con-
> tains ourselves (or only insignificant part of ourselves), for it forms a "social"
> context into which we are not integrated. So, the problem becomes that of
> bringing our life back into contact with our culture, making it a living culture
> once again. To achieve this, we shall first have to kill "the respect for what
> is written down in black and white"... To break up our language so that it
> can be put together again to re-establish contact with "the absolute", or, as I
> should prefer to say, "with multiple reality"; it is imperative to "push human
> beings again towards seeing themselves as they really are".
>
> (Ionesco 1958)

There was a shift in the communication form, and stark visuals came to be used in theater to communicate something which the spoken word would kill with its constitution. Absurd Theatre, Theatre of Cruelty, Immersive Theatre, Theatre of the Oppressed, Performance Art, Expressionist Theatre, and Physical Theatre were creating a visual vocabulary in place of the written one or to enhance the minimal verbal communication. Written and spoken language were becoming a barrier, more than a means of communication. The language was concealing rather than revealing, very often the act of labeling, defining, andf constituting with the written word was widening the gap of "what is being said" to "what is to be said". The word, which became "not a strong enough tool to reveal inner dialogue" (Meyerhold 1969, p. 25) was replaced with plastic movement. It was the pattern of the actors' movements which formed the scene that helped the spectator not only to observe the development of the plot but also to delve into the subtext. Theater was moving towards becoming a synesthetic experience from a cognitive or intellectual one. It was attempting to discuss the "being" and language was falling short of it.

Visual vocabulary came to use in myriad ways to reveal the subtext of what was embedded between the lines. Gestural hieroglyphics came to be used as a means of communicating the unsaid and unspoken territories of the unconscious. The sce-nography was developing in different theater practices across the world. Theater makers such as Tadeusz Kantor, Peter Handke, Sergei Eisenstein, and many others worked in creating a visual sensory experience in the shared space. Their work formed the approaches, where the invisible was felt. The importance of visual imagery as a sense-making element of the performance increased significantly, and the stage elements acquired the qualities of a character. Spontaneity was favored and artists' bodies found as much importance as their voices. There was a strong urge to do away with making theater that is highly verbose as often verbal theater failed to explain the absurd, the ephemeral, and the visceral.

> Where does our investigation get its importance from, since it seems only to destroy everything interesting; that is, all that is great and important? (As it were, all the buildings, leaving behind only bits of stone and rubble.) What we are destroying is nothing but a house of cards, and we are clearing up the ground of language on which we stand.
>
> (Wittgenstein 1998, p. 118)

Theater is, therefore, not only a pre-mediated and carefully written dramatic play, but also an experience of embodied space felt through various sensual, visual, and visceral ways. One of the most important features of such performances is the marked shift of focus from the actor playing the role or a character on the stage, to the experience of a shared social reality/space, the collective experience of "being-in-the-theatre". "This is the anxiety that roils and percolates, mixed with all the sadness and futility. What theater people do is put on a show; what audience members do is gather. It's ritual; it's reflex. It is also, in any conventional sense, largely inoperable right now" (Hughes 2020).

Is it possible to create this "shared experience" of the "ublime and the visceral" through digital platforms? Is it possible to create the ambiance of live theater through live streaming? Is it possible to feel the same shared reality with live telecast? Is it possible to transmit the silence of an auditorium, the pregnant pauses, the beauty of breath, via virtual platforms? Is it possible to take the spectator on an inner voyage with online theater?[8] Is it to say that Cine Plays don't work and something is inherently wrong with live streaming of plays, be it on a national or international scale?

> I think for those who can watch it online, I think it's a good thing, but it's kind of like, watching a movie on TV is great, but going to a movie theatre is exceptional and then you go to live theatre is the greatest. I mean, you see everybody, action, life, all the mistakes, everything, you see it 3D. It's awesome and there's just to be the pinnacle of an experience of the entertainment is the theatre.

says Ric Stiegman, board member of Stained Glass Theatre. (Rivera 2020) The online platforms of the digital world are not equipped to provide the shared space that theater space did, where objects become characters and human beings participate in a process of freeing themselves from the shackles of uncontrolled reality. The collective participation on digital platforms lacks the cohesive spirit that is created in the physical-psychic theater space. Digital platforms provide anonymity to the viewers rather than solidarity. Therefore, theater for its very own reason of being (*Dasein*) a shared space will not be malleable enough to suit digital platforms. It's an art form and a business that depends on creating emotional experiences for those present in the space. Arts journalist Laura Collins-Hughes laments the death of theater. She describes her experience of watching the filmed version of Hamilton as "The Hamilton[9] movie, a thrilling and democratizing testament to the power of stage performance, can't capture the soul of theater, because that soul lives in the room". (Hughes 2020)

Theater is a living organism and it is a social body formed by hundreds of those collected in theater, thinking and reflecting at the same time, to the same experience in a similar and yet unique way. Theater is a live experience, a breathing art, a sacred space and the truth is that none of this can be replicated, adjusted, or altered in any form to suit digital media. The lungs of this organism are interconnectedness, without this socializing, the theater will find it difficult to breathe. Theater is a language of the body, the voice, the gestures, a magic spell woven by the human soul and only comprehensible to all those present in that sacred space. This magic of theater cannot be created on digital platforms. Even when it comes to films, the festival director of Cannes Film Festival Thierry Fremaux is hesitant and says it's impossible to move to the digital platform. He believes "Directors of 'films' are driven by the idea of showing their movies on a big screen and sharing them with others at events like festivals, not for their works to end up on an iPhone" (Keslassy 2020)

With an uncertain future and the unending lockdown, the theater fraternity-like others, are finding it impossible to comprehend even the present. Theater is a live art and nothing is living anymore. Theater companies can't pay their people for work they have not done. Also, do theater companies in India have capital? Therefore, it's becoming impossible to not lay off people to preserve capital[10]. The concern is to be able to find these artists and resources who simply believe in passion and give their best of abilities to make theater possible. There are innumerable folk theater groups of Jatra, Bharud, Dashavatar, Tamasha, Kathakali, Theeyam, Pandavani, Yakshagana, Maanch, Nautanki, Bhavaai, Bhaona, Swang, etc. and innumerable small theater companies in the metropolitan cities of the country who have zero capital and function based on the per show. Michael Strickland, founder of the Lighting Production Company, best puts it: "Each day I discover that few people understand that live entertainment production firms and their people are sitting at zero income." (Rivero 2020)

Towards a Faint Future

"So, it's not overdramatic to speak of grief, a freighted word that we associate most with death, but that is simply the sorrow that comes with heavy loss. For some of us who depend on the theater for sustenance—creative, spiritual, economic, all of the above—that is the term to describe what we feel in this time of limbo". (Hughes 2020) The impact of COVID-19 lockdown on society is unprecedented and nobody can say precisely when we will return to normal public life. The lockdown time of COVID-19 has plagued the world of theater with uncertainty and a dense foggy future. If a human is a social animal and social distancing is the new normal, without the social what's left is only animal. Theater is possible because of the coming together of people. Even if social distancing norms are followed, a show cannot run for one-third of the auditorium capacity. Theater always served as a platform to talk about injustice. Although theater is an art form to express the abject poverty, grief, injustice, and alienation, today theater itself suffers from an inexpressible syndrome. The artist is left feeling an emptiness, a void about the future, and anxiety about the probability of one. COVID-19 is an epistemological crisis of the contemporary world and an ontological crisis of theater. Though there is also a possibility of a virtual theater,[11] once the live element is taken out, it ceases to be theater; it will be a newer form for a newer medium. Very possibly, it can be a cost-effective medium to create theater, where producers don't need to worry if the auditorium will go full house. Also, the audience might find it convenient to sit at home and enjoy this new theater without having to wade through the traffic of the maximum city, saving time, energy, and probably even ticket cost. Theater artists might start packaging new theater for these newer times. But 'for how long, is a question that none can answer or predict for now. If theater turns virtual then how different is it from cinema? Further, "being-in-the theater" loses its existence without the theater space. The shared experience of living the unlived life no more exists; making life a tedious affair with the abject absurdity of the world relegates us to confinements and caged existence. Further, theater isn't only about actors, it's a life lived in the shadows: thankless, unseen, and hidden away in the process of making a play. From set designers to makeup artists, musicians, costume designers, backstage, logistics team, graphic artists, director, writer, scenographer, dancers, light-person and several innumerable people who multitask in this resource-deprived art form, making the most of whatever they could find, are drowned in financial worry and loneliness. For an art form that thrives on collaboration, the very act of socially distancing from people is an act of severing their umbilical cord to the world. It's not just theater, it's a living ecosystem. Distancing is depriving them of their living existence, "being-in-the-theatre" thus, creating an ontological crisis of theater. Poetry, painting, writing, composing music are largely individual arts that can continue in isolation. But theater exists because of the world that we inhabit, and theater is possible because it is a collaborative art that can only happen "in being with others/the world". Theaters will possibly open at full capacity and the audience may come back to theaters but in that long gap of months and years, would it alter our lifestyle patterns to such an extent that going out especially for drama performances may not be an easy decision? Will the inertia created in the everyday life of the pandemic hold the audience back from going to theaters? OTT (OTT stands for "over-the-top" and refers to technology that delivers streamed content via internet-connected devices) and digital platforms have started creating extensive content for the audience sitting at home, in fact, the films are now released on such digital platforms. If that is the case, then how many people are going to move out of the comfort of their home to watch plays. Further, will it now require veteran actors and even celebrities to act in plays so that the audience comes to such plays, but will it then affect the democratic space of theater? How will the smaller theater companies survive? Most importantly, what is the future of experimental theater vis-à-vis commercial theater? Many such questions hang on the precipice of new normal life and life post-COVID-19. Also, the question is still unanswered as to whether we have moved beyond COVID-19 or if the shadow of the outbreak is still lurking in the dark to pounce on our existence and bring everything else to another comma. The written theater suffers but certainly, the suffering of physical theater, experimental theater, non-scripted dramas, and devised performances is lamentable. Will theater companies and audiences once again risk themselves into the world of the sensory and the physical?

Will digital theater provide theater for the senses? Theater is a fresco in motion and is made on a stage in such a way that it cannot be moved. "The Last Judgement" of Michelangelo can be seen at home in printed form or on a computer screen, or even in 360 virtual reality (VR), but is it the same experience as seeing it in person at the Sistine Chapel? Theater is a breathing and living art made up of life. This fresco cannot be moved anywhere else. We can only hope for the interconnectedness of beings once again. Time and again we could be filled with grief over our losses and enraged by the apathetic nature of political leaders, but once again we must dream of a shared reality, for there could be a beacon of hope that pierces through that void, in the belief that when all this is over, we shall be all dressed up in the most intoxicating colors, on a phantasmagorical set, performing to an invigorating audience.

Notes

1 On March, 24 2020, the Government of India under Prime Minister Narendra Modi ordered a nationwide lockdown for 21 days, limiting movement of the entire 1.3 billion population of India as a preventive measure against the COVID-19 pandemic (Gettleman, Jeffrey, and Schultz 2020). It was ordered after a 14-hour voluntary public curfew on March 22, followed by the enforcement of a series of regulations in the country's COVID-19 affected regions. The lockdown was placed when the number of confirmed positive coronavirus cases in India was approximately 500. However, the lockdown for performing arts began much earlier than the rest of the sectors. From March 13, 2020, Chief Minister of Maharashtra Uddhav Thackeray announced that the government has invoked the Epidemic Diseases Act of 1897 to tackle the virus outbreak and theatres and gyms were to be shut in Mumbai along with five other cities in Maharashtra due to the coronavirus until further notice. From March 13, 2020 until now stages have been empty, devoid of any shows or even rehearsals; the ghost light is left on for the stage in the hope that one day artists and audiences will return to the theater.

2 "The scene is affected as much as possible", said Grütters (of The Christian Democratic Union of Germany) to the Redaktions Netzwerk Deutschland (Tuesday). The damage caused by more than 80,000 canceled events alone is estimated at 125 crores. She hopes that with the aid package passed by the Federal Cabinet on Monday "everyone will survive".

3 A small group of independent artistes and individuals working with the arts, namely Aneesh Pradhan (musician and scholar), Arundhati Ghosh (cultural practitioner), Mona Irani (producer and casting director), Rahul Vohra (actor, director and arts consultant), Sameera Iyengar (cultural practitioner), and Shubha Mudgal (musician) have come up with a plan to raise Rs. 35 lakhs through a campaign titled ADAA (Assistance for Disaster Affected Artistes). Other than ADAA, Prasad Kambli is working towards gathering donations for supporting the Marathi Theatre makers and technicians. There are several such independent efforts made to support the artists at an individual level such as Theatre Dost. However, there is no initiative from the Government of India.

4 However, this was a short-lived experience. With the second wave of COVID-19, theaters were shut only to be opened again in October 2021 and to be shut again by December 2021. In short, theaters resumed only for about two months each time that they reopened in 2021. Also, it nearly takes two months minimum for most theater companies to create a play. The uncertainty of time and life during COVID-19 only brought old productions to stage, besidesthan some exceptions. Some theater companies tried putting out digital productions.

5 "Index", Etymonline, Accessed May 2, 2020, www.etymonline.com/word/theatre.

6 "Even today, there are more than 1,500 play performances in a month in the four main languages: Hindi, English, Gujarati and Marathi (you can now add Telugu, Kannada and Konkani to this list). This beats the monolingual theater culture of New York or London or Berlin, hands down. The top Marathi and Gujarati plays net Rs. 2.5 lakh at the box office for a single show', stated Ramu Ramanathan in an article in *Livemint* in 2015. It's been more than 90 days since theaters shut down in Maharashtra, the question is distressing— what about these 3000 play performances? If this question is extended to India, the question leaves us staring into a void.

7 Most of the artistes, rather almost all in India, are paid as per the number of play performances. With no revenue for the last three months, a handful of the actors who were capable of learning the digital technology did create a play or two at home, and some read poems, *nazms*, short stories, and plays online. Some of these digital performances were ticketed through Insider or BookMyShow, and some were free. However, most of them who used this platform were veteran actors from Hindi, Marathi, and English theater. Many theater companies from Maharashtra remain silent in the hope of returning to the real stage one day. There are thespians who have no choice but to pause for now, and there are those who are finding alternative ways to make and spread theater. There are artists who are adapting their tools of theater to suit new mediums, but how long would it be successful? Only time will tell!

8 There were attempts made by small and big theater companies to put out online productions. For instance, The National Centre for the Performing Arts' (NCPA's) NCPA@ home series, showcasing the best of their plays and musical performances, is a step in that direction. They believed that going digital is helping theater groups not only reach their patrons, but also patrons of the art form across the globe who haven't ever attended a concert or play in person at the NCPA. In such a way, a new audience is also there in the making; however, this new audience is not really the ones who turned up at auditoriums and theater spaces to watch plays. Some thespians are optimistic that digitization will make theater more accessible to the audience while also encouraging more experiments in this field where different interfaces can be created between the audience and performers through digital platforms. 2020 and 2021 saw such experiments but all of them lived a short life and once theaters opened up, they ceased to exist. This raises another question of whether digital theater is temporary in a nation like India which thrives on oral literature and visual communication. Ranga Shankara in Bangalore ran their annual theater festival online as a ticketed event and the response to the program was disappointing. Samyuktha, head of programming at Ranga Shankara, run by theater veteran Arundhati Nag in Bangalore, said they had not even thought of going online until the pandemic hit. Unsure of what to do next, they took a while to stage a big production online. The festival reached around 1,500 people for the event which ran for about seven days, as each film was showcased for seven days. The global audience was negligible considering the number. The organizers were baffled too with such a poor response.

9 Hamilton is the musical premiered on Broadway in 2015. A filmed version of it is streaming on Disney$_+$.

10 On the scale of large theater festivals, the organizers of the 15th edition of the Mahindra Excellence in Theatre Awards (META) announced that the festival, originally due to take off in March 2020, was to be been postponed. Similarly, the Akhil Bharatiya Natyaparishad announced via a widely circulated official communique, that Marathi

Natya Sammelan 2020 has been postponed. As far as the world is concerned, experts predict that COVID-19 will cut Rs 1.2 crore out of the entertainment industry in the United States alone. Global entertainment giant Cirque du Soleil shut down 44 shows worldwide and did not reopen until January 2021. COVID-19 has far reaching impacts on Indian theater and the world at large. However, with the UK and the US the coping mechanisms are different. The National Theatre London has moved on to livestreaming plays for free on Youtube and seeking donations. So is the case with Complicite, Schaubühne, Plays in the House, Martha Dance Company, Irish Repertory Theatre, and The Metropolitan Opera, etc. Some of them are offering it free for viewing and some are ticketed ranging from Rs. 750 to Rs. 1900.

11   From the National Theatre in the UK to the Bolshoi Theatre in Russia, some of the greatest arts institutions began to stream recordings of their classic shows online, mostly free, for audiences across the globe. The discovery of Zoom led to experiments such as transcontinental dramatic readings and performances. Actors began to upload performances in quarantine. In India, after a plethora of rushed and forgettable plays on YouTube, a number of experiments emerged that will set the foundation of theater in 2021 and beyond (Nath 2020).

Bibliography

Adler, Stella, and Howard Kissel. 2001. *Stella Adler: The Art of Acting*. New York: Applause Books.

Artaud, Antonin. 1958. *The Theatre and Its Double*. Translated by Mary Richards. New York: Groove Press.

Artaud, Antonin. 1976. *Selected Writings*. Translated and edited by Susan Sontag. Los Angeles and Berkley: University of California Press.

Brown, Kate. 2020. "Germany Has Rolled Out a Staggering €50 Billion Aid Package For Small Businesses That Boosts Artists and Galleries-and Puts Other Countries to Shame." *Artnet News*, March 27, 2020. news.artnet.com/art-world/german-bailout-50-billion-181 5396

Day, Maren. 2017. "How Does the (Digital) Theatre of the Future Look Like?" *The Theatre Times*, August 15, 2017, https://thetheatretimes.com/how-does-the-digital-theatre-of-the -future-look-like/

Heidegger, Martin. 1962. *Being and Time*. Translated by John Macquarie and Edward Robinson. Oxford: Blackwell.

Hughes, Laura. 2020. "Digital Theater Isn't Theater. It's a way to mourn its Absence." *New York Times*, July 8, 2020, https://www.nytimes.com/2020/07/08/theater/live-theater -absence.html

Ionesco, Eugene. 1958. "Ni un dieu, ni un demon", *Cahiers de la Compagnie Madeleine Renaud*. Paris: Jean-Louis Barrault.

Jeffrey, Gettleman, and Kai Schultz. 2020. "Modi Orders 3-Week Total Lockdown for All 1.3 Billion Indians." *New York Times*, March 24, 2020, https://www.nytimes.com/2020 /03/24/world/asia/india-coronavirus-lockdown.html

Johnston, Daniel. 2006. "Overcoming the Metaphysics of Consciousness: Being / Artaud." In *Proceedings of the 2006 Annual Conference of the Australasian Association for Drama*, June 20, 2006. University of Sydney: Australasian Association for Drama, Theatre and Performance Studies, http://hdl.handle.net/2123/2527

Keslassy, Elsa. 2020. "Cannes Film Festival Won't Go Virtual If All Else Fails." *Variety*, April 9, 2020, variety.com/2020/film/global/cannes-film-festival-wont-go-virtual-coron avirus-1234572974/

Lewis, Helena. 2020. "When Will We Want to Be in a Room Full of Strangers Again?" *The Atlantic*, May 12, 2020, https://www.theatlantic.com/international/archive/2020/05/ theater-survive-coronavirus-art-west-end-broadway/611338/

Meyerhold, Vsevolod. 1969. *Meyerhold on Theatre*. Translated by Edward Braun. London: Methuen and Co Ltd.

Nath, Dipanita. 2020. "With the Stage Locked Down, a New Art form Emerged During the Pandemic — The Digital Theatre." *The Indian Express*, December 31, 2020, https://indianexpress.com/article/lifestyle/art-and-culture/pandemic-lockdown-digital-theatre-7127694/

News. 2020. "Coronavirus Impact: Sangli 100th Marathi Drama Conference Will Be Postponed." *Bahujannama*, March 13, 2020, bahujannama.com/sangli-100th-marathi-drama-conference-will-be-postponed/

News. 2020. "Grütters Want to Save Artists in Crisis." *Farnkfurter Allgemeine,* March 24, 2020. www.faz.net/aktuell/feuilleton/corona-monika-gruetters-will-krisengebeutelte-kuenstler-retten-16693838.html?fbclid=IwAR3Sb8TUwLDSrvkA1oM0MW_Bmw_gXhsVDpF0FHA-OxYklb0rsvhvlC6Udeg

News. 2020. "Theatres Are 'Clinging on' but Face Precarious Future." *Head Topics*, May 14, 2020, headtopics.com/uk/theatres-are-clinging-on-but-face-precarious-future-13021793

News. 2020. "Theatres, Gyms to Be Shut-in Mumbai, 5 Other Cities in Maharashtra Over Coronavirus." *Hindustan Times*, March 13, 2020, www.hindustantimes.com/india-news/maharashtra-govt-orders-closure-of-theatres-gyms-malls-amid-coronavirus-outbreak/story-zSgbo7zDo698YpzudILHmJ.html

Parks, Mary Alice. 2020. "Coronavirus May Have Devastated the Theatre World Artists Are Adapting." *ABC News Network*, March 26, 2020, abcnews.go.com/Business/coronavirus-devastated-theatre-world-artists-adapting/story?id=69750362

Puchner, Martin. 2014. "The Problem of the Ground: Martin Heidegger Site-Specific Performance." In *Encounter in Performance Philosophy*, ed. Laura Cull and Alice Lagaay. London: Palgrave Macmillan.

Ramanathan, Ramu. 2015. "Theatre Is Mumbai, Mumbai Is Theatre." *Livemint*, August 14, 2015, https://www.livemint.com/Leisure/NlibUTuqx4xhJtLaz3Z9wN/Theatre-is-Mumbai-Mumbai-is-theatre.html

Read, Peter. 2017. "Done with the Judgement of God: The 'Prolonged Ontological Crisis' of Antonin Artaud." *TLS. Times Literary Supplement*, no. 5976, October 13, 2017. https://www.the-tls.co.uk/issues/october-13-2017/

Rivera, Michael. 2020. "Devoid of Expression: COVID-19's Impact on Theatre." *The Chart Online*, May 01, 2020, https://www.thechartonline.com/the_arts/devoid-of-expression-covid-19-s-impact-on-theatre/article_63a60b6e-8bcd-11ea-8585-af1fe56f5b2a.html

Rivero, Nicholas. 2020. "Our Industry Isn't Coming Back like Yours Is." *Medium*, May 14, 2020. https://medium.com/swlh/our-industry-isnt-coming-back-like-yours-is-4cbf261194e1

Sahani, Alka. 2021. "As Covid Downs Curtain on Stage, TheatreDost Helps Mumbai Artistes, Backstage Workers." *The Indian Express*, July 17, 2021, https://indianexpress.com/article/cities/mumbai/as-covid-downs-curtain-on-stage-theatredost-helps-mumbai-artistes-backstage-workers-7409744/

Sahani, Kivleen. 2021. "When Theatre Goes Online." *The Citizen*, July 2, 2021, https://www.thecitizen.in/index.php/en/newsdetail/index/16/20565/when-theatre-goes-online

Sarkar, Badal. 2003. *On Theatre*. Seagull Books.

Sircar, Badal. 2009. *On Theatre: Selected Essays.* Calcutta: Seagull Books.

Spasskaia, Margarita. 2018. "The Formation of the Visual Theatre Aesthetics: Theatre Practice and Experiments of the Russian Avant-Garde in the 1900–1930s." *Vestnik of Saint Petersburg University Arts* 8, no.4: 593–604.

Wittgenstein, Ludwig, and Gertrude Anscombe. 1998. *Philosophical Investigations*. Oxford: Blackwell.

Part II

Mental Health and the COVID-19 Pandemic

6 Rational Self-Management in the COVID-19 Pandemic

Anjali Joshi

> People and things do not upset us. Rather, we upset ourselves by believing that they can upset us.

The quote by the eminent American psychologist, Dr Albert Ellis, serves as a beacon for us, especially when we strive to adapt to a new normal brought on by the unprecedented COVID-19 pandemic. The outbreak has not only impacted our physical health but also created a lasting impact on our mental health. In response to the real or perceived threat of this virus, there is a huge increase in coronavirus stress in the general population. Mental health professionals face a major challenge in preventing its adverse impacts on our mental well-being. One model that preserves our mental health and which could be a savior at such a trying moment is "Rational Emotive Behavior Therapy" (REBT). The aforementioned quote by Ellis, the founder of REBT, is the cornerstone of REBT. He founded REBT in 1955 and for the last 65 years, it has become a leading cognitive behavioral approach to counselling and psychotherapy. Today, it has reached every nook and cranny of the world and is being used effectively in many areas of life.

REBT liberates people from their own handicapping attitudes and helps them build lasting emotional well-being. Many times, our practical problems get smothered by unnecessary self-defeating emotions and instead of the transition from "problem" to "solution", we regress from "problem" to "problem compounding". REBT educates people on how to solve practical problems objectively and rationally without getting engulfed in the whirlwind of self-destructive emotions and behavior. In short, it trains people for rational self-management. The philosophy underpinning REBT is so profound that if we imbibe it, it will help us sail through the pandemic with minimum disturbance.

When it comes to the pandemic and its impact on mental health, the common notion is that the pandemic causes our emotional disturbance. REBT differs radically from this common-sense approach that events cause disturbances in us. It counterattacks this notion by claiming that the same pandemic does not cause the same disturbance in all. Some people get more disturbed, while others get less disturbed, and yet others remain unaffected. It signifies that, more than external events, the meaning we assign to them determines our emotions. Hence, REBT postulates a cognitive-emotive interface. It claims that cognition is a crucial determinant of human emotions. It states that we don't just become disturbed by

DOI: 10.4324/9781003304517-9

traumatic events in our life; we also choose to be upset about them. Ellis (2001) says, "You are a chooser, a constructor of how you react psychologically, and you can choose to refuse to create your upset and to work toward more helpful ways of reacting" (p.15).

We have numerous beliefs, cognitions, thoughts in our minds. REBT makes a distinction between beliefs. Some beliefs are constructive and help us in accomplishing our goals, while others are destructive and divert us from our goals. Constructive beliefs are called "rational beliefs", while destructive beliefs are called "irrational beliefs" in REBT. Irrational beliefs include cognitive distortions such as exaggeration, oversimplification, overgeneralization, invalidated assumptions, and absolutistic notions. REBT stresses that a key cause of our emotional disturbance lies in irrational beliefs.

REBT not only describes the cause of our disturbance but also offers techniques to alleviate it. The most common technique used in REBT is the disputation of irrational beliefs. It consists of asking several questions to challenge the inaccuracy of these irrational beliefs. Questions such as "Where is the evidence? Why must it be? How can you prove it?" are frequently employed. At the same time, rational counterparts are also presented to distinguish between absolutistic demands and non-absolutistic desires.

As a result of rigorous disputation, we realize that our beliefs are irrational, and we begin to replace irrational beliefs with rational beliefs. When the needless and harmful emotional turmoil in our minds subsides, we embrace a new philosophy of life. When we reach this stage, we not only solve the current problem but also develop a rational approach towards self-management which is long-term and not symptomatic or palliative. In Ellisian language, we not only feel better, but we get better as well.

REBT can be understood via a simple conceptual model. It is known as the ABCDE framework. This framework is elaborated in Figure 6.1.

Let us discuss a few cases with whom this framework has been instrumental in overcoming emotional distress during the pandemic.

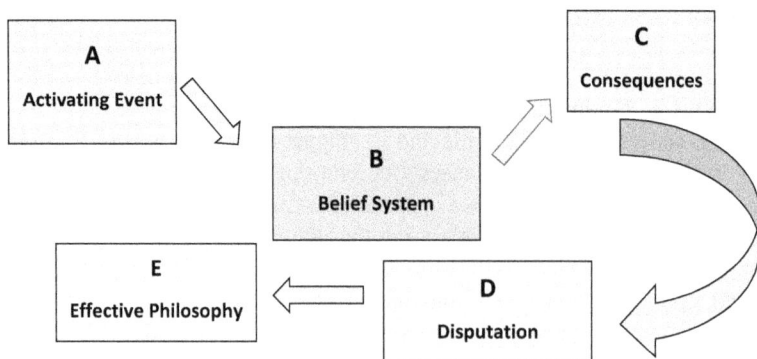

Figure 6.1 ABCDE Framework of REBT

My first case; we will call him Sameer. He watched a news report on TV that a new variant of the coronavirus discovered in the second wave was more devastating than the first, mortuaries were overflowing with the dead, while relatives wailed outside. He was very anxious about what would happen if he were infected and died. He was terrified that everyone around him would be infected and spread the disease to him. He was checking himself several times a day to see if he had a temperature.

Let us take a look at how I analyzed Sameer's emotional disturbance from the REBT point of view. In REBT "A" stands for *activating event*, that is, the event that contributes to our emotional distress. The emotion that arises in our mind about that event and the behavior that we follow is called "C". "C" stands for emotional and behavioral *consequences*. In Sameer's case, "A" was the news on TV and "C" was his anxiety and the behavior of checking his body temperature several times a day. We commonly believe that the news on TV is the cause of Sameer's anxiety, that is, "A" (TV news) is the cause of "C" (anxiety). REBT, however, advocates the verification of the veracity of this common belief.

To know more about "B", that is, *belief system*, we will see my two other clients who were also distressed during the same time. Let us call them Aditya and Nisha. Both watched the very same news that Sameer had seen on TV, but their emotions were not the same as those of Sameer's. Upon watching the same news report, Aditya was angry at people as he thought that the second wave was fueled by their negligence, such as not following social-distancing protocols or visiting public places without caution. He began yelling at everyone whose masks had slidden off their noses even slightly or if they had failed to maintain adequate social distancing. Nisha also watched the same news as Sameer and Aditya, but her emotions were different. She was depressed with the thought that the pandemic had been going on for a long time, and since the situation was deteriorating day by day, she wouldn't be able to handle it. She was gloomy and sad and began to withdraw from social interactions.

Let us have an elaborate discussion on these three cases from the REBT perspective. REBT states that if the news on TV (A) is the cause of Sameer's anxiety and behavior (C), then everyone other than Sameer, for example, Aditya and Nisha who had seen the same news should be anxious. Similarly, in Aditya's case, if the TV news (A) is the cause of his anger, everyone other than him who watched the same news should have felt angry. In Nisha's case as well, if she would have depressed because of watching the news, everyone who watched it should have been depressed. However, this did not occur. Even though everyone had watched the same news, their emotions were all different. In short, while "A" was the same in the cases of Sameer, Aditya, and Nisha, their "C" was different. This suggests that, contrary to popular belief, "A" is not the cause of "C".

Commenting on what the cause might be, REBT states that the real cause of their emotional disturbance is a process that occurs between "A" and "C". This process addresses what they spoke in their mind while watching the news. This process happened so quickly, at a breakneck speed, that they did not even realize it. REBT names this process "self-talk". Self-talk refers to the ongoing conversations we have with ourselves. Self-talk is a psychological term that indicates everything that a person says to himself. We express our deeply rooted underlying beliefs to ourselves via words, phrases, and sentences used in self-talk.

In Sameer's case, his self-talk was "What if I've been infected with the virus and am about to die? It will be terrible! I can't stand this!" The news must have ended in about five to ten minutes but Sameer's anxiety, on the other hand, lingered in his mind for several hours. This indicates that his anxiety stems from what he told himself (self-talk) rather than the news he watched. He repeated these sentences to himself over and over again. As a result, he became more anxious. The anxiety caused him to constantly check his body temperature.

Aditya and Nisha went through a similar process. While watching the news, they too talked quickly in their minds. Their self-talk, however, was not the same as Sameer's. Aditya's self-talk was "People around me are so selfish! Can't they understand that by not adhering to the norms of social distancing and masks, they are spreading the infection and endangering the lives of others?" This self-talk caused him to become enraged and yell at others. In Nisha's case, her self-talk was "The situation is so awful! The pandemic will not go away anytime soon, and the prospect of having to live with it for the rest of my life is disheartening". These sentences contributed to her depression and her behavior to restrict her social interactions.

This raises the question of why, even though the event is the same, three of them have distinct self-talk? REBT states that the answer lies in their *belief* system (B). According to REBT, *belief* (B) is the individual's meaning or evaluation of the activating event. Since the three of them have given different meanings to the same event, their self-talk, as well as their emotions and behavior, were all different. Self-talk is the manifestation of beliefs.

REBT says that there are a variety of irrational beliefs that lead to emotional distress. Ellis (1994) has summarized them into 12 generic irrational beliefs (See Appendix 1). A major component of these irrational beliefs is rigid demandingness. It is manifested in the form of absolutistic *musts* or *shoulds*. According to REBT, these dogmatic demands are at the core of our disturbance. Ellis has classified them into three major heads. They are called the main categories of *musturbatory* beliefs. *Musturbatory* beliefs touch on believing that something *must* or *must not* happen. We often indulge in musturbation in three ways. These ways represent three categories of *musturbatory* beliefs. The first category represents "I", i.e., "we believe that I *must* or *must not* do something". A second category represents "Others", i.e., "we believe that others *must* or *must not* do something". A third category represents' the situation around us, i.e., "we believe that the situation around us *must* or *must not* be like this". The beliefs which Sameer, Aditya, and Nisha are holding represent these three categories. Sameer's irrational beliefs fall into the first category of *musturbatory* beliefs, i.e. "I", while Aditya represents the second category, i.e., "others", and Nisha holds the third category, i.e., "situation". Before we dwell on their beliefs in-depth, let us see three *musturbatory* ideologies as described in REBT.

Musturbatory Category 1—Refers to "I". I *must* be perfect and *must* be approved by others.
Musturbatory Category 2—Refers to "others". Others *must* be kind and just to me.

Musturbatory Category 3—Refers to the "situation" around a person. The situation around me *must* be easy.

Let's look at the different beliefs Sameer, Aditya, and Nisha were holding in their minds and see which *musturbatory* category they belonged to.

Sameer's belief was "I *must not* have the coronavirus infection and if I have it, it would be *terrible,* and I *can't stand* it" (*Musturbatory* Category 1).

Aditya's belief was that during the pandemic, people *should not* be careless and *should* take precautions to avoid spreading it to others (*Musturbatory* Category 2).

Nisha's belief was "The pandemic *should never* have lasted this long. It's *awful* and if it continues, I *won't be* able to bear it any longer" (*Musturbatory* Category 3).

We have earlier seen how beliefs are manifested by our self-talk. Hence, self-talk is a major tool used in REBT to detect our irrational beliefs. If you look closely at the self-talks of Sameer, Aditya and Nisha, you will discover that they are consistent with their beliefs. This means that self-talk originates in beliefs. Because the beliefs of all three are different, their self-talks are also different. As a result, their feelings and behaviors are also different. In a nutshell, their beliefs (B) towards the news are the real cause of their feelings and behaviors. REBT postulates that the real cause of "C" (consequences) is "B" (beliefs) and not "A" (activating event). This is a key insight into the REBT doctrine. Figure 6.2 will demonstrate this.

When Sameer, Aditya, and Nisha gained this insight, I progressed to the next letter of the ABCDE framework, "D". "D" stands for *disputation* of the beliefs that create self-destructive emotions and behavior. These beliefs are "*irrational beliefs*". Every emotional disturbance, according to REBT, is caused by an irrational belief that we need to identify and challenge. Irrational beliefs are challenged

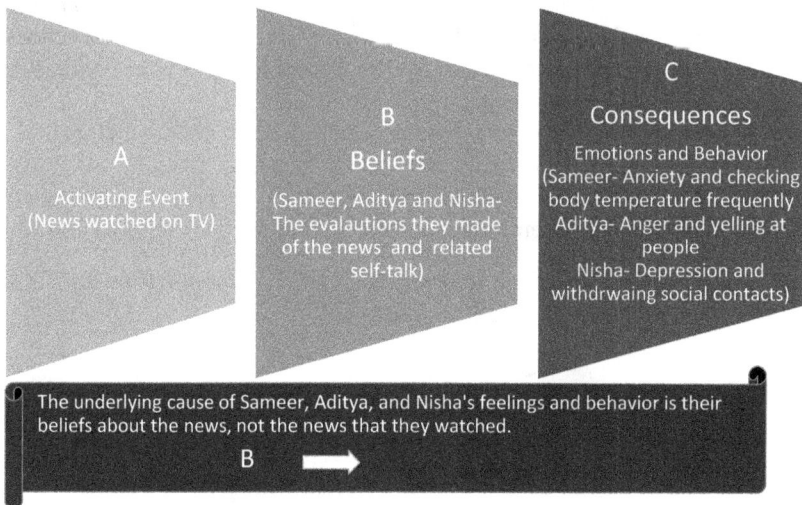

A	B	C
		Consequences
	Beliefs	Emotions and Behavior
Activating Event		(Sameer- Anxiety and checking
(News watched on TV)	(Sameer, Aditya and Nisha-	body temperature frequently
	The evalautions they made	Aditya- Anger and yelling at
	of the news and related	people
	self-talk)	Nisha- Depression and
		withdrwaing social contacts)

The underlying cause of Sameer, Aditya, and Nisha's feelings and behavior is their beliefs about the news, not the news that they watched.

B ➡

Figure 6.2 Analysis of Emotions and Behavior

and cross-examined at the "D" stage. The "D" stage involves forcefully and persistently confronting irrational beliefs. Let us take a look at how Ellis (1995) depicts a rigorous disputation of irrational beliefs in the book *How To Stubbornly Refuse To Make Yourself Miserable About Anything – Yes, Anything!*

> When you have discovered some of your unscientific beliefs with which you are creating emotional problems and making yourself act against your own interests, use the scientific method to challenge and dispute them. Ask yourself:
>
> Is this belief realistic? Is it opposed to the facts of life?
>
> Is this belief logical? Is it contradictory to itself or my other beliefs?
>
> Can I prove this belief? Can I falsify it? Is there any sense in my holding it if it is unfalsifiable?
>
> Does this belief prove that the universe has a law of deservingness or undeservingness? If I act well, do I completely deserve a good life, and if I act badly, do I totally deserve a bad existence?
>
> If I continue to strongly hold the belief (and to have the feelings and do the acts it often creates), will I perform well, get the results I want to get and lead a happier life? Or will holding it tends to make me less happy?
>
> (pp. 36–37)

The "D" stage of the ABCDE framework is very crucial in REBT. It aims to demonstrate to us how our irrational beliefs cause disturbances and to persuade us to embrace rational ones instead. The "D" stage is completed when irrational beliefs are replaced by rational beliefs.

Sameer, Aditya, and Nisha were all emotionally disturbed, displaying unhealthy emotions, namely, anxiety, anger, and depression. It shows that their beliefs at the "B" stage were irrational. REBT proposes two main criteria of rational beliefs that are used in disputation. The first criterion of rational beliefs is that they are based on facts (factual) and the second is that they benefit us in the long run (functional). Irrational beliefs, on the other hand, are unrealistic and cause emotional distress, thereby not beneficial in the long run.

Let us see how I counseled Aditya and Nisha in disputing their beliefs at the "B" stage. They brainstormed and practiced disputation questions based on the aforementioned two criteria. The result of this exercise was the creation of disputation questions that challenged their irrational beliefs. Some of them were as follows:

Sameer: Irrational belief—I *must not* have coronavirus infection and If I have, it would be *terrible,* and I *can't stand it.*

Disputation Questions

- Why *must I not* have it? Why I am the exception? (Factual)
- If it can happen to others, why *must it not* happen to me? (Factual)
- Is there any assured way that I can completely prevent myself from getting it? (Factual)

- If I have it, will it be so *terrible* or will I make it *terrible*? (Factual)
- What do I mean by *terrible*? Is it the end of the world if I have the infection? (Factual)
- Isn't it true that no one should have recovered from the coronavirus infection if it is the end of the world? Is it supported by evidence? (Factual)
- *Terrible* is extreme adversity. Is it extreme adversity? There are a lot of things that are worse than the coronavirus infection. What would I call them if I thought this was *terrible*? (Factual)
- *Can't* implies impossibility. Is it impossible to stand this? If so, how do others stand in this situation? (Factual)
- Suppose I have no choice but to endure this infection, do I still not have a choice of standing it whiningly or gracefully? (Factual)
- Isn't this sentence going to make me even more upset? (Factual)
- Won't this sentence make me even more distressed? If I say this to myself, will it not increase my disturbance even more? (Functional)
- Will telling this to myself help me take any constructive steps towards preventing an infection, or will it cause me to engage in unwarranted behavior?

Aditya:Irrational belief—In the pandemic, people *should not* be careless and *should* take precautions to avoid spreading it to others.

Disputation Questions

- Is there any compulsion on them why they *should* not do so? (Factual)
- Are there any absolute necessities in human behavior? (Factual)
- Are they not free to behave as they wish to? (Factual)
- Is there any law of the universe that compels them to behave in any specific way? (Factual)
- Is there any way to control other people's behavior? (Factual)
- Is this thinking going to help me to change other people's behavior? (Functional)
- Will telling myself this help me take any constructive step to raise public awareness and prevent contagion? (Functional)
- Will I not nurture negative emotions against other people if I say this to myself, hindering my attempts to enhance public awareness and prevent contagion? (Functional)
- Will this thought make me less tolerant of people who act in ways that differ from mine? (Functional)

Nisha:Irrational belief—The pandemic *should never* have lasted this long. It's *awful* and if it continues, I *won't be* able to bear it any longer.

Disputation Questions

- Who am I to decide what *should* happen and what *should not* happen in the world? (Factual)
- Do I possess any special power to control the conditions in the world as per my wishes? (Factual)
- Do I have the authority to declare in an absolutistic way that the pandemic *should never* have lasted this long? (Factual)
- Is it *awful* or is it unpleasant? (Factual)
- Am I not magnifying the situation by calling it *awful*? (Factual)
- The word *"won't"* denotes inability. Is it referring to being unable to bear the situation or the difficulty in bearing it if it continues? (Factual)
- What evidence do I have that I *won't* be able to take it much longer? (Factual)
- Will this thought help me in devising a strategy to deal with the situation? (Functional)
- Will this thought not to make me less tolerant of frustrating situations? (Functional)
- Will this thought not make me less confident in my ability to deal with tough situations in the future? (Functional)

When Sameer, Aditya, and Nisha asked themselves such questions at the "D" stage and scrutinized their replies, they realized that their beliefs were not based on facts. They were unrealistic and were not helpful to them in the long run. They were, in fact, exacerbating their emotional distress. They recognised how critical it was to cultivate rational beliefs rather than irrational beliefs.

Disputation is a cognitive technique used in REBT. It is used to modify our cognitions. Along with cognitive techniques, emotive and behavioral techniques are also used. Emotive techniques are used to modify our unhealthy emotions. Behavioral techniques are used to modify self-defeating behavior. Hence, along with disputation, I used emotive and behavioral techniques on Sameer, Aditya, and Nisha. One of the prominent emotive techniques used in REBT is Rational Emotive Imagery (REI). Let us see how I helped Sameer, Aditya, and Nisha with REI.

REI has two parts. In the first part, I asked them to visualize the situation that caused disturbing emotions in their mind (unhealthy emotion). I encouraged them to connect with their true emotions they experienced at the time of the incident and allowed them to experience them fully. When I moved to the second part, I asked them to visualize the same scenario, but this time I urged them to substitute healthy emotions in the place of unhealthy emotions. A premise of REI is that a change in emotion is possible only when we bring a change in its underlying self-talk. As a result, disputation happens automatically. I asked them to practice REI once a day for a month until they become accustomed to replacing unhealthy emotions with healthy ones.

I assisted Sameer, Aditya, and Nisha in developing new rational beliefs using these techniques. Sameer's new belief was "I wish to not have the coronavirus infection but there is no reason why I *must not* have it. Even if I have it, it would be inconvenient, but not *terrible* and though it is difficult to stand, there is no evidence to say that I *can't* stand it". Aditya developed a rational belief that "in the pandemic, it would be better if people were more cautious and took care to prevent spreading it to others but demanding that they *should* do it is unrealistic". Nisha's rational belief was that "it would have been preferable if the pandemic had not lasted as long as it did but demanding that it *should never* have happened is unrealistic. Even if it happened, it would be disadvantageous, but not *awful*, and if it persists, it will be tough to bear, but it is unjustifiable that I *won't* be able to bear it".

Sameer's self-talk changed when he obtained the rational belief. He told himself that, while he didn't want to be infected, it was unreasonable to demand that he *must not* get it. He considered the coronavirus to be inconvenient, but not *terrible*. Furthermore, if he had to face this condition, he began telling himself that he could handle it, no matter how difficult it would be. Aditya's self-talk also changed as he developed a rational belief. He began telling himself that, while he preferred that people would be more cautious and take all precautions to avoid spreading the illness, he would refrain from imposing absolutistic demands on them that they *should* do so. He started telling himself that he would be more accepting of others and would devote his energy to raising public awareness about the social behavior around the disease. Nisha's self-talk also changed as she obtained a rational belief. She realized that her demand that the pandemic *should never* have lasted as long as it did, even if she wanted it not to, was irrational. She began telling herself that even if the pandemic lasted for a long time, it would not be an *awful* situation, and she would handle it gracefully.

When they practiced these new self-talks, there was a change in their emotions and behavior. Sameer expressed "concern" (healthy emotion) about the corona-virus infection, but he did not appear to be anxious (unhealthy emotion). He was taking the necessary precautions to avoid it, but he had given up the habit of con stantly checking his body temperature. Aditya was irritated (healthy emotion) by people's carelessness, yet he did not become angry (unhealthy emotion) at their actions. He also ceased yelling at others who did not adhere to the social norms of the pandemic. Though Nisha was frustrated (healthy emotion) due to the prolonged pandemic, she was not feeling depressed (unhealthy emotion) about it. She also started engaging with other people in her network and was becoming more hopeful.

To help them behave following their newly acquired rational beliefs, I used a behavioral technique called "Acting on rational beliefs". I asked them to make a conscious effort to act as if they only have rational beliefs. I persuaded them to act rationally as much as they could. Their efforts to incorporate rational beliefs into their behavior gradually resulted in a shift in their irrational beliefs and inspired them to continue to do the desirable tasks.

When there was a desirable change in their self-defeating feelings and behav-ior, they progressed to the last stage of the ABCDE framework, that is, "E". "E" stands for *effective philosophy* of life. This stage provokes the person to look at his or her life from a new perspective. It does not end with the resolution of the current

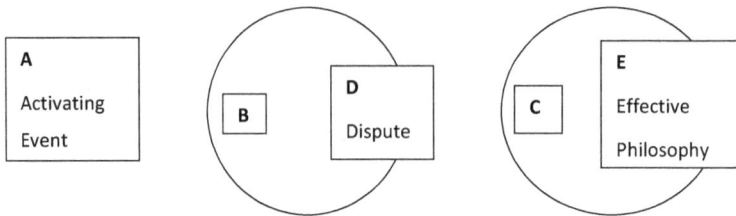

Figure 6.3 A Method of Solving Emotional Problems. *Source: Joshi, A. & Phadke, K. (2018).*

emotional issue; rather, it provides the person with broader insights that he or she can apply throughout their life. It helps in the adoption of a rational philosophy of life.

Figure 6.3 shows how the ABCDE framework can be used to address emotional disturbances.

The following are a few examples of broader insights acquired by Sameer, Aditya, and Nisha at stage "E":

- "*Musts*" and "*Shoulds*" are absolutistic demands that cause emotional disturbance. I can use wishes or desires instead of "*musts*" or "*shoulds*".
- I will not label adversity as "*terrible*" or "*awful*". By labeling them I amplify the severity of the adversity. I can refer to them as "unpleasant" or "inconvenient" instead.
- I will learn to be more tolerant of myself, others, and the situation. Tolerance entails accepting them even though they do not meet my expectations.

At the end of the "E" stage, Sameer, Aditya, and Nisha got enlightened on the causes and remedies of their emotional disturbances and they were ready to deal with any calamity that arose in the future.

The letter "E" is the final stage in the ABCDE framework. It completes the REBT process. The rational self-management adopted at this stage will be useful to Sameer, Aditya, and Nisha in their later life as well. Even if they get emotionally disturbed again, they have learned how to use the ABCDE framework to overcome their self-destructive emotions.

The "E" stage entails philosophical restructuring. In the following steps, (Ellis, 1976, p. 29) we can check the progress of Sameer, Aditya, and Nisha at the "E" stage.

1. They can fully acknowledge that they create, to a lesser or greater extent, their disturbances.
2. They can see clearly that they do have the ability to change these disturbances significantly.
3. They understand that what we usually call "emotional problems" stem mainly from irrational beliefs.

4. They clearly perceive these beliefs and dispute them.
5. They realize that they need to work hard in emotive and behavioral ways to counteract these beliefs and the unhealthy feelings and actions to which they lead.
6. They reuse and re-practice REBT to uproot and change disturbing consequences for the rest of their lives.

The ABCDE framework used in REBT is so effective that it is utilized not only to treat anxiety, anger, and depression but also to treat a variety of other unhealthy emotions that might impair one's mental health. No matter what the calamity is, it does not have the inherent power to upset you. REBT teaches you how to effectively manage your thoughts, emotions, and behavior in the face of adversity. Commenting on how we can make ourselves happier and less disturbed, Ellis (1999) asserts,

'You largely bring on your own emotional disturbances by choosing, both consciously and unconsciously, to think irrationally, to create unhealthy negative feelings, and to act in self-defeating ways. Fortunately, therefore, you can choose to change your thinking, feelings, and behaviours to undisturb yourself. If you do so in a forceful, persistent manner, by using REBT techniques, you can make yourself considerably less disturbed-that is, less anxious, depressed, enraged, self-hating and self-pitying- and sometimes to do so in a short period of time. They aren't magical or miraculous. But they definitely can help!

(p.175)

If you keep these words in your mind all the time and continue to practice REBT, it will assist you in rational self-management, not only during the pandemic but also during future turbulent times.

References

Ellis, A. (1976). Toward a new theory of personality. In A. Ellis & J.M. Whiteley (Eds), *Theoretical and Empirical Foundations of Rational-Emotive Therapy* (p. 29). Brooks/Cole, Monterey, CA.

Ellis, A. (1994). *Reason and Emotion in Psychotherapy- A Comprehensive Method of Treating Human Disturbances Revised & Updated.* Carol Publishing Group, NY.

Ellis, A. (1995). *How To Stubbornly Refuse To Make Yourself Miserable About Anything – Yes, Anything!* Carol Publishing Group Edition, pp. 36–37.

Ellis, A. (1999). *Make Yourself Happy & Remarkably Less Disturbable.* Jaico Publishing House, Mumbai, p. 175.

Ellis, A. (2001). *Feeling Better, Getting Better, Staying Better-Profound Self-Help Therapy for Your Emotions.* Impact Publishers, CA, p.15.

Joshi, A. & Phadke, K. (2018). *Rational Emotive Behaviour Therapy Integrated.* Sage Publications, New Delhi, p. 35.

Appendix 1

Table 6.1 is a list of twelve generic irrational beliefs. In this list, irrational beliefs are presented on the left side and corresponding rational alternatives are shown on the right side.

Table 6.1 Irrational Beliefs and Rational Beliefs

No	Irrational Beliefs	Rational Beliefs
1	It is a dire necessity for an adult to be loved by everyone for everything he does.	It is better to concentrate on one's own self-respect, on winning the approval of others for practical purposes (such as job advancement), and on loving rather than on being loved.
2	Certain acts are wrong, or wicked, or villainous, and therefore people who perform such acts should be severely punished.	Certain acts are inappropriate or antisocial, and that people who perform such acts are invariably stupid, ignorant, or emotionally disturbed.
3	It is terrible, horrible, and catastrophic when things are not the way one would like them to be.	It is too bad when things are not the way one would like them to be, and one should certainly try to change or control conditions so that they become more satisfactory, but if changing or controlling uncomfortable situations is impossible, one had better become resigned to their existence and stop telling oneself how awful they are.
4	Much human unhappiness is externally caused and is forced on one by outside people and events.	Virtually all human unhappiness is caused or sustained by the view one takes of things rather than the things themselves.
5	If something is or may be dangerous or fearsome one should be terribly concerned about it.	If something is or may be dangerous or fearsome, one should frankly face it and try to render it non-dangerous, and when that is impossible, think of other things and stop telling oneself what a terrible situation one is or may be in.
6	It is easier to avoid than to face life's difficulties and self-responsibilities.	The so-called easy way is invariably the much harder way in the long run and the only way to solve difficult problems is to face them squarely.
7	One needs something other or stronger or greater than oneself on which to rely.	It is usually better to stand on one's own feet and gain faith in oneself and one's ability to meet difficult circumstances of living.
8	One should be thoroughly competent, adequate, intelligent, and achieving in all possible respects.	One should do rather than always try to do well, and one should accept oneself as a quite imperfect creature who has general human limitations and specific fallibilities.

(Continued)

Table 6.1 Continued

No	Irrational Beliefs	Rational Beliefs
9	Just because something once strongly affected one's life, it should indefinitely affect it.	One should learn from one's own past experiences but not be overly attached to or prejudiced by them.
10	It is vitally important to our existence what other people do, and that we should make great efforts to change them in the direction we would like them to be.	Other people's deficiencies are largely their problems and putting pressure on them to change is usually least likely to help them do so.
11	Human happiness can be achieved by inertia and inaction.	Humans tend to be happiest when they are actively and vitally absorbed in creative pursuits or when they are devoting themselves to people or projects outside themselves.
12	One has virtually no control over one's own emotions and that one cannot help feeling certain things.	One has enormous control over one's emotions if one chooses to work at controlling them and to practice saying the right kind of sentences to oneself.

Source: Ellis, A. (1994). Reason and Emotion in Psychotherapy—A Comprehensive Method of Treating Human Disturbances Revised & Updated. Carol Publishing Group, NY.

7 The COVID-19 Pandemic and Rumor

The Indian Story

Braj Bhushan

Pandemic and Psychology: A Brief Overview

Human history has witnessed mass death and survival risk due to infectious diseases in the past. However, this piece of history does not remain in our conscious memory until brought forward by scholarly writings. They do not exist in public discourse. For instance, the plague of Athens (430–427 BCE), the Black Death of the 14th century, and the influenza pandemic (1918–19) were nowhere part of public discourse and were highlighted only in scholarly writings. Although all of them accounted for massive loss of human lives, they did not become part of the public discourse during COVID-19.

Rumor

During the COVID-19 period, we heard all kinds of stories. Some of them were true while most of them were misinformation propagating through gossip, either in person or through social media platforms. Although apparently looking alike, Gluckman (1963) has differentiated between rumor and gossip. Rumor has been defined as "an unverified proposition for belief that bears topical relevance for persons actively involved in its dissemination" (Rosnow & Kimmel, 2000, p. 122). Bordia and DiFonzo (2004) characterize it as "fleeting temporal phenomena" that are "purportedly … factual but lack authenticity" and "leave no trace".

Psychologists have focused on rumor research on and off. Three amazing old works on rumor originated from India and can be found in the *British Journal of Psychology*, two by Prasad (1935, 1950) and the third by Sinha (1952). While Prasad (1935) studied rumors surrounding the property damage and human loss in Patna (the present capital of the state of Bihar, India) during the Great Indian Earthquake of 1934, Sinha (1952) studied rumors during the 1950 landslide on the Darjeeling-Siliguri road in the north part of the state of West Bengal, India. In his other classic study, Prasad (1950) compared rumors collected from the field with those collected from the newspapers and historical accounts to find similarities in the theme across time and culture. He emphasized a multilevel phenomenon with emotion and cognition on one hand and group and culture on the other, thus propagating rumor. Although Jadunath Prasad of Patna University happens to be the front runner in rumor research in the world, the present generation of social

DOI: 10.4324/9781003304517-10

psychologists in India did not study it during the COVID-19 pandemic. Even at the global level, rumor research reached its peak during World War II and eloped from the mainstream after that. It was revisited by a few researchers during the COVID-19 crisis.

Almost all of us have experienced how the information/misinformation reached us during the COVID-19 period. Rumors sprout in ambiguous situations. Lack of credible information from the concerned agencies make situation cognitively challenging and thus become a breeding ground for rumors. Further, personal relevance provides fertile ground for its growth. This is what we saw during the COVID-19 pandemic. The information about the infection, preventive measures, testing mechanism, credibility of test reports, and so forth was highly fluid and many a times even contrasting. Hence, the situation became conducive enough to breed rumors.

Lack of cognitive clarity also makes us anxious or fearful of the situation and the intensification of the situation facilitates the spread of rumors as it is instrumental in venting the anxiety (Rosnow, 1991). Based on their anxiety-inducing ability, rumors are classified as dread or wish rumors (Rosnow, Esposito, & Gibney, 1988). They differ in their inherent nature. While dread rumors have to do with unwanted fear, wish rumors contain optimism, thus looking for desirable consequences. This has a resemblance with upward and downward counterfactual thinking. According to Rosnow et al. (1988), dread rumors propagate faster than wish rumors irrespective of the significance and belief in them (Walker & Blaine, 1991). Dread rumors are associated with unwanted fear and the unfolding of COVID-19 in India and elsewhere saw heightened fear of the unknown mixed with ambiguity. This provided a conducive breeding environment for the rumors.

One can shift the blame of the spread of rumors to the situational factors, but an obvious question that comes to mind is—why do people participate in spreading rumors? Walker (1996) suggests that by participating in a rumor mill, the given individual is able to reduce the "loss of control". The perception of loss of control is an integral component of terrifying events. Hence, it becomes amply clear that fear and its by-products have a key role in the rumor mill.

It is also interesting to examine the flow or transmission of a rumor. Krull and Anderson's (1997) model (Figure 7.1) explains the processes involved in it.

Bordia and DiFonzo (2004) have claimed that Krull and Anderson's model explains intrapersonal processes and adapted it to interpersonal process. The explanation given by them is illustrated in Figure 7.2.

Explaining the transmission of rumor, Allport and Postman (1947) have highlighted three steps—leveling, sharpening, and assimilation. They found a loss of 70% of the information, thus resulting in levelling of the information; transmission of select details, thus sharpening the information; and assimilation resulting in a distorted narrative due to "unconscious affective and intellectual motivation". However, this serial reproduction procedure has been criticized by a few researchers (Buckner, 1965; Rosnow, 1980; Shibutani, 1966) suggesting rumor transmission to be an exchange in the real-life scenario (Buckner, 1965; Caplow, 1947; Firth, 1956; Rosnow & Fine, 1976).

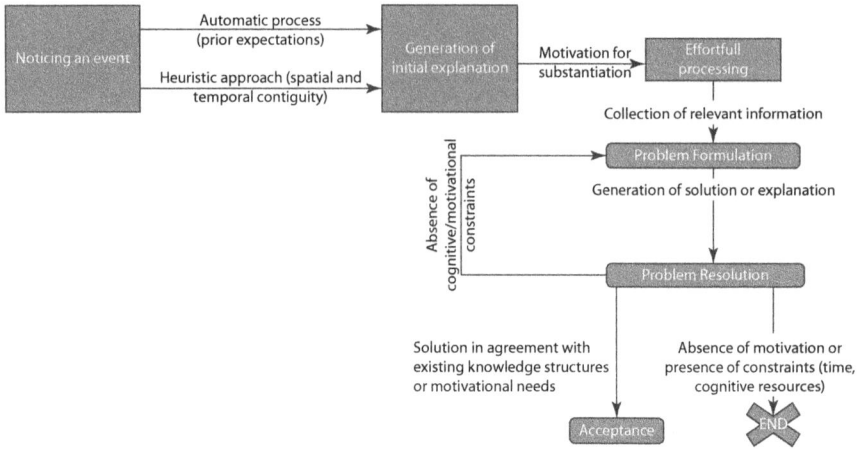

Figure 7.1 Illustration of Krull and Anderson's Model (1997)

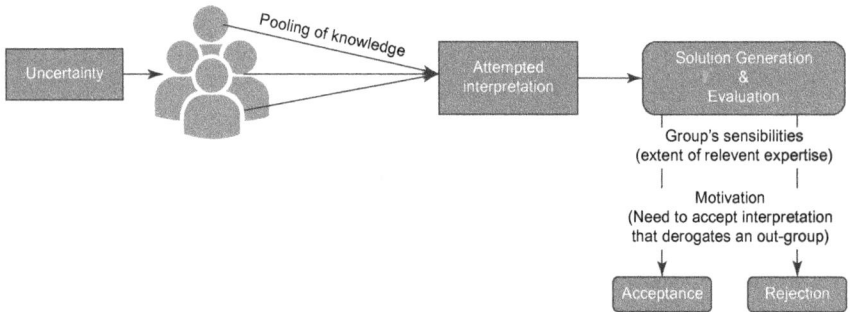

Figure 7.2 Illustration of Adaptation of Krull and Anderson's Model by Bordia and DiFonzo (2004).

Empirical examination of rumor is full of challenges. Bordia and Rosnow (1998) have proposed a computer-mediated communication network, Rumor Interaction Analysis System (RIAS), comprising of 14 categories of statements—prudent, apprehensive, authenticating, interrogatory, providing information, belief, disbelief, sensemaking, directive, sarcastic, wish, personal involvement, digressive, and uncodable. These categories show the nature and pattern of statements involved in rumor transmission. Prudent statements (Pr) are cautionary to evade accountability for whatever is being said. Apprehensive statements (Ap) express threatened feelings inclusive of fear, dread, anxiety, or apprehension related to the rumor. Authenticating statements (Au) express declarations with credibility. Interrogatory statements (I) consist of questions seeking information. Providing information (Pi) are similar to interrogatory statements and comprise of material relevant to the given rumor. Belief statements (B) reflect belief of the person in the given rumor. Absence of such belief is disbelief statements (Di). Sensemaking statements (SM) indicate the process of drawing inferences in order to solve the problem at hand. Directive statements (Dr) are announcements suggesting a course of action. Sarcastic statements (S) ridicule the beliefs of others. Wish statements (W) carry optimism. Personal involvement (P) statements pronounce one's experiences with respect to the given rumor. Digressive statements (Dg) are not directly related to the original rumor. According to Bordia and Rosnow (1998), sensemaking statements dominate rumors (above 17%), both wish and dread rumors, in the first quarter. In the case of dread rumors, it dominates in the first quarter, increases until the third quarter, and then declines, thus indicating that rumors are processed upon receiving to check for the truth using decision rules and heuristics.

Of the three major studies cited above, Allport and Postman's (1947) study was in response to wartime needs whereas the study by Prasad (1935, 1950) and Sinha (1952) was against the backdrop of a natural disaster. They were not with respect to any pandemic. The others have to do with the transmission of rumors. So, the recent studies of rumor deserve special attention as they were conducted during the period of COVID-19 and were assisted by modern-day tools and techniques.

COVID-19, Infodemic, Rumor, and Vaccine Hesitancy

Our COVID-19 response started with lockdown and quarantine and extended to contact tracing, surveillance, and testing before the doors were opened for the public vaccination drive. It was at this point when large scale vaccine hesitancy was realized. In 2019, the World Health Organization (WHO) recognized vaccine hesitancy as one of the top ten threats to global health. Based on the findings of her Vaccine Confidence Project, Larson (2020) identified the following factors that affect the vaccination drive—"rumor, dignity, distrust, risk, emotional contagion, choice, the power of beliefs over facts, and the power of stories over data" (cited in Gellin, 2020, p. 303). Larson (2020) argues that "we don't have a misinformation problem, we have a relationship problem" (cited in Gellin, 2020, p. 304) suggesting that unlike misinformation, underlying distrust cannot be deleted. She advocates attention to the rumors surrounding vaccination instead of countering and dismissing them. Thus, what was put on the backburner after World War II has once again come to the focus of attention.

The earlier section highlighted rumor transmission. One can take a critical set, an uncritical set, or a transmission set in relation to a rumor. Adopting the critical set would imply using the critical ability to parse out false information and see the truth. The reverse would happen when one adopts an uncritical set. In the transmission set, the critical ability is immaterial. The laboratory experiments of rumor usually adopt the transmission set, but how do messages float around in the present times? According to the Royal Society for Public Health (Durant, 2019), two-fifth of their respondents received vaccination related negative messages from the social media. Stecula, Kuru, and Jamieson (2020) have reported social media as a dominant source of vaccine-related misinformation resulting into vaccine-hesitancy.

Tedros Adhanom Ghebreyesus, the Director-General of WHO, referred to "infodemic" claiming that fake news "spreads faster and more easily than this virus".

An infodemic has been defined as "an overabundance of information—some accurate and some not—that makes it hard for people to find trustworthy sources and reliable guidance when they need it" (Islam et al., 2020, p. 1621). The retrospective COVID-19 related infodemic reports on sources such as newspapers, social media sites, fact-checking agency websites, and websites for television networks between December 31, 2019, and April 5, 2020 were studied by Islam et al. (2020). They found rumors to be most prevalent among all kinds of infodemics. This study found that the rumors ranged from the illness, it's transmission, and mortality to means of infection prevention and control measures. This was the time when India had started witnessing COVID-19 cases, and the first phase of lockdown was imposed. What did we observe here?

India experienced the first three-week countrywide lockdown starting March 25, 2020, which got extended twice, first until May 3 and then until May 17. This was the first-ever experience forced confinement within a defined space for people who kept receiving COVID-related information either through mass media or social media platforms. It was the latter that became a major source of rumor transmission. This step appeared effective in its first week but then three broad kinds of events were reported—the news of the congregation of thousands of visitors in Nizamuddin headquarters of the Tablighi Jamaat between March 13 and 24, 2020 in New Delhi, statements by few politicians correlating belief to the spread of COVID-19, and physical attacks on frontline workers in different parts of India. The press conference of the health ministry linked the mid-March Tablighi Jamaat event to the total confirmed cases of COVID-19. According to them, these attendees constituted 29.8% of the total coronavirus cases in India (at that point in time). Also, there were socio-political developments around that time in the aftermath of the enactment of the Citizenship Amendment Act (CAA). Select areas saw more than a month-long protest. While the focus of mainstream media also shifted during that time, there was an overflow of messages on social media. It could have been interesting to examine how the interplay of these three factors affected rumors during the nearly two-year COVID-19 period, but this did not attract the social psychologist in India. As a result, we have to look at reports from other studies.

A close look at them suggests that they were mostly belief-related information running close to the traditional knowledge, thus making acceptability easy. For instance, using sodium chlorite solution acid (Spencer, 2020; Vrajlal, 2020) with citric, or drinking bleach or alcohol to increase immunity (Victoria Knight of Kaiser Health News, 2020). Country-specific infodemics included using tea and cow urine or dung in India (BBC Reality Check Team, 2020), camel urine with lime in Saudi Arabia (Cable, 2020), and medicinal plants in Africa. A media report (India Today, 2021) highlighted the rumor in rural India that "those who take the jab die". Although every piece of information is not blindly accepted, misperceptions that align with one's belief, attitude, and group identity are. Earlier studies have shown the effect of health literacy on believing misinformation. The boycott of the polio vaccine in Nigeria, Pakistan, and Afghanistan (Aylward & Heymann, 2005; Hussain, Boyle, Patel, & Sullivan, 2016) is an example of this. Even certain areas in Western Uttar Pradesh in India had shown a similar trend and the government had to rope in religious leaders to overcome the rumor that the polio vaccine was a means of birth control.

Coming back to rumors during the COVID-19 period, India was the source of 13% of such rumors and conspiracy theories, slightly less than the United States (15%) and more than Brazil (12%). According to this study, these rumors came in three waves—between February–May 2020, June–September 2020, and 16 October to 20 November 2020. Of them, the second wave had the highest number of rumors.

Another study by Islam et al. (2021) reviewed the online rumors from 52 countries. Besides television and newspaper websites and social media, the team also looked at sources such as Google, Google Fact Check, Youtube, fact-checking agency websites, and television. The researchers classified them as true, false, misleading, or exaggerated information and found that of the total 637 pieces of information, 91% were rumors whereas the remaining 9% were conspiracy theories. 36% of the rumors were related to vaccine development and availability, 20% to morbidity and mortality, and 8% to safety and efficacy. The researchers suggested that there is a likelihood that rumors and conspiracy theories contributed to vaccine hesitancy.

The decision to get vaccinated involves computing the risk-benefit ratio amidst uncertainty. These are the essential ingredients of rumors as well (Larson, 2020). The Wellcome Global Monitor survey (2018), covering over 140 countries, reflects the trust-distrust ratio in scientists and vaccines. Only 72% of the respondents expressed their trust in scientists, leaving behind 28% distrust. Similarly, while 79% thought the vaccine to be safe, 21% did not. 84% of respondents thought the vaccine to be effective, while 16% did not (cited in Gellin, 2020).

This hesitancy was reported from several parts of India. There were reports of villagers running away from their villages upon the arrival of the vaccination team (Hindustan, June 4, 2021) and attacks on the vaccination teams (The Indian Express, 25 May, 2021). In one instance, the villagers even jumped into the river to escape vaccination (Time of India, 25 May, 2021). In all these cases, rumors played a crucial role. The villagers jumped into the river because of the rumor that the vaccine meant for them was poisonous. As mentioned earlier, *India Today* magazine highlighted the rumor floating in rural India that "those who take the jab die".

Studies have found that exposure to information, whether true or not, is crucial to believing it. Fazio et al. (2015) found greater acceptance of "illusory truth" in students for claims such as "The Atlantic Ocean is the largest ocean on Earth" simply because of their random exposure to it. The same applies to news from low-quality outlets (Prior, 2005). Besides the exposure effect, absence of cognitive scrutiny and reliance on intuitive thinking works in favor of misperceptions. In the case that the information comes from trusted sources, the acceptance increases. This is because "many use source identity as a heuristic for accuracy" (Nyhan, 2020, p. 226).

Islam et al. (2021) has also highlighted a political-economic motive in India suggesting availability of vaccine for those voting for the ruling party. At least two leaders belonging to two different political parties released statements doubting the efficacy of the vaccine. One of them had even ruled a state for five years. Following this, several other local leaders started repeating this and got publicized in newspapers and television.

Overall, right from the unfolding of COVID-19 to the ongoing mass vaccination drive, the scenario in India and elsewhere was ambiguous with a great degree of perceived loss of control. On one hand, the virus was coming in several variants, on the other hand, there was no means for cognitive scrutiny. This facilitated reliance on intuitive thinking. Mixed with socio-cultural beliefs and political-economic motives, rumors propagated well and could be significantly sustained to impact vaccination hesitancy. Rumor serve our "cognitive and emotional urge[s] to understand and comprehend" events in our surroundings (Allport & Postman, 1948, p. 206). With the new information correlating blood clot and heart conditions to COVID-19 vaccines and the new variants surfacing here and there in the world, one can only imagine the upcoming developments and challenges in the future.

What Next?

It is amply clear that this pandemic has resulted into psychological burden (Abdoli, 2020), but the scientific community has responded to the infodemic. However, there seems to be a pattern in this response with few bits and pieces missing. Between January and March 2020, at a time when COVID-19 was gaining momentum, there was also a steep rise of 900% in fact checks (Brennen et al., 2020). However, this was limited to fact-checks in the English language only. There is no estimate of the language independent volume of misinformation or fact-checks. Overcoming such linguistic barriers to create and store rumor data is the need of the time. Availability of relevant data sources is key to analyses of such misinformation. As of now, FactCheck .org (Brooks, 2020) and Poynter.org (Neil Brown, 2020) seem to be the biggest sources of COVID-19 related rumor data. A careful look at the rumor datasets such as Qazvinianetal, KWON, MediaEval dataset, RUMDECT dataset, RUMOUREVAL dataset, and PHEME dataset, etc. shows that overall Twitter/X has been the generous choice of the researchers. Even for COVID-19, the available datasets have largely gathered data from social media sites, such as COVID-19 associated Tweets, CoAid, the COVID-19 healthcare misinformation dataset, and others. The rumors that spread through word-of-mouth, a prevalent practise in collectivist cultures, has remained uncaptured. The social scientists who gather primary data for their study can be a great source of help in this regard. Thirdly, techniques adopted to analyze the data also seems to be an important issue. Modeling and prediction seems to be popular buzz words and the front runners are mostly the experts of engineering sciences.

Cheng et al. (2021) have developed web crawlers for automated data extraction from Google browser and Twitter/X. They labeled the emotional content of the rumor and its context. The data was subjected to veracity and stance classifications and sentiment analysis to compute the long-range correlation using the Detrended Fluctuation Analysis. This time series analysis indicates rumor popularity. Finally, they used a connected neural network to conclude that certain lexical and syntactic features can distinguish between a true and fake statement.

Lao et al. (2021) have emphasized on simultaneous looks at the linear temporal sequence and the non-linear diffusion structure, thus accommodating content of the claim, social context, as well as the temporal information. They have proposed Rumor Detection with Field of Linear and Non-Linear Propagation (RDLNP) which can help unfurl dissemination of rumors on social media and the response of the community.

To reiterate, for rumor datasets, modeling and prediction seem to be the current trend of data analysis (Cheng et al., 2021; Lao et al., 2021; Pathaka et al., 2020). This was a wonderful opportunity for the psychologists in India to empirically study the nature of rumors, means of transmission, and their relative impact on vaccine hesitancy. Alas, they missed the bus. They seem to have moved to the back bench. A whole lot of facts are left unattended by those who have opted for modeling and prediction. For instance, thousands of visitors had congregated in Nizamuddin headquarters of the Tablighi Jamaat between March 13 and 24, 2020 in New Delhi, and this was projected to be linked to the total confirmed cases of COVID-19 (29.8%) at that point in time. Another religious congregation, the Haridwar Kumbh, was held during April 1 to April 30, 2021 (the notified period) and according to the official sources 34.76 lakh devotees took a holy dip in the Ganges River during this period. The organizers claimed to have taken 5,555,893 swab samples of the devotees of which 17,333 tested positive. These two events took place at an interval of a year and had to do with two different religious groups, the Muslims and the Hindus. Both the events had generated a whole lot of posts on social media with apparent attitudinal bias. The content of those claims, their context, and the temporal information could have been analyzed. Even other moderating factors could have been identified and empirically tested.

Let us take another example. We have succinctly looked at the work of Prasad (1950) where he compared rumors collected from the field with those collected from the newspapers. The same can be replicated in the current scenario. Field data can be generated from those who ran away from their villages or jumped into the river during the visit of the vaccination team. Following Prasad (1950), one can find similarities in the theme across time and event. This very study has the potential of becoming one of its kind as the majority of the recent studies have banked on tweets and inputs from other social media platforms.

These are only teasers to pique the urge in social scientists, especially psychologists, to carry forward the legacy established by pioneers such as Jadunath Prasad and significantly contribute to the scientific knowledge and healthcare management.

References

Abdoli, A. (2020). Gossip, rumors, and the COVID-19 crisis. *Disaster Medicine and Public Health Preparedness, 14*(4), e29–e30. https://doi.org/10.1017/dmp.2020.272

Allport, G., & Postman, L. (1948). *The Psychology of Rumor*. New York: Henry Holt & Company. https://doi.org/10.1177/000271624825700169

Allport, G.W., & Postman, L.J. (1947). *The Psychology of Rumor*. New York: Holt Rinehart and Winston.

Aylward, R.B., & Heymann, D.L. (2005). Can we capitalize on the virtues of vaccines? Insights from the polio eradication initiative. *American Journal of Public Health, 95*(5), 773–777. https://doi.org/10.2105/AJPH. 2004.055897

BBC Reality Check Team. (2020). Coronavirus: Does drinking tea help? *BBC News*. Delhi: BBC News.

Bordia, P., & DiFonzo, N. (2004). Problem solving in social interactions on the internet: Rumor as social cognition. *Social Psychology Quarterly, 67*(1), 33–49. https://doi.org/10.1177/019027250406700105

Bordia, P., & Rosnow, R.L. (1998). Rumor rest stops on the information highway: Transmission patterns in a computer-mediated rumor chain. *Human Communication Research, 25*(2), 163–179. https://doi.org/10.1111/j.1468-2958.1998.tb00441.x

Brennen, J.S., Simon, F.M., Howard, P.N., & Nielsen, R.K. (2020). *Types, Sources, and Claims of Covid-19 Misinformation*. Reuters Institute.

Brooks, K.H.J. (2020). Factcheck.org: A project of the Annenberg public policy center. https://www.factcheck.org

Buckner, H.T. (1965). A theory of rumor transmission. *Public Opinion Quarterly, 29*, 54–70. https://doi.org/10.1086/267297

Cable, T. (2020). *CDD Fact Check: Can Camel Urine, Lime Cure Coronavirus? The Cable*. Abuja: The Cable Newspaper.

Caplow, T. (1947). Rumors in war. *Social Forces, 25*, 298–302. https://doi.org/10.2307/3005668

Cheng, M., Wang, S., Yan, X., Yang, T., Wang, W., Huang, Z., Xiao, X., Nazarian, S., & Bogdan, P. (2021). A COVID-19 rumor dataset. *Frontiers in Psychology, 12*, 644801. https://doi.org/10.3389/fpsyg.2021.644801

Durant, W. (2019). How do we respond to the challenge of vaccine misinformation? *Perspectives in Public Health, 139*(6), 280–282. https://doi.org/10.1177/1757913919878655

Fazio, L.K., Nadia, M.B., Payne, B.K., & Marsh, E.J. (2015). Knowledge does not protect against illusory truth. *Journal of Experimental Psychology General, 144*(5), 993–1002. https://doi.org/10.1037/xge0000098

Firth, R. (1956). Rumors in a primitive society. *Journal of Abnormal and Social Psychology, 53*, 122–132. https://doi.org/10.1037/h0044891

Gellin, B. (August 1–7, 2020). Why vaccine rumours stick—And getting them unstuck. *Lancet, 396*(10247), 303–304. https://doi.org/10.1016/S0140-6736(20)31640-8

Gluckman, M. (1963). Gossip and scandal. *Current Anthropology, 4*, 307–316. https://doi.org/10.1086/200378

Hindustan. (June 4, 2021). https://www.livehindustan.com/uttar-pradesh/siddhart-nagar/story-when-the-vaccination-team-arrived-the-villagers-closed-the-doors-women-imprisoned-in-the-house-men-ran-away-from-the-village-4090268.html

Hussain, S.F., Boyle, P., Patel, P., & Sullivan, R. (2016). Eradicating polio in Pakistan: An analysis of the challenges and solutions to this security and health issue. *Global Health, 12*(1), 63. https://doi.org/10.1186/ s12992-016-0195-3

India Today. (June 2, 2021). https://www.indiatoday.in/coronavirus-outbreak/story/-those-who-take-the-jab-die-rumours-mar-covid-vaccination-drive-rural-india-rajasthan-bihar-uttar-pradesh-madhya-1809812-2021-06-02

Islam, M.S., Kamal, A-H.M., Kabir, A., Southern, D.L., Khan, S.H., Hasan, S.M.M., et al. (2021). COVID-19 vaccine rumors and conspiracy theories: The need for cognitive inoculation against misinformation to improve vaccine adherence. *PLoS One, 16*(5), e0251605. https://doi.org/ 10.1371/journal.pone.0251605

Islam, M.S., Sarkar, T., Khan, S.H., Mostofa Kamal, A.H.M., Hasan, S., Kabir, A., Yeasmin, D., Islam, M.A., Amin Chowdhury, K.I., Anwar, K.S., Chughtai, A.A., & Seale, H. (2020). COVID-19-related infodemic and its impact on public health: A global social media analysis. *The American Journal of Tropical Medicine and Hygiene, 103*(4), 1621–1629. https://doi.org/10.4269/ajtmh.20-0812

Krull, D.S., & Anderson, C.A. (1997). The process of explanation. *Current Directions in Psychological Science, 6(1)*, 1–5. https://doi.org/10.1111/1467-8721.ep11512447

Lao, A., Shi, C., & Yang, Y. (2021). Rumor detection with field of linear and non-linear propagation. *WWW '21: Proceedings of the Web Conference, 2021*, 3178–3187. https://doi.org/10.1145/3442381.3450016

Neil Brown, K.M. (2020). The coronavirusfacts/datoscoronavirus alliance database. https://doi.org/10.1093/database/baz138. https://www. poynter.org/ifcn-covid-19-misinform ation/

Nyhan, B. (2020). Facts and myths about misperceptions. *The Journal of Economic Perspectives, 34(3)*, 220–236. https://doi.org/10.1257/jep.34.3.220

Pathaka, A.R., Mahajana, A., Singha, K., Patila, A., & Nair, A. (2020). Analysis of techniques for rumor detection in social media. *Procedia Computer Science, 167*, 2286–2296. https://doi.org/10.1016/j.procs.2020.03.281

Prasad, J. (1935). The psychology of rumour: A study relating to the great Indian earthquake of 1934. *British Journal of Psychology. General Section, 26(1)*, 1–15. https://doi.org/10.1111/j.2044-8295.1935.tb00770.x

Prasad, J. (1950). A comparative study of rumors and reports in earthquakes. *British Journal of Psychology, 41*, 129–144. https://doi.org/10.1111/j.2044-8295.1950.tb00271.x

Prior, M. (2005). News vs. entertainment: How increasing media choice widens gaps in political knowledge and turnout. *American Journal of Political Science, 49(3)*, 577–592. https://doi.org/10.1111/j.1540-5907.2005.00143.x

Rosnow, R.L. (1980). Psychology of rumor reconsidered. *Psychology Bulletin, 87*, 578–591. https://doi.org/10.1037/0033-2909.87.3.578

Rosnow, R.L. (1991). Inside Rumor: A Personal Journey. *American Psychologist, 46*, 484–496. https://doi.org/10.1037/0003-066X.46.5.484

Rosnow, R.L., Esposito, J.L., & Gibney, L. (1988). Factors influencing rumor spreading: Replication and extension. *Language and Communication, 8*, 29–42. https://doi.org/10.1016/0271-5309(88)90004-3

Rosnow, R.L., & Fine, G.A. (1976). *Rumor and Gossip: The Social Psychology of Hearsay.* New York: Elsevier.

Rosnow, R.L., & Kimmel, A.J. (2000). Rumor. In A.E. Kazdin (Ed.), *Encyclopaedia of Psychology*, Vol. 7. New York: Oxford University Press.

Shibutani, T. (1966). *Improvised News: A Sociological Study of Rumor.* Indianapolis: Bobbs-Merrill.

Sinha, D. (1952). Behaviour in a catastrophic situation: A psychological study of reports and rumours. *British Journal of Psychology. General Section, 43(3)*, 200–209. https://doi.org/10.1111/j.2044-8295.1952.tb00343.x

Spencer, S.H. (2020). Fake coronavirus cures, Part 1: MMS Is Industrial Bleach. https://www.factcheck.org/2020/02/fake-coronavirus-cures-part-1-mms-is-industrial-bleach/. Accessed April 4, 2020.

Stecula, D.A., Kuru, O., & Jamieson, K.H. (2020). How trust in experts and media use affect acceptance of common anti-vaccination claims. *The Harvard Kennedy School Misinformation Review, 1(1)*. https://doi.org/10.37016/mr-2020-007.

The Indian Express. (25 May, 2021). https://indianexpress.com/article/india/officials -attacked-in-madhya-pradesh-village-over-vaccine-hesitancy-two-arrested -7328923/

The Time of India. (25 May, 2021). https://timesofindia.indiatimes.com/india/villagers -jump-into-river-to-evade-covid-vaccine-shots/articleshow/82927966.cms

Victoria Knight of Kaiser Health News. (2020). COVID-19: Beware online tests and cures, experts say. *The Guardian.* Surry Hills, NSW: The Guardian.

Vrajlal, A. (2020). Chinese-Australians facing racism after coronavirus outbreak. https://www.huffingtonpost.com.au/entry/ coronavirus-australia-racism_au_5e33a522c5b6f 2623326d72b. Accessed April 4, 2020.

Walker, C.J., & Blaine, B. (1991). The virulence of dread rumors: A field experiment. *Language and Communication*, *11*, 291–297. https://doi.org/10.1016/0271-5309(91)90033-R

Walker, C.J. (1996). Perceived control in wish and dread rumors. Presented at the annual meeting of the Eastern Psychological Association, March, Washington, DC.

8 Creative Responses to the COVID-19 Pandemic

Shared Stories of Disabled Young People, Caregivers, and Mental Health Practitioners from Mumbai, India

Jill Sanghvi and Jehanzeb Baldiwala

Introduction

The COVID-19 pandemic has affected all strata of society, without discrimination. However, in this time, young people with developmental disabilities have been identified as a particularly vulnerable group. Working in partnership with the caregivers of young people with developmental disabilities, the authors have sought to respond to the COVID-19 pandemic by transforming practice. This involved witnessing and co-creating stories of resilience, courage, and creativity.

The authors are mental health practitioners, aligned to narrative ideas and practices (White & Epston, 1990), who engage in therapeutic conversations with disabled children and caregivers. They also collaborate with other practitioners and hold spaces of solidarity. The intention of writing this chapter is to make visible the idea that people are always responding in creative ways that make it possible for them to experience hope and navigate difficult times in their lives. The authors draw upon this understanding from narrative ideas and practices (White & Epston, 1990) that propose that stories of hope and resilience always exist but often get subjugated when the problem stories take center stage.

First reported in Wuhan, China, in late 2019/early 2020, the coronavirus spread rapidly across the world, affecting large numbers of people, especially those from vulnerable groups, and resulting in deaths. India has not been immune to the effects of this global crisis. Mumbai, a metropolitan city, home to 23.598 million people (Mumbai Metropolitan Region Development Authority, 2021), is India's financial capital. It has the busiest airports, seaports, and is the major hub for business and manufacturing. These features contribute towards a city that is densely populated. A large portion of this population is migrants from other parts of the country who come seeking employment, and often live in congested conditions that include slum settlements. Mumbai is also the point of entry for many Indians who have been living internationally. The mobile population, coupled with the lack of preparedness, poor sanitation, lack of medical facilities and resources (e.g., masks, oxygen cylinders), led to the virus rapidly spreading, as exposure among

DOI: 10.4324/9781003304517-11

Mumbai inhabitants was high (Grover & Singh, 2020). The city was thus a hotspot of COVID-19 infection.

One of the responses to control the spread of the virus was imposing lockdowns on populations. This measure was first announced in India in March 2020. For many people, it was unexpected and people were given little time to prepare. However, as one of the most densely populated cities in the world, Mumbai struggled to flatten the curve of the spread despite severe lockdown. The Indian Government's response to dealing with the COVID-19 pandemic was immediate, but there was a lack of planning and coordination given the scale of the implementation of lockdown (Kumar & Choudhury, 2021).

The suddenness of the lockdown did not allow people time to prepare, certainly not caregivers of young people with developmental disabilities. Disasters and emergencies disproportionately affect those who are part of the disabled community everywhere in the world. The COVID-19 pandemic was no different. Disabled people faced many hardships and the lockdown measures taken by governments meant people with disabilities were excluded and their needs often not considered (Shakespeare et al., 2021). Disabled people who needed to access healthcare or pharmacies were unable to do so. Cancellation or postponement of regular healthcare or rehabilitation differentially impacted them due to their additional health needs. For example, if their wheelchair or hearing aid remained not prescribed, did not receive the required maintenance, or was unrepaired, it made them dependent on family, if present, or those around them. Mandatory use of facemasks makes recognition for autistic people difficult and lip reading impossible for deaf people (Cullinane & Montacute, 2020). Additionally, being restricted to the home and elevated stress of family members increases the risk of physical or sexual violence and abuse in general, and children and adults with disabilities become more vulnerable (Jones et al., 2012), Increased isolation and uncertainty of what will happen as well as fear of illness have also led to the mental health of disabled people being affected. The economic fallout of the pandemic scenario is greatest on those who are poorest, especially those that live in low and middle-income countries (Kumar & Choudhury, 2021), where there are no social nets or welfare from the state available. This once again means disabled people depend on families/charity for financial support. People experienced anxiety due to fear of infection, changing lifestyles, and isolation from loved ones. People from diverse intersections of caste, class, gender, sexuality, and ability experienced the pandemic in different ways. Some disabled young people spoke a lot about disconnection from friends and the loss of their peer group; while other young people witnessed an increase in violence in the home, experienced financial insecurity due to loss of jobs of their parent/s, and loss of school as a safe space.

All of these experiences led to an increased need for the services of mental health workers. People were looking for answers and information about what to expect as well as hoping for support in managing anxiety, isolation, and elevated levels of distress. Clients were asking for longer sessions; and often, checking in on clients became more frequent. It became harder to set boundaries between personal and professional time. Interactions that were formerly face-to-face shifted to phone calls and video calls, and practitioners had to learn to use these ways of interaction to continue to support people who accessed services. Often, families were facing loss, coping with illness, and had many difficulties which hampered payment of fees, and workers were creating sliding scales in response. There were several requests to be part of helplines and support services. Mental health practitioners were also juggling with their own experiences of anxiety, illness within families, and other personal situations as a result of the pandemic.

While the uncertainty and unpredictability of the situation brought challenges, it also opened up a myriad of possibilities. This article explores how we, as therapists, sought to bring those possibilities to light and use them in practice to give people hope in uncertain times.

Understanding Disability in the Indian Context

There has been an enormous volume of research on autism (Huws & Jones, 2010, 2011) in the last two decades (Wolff, 2004) that has primarily focused on the medical characteristics and psychological consequences. The majority of this research has been from the West, with very little research done in an Indian context. In general, the mental health of young people and their families remains a much-neglected aspect in the research being done in India (Sanghvi, 2021). While there is increasing awareness of mental health and a growth in organizations providing services for families and persons with autism, there is still a long way to go (Lake et al., 2014). Within the Indian context, most of the research on autism is intervention-based (Divan et al., 2015; Manohar et al., 2019; Nair et al., 2014) resulting from medical discourses surrounding autism that often point to a deficit model. It has focused on understanding the needs of families and young people with autism, with the underlying assumption that research will support the building of a treatment plan to fix the "problem" (Sanghvi, 2021).

Ghai (2015) highlighted how disability for both men and women in the Indian context is not a singular marker and that it has to be positioned in multiple contexts, which contain many other markers of difference and inequality such as poverty, caste, class, gender, and rural-urban divide. Within India, generalizations have been made for understanding disability due to which narratives have been created which tend to exclude important features of disabled people's lives and of their knowledge (Ghai, 2015). Hence, families in India are often under stress and hard-pressed to care for the life-long needs of children with disabilities; especially because of the paucity of services, infrastructure, and social attitudes towards disabled persons (Vaidya, 2016). The caregiving role of the family is thus deeply enmeshed within economic as well as in cultural and social expectations (Vaidya, 2016). For example, families construct and change their routines around persons with autism, which may set them apart from the rest of the society (Vaidya, 2009).

Vaidya (2009) noted that interactions between families and the wider community were fraught with tensions; neighbors were, on the whole, concerned but cautious, and strangers often reacted with curiosity, amusement, or ridicule to odd behaviors exhibited by the child. While children with severe symptoms were regarded as deranged or mad, the mildly affected or high-functioning children managed to "pass", usually with difficulty. Mothers experience a lot of isolation as they spend most of their time traveling to therapy sessions, in therapy sessions, and coping with household chores (Krishnamurthy, 2008). However, this social perspective of what it means to live with autism and other disabilities is largely missing from the Indian research.

Working with Children and Families with Developmental Disabilities

Most interventions in the Indian context are focused on parent and child training programs (Juneja et al., 2012) as ways of "fixing" behaviors and social skills associated with autism. These training programs, often based on the deficit model, draw heavily from the medical discourses to "fix" what does not fit with how to live in society. The message that goes out to the children and families is that they are not on par with other children or that they are less than other children, and that they may not be included in "normal" social activities. Such messages can bring feelings of shame and social isolation for families. Due to the dominant discourses that emphasize disability as something that needs to be fixed, parents are not able to look at disability as an advantage.

Parental perspectives often differ from traditional scientific/professional viewpoints because parents have been shown to find meaning that may not always resonate with medical narratives. An investigation of what matters to parents in their everyday lives of different cultures is also necessary (Desai et al., 2012). This understanding points to a direction of finding out more about the alternative stories of disabilities which may be experienced by individuals and their families in their everyday lives but may not be visible to society. Fathers, culturally, are not vocal about their emotions and often spend longer hours at work, feeling the pressure to earn more money for a child who may be dependent on them for a long time (Krishnamurthy, 2008). The literature reviewed offers positive accounts of narrative therapy as a modality to support children and young people who are experiencing developmental disabilities and emphasizes including the family in conversations within the Indian context.

An earlier study from 2017 explored the impact of sharing experiences of fathering by creating a support group for fathers of children with disabilities using narrative therapy. The authors identified that fathers needed a space to share their narratives of fathering a child with a disability in an Indian context and brought forward the importance of including fathers in conversations about children's well-being and care (Shetty et al., 2017). A more recent study conducted to understand the experiences of children with developmental disabilities and their families receiving narrative therapy in Mumbai also shared positive accounts of the approach. Collaborative practices made it possible for young people and their families to experience a sense of agency and control in their lives and made visible possibilities for immediate and future actions that fit with preferred ways (Baldiwala & Kanakia, 2021).

Narrative Ideas and Practices

Narrative practices are used as a respectful non-blaming approach to counseling, as well as for engaging with communities. It proposes the idea that people are the expert in their own lives (Morgan, 2000; White, 2007; White & Epston, 1990). Narrative practitioners view problems as external from people and believe people have many skills, commitments, beliefs, values, and abilities that make it possible for them to decrease the influence of problems in their lives (Carey & Russell, 2003). Narrative therapy also emphasizes the importance of culture, histories of community, and people's own lived experiences in the shaping of their identity (White & Epston, 1990). Fundamental to narrative practices is the understanding that people are born into stories, and these stories shape their social realities (Combs & Freedman, 2004).

As an approach, narrative practices challenge the idea that mental health practitioners have to reach a single truth about any person or community by delving into ideas about the true self or inner self. Instead, it encourages therapists to be curious about the stories that people choose to share and tell, and to support people in reauthoring these stories in preferred ways (White, 2004). It draws attention to the idea that we exist amongst discourses and these discourses have shaped the way we perceive our social world to be. Discourses go on to gain status as being the only "truth" and dominate how we define our social world and ourselves. Alternative discourses tend to be marginalized and subjugated; however, they can still challenge dominant discourses (Sanghvi, 2021).

Drawing upon post-modern ideas, narrative practices rest on the belief that our identities are socially constructed. This allows us to shift from centering individuals and their actions to centering relational processes (Hoffman, 2007). In addition to shifting our stance as therapists, this difference in approach influences how we imagine contexts for healing (McNamee, 2009) and legitimizes communal practices as an alternative to clinical practice (Sax, 2011). Literature on resiliency and trauma experiences explores alternative accounts of responding in events that are traumatic such as solidarity, joy, friendship, love, generosity, spontaneous acts of courage, and peoples' resourcefulness (Solnit, 2009). Family and collective level interactions that rebuild family and community agency and resilience along with the use of cultural practices and school-based programs help rekindle community processes (Somasundaram & Sivayokan, 2013). Narrative approaches view strengthening webs of connection and community supports as an integral part of therapeutic work (Sax, 2013).

As mental health practitioners who engage in the practice of narrative therapy (White, 2007), we were keen to listen to stories that helped disabled young people and caregivers through these difficult times. What was happening in the world that was bringing anxiety to them? How were they managing the stresses in their lives? This line of questioning often reveals stories of negotiations between individuals who take initiative, and an environment with crisscrossing resources in myriad and unpredictable combinations that bring endless possibilities (Unger, 2005). We hold on to the idea that our role as narrative practitioners in these conversations is to be open to hearing about those stories that make visible and thicken agency, resilience, and resourcefulness of people. In this way, conversations of hoping and coping come forward, offering more space, in place of conversations that explore problems. This kind of stance, curiosity, and double witnessing for stories about the steps undertaken to move toward preferred ways of living allow us to co-create stories of lives as lived well despite difficulties and hardship.

Shankar's Story

Shankar was 19 years of age when the pandemic started. He is autistic and lives with his parents in Mumbai. One of the things that Shankar really loved was being independent and spending time alone at home while his parents were at their work-place. He enjoyed going to school. With the imposition of lockdown his entire routine changed. His parents worked from home and his own school was closed in March. There was a lot of despair because he had been looking forward to celebrat-ing his birthday and cutting cake with his teachers at school. One of the things that Shankar is passionate about is stationary. He loved going to stores, browsing and selecting pens and other items. Once a month he looked forward to a stationary buying day. Additionally, when there was a lot of anxiety, he could buy a few pens and feel a bit calmer. During the lockdown, stationary was not an essential item, and stores were closed indefinitely. He was unable to do these little things that meant so much to him. In addition, there was no clarity of the period of lockdown. It would be announced for three weeks at a time and at the end of every three-week period, it would be further extended. This increased the anxiety tremendously for him. There was a lot of ambiguity regarding services and no public transport was available which made any predictability regarding accessing therapy in person impossible. People were moving slowly to using the online medium to access edu-cation and therapy, but it took three months for everyone to transition. These and many other changes led to extreme distress for Shankar and his family.

Narrative ideas allowed us to locate the problem in the unpredictability of the pandemic and the city's responses to the situation, as well as the loss of routines and things to which Shankar was looking forward. In identifying these factors that were bringing anxiety we were able to co-create plans together that reduced the anxiety and brought him peace, calm, and happiness, which was what Shankar wanted for himself and his family. Co-research took us back to old practices and rituals. Some of these included writing the plans for the day, notes from conversations with the therapist that he could take back and read when he wished to, exploring shop-ping online once delivery opened up, and having a physical exercise routine every morning and evening. Among many other ideas in which Shankar engaged, he also found a new passion for researching recipes and baking or cooking with his mom. One of the things that stood out was the caregiver's understanding of Shankar's responses. She came up with the idea of bringing more predictability with respect to when Shankar would be able to resume in person therapy, celebrate his birthday with teachers, or visit his grandmother by selecting a date a few months away and sharing this with Shankar.

Through conversations with Shankar, what became more visible were his hopes for calm, peace, and happiness. He discovered skills that he had to bring these hopes into his life. His experiments with cooking continued, and he began selling brownies. He also helped with the household cooking and assisted his parents with daily chores within the home. He walked indoors and eventually went for walks in the garden and exercised in the mornings. He started traveling alone for his classes to college when the lockdown lifted. He learned to tell his mind things such as "college will open soon" to bring calmness. He began with taking a few steps and then more steps that allowed him to "go ahead in life" and have the "good life" he preferred. As conversations continued, it became possible to listen to the depth and richness of each story. Understanding that there are multiple voices in a story and many connections across time cements the idea that a story never ends and that it gets richer as time goes by.

Expanding the Narrative

Other caregivers of children with developmental disabilities shared their constant fears and anxieties related to themselves and their families, especially their children; for example, the fear of contracting the virus and what that would mean for their caregiving responsibilities of their children. Other anxieties included their children's well-being, finances, meeting the basic needs of the family, and concern over the termination of therapy sessions and whether their child would regress. Specific difficulties related to their child included coping with the child's "behaviors", engaging their children throughout the day due to an overwhelming workload at home and at work, and concerns related to their child's ability to keep up with schoolwork and the increased use of screen time. Caregivers expressed a feeling of isolation from being unable to connect physically with their community, which offers fundamental support in their lives. These conversations gave voice to caregivers' sense of helplessness; however, we also witnessed their resilience.

As mental health practitioners who engage in the practice of narrative therapy (White & Epston, 1990), we were curious to listen to and make visible stories that supported disabled young people and their caregivers through these difficult times. We were also interested in how mental health practitioners were responding to these challenges and continuing to support people. Our stance of curiosity and the questions and responses as practitioners were situated in our alignment to narrative ideas and practices. This inquiry and curiosity extended to other children and caregivers, and their responses too offered multiple stories of what the lockdown has made possible for them. Some of these included:

1 *Spending time with families.* Caregivers welcomed this time of lockdown to extend support to each other and redefine relationships. For example, the current situation made it possible for fathers to spend time playing with their children and be involved in their daily activities. Being able to support their children with attending online school also generated feelings of security and comfort for those children who had experienced increased anxiety during non-pandemic times (from bullying, sensory overload, keeping up with what the teacher and classmates are doing, which can be hard when experiencing a

learning disability). Experiencing less anxiety gave caregivers an opportunity to explore new skills of their children.

2 *Discovery of skills.* Caregivers used this time to uncover skills lost with time or engage in the development of new skills such as meditation, yoga, art, cooking, music, etc. Being at home allowed them to have more conversations with each other, connect with friends and families, and exchange ideas, read books, or look up ideas on the internet. One family discovered making fun videos of themselves as a way of coming together.

3 *Continuing therapy at home.* During this period, caregivers shared how they figured out creative ways to engage children and simultaneously continue to work on their therapeutic goals. For instance, caregivers reflected on how including children in chores like cutting vegetables built on their skills for daily living and became a way to share the workload. Another parent presented the disabled young person with different beans and pulses mixed together in a bowl and gave them the task of separating the ingredients into smaller containers as a way to practice fine motor skills.

4 *Prioritizing values.* Another creative response to the COVID-19 pandemic came through finding a way to continue holding on to what they considered important. Some the questions we were interested in included: what were they doing to stay close to what was important to them and what were some of the things or people who supported them? Disabled young people and caregivers shared about prioritizing what they want to hold on to, their hopes and values as a family and how this allowed them to let go of things that were not as important and were potentially coming in the way of their hopes and values. For example, one mother of an autistic young person spoke about how maintaining peace in the house and everyone being happy was most important to her, and so she chose to let go of struggling with allowing her daughter additional screen time. In this action of letting go she felt she maintained a state of calm which permeated across the family.

Responses of Mental Health Practitioners

The current situation has also called upon us, as workers, to develop creative ways to continue partnering with and supporting families. As mental health workers, the creative ways in which caregivers have responded to these new circumstances have inspired us to co-create and hold spaces to support these little and "little big" ways of navigating current times.

Making possible leisure spaces: An online format where young people experiencing developmental disabilities can come together and "chill" has seen enthusiastic attendance and been widely appreciated. Families come together to witness each other dance, play musical games, do crafts and use colours; but, most importantly, to connect with friends. The feeling of partnership and engaging with peers reduces the sense of being alone (Law et al., 2002) and in this space, children are able to put aside fear, share laughter, and feel uplifted. Caregivers have experienced support and reassurance that their children can connect with their therapists and other young people.

Connecting caregivers: Caregivers have greatly appreciated spaces to explore leisure and connection with others through the opportunity to do something fun and relaxing with a group of caregivers who share a similar lived experience. In the caregiver groups, vibrant exchanges of ideas and "jugaad" or life hacks on how to continue therapy goals using daily chores, how to get deliveries of food, who to contact for medications or permissions for moving during lockdown are all explored.

Using books: Books support both children and caregivers in initiating conversations about what has been hard (Heath et al., 2017). They also make it possible to express things which may be hard to share (e.g., worries) and can provide newer possibilities for people to respond. Both children and caregivers have shared that being able to exchange information and understand a situation better, contributes to a sense of agency over the context. This brings a feeling of knowing what ones' choices are, thereby reducing the sense of unpredictability. Books like *Ruby's Worry* by Tom Percival make it possible for children to imagine, draw, and create what "worry" may look like for them. When they read the different ways that the character is responding to worry, they may resonate with her and discover new ways of managing worry in their own lives.

Establishing new rituals and practices and reclaiming old ones: The COVID-19 pandemic has offered many disabled young people, their caregivers, and mental health practitioners the opportunity to reflect on their ways of being in the world. We witnessed a reclaiming of old rituals and practices and the co-creation of new ones that brought a sense of certainty and connection and made it possible for people to experience joy in the moment, or a sense of stability, a feeling of being grounded or having a sense of agency. Some families decided on having a fixed bedtime or mealtimes, a bath or exercise routine etc., while others focussed on creating family time to play together, involving each member in chores or assigning different chores to each member of the home, and including everyone by giving each member an opportunity to choose a movie or the fun activity for the day.

Leaning in—Responses by Practitioners for Practitioners

The literature around narrative practices in supporting professionals and practitioners emphasizes our collective sustainability. It has the intention to build solidarity and an orientation of social justice. At the center of the conversation are principles including centring ethics, creating solidarity, addressing power, finding ways to create collective sustainability, critically engaging with language, and structuring safety (Reynolds, 2010).

Narrative practices underline the performance of therapist identities in ways that can provide therapists with an antidote to despair and fatigue (White, 2007). Engaging in practices like remembering conversations, coming together for definitional ceremonies, identifying the influence that therapeutic interaction can have on practitioners, and expressing this to our clients can help to reinvigorate the work and lives of practitioners and re-imagine despair/burnout (White, 2007).

One of the challenges that we came across during these two years has been not feeling very hopeful. There were days when it was hard to see the relevance of one's actions and nothing made sense or felt important. These thoughts are not all-consuming, but they can be consuming and almost in contrast to these was another thought, the thought that if we feel it, others who are witnessing stories must have similar moments. And as they navigate the territories between hope and hopelessness, they must be discovering creative ways to nourish hope and continue on.

Multiple gatherings were held where practitioners could come together. The idea of these collective care spaces was to create a safe space to share, to make visible skills and ways people were responding, share small happiness, brainstorm ways to reduce the influence of the many problems present in the context, and witness each other's stories in ways that we experience resonance and are linked together as a community, building solidarity and a sense of being connected.

These gatherings were often two-hour meetings on Zoom that were open to all workers who were supporting individual's, families', and communities' mental health and wished to participate. Two or three mental health workers volunteered in turn to facilitate these conversations. Numbers of participants logging in ranged from 10 to 50 in the different groups that came together and were mostly from Mumbai and Kolkata. The gatherings usually started with a game and a prompt to think about what people value or believe is at the heart of their work followed by a conversation about some ways that they have discovered/tried to respond to these times in the pandemic. There was also an effort to stay curious and inquire more into ways that people hold on to hope and well-being and the actions as well as beings that support them in doing so. Conversations ended with asking the group to reflect on or think of a word/phrase/metaphor/image/poem/song/sensation that might allow them to keep these responses close to them and make it possible to continue to respond and do the things they were doing.

These gatherings included conversations and sometimes silence and tears. Participants responded in so many different ways that were rooted in their histories and lived experiences. They located hope in "little big" actions and steps they were taking, in being close to nature, and in acts of solidarity with each other. A lot of sharing and expressing despair and hope were made possible through sharing poetry and children's picture books and singing together. As people exchanged their anecdotes and stories, we rescued the words and captured them through poetic documentation or illustration with the intention of having something for people to hold on to beyond the community gatherings. These documents acted as a testimony to workers' creative responses to the distress, their acts of collective care, and a reminder of the possibility to keep hope available.

Conclusion

To conclude, this study analyzed the creative responses offered by disabled young people, caregivers, and mental health practitioners, which have been drawn from the authors' experiences during the COVID-19 pandemic. This study shows the pandemic brought many difficulties; however, as therapists, holding the belief that people are always responding allowed many stories of hope and resilience to become visible. During the challenging days of the pandemic, everyone maintains that people have many skills and know-how and are active participants in holding on to what is important to them.

References

Baldiwala, J., & Kanakia, T. (2021). Using narrative therapy with children experiencing developmental disabilities and their families in India: A qualitative study. *Journal of Child Health Care*. https://doi.org/10.1177/13674935211014739

Carey, M., & Russell, S. (2003). Re-authoring: Some answers to commonly asked questions. *International Journal of Narrative Therapy and Community Work, 3*, 60–71.

Combs, G., & Freedman, J. (2004). A poststructuralist approach to narrative work. In L. E. Angus & J. McLeod (Eds.), *The handbook of narrative and psychotherapy: Practice, theory and research* (pp. 137–156). Sage. https://doi.org/10.4135/9781412973496.d11

Cullinane, C., & Montacute, R. (2020). *COVID-19 and social mobility impact brief # 1: School shutdown*. The Sutton Trust. https://www.suttontrust.com/our-research/covid-19-and-social-mobility-impact-brief/

Desai, M. U., Divan, G., Wertz, F. J., & Patel, V. (2012). The discovery of autism: Indian parents' experiences of caring for their child with an autism spectrum disorder. *Transcultural Psychiatry, 49*(3–4), 613–637. https://doi.org/10.1177/1363461512447139

Divan, G., Hamdani, S. U., Vajartkar, V., Minhas, A., Taylor, C., Aldred, C., Leadbitter, K., Rahman, A., Green, J., & Patel, V. (2015). Adapting an evidence-based intervention for autism spectrum disorder for scaling up in resource-constrained settings: The development of the PASS intervention in South Asia. *Global Health Action, 8*, 27278. https://doi.org/10.3402/gha.v8.27278

Ghai, A. (2015). *Rethinking disability in India*. Routledge.

Grover, A., & Singh, R. B. (Eds.) (2020). Geographical background: Delhi and Mumbai. In *Urban health and wellbeing: Indian case studies* (Chapt. 3, pp. 63–101). Springer.

Heath, Y., Smith, K., & Young, E. L. (2017). Using children's literature to strengthen social and emotional learning. *School Psychology International, 38*(5), 541–561. https://doi.org/10.1016/j.dhjo.2021.101064

Hoffman, L. (2007). The art of "witness": A new bright edge. In H. Anderson & D. Gehart (Eds.), *Collaborative therapies: Relationships and conversations that make a difference* (pp. 66–79). Routledge.

Huws, J. C., & Jones, R. S. (2010). 'They just seem to live their lives in their own little world': Lay perceptions of autism. *Disability & Society, 25*(3), 331–344. https://doi.org/10.1080/09687591003701231

Huws, J. C., & Jones, R. S. (2011). Missing voices: Representations of autism in British newspapers, 1999–2008. *British Journal of Learning Disabilities, 39*(2), 98–104. https://doi.org/10.1111/j.1468-3156.2010.00624.x

Jones, L., Bellis, M. A., & Wood, S. (2012). Prevalence and risk of violence against children with disabilities: A systematic review and meta-analysis of observational studies. *The Lancet, 380*(9845), 899–907. https://doi.org/0.1016/S0140-6736(12)60692-8

Juneja, M., Banerjee Mukherjee, S., Sharma, S., Jain, R., Das, B., & Sabu, P. (2012). Evaluation of a parent-based behavioral intervention program for children with autism in a low-resource setting. *Journal of Pediatric Neurosciences, 7*(1), 16–18. https://doi.org/10.4103/1817-1745.97612

Krishnamurthy, V. (2008). A clinical experience of autism in India. *Journal of Developmental & Behavioral Pediatrics, 29*(4), 331–333. https://doi.org/10.1097/DBP.0b013e3181829f1f

Kumar, S., & Choudhury, S. (2021). Migrant workers and human rights: A critical study on India's COVID-19 lockdown policy. *Social Sciences & Humanities Open, 3*(1). https://doi.org/10.1016/j.ssaho.2021.100130

Lake, J., Perry, A., & Lunsky, Y. (2014). Mental health services for individuals with high functioning autism spectrum disorder, *Autism Research and Treatment*, Article ID 502420. http://dx.doi.org/10.1155/2014/502420

Law, M., King, S., Stewart, D., & King, G. (2002). The perceived effects of parent-led support groups for parents of children with disabilities. *Physical & Occupational Therapy in Pediatrics*, *21*(2–3), 29–48. https://doi.org/10.1080/J006v21n02_03

Manohar, H., Kandasamy, P., Chandrasekaran, V., & Rajkumar, R. (2019). Early diagnosis and intervention for autism spectrum disorder: Need for pediatrician–child psychiatrist liaison. *Indian Journal of Psychological Medicine*, *41*(1), 87–90. https://doi.org/10.4103/IJPSYM.IJPSYM_154_18

McNamee, S. (2009). Postmodern ethics. *Human Systems*, *20*(1), 57–71.

Morgan, A. (2000). *What is narrative therapy? An easy-to-read introduction*. Dulwich Centre Publications.

Mumbai Metropolitan Region Development Authority. (2021). Retrieved from https://mmrda.maharashtra.gov.in/about-mmr

Nair, M. K. C., Russell, P. S. S., George, B., Prasanna, G. L., Bhaskaran, D., Lenna, M. L., Russell, S., & Mammen, P. (2014). CDC Kerala 9: Effectiveness of low intensity home based early intervention for Autism Spectrum Disorder in India. *Indian Journal of Pediatrics*, *81*(Supplement 2), 115–119. https://doi.org/10.1007/s12098-014-1474-8

Reynolds, V. (2010). A supervision of solidarity. *Canadian Journal of Counselling*, *44*(3), 246–255.

Sanghvi, J. (2021). *Bringing forward voices of young people with autism in India* [Unpublished, Doctoral thesis, Vrije Universiteit Brussel]. Belgium.

Sax, P. (2011). Neighborly ways of being and paradises in hell: Communal practices that support naturally occurring communities. *The Journal of Systemic Therapies*. http://www.narrativeapproaches.com/neighborly-ways-of-being-and-paradises-in-hell-communal-practices-that-support-naturally-occurring-communities/

Sax, P. (2013). Reclaiming community out of personal catastrophe: Communal practices that build on naturally sustaining webs. *Journal of Systemic Therapies*, *32*(1), 30–42.

Shakespeare, T., Ndagire, F., & Seketi, Q. E. (2021). Triple jeopardy: Disabled people and the Covid 19 pandemic. *The Lancet*, *397*(10282), 1331–1333. https://doi.org/10.1016/S0140-6736(21)00625-5

Shetty, R., Baldiwala, J., & Vasunia, T. (2017). The I'm-perfect fathers group: A gathering of fathers of children with disabilities. *Indian Journal of Occupational Therapy*, *49*(1), 29–33.

Solnit, R. (2009). *A paradise built in hell: The extraordinary communities that arise in disaster*. Viking.

Somasundaram, D., & Sivayokan, S. (2013). Rebuilding community resilience in a post-war context: Developing insight and recommendations - A qualitative study in Northern Sri Lanka. *International Journal of Mental Health Systems*, 7, Article No 3. https://doi.org/10.1186/1752-4458-7-3

Ungar, M. (2005). A thicker description of resilience. *The International Journal of Narrative Therapy and Community Work*, *3/4*, 89–96.

Vaidya, S. (2009). *A sociological study of families with autism in Delhi: Issues and challenges*. Paper presented at the Asian Pacific Autism Conference, Sydney, Australia.

Vaidya, S. (2016). *Autism and the family in urban India: Looking back, looking forward*. Springer.

White, M., & Epston, D. (1990). *Narrative means to therapeutic ends*. W. W. Norton.

White, M. (2004). Folk psychology and narrative practices. In L. E. Angus & McLeod (Eds.), *The handbook of narrative and psychotherapy: Practice, theory, and research* (pp. 15–51). Sage Publications, Inc.

White, M. (2007). *Maps of narrative practice*. Norton.

Wolff, S. (2004). The history of autism. *European Child & Adolescent Psychiatry*, *13*(4), 201–208. https://doi.org/10.1007/s00787-004-0363-5

9 Mental Health of Students of Higher Education in Maharashtra During the COVID-19 Pandemic

A Preliminary Study

Juhi Deshmukh, B.R Shejwal, Satishchandra Kumar, Dave Sookhoo, Abhijeet Chore, and Shweta Sahasrabuddhe

Introduction

Novel coronavirus, a global crisis, unlike any other catastrophe witnessed by the entire world in the last 75 years has heightened human suffering, killed people, and has backtracked societies and countries. Much more than a health crisis, it manifested as a human, economic, and social crisis (United Nations, n.d.).

Coronavirus impacted everyone from the grassroot levels to the most powerful economies in the world and even today no one is immune. From healthcare system to banking and from food supply chain to education, every sector has faced the brunt of this calamity. The unprecedented healthcare demand during the volatile global outbreak of COVID-19 almost collapsed the entire healthcare systems globally without any exemption and more so in the developing countries. Malik (2022), in an integrated review approach, found that factors such as frail infrastructure, deficit financing, lack of transparency, and meager healthcare management resulted in aweak and fragile healthcare system in India. India reported 30,134,445 COVID-19 cases and 393,310 deaths during the two COVID waves. The nature of mental health concerns also varied between the two waves of the pandemic due to the differences in the severity of infection and death toll (Sv Lathabhavan & Ittamalla, 2021).

As the pandemic was leaving deep scars around the globe, India, with around 91% of the total workforce from the informal sector, was able to foresee the depth of the socioeconomic hit that could be caused shortly by the pandemic (Pothan, Taguchi & Santini, 2020). The worst part of the inescapable countrywide lockdown was that it concurred with the country's peak harvesting time of a variety of crops of the season. Local food systems are fragile in a country like India and it worsened amid the lockdown. Temporary workers in cities had no alternative than to leave and get back to their villages which was the only hope for survival.

DOI: 10.4324/9781003304517-12

The ordinary lives of youth in India took a U-turn with the lockdowns imposed one after another to enforce social distancing. Unusual learning platforms, soaring unemployment, disproportionate online learning conditions of students, isolation, return to domestic work for girls from disadvantaged backgrounds, fear of missing out, and thrust of technology has left deep scars on the youth of India (Farcis, 2021; Deniz, 2021; Monteith et al., 2021).

The Indian education system for centuries has been dominated by classroom education, however the pandemic scenario made it very difficult to run the education system in the traditional way. All educational activities like teaching, assessment, admissions, entrance examinations, and even internships are being conducted online during this period. But the fact remains that not all the students could benefit equally from the same due to several reasons like lack of high-speed internet access, and limited network data, power supply, and technological gadgets (Rawal, 2021). Also teaching and learning efficacy of online teaching has been found to be less preferred. Lack of facilities, infrastructure, technical tools, and internet access are the major drawback for conducting online sessions (Bao, 2020; Naik, Deshpande, Shivananda, Ajey & Patel, 2021)

The available studies and data raise a few concerns, like after almost two years of facing the pandemic are we better prepared with the facilities and infrastructure not only in the urban areas but also in the rural areas? And after these trying times have we figured out an approach to assess the mental health of students, especially the ones who are more vulnerable to the situation?

The 75th report of the National Sample Survey Office (NSSO) for 2017–18 highlights some of the major challenges that may have been causal factors in jeopardizing the education system during COVID-19. The survey reveals that only 4% of rural households and 23% of urban households possessed computers which include all desktops, laptops, palmtops etc. The report mentioned that the percentage of households having internet facilities stands at 23.8% with rural availability at 14.9% and urban at 42%. Reports mention that only 12.5% of students had access to smartphones. In urban areas on average 33.6% of people in the age range 15–29 years, and 20.4% in the age group of 15–59 years could operate a computer. These numbers sink starkly for the rural areas where, on average, only 23.7% of people in the age group of 15–29 years can use computers, moreover only 27.6% of the female population can use computers compared to 39% of the male population (Gupta, 2019; Sahni, 2020).

Given the above facts, is our resort to policies of online education a correct step? Do we have any plans and policies to cater to the mental health of these youth who are already vulnerable and facing such massive devoid? How are we preparing, coping, and planning for recovery of not only the physical health but also the mental health of the youth?

The mental health challenges posed by the coronavirus don't end here. At one end, the mere availability of computers and internet is a challenge, on the other end dubious internet use has increased profoundly over the past few years and COVID-19 pandemic lockdowns have augmented the phenomenon globally. Reports indicated that Microsoft's game servers saw ten million users during 2020 (Noah,

2020). This reflects how the gaming industry thrived during the pandemic. During 2020, BBC and Netflix recorded 16 million new subscribers which was almost 100% higher than the earlier year (Zoe, 2020).

The concern here is that for years there has been a debate on the excessive usage of and addiction to the internet and DSM has proposed Internet Gaming Disorder (The "gamers" play compulsively, to the exclusion of other interests, and their persistent and recurrent online activity results in clinically significant impairment or distress) as an addictive disorder also known as pathological internet disorder (American Psychiatric Association, 2013). Why then, has no psychoeducation or sensitization been provided to the youth regarding the excessive internet use which is no more a choice but a condition during multiple COVID-19 lockdowns? Or has it been a presumption that the youth who eventually are left with no choice but to use internet for almost six hours on online education during lockdowns will not get the urge to use any other online medium (gaming, shopping, watching, chatting or even pornography) for leisure?

On one hand where internet addiction is considered as a disorder the National Association of Software and Service Companies (NASSCOM) reports that students are spending 50% more time online than they would have before the COVID-19 pandemic (Das, 2020). There have been a growing number of evidences which verify that youth, the deepest asset of our country, is falling prey to online gaming, pornography, reckless online shopping owing to outstretched periods of staying at home. They have habituated to this lifestyle and developed a dependence on the internet as an essential part of their lives (Kakoor & Bashir, 2021; Jebaraj, 2021; Amin, Griffiths & D'souza, 2022).

Taking the above into account it is critical to recognize the importance of considering the mental health perspective while making policies that involve the youth of the country. It is of cognizance to sensitize and psychoeducate the youth before they open this Pandora's box of technology which surely can enable them but it can limit them too. It's equally paramount to plan to equip the primary and tertiary level support for the youth during testing times, which can be done through thorough family therapy and support group interventions. As Melinda Gates has rightly quoted "This pandemic has magnified every existing inequality in our society – like systemic racism, gender inequality, and poverty," (Ford, 2020); it's of prime relevance to ensure that mental health is of equal concern and that we take steps for its prevention and management.

Method

The aim of this study was to explore the mental health of students in the state of Maharashtra during the COVID-19 pandemic. The population of students drawn from rural and urban backgrounds were compared on Depression, Stress, Anxiety, Grit and Well-being. The study was carried out to bring to light the differences between the two groups during the pandemic. The literature previously studied suggested that a significant difference would be found between the two populations.

Sample

The sample consisted of 325 respondents from the age group of 18 to 24 years of age drawn from approximately 100 different villages, towns, and cities in the Indian state of Maharashtra. The students were from different streams and academic backgrounds of private and government colleges. Sampling technique used was purposive snowball sampling.

Inclusion criteria:

- 18 to 24 years of age
- Pursuing a full time degree course being conducted online
- Residing in the state of Maharashtra, India

The characteristics of the population are as represented with a pie chart below.

Data Distribution

The criteria of rural urban population classification for sampling have been defined as per the rural urban classification census of Government of India 2021.

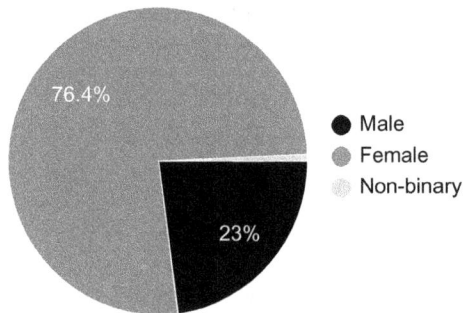

Figure 9.1 Diagrammatic Representation of Gender Distribution

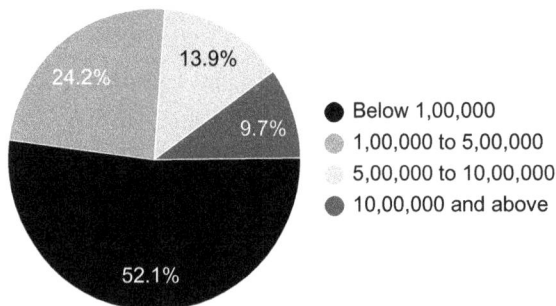

Figure 9.2 Diagrammatic Representation of Annual Income Distribution

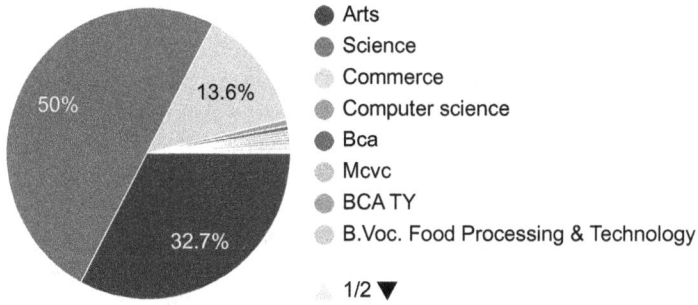

Figure 9.3 Diagrammatic Representation of Stream Distribution

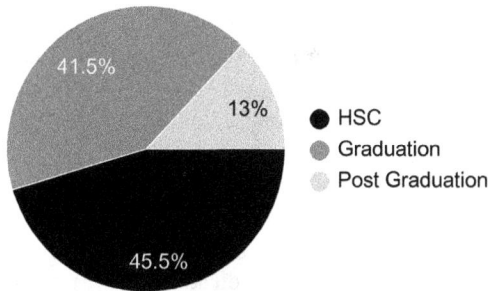

Figure 9.4 Diagrammatic Representation of Education Spectrum

Measures

1. Demographic data

Demographic data were collected using a form specifically for the purpose. Participants were asked to provide their age, gender, year of study, faculty, ethnicity, family support, marital status, living arrangement (parents, hall of residence), and whether they were first in the family to attend university education.

2. General health WHO-5

The WHO-5 instrument is a 5-item self report that assesses wellbeing, over the past two weeks on a 6-point Likert-type scale from 0 (not present) to 5 (constantly present). The range of scores on the WHO-5 can be from 0 to 25. The scoring principle states that the raw score ranging from 0 to 25 is multiplied by 4 to give a final score between 0 and 100, with 0 representing the worst and 100 representing the best imaginable well-being, respectively. A score below 13 will be indicative of poor well-being and the need to test for depression. In a systematic review that included 213 studies, Topp, Ostergaard, Søndergaard and Bech (2015) found that the WHO-5 demonstrated construct validity, was high on clinometric validity, and can be used asboth a screening for depression and as an outcome measure in clinical trials. The WHO-5 has been translated in well over 30 languages and successfully applied across a wide range of study fields in studies in different regions of the world (Sischka et al., 2020; Topp et al., 2015). Although a measure of well-being, the WHO-5 has been shown to be an equally valid measure of depression (Krieger et al., 2014). These researchers compared the validity of the WHO-5 with other established measures of depression, such as the Beck Depression Inventory-II (BDI-II) and Hamilton Depression Rating (HAM-D). Krieger et al. (2014) concluded that the WHO-5 can be used in the context of depression research. Similarly, Ghazisaeedi et al. (2021) assessed the validity and reliability of the WHO-5 in comparison with the patient health questionnaire - 9 (PHQ-9) and patient health questionnaire - 2 (PHQ-2) among 400 Iranian students who also completed The Beck Depression Inventory (BDI-13). They reported an internal consistency value of .94 for the WHO-5. Hence, the use of the WHO-5 in the study was clearly justifiable and provided an opportunity for further validation in a non-European population.

3.   The Depression, Anxiety and Stress Scale (DASS-21)

The Depression, Anxiety and Stress Scale (DASS-21) is a set of three scales designed to assess states of depression, anxiety, and stress (Appendix). Each scale contains seven items, divided into subscales with similar content. Each item includes a statement and four short response options to indicate severity, ranging from 0 ("Did not apply to me at all") to 3 ("Applied to me very much, or most of the time"). The total score of each scale is multiplied by 2 to yield equivalent scores to the full DASS-42 (Lovibond & Lovibond, 1995). Cut-off scores derived from a set of severity ratings proposed by Lovibond and Lovibond (1995) were utilized. The DASS-21 has been used extensively (Patten & Vaterlaus, 2020; Shaw et al., 2017) and translated in several languages, for example, in Nepali (Tonsing, 2014) and across cultures (Oei et al., 2013). The reliability of DASS-21 remained stable with alpha values above 0.8 as reported in several studies (Lee, 2019; Johnson et al., 2018).

The DASS-21 has been used extensively in studies (Bhullar, White & Phillips, 2013; Johnson et al., 2017; Lee, 2019). Studies reporting the factor structure of DASS-21 have reported confirmation of the three-factor structure (Henry and Crawford, 2005; Mellor et al., 2015; Johnson et al., 2018; Shaw et al., 2017).

4.   Perceived Stress Scale (PSS)

The Perceived Stress Scale (PSS) (Cohen, Kamarck, & Mermelstein, 1983) was selected because it is one of the most widely used psychological instruments for measuring perception of stress (Appendix). The PSS-10 has 10 items and measures the degree to which the individual appraised as stressful the situations they experience in their life. The items in the PSS are of a general nature and relatively free of content specific to any subpopulation group. They ask about respondents' feelings and thoughts during the last month, which are designed to gauge how unpredictable, uncontrollable and overloaded respondents find their lives. For example, "In the last month, how often have you been upset because of something that happened unexpectedly?" and "In the last month, how often have you felt that things were going your way?" Response options include 0 = never, 1 = almost never, 2 = sometimes, 3 = fairly often and 4 = very often. Higher scores indicate higher levels of perceived stress. The PSS has been paired with tools to assess effects of mindfulness interventions (Trammel (2018). The PSS showed good internal reliability, with Cronbach's α for pre-test PSS, α = .307 and post-test PSS, α = .077 for this study. In their study, Samaha and Hawi (2016) reported scores for this scale ranging from 6 to 34, and the Cronbach alpha coefficient was .87. In a study of 534 UK university students, Donovan et al. (2017) examined the factor structure, composite reliability, convergent validity, and gender invariance of the PSS-10. They tested four distinct models using confirmatory factor significant mean differences between genders. The internal consistency reported was 0.88 for the PS total factor and 0.70 for Coping, whilst the composite reliability for the Distress factor was low at 0.10.

The findings of the above studies support our choice of the PSS-10 as a measure of perceived stress among students in our study.

5.   The Short Grit Scale (Grit-S))

The Short Grit Scale (Grit-S) retains the two-factor structure of the original Grit Scale, namely perseverance of effort (six items) and consistency in interest (six items) (Duckworth, Peterson, Matthews, & Kelly, 2007) with four fewer items and improved psychometric properties. It is a 12 item questionnaire with a 5 point Likert scale. The Grit Scale is self-scored (paper/pencil version), Scores range from 1 (not at all gritty) to 5 (extremely gritty). Psychometric evidence is based on approximately 1500 adults and internal consistency estimates (Cronbach's alpha) for the Grit Scale was 0.85 (Duckworth et al., 2007).

Procedure

The proposal was approved by the Ethical Committee, Savitribai Phule Pune University. The necessary permissions from different colleges and universities across Maharashtra were taken and data was collected from the students according to the sample frame using a Google form. Informed consent was taken and a background of the study was provided before data collection.

The data collected was scanned for outliers using box plots and the final sample was put to data analysis using Excel 23 and SPSS V27.

Results

The data of 325 students was gathered from different cities and villages across Maharashtra consisting of students in the age range of 18 to 23. The data was scanned for outliers and a workable data for the sample of 317 students was analyzed. Pearson's Product Moment Correlation and Student's t Test was used to analyze the pilot data.

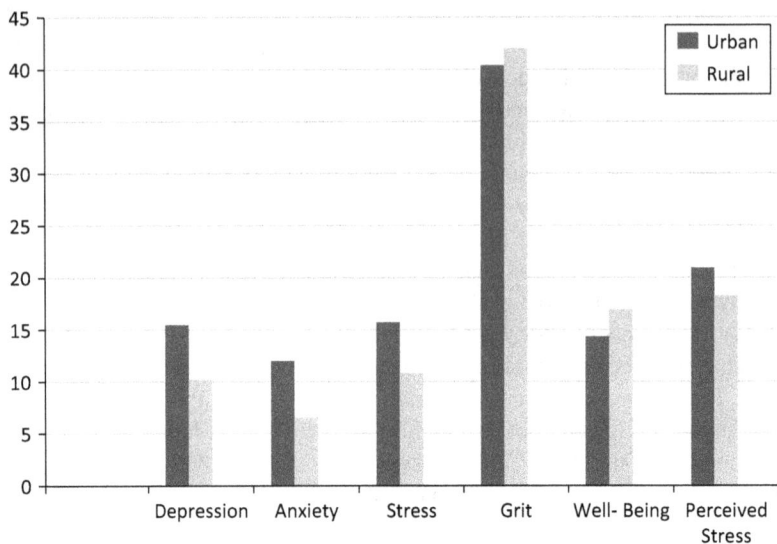

Figure 9.5 Difference between Urban and Rural Population

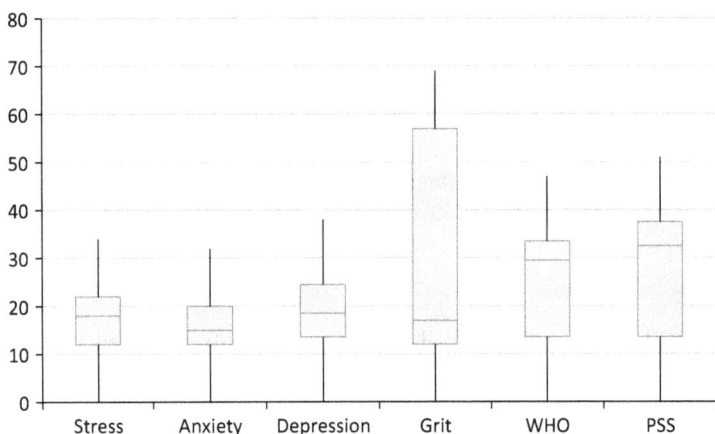

Figure 9.6 Outliers From the Data of 325 Were Eliminated Using Box Plots

The descriptive data set for the obtained results show the trends prevalent among the population studied. A noticeable difference among the selected variables can be seen among the students from urban and rural populations. A detailed description of the obtained results is as follows.

Depression between the students from urban and rural areas was studied. It was found that the mean of urban students was 7.72 and the mean of rural students was 5.10. This shows that the mean value of the urban population is very significantly higher than that of rural population. The t-test value is 3.9 with a degree of freedom

Table 9.1 Mean and T-value for Urban and Rural Students on Depression, Anxiety, Stress, Grit, Well Being, and Perceived Stress (N=317).

	Depression		Anxiety		Stress		Grit		Well being		Perceived Stress	
	Urban	Rural	Urban	Rural	Urban	Rural	Urban	Rural	Urban	Rural	Urban	Rural
Mean	7.72	5.10	5.99	3.28	7.84	5.42	40.37	41.99	14.30	16.91	20.91	18.25
N	165	152	165	152	165	152	165	152	165	152	165	152
df	315		315		315		315		315		315	
t value	3.90**		5.01**		3.83**		−2.35**		−4.30**		3.62**	
p value of significance (p < 0.01)	1.96		1.96		1.96		1.96		1.96		1.96	

** Significant at 0.01 level of significance

(df) of 315 and is significant at 0.01 level. This means that there is a significant difference with respect to depression levels among the urban and rural students.

Anxiety between the students from urban and rural areas was studied. It was found that the mean of urban students was 5.99 and the mean of rural students was 3.28. This shows that the mean value of the urban population is very significantly higher than that of the rural population. The t-test value is 5.01 with a df of 315 and is significant at 0.01 level. This means that there is a significant difference with respect to anxiety levels among the urban and rural students.

Stress between the students from urban and rural areas was studied. It was found that the mean of urban students was 7.84 and the mean of rural students was 3.83. This shows that the mean value of the urban population is very significantly higher than that of the rural population. The t-test value is 3.83 with a df of 315 and is significant at 0.01 level. This means that there is a significant difference with respect to stress levels among the urban and rural students.

Grit levels between the students from urban and rural areas were studied. It was found that the mean of urban students was 40.37 and the mean of rural students was 41.99. This shows that the mean value of rural population is significantly higher than that of urban population. The t-test value is -2.35 with a df of 315 and is significant at 0.01 level. This means that there is a significant difference with respect to grit levels among the urban and rural students.

Well-being levels between the students from urban and rural areas were studied. It was found that the mean of urban students was 14.30 and the mean of rural students was 16.91. This shows that the mean value of the-*rural population is significantly higher than that of the urban population. The t-test value is -4.30 with a df of 315 and is significant at 0.01 level. This means that there is a significant difference with respect to well-being among the urban and rural students.

Perceived stress levels between the students from urban and rural areas were studied. It was found that the mean of urban students was 20.91 and the mean of rural students was 18.25. This shows that the mean value of the urban population is significantly higher than that of rural population. The t-test value is 3.62 with a df of 315 and is significant at 0.01 level. This means that there is a significant difference with respect to perceived stress among the urban and rural students.

Table 9.2 Correlation Matrix

Variables	Correlation Matrix						Cronbach Alpha
	Grit	Stress	Anxiety	Depression	WHO	PSS	
Grit	**1**						**0.57**
Stress	**−0.28****	1					**0.91**
Anxiety	**−0.23****	0.81	1				
Depression	**−0.34****	0.85	0.81	1			
WHO	**0.39****	-0.48	-0.45	-0.52	1		**0.82**
PSS	**−0.40****	0.70	0.63	0.80	-0.61	1	**0.70**
N= 317							

** Significant at 0.01 level of significance

The correlation matrix for all the variables was done. The correlation co-efficient indicate strong correlations between the variables in the study. Stress, anxiety and depression along with perceived stress show a strong positive correlation. These variables were also seen having a strong negative correlation with grit and well- being

Discussion

This research was a part of a pilot study where differences among students living on the urban and rural areas of Maharashtra were studied with respect to depression, anxiety, stress, grit, perceived stress and wellbeing. The results of this study have shown interesting trends.

India's youth force is spread over scattered demographics, each region state and the developmental condition of these demographics bring along a completely different set of challenges. The sociocultural thread that fosters the quality of the social support that is available also plays a vital role in the mental setup of the youth. The impact that has been inflicted on the youth population has been called systematic, deep, and disproportionate as reported by the International Labor Organization in the 2020 Youth and Pandemic Global Report. The report tries to account for the global economic, social, and educational crisis that came in as part of the pandemic. The widespread impact of the pandemic was felt across populations and it was also found to be varied in its impact depending on the population. It is reported that 17% of youths aged 18–24 who participated in the study lost a job during the course of the pandemic and an alarming 35% of employees witnessed a reduction in their income in the UK (Gustafsson, 2020). An even higher number of 58.5% of people aged 15–24 who were surveyed in India reported to have lost a job during the period from December 2019 to April 2020, highlighting the magnified impact of the pandemic in the highly populated country. There also seems to be a scenario where the urban population has suffered more in terms of employment as the agricultural sector in the country has remained largely unaffected during the pandemic and special government schemes have safeguarded incomes and compensation for losses if any (Farcis, 2020). The rural areas also tend to have a scarcer population and hence it has remained relatively untouched as far as the COVID-19 pandemic is concerned.

The youth was in the forefront of the unforeseen emergency and they have been bearing the brunt of the changes in all walks of life. Life has particularly been hard for people who have been undergoing a transition during this period. And one such population has been students across the globe. The major transition that occurred globally in terms of education was the shift on the modality of the delivery. Students in major cities who studied in well-established universities found it easier to keep the academic momentum going whereas a different section of the population had a starkly different story to tell. It is reported that in the Mysore region of southern India, as high as 43% of students in public universities were no longer following their bachelor's degree courses in December 2020. The drop-out rate for girls has been as high and alarming as 65% (Farcis, 2020). This massive divide can be attributed to various factors including access to available infrastructure, pro activeness of the universities, and the relative socio-economic condition of the student. For other students who have been able to shift online to continue their education the problems have been of a different nature. Isolation, depression, and stress have been commonly reported among online education seekers (Chaudhary, 2021).

Students have reported problems that have risen not only due the uncertainty that has come to the fore due to the pandemic but also due to the physical and health challenges that have come as a by-product of the altered way of living and learning. Students have had multiple complaints including headache, backache, watering of the eyes, not feeling involved, and screen fatigue (Pandya, 2021). Evidently, the effect of the pandemic has been multifold in nature. One other challenge that students have faced, is the stigma surrounding the quality of education and assessments that they have undergone. They have very infamously been named as the "Corona batch" and "Covid batch" and that might be detrimental to their academic and professional future. The presumption that online education is not as effective as offline education seems to be a well-accepted truth. The students of the current batches especially in standard X, XII, and the final year of their graduation and post-graduation programs run the risk of developing a belief that they have received substandard education due to the online modality.

Through this preliminary investigation which has been held on a sample of 317 students in Maharashtra it is evident that the mental health of the youth from different parts of Maharashtra even during a pandemic never plummeted to an alarming stage. The overall levels of stress, depression, anxiety, and perceived stress remained below thresholds whilst grit and wellbeing thrived. Even though these results are preliminary they were obtained through a study held on a population that had a direct academic implication due to the pandemic and came from various socio-economic backgrounds and hold significance in providing an overview of the prevalent scenario in the midst of the pandemic. The relatively lower levels of stress, depression, and anxiety among the said population could be attributed to the increased awareness about mental health among the student population (Moghe, Kotecha, & Patil, 2020).

Among the relatively lower scores on the distress variables used in the study, it may be worthwhile to note the significant differences that have been found among the rural and urban populations. The rural population had lower scores on stress, depression, anxiety, and perceived stress. Interestingly, the urban student population, seemingly more equipped with technology, access to infrastructure, connectivity, and other means of entertainment, scored higher on the distress variables as compared to the sister population from the rural areas. These findings challenge the perspective that views the rural academic and mental setup as inchoate. In addition to this, the rural population also showed significantly higher scores on grit and well-being. This shows that the rural population is neither operating from a position of lacuna nor perturbation, but in fact, making the most of the available resources. These findings could be due to the fact that the rate of unemployment affected the urban population more than the rural population as agriculture was a sector that thrived even during the pandemic. Furthermore due to the lower population density in the rural area, the spread of the virus was not as pronounced as in the urban areas as the rural areas have seen a consistently low fatality rate (Radhakrishnan, 2020). Even though these findings need further exploration through supplementary data collections to be able to expound the causes for the same, the present trend is remarkable.

Conclusion

The primary exploration of the mental health of students staying in the rural and urban areas of Maharashtra during the pandemic has shown interesting results. The comparisons done on these sets of population revealed that the rural population experienced lesser distress during the pandemic as compared to their urban counterparts and at the same time they also showed higher levels of grit and well-being. Further exploration of the underlying causes for the same and the qualitative differences will be the focus of the next part of the study.

References

American Psychiatric Association. (2013). *Diagnostic and statistical manual of mental disorders* (5th ed.). https://doi.org/10.1176/appi.books.9780890425596

Amin, K. P., Griffiths, M. D., & Dsouza, D. D. (2022). Online gaming during the COVID-19 pandemic in India: strategies for work-life balance. *Int J Ment Health Addiction*, 20, 296–302. https://doi.org/10.1007/s11469-020-00358-1

Bao, W. (2020). COVID-19 and online teaching in higher education: A case study of Peking University. *Human Behavior and Emerging Technologies*, 2(2), 113–115.

Chaudhary, A. P., Sonar, N. S., Jamuna, T. R., Banerjee, M., & Yadav, S. (2021). Impact of the COVID-19 pandemic on the mental health of college students in India: Cross-sectional web-based study. *JMIRx Med*, 2(3), e28158.

Cohen, S., Kamarck, T., & Mermelstein, R. (1983). A global measure of perceived stress. *Journal of Health and Social Behavior*, 24(4), 385–396.

Das, P. (2020). Students are spending 50 percent more time online due to COVID pandemic, finds NASSCOM report. *Exdex Live, Indian Express*. Retrieved from https://www.cdcxlive.com/news/2020/oct/13/students-are-spending-50-per-cent-more-time-online-due-to-covid-pandemic-finds-nasscom-report-15187.html

Deniz, M. (2021). Fear of missing out (FoMO) mediate relations between social self-efficacy and life satisfaction. *Psicologia: Reflexão e Crítica*, 34, 28. https://doi.org/10.1186/s41155-021-00193-w

Duckworth, A. L., Peterson, C., Matthews, M. D., & Kelly, D. R. (2007). Grit: Perseverance and passion for long-term goals. *Journal of Personality and Social Psychology*, 92(6), 1087.

Farcis, S. (2021). India's Youth: Hit hard by the pandemic. *The UNESCO Courier*. Retrieved from https://en.unesco.org/courier/2021-2/indias-youth-hit-hard-pandemic

Ford, L. (2020). Covid has magnified every existing inequality' – Melinda gates. *The Guardian*. Retrieved from https://www.theguardian.com/global-development/2020/sep/15/covid-has-magnified-every-existing-inequality-melinda   gates?utm_term=Autofeed&CMP=twt_gu&utm_medium&utm_source=Twitter#Echo box=1600146858

Ghaziseedi, M. et al. (2021).Validity, reliability, and optimal cut-off scores of the WHO-5, PHQ-9, and PHQ-2 to screen depression among university students in Iran. *International Journal of Mental Health and Addiction*, 20, 1824–1833.

Gupta, S. (2019). NSO survey finds big rural-urban divide in computer, internet use. *Times of India*. Retrieved from NSO survey finds big rural-urban divide in computer, internet use | India News - Times of India (indiatimes.com)

http://www.apa.org/helpcenter/stress-kinds.aspx. Accessed February 11, 2010.

https://india.unfpa.org/en/topics/young-people-12

https://swachhindia.ndtv.com/world-mental-health-day-2020-in-numbers-the-burden-of -mental-disorders-in-india-51627/

Jebaraj, P. (2021). Gaming disorder increases during pandemic. *The Hindu*. Retrieved from https://www.thehindu.com/sci-tech/health/gaming-disorder-increases-during-pandemic/ article36812568.ece

Karoor & Bashir. (2021). The pandemic of pornography. *Kashmir Observer*. Retrived from https://kashmirobserver.net/2021/06/11/the-pandemic-of-pornography/

Krieger, T. et al. (2014). Measuring depression with a well-being index: Further evidence for the validity of the WHO Well-Being Index (WHO-5) as a measure of the severity of depression. *Journal of Affective Disorders*, 156, 240–244. https://doi.org/10.1016/j.jad .2013.12.015

Lovibond, P. F., & Lovibond, S. H. (1995). The structure of negative emotional states: Comparison of the Depression Anxiety Stress Scales (DASS) with the beck depression and anxiety inventories. *Behaviour Research and Therapy*, 33(3), 335–343.

Malik, M. (2022). Fragility and challenges of health systems in pandemic: Lessons from India's second wave of coronavirus disease 2019 (COVID-19). *Global Health Journal*. https://doi.org/10.1016/j.glohj.2022.01.006

Monteith, S., Bauer, M., Alda, M. et al. (2021). Increasing cybercrime since the pandemic: Concerns for psychiatry. *Current Psychiatry Reports*, 23, 18. https://doi.org/10.1007/ s11920-021-01228-w

Naik, G. L., Deshpande, M., Shivananda, D. C., Ajey, C. P., & Manjunath Patel, G. C. (2021). Online teaching and learning of higher education in India during COVID-19 emergency lockdown. *Pedagogical Research*, 6(1), em0090. https://doi.org/10.29333/ pr/9665

Noah, S. (2020). The Giants of the Video Game Industry Have Thrived in the Pandemic. Can the Success Continue? *The Washington Post*. Retrieved from https://www .washingtonpost.com/video-games/2020/05/12/video-game-industry-coronavirus/ Google Scholar

Pandya, A., & Lodha, P. (2021). Mental health of college students amidst COVID-19: Implications for reopening of colleges and universities. *Indian Journal of Psychological Medicine*, 43(3), 274–275.

Pothan, P., Taguchi, M., & Santini, G. (2020). *Local food systems and COVID-19; A glimpse on India's responses*. Food and Agricultural Organization of The United Nations. Retrieved from https://www.fao.org/in-action/food-for-cities-programme/news/detail/en /c/1272232/

Radhakrishnan, V., Sen, S., & Singaravelu, N. (2020, September 19). Data | Lower COVID-19 fatality rate in rural areas not necessarily due to lower share of co-morbidities among rural population. Retrieved from https://www.thehindu.com/. https://www.thehindu .com/data/data-lower-covid-19-fatality-rate-in-rural-areas-not-necessarily-due-to-lower -share-of-co-morbidities-among-rural-population/article32620632.ece

Rai, A. (2020). Is India ready for online education? – Evidence from the national sample survey's 75th round survey. Vidhi. Reterived from Is India Ready for Online Education? – Evidence from the National Sample Survey's 75th Round Survey (vidhilegalpolicy.in)

Rawal, M. (2021). An analysis of COVID-19: Impacts on Indian educational system. *Educational Resurgence Journal*, 2(5). Retrieved from 35-40.pdf (dypvp.edu.in)

Sahni, U. (2020). COVID-19 in India: Education disrupted and lessons learned. *Brookings*. Retrieved from COVID-19 in India: Education disrupted and lessons learned (brookings .edu)

Samaha, M., & Hawi, N. S. (2016). Relationships among smartphone addiction, stress, academic performance, and satisfaction with life. *Computers in Human Behavior*, 57, 321–325.

Sischka, P. E., Costa, A. P., Steffgen, G., & Schmidt, A. F. (2020). The WHO-5 well-being index–validation based on item response theory and the analysis of measurement invariance across 35 countries. *Journal of Affective Disorders Reports*, 1, 100020.

SV, P., & Lathabhavan, R. (2021). What concerns Indian general public on second wave of COVID-19? A report on social media opinions. *Diabetes & Metabolic Syndrome: Clinical Research & Reviews*, 15(3), 829–830. Retrieved from https://www.sciencedirect .com/science/article/pii/S1871402121001132

Tonsing, K. N. (2014). Psychometric properties and validation of Nepali version of the Depression Anxiety Stress Scales (DASS-21). *Asian Journal of Psychiatry*, 8, 63–66.

Topp, C. W., Østergaard, S. D., Søndergaard, S., & Bech, P. (2015). The WHO-5 well-being index: A systematic review of the literature. *Psychotherapy and Psychosomatics*, 84(3), 167–176.

United Nations. (2020). United Nations comprehensive response to COVID-19: Saving lives, protecting societies, recovering better. Retrieved from https://www.un.org/sites/ un2.un.org/files/2020/10/un-comprehensive-response-to-covid-19.pdf

Zoe, T. (2020). Netflix gets 16 million new sign-ups thanks to lockdown. *BBC*. Retrieved from https://www.bbc.com/news/business-52376022

Part III
The COVID-19 Pandemic
Resilience and Setbacks

10 Tears, Resilience, and a Pandemic

A Visual (Semiological) Journey

Rashmi Lee George

Introduction

Visual art is a form of expression that produces objects such as drawings, paintings, sculptures, ceramics, and poetry. Similarly modern visual arts use technology and produce photography, video, filmmaking, and architecture. Art is associated with the era and period. When COVID-19 swept across nations, leaving many dead and orphaned, people used visual art as one of the mediums to express their emotions. During COVID-19, people continued to create photographs, Instagram images, murals, graffiti, videos, and paintings. This is not a novelty of this century; it has been done before. When the Black Death, or the Bubonic Plague, wreaked havoc, along with evidence of mass graves, church registers, and official documents, there remain visual artifacts such as murals, frescoes, and paintings pertaining to these pandemics of yesteryears. Jagdip Jagpal, Fair Director, India Art Fair says, "Taken in conjunction with other historical documentation, [such works] serve as a visual record of a particular point of view, in the same way that literature, music and theatre reveal the human condition during trying times" (Kumar The Hindu). This chapter examines visual arts that were produced during times when the world went through a health crisis, both in the past and present, through a semiological lens. This chapter is divided into three sections. The first section discusses the fragile nature of human existence. The second section enumerates the paradox of being a frontline worker and the message of masks. The third section analyses the corollary of the pandemic in the environment and our lives.

The chapter uses a visual research method (VRM) which incorporates visual elements such as maps, drawings, photographs, videos, as well as three-dimensional objects, into the research process (Webb and Bedi 1). In this chapter, 29 paintings and murals are examined from around medieval, renaissance, and COVID-19 times. Even some select folk-art medium form part of this discourse. The selected paintings and murals refer to the pandemic in one (era) or the other (art form) and hence they find a place in this chapter. The method of analysis of these visual arts is situated within the theory of semiology which "confronts the question of how images make meanings head on … semiology offers a very full box of analytical tools for taking an image apart and tracing how it works in relation to broader systems of meaning" (Rose 70). The main postulant of this theory was Swiss linguist Ferdinand Saussure who sought to understand how words in a language-linguistic

DOI: 10.4324/9781003304517-14

system mean what they mean (Pooke and Newall 92). He attempted to comprehend the construction of signs and their meaning instead of particular languages.
He identified two aspects of the linguistic signs: the actual spoken or written word
which is the signifier or the physical element and the idea of the sign or mental
image known as the signified. The signifier and the signified are interdependent
yet separate (Pooke and Newall 93). Saussure's work and theories are concerned
with language, however, the essence of his work can be applied to sign systems
across media and communication, including images and art (Pooke and Newall
93, 94). Saussure creates a division of language into langue and parole, and it is an
important distinction in structuralism. Langue refers to the system of language, the
rules and conventions that organize it. Parole refers to the individual utterance, the
individual use of language (Storey 244). This theory is used to analyze the visual
medium in this chapter.

Roland Barthes uses Saussure's semiological model—the schema of signifier/
signified = sign—in his essay "Myth Today" and adds to it a second level of signification (Storey 254). As mentioned earlier, the signifier "skeleton" produces the
signified "skeleton": a human structure constructed of bones. Barthes would regard
this as the primary level of signification. However, in the secondary level of signification the skeleton may signify danger or death. Barthes calls the primary signification "denotation" and the secondary signification "connotation" (Storey 254). He
asserts that meanings are created for mass consumption at the level of secondary
signification or connotation. This is due to the polysemic nature of signs—these
signs have the propensity to signify multiple meanings (Storey 255). The transition
from denotation to connotation is possible because of the store of social knowledge
(a cultural repertoire) upon which the reader is able to draw when he or she reads
the image. Without access to this shared code (conscious or unconscious) the operations of connotation would not be possible. To continue the example of the "skeleton", it is a shared idea that a "skeleton" connotes death or danger. Such shared
knowledge can differ from one culture to another, and from one historical moment
to another. For instance, the skeleton could refer to a ghost who must be rejected in
some cultures, whereas in some others they will be welcomed as the return of their
ancestors. Cultural differences might also be marked by differences of class, race,
gender, generation, or sexuality (Storey 264). The variation in reading is not cha-
otic, it depends on the different kinds of knowledge—practical, national, cultural,
aesthetic—invested in the image by the reader (Storey 265). It was Barthes who
insisted that regardless of the authorial intention, any listener or viewer could freely
interpret any sign or image (Pooke and Newall 100). He suggested the idea of the
"death of the author" based on this theory. This chapter applies Saussure's ideas of
sign, signifier, and signified along with Roland Barthes's addition of primary and
secondary signification to the images related to the pandemic seen hereafter.

Fragility of Human Existence

Fragility of human existence is reiterated through the vulnerability of humanity in
the face of various human-made and natural disasters. Epidemics and pandemics

accentuate the fragility and vulnerability still further. This section tries to under-stand the timestamping of death in the context of the health disasters that struck the world. Additionally, it discusses issues that are reminders of life and finally it focuses on the sufferings of the migrants who get uprooted due to the pandemic.

The Timestamping of Death and Reminders of Life

The murals and paintings have timestamped the events of any given age because they depict the reality of the times. This section showcases seven paintings that have emerged from the recurrent Bubonic Plague (also referred to as Black Death in the fourteenth century) in Europe along with a current photograph to indicate the aftermath of COVID-19. The trauma of the pandemic caused by the corona-virus will be similar to the residual trauma that remained after the Black Death in Europe. The impact of the Black Death resonated in many walks of life. One of the most visible areas is art. The Black Death kept returning for more than 300 years—the plague became a regular phenomenon in Europe (Stanska Daily Art). According to Sardis Medrano-Cabral, "The trauma of the Black Death gave rise to the most popular artistic channel for the representation of death, the Dance of Death" (Medrano-Cabral Montana).

The Black Death and the Bubonic Plague intensified the concept of Danse Macabre which was prevalent in the form of drama, poetry, music, and visual arts from the Late Middle Ages. As a medieval allegory, it propounded the idea of an "all-conquering and all-equalizing power of death" (The Editors Britannica). It was conventionally agreed that the signifier is the skeleton visible in the image, and the signified is a sign of death. The connotation of the image is also linked to the folk superstition repre-sented by the skeletons themselves, or them accompanying the living. It further had a second social and spiritual lesson, that death is always coupled with the living. In the Dance of Death, the corpses often tug or draw the living to death (Cohen 1982 as quoted by Sardis Medrano-Cabral). During the COVID-19 crisis, people have lived and continue to live in the shadow of Death. It is a reminder of the Danse Macabre of the twenty-first century where death haunts both the rich and the poor alike.

Giacomo Borlone de Burchis's the *Triumph of Death* with The Dance of Death shows the power exuded by Death who stands with two scrolls. Flanked on both sides are two fellow skeletons who are killing people. People can be seen begging for mercy, offering them gifts but Death does not relent. Likewise, the COVID-19 era will be remembered along with visuals of people begging for beds and oxygen in hospitals.

In the *Dance of Death* by Michael Wolgemut the skeletons are seen dancing in the form of a lively farandole, a lively dance in which the dancers join hands and wind in and out in a chain. The depiction of skeletons playing music was a common one (Horvat Web).

The Dance of Death or Danse Macabre played the role of *memento mori*, the symbolic trope that everyone must die.

> Strictly speaking, it is a literary or pictorial representation of a procession or dance of both living and dead figures, the living arranged in order of their

rank, from Pope and Emperor to child, clerk, and hermit, and the dead leading them to the grave.

(The Editors Britannica)

The Danse Macabre murals and paintings were frequent and therefore they are the
langue in Saussure's terms and the individual Danse Macabre paintings are the
parole. The langue and the parole could accommodate differences which would
contribute to the difference in their meanings.

Arnold Boecklin, a Swiss symbolist painter, portrays the personification of Death
in *The Plague*. Death rides on a winged creature, flying through the streets of a medieval town. Death seems to be in control of its own path and will strike disaster in
its way. He uses this person as a signifier of the signified death and decomposi-
tion. Arnold Boecklin was deeply interested in the nightmares of war, pestilence, and
death. *The Plague* also uses a different signifier to convey the idea of death.

Bruegel's apocalyptic work called *Triumph of Death* is an intense visual of
Death capturing everyone and almost the end of life on earth. The background and
foreground overflow with the presence of the skeletons who represent death. The
middle-ground shows a skeleton on a horse with a scythe (Anneberg Learner Web)
like that of the Grim Reaper representing death. The myriad roles performed by the
skeletons shows their reach among humans. They do not leave any human alone
and it is a sign of the Danse Macabre idea of death being a constant companion in
human existence. The signifiers and signified culminating in the sign of death in
this painting are common knowledge. It is this shared knowledge about the persis-
tence of death that makes this painting a compelling one. The pestilences in those
times would have externalized this feeling of being constantly chased by death.

The much criticized and much honored photographs of mass cremations in
Delhi by the Pulitzer-Prize winning Indian photo-journalist (late) Danish Siddiqui
are a harsh reminder of the *Triumph of Death* by Pieter Bruegel the Elder. His
photograph became a signifier of the number of deaths in the second wave of the
novel coronavirus.

The sight of a Plague Doctor in the costume that appears in the picture would
have been a common sight during the Plague.

> The costume consisted of an ankle length overcoat, a bird-like beak mask
> filled with sweet-or-strong-smelling substances, along with gloves and boots.
> The mask had glass openings for the eyes. Straps held the beak in front of the
> doctor's nose which had two small nose holes and was a type of respirator.
>
> (Phillips 2013)

The beak could retain dried flowers such as rose or carnations, various herbs such
as mint, spices, camphor, or a vinegar sponge. The objective of the mask was to
occlude bad smells of the plague. The wooden cane was used to examine patients
through physical distancing. It was further used to remove the clothing from plague
victims. They would also be used to point out areas that needed medical attention.

The primary signification of the Plague Doctor is a sense of relief; however, the
secondary signification is that of terror too. His appearance indicated the presence

of a patient afflicted with plague. His presence too thus also became an imminent threat just like the sound of an ambulance and the sight of containment zones during the COVID-19 times that this contemporary era has witnessed.

Reminders of Life—A Trail of Tearful Migrations

Art created during the pandemic showcases people's ability to mirror their perspective of the reality around them. While the murals mainly from the Black Death/ Bubonic Plague times were reminders of the fragility of human existence, the murals as part of the street art in 2020–2021 are reminders of the life-givers. This section focuses on three select paintings by Dhruvi Acharya and its thematic counterpart in folk art.

Dhruvi Acharya captures the plight of the migrant workers who were caught off-guard in the midst of the lockdown. Their response to the lockdown shook the consciousness of the nation and exposed the thoughtlessness of an administration that lacked the foresight to anticipate the "Trail of Tears" that the workers undertook. "The Trail of Tears" was the forced removal of the Native Americans from the Southeast of the Mississippi to the West of the Mississippi (Pauls Britannica). The "Trail of Tears" of the Indian sub-continent during the lockdown captured the imagination of the folk artists too. Three paintings from three different origins showcase the plight of the migrants during the lockdown in India. These paintings, besides denoting the crisis of the migrant workers, also point to the dearth of foresight and vision in the people who could not see their definite problems.

Acharya's watercolors entitled "Painting in the Time of Corona" are a collection of artworks that were done on each day since the announcement of the Janta Curfew in March 2020. Her nearly surreal watercolor series is numbered as per the days of the lockdown. Her protagonists are recognizably women and men who are surrounded by thought-bubbles, open-mouthed flowers which appear to grin or to look shocked. The use of colors in the collection is nearly common— blue and red are used frequently. They present a grim and bleak tone used indisputably to demonstrate the gloomy moments of the pandemic. "I am basically painting what I feel, read, think about, see and hear", says Acharya.

> So, the ideas I'm trying to explore through these paintings range from loneliness, isolation, the plight of the daily wage labourers, the birds and animals who have almost found a new life in the absence of humans, and the newfound fear of the virus, and of human touch itself.
>
> (Basu Architecture)

In the Painting in the Time of Corona, Lockdown Day 9, 2 April 2020, Mumbai. Acharya shows men and women with and without masks. They are evidently people in transit. During the lockdown, the migrant workers were left stranded. Lack of employment and inability to pay rent, and the fear of the pandemic compelled the migrant laborers to return home to the far-flung corners of India. Since the inter-state trains and other modes of transportation were halted, many walked for days on end to reach their native places. This was one of the problems caused by the sudden announcement of the lockdown. Unprecedented numbers, akin to the exodus during the partition of India, were seen in the mass exodus of people moving from the metropolis to their homes.

Many folk artists adapted their folk-art forms to capture the themes of the pandemic—one of them being migration. Kalyan Joshi, who is an exquisite phad painter, has put together the different aspects of migration in *Migration in the time of COVID-19*. "Phad" refers to a type of scroll painting made using bright and subtle colors. The outlines of the painting are first drawn using blocks and later filled with colors (Nayanthara 14). Kalyan Joshi, with the aid of natural colors on textile, showcases the desperation of families, carrying their possessions and children, walking back to their villages (Bhuyan Mint).

"COVID" by Mahesh Shyam, a Gond artist, manifests the hardships of the migrant workers. He depicts them as having collapsed by the wayside. Through the use of vibrant colors and the portrayal of the local flora, fauna, Gods, and Goddesses (Mehal Expressions) the Gond artists capture an all-encompassing image of their society. Thus also, during the pandemic, the lockdown-induced-migration in all its horrors is painted by Mahesh Shyam. The movement of the migrant workers from various metropolises to the villages was a cry to leap into life at least in their native places because the urban centers had become hostile due to lack of employment. There was no money to support their daily needs and in their despair and longing to be home they trudged kilometers and kilometres to reach homes along with their families which included children. These paintings in their colorful sequence perhaps alleviate the sufferings that they might have experienced. Many stories of untold miseries appeared in the newspapers of people dying on the roads due to heart attacks and various accidents. These paintings reflecting the "Trail of Tears" will stay as a footprint for posterity to explore when the latter wish to look at the history of the period. Sometimes, the official versions are so marred by lies and bogus data that such works of art will become sources to corroborate the veracity of events in history.

The timestamping of death and the reminders of life through the mobility of the migrant workers during a pandemic that was raring to kill everyone speaks volumes about the catastrophe that one encountered during the COVID-19 crisis. The ethereal quality of human life was further shaken by the vulnerability one experienced due to inadequate healthcare infrastructure and lack of employment. The urban spaces had become hubs of death and destruction and since transportation had stopped, people had no choice but to walk for days together to reach their homes. Thus, the paintings of the omnipresence of death and compelled migrations due to unemployment and unsafe situations are the hallmarks of the COVID-19 times. Despite the negatives, human resilience enabled people to survive. One of the groups that need to be mentioned is the frontline workers.

(Un)Masking the Frontline Workers

This section discusses the actions taken during COVID-19 along with the actors involved during the COVID-19 pandemic. It firstly deals with the art used to communicate the effective utilization of masks to prevent the virus. Secondly, it discusses the depiction of the role of frontline workers through the medium of visual art.

The Message of the Masks: Classic and Folk

The pandemic of the twenty-first century will be remembered for its reiteration on various protocols and the punishments that were determined should one violate those norms. The work of art in this section showcases the importance of following COVID-19 protocols such as using masks, washing of hands, and maintaining social distance. Almost every other country in the world stressed these restrictions and protocols. Both classic and folk arts (showcased in this section) have engaged in pleading with the masses to mask-up in order to prevent the spread of the coronavirus. Additionally, the pandemic compelled artists to re-imagine and adapt classical work in contemporary times. Such contemporary inventive pieces are showcased in this section. While being creative, these forms also reminded people about their duty to prevent the spread of the virus.

Thanks to the Canada-based Genevieve Blais's Instagram page on Plague history, which she created to recreate iconic pieces of art, there has been a rise of those works in the form of murals in the streets of Mumbai. Some of Bais's works include

> the *Mona Lisa*, her ominous smile hidden behind a mask, a self-portrait of Dutch impressionist artist, Vincent Van Gogh, both ears intact securing the mask in place, *The Lovers* by Gustav Klimt, seen masked and embracing, which she cleverly corrected wasn't social distancing, the Statue of Liberty, Johannes Vermeer's *Girl With A Pearl Earring*, *The Scream* by Edvard Munch, muffled by a mask, Michelangelo's *Creation of Adam*, cleverly captioned that God too is practising social distancing, to name a few.
>
> (Jamal Hindustan Times)

The streets of Mumbai saw Western/European classical art with masks urging people to wear masks. These classics served to bridge the gap between the East and the West while facing the dreaded coronavirus. It was an opportunity for art to unite the world against the attack of the virus. Not only classical art, even pop art images of Marilyn Monroe adorned the streets of Mumbai. Further, folk art forms too were used to convey the message of social distancing and the importance of masks and handwashing. The creative artwork that was on display vociferously urged people to comply with mechanisms to prevent the coronavirus. These images are additionally significant because they are images conveying a message rather than words explaining a message. It is a visual illustration rather than a verbose text and hence it conveys more impact in connecting with the people.

During the COVID-19 crisis, apart from the murals in the streets, many folk artists in India released paintings to convey the message of social distancing and hygiene. India's prominent folk artists have released a series of paintings to spread the message of social distancing and hygiene (Tilak BBC). Minhazz Majumdar, a Delhi-based writer, designer, and curator specializing in Indian traditional arts, says, "I realised that for each artist, creating a pandemic-related work meant different things. For some, it was therapeutic, as it offered a way to make sense of things. For others, it was a way of recording and documenting these times" (Bhuyan Mint). Furthermore, she conveys to Bhuyan from *Mint* that, for the first time in history, the pandemic compelled the folk and tribal artists across India to create art based on the theme of the pandemic.

According to Laila Tyabji, the chairperson of Dastkar, India's prominent society for crafts and craftspeople, "Though many fear the impact of COVID-19 may be the end of craftspeople, it is their creativity and resilience that could save them" (Tilak BBC). Since March 2020, many folk artists have been producing folk art that communicates the "messages of social distancing, wearing face masks, washing hands with soap and avoiding group travel" (Tilak BBC). For instance, even the Gods cover their faces with masks during COVID times in the Pattachitra art created by Apindra Swain. The Pattachitra art or cloth form as they are known emerges from Odisha. They are known to depict stories of the famous Jagannath temple of Puri. Renowned for the use of vibrant colors such as red, ochre, indigo, green, black, and white obtained from natural sources like hingular (cinnabar, ore of mercury), haritala (yellow orpiment), lampblack, and shells. These paintings are created in the form of scrolls (Nayanthara 16).

Ambika Devi, a multiple-award-winning artist from Rashidpur village in the northern state of Bihar, uses a folk-art form called Madhubani which is eponymous with a district in the state. Natural pigments are used for color. It is an art passed on for generations together within a compact geographical area. Ambika Devi's art showcases the contemporary relevance of the Madhubani painting. In these pieces, she shows people wearing face masks following instructions on hand washing and maintaining social distancing at village markets.

In order to emphasize the notion of "social distancing," a graphic artist based in Mumbai, (who prefers to go by her account name Smishdesigns for the creative freedom it offers) chooses to present a rendition of Raja Ravi Varma's *Urvashi and Pururavas* with a heavenly nymph wearing a face mask and flying away from her beloved husband saying, "Social distancing" (Joshi & Dhawan The Times). She has reinvented characters from classical paintings within the scope of contemporary times. She depicts Mughal lovers embracing with their masks on.

Celebrating the Frontline Workers

The frontline workers such as doctors, nurses, community health workers, sanitation workers, police, volunteers, and ambulance drivers stood their ground to help the state in coping with the pandemic. Many lost their lives in their combat against the novel coronavirus. They even took a lot of flak from the common people who refused to follow the COVID-19 restrictions such as wearing masks or sanitizing themselves. The four pieces of paintings and murals recognize the magnitude of the efforts contributed towards the general well-being of the community.

Dhruvi Acharya shows a person in an outfit that looks strikingly like a Personal Protective Equipment (PPE) kit that was in the news. PPE kits were inadequate in supply and therefore unavailable to the frontline workers. The importance of PPE kit cannot be overemphasized enough. Acharya's *Painting in the Time of Corona Lockdown Day 20, 13 April 2020* thus captures the spirit of the lockdown through her paintings. While Dhruvi Acharya almost rewards the PPE wearer with flowers that appear pleasant instead of the grim appearance they showcase in other paintings.

Duyi Han, the creative director of Doesn't Come Out, a design studio in New York and Los Angeles, created a series called *Saints Wear White* in a chapel in Wuhan, where the coronavirus originated. A trained architect from Cornell University, he has roots in Wuhan where his grandparents live. His piece is inspired by the church frescoes and murals. He created the piece to pay tribute to the service rendered by the medical workers. "I love fresco paintings as an art form. They are powerful in evoking the emotion of respect and the sublime. I use it to show respect and to advocate for these medical workers" says Han (Chaves, The National). He further hopes that the mural in a church in China will demolish the stereotypical cultural assumptions of the Western and global viewers concerning China. It will further focus on the medical fraternity instead of the country itself as an exotic location, especially at a time when "the disease invokes racism and xenophobia" (Khanna Architecture).

The visual art created by Dhruvi Acharya, Rohan More, Duyi Han, and Tommy Fung explores different issues pertaining to the lockdown during the COVID-19 pandemic. They either reflect the reality or create interpretative visual texts that emerge from the lockdown. The impact of the lockdown on animals and the environment in particular, paying tribute to the frontline medical workers or encapsulating the fear and terror caused due to the pandemic, these artists have aced their styles with their contribution to the visual creative sphere. Likewise, folk artists too have managed to display their art within the context of the pandemic. For example, Swain passes on the message "Stay Home" through Pattachitra. It has all the features of a Pattachitra style; however, instead of Gods and Goddesses, it showcases frontline workers.

Mumbai saw the rise of many murals depicting the frontline workers such as Mural on Frontline Workers. The messages during COVID-19 through the murals were imbued with a tone of gratitude. They were reminders of the work done by the frontline workers such as the medical/para-medical staff, the police, journalists, sanitation workers, and so on.

Art never ceases. The art from centuries ago and the current pandemic are testimony to the resilience of the people who have not stopped creating art. They have re-negotiated, re-imagined, and re-inscribed their art into the world despite the pandemic.

Corollary of the Pandemic

The proposition that follows the pandemic reveals surprising facts about human existence and its impact. Locked-out of the environment and pandemic; the eequalizer is corollaries to the effect of the pandemic. They remind, once again the detriments caused by human greed and the helplessness of humanity in front of the pandemic.

Locked-Out of the Environment

"Locked-out of the environment" is a reference to the disappearance of humankind from the natural environment. This change enabled the animals to thrive in the environment. Two photos used in this section further elucidate this idea.

Acharya in her painting showcases humans and wild and domesticated animals (aerial, terrestrial and aquatic) in one frame. During the lockdown there were constant reference to sighting of animals in various uncharted locations. This was a phenomenon world over. Roy from *Down to Earth* reports,

> While Sambar deer wandered on the roads in Chandigarh, a small Indian civet was spotted on a zebra-crossing in Kerala. A herd of spotted deer explored the streets of Haridwar without the fear of being killed by moving vehicles. There was an increase in the number of flamingos congregating in Mumbai, according to news reports. It seemed wild animals took pride in allowing city folks to glorify their appearances. The now pristine beaches across the country's coastline became hatching grounds for tiny Olive Ridley turtles, while critically endangered Ganges dolphins made a return to the ghats of Kolkata .

This painting is an attempt to showcase the importance of coexisting peacefully with the human and non-human stakeholders. Acharya juxtaposes humans with and without masks and seamlessly portrays various animals and birds in one painting. She writes in *Vogue*, "And I do hope, when we do come out on the other side, that we prioritise health, family, the environment, science and education above weapons, war, religious fanaticism, mindless 'development' (read destruction) and production" (Vogue, 2020).

Another artist who showcased the impact of the lockdown on the non-human world is Rohan More, a contemporary visual artist known for his tongue-in-cheek series on hype culture called "Vilayti Shauk". According to Rohan More, the artwork *The Captor is now the Captive* conveys the irony of the lockdown in India. He says,

> As humans I think we're beings of subjugation, and animals often bear the brunt of that. Now that we are confined to our homes, the earth finally has space to breathe and animals are hopefully getting a break from relentless human activity. That's what I wanted to communicate through the artwork: that, for once, the captor is now the captive.
>
> (Khanna, Architecture)

Pandemic—the Equalizer

The Danse Macabre series reiterate the constancy of death. It is a reminder of how death comes to everyone irrespective of their class, gender, or race. The pandemic has made people realize the sense of alienation and isolation that one could experience when one is afflicted with the virus. The isolation from family and friends while one is either in home-isolation or in the hospital is gruesome, especially if the healthcare is lacking in infrastructure and supporting medical and para-medical staff. The three art pieces in this section present the varied situations during a pandemic that can affect human existence.

Acharya, through her *Painting in the Time of Corona, Lockdown Day 35, 28 April 2020, Mumbai*, represents many people from different walks of life. The open-mouthed flowers seem to be howling in terror due to the trying time that the world finds itself in. It also shows women who could perhaps be employed outside. The expressions on the faces of the women seem to suggest they are waiting in anticipation of something during the pandemic. Everyone, in other words, is affected by the pandemic one way or another.

Acharya shows a woman who is afflicted with COVID-19 in *Painting in the Time of Corona, Lockdown Day 14, 07 April 2020, Mumbai*. The posture of the woman lying on the bed shows the extent of her illness. Further, the color of her skin is in contrast with the background and hence she gets foregrounded in the painting. The depiction of the respiratory tract and the use of red and blue in its most accentuated state signify how the pandemic strikes people. It presents the fear that coronavirus generates among people.

Tommy Fung, a graphic designer and photographer from Hong Kong, used digital art to create a surreal representation of the fear generated among people due to the coronavirus (Fig 29). He uses Photoshop as a tool to create his work *Facehugger*, which is inspired by the James Cameron film Alien. His desire to recreate elements of film in his portrayal of everyday life in Hong Kong motivated him to create the passenger with a grotesque facehugger. He says,

> Since the virus outbreak, people in Hong Kong have been wearing all kinds of face masks on the street—surgical, N95, gas masks, DIY, etc. That's why I wanted to create an image of someone using a very scary one; you don't know if he's wearing a new type of mask or if he just got a new kind of infection.
>
> (Khanna, Architecture)

Conclusion

Art has always provided the much-needed sense of relief and calm in the midst of any disaster. Hence, be it the novel coronavirus or the Black Death or the Bubonic Plague which have left many dead and traumatized, these pandemics have not left humans bereft of emotions that produce art. The murals and paintings of medieval times and the contemporary era have mirrored social reality to such an extent that they could be studied as texts that reveal facts about history. A study of the visual texts alone can yield a large amount of information about the times. The paintings on the traumatic migration during the pandemic in India or the frontline workers speak volumes about the plight of the common people who were displaced and compelled to face the novel coronavirus. The paintings and murals have a place in history because they privilege the frontline workers who took on the mantle of saving the human race. It does not discriminate. Lastly, the pandemic was once again a reminder about the extreme caution one needs to ensure in order to protect oneself and one's neighbor.

Bibliography

Akundi, Sweta, "Discover Quarantine Art, now surfacing on social media to raise spirits." *The Hindu*, 23 March 2020, https://www.thehindu.com/entertainment/art/discover -quarantine-art-on-social-media-to-raise-spirits/article31143614.ece. Accessed 09 February 2022.

"Art through time: A global view." *Anneberg Learner*, https://www.learner.org/series /art-through-time-a-global-view/death/triumph-of-death/#:~:text=Painted%20by %20Bruegel%20around%201562,vision%20of%20death%20and%20destruction. Accessed 09 February 2022.

Basu, Rituupriya, "Artist Dhruvi Acharya's watercolours, which are up for sale, are helping tide over this crisis." *Architecture and Design Magazine*, 28 April 2020, https://www .architecturaldigest.in/content/chemould-prescott-road-mumbai-open-sale/. Accessed 09 February 2022.

Bedi, Shailoo and Jenaya Webb, eds. *Visual Research Methods: An Introduction for Library and Information Studies*. Facet Publishing, 2020.

Bhuyan, Avantika, "Folk artists as record-keepers of the pandemic." *LiveMint*, 3 July 2021, https://lifestyle.livemint.com/how-to-lounge/art-culture/folk-artists-as-record-keepers -of-the-pandemic-111625246234414.html. Accessed 09 February 2022.

Böcklin, Arnold, "The Plague by Arnold Bocklin." *World History Encyclopedia*, 19 June 2018. Web. 08 February 2022.

Britannica, The Editors of Encyclopaedia. "Dance of death." *Encyclopedia Britannica*, 28 May 2008, https://www.britannica.com/art/dance-of-death-art-motif. Accessed 04 February 2022.

Chandler, Daniel, *Semiotics: The Basics*, Routledge, 2007.

Chaves, Alexandra, ""How can I offer something positive in this situation?": How artists are taking on the coronavirus outbreak." *The National*, 5 March 2020, https://www .thenationalnews.com/arts-culture/art/how-can-i-offer-something-positive-in-this -situation-how-artists-are-taking-on-the-coronavirus-outbreak-1.988201. Accessed 09 February 2022.

"COVID-19 murals: From Mona Lisa to Van Gogh, Mumbai's artists are putting masks on pop culture icons." *Mid-Day*, 09 June 2021, https://www.mid-day.com/lifestyle/culture /photo/COVID-19-murals-from-mona-lisa-to-van-gogh-mumbais-artists-are-putting -masks-on-pop-culture-icons-91987/2. Accessed 09 February 2022.

Horvat, Robert, "The dance of death." *Rearview Mirror*, 5 November 2013, https://rear -view-mirror.com/2013/11/05/the-dance-of-death/. Accessed 09 February 2022.

Jamal, Alfea, "Masked Mona Lisa, Van Gogh, Frida Kahlo: Artist recreates famous paintings with coronavirus era twist." *Hindustan Times*, 18 August 2020, https://www .hindustantimes.com/art-and-culture/masked-mona-lisa-van-gogh-frida-kahlo-artist -recreates-famous-paintings-but-with-coronavirus-era-twist/story-yi36ddLzhB3siqp 8hOvhbJ.html. Accessed 09 February 2022.

Joshi, Sonam and Himanshi Dhawan, "Coronart: How isolation is inspiring artists." *Times of India*, 1 May 2020, https://timesofindia.indiatimes.com/india/coronart-how-isolation -is-inspiring-artists/articleshow/75444380.cms. Accessed 09 February 2022.

Khanna, Jasreen Mayal, "How the global art world is responding to the COVID-19 lockdown." *Architecture and Design Magazine*, 11 April 2020, https://www .architecturaldigest.in/content/how-the-global-art-world-is-responding-to-the-COVID -19-pandemic/. Accessed 09 February 2022.

Kumar, Surya Praphulla, "When Indian folk art finds a viral muse." *The Hindu*, 02 June 2020, https://www.thehindu.com/profile/author/Surya-Praphulla-Kumar-4959/. Accessed 10 February 2022.

Maurya, Ratnesh, "How artists across India are reacting to life with COVID-19." *The News Strike*, 26 April 2020, https://thenewsstrike.com/how-artists-across-india-are-reacting-to -life-with-COVID-19/. Accessed 09 February 2022.

Medrano-Cabral, Sardis, "The influence of plague on art from the late 14th to the 17th century." Montana State University, https://www.montana.edu/historybug/yersiniaessays /medrano.html. Accessed 09 February 2022.

Mehal, Zeina, "Gond paintings - Capturing the life and essence of one of India's largest tribes." *Expressions: The Artisera Blog*, 3 October 2016, https://www.artisera.com/blogs /expressions/gond-paintings-capturing-the-life-and-essence-of-one-of-india-s-largest -tribes. Accessed on 02 February 2022.

Nayanthara, S., *The World of Indian Murals and Paintings*, Chillibreeze, 2006.

Pauls, Elizabeth Prine, "Trail of tears." *Encyclopedia Britannica*, 30 November 2021, https://www.britannica.com/event/Trail-of-Tears. Accessed 09 February 2022.

Phillips, Alice M., *The Black Death: The Plague*, 1333–1770, 2013, https://hosted.lib.uiowa .edu/histmed/plague/. Accessed 08 June 2024.

Pooke, Grant and Diana Newall, *Art History: The Basics*, Routledge, 2008.

Quinn, Alana, "Duyi Han: The Saints wear white." *Issues in Science and Technology* 37, no. 2 (Winter 2021): 6–7. https://issues.org/duyi-han-digital-art/. Accessed 09 February 2022.

Rose, Gillian, *Visual Methodologies*, Sage Publications, 2001.

Roy, Suranjita, "Wildlife during a pandemic: The other side of the coin." *Down To Earth*, 29 July 2020, https://www.downtoearth.org.in/blog/wildlife-biodiversity/wildlife-during-a -pandemic-the-other-side-of-the-coin-72547. Accessed 09 February 2022.

Stanska, Zuzanna, "Plague in art: 10 paintings you should know in the times of coronavirus." *Daily Art Magazine*, 9 March 2020, https://www.dailyartmagazine.com/plague-in-art-10 -paintings-coronavirus/. Accessed 09 February 2022.

Storey, John, *Cultural Theory and Popular Culture: An Introduction*, Routledge, 2012.

Tilak, Sudha G., "Gods in face masks: India's folk artists take on COVID-19." *BBC*, 2 May 2020, https://www.bbc.com/news/world-asia-india-52464028. Accessed 09 February 2022.

"3 Artists share their personal experience in self-isolation and what life will be like post the pandemic." *Vogue*, 16 June 2020, https://www.vogue.in/magazine-story/3-artists -share-their-personal-experience-in-self-isolation-and-what-life-will-be-like-post-the -pandemic/. Accessed 09 February 2022.

11 Air India's Response to the COVID-19 Pandemic

Seema Rawat

Introduction

First reported in Wuhan (China) in December 2019, COVID-19, or coronavirus as it was initially named, had spread to 215 countries across the globe within a few months. As Indian cases of reported COVID-19 cases went from a mere 3 cases on February 22, 2020, to becoming the third country after Brazil and the United States to cross a million confirmed cases by the end of June, the country too went into lockdown from March 22. Televised as an address by its Prime Minister, the announcement brought the country to a standstill. This abrupt closure meant enormous hardship to several groups including migrants and was viewed critically as a "shambolic" (Ganguly 2020) and insensitive to the socio-economic context of India (Ghosh 2020), tough and timely (PTI 2020) though undeserving of the the unique challenges of the Indian context (Lancet 2020). The closure of borders engaged early before virus transmission in the country's population followed by mandatory lockdown, and isolation until the entire country is vaccinated, did spare island countries such as New Zealand, the loss of lives. Worldwide, governments took the stance of phased lockdowns and continued to do so even after two years as the virus mutated and eluded the control brought about by vaccinations.

In the Indian context though, even as the government directed a ban on international flights on March 22, 10 days after the first death in Kerala of a returning student from Wuhan, the impact of COVID-19 has been profound with 492,327 casualties and 40,622,709 in 2 years since January 2020 (WHO 2022). The frontline health workers struggled to respond as the health infrastructure was strained to breaking point. The lockdowns did slow the spread of the infection but they also had grave economic consequences. The aviation industry worldwide has suffered immensely, its airlines and airports face unto $415 billion annual losses potentially (ICAO 2022). However, it has also contributed to the spread of the virus, turning it from a local epidemic to a global pandemic (Sun et al. 2021, Budd et al. 2009) as flights continued to operate internationally even as the World Health Organization declared it a pandemic on March 11, 2020.

The fear of the disease led to an unprecedented decrease in passenger demand and, coupled with the countrywise ban, it completely halted the operations (Sun

DOI: 10.4324/9781003304517-15

et al. 2020a). The demands of stranded citizens to be brought back to their home countries built pressure on their governments to open the airspaces to facilitate them. The national carrier of India, Air India, and its crew, both pilots and cabin crew, operated evacuation flights to bring the stranded citizens and the diaspora into India through first the evacuation flights, then the Vande Bharat Mission along with the "Air Bubbles" or the bilateral flights between certain countries and India. This was supplemented with cargo flights bringing in medicines, protective equipment, and other essential supplies. This was at a great loss to it as for the first time, during such humanitarian effort, it lost several employees as they continued to operate flights before, during, and after the imposed lockdowns as the pandemic raged with its multiple waves. Their sense of duty, service, and hospitality has been seen as a commercial transaction, and their representation is normalized. The flight duties can be regarded as something that might be both lived and embodied and so, experienced (Heidegger 1988).

Several recent studies investigate the role of air transportation (and other modes) in the spread of COVID-19 (Christidis & Christodoulou 2020; Gilbert et al. 2020). The experiences of the flight crew as they navigated this contagion of air and the space of their work, however, has not been studied.

It is important, therefore, to reflect upon how we come to "know" about flight and cabin crew experiences of operating these flights and the vagaries of the complex social and cultural spaces in which they live and work so that we can explore new ways of "knowing" in relation to broader social science discourses.

Indian Aviation

In 1911, Allahabad (now Prayagraj in the State of Uttar Pradesh) was the site of the first commercial flight but the true genesis of Indian commercial aviation lay in the first commercial airline Tata Airlines' maiden flight piloted by JRD Tata, in a single engine De Havilland Puss Moth from Karachi to Bombay in October 1932. Soon, Indian Trans Continental Airways, Madras Air Taxi Services, Indian National Airways (1932–1934), and Deccan Airways (1945) started operations. In 1946, Tata Airlines was rechristened Air India ("Wings For A Nation | Tata group", 2022) with its strategy built around its host "Maharaja" image, which symbolized the new exotic, glamorous India and the era of international flights began in 1946. However, with the passing of the Air Corporations Act in 1953, all the existing airlines were "nationalized" and merged into two airlines—Indian Airlines (domestic operations) and Air India International (international operations). The "open skies" policies after the liberalization of the Indian economy again saw an influx of private airlines, though most did not survive, they set the ground for the current airlines. The national carriers continued reinventing themselves as aviation became more affordable and accessible. They are privatized now and with this disinvestment, have lost the status of a public sector undertaking (The Hindu, January 2020). However, they are reverting back to the Tata fold, thus completing a full cycle.

Historical Evacuations

Air India not only provided the initial impetus to civil aviation in India, it was also the flag bearer of the national pride and ambition represented by the geopolitical reach (Adey 2006; Butler 2001). Long before the Vande Bharat mission, a humanitarian effort to repatriate stranded Indian nationals during Covid 19 was launched by the Ministry of Civil Aviation, Government of India, Air India, the national carrier, had evacuated stranded Indian nationals. This included its largest-ever civilian airlift of 110,000 people from the Persian Gulf in 1990 during the Iraqi invasion of Kuwait. As the national carrier, it is tasked with such perilous endeavors, with its civilian flight crew flying into unsafe airports alongside India's defense forces (Table 11.1).

Evacuations during the COVID-19 Pandemic

As the world grappled with the initial anxiety of the outbreak of the virus, the Indian students in its epicenter, Wuhan, made fervent appeals to be brought back home. The city, however, was on complete lockdown. Air India, with special permission from the Chinese authorities, flew two 747 aircrafts on consecutive nights into Wuhan on January 31 and February 1. These flights, operated by the same set of 15 cabin crew and four pilots, included engineering, commercial, and support staff. As little was known about the disease at the time, a contingent of doctors accompanied the flight to screen the 647 evacuees, and the director of operations at Air India was on board to direct the operation. These were followed by an evacuation flight to repatriate the stranded passengers of the cruise liner "Diamond Princess' and a flight by the Indian Airforce carrying medical supplies to Wuhan and bringing 76 Indians and 36 foreign nationals back (Business Line 2020). These operations were treated as medical emergencies and were fully supported by the Indian Government, who also financed the evacuations of 842 Indians and 48 foreign nationals.

Lifeline Udaan and Vande Bharat Mission

Urgent appeals to evacuate stranded citizens and diaspora nudged the government to begin the evacuation under the banner of Vande Bharat Mission and it continues in addition to "Air-bubble" bilateral flights between specific countries (Table 11.2). Air India deployed its aircrafts and crew to operate these flights under direction and within the restrictions imposed by the Ministry of Civil Aviation (MOCA). Envisaged as a purely civilian initiative, there were non-scheduled commercial flights with no financial support or subsidy by the government, neither for the airlines nor for the passengers (Mitra 2021) but the monitoring was conducted by the Ministry of External Affairs (MEA). The evacuation operation phase involved the airlift of evacuees from different countries by airline officials and their transportation to India. Operated in 16 phases since May 7, 2020, each phase lasted 10 to 61 days, 51,473 flights were operated, and

Table 11.1 Evacuations by Air India

Year	Evacuated FromNia	Total Evacuees	Agencies Involved
2015	Iraq	7,000/ NA	Chartered and scheduled Iraqi Airways aircrafts, mainly out of Najaf
July 2005	Yemen	6,710/NA	Chartered Air India (AI) planes, 17 flights from Sanaa to Djibouti + Indian Air Force (IAF).
2014	Libya	3,600/5,600	chartered ferry + Chartered AI flights
2014	Ukraine	1,000/NA	Special AI flights
2011	Yemen	700-800/NA	Special AI flights
2011	Libya	16,400/18,000	Chartered 4 AI and 2 commercial aircrafts (Jet Airways and Kingfisher Airlines) and 2 passenger ships. IAF: IL-76 (Sirte to Cairo: 186 evacuees). IN: INS Jalashwa, INS Mysore, and INS Aditya.
2011	Egypt	700/3,600	Special AI flights
2006	Lebanon	2,300/ 12,000	Chartered AI planes from Cyprus + IAF+ Naval Support
2003	Kuwait	3,500/300,000	Special AI flights.
1996	United Arab Emirates	60,000/NA	Extra flights by AI.
1994	Yemen	1,700/7,000	Special AI flights + IAF
1990	Kuwait/Gulf	170,000/200,000	Special AI flights + Naval Support
1986	Yemen	800/3,000	About 350 Indians evacuated from Aden at government cost. Another 425 reached:pjibouti on their own and evacuated from there to India.
1980	Iraq	11000/ NA	Special AI flights + Naval Support
1962	Mozambique	2,300/ 2,400	Chartered passenger ships

Source: Compiled from Ministry of Civil Aviation

Table 11.2 Air India Group—Vande Bharat Mission

Phase	No. of Flights	No. of Passenger's Carried
Total of Phase 1 (10 days)	128	16,270
Total of Phase 2 (29 days)	650	75,297
Total of Phase 3 (25 days)	910	132,820
Total of Phase 4 (31 days)	1,275	167,176
Total of Phase 5 (31 days)	1,472	199,013
Total of Phase 6 (61 days)	3,596	446,559
Total of Phase 7 (61 days)	4,744	663,027
Total of Phase 8 (59 days)	5,596	814,532
Total of Phase 9 (31 days)	3,036	446,432
Total of Phase 10 (61 days)	4,646	496,889
Total of Phase 11 (61 days)	3,826	358,806
Total of Phase 12 (31 days)	2,536	311,462
Total of Phase 13 (30 days)	3,044	406,173
Total of Phase 14 (31 days)	3,610	531,899
Total of Phase 15 (61 days)	8,234	1,293,086
Total of Phase 16 (30 days)	4,170	547,109
Total of Phases 1 to 16	**51,473**	**6,906,550**

Source: Compiled from Ministry of Civil Aviation

more than 6,906,550 passengers transported (MOCA January 2022). Though the registration before the flights and the rules of quarantine was disadvantages to a section of citizens and diaspora including single and separated women and migrants (Mitra 2021), this was the only thread which connected families and facilitated travel in highly contagious times.

Theoretical Framework

Aviation facilitates movement with the cabin and cockpit crew working as the aircraft slices the air and shrinks the distances. This movement centers the work they do, controls their lives, and impacts their social relations. In the theoretical frameworks which have informed the studies of mobile work, "mobilities turn" (Sheller & Urry 2006) is the growing focus on the economic-social world being propelled by movement and flow informed by a "networked" life (Hannam et al. 2006). "Mobilities" refers to a social science which conceptualized all movement whether blocked or potential, voluntary, temporary place making, as representative of the political, economic, and social relations. The mobilities paradigm provided a theoretical framework to understand not only the spatial rootedness but the movement and the interplay of the stillness with it. The five mobilities that Urry (2007) proposed were the following practices—the corporeal travel of people; movement of objects; imaginative travel; virtual travel; communications, both analogue and digital. It is not a simple fact of travel but of the "contested world of meanings and power" (Cresswell 2006).

The contested role of work, as it can be a job, a career, or even a calling (Warhurst & Nickson, 2007) as well as the blurring between work and non-work, can become important as the employee looks for ways to reconcile work and identity either by using work to define themselves or by discounting its importance in their lives (Crang 1997). The mobilities framework concedes space for exploration of the transitory lives of the mobile worker: "it is not just how people make knowledge of the world, but how they physically and socially make the world through the ways they move and mobilise people, objects, information and ideas" (Büscher & Urry 2009) that allows us to construct new knowledge.

It is this framework that allows for the exploration of the flight experiences of the crew as they experience travel during the pandemic.

Methodology

A constructivist approach is vital to understand the "unheard voices" of those who are mobilized to work during the pandemic at the forefront, and qualitative approaches are better in that regard. According to Lincoln and Guba, the purpose of a qualitative study is to "accumulate sufficient knowledge to lead to understanding" (1985). The study acknowledges that the method can generate and shape theory, just as theory can generate and shape method. There is a back-and-forth character in which concepts, conjectures, and data are in continuous interpretation (Van Maanen et al. 2007).

To understand the pandemic from the perspective of the crew, the research initiated the question addressed in the next section.

How Did Its Crew Experience the Evacuation Flights?

To explore this, the pilots and cabin crew of Air India who operated the evacuation and Vande Bharat flights were engaged with. As an insider who had worked in aviation, the initial participants were known to me, and they then became the gatekeepers who connected me to their colleagues. This study adopts the approach as suggested by Merriam (2002) in which the researcher first approaches participants from whom she could substantially learn from (Polkinghorne 2005) and those who were "information rich cases" (Patton 1990). Memos were created on free-flowing conversations with the crew and their families. Interactions occurred over a span of 12–14 months from December 2020 to January 2022, ebbing with each wave of COVID-19. I spoke with them multiple times and these free-flowing interactions gave me an "emic" view of the lived experiences. Responses were also sought via text messages with questions such as "Why did you operate these flights?" and "How did your family and community respond?" These memos and responses were substantiated with company circulars, government reports, televised interviews, and press releases.

Lived Experiences of the Crew

Supererogation

The Wuhan evacuation flights in the early days of the pandemic were a response to the desperate appeals of young Indian students. With an air of suspenseful fear and a forceful response by governments to close their borders and cutoff all travel connections with China, Wuhan was like a leper to be shunned. The response from Air India astonished all.

> The national carrier once again comes to the rescue – this time to evacuate Indians from Wuhan, the site of the outbreak of coronavirus. This mission begins today with a Jumbo 747 operating between Delhi and Wuhan. Jai Hind!
>
> (Ashwini Lohani CMD Air India Twitter 30th January 2020)

This was not an insular perspective. The idea of the rescuer, who at her own peril would do her duty for the nation, is reinforced through the invoking of a patriotic "*Jai Hind*" (Glory to India). The history of earlier evacuations was recollected by the crew who speak of their role as the rescuer in Kuwait, Sana'a and the more recently from Iraq and Libya. "Going beyond the call of duty" identifying themselves as "the second line of defense" in this proxy war against the spread of the virus, the crew who operated the first evacuation flight were cognizant of their duty towards their family who were fearful of contracting the virus. The courage it took to operate in the ambiguous early days of the pandemic was linked to that of a soldier at war, who overcomes his fear.

> As we approached the city, the skies were silent. The airport looked like a graveyard of aircrafts and we waited a while at the tarmac for any signs of life to emerge from the terminal. It was quite unnerving, maybe 100 aircrafts parked, sealed, and the airport was totally dark. There was one person on the ground standing there, we were there on ground for 7 hours, as no one approached the aircraft.
>
> The doctors were able to screen the passengers only at entrance to the aircraft, it was not according to the plan whereby the terminal building could be used for this. We were to stay briefly at Wuhan, but it took 7 hours. That is when we came to know that the students were allowed to leave their university after the aircraft had left Delhi. They came by road to Wuhan then into another facility for holding and then at airport. At all these three places they were checked for signs of COVID.
>
> Why did we do it? Simply as it's our national duty. I feel a strong nationalist feeling, representing the country, ours is not to ask, just like that line from Lord Byron [it is Lord Alfred Tennyson], ours is not to ask but to do and die.
>
> (Air India Pilot who operated the Wuhan evacuations in conversation December 2021)

Invoking Lord Tennyson's war poem *The Charge of the Light Brigade*, "Someone had blundered:/ Theirs not to make a reply,/ Theirs not to reason why,/ Theirs but to do and die:/ Into the valley of Death/ Rode the six hundred.", reinforces the identity the crew has adopted to rationalize the moral dilemma of protecting themselves and their families and their duty to operate the flights. The nationalistic pride was expressed by several crew members as the main motivation to operate, as they equated the status of the national airline to be the protector and carrier of national pride.

Duty is also towards the fellow citizens who are in need of urgent help. As borders closed, these flights then were the only way home. Recognizing that the operations of the flights would stop if they did not agree to fly, the narrative of a pragmatic professional who is steadfast towards his obligation takes center.

> Job needs to be done. Can't let the people who depend on us down.
>
> (Airline Crew, has worked for 31 years, text message January 2022)

> It is a service to the passengers. Helping people to meet their close ones during such tough times.
>
> (Airline crew, has worked for 7 years, text message January 2022)

The professional identity of the pilots was a glue which bound them together. The obligation was also towards their own kind. As aviation crew and staff, the fear of contamination was high, and not all were equipped with protective gear, or had the flexibility of refusing to work. The isolation also led to a shared understanding of the experience.

> There is a lot of brotherhood/sisterhood. We help each other. In the early days when cargo flights had also begun, I say that the Spicejet pilot had nothing. (I asked) Where are your PPEs? They had none. So we gave it to everybody. At the airport the healthcare person has to take our temp[erature]. He was scared. So we take the thermometer and do it ourselves.
>
> (Air India Pilot worked for 24 years, in conversation July 2021)

Some acts are supererogatory, that is, above and beyond the call of duty. But if doing one's duty diligently is the best that can be, then how can some acts be better than the best? The conflicts of obligations, one to family and self, the other to the job, fellow human beings, and the country, lead to a struggle. The denial of this moral dilemma "flies at the face of experience" (LaFollette 2013).

Solicitude

The anxiety of jeopardizing the family's health, or falling prey to the virus themselves was a common experience for most. The safety protocols created ensured regular testing before and after operating the flight. While detailing the experience of operating in PPE, the crew acknowledged its use but also spoke of the discomfort it brought.

> Our briefing is normal, evacuation norm is 90 sec[onds] but … how to do it in a PPE, as no practice "fear is good, panic is bad" So jump into a PPE … Remain in that 16–17 hours, go in uniform, change into a T shirt. Wear PPE and remain in it … later dispose it off.
>
> (Air India Pilot, has worked for 14 years, in conversation August 2021)

The protocols also meant quarantining for a long period of time, isolated while waiting for the results to come. The facilities for quarantining were not the same in all cities and the stay in a guest house, being all alone, was not just physical but a mental strain.

> In fact, I called up one of my seniors and confided in him (by sharing) my phone password and insurance details in case something happened to me because I didn't want my family to panic; operating flights during COVID in PPE kits and masks was stressful. The most challenging thing was fighting the unknown enemy without compromising flight safety and the safety of the passengers along with fighting the fatigue and jet lag.
>
> (Capt. Dhillon, Air India Pilot, Outlook 2021).

When families contracted COVID-19, were hospitalized and needed support, this isolation brought about by quarantine added to the stress.

While returning, it was so challenging to keep the thoughts of my family's well-being aside and concentrate on my flying with 100% efficiency without compromising the safety of about 500 passengers.

(Capt. Suri, Outlook 2021)

The anxiety was due to the pandemic but it was compounded by protocols around aviation and travel. With an average of 2–3 flights per week, even during the height of the second wave, the crew went through multiple quarantines, testing, and isolations. Even this did not protect them for contracting the virus. Using humor as a way of masking the risks that they took, a pilot compared himself to the story of King Chandragupta who was given slow doses of poison by his advisor Chanakya, so that his body became immune to it (Air India Pilot in conversation, January 2022).

It was a known risk that I had undertaken. I was cautious in the beginning later on became comfortable.

(Airline Cabin Crew, has worked for 18 years, text message January 2022)

There has been no training, counseling, or even recognition of the impact this prolonged anxiety has on the health of the airline crew. The stringent standards of a fit body required of the airline crew impose a culture of silence around any frailties.

A pilot is as good as his last medical.

(Air India Pilot, has worked for 24 years, text message January 2022)

The Air India crew members who brought hundreds of stranded Indians back home experienced being stigmatized by their neighbors when their homes were stamped "quarantined" (Upadhya 2020).

The mobile workers were not given the status of frontline workers and were operating the flights in a compressed space of the aircraft with close proximity to the passengers.

Conclusion

This study has shown that the crew is resilient but also disappointed. The wisdom that comes with experiencing these life-altering events provides a perspective to understand what organizational resilience (or lack of) could be (Meyer 1982). The neo-liberal forms of government put the onus on the individual to govern themselves in appropriate ways. By taking a distance, the government encourages the idea of active citizenship, whereby people, rather than relying on the state, take responsibility for their own social and economic well-being (Joseph 2013). In particular, it focuses on the risk and security aspects of this by encouraging preparedness and awareness as individual actions thus constructing governable spaces where the power relations and hierarchies are hidden but still at play (Davis 2011).

The culture of authentic hospitality was built into the national carrier from its inception through its founder JRD Tata, who started India's first airline, Air India's precursor Tata Airlines in 1932, and it has become the signs and symbols, shared practices, and underlying assumptions of this organization. Though significant shifts in the context of business operations such as the deep upheaval to the aviation sector worldwide may necessitate the organizations to realign their culture (Meyer 1982), some elements can be the "toolkit" around which new cultural ethos can take shape to better respond to altered realities, and the new views can support these deeply entrenched values (Spicer 2020).

The shocks that aviation faces, be it the economic downturns or the 9/11 attacks, have pruned the industry and given opportunity for new airlines to emerge. Air India has received jolts of privatization, of COVID-19-induced economic difficulty, and an increasingly transactional, commercialized aviation space where its cultural elements embodied in the pot-bellied Maharaja are a misfit. The cultural embeddedness of sacrifice, duty, and resilience to stay on the path have been tested and are found straining. In light of governmental apathy and societal snub, if these values have to endure, recognition of this superhuman effort, providing succor to wounded emotions and formulating a sustainable strategy to deal with the concerns of globally dispersed Indian citizens and diaspora, is crucial.

References

Adey, P. (2006). Airports and air-mindedness: Spacing, timing and using the Liverpool Airport, 1929–1939. *Social & Cultural Geography*, 7(3), 343–363.

Banerjee, D., Sathyanarayana Rao, T. S., Kallivayalil, R. A., & Javed, A. (2021). Psychosocial framework of resilience: Navigating needs and adversities during the pandemic, a qualitative exploration in the indian frontline physicians. *Frontiers in Psychology*, 12, 775.

Budd, L., Bell, M., Brown, T. (2009). Of plagues, planes and politics: Controlling the global spread of infectious diseases by air. *Political Geography*, 28 (7), 426–435.

Büscher, M., & Urry, J. (2009). Mobile methods and the empirical. *European Journal of Social Theory*, 12(1), 99–116.

Butler, D. L. (2001). Technogeopolitics and the struggle for control of world air routes, 1910–1928. *Political Geography*, 20(5), 635–658.

Christidis, P., & Christodoulou, A. (2020). The predictive capacity of air travel patterns during the global spread of the COVID-19 pandemic: Risk, uncertainty and randomness. *International Journal of Environmental Research and Public Health*, 17(10), 3356.

Crang, P. (1997). Performing the tourist product. In C. Rojek & J. Urry (Eds.), *Touring Cultures: Transformations of Travel and Theory* (pp. 137–154). Routledge.

Cresswell, T. (2006). *On the Move: Mobility in the Modern Western World*. Taylor & Francis.

Davies, J. S. (2011). *Challenging Governance Theory: From Networks to Hegemony*. Policy Press.

Ganguly, S. (2020). Mangling the COVID crisis- Indias response to the pandemic. *The Washington Quarterly*, 43(4), 105–120.

Ghosh, J. (2020). A critique of the Indian government's response to the COVID-19 pandemic. *Journal of Industrial and Business Economics*, 47(3), 519–530.

Gilbert, M., Pullano, G., Pinotti, F., Valdano, E., Poletto, C., Boëlle, P. Y., … Colizza, V. (2020). Preparedness and vulnerability of African countries against importations of COVID-19: A modelling study. *The Lancet*, 395(10227), 871–877.

Hannam, K., Sheller, M., & Urry, J. (2006). Mobilities, immobilities and moorings. *Mobilities*, 1(1), 1–22.

Heidegger, M. (1988). *The Basic Problems of Phenomenology* (Vol. 478). Indiana University Press.

ICAO. (2022). Effects of novel coronavirus (COVID-19) on civil aviation: Economic impact analysis. ICAO. Retrieved from https://www.icao.int/sustainability/Documents/COVID -19/ICAO%20COVID%202022%2002%2015%20Economic%20Impact%20Toru %20Hasegawa.pdf

Joseph, J. (2013). Resilience as embedded neoliberalism: a governmentality approach. *Resilience*, 1(1), 38–52.

Knox, H., O'Doherty, D., Vurdubakis, T., & Westrup, C. (2008). Enacting airports: Space, movement and modes of ordering. *Organization*, 15(6), 869–888.

LaFollette, I. H. (2013). *The International Encyclopedia of Ethics*. Wiley-Blackwell.

Lancet, T. (2020). India under COVID-19 lockdown. *Lancet (London, England)*, 395(10233), 1315.

Lincoln, Y. S., & Guba, E. G. (1985). *Naturalistic Inquiry*. SAGE.

Merriam, S. B. (2002). Introduction to qualitative research. *Qualitative Research in Practice: Examples for Discussion and Analysis*, 1(1), 1–17.

Meyer, A. D. (1982). Adapting to environmental jolts. *Administrative Science Quarterly*, 27(4), 513–557.

Mitra, P. (2021). The Vande Bharat Scam: Women, social standing, and evacuation flights to India under Covid-19. *Journal of Comparative Literature and Aesthetics*, 44(1), 79–91.

Patton, M. Q. (1990). *Qualitative Evaluation and Research Methods*. SAGE Publications, inc.

Polkinghorne, D. E. (2005). Language and meaning: Data collection in qualitative research. *Journal of Counseling Psychology*, 52(2), 137.

PTI. (2020, April 14). Who lauds India's 'tough and timely' actions against coronavirus. *The Hindu*. Retrieved October 12, 2021, from https://www.thehindu.com/news/national /who-lauds-indias-tough-and-timely-actions-against-coronavirus/article31338150.ece

Sheller, M., & Urry, J. (2006). The new mobilities paradigm. *Environment and Planning A*, 38(2), 207–226.

Spicer, A. (2020). Organizational culture and COVID-19. *Journal of Management Studies*, 57(8), 1737–1740.

Sun, X., Wandelt, S., & Zhang, A. (2020). How did COVID-19 impact air transportation? A first peek through the lens of complex networks. *Journal of Air Transport Management*, 89, 101928.

Sun, X., Wandelt, S., Zheng, C., & Zhang, A. (2021). COVID-19 pandemic and air transportation: Successfully navigating the paper hurricane. *Journal of air Transport Management*, 94, 102062–102062.

Upadhya, P. (2020, March 23) Facing discrimination for flying during Covid-19 outbreak, says Air India staff. *India Today*. Retrieved from www.indiatoday.com

Urry, J. (2007). *Mobilities*. Cambridge: Polity.

Van Maanen, J., Sørensen, J. B., & Mitchell, T. R. (2007). The interplay between theory and method. *Academy of Management Review*, 32(4), 1145–1154.

Warhurst, C., & Nickson, D. (2007). Employee experience of aesthetic labour in retail and hospitality. *Work, Employment and Society*, 21(1), 103–120.

World Health Organization. (2022, January 22). India: Who coronavirus disease (covid-19) dashboard with vaccination data. World Health Organization. Retrieved January 22, 2022, from https://covid19.who.int/region/searo/country/in

12 Finding Hope and Solidarity Through Camus and Derrida During COVID-19

Biraj Mehta Rathi

[1]Critique of Medical Model: Camus' Existential Perspective and Humanistic Psychology

Crisis such as pandemics, expose the vulnerable and helpless nature of human existence. Thus, they formed a backdrop to many Greek narratives.[2] They served as a framework for the evolution of the plot or formed a backdrop to the unfolding of the personal tragedy of the protagonist. Plagues were generally described as a result of tragic faults of human nature or bad leadership. At the start of Sophocles' *Oedipus The King*, the city of Thebes is described as suffering from a terrible plague, crops failing, and women and children dying (1982, lines 1–55). The cause as we know is Oedipus' tragic fate of murdering his father. Thucydides, the Greek historian, describes the devastation caused by plague in the seventh chapter of his work, *The History of the Peloponnesian War*. He describes it as a state where the Athenians were completely unprepared. Neither physicians nor sacrifices to Gods and divinations could successfully stop the misery. Sick people died of bad governance, isolation, neglect, lack of shelter, diseases spread from improper burials, lawlessness, and looting (Thucydides 2012, 241–273). Yet, such misery did not stop Athenians from embarking on war with Sicily, nor Oedipus' sons from raging a civil war. Thus, epidemics and plagues made an ideal backdrop for making sense of human faults and exposing human vulnerability. The Greek tragedies bring to light the indifferent nature of the natural and divine forces. Since there is no cosmic order and universe is unsympathetic, human beings are doomed to suffer and die. In almost all of Camus' writing too, death, alienation, indifference of the universe, and absurdity of life constitute the key themes. Death is viewed as the only authentic possibility of human existence, it is all pervasive and is understood as the end of all creation as well as value of life. Understanding life would consist in an understanding of dying every moment of life, thus one ascribes meaning to life through an understanding of death. Life, for Camus, is absurd. Absurdity is the fundamental disharmony and the tragic incompatibility of human existence. It is the product of collision and confrontation between human desire for order, meaning, and purpose to life. Human beings desperately seek hope and meaning in the hopeless and meaningless world. They seek clarity and transcendence and they realize that the cosmos does not offer it, thus they are fated to inhabit a cosmos that is indifferent (Camus 1991, 91–92).

DOI: 10.4324/9781003304517-16

In the collection of stories published as *The Myth of Sisyphus*, Camus explains the purpose of life. Sisyphus was condemned to roll a stone up the mountain knowing that the stone will roll down again. Sisyphus would prefer death to this task but not so in Camus's myth. The myth stands for living the absurd, living in a total lack of hope (which is not the same as despair), a permanent reflection (which is not the same as renunciation), and a conscious dissatisfaction (which is not the same as juvenile anxiety). For Camus, Sisyphus is the ultimate absurd hero.[3] *The Plague* too appears as a chronicle of heroism in the face of tragic incompatibility of human existence. The last paragraph of Camus' novel *The Plague* suggests that plague is an undeniable part of life. Dr. Bernard Rieux, the protagonist, claims that "the plague bacillus never dies or disappears ... it can lie dormant for years" (2010, 297). Camus is critical of all religious discourses, as they cannot justify human suffering or rationalize the mortality imposed upon every human. Dr. Rieux asks his stranded visitor Jean Tarrou, "mightn't it be better for God if we refuse to believe in Him and struggle with all our might against death, without raising our eyes towards the heaven where he sits in silence?" (Camus 2010, 124). Thus, the plague assists people to understand that personal suffering is vain. It suggests that the only way out is to embrace the omnipresence and omnipotence of the plague through acts of altruism and heroism, "healers", as Dr. Rieux calls them (Camus 2010, 296). Thus, the novel also highlights the importance of hope, solidarity, and empowers people to respond to plague by enduring its absurdity with courage and resilience. Such acts of heroism are displayed in the novel by Dr. Bernard Rieux, the volunteering anti-plague sanitation squads formed by Tarrou, a visitor to Oran and Joseph Grand, a municipal clerk of Oran. They, along with volunteers, fight plague by helping others even though the struggle is futile in the face of certain death. Grand's quest for a perfect manuscript for his novel is as hopeless as his struggle to fight the plague (Camus 2010, 45). It illustrates that the only way of dealing with the absurdity is to keep struggling against inadequacies of language, tyranny of plague, and create one's own meaning and happiness from that struggle.

Camus' novel also discusses the experience of exile and imprisonment. After a long period of denial, the authorities take note of the rising deaths and quarantine the town of Oran (Camus 2010, 60). People are left stranded, without resources and some separated from their loved ones. Camus describes the townspeople feelings that range from denial, plans to escape from Oran and rejoin with their loved ones or later live hopelessly in the illusion of sadness, disappointment, and longing. The townspeople suffer a similar pain of epidemic and experience comparable kinds of exile and imprisonment, yet they feel alone in their suffering (Camus 2010, 63–64). Only those who accept the plague's power and their own state of exile are able to find a personal sense of meaning and freedom. As healers, Dr. Rieux, Tarrou and Grand exhibit empathy, love, and solidarity.[4] They exhibit life-affirming values of hope in the most irreducible and impossible situations. The absurdity of the situation brings one to realize that we are interconnected. Though one cannot escape being a victim, one can build solidarity by sharing suffering and, thus, escaping the exile and loneliness. *The Plague* brings to light our inherent incompleteness and the futility of medical, political, or religious models in dealing with it. Such an inquiry is important to counter medical discourses that currently dominate considerations of the pandemic.

As analyzed by Michel Foucault, medical discourses of pandemic objectify the human subject,[5] firstly, through the mode of inquiry which medicalizes bodies and is given the status of sciences; secondly, objectification of the subject through dividing practices of creating opposites (in this case healthy vs. sick) and lastly, how people turn themselves into subjects as they identify themselves with the definitions provided by the sciences (Foucault 1982, 777–778). The impact is dehumanizing as the human subject is systematized and homogenized into various forms of rationality that generalize, define, and organize people and societies in ways that are deterministic and over which people have no control. It is worse, as Foucault explains, when one is "blackmailed"(1997, 119) into taking sides where either one submits to this determinism or one rejects it. Instead of the quest for systematized universal truths, Foucault makes a case for discourses that make room for the possibility of a reflective relation to the present, a practical critique that allows transgressing the normative borders and allows one to probe historically into the events that have made us who we are (Foucault 1997, 120). This is Foucault's notion of bio-politics that becomes most relevant to counter the dominating medical discourses of pandemic.[6]

Foucault, in his work "The Politics of Health in the Eighteenth Century" in *Power/Knowledge: Selected Interviews and Other Writings 1972–1977* discusses a form of politics that is born out of medical practices. Though, both are thought of separately, medical politics or politics of health defines all other politics (as seen in times of the COVID-19 pandemic too). His essay highlights the birth of hospitals and medical centers and the political power that builds around it. The eighteenth century saw the development of a medical market in the form of private clinics, experts offering specialized medical attention, and the growth of individual and family demand for healthcare. Clinical medicine centered around individual examination, diagnosis, and therapy, simultaneously building the idea of disease as a political and economic problem for social communities which governments must seek to resolve as a matter of overall policy (Foucault 1980, 166). Apart from the state apparatus, there were religious groups, charitable organizations that operate like agencies of surveillance of one class over the vulnerable sick class that are posed as a potential sources of collective danger. Academia of the nineteenth-century societies produced quantifiable knowledge of diseases and state participation in health of population takes the form of objective policies and collective control measures (Foucault 1980, 167–168).[7] One of them is the control of the urban space, it's developments, constructions, and institutions are considered a deciding factor for mortality of its inhabitants and thus, it is converted into a medicalizable object through concentrated urban policies. They are reflected in the authoritarian medical intervention in spaces considered as breeding grounds such as prisons, harbors, installations, the hospital where non-citizens and beggars may mingle together in an already inadequate medical set up. Thus, medicine, rather than as art of health or skill of curing, assumes an important place in the administrative system, where the doctor and the clinic becomes an advisor for social governance, their role in observing, correcting, improving, and maintaining social order of the social body becomes increasingly important. It gives them a politically privileged position for all matters (not merely concerning disease) including food, drink, sexuality, productivity, clothing, and the layout of habitat. Lifestyles comes to be dominated by medical interpretations of health and hygiene leading to surplus power, surveillance, and control (Foucault 1980, 177). Hospitals become centers that do not merely cure the social and individual bodies of diseases; it becomes a center of power that brings in moral servitude as it generates clinical knowledge, medical classifications, techniques, and therapeutic efficiency that comes to organize the urban social and economic spaces, the family, and the physical bodies of individuals (Foucault 1980, 179–180). This analysis remains relevant to describing the current pandemic as world governments, assisted by medical practioners, impose authority on entire populations by eradicating all values of liberty under the pretext of protection and survival. Medical approaches to pandemics reduce the human beings to mere biological bodies who can be examined and exploited. Such discourses do not do justice to existential concerns of death, isolation, identity, freedom, responsibility, and futile attempts to create ultimate meanings in a meaningless world. Ignoring these concerns only serves to deepen the psychological conflicts that are associated with them and society at large. Thus, existential humanistic psychology and phenomenological approaches to pandemics appear as urgent counter responses to understanding the pandemic.

Contrary to positivist psychology that aims at exhaustively determining the elements of human consciousness as physico-chemical processes (with reference to anatomical structures and it's different causal connections with the physical world), existential and humanistic psychology concerns itself with the lived experiences of people and their basic concerns of human existence. It examines people's engagement with their positions in the world and their conception of human existence. Influenced by the philosophical tradition and artistic expressions of thinkers such as Kierkegaard, Nietzsche, Heidegger, Dostoevsky, Kafka, Sartre, Simone de Beauvoir, Camus, Ionesco, and Beckett (to name a few), existential psychologists have rejected the use of experimental laboratory methods in psychology (oriented towards natural sciences), preferring instead to analyze people's subjective experience and personal phenomenology.[8] Scientific theories that reduce human behavior to deterministic terms of mechanisms (functions), run the risk of constricting or forming narrow definitions of human conditions that come to determine the society. They construct structures of exclusions (such as asylums, rehabilitation centers and clinics) where situations such as anxiety, depression, and alienation are perceived as being contrary to forms of rationality productive for the society, rather they get categorized as clinical conditions that are believed to require medical attention or therapy. Foucault in his work *Madness and Civilization: A History of Insanity in the Age of Reason*, further explains how medical and therapeutic models tend to concentrate on individual personalities (and their traits) rather than structures of exclusions, thus, they form discourses that control and define lives of individuals in subtle and powerful ways (1988, para. 240–241). Humanistic and existential psychology on the other hand, attempts to understand how the conscious and unconscious interact with the concrete world (of physical realities) thereby concealing or revealing motivational conflicts that have existential implications for people. Influenced by the twentieth-century phenomenological, existential, and literary movements, humanistic psychology of thinkers strived to understand people's existential struggles and their associated anxiety and alienation not as dysfunctional, but rather as an inevitable consequence of the human condition. Thinkers such as Otto Rank, Rollo May, and Victor Frankl Irvin Yalom (to name a few) emphasized on understanding people's struggles to understand the meaning and significance of life which empowers them to achieve a new freedom and responsibility to act. Their philosophies were influenced by existential philosophies as well as phenomenological traditions that describe the structures of experience, in particular consciousness, the imagination, relations with other persons, and the situatedness of the human subject in society and history.[9]

Emphasizing on the human subject, Karl Otto Rank's *Will Therapy* sought to use the person's creative will as a vehicle for transformation and psychological growth. Rank aims to lift the therapeutic processes as an intellectual training as it is reductive in nature.; for example, Sigmund Freud reduces one's actions and motivations to repressed sexuality, as Karl Jung reduces awareness to unconscious made conscious. These are limited as they subordinate the actual moment of experience to a troublesome phenomena accompanied by unavoidable mechanisms of resistance, hence in need for rectification. Rank emphasizes that the value of the therapeutic experience, like that of every real experience, lies in its spontaneity and uniqueness which constitutes the value of the therapeutic technique (Rank 1945, 5). Rollo May, in Chapter 1 "The Origins and Significance of the Existential Movement in Psychology" of his book *Existence: A New Dimension in Psychiatry and Psychology* explains that existentialists are centrally concerned with rediscovering the living person as the one that experiences the real situations of the world. Moving away from concerns of isolated psychological reactions themselves and theories that compartmentalize and dehumanize modern culture, Rollo makes references to thinkers like Freud, Kierkegaard, Heidegger, Nietzsche, Sartre, Kafka, and Camus, and artistic expressions of Picasso and Van Gogh to emphasize understanding human beings within their structures of existence as well as their capacity of self-realization and rising to their full potential (May 1958, 3–36). Thus, the fundamental contribution of existential therapy is to understand a person within the cultural, historical, and physical constructions of existence, not to deny the specific behavior patterns or the validity of the dimensions of the psychological but to resist the temptation to reduce human behavior to a bundle of drives and tendencies (May 1958, 39). Victor Frankl, pioneer of existential psychotherapy, developed logotherapy, which focuses on the importance of finding meaning in life. Whereas psychoanalysis focuses on self-centered introspective and retrospective ways of reinforcing neurosis, logotherapy focuses on having the person confront and reorient herself towards the future. This is believed to be an effective as well as a humane way to have the person become aware of one's own life meanings that can contribute much to one's own ability to overcome their fear and neurosis. Victor Frankl explains that the theory is called logotherapy as the name denotes meaning. It focuses on the nature of human existence as well as on human being's search for meanings. According to logotherapy, this striving to find a meaning in one's life is the primary motivational force, thus Frankl focuses on the will to meaning in contrast to the Freudian principle of pleasure principle as the driving force. According to Frankl, the will to meaning is the primary factor that drives the human condition; its meaning is unique and can only be fulfilled by the self. The resulting actions are not mere defense mechanisms, rather they are human endeavors driven by the passion to live (and even die) for the sake of ideals and values. Failures are perceived as existential problems rather than conflicts arising from instincts and desires (Frankl 1968, 39).

Irvin Yalom's concept of "existential psychodynamics" (1980, 6) emphasizes the conflict that flows from the individual's confrontation with the "givens of existence" (Yalom 1980, 8)—those that are inescapable parts of the human being's existence in the world. The same is discovered through personal reflection, a certain bracketing from the everyday world. Upon deep reflection, one confronts ones own "situations" (Yalom 1980, 8) in the world, one's own boundaries, possibilities, and the "deepest structures" (Yalom 1980, 8), of one's own existence. This process of reflection is often catalyzed by certain urgent experiences. He calls them the boundary situations, which include experiences as a confrontation with one's death, choices one makes, as well as the collapse of some fundamental meaning-providing schema (Yalom 1980, 7–8). His book *Existential Psychotherapy* mainly deals with four ultimate concerns: death, freedom, isolation, and meaninglessness. These become the main ideas that are used by existential psychotherapists. It replaces the Freudian idea of individuals being driven by impulsive drives; rather, it makes a claim that the therapist has far more legitimacy if he or she views the individual primarily as a fearful and suffering being in the world who strives for meaning in a world devoid of one (Yalom 1980, 8–9). Only by making one's own self vulnerable to this absurdity can one sustain oneself. As discussed earlier in the chapter, the central characters of the novel, Rieux, Rambert, and Tarrou, live and struggle in the way that Camus and advocates of existential psychotherapy explain. They recognize the absurd (the power of the plague and their own inevitable doom) but still work ceaselessly against it, finding meaning in healing others.

Yet, Camus' *The Plague* must be engaged with critically as one can question the certainty with which the central character and narrator Dr. Rieux can claim commonality and solidarity of the experience of love, exile, and suffering among all fellow citizens. At the start of the novel, Dr. Bernard Rieux discloses himself as the impartial narrator, an unknown person who was closely involved with what is to be narrated (Camus 2010, 4). For the reader, Dr Rieux's impartial narration as well as active participation in the epidemic frames the case for a collective experience of the plague; it is this "impartiality" that must be scrutinized. While the novel was originally written as an allegory for the German occupation of France during World War II, Camus/Dr. Rieux never mention the impact of the epidemic on non-French Algerian communities. This omission of the experience of the colonized brings to light the challenges of the claim of being an impartial observer and simultaneously an involved agent. It explains that an examination of the researcher's own mental and physical well-being, social relationships, and livelihood would be equally important to scrutinize so as to identify inequalities in our societies and give voices to those who have been marginalized in the first-person narratives. Derrida's philosophy of deconstruction proves relevant to uncover those that are "othered" (due to inequalities); towards a more inclusive version of building hope and solidarity. The second section examines the relevance of Derrida's philosophy of deconstruction and application of concepts such as autoimmunity and unconditional hospitality towards prospects of solidarity, those beyond the phenomenological existential perspectives and therapeutic model.

Derrida's Notion of Autoimmunity and Hospitality: A Deconstructive Intervention to Pandemic

This section of the chapter makes a case for humanistic intervention following Derrida's philosophy of deconstruction and notion of autoimmunity and hospitality. Derrida discusses this logic of autoimmunity in "Philosophy in a Time of Terror: Dialogues with Jürgen Habermas and Jacques Derrida" and in his work *Rogues*. His notion of autoimmunity implies a self-destructive tendency whereby an organism works to destroy its own protection by working against its own immunity. He suggests this in the context of explaining wars, terrorism, and nationalism. He believes that such nationalism contains its own internal logic of destruction, the only way would be to drop guard and explore the possibility of turning enemies into allies. This alone can ensure peace. (Borradori 2003, 150–154). This concept is relevant here as the essay suggests that the only way to challenge the pandemic is not quarantine and isolation measures. However certain the sickness may be, the only way to challenge it is by building solidarity and working towards serving those who suffer from it (as illustrated in the novel *The Plague*).

Derrida uses it in the context of explaining wars and terrorism waged by nation states but the establishment of a metaphorical relationship between the human body and the body politic is relevant here. To conceptualize the political body as a living body is one of the most prominent features of political and nationalist discourses. It theorizes the biological health as analogous to the health of the political body, thus state control over the health of individuals becomes a moral norm.[10] This explains and justifies quarantine as the state response to pandemics. As Camus in the novel explains, "Thus the first thing that plague brought to our town was exile" (Camus 2010, 67). The town exiled from the rest of the world for fear that the plague can spread to the rest of the world; further, it also isolates people from one another as they fear that their neighbors may infect them (Camus 2010, 71). Deprived of communities, people are alienated from themselves. Further, Camus explains the futility of the system of patrols instituted in the novel; they are on duty to kill the cats and dogs that they believe are possible carriers of infection (Camus 2010, 108). Dogs and cats become scapegoats that human societies can blame, as the actions of patrolling groups do not prevent or slow down the spread of plague in any way. They only increase the nervous tension already existing in the town. In contrast, those who enrolled in the anti-plague squads, too, gained no great merit, yet they knew that it was the only thing to do. These groups enabled townsfolk to come to grips with the disease and convinced them that fighting plague was the concern of all.

This makes a case for Derrida's notion of autoimmunity that he uses to subvert the ideology of nationalism and borders. Derrida uses the term autoimmunity to describe a gesture of self-defense or self-preservation that in fact leads to that thing's destruction. It enables an exposure to the other, importantly for Derrida, the logic of autoimmunity reveals that absolute immunity is impossible: in an attempt to achieve absolute protection, destruction ensues.[11] In *The Plague*, the sanitation squad put up by people does not necessarily achieve anything worthwhile, yet by accepting the destruction in the universe, people build a community by creating a group that mutually accepts death. Though people in Oran already know that they will be killed by the plague, the squad helps people come to terms with this predicament and encourages them to do their best to fight it. By making themselves vulnerable, many get infected. Joseph Grand, Othon, the judge who recovers but requests to be posted back in quarantine facilities to help others (Camus 2010, 249), Raymond Rambert who eventually joins the anti-plague squad (2010,199) and Tarrou, eventually dies of disease (2010, 277), are heroic in dropping their immunity guard and finding meaning in healing others. This seems to be the only way to fight the random destruction caused by plague. Not only do they exhibit Derrida's logic of autoimmunity but also his philosophy of embracing unconditional hospitality.

The logic of autoimmunity requires unconditional hospitality, opening up to the future in a way that we risk everything. In his essay "On Hospitality" Derrida explains unconditional hospitality as compromising one's self and accepting the other with its hostility. This is also used in the context of suggesting peace among nation states that wage wars. The concept is relevant here as pandemics bring lockdowns and people become selfish in protecting themselves. Closely tied with the concept of immunity, it suggests a way of building collaboration and solidarity to counter the pandemic. In his work *Rogues*, Derrida states that it requires autoimmunity, the possibility of suppressing one's immune relations in order to allow contact with the outside world (Derrida 2005, 35). It is a constant negotiation with what seems to threaten one's security, as that is the only chance of a peaceful future (Thomson 2007, 77–78). In his essay "On Hospitality", Derrida explains it as an *aporia*, a puzzle or a paradox that harnesses an impossible reconciliation between two contradictory imperatives. Firstly, the imperative contained in hospitality is to welcome the other in an absolute unconditional sense (before one is aware of knowledge or recognition of names and identity). The second imperative is to welcome the other in an absolute unconditional sense. Derrida states that pure unconditional hospitality does not consist of an invitation (that is one is welcomed on the condition that one adopts (and not disrupts) the laws and norms of the territory). Pure unconditional hospitality opens to someone who is neither expected nor invited, to the one who arrives as a foreign visitor, a new arrival, non-identifiable and unforeseeable, an absolute other (Derrida 2003, 211–212). It is building an ethical relation that is transgressive in its overcoming of all barriers, towards building a hospitality of care for those who suffer. Self-protection makes the self more vulnerable, yet, it is precisely in performing unconditional hospitality, as an inherent openness to the possibility for the other (death) to arrive, that one finds freedom and meaning. Thus, autoimmunity not only entails the potential destruction of the self, it is also where the self is always compromised (Derrida 2005, 36).

Yet, as explained in the previous section, Camus' *The Plague* does not address the nature of pandemic sufficiently. The pandemic not only reveals human vulnerability and interconnectedness, it also brings to light pre-existing social, economic, political, and health inequalities in our communities. They expose the unacknowledged assumptions that are impediments to understanding experiences of other people and communities. The unguarded subjectivity of Dr. Rieux lacks reflexivity, positionality, and an iterative[12] process that would lend legitimacy to the assumption of a shared experience. As explained by Derrida, the process of iteration is that of repetition, one can repeat what one can identify and to identify one has to be able to repeat them, thus, iterability undermines the context as the final governor of meanings. Thus, iterability is the logical possibility of a functioning beyond the live present context or an empirically determined location (Derrida 1982, 315). While at one level, the experience of love, exile, and longing in *The Plague* seems relatable and communicable in contemporary crisis of the pandemic, yet, in its inadequacy to explain its origins in social, political, and economic inequalities it lacks the force needed to build an inclusive morality of solidarity. The pandemic revealed pre-existing fault lines of our community struggling with inadequate habitats, insecure working conditions, insufficient infrastructure, uncertain livelihoods, inaccessibility of state-provided relief, public distribution system, and economic deprivations of social security, cash transfers, and loans during the pandemic. The gaps are widened with the intersection of gender, religion, class, caste, and disabilities. The current crisis of COVID-19, thus, appears as what Derrida would call an "event" (Derrida 1982, 326), an unexpected, surprising rupture in/to the structure itself.

Derrida's notion of deconstruction is a useful intervention here. It refutes the idea that all phenomena are reducible to operation of systems and its through structures constructed that we come to have total control over our environment. Traditionally, all systems and structures have been oriented towards a center. A centre marks a fixed origin, a point of presence and reference (metaphysical notions of God, essence, substance, ideas, and consciousness are examples of the same). The function of this center is not only to orient and balance but it also plays the role of the organizing principle in a structure that limits the free play (recreation and reinventing) of structure. This center, Derrida explains, is paradoxically at the center of the theory (since it is the foundation of theory) as well as outside it (it is exceptional). "The centre is at the centre of the totality, and yet, since the centre does not belong to the totality (is not part of the totality), the totality has its centre elsewhere" (Derrida 2000, 89). Thus, the center that governs the structure, also escapes structurality (being the governing power of structure). Centered structurality is based on the idea of fundamental immobility and certainty where substitution, repetition, and transformation are no longer possible or remain limited within a structure (2000, 89–90). This centering that is questioned is described by Derrida as an "event" that is a point of rupture or discontinuity in the history of center. As an antithesis to the traditional theories, the need for a center as a natural, fixed site and as constituting a structure is questioned and examined.

The pandemic here appears as an "event" that exposes the fact that structures are not beyond history or people. Structures are organized by human experience, interpretations, desire, and behaviours. Structures are both what they seem and what they do not. Structures are fragmented, punctuated by absences, containing an excess of words and ideas which, if acknowledged would threaten to undermine the structures as a whole. Deconstruction thus helps perceive how structures (in this case political state, healthcare, and systems of social services, criminal justice, and policing) were constructed. It appears as an affirmation of the experiences or ideas that have been left out to ensure that the system looks solid and secure. It is witnessing how, by virtue of something being absent, the structures made themselves stable and fixed. The "event" then unexpectedly makes visible those that have been silenced (Derrida 1982, 327). By listening and responding to these "othered" voices and experiences, one can aspire to building a better and inclusive world of hope, care, justice, and solidarity.

In Camus' *The Plague*, Dr. Rieux becomes the spokesperson of the struggles of people of Oran. The vulnerable of the town, represented by Dr. Rieux as victims of plague, are a heterogeneous group. The novel describes M. Michel, the doorkeeper of the building where Dr. Rieux works. He was the first to be distressed by the appearance of dead rats as well as fall victim of the plague. The elderly Dr. Rieux's mother appears as a figure of stability, peace, and kindness, an asthma patient who makes up stories about the plague, Oran and its people and Dr. Castel, an elderly colleague of Dr. Rieux's who works towards developing an anti-plague serum. The administration includes M. Othon, the strict police magistrate who grows gentle with the death of his son, the Prefect of Oran who refrains from taking action to not alarm the town people, Mercier who is in charge of pest control for the city, the criminal underground Gonzalez, Garcia, Raoul, Marcel, and Louis who can offer safe passages in exchange of a fee to sneak people out of city limits. There is mention of few women—Dr. Rieux's wife who leaves for the sanatorium just before the plague strikes, Jeanne, the municipal clerk, and Joseph Grand's ex-wife who left him. Apart from them, there are the two visitors, Tarrou and Rambert, who join the doctor in the anti-plague struggle. Tarrou organizes an anti-plague sanitation squad and plays an equally important role along with the other sanitation squads in countering the plague. There are two anomalies, the man who lures cats and then spits at the cats each day, and Cottard, the man who lives in hiding for an unknown crime committed. He welcomes the plague as his feeling of loneliness and exile is now shared by all and goes insane out of rage when the plague ends and things return to normalcy. Both of them illustrate the absurdity and meaninglessness of the universe; in this case Dr. Rieux's universe which consists of French people.

Applying Derrida's philosophy of decentering, Dr. Rieux's narrative lacks mention of disadvantaged groups of any urban setting, such as street dwellers, migrants, the daily wage earners (to name a few) who live with severely compromised rights, inhabitable habitats, no social securities, and the other deprivations of Algerians caused by French colonization in general. There's description of the prison houses, graveyards, coffin maker's workshops, and sanitation squads with little description of inner and outer worlds that are disadvantaged because of their position in community. One is invited to imagine the pain and struggle through characters of Dr. Rieux's world is collective; as the plague strikes each one without discrimination. Their absence gives legitimacy to Dr. Rieux's/Camus' cosmos of absurdity and meaninglessness within which the actors rise in Sisyphian spirit to build hope and solidarity without being immediatelyconcerned with the new unequal normal that may be building or the fissures that led to the plague in the first place. Thus, while Dr. Rieux's intervention in the "event" effectively exposes the non-humanistic exclusive practices of the state, religion, and medicine, it paradoxically reinforces its own exclusions. The same can be illustrated with the contemporary context of the pandemic.

The coronavirus brought to light the inadequacy of the justice frameworks especially in the areas of health, food, education, social securities, personal safety, and public distribution welfare schemes. Besides public health infrastructure, national and internal policies have evolved in a way that has developed a consensus of inequality. The world witnessed one of the worst lockdowns with thousands losing their livelihood, and growing panic over testing and treatment. Fake products and black marketing of everything from masks and sanitizers to daily essentials, people falling prey to faulty treatments and excess of misinformation dismantled the already fragile socio-political infrastructure of the human ecosystem that has been steadily neglected and made vulnerable. Stigma, xenophobia, and panic in interpersonal, social, and political domains deepened fissures (beyond repair) that added to the struggles of coping with the mortality threat posed by the virus. Further, it pushed people in what was considered "safe spaces" and left unaccounted the resulting gender-based violence, violence against children, the elderly, and the disabled.[13] Class-based inequalities became stark as the migrants, daily wage earners, vendors, domestic help, and agricultural laborers were left to the mercy of callous government relief packages (more of token) that are not in sync with the mass reality of starvation, inaccessibility to loan provisions, and absence of real emergency mitigation measures. In India, this resulted in mass movement of people to return to their home villages from cities in desperate situations. Some traveled large interstate distances on foot, cycled (or any means available) with no assurance of food or water supplies, falling prey to conditions like heat strokes, starvation, or diseases like cholera and diarrhea. The sanitizing process of the urban centers was thus much more than a hygiene-related cleansing process. Rather than the forced evictions from "sanitised" city streets of the vulnerable urban poor who were thrown into worse distress situations threatening their entire existence.

Worldwide, the pandemic exposed the underfunded and aging health systems across the capitalist world. Despite government efforts to take care of global stock markets and declining trade due to "de-globalisation", economic activities spiraled into recession as industrial production declined, unemployment increased, and millions of businesses struggled for survival. The failures of the economic neoliberal policies of minimal state intervention and free-market ideology became stark as government assistance became urgent to bail out private enterprises. Excessive pressure on poorly sponsored public healthcare services, inadequate functionality of privatized health services, as well as the inefficacy of existing welfare systems exposed the inability of private capital to effectively respond to the severity of the pandemic. In order to avoid a total collapse of health systems, governments resorted to extreme measures such as national lockdowns. A sense of patriotic solidarity is propagated to prevent revolt and ensure compliance with the guidelines. Through the streaming of information on mainstream media and restrictions on the movement of people, a system of social discipline is imposed that has changed employment and education patterns across the world (Constantinos 2021, 285).

A new trend with changes in technology has established part-time jobs, subcontracting, and working from home as the "new normal" that has important implications on productivity, mental state, and patterns of consumption and behavior. Social distancing has ushered in a harsh environment of pessimism that is constantly reinforced by serious public health threats and public emergencies. Under the same pretext, authoritarian practices of restrictions on fundamental rights, movement of people, and goods have also deepened the already existing refugee crisis. Contrary to the facts of failure and inefficiency of the state, it is promoted as an indispensable sovereign, dynamic, and authoritative power that offers protection and treatment services. It is propagated as an advanced political state that has embraced the challenges of the pandemic by implementing measures based on scientific authority. New social boundaries are defined so that the society embraces the "new normal" that effectively hides the criminal lapses of a badly run state that led to the crisis in the first place (Constantinos 2021, 285–286). Proclaiming the pandemic as an unusual event it becomes imperative for all to join together in solidarity, even though the battle clearly spells a class character (and its intersectionality with gender, caste, religion, disability). It is the poor, working class and their immediate families exposed to the most harmful health, economic, and social consequences of the pandemic. They risk their lives without any protection to facilitate a return to "normalcy", one that is primarily a business opportunity promoted by the capitalist motto of continuing production and maximizing profits. Thus, though the pandemic seems like it affects one and all without discrimination, it is not without unequal impact and consequences. The battle is not fought together in solidarity; rather, it is those who are rendered vulnerable by preexisting economic and social conditions. The workers that suffer the most, weighed down by the burden to bring things to "normalcy" while the privileged capitalize on their position and build profits.

Camus' *The Plague* or the humanistic psychological theories do not do sufficient justice to combat the complex situation discussed. The novel ends with the plague mysteriously disappearing (as mysteriously as it appeared) and Dr. Rieux reinforcing the absurdity and Sisyphian spirit of heroism with his proclamation of the plague microbe never dying rather only lying dormant to rise to its destruction again (Camus 2010, 297). Such a proclamation does make an important case for existential hope and solidarity as a response to the challenge posed by the pandemic. Though medical interventions are indispensable, *The Plague* emphasizes on human ability to use one's own personal impulses to find wisdom, growth, healing, and fulfillment. It reminds us that we are not autonomous and that our actions affect others and the world around us, thus breakdowns and crisis require humanistic intervention. In difficult times of the pandemic the existential approach prompts us to evaluate the success of medical and political practice and calls for prioritizing the ethical responsibility of crossing the threshold of securing immunity towards embracing human vulnerability and being hospitable to the other. Yet, the project demands looking at social realities beyond existential and therapeutic model, it demands a deconstructive intervention. It aims to expose the *aporias* (unresolvable contradictions) within discourses which are understood as meaningful structures. It does not leave fully intact the object of study, it starts from the close reading of the text in the question (in this case existential expression of the pandemic) and the purpose is not to re establish its coherence but to show its limits so as to subvert it. In its subversion also lies the paradox of reinforcing the very forces it aimed to destabilize (Thomson 2003, 5–6). This, according to Derrida is inescapable as there can be no ultimate reference point outside the structured discourses, the critique of it contains the assumptions it strives to reject and the power of the "centre ordered structures" is restored and reinforced in the very act of destroying it (Derrida 2000, 91). Yet, in its iterability, in its repetition lies the scope for its rectification, of exposing those "absences" that are deliberately erased so as to rebuild a more inclusive discourse. An inclusive understanding of building solidarity and hope in pandemic would involve witnessing the fractured foundations of our civic state that led to the experience of loss and pain; without these considerations one would fail to acknowledge the true nature of pandemic which calls for an urgent responses to care, justice, and change.

Notes

1 A shorter version of this paper is published in the University of Mumbai journal *Sambhashan*, Inaugural Issue, Vol. 1, Issue No.1, May 2021. I am grateful to Prof. Mahadevan for this opportunity and her insights, though all faults in the chapter are purely mine.

2 Nietzsche in his work The Birth of Tragedy explains that myths instill life affirming attitudes that he describes as "pessimism of strength" (2007, 4). The significance of tragedy is that the tragic sense of life can be overcome by justifying life as desirable despite its dark moments.

3 He was sentenced for the crime of loving life too much; he defied the gods and fought death. The gods thought they found a perfect form of torture for Sisyphus. He would constantly hope for success, that the stone would remain at the top of the mountain. This, the gods thought, would forever frustrate him. Yet, defying the gods, Sisyphus is without hope. He abandons any illusion that he might succeed at the assigned task. Camus thus considers him a hero. Sisyphus begins to view his ability to do the task again and again, to endure the punishment as a form of victory (Camus 1991, 182–184).

4 Contrasted by characters like Raymond Rambert, a journalist stranded in Oran devises a plan to escape the city to join his lover in Paris after city officials refused his request to leave. He befriends some criminals so that they may smuggle him out of the city (Camus 2010, 102–106). Another character, Father Paneloux, uses the plague as an opportunity

to advance his religious philosophy by suggesting that the plague was an act of God for the citizens' sinful nature (Camus 2010, 94–95). Living in denial of the absurdity of the situation is philosophical suicide (Camus 1991. 48, 61)

5 The following is Foucault's analysis of the self and power in his work "The Subject and Power". Though his philosophy never made direct references to the pandemic, his analysis of infectious diseases as modes of thought that organize societies is relevant to the current context.

6 An informative overview of the editorial conditions of the lecture course found in Mike Gane, *Foucault on Governmentality and Liberalism, Theory, Culture & Society* 25(7–8) (2008): 353–363.

7 This has its first effect in the organization of the family. The family becomes the link between health of its members and the society at large. It encourages a private ethic of good health as the duty of parents towards all needing care; as prescribed by the state. Thus, the family is "medicalized"(Foucault 1980,175), values of respecting one's health, health of other members, access to the market where supply and demand for medical care take place simultaneously with state authority and its intervention through the insti-tutionalization of all services come to characterize the family and hence its medicaliza-tion (Foucault 1980, 175–176).

8 Existential concerns are a major force in human behavior, and ignoring these con-cerns only serves to deepen the psychological conflicts that are associated with them. Existential concerns of death, isolation, identity, freedom, responsibility, and one's desire for ultimate meaning have a deep impact on people's life. Strict measurable, cog-nitive, and objective methods are inadequate to explain the same.

9 Twentieth-century thinker, Edmund Husserl's theory of phenomenology emphasized the need to set aside theoretical assumptions and describe immediate experiences of phenomena themselves. He emphasized the intentional nature of human mental activ-ity. Psychic acts are intentional because they are oriented or directed toward some spe-cific situation or object beyond themselves and can be meaningfully understood only in that context. Thus, consciousness is not merely internal; it is an involvement of the subject with the object of perception. Through intentionality, the human and experi-ential world interact and co-create the external world/phenomena. Martin Heidegger combined Husserl's phenomenological method of detailed study of mental acts with an examination of the structure of human existence. In *Being and Time*, he described the human being as a being in the world; that is, human beings discover themselves through their facticity and historical situations. Heidegger also discusses human beings as beings towards death; that is, human beings discover their completeness in their awareness of their deaths. Merleau-Ponty in his work *Phenomenology of Perception*, defined the phenomena of the mental as the structure of behavior. He uses the theories of the Gestalt psychologist Kurt Goldstein's investigations of neurologically affected individuals to explore the organization of human movement and the embodied self's relationship to the environment. For Husserl, Heidegger, and Ponty, neurophysiological processes sepa-rate from the contexts and situations cannot sufficiently explain human behavior (Moss 2015, 9–10). Phenomenological theories along with the existential themes (discussed in the context of Camus' *The Plague*) influenced twentieth-century existential humanistic psychology.

10 Plato does so in his work *The Republic* (2003, 427d–449a) and Thomas Hobbes in his work *Leviathan* (1973, 100–105).

11 Derrida explains this in the context of nation states. Since nation states remain uncom-promising about their borders, they remain threatened internally by their own logic. He suggests that if democracy were absolutely immune from compromise, it would be abso-lutely sovereign, inert, and hostile to the other. Autoimmunity, paradoxically nurtures a democratic culture of openness towards the possibility of infinite alteration, reworking and re orientation (Derrida 2005, 33–34).

12 In 1971, the *Societies De Philosophie De Langue Francaise* organized a colloquium where Derrida delivered a lecture titled *"Signature, Event, Context"* and he raised the question of whether the word communication can communicate. Communication in language or discourse implies a transmission from one person to another. It signifies something in transit. It's signifiers can relate to many signifieds, thus threatening it unless it is limited by a context. Derrida explains that communication, such as writing, is cut free from its sender and its addressee. Thus, a third party can decipher it, identify its marks, and use it (1982, 315–316). Therefore, language must be iterable, repeatable, yet repeatable with a *différance* or rearticulation/repetition; thus, it can never be neutral (Derrida 2002,441).

13 The following is the summary from P. Sainath's "What We Should Do About Covid-19?: The Government's 'Package' Responding To the Crisis Is a Blend of Callousness and Cluelessness", published by *People's Archive of Rural India*. Accessed: URL https://ruralindiaonline.org/en/articles/what-we-should-do-about-covid-19/ on January 11, 2022 at 15.22pm.

Works Cited

Borradori, Giovanna. 2003. *Philosophy in a Time of Terror*. Chicago: University of Chicago Press.

Camus, Albert. 2010. *The Plague*. London: Penguin Books.

Camus, Albert. 1991. "Myth of Sisuphus." In *Myth of Sisyphus and Other Essays*. Translated by Justin Obrien, 8–103. Vintage. Apple Books.

Constantinos Alexiou. 2021. "Covid-19, Capitalism and Political Elites: The Real Threat to Humanity." *Human Geography*, Vol. 14, No. 2, pp. 284–287. https://journals.sagepub.com/doi/full/10.1177/19427786211012671 Accessed on 11 January 2022 at 16.12pm.

Derrida, Jacques. 2002. "Différance." In *The Phenomenology Reader*. Edited by Dermot Moran and Tim Mooney, 441–464. London: Routledge.

———. 2003. "Hospitality." In *The Derrida Habermas Reader*. Edited by Lasse Thomassen, 208–230. Edinburgh: Edinburg University Press.

———. 2005. *Rogues*. Translated by Pascale-Anne and Michael Naas. Stanford, CA: Stanford University Press.

———. 1982. "Signature Event Context." In *Margins of Philosophy*. Translated by Alan Bass. The University of Chicago Press. https://1lib.in/book/783819/9b8b02 Accessed on 8 January 2022 at 8.06am.

———. 2000. "Structure, Sign and Play In The Discourse of Human Sciences." In *Modern Criticism and Theory: A Reader*. 2nd Edition, Edited by David Lodge and Nigel Wood, 88–103. Harlow: Longman.

Foucault, Michel. 1988. *Madness and Civilization: A History of Insanity in the Age of Reason*. New York: Vintage Books.

———. 1980. "The Politics of Health in the Eighteenth Century." In *Power/ Knowledge: Selected Interviews and Other Writings 1972–1977*. Edited by Colin Gordon. Translated by Colin Gordon, Leo Marshall, John Mepham, Kate Soper, 166–182. New York:Pantheon Books.

———. (Summer, 1982). "The Subject and Power." *Critical Inquiry*, Vol. 8, No. 4: pp. 777–795. Accessed from URL: http://www.jstor.org/stable/1343197 Accessed 10 January 2021, 13.04pm.

———. 1997. "What Is Enlightenment?" In *The Politics of Truth*, Edited by Sylvère Lotringer and Lysa Hochroth, 101–134. New York: Semiotext(e).

Frankl, Victor Emil. 1968. *Man's Search for Meaning: Basic Concepts of Logotherapy*. Translated by Ilse Lasch. https://1lib.in/book/1284263/910461 Accessed on 3 January 2022 at 12.50pm.

Gane, Mike. 2008. "Foucault on Governmentality, and Liberalism." *Theory, Culture and Society*, Vol. 25, No. 7–8, pp. 353–363.

Hobbes, Thomas. 1973. *Leviathan*. London: J. M. Dent and Sons.

Moss, Donald. 2015. "The Roots and Genealogy of Humanistic Psychology." In *The Handbook of Humanistic Psychology: Theory, Research and Practice*. Edited by Kirk J. Schneider, J. Fraser Pierson, and James F.T. Bugental, 3–18. Sage.

Nietzsche, Frederick. 2007. *The Birth of Tragedy and Other Writings*. Edited by Raymond Geuss and Raymond Spiers. Cambridge: Cambridge University Press.

Plato. 2003. *The Republic*. Translated by Desmond Lee. London: Penguin Classics.

Rank, Otto. 1945. *Will Therapy*. Translated by Jessie Taft. Philadelphia: Pennsylvania School of Social Work. https://1lib.in/book/2556715/4446b8 on 3rd January 2022 at 12.42pm.

Rollo May. 1958. "The Origins and Significance of the Existential Movement in Psychology." In *Existence: A New Dimension in Psychiatry and Psychology*. Edited by Rollo May, Ernest Angel, Henri, and F. Ellenberger, 3–36 New York: Basic Books Inc. Publishers.

Sophocles. 1982. *Oedipus The King*. Edited by R.D. Dawe. Cambridge: Cambridge University Press.

Thomson Alex. 2007. "Derrida's Rogues: Islam and the Futures of Deconstruction." In *Derrida Negotiating the Legacy*. Edited by Madeline Fagan, Ludovic Glorieux, Indira Hasimbegovic, and Marie Suetsugu, 66–79. Edinburgh: Edinburgh University Press.

Thucydides. 2012. *The History of the Peloponnesian War*. Translated by Richard Crawley. Duke Books, Apple Books.

Thomsassen, Lasse. 2003. "Introduction: Between Deconstruction and Rational Reconstruction." in *The Derrida – Habermas Reader*. Edited by Lasse Thommassen, 1–10. Edinburgh: Edinburgh University Press.

Yalom, Irvin. 1980. *Existential Psychotherapy*. New York: Basic Books.

13 EPFO to e-EPFO

Transformational Journey of a Service

Mridula Ghai, Nilendu Mishra, Ajay Kumar,
and Ghazala Ali Khan

Introduction

The Mandate of Social Security

Social security, as defined by the International Social Security Association (ISSA) under the International Labor Organization (ILO), is any program established by legislation, or any other mandatory arrangement, that provides individuals with basic income security when faced with contingencies of old age, survivorship, incapacity, disability, unemployment etc.

The first rudimentary social security programs were launched in Europe in the late-nineteenth century. Since then, social security has emerged as a key concept in world development, expanding in both coverage and scope, supported by international covenants, and the recognition of social security as a basic human right in the Universal Declaration of Human Rights. Social security thus creates an element of security in an economic environment that creates insecurity (Baker & Weisbrot, 1999). In developing countries like India, social security is best understood as pro-poor measures that can be promotional, aiming to augment income, such as the Mahatma Gandhi National Rural Employment Guarantee Act 2005 (MGNREGA), preventive, aiming to forestall economic distress, such as Provident Funds, and protective, aiming to ensure relief from certain external shocks, such as remuneration in the case of injury or death of a primary breadwinner (Sarkar, 2004).

However, in a world of rapid technological change, at the present time, the labor market is undergoing radical transformations that are upending many of the known assumptions about work and careers (Brynjolfsson and McAfee, 2014; Stiglitz, 2015). The numbers in the vulnerable population are increasing, not only as the ranks of the uninsured grow, but as the population ages (AJMC, 2016). Economic growth has helped reduce the incidence of absolute poverty, but less so in unequal countries, and threatens to stall progress against poverty by attenuating growth prospects (Ravallion, 2014). The havoc caused in the last couple of years by the pandemic has brought out in sharp relief, the extent to which the wealth and resources of the world are unequally apportioned. Unfortunately, as bad as inequality had been before the pandemic, the post-pandemic world could experience even greater inequalities unless governments do something (Stiglitz, 2020).

The financial, fiscal, and economic affordability and sustainability of social protection systems has become a major concern for countries. Social security

DOI: 10.4324/9781003304517-17

represents an investment in a country's "human infrastructure" no less important than investments in its physical infrastructure. Universal coverage, access to basic services, full and comprehensive health coverage, and access to primary and tertiary education are now recognized as bare minimums that all countries of the world should strive to provide to their citizens. The concept of "decent work" affording dignity as well as a minimum living wage, work-related rights, protections as well as unemployment cover, is now not merely "aspirational", as per Bluestien et al. (2016), but is being increasingly adopted and applied in developing countries in a bid to afford better accountability towards citizens and take care of poor and vulnerable sections.

The Indian economy, being a developing one, has a well-intentioned social security system in place. However, it has been constrained in the years past by an unwieldy population, and scarcity of finances and resources. Informal workers have been left out of coverage due to structural constraints, and now, new and platform-based work relations have also rendered the new age workers vulnerable. However, Weber (2018) believes that in spite of the changing and flexible character of platform work, extending social security is feasible—if one is ready to explore new avenues. With the growth of the economy, the government is also determined to provide comprehensive social security to all through promulgation of the new code on social security, and registration of gig workers as well as informal workers within its ambit.

The Organization

The Employees Provident Fund Organization (EPFO), under the Ministry of Labor and Employment (MOLE), is India's flagship social security organization providing comprehensive cover to the country's private organized sector of establishments employing 20 or more workers. It is one of the largest Social Security organizations in the world in terms of clientele and the volume of financial transactions undertaken,[1] maintaining 24.77 crore accounts, with 5.8 crore active contributing members and over 67 lakh pensioners.[2] With a total corpus of Rs. 13.87 lakh crores, it is the world's eighth-largest pension fund. In terms of physical presence, it has 138 regional offices, under 22 zone level offices, and 117 district offices.

EPFO administers the Employees' Provident Funds & Miscellaneous Provisions Act 1952 and the three schemes framed thereunder, namely, the Employees Provident Fund Scheme 1952, The Employees' Pension Scheme 1995, and the Employees Deposit Linked Scheme 1972. The benefits include a retirement corpus allowing for partial withdrawals for education, marriage, illness, and house construction, monthly pensionary benefits on superannuation, disability, survivorship benefits for spouse and dependent children, and deposit linked life insurance cover for death in service with a benefit amount of 20 times of the wages, up to Rs. 7 lakh. Given the Indian social milieu, the bulk of the benefits are designed keeping in view old-age security and survivorship benefits. The accumulated corpus with interest is tax-free on pay out, providing safety along with higher returns on savings. The pension scheme is unique in the sense that it is a defined benefit scheme, with the entire contribution being funded from the employer's side. It is for these reasons that EPFO has been considered the mainstay of social security for economically weaker sections since its inception in 1952.

However, the organization, with its cumbersome legacy records, has struggled to keep pace with changing times. Slow pace of computerization and backlogs of old, decrepit, and often incomplete records, had been putting a strain on offices grappling with staff shortages and infrastructural constraints. Modernization, computerized settlement, and online functioning happened, albeit at a slow pace. Even though online claim filing and settlement had been introduced way back in 2017, there was very low take-up initially, due to beneficiaries' lack of technological knowledge and resistance to change. In the first 6 months, only about 3% of claims were filed online. With sustained effort, however, the number of claims preferred online went up to over 90% of total claims by the end of March 2020. This preparation proved invaluable during the pandemic when offline claim filing had been rendered impossible. The pandemic, in fact, provided the launchpad and the necessary impetus for fast-tracking the digitization of the organization.

The Pandemic

When the COVID-19 pandemic struck, jobs and services across the country were crippled, and workers were badly affected, not only through lack of preparedness, but also economically. Predominantly the economically weaker sections were affected more. It was reported in a survey that around two-thirds of respondents in the period reported either losing employment during the lockdown or witnessed a decline in earnings (Kesar et al., 2021). Unemployment rose post-pandemic to more than three times what it was in 2018, and although it has fallen to pre-COVID-19 levels, wages have fallen sharply (Mehrotra and Parida, 2021). COVID-19 has, in particular, exposed informal workers to great hardship, and another catastrophe will push workers drastically into poverty (Mehrotra, 2021). Bertrand, Krishnan, and Schofield (2020) analyzed data collected by Centre for Monitoring Indian Economy (CMIE) as part of its Consumer Pyramids Household Survey (CPHS) and found that 84% of households have reported a decline in income since the lockdown.

It was at this time when the workers were reeling with lockdowns leading to a loss of earnings, that EPFO stepped in. Having been designated an organization providing "essential services", EPFO's 138 regional and all associated subordinate offices remained functional throughout the pandemic. However, the initial phase of working was very difficult internally for the organization, as there were numerous pain points. Not only was the staff required to dispose of the regular workload of final settlement, pension, and advance cases while the nation was in lockdown, they also had to handle the additional workload of COVID-19 advances mandated by the government, to provide relief in the form of liquidity to the members not getting salaries due to the closure of workplaces. Facing lockdown restrictions, shut-down of public transport, rostering requirements, closure of workplaces due to outbreaks and quarantines, the staff in all offices across the nation continued working, often in crisis mode, through the pandemic. While other businesses and economic activities were either closed or people were facilitated to work from home, EPFO staff continued working in a physical mode, in staggered shifts complying with the government's safety mandates, not getting a break from punishing workloads and deadlines of settlements. This was also the time when they worked without vaccines, with a shortage of masks and sanitizer, and no tested protocols of treatment should they get infected.

Impetus to Change

EPFO, until a few years back, like any other government organization, grappled with physical files, non-digitized records, and manual settlement of paper claims while being severely resource- and staff-constrained. New recruitment was not happening, and the older workforce was retiring in droves every month, leaving the organization staring at a heavy staff crunch.

Ironically, the crisis helped power the digital transformation of the organization. The pandemic forced the organization to devise new ways to deal with the unprecedented situation. The entire functioning of the organization, including the claim statement, was required to be shifted to an online mode. Members were required to be facilitated to receive money and pensions without being made to venture out of their homes. Digital platforms on mobile phones had to be utilized, and awareness had to be created about their use and the leadership of the organization rose to the occasion. Fast tracking digitalization and brainstorming to devise new ways to increase outreach, new avenues, and benchmarks of service delivery were laid down to augment the existing processes, and unknowingly, higher standards in customer service began to be laid down and implemented. Technology made many things possible. Following were the broad initiatives adopted towards this end.

EPFO had introduced the facility of submitting online claims in May 2017, and by March 2020, more than 90% of claims were being filed online. This proved

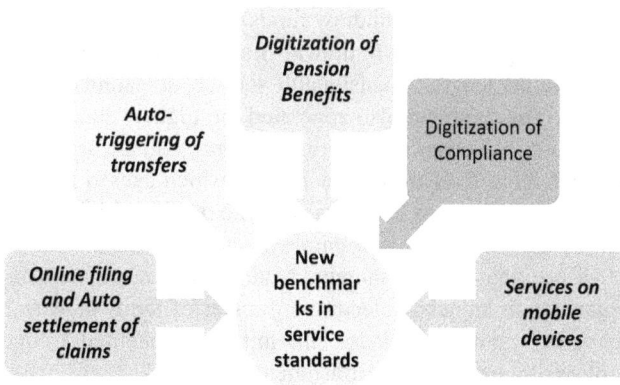

Figure 13.1 Auto-settlement of Claims

Exponential growth in online claim settlements (in Lakh)

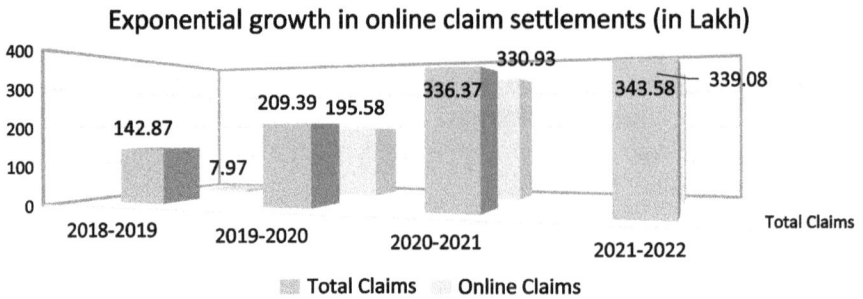

Figure 13.2 Exponential Growth in Online Claim Settlements (in Lakh)

invaluable in settling claims during pandemic restrictions. The following graph illustrates the progress made in moving from paper claims towards online claims.

During the pandemic and faced with the extra workload of COVID-19 advances amid staff shortage and government-mandated safety protocols, the department fast-tracked its *next level* of innovation, of system-driven auto-claim settlement for accounts which were Know Your Customer (KYC) compliant, by linking the member's Universal Account Number (UAN) with KYC details. This module had been introduced on a pilot basis at selected offices towards the latter part of 2019. During March 2020, with the onset of the pandemic and consequent lockdown, this facility was scaled up and launched pan India. It ensured seamless extension of service to subscribers who were grappling with liquidity problems while fulfilling the government directives and 1.06 crore claims have been settled so far through auto-mode.

Online and Auto Triggered Transfers

Transfer of funds between accounts is a cumbersome process requiring multiple points of verification. Long processing time and high return ratio have over the years encouraged employees to withdraw funds instead of seeking transfer to their new accounts. These premature withdrawals not only deplete the retirement corpus, but also reduce the length of pensionable service, defeating the whole purpose of social security. This problem also generated the highest number of grievances on the grievance portal. Towards mitigating this problem, the organization simplified transfers, launching the auto-trigger facility which caused funds to get automatically transferred to the new accounts once the details of the member had been matched between the old and the new employers.

In respect of exempted establishments having their own Provident Fund (PF) trusts, the organization launched electronic transfer of funds in May 2019, doing away with physical transfer of funds. This initiative benefited around one crore members employed in exempted establishments.

Every pensioner is required to submit a life certificate once a year in November for the pension to be continued. This process earlier involved pensioners having

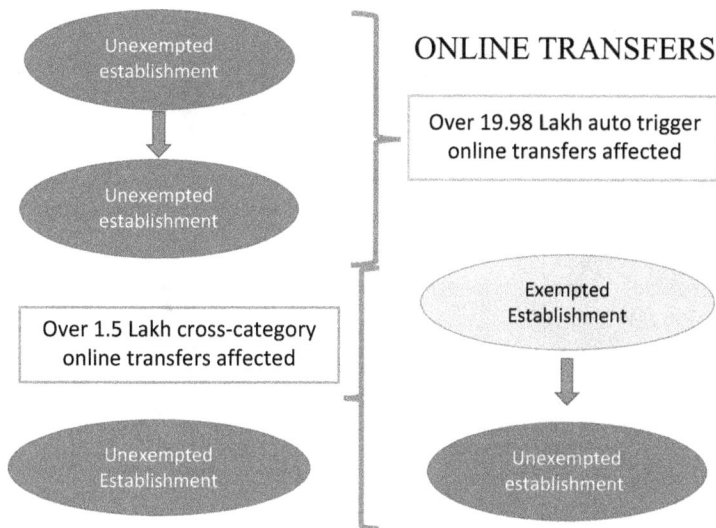

Figure 13.3 Digitization of Pension Benefits

to travel long distances and wait in queues at their bank branches to submit their life certificates, which would at times get misplaced. This caused avoidable inconvenience and resulted in a large number of grievances on account of the stoppage of pensions. A key policy change was made with the introduction of digitally filed life certificates called *Jeevan Praman Patras* (JPP), a Government of India initiative implemented by EPFO. Pensioners have now been enabled to submit life certificates in digital form, anytime during the year, instead of in November, as was the practice earlier. Over three lakh service centers have been engaged to capture biometrics and facilitate filing the life certificates. Also, by integrating the JPPs with the DigiLocker initiative of the government, the same is now accessible to them on their mobile phones on DigiLocker as well as through the Unified Mobile Application for New-age Governance (UMANG) app.

Government of India's Unified Mobile Application for New-age Governance (UMANG) application offers a single platform for all citizens to access a range of e-government services on their mobile phones. This platform was made use of by EPFO to extend services to subscribers. EPFO offers more than 16 services through the UMANG app, and many more are in the process of being added.

The app witnessed a 180% jump in claims filed on the UMANG app to 11.27 lakh during the COVID-19 period from April to July 2020. With social distancing and restrictions due to the pandemic, UMANG has become the preferred mode of accessing services. EPFO is the single largest user of both UMANG and *Jeevan Praman Patra* initiatives. DigiLocker and facilities of common service centers of MeitY are also being extensively used by EPFO.

Employee Centric Services	Employer Centric Service	General Services

Request for Covid advance Form 10C
View Member Passbook
Raise Claim
Track Claim
UAN activation
UAN Allotment
Register Grievance
Send Reminder
View Status
	Get Remittance Details by Establishment ID
	Get TRRN Status
		Search Establishment
		Search EPFO
		Account details on SMS
		Account details on Missed Calls
		eKYC Service-Aadhaar SEEDING
		Pension Service
		  Jeevan Pramaan
		  View Passbook
		  Download Pension Payment Order

Figure 13.4 Employee Centric Services and General Services

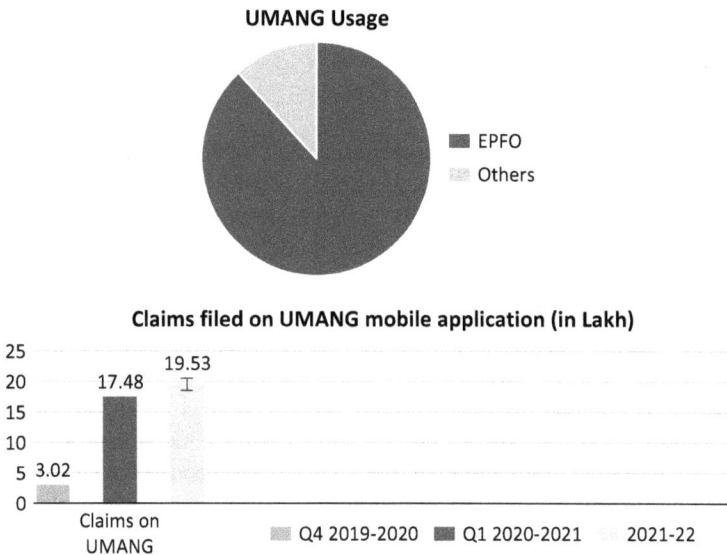

UMANG Usage

EPFO
Others

Claims filed on UMANG mobile application (in Lakh)

3.02   17.48   19.53

Claims on UMANG

Q4 2019-2020   Q1 2020-2021   2021-22

Figure 13.5 UMANG Usage and Claims

Digitization of Compliance

E-inspections were introduced as part of pandemic-driven emergency measures, but they have proved to be futuristic and efficient, ensuring transparent compliance. 7A[3] proceedings and e-inspections have made compliance faceless and efficient. Virtual hearings have been appreciated for increasing ease of compliance.

Addition of other e-services has been and continues to be a work in progress. EPFO has partnered with C-DAC, a premier R&D organization of the Ministry of

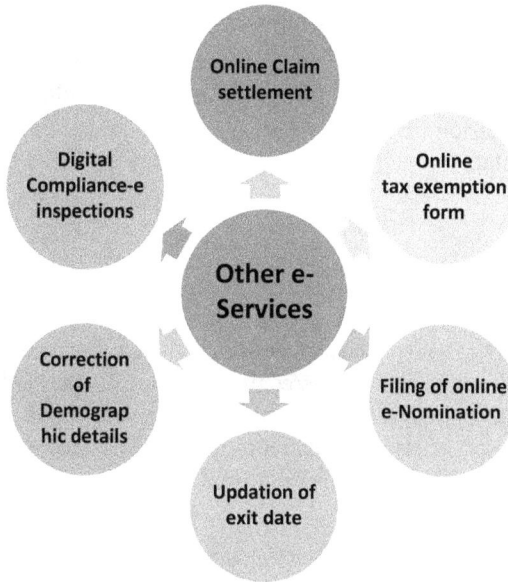

Figure 13.6 E-services Provided by EPFO

Electronics and Information Technology (MeitY) to find innovative solutions to everyday problems. Underpinning all digital solutions however, is the correct identification of members through a fool-proof KYC system. The e-services provided by EPFO are given in Figure 13.6.

Pathways to Change

Change requires vision, mandate, and will. Ably led from the front, dedicated officers and staff operated with intention to serve during the pandemic. Real-time monitoring through dashboards, leveraging the power of technology, and periodic review for course-correction, propelled the journey forward.

Leveraging Technology

Auto settlement of claims, multilocational claim settlement, and work-from-home (WFH) modalities were all made possible through imaginative use of technology. Moving away from bureaucratic mindsets and embracing unconventional methodologies was possible only due to the exigencies of the pandemic. Also, availability of ready-to-use digital platforms increased exponentially the reach of services. Not wasting time in reinventing the wheel, the government initiated digital platform of UMANG was made use of by the management, and EPFO services were seamlessly integrated on it. This saved the organization considerable time and cost.

Pilot Testing Before Scaling up of Initiatives

All components of digitization were pilot tested in select offices for robustness before being scaled up nationally. Best practices were identified and replicated to make informed decisions. By the time the pandemic struck, EPFO had completed pilot projects on auto-claim settlement which could be upscaled immediately.

Service Centred Mindset

Recognizing that the pandemic was rapidly unfolding an unprecedented human tragedy, and that just a professional approach would not work, EPFO tried to sensitize and motivate its staff to understand and implement the fundamental shift of perceiving their jobs as a service to humanity. Overcoming fear, and despite hardships, infections, and casualties, the employees of the organization carried on with their work, unmindful of personal safety and without protest. This service mindset, of working for the greater good was the main reason behind the organization's success story.

Out of the Box Thinking: Multi-Locational Claim Settlement and Work-From-Home Modalities

Recognizing that some offices faced a heavier load than others, and that lockdowns affected different regions differently, the idea of multilocational claim settlement was conceived. Offices less affected by COVID-19 in tier two and three cities were looped in to handle the excess workload of larger offices like Bandra and Gurgaon. Reallocation of workload also led to work rationalization, enhancing productivity. EPFO also adopted the modality of limited WFH and simplification of KYC updating processes to fast-track claim settlement.

Effective Outreach and Communication

EPFO took steps to keep two-way communication open throughout the pandemic. Recognizing the difficulties being faced by members in preferring claims remotely, as well as with a view to increase outreach, "Meet the CPFC" seminars were organized in metro cities to initiate direct interaction with industry leaders and facilitate them in extending services to their workers and to educate them about the initiatives taken by EPFO. In addition, webinars were organized with Confederation of Indian Industry (CII) and Federation of Indian Chambers of Commerce & Industry (FICCI), joint committees were formed to formalize system improvements, and new employers onboarding webinars were also conducted. Thousands of educational webinars were organized disseminating information regarding EPFO services and how to avail of them. Suggestions and feedback of participants were incorporated in policy decisions to enhance ease of doing business for employers and ease of access for subscribers.

The PRAYAAS initiative is an outreach program as an endeavor to release pension on the day of superannuation. Webinars are conducted by field offices inviting members superannuating within three months. The purpose of these webinars is to educate the members and their employers so that they can submit pension claims complete in every respect and EPFO can issue pensions on the day of superannuation to such members.

EPFO: Then vs Now

Claim Settlement in Record Time

The EPF Act and schemes mandate a claim settlement time of 20 days. Online and auto mode of claim settlement has made three-day claim settlements possible. Despite COVID-19 pandemic restrictions, EPFO was able to settle 74.62 lakh claims during April to July 2020. The claim-settlement rate in these 4 months was 26% higher than what it was in the same period in the previous year.

Successful Fulfilling of Government Mandate

In view of the distress and liquidity crisis caused by the pandemic, the EPF Scheme was amended allowing for a non-refundable advance of up to 75% of the member's total PF contributions. This special COVID-19 advance became part of Pradhan Mantri Garib Kalyan Yojna (PMGKY) announced by the government. During the period between March and July 2020, more than 30 lakh members made such withdrawals of about Rs. 8000 crores. Further, a benefit of Rs. 1927 crore was given to 42.62 lakh subscribers working in about 2.66 lakh establishments. Also, almost 56% of the COVID-19 related claims were settled through the auto settlement mode without any human intervention.

Increased Productivity

Despite constrained manpower deployment, the average monthly claim settlement increased to 20.60 lakh per month from 17.45 lakh per month during pre-COVID-19 times. This marked a 24% increase in productivity even with a decrease in staff deployment by 34%. The cumulative effect was to the tune of 87% increase in productivity as far as claim settlement was concerned.

Enhanced User-friendliness of Services

The grievance redressal portal has been revamped to be more responsive to complaints, and resolve them in real time. Interfaces for updating and correction of demographic data mismatches, coding in job exit dates through electronic devices from home, and a facility for filing e-nominations etc. are some other mechanisms through which EPFO is removing red-tapism and pain from routine tasks. Another legacy problem, of members depending on employers for verification and forwarding of claims, has also been resolved through KYC seeding. The relationship between EPFO and its members is now direct and close-knit due to the e-initiatives.

Carrying the customer friendliness mandate forward, in January 2021 a Common Services Centre's Virtual Contact Centre (CSC-VCC) was implemented which has features like call recording and monitoring, real-time dashboard, call-back and SMS facilities, feedback from stakeholders, and provision for detailed reports. The capacity of the call centre has been continuously increased, and approximately 4000 calls are replied to. The call center facility has also been extended to zonal offices in vernacular languages. Social media handles at Facebook and Twitter/X are also being increasingly utilized to provide information and guidance as well as resolve issues.

Disaster Proofing of the Organization

The initial impact of the Covid-19 was high in cities like Mumbai, Delhi, Gurugram, Chennai, Bengaluru, which had high claim receipt, and increased additional receipt of COVID claims. To handle this high workload, EPFO launched a multi-location claim settlement facility which gave EPFO wherewithal to settle online claims from any of its regional offices, across the country. This allowed offices with lesser workload to share the burden of offices that have accumulated a higher level of pendency, due to COVID-19 restrictions and also enabled fast-tracking of the settlement process.

This facility has gone a long way in not only mitigating the present crisis but also disaster-proofing the organization going forward for future calamities as well. For reasons of any natural disaster such as floods, earthquake, epidemic or for any other reason if there is a shutdown in part of the country, the work in EPFO offices will not stop.

Planning for the Future

The success of the e-initiatives has emboldened EPFO to now plan for the future with renewed vigor and enthusiasm. EPFO has its data centers at Gurugram, Secunderabad, and New Delhi, where the process for replacing the old software and hardware has been initiated with the technical support of Center for Development in Advanced Computing (C-DAC). Railtel Corporation has been roped in for the data center management and global network operation center management. The network bandwidth is also being increased so that the stakeholders do not face problems of slow speed while accessing the various online services provided by EPFO.

The feedback received from members through the EPFiGMS is also being analyzed on regular basis so that remaining bottlenecks in service areas can be removed. The call center services are also being augmented to include more Indian languages so that members of different states are able to get updated information in their mother tongue.

Covid-19 has forced establishments to increase their remote workforce. This has provided a window of opportunity to hackers, as more and more people are online throughout the day. In fact, last year's data shows that most of the data breaches that took place were due to hacking of mobiles and IoT devices. Nowadays, these devices have become a necessity and are available in plenty at workplaces around the world. Accordingly, EPFO is setting up a Security Operation Center at the National Data Center in Dwarka, New Delhi to ensure that its systems are monitored 24 x 7 and adequate security measures are put in place to counter the emerging cyber security threats. Further, the technical team of EPFO is always in touch with the Indian Computer Emergency Response Team (CERT-In) to counter any emergent threats.

EPFO, through the initiatives mentioned above looks forward to the future with new hope. It will endeavor to set new standards of service delivery to all its stakeholders and try to move towards the ultimate goal of universal social security coverage to the working population in India.

Aspirational Vision for the Future of Social Security in India

The government is already looking forward to universalizing social security for all citizens, particularly the weaker sections, and aligning the benefits provided with international standards. ILO's Social Security (Minimum Standards) Convention, 1952 (No. 102) sets out the benchmark for social security benefits and the conditions under which they are granted. Convention 102 is built on the idea that there is no right model for social security, social security grows and evolves over time, and that social security policies should reflect countries' social and cultural values, their history, their institutions, and their level of economic development.

The Social Protection Floors Recommendation, 2012 (No. 202) provides guidance on introducing or maintaining social protection floors and on implementing social protection floors as part of strategies to extend higher levels of social security to as many people as possible, in accordance with the guidance set out in ILO social security standards. There should be provisioning for a basic minimum social protection floor, in terms of ILO Convention No. 202, for poor and disadvantaged workers, while striving for enhanced contributory benefits to higher-income individuals.

The United Nations Sustainable Development Goal (SDG 1.3) recommends the implementation of nationally appropriate social protection systems and measures for all, including floors, and by 2030 achieve substantial coverage of the poor and the vulnerable. The adoption of the 2030 Agenda for Sustainable Development by all UN Member States has reaffirmed the global commitment, which prioritizes social protection as a means to achieve several SDGs. Most prominently, SDG 1.3 calls upon countries to implement nationally appropriate social protection systems for all, for reducing and preventing poverty.

In accordance with the above international guidelines, the social security milieu of the nation in the coming decades should be looking to broadly cover economically weaker sections under social protection programs, while looking at contributory coverage with higher benefits for the better-off formal sector workers. We should also be looking to align our goals with the decent work minimum standards of ILO as applicable to India, and look to provide safe and dignified working conditions to all workers. The following figure, sourced from the ILO website, is an indicative framework of the way forward for social security in India.

Social Security is required to be designed keeping a close eye on developments well into the future, beyond our own likely life expectancies. It is required to be re-imagined to become better, more inclusive, and broader based. Following avenues are aspirational for the nation to take the lead in the social security arena:

- Universalization of Social Security: outreach to the last person, full range of benefits
- Ease of access, Remote assistance and App-based support
- Re-thinking of disability and efforts to make society more sensitized and inclusive.
- Gender sensitivity, parity, and improved the treatment of women, children, and elderly populations.

Providing social security to unorganized sector workers will be challenge as well as the key to India becoming a global leader as well as a manufacturing hub.

Notes

1 EPFO Website https://www.epfindia.gov.in
2 EPFO 67th Annual Report 2019–20
3 In the employees Provident Funds, Section 7A is the provision under which PF commissioners (who are vested with the powers of a civil court), can initiate an inquiry, by order, to determine (i) the applicability of the EPF Act to an establishment in case of a dispute; and (ii) to determine amounts due from any employer under the EPF Act and its schemes.

Bibliography

AJMC. (2006). "Vulnerable Populations: Who Are They?" *American Journal of Managed Care*, Volume 12, Issue 13 Suppl, pages 48–52. https://pubmed.ncbi.nlm.nih.gov /17112321

Baker, D., and M. Weisbrot (2001). *Social Security: The Phony Crisis*. University of Chicago Press.

Bertrand, M., K. Krishnan, and H. Schofield (2020). "How Are Indian Households Coping Under the Covid 19 Lockdown? 8 Key Findings". https://www.chicagobooth.edu/research /rustandy/blog/2020/how-are-indianhouseholds-coping-under-the-covid19-lockdown

Blustein David, L., O. Chad, A. Connors-Kellgren, and A. J. Diamonti (2016). "Decent Work: A Psychological Perspective". *Frontiers in Psychology*, Volume 7. https://www .frontiersin.org/article/10.3389/fpsyg.2016.00407,   DOI=10.3389/fpsyg.2016.00407, ISSN=1664-1078

Brynjolfsson, E., and A. McAfee (2014). *The Second Machine Age: Work, Progress, and Prosperity in a Time of Brilliant Technologies*. W. W. Norton & Company.

Centre for Sustainable Employment, Azim Premji University. (2020). "Azim Premji University COVID-19 Livelihoods Survey". https://cse.azimpremjiuniversity.edu.in/ covid19-analysis-of-impact-and-relief-measures

Employees' Provident Fund Organisation (EPFO), Annual report 2019–20. https://search
.epfindia.gov.in/Annual_Reports/AR_2019-20.pdf

Employees' Provident Fund Organisation (EPFO), Ministry of Labour and Employment,
Government of India, Website https://www.epfindia.gov.in/site_en/index.php

Employees' Provident Fund Organisation (EPFO), Ministry of Labour and Employment,
Government of India, Booklet, "Response to Covid-19". Published 2020.

Employees' Provident Fund Organisation (EPFO), Ministry of Labour and Employment,
Government of India, Booklet, "Response to COVID-2.0". Published November 2021.

Employees' Provident Fund Organisation (EPFO), Ministry of Labour and Employment,
Government of India, Booklet, "Nirbadh: Seamless Service Delivery, EPFO to e-EPFO".
November 2021.

ILO. (2020). *ILO Monitor: COVID-19 and the World of Work.* Second edition. International
Labour Organisation. https://www.ilo.org/wcmsp5/groups/public/---dgreports/---
dcomm/documents/briefingnote/wcms_740877.pdf

Kesar, S., R. Abraham, R. Lahoti, P. Nath, and A. Basole (2021). "Pandemic, Informality,
and Vulnerability: Impact of COVID-19 on Livelihoods in India." *Revue Canadienne
D'études Du Développement*, Volume 42, Issue 1–2, pages 145–164. https://doi.org/10
.1080/02255189.2021.1890003

Mehrotra, S. (2021). "An Alternative Fiscal Package to Mitigate India's COVID Economic
Crisis." *Indian Economic Journal*, Volume 69, Issue 3, pages 553–567. https://doi.org
/10.1177/00194662211021366

Mehrotra, S., and J. K. Parida (2021). "Stalled Structural Change Brings an Employment
Crisis in India." *Indian Journal of Labour Economics*, Volume 64, Issue 2, pages 281–
308. https://doi.org/10.1007/s41027-021-00317-x

Ravallion, M. (2014). "Income Inequality in the Developing World." *Science*, Volume 344,
Issue 6186, pages 851–855. https://doi.org/10.1126/science.1251875

Sarkar, S. (2004). "Extending Social Security Coverage to the Informal Sector in
India." *Social Change*, Volume 34, Issue 4, pages 122–130. https://doi.org/10.1177
/004908570403400410

Stiglitz, J. (2020). *Point of View: Conquering the Great Divide.* COVID-19 and Global
Inequality- International Monetary Fund F&D Finance & Development Magazine 17–
19, 0057(003). https://doi.org/10.5089/9781513544595.022.a005

Weber, E. (2018). "Setting out for Digital Social Security". Research Department Working
Paper No. 34, International Labour Office Institute for Employment Research. 1–8.

World Social Protection Report 2017–19. (2020). "Universal Social Protection to Achieve
the Sustainable Development Goals". International Labour Organization.

14 The Concept of *Seva* in Sikhism and Its Relevance in the COVID-19 Pandemic

Ravinder Kaur Cheema

Concept of *Seva* in Sikhism

The word *Seva* or "selfless service" or "volunteerism" is performed by a Sikh individual without any expectations of reward or benefits in return. The person who performs this kind of *Seva* is called "*Sevadar*". In Sikhism, *Seva* is treated as a noble activity as it morally, ethically, and spiritually uplifts the concerned "*Sevadar*". As is well known, the Sikh prayer ends with "*Sarbat da Bhala*" which means "well-being of all"; the Sikh community reaches out to serve the entire humanity without any discrimination. Sikhism professes universal love and promotes compassion.

A glance over the traditional society of India reveals that the concept of *Seva* was well known to the people. A sociological perspective of *Seva* points out clearly that *Seva* is worship of Gods to be performed only by the upper caste Brahmins and the lower services are to be performed by the lowest in the caste structure.[1] In Sikhism, however, caste distinctions have no place and God is not apart from the creation. "He pervades in His creation", and in fact, the aim of worshiping God is accomplished by performing *Seva*.[2]

In his chapter, Dipankar Gupta states that all religions may be professing love and encourage altruism and compassion but Sikhism does something more than that; perhaps no other religious denomination does. He elaborates that it is in Sikhism alone that service to others is an important aspect of devotional practice for the laity. Not denying the fact that other religions do have saints, healers, and preceptors too, yet in Sikhism alone it is the laity and not the virtuosos. It is the everyday worshiper and not the ordained priests who are the heroes. In Sikhism, it is not the great, the gifted, or the sage who serve ordinary people but it is ordinary people who serve the ordinary people.[3]

A typical psychological viewpoint tries to measure the benefits of *Seva* and conclude that "if the motive of the person is to receive or get those benefits by volunteering, they may not see those benefits".[4] A generally accepted notion is that selfless service can be done only if a person is selfless. In his article Prof. Johnson tries to find out whether selflessness is an inherent characteristic of human personality or could be through certain prescribed methods. To prove it, he does quote Prof. John L. Holland, a well-known psychologist and his six personality types, viz. Social, Realistic, Investigative, Artistic, Enterprising, and Conventional.[5] Prof.

DOI: 10.4324/9781003304517-18

Holland gave equal importance to all six personality types. He states that each personality with a different set of values is attracted towards specialized professional roles considered essential for a sustainable society.[6]

Dr. Johnson's research analysis on the topic points out that the advocates of *Seva* do not necessarily force themselves into selfless service. *Seva*, not done in a selfless manner, may not result in positive outcomes. To him, all types of *Seva* offered should be aiming at bringing a change in the society without any expectation.[7]

Argument

While understanding the concept of *Seva* from different perspectives, it can be argued that the practice of *Seva* in Sikhism is entirely different from all other practices of services. The incidences since the Guru period reflect the selfless *Seva* (nishkam seva) and are essence of the values inculcated amongst the people of the times. Since then, the Sikhs performed *Seva* on occasions when needed in the society. This argument has been justified by tracing various events in history when Sikhs have taken up performing *Seva*. *Seva* is a part and parcel of the Sikh's life and it is to be practiced with modesty and humbleness. The approach towards performing *Seva* by Sikhs is different as it is not only to be performed during the times of need but also in our day-to-day life; it is by the rich as well as the poor and for the rich, poor, and the needy in the society without any discrimination. Another notable feature of *Seva* is that it can be performed by the young for the old or vice versa, for the friend or a foe, and above all, it should not be announced or cited. The daily Sikh prayer ends with "Sarbat da Bhala" which means "seeking the well-being of all"; the Sikh community reach out to serve the entire humanity without any discrimination promoting universal love and compassion. Guru Nanak preached "one should cultivate true humility and be of service to others".[8] The evolution of this concept in Sikhism can be traced through the Sikh scriptures and is inspiring.

Historical Perspective of *Seva* in Sikhism

In Sikhism, the institution of *Seva* is associated with the arrival of Guru Nanak. Many scholars and historians point to the capital investment of Rs. 20 by Nanak. The anecdote explains how Nanak's father gave him Rs. 20 to start a business. On his way to the nearby town to buy the merchandise, he saw a group of men, dressed shabbily and perhaps starved for many days. Looking at their plight, Nanak purchased clothes and eatables to feed the hungry flock. He might have been rebuked immensely by his father but it laid down the foundation of *Seva* in the Sikh community. It reflects that the Guru initiated the concept of *Sacha Sauda* which is the true and fair deal of Rs. 20 more than 500 years ago.[9]

The primary teaching of *Sacha Sauda* was a revolution in itself that emphasized the importance of help provided where needed the most, without any prejudice or discrimination. This practice started by Nanak was popularized by all His successors during their period and has been further witnessed in Sikh history and the sub-continent, heavily polarized by caste and religion.

Guru Angad Devji, the second Guru, and his wife Mata Khivi, in particular, was known for preparing the *langar* (community kitchen) for the congregation. Mata Khivi herself served the *langar* and hence she is the only one whose name is mentioned in the Sikh Holy Scripture *Sri Guru Granth Sahib* for her dedicated service. In the words of Balwand – the ballad:

> Balvand khīvī nek jan jis bahuṭī chhāo paṭrālī
> Langar daᵒulaṭ vandīai ras amriṭ khīr ghiālī.

Balwand says that Mata Khivi is a noble woman who gives a soothing, leafy shade to all. She distributes the bounty of the Guru's *langar*; the kheer (rice pudding) and ghee is like sweet ambrosia.

The *langar* was served without any consideration of caste, race, religion, etc. The idea of *Seva* in Sikh tradition does not place any importance to the rich and the influential; rather, it is an ordinary people serving the ordinary.

> Neecha Andar Neech Jaat, Neechi Hu Att Neech,
> *Nanak Tin Ke Sang Saath, Vadiya Sio Kya Rees.*[10]

It means that the Guru was more compassionate towards the underprivileged and socially deprived section of the society.

Even when Emperor Akbar visited Guru Amar Das, the third Guru at Goindwal *Sahib*, about 40 kms from Amritsar in the 1560s, he was told to partake in the *langar* first and then meet him. King Akbar sat crossed-legged in a *pangat* (people seated in a row) with others, partook of the *langar*, and then met the Guru for conversation. In fact, Guru Amardas popularized this institution and made it a rule that people wishing to see him should first partake in the *langar*.

The Guru says,

> Jāṭ kā garab na karīahu koī.
> Barahm binde so barāhmaṇ hoī. ||*1*||[11]

The Guru emphasized that no man should take pride in his birth or caste as the true Brahmin is the one who knows God.

The later Gurus; Guru Ramdas, the fourth Guru, and Guru Arjan Devji, the fifth Guru, are known for various community work. The fifth guru, Arjan, built a leprosy home and a tank at Tarn Taran. Harmandir Sahib (generally referred to as the Golden Temple) was built by the fourth Guru in the midst of the huge *sarovar* (tank). Many new towns were built, which today are known for their historical and religious importance. The seventh Guru, Har Rai, created a herbal garden in Kiratpur that had medicinal herbs and it is said that the Mughal crown prince Dara Shikoh got cured by these herbal medicines under the Guru's observation.

Gurdwara Bangla Sahib, in New Delhi, is associated with the visit of Guru Harkrishan, the eighth Guru. In 1664 during his stay there, a large number of people suffered due to rapidly spreading smallpox. The Guru along with his followers attended to the sick to redress their suffering. It must be noted that the Guru himself died due to this deadly disease.[12]

In the battles fought by Guru Gobind Singh, the tenth Guru, one of his followers named Bhai Kanhaiya would enter into the battlefield with his mashk (a goatskin water carrier) and served water to the wounded soldiers irrespective of which group they belonged to (own or enemies).

When other Sikhs complained about him feeding and serving the enemy, he replied to the Guru that, "I see you everywhere, I see people suffering. I saw no Mughals or Sikhs in the battlefield, I only saw the Guru's face in every soldier. The Guru was pleased with his reply and also encouraged him to apply medicines on the wounds of all fallen soldiers.[13] The Sikhs do believe that Bhai Kanhaiya should be regarded as the forerunner of the foundation of the Red Cross.[14] Bhagat Puran Singh, who founded the Pingalwara, continued serving the destitute and opened a leprosy home in Amritsar and is truly regarded as the core of a great humanitarian movement. He worked towards providing the medical treatment to the poor and the helpless patients particularly to those who were unable to get admitted in the hospital.

Epidemics have always been part of human life since time immemorial, the world over and especially in India. Those were the times when medical facilities were few and not easily available. At the closure of the year 2020 the world fell victim to the coronavirus that has left unaccounted numbers homeless, jobless, and fighting to save their lives from this dreadful COVID-19. A large number of people were in dire need of getting health facilities, food, and shelter.

India too has been at the receiving end, standing second as far as suffering and deaths are concerned. There was an enormous demand for hospitals and healthcare centers with facilities for COVID-19 patients as the number of COVID-19 positives was increasing rapidly. However, as the government announced a lockdown in many regions with the closure of educational institutions, transportation, and workplaces, etc., people faced difficulties in their daily survival. People, along with their families, started moving from the cities to their hometowns for a safer life. The government responded, though late, to deal with the situation which was becoming unmanageable. There were huge crowds at the bus depots and railway stations and a lot of miscommunication through social media leading to a lot of commotion. In this situation, people started walking, and they walked long distances, some carrying their children and elderly parents. What added to their misery was hunger and death. Such a scenario was indescribably terrible.

The need of the hour was the support from society to help these people with food, transport, and health facilities. The multifold increase in COVID-19 cases put an onus on the State and Central Governments to increase health-related infrastructure. At such times, humans also rely on the teachings of religion to find relief and solace.

The Sikh community has always led from the front during difficult times or crises that arose in our society or perhaps anywhere in the world. Sikhs have served the people during natural disaster, through health services, education services, providing food, shelter and so on. The teachings of Sikh Gurus have been a guiding force that embodies the spirit of the Sikh community. The Sikh faith that spread in the medieval period in Punjab has innumerable instances of the Sikh Gurus serving the sick and the needy.

In the 2019 pandemic crisis, the Sikh community rose to the occasion and opened up the *gurdwaras* for COVID-19 centers and *langar* (community kitchen services). Many individual Sikhs and many Sikh organizations took up the responsibility to serve the affected, initially the migrants, and later those who needed medical help. Food and other essentials were distributed on the highways and railway stations. A large number of *gurdwaras* and Sikh organizations have been kind enough to do this *Seva*. Selfless *Seva* in Sikhism is regarded as service to God.

In the modern times too, the Sikhs have made landmark contributions towards serving the society in the form of establishing institutions of social service which are discussed further in the chapter. One important institution that stands today as a number one institution, was an initiative by Rajkumari Amrit Kaur towards establishing an institution of postgraduate medical education in India. It was during the period of the Nehru Government that the All India Institute of Medical Sciences (AIIMS) was established and the actual driving force behind it was Rajkumari Amrit Kaur. She was India's first Health Minister in Prime Minister Nehru's First Cabinet. Funds were the issue to build AIIMS, so she was instrumental in acquiring a huge amount from the New Zealand Government. Over the years, she rallied around and was successful in getting donations from international bodies like the Rockefeller Foundation, and the Ford Foundation, as well as from the governments of Australia and West Germany, as well as from the Dutch Government.

Besides laying the foundation of AIIMS, she also founded the Indian Council of Child Welfare and became its first president. She was President of the Indian Leprosy Association, the Tuberculosis Association, and Vice-President of the International Red Cross Society. She led the Indian delegation to the World Health Organization (WHO) for four years and was President of the WHO assembly in 1950. Her largest campaign as Health Minister though, was against Malaria. "At the height of the campaign, in 1955, it was estimated that 400,000 Indians who otherwise would have died, had been saved by mitigation of malaria in their districts", says the New York Times obituary.[15]

Seva as Depicted in Sri Guru Granth *Sahib*

The word "*Seva*" and its importance has been quoted 1,510 times in *Sri Guru Granth Sahebji*.[16] These verses related to *Seva* explain the meaning, benefits, and the ways to perform *Seva*. A few verses are quoted below to understand the concept:

> Sevā karat hoe nihkāmī,
> Tis kao hot parāpat suāmī.[17]

This means that if we perform service selflessly without the thought of a reward, we shall realize the Lord.

Seva of this kind will certainly lead to liberation. However, selfless *Seva* is critical in making this action meaningful.

> Sukh hovai sev kamāṇīā.[18]

This means that you shall find peace doing *Seva*.

When a person performs *Seva*, the mind should not wander about; they should recite *Gurbani*. In this process of performing *Seva,* the person should not carry any ego or pride.

There is a very significant verse which says:

> vich dunīā sev kamāīai
> Tā dargeh baisan pāīai.[19]

It means that the person performing *Seva* in the midst of this world, will get a place of honor in the court of the Lord.

> Har kī tum sevā karahu dūjī sevā karahu na koe jī.
> Har kī sevā te manhu chindiā fal pāīai dūjī sevā janam birthā jāe jī. ||1||[20]

The Sikhs are supposed to have firm faith in God while serving humanity; they serve God through them.

To attain spiritual life, *Seva* is essential in Sikhism, and the Sikhs always pray and crave for a chance to serve the people. Guru Arjan Devji, the fifth Guru, says, "I beg to serve those who serve You".[21] And Guru Amardas expressed that individuals will find solace while performing *Seva.*[22] In another verse, Guru Arjan Devji explains, "Human beings who do not do good deeds to others are worthless". Bhai Gurdas, a spiritual thinker and writer who wrote *Sri Guru Granth Sahib* as revealed to him by the fifth Guru, endorses this by saying that "without service to others, hands and feet of any individual are disdainful and all other activities are worthless".[23]

Seva with a selfish motive is of no use, and people who practice this suffer great pain and lose this human life in vain. While self-auditing the life of an individual without *Seva*, the Guru prays to the Lord as:

"Neither have I practiced meditation, self-discipline, self-restraint not righteous living. Neither I have served the holy people; nor recognized the Supreme Lord. Says Nanak, my actions are contemptible. O Lord, I seek thy protection, protect, preserve, sustain me". [24]

The Guru emphasizes on selfless *Seva*:

> Sevat sevat sadā sev terai sang basat hai kāl
> Kar sevā tūṅ sādh kī ho kātīai jam jāl. ||1|| [25]

This means that we serve and serve the Lord forever; death hangs over your head. So we should do *Seva*, selfless service, for the Holy saints, and the noose of death shall be cut off.

Seva of mankind is all greatly emphasized in *Gurbani*. The Guru explains that if anyone has mercy on any soul, this is better than the pilgrimage of 68 religious places and all donations made by him. The Guru further says:

"O Lord, make me the slave of Lord's slaves; the best service is the service of human beings". [26]

By doing selfless service a person is transformed into a *"Sevak"* and the *Sevak* has a lot of importance in *Gurbani*.

> *Sevak kao sevā ban āī*
> *Hukam būjh param paḍ pāī.*[27]

Thus explaining that the servant's purpose is to serve and by obeying the Lord's command, the supreme status is obtained.

In the words of Kabir;

> Kehkabeer ab jaaniaasa(n)tan ridhaimajhaar ||
> sevak so sevaabhalejeh ghat basaimuraar ||4||1||12||63||[28]

It means that Kabir has understood that the Lord dwells within the hearts of His saints and that the servant who performs the best service is the servant whose heart is filled with the Lord.

Thus, the term *"Seva"* is well defined in not only the *Gurbani* contained in *Sri Guru Granth Sahib* but also finds ample space in every kind of Sikh religious literature. Therefore, *Seva* can be regarded as a distinct and unique feature of Sikhism. *Seva* is not an act to glorify oneself. In a real sense, performing *Seva* helps to achieve one's well-being, particularly for the people who are otherwise quite depressed and disturbed.[29] It can thus be concluded that the motto of *Seva* is service to humanity. The Gurus instructed their followers to serve the underprivileged and downtrodden. "The poor man's mouth is the depository of the Guru". You serve God through them. "The grain, O God, is your own gift. Only the *Seva* is mine which please be gracious enough to accept".[30]

In the Sikh way of life, the *Seva* is considered the prime duty of the householder. Bhagat Kabir is quoted in the hymns of *Sri Guru Granth Sahib* as follows:

> *Kabīr jā ghar sādh na sevī°ah har kī sevā nāhi*
> *Ŧe ghar marhat sārkhe bhūṭ baseh ṭin māhi. ||192||*[31]

It means that those houses in which neither the Holy nor the Lord are served— those houses are like cremation grounds; demons dwell within them.

Thus, *Seva* in Sikhism must be:

- without *nishkam* (desire)
- *nishkapat* (guileless)
- with *nimrata* (in humility)
- with *hirda shudh* (with purity of intention)
- *chitlai* (with sincerity)
- by *vichon aap gavae* (in utter selflessness)[32]

Such a kind of *Seva* for the Sikh will lead to a life of dignity and *mukti* (liberation). Humanitarian service is thus the Sikh ideal of *Seva*.

Types of *Seva*

An individual can perform *Seva* in three ways, namely "*Taan*", "*Maan*" and "*Dhan*". *Taan se Seva* is the *Seva* done through physical means and is considered to be the highest of all which every able-bodied Sikh is expected to do. Bhai Gurdas, a spiritual thinker and writer, wrote *Sri Guru Granth Sahib* as revealed to him by the fifth Guru. Guru Arjan Devji writes that "curses are the hands and feet that do not engage in *Seva*".[33] Unfortunately, in traditional Hindu society, the work involving physical labor was given to the lowest of the low castes. But it was in Sikhism that manual labor was sanctified and dignity of labor was established. It is rather institutionalized.

Physical *Seva* involves doing manual work such as cleaning the *gurdwaras*, washing the utensils, caring and up-keeping the shoes of the *sangat* (congregation), cooking food in the community kitchen (*langar*), and many more such jobs. The Sikhs take part in "*Kar Seva*" which is serving the house of God, such as constructions or renovations of *gurdwaras*, hospitals, ponds, and *dharmashalas*, etc. Another important *Seva* is serving fresh, clean drinking water to the people and to the animals too. Such a water–dispensing stand is called a *chhabeel*.

Voluntary service is offered at hospitals or institutions serving the aged, orphans, differently abled, and the sick. The Sikhs are the first ones to reach such places which are affected by natural calamities like flood, famines, earthquakes, or any deadly outbreaks such as coronavirus etc.

The second type of Seva is through "Maan" (Mind)

This involves the use of one's talents such as creativity, communication, managerial, and others for the welfare of mankind. *Taan se Seva* is the first type of seva done through physics means this kind of *Seva* aims at finding different ways to serve humanity with love and compassion and in a way serve God through men.[34] The persons in this category of *Seva* provide free academic or religious education. Surgeons, specialists, physicians, engineers, architects, musicians, and many other professionals help individuals or institutions. Voluntary research undertaken in any field that can help save any living being or the environment can also be regarded as *Maan se Seva*, for example, awareness activities about protecting the environment. Sri Guru Har Rai Guru, the seventh Guru, was a great environmentalist.

The third category of *Seva* is through "*Dhan*" (wealth). It is a service through material means or philanthropy (*daan*) and donations, etc. The Sikhs are expected to donate one-tenth of their income, called *dasvandh*, to charity. This kind of *Seva* also involves helping others in times of financial difficulties, giving, through charity work or money, to the poor. The offerings made to the Gurus and *dasvandh* are used mainly for maintaining the *gurdwaras*, towards *langar*, and other social welfare projects.

It is however to be noted that when Sikhs step out to help others they do not do it as charity, but as service first. Charity is not uppermost in their minds as it may be in other religions. Service is more immediate. As Dipankar Gupta states that, the donations that Sikhs make before the Book is not marked by grandstanding of the kind that other events are. The money slipped unannounced and with no fanfare into the collection box. Who has given how much is not known… and that is what makes this act a commendable egalitarian one. [35] (Book here the means the Holy Granth, *Sri Guru Granth Sahib*.)

Significance of *Seva*

What Does One Learn and Gain from Seva?

Performing selfless service has its own significance. It plays an important role and has many benefits. Here the benefits are not in the form of a reward; rather, it has to be understood that the one who does the *Seva* actually achieves satisfaction in giving relief to the grieved, attains happiness, learns to give up ego, learns to feel the pain of others, understands the importance of life, reduces stress, learns to manage emotional disturbance… and above all, one learns sharing and spreading happiness ….

As Sri Sri Ravi Shankar rightly points out, the joy of serving others gives much more satisfaction than the joy of getting something.[36]

Apart from the above, selfless service improves one's morale, self-confidence, self-esteem, health, sensitivity, and discipline. Such an individual obtains peace and pleasure, and the true *Sevadars* are assured of an honorable place in the Court of God. Selfless service endows upon them spiritual benefits and eliminates the fear of death.

Seva helps the Sikhs to become *Gurmukh* (attached to God) as it helps them to inculcate five virtues, namely truth and truthful living, compassion and patience, contentment, humility and self-control, love, and wisdom and courage.[37]

Understanding *Seva* from another perspective is equally important to mention. This *Seva* has relevance to the mistakes or wrongs committed by a Sikh. Mistakes which are generally treated as contrary to the established socio-religious norms can be redeemed by appearing before the *Akal Takhat* (The Supreme Religious Seat of the Sikhs). The mistakes or wrongs done such as blasphemy, remarks against the Gurus, and intentional wrong interpretation of *Gurbani*, or breaking the religious norms while practicing certain social activities come under this purview. Persons committing such mistakes appear before the constituted body to ask for forgiveness. The body takes the decision as per the established principles and pronounces the punishment—which is generally a *Seva*. This *Seva* includes cleaning, polishing shoes, or cooking in the community kitchen. The wrongdoers accept this with folded hands and bowing heads.

Sikh's *Seva* at Its Peak during COVID-19 Pandemic

All institutions or individuals need to be given due credit for the type of their services, however it is not possible to list all. A few examples discussed below are an eye-opener as to what extent the Sikh community does selfless service not only during crises but even in normal times.

Gurdwaras have been the epitome of service and brotherhood. In Delhi, many *gurdwaras* served food to a large number of people who suffered on account of lockdown due to the COVID-19 pandemic. The famous *Bangla Sahib Gurdwara* in Delhi had been preparing *langar* for more than 40,000 people on a daily basis as per the request of the Delhi Government. Around 60 *Sevadars* worked from 5 o'clock in the morning to prepare and serve the food.

In March, *Majnu Ka Tila*, a historic *gurdwara* in Delhi, was converted into a quarantine center. Around 200 migrants from Punjab, Rajasthan, and Maharashtra were given shelter as the Delhi Government had sealed all borders. Even *Motibagh Gurdwara* and *Rakab Ganj Sahib Gurdwara* came forward to provide shelter to the healthcare workers. The *gurdwaras* assured that the chain of food supply did not halt as they made arrangements for more. *Gurdwara Gobind Dham* at Ahmedabad also helped the needy and the poor. The President of the Dham mentioned that anyone who came there with an empty stomach will be fed.[38]

It is notable that the Sikh community serves the people without any fear of their own health and this reflects in their service to humanity in the time of crisis. The Sikhs did not think for a moment that they were serving the people of other communities or religion. COVID-19 had destroyed the lines of division between the communities or religious groups. It can be exemplified as follows: when nearly 40 students who belonged to Uttar Pradesh and Bihar were held up in a *Madrasa* in Punjab, people at *Gurdwara Haa Da Naara Sahib* in Malerkotla (Punjab) acted promptly and provided food to the hungry students. Not only food, they also arranged the utensils as the Madrasa didn't have them. To this act of the *gurdwara* committee, the *Maulvi* at the *Madrasa* expressed his gratitude for their service. Apart from this, the *gurdwara* in this region served *langar* to around 1000 needy and poor people every day. They were helped by the local women or *sewadars* to prepare *langar* for the residents on a daily basis. Another *gurudwara* in the same region took the responsibility of providing meals to migrant labourers who were stuck in the nearby areas due to the COVID-19 lockdown.[39]

As NDTV commented, the Sikh community had not only fed the poor but also arranged the oxygen *langars* and assured every kind of free medical help, including ambulance services, during the COVID-19 crisis. Along with the Delhi Sikh Gurdwara Management Committee (DSGMC), NDTV launched a special fundraising campaign named "*Dil Se Sewa* – Helping India Breathe" that came as a ray of hope in times of distress. As India was entering into the second wave of the COVID-19 pandemic, the campaign aimed at providing the urgently needed support to the COVID-19 patients.

The funds raised were used for all essential services required to help the patients suffering with COVID-19. Funds were also used to improvise the infrastructure such as a newly created COVID-19 care facility, free ambulance service, free dialysis, the low-cost MRI and CT Scan center, and the "dawakhanas" that provide medicines at reasonable rates, among others.

Vikramjit Sahney, Chairman of Sun Foundation and International President of the World Punjabi Organization, came up with the first-ever mobile coronavirus testing clinics and ambulances. These services reached the containment zones in Delhi and villages of Punjab. They also supported the *langar Seva* together with DSGMC. Oxygen shortage was managed by arranging 500 oxygen concentrators, along with Sun Foundation and the support received from Steve Gupta, Chairman of the Gupta Family Foundation (Toronto).

H.S. Kandhari, CEO, Ponty Chadha Foundation with its staff helped the *gurdwara* teams with supply of food and essential medical help for the patients. An important area in which the foundation assisted was helping the people at cremation grounds in Bulandshaher. They also organized three campaigns in Punjab for vaccination.[40]

Worldwide, the Sikh community has never restricted itself from helping or rescuing people in distress and has never been seen discriminating on the grounds of caste, creed, religion, or region as far as service to the society is concerned. The compassion of the community is noteworthy.

The Delhi Sikh Gurdwara Management Committee (DSGMC) has been in the forefront performing *Seva* during the pandemic in Delhi. The *Gurdwara Rakabganj Sahib* in central Delhi set up Sri Guru Tegh Bahadur Covid Care Centre in 10 days with the capacity of catering to around 70 patients. It radiates order, control, empathy, and calm. The facility included an oxygen concentrator attached to each bed and meals planned by a dietician. Extending its support to this Covid center, the Delhi Government assured to provide an intensice care unit (ICU) bed in emergency at Lok Nayak Jay Prakash (LNJP) hospital. Around 50 doctors and 24 nurses were assigned to this Covid care center, by the government, including 10 volunteers assisted the patients coming back from all across the National Capital Region (NCR). At this center, care was also taken of those patients who did not have anyone back home to take care of them after discharge.

The volunteers of DSGMC turned six *gurdwaras* into places of healing and recovery, arranging oxygen, food, and free treatment for anyone who needed help. Manjinder Singh Sirsa, President, DSGMC, stated that as the virus spread rapidly, they received 5,000 calls each day from people in complete distress asking for beds and oxygen, thus immediately the oxygen *langar Seva* was started. Oxygen was brought in from the neighboring states of Haryana and Himachal Pradesh, even cities such as Raipur and Meerut. During the day, the volunteers prepared the *langar* and at night drove hundreds of kilometers to deliver the oxygen cylinders.

To the question about managing such a mammoth task, the President, Mr. Sirsa, replied that "Sikhism is not (just a) religion but a way of living. There is a passion for service that comes with faith". He appreciated the team of 300 volunteers and 1800 DSGMC employees who worked day and night to help the affected people. Over 100000 food packets were distributed daily during the pandemic. Donations poured in from all over the world to the extent that an oxygen plant was shipped to be set up at *Gurdwara Bala Sahib* in Sarai Kale Khan. The committee seems to be preparing for the third wave as well, aiming at having a 100-bed hospital with an ICU facility, including ventilators and BiPAP machines (BiPaP is a machine that helps puts pressure to push air into your lungs). This exemplifies extremely commendable *Seva* performed by the DSGMC.[41]

In Mumbai, the commercial capital of India, the Sikh community members organized *langars* (free kitchens). Sri Guru Singh Sabha Gurudwara at Dadar has always been a serving center for cancer patients. During the COVID-19 pandemic, they distributed free mini oxygen cans and cylinders to the patients. A *gurdwara* at Kharghar, near Navi Mumbai, distributed free mini oxygen cans to the people at their homes. They also procured oxygen cylinders in an emergency for those who were not able to get them. The services were available 24/7. Hemkunt Foundation also helped the local *gurdwaras* of Mumbai in procuring oxygen cylinders. Besides this, ration packets were also distributed to the people. Even today, many *gurdwaras* continue serving *langars* and rations to the needy. *Gurdwaras* all over Maharashtra fed around 2 million people in just 10 weeks during the COVID-19 crisis.[42]

Selfless Service by Kalgidhar Society at Barusahib (Himachal Pradesh)

Noteworthy *Seva* has been performed by the Kalgidhar Society at Baru Saheb not only during COVID-19 times but always. It is a center which imparts free education to the children of backward hilly rural areas. The Society offers employment on a preferential basis to the masses of this backward area to enable them to achieve their daily basic needs.

Statistics reflect on the number of people helped with services such as charitable hospitals, rehabilitation centers, medical camps, home for widows and the destitute, senior citizen services, orphanages, and disaster relief which changed their lives. Following is the data for the same seventy-thousand students, 4,172 teachers/ professors, 288,000 patients, 6,450 orphans and other poor children, 378 senior citizens, 1,200 widows and needy women, 5,119 addicts and their families, 9,822 earthquake victims affected in Kashmir. The aim of the Society is to build superior human character and high moral values leading towards establishing permanent world peace.

During the pandemic, the Society served around 350 houses every week. A door-to-door campaign in Lana Bhatla village (Baru Sahib) providing *langar*, free sanitizers, and facemasks was of great relief.[43]

Shaheed Bhagat Singh Sewa Dal (SBS Foundation)

For more than 25 years, the SBS Foundation has been providing medical services to the underprivileged. Free cremations or burials for the poor and the homeless, and all kinds of welfare services were offered during the COVID-19 crises and in regular times too. The yeoman service by the SBS Foundation was when they came forward to cremate the bodies of those who died due to coronavirus. Importantly, the services of the foundation commenced in September, which was the peak of the first pandemic wave in the country. In a day, the volunteers cremated about 10 bodies and during the devastating second wave, more than 120 cremations were done daily.

The situation was getting worse as the deaths were rising and parking lots were used to accommodate the bodies in Delhi. As per Reuters, the Muslim graveyards started running short of space and hence some Muslims cremated their loved ones.

A temporary cremating facility was arranged at Seemapuri crematorium to meet the needs of the rising COVID-19 deaths. During this service of cremation, many of the SBS volunteers tested positive for coronavirus, but they continued the service with the help of the public. Mr. Jeet, the Chairperson of the SBS Foundation, keeping up the spirit of *Seva,* mentioned that they were scared and aware of the risks they faced while doing this work. They were prepared to give their lives to this cause but not let down the nation. That was the spirit of the *Sevadars* during the Covid-19 crisis.

The entire work by the volunteers is unimaginable. They built funeral pyres, cremated the bodies, and further cleared the area to continue the process. They worked tirelessly without even water breaks, when the temperatures rose above 107 degrees Fahrenheit. Mr. Jeet mentions the ghastly feelings experienced by the volunteers each day while performing the cremations. They tried to give each body the dignity it deserved. It was an extremely hard time for the SBS volunteers but while performing this *Seva* they felt that they were able to be with the person in his last journey and felt very connected to their souls, giving them peace.[44]

Continuity of Services rendered by Sikh Individuals and NGOs

Besides the *Seva* during the pandemic crisis, the Sikhs have been rising to almost every crises in India and the world, be it any fellow being in any situation. To mention a few:

Gurdwaras were opened for shelter, food, and safety to riot victims in Delhi. Two Sikh brothers served tea and *langar* to Citizenship Amendment Act (CAA) protestors at India Gate, Delhi.

A helping hand was extended to the flood-affected in Assam by the *Gurdwara Singh Sahib Sabha* in 2015, making sure no one was left out. Similarly, in 2019, the Delhi Sikh *Gurdwara* Management Committee provides *langar* to flood-hit victims in Uttarakhand.

As we know the turban is a symbol of identity for the Sikhs. A unique example of *Seva* must be mentioned here. In Chandigarh, a drowning man was saved by two Sikhs using their turbans. Floods hit Mumbai city in 2006, and thousands were stranded on roads and railway stations. The Sikh volunteers fed the stranded people who had nowhere else to go. Many *gurdwaras* were opened for their shelter too.

At the international level too, the Sikh community has been extending their *Seva* to the needy on every occasion of crisis.

The UK-based organization, Khalsa Aid, founded in 1999, is one of the biggest Sikh organizations that caters to the poor and the needy worldwide, particularly in disaster-hit areas. Many times while performing this *Seva*, they have put their own safety in danger. Khalsa Aid came to the rescue of the people of Maharashtra, affected by drought in 2016. They purchased water at higher rates to provide it to drought-hit regions of Maharashtra.

In the conflict between Iraq and Syria, Langar Aid volunteers—which is an extension of Khalsa Aid—arranged *langar* for nearly 15,000 refugees at the Iraq-Syria border.

The *Seva* by United Nations-affiliated group named UNITED SIKHS is commendable. The Paris terror attack of 2015 left the city shocked and shattered. The organization came to the rescue of the people seeking shelter, food, and safety along with arranging free rides for Parisians and organizing blood donation drives for the needy.

The turban is the pride and respect of the Sikhs and should not be removed in public or touched by anybody. However, in a situation of saving anyone's life it's a selfless *Seva*. Here is one example of *Seva* performed by a young 22 year old Sikh, Harman Singh from Auckland, who rescued a child using his turban to control the child's bleeding head in an accident. Harman did exactly what was needed at that time without a thought of whose child it was.[45]

UNITED SIKHS provided humanitarian aid in the Chamrang Road fire at Amritsar, that destroyed around 80 makeshift shacks of 300 daily wagers who migrated from Bihar. They started a hotline to serve those in need during the COVID-19 pandemic.[46]

In Delhi, 381 people died after being infected by the COVID-19 virus. Mr. A.N. Yadav, 70-year-old, was one of those who died at his home in the city's Ranibagh area. Devender and Pritam, from the UNITED SIKHS helped this family to cremate the dead. Devender went on to make arrangements for the funeral and Pritam with great difficulty managed to bring the body down from the second floor of their building. They both have done this selfless *Seva* more than 300 times. There were many who could not afford funerals for their dear ones. Devendra and Pritam ensured a dignified funeral for such, irrespective of their religion.[47]

The Hemkunt Foundation, set up in 2010, provided thousands of oxygen cylinders free of cost to COVID-19 patients who were facing breathing difficulties. The foundation has worked across states in India and internationally, even providing humanitarian aid to the Philippines in the aftermath of the Taal Volcano eruption.[48]

A very heart-touching incident occurred with one woman migrant worker named Shakuntala, who was traveling on foot from Nashik in Maharashtra to Satna in Madhya Pradesh. She gave birth to a baby on the roadside on May 12. Her husband Rakesh Koul told TOI that the journey was extremely laborious but they witnessed extreme kindness on the way. "A Sikh family gave clothes and essentials for the newborn baby at Dhule", he said. He and the others lost their jobs as industries shut down in Nashik in the COVID-19 lockdown.

The Sikhs did reach new heights through the pandemic by taking a call on the need for the importance of medical colleges and hospitals in the future. Gurdwara Abchal Nagar Nanded Sahib announced that they had received enough donations in the last 50 years to take up this task to serve the society.[49]

Conclusion

The concept of *Seva* in Sikhism provides us an opportunity to understand and discipline our inner selves and shows us the path that can be adopted to perform selfless service. The spirit of *Seva* is the key element in the process of reorganizing ourselves and extending our services towards the upliftment of the downtrodden and the needy. It also teaches us to stand up and serve selflessly during any crisis that emerges, as serving mankind is worshiping God. Thus, we find a large number of Sikh volunteers dedicated to selfless service in any situation with humility. There are numerous examples of the Sikh community rising to the occasion from the Rohingya crisis in Myanmar to the Paris terror attacks. They have served in the farmers' marches in India to the protests in America against George Floyd's killing. Worldwide, the community has practiced this tradition to help people in their difficult moments.

The organizations along with NDTV in its fundraising campaign did attract a large number of people from varied fields who appreciated the initiative, appealed, motivated, and inspired people to come forward to contribute and also contributed themselves in whatever way they could.

The *Seva* of oxygen and beds was a lifesaver for the unwell and also raised the hope and confidence amongst the affected. This and any other kind of *Seva* should be a part of every individual's life and be an example to emulate by generations to come. *Seva* is an experiential learning in itself and helps in awakening the inner self of an individual to work towards bettering the society in times of crises and otherwise too. As rightly responded by Sri Sri Ravi Shankar to the Dil Se Sewa telethon, it is time to wake up the valor in us to help others in this challenging time.

The Sikh community is proud of all the *Sevadars*, seeing them practice what the Sikh Gurus preached. The "*Sarbat da bhala*" principle ingrained within the Sikh faith is quite visible through the *Seva* performed in difficult times. Selflessness of *Sevadars* is impressive as it ends the ego in an individual. They perform *Seva* for everyone with dignity and grace. In the COVID-19 pandemic, the Sikhs *Sevadars* acted with empathy, compassion, and responsiveness, making a difference in the lives of the COVID-19 affected people.

In apt words Dr. Prannoy Roy comments on what *Seva* means to us:

> Nothing is more inspiring, nothing is more genuine, nothing has more impact on the current suffering in society and nothing makes all of us more proud of our country than the Kar Sewa – all across India and across the world. All of you who are risking your own lives – working tirelessly among the people in areas which are COVID infected – you could be infected at any moment but you carry on and that's the essence of Chardi Kala. Fearless; living life in the present, caring for others and not thinking about dangers in the future. This "sewa" by the Sikh community is for everyone – equally.[50]

A Sikh is always willing to endure pain and suffering in order to provide comfort and facility to others. He does not want another person to suffer through him.

The Guru says:

> *Kām na bisrio kroḏẖ na bisrio lobẖ na cẖẖūtio ḏevā*
> *Par ninḏā mukẖ ṯe nahī cẖẖūṯī nifal bẖaī sabẖ sevā.* ||*1*||
>
> (SGGS, p. 1253)

This indicates that if you have not shunned lust, you have neither forgotten anger nor avarice. You have not abandoned slander of others, and if all these vices are your friends, then your service or *Seva* is fruitless.

The Chapter can be concluded with the learnings from *Seva* as stated in an article titled "Neither a Shield, Nor a Sword" by T. Sher Singh. It is vital that we should be wholeheartedly involved in performing *Seva* without any expectation or any kind of return benefits. Further, while performing *Seva* one must believe that it is not one's right to do so and at the same time if we try to snatch it from others, it can never be regarded as *Seva*. Appreciation or criticism should not ever drive us away from performing *Seva*. Finally, the *Seva* performed should not ever be mentioned to others or one must never take pride in it. *Seva* helps the human being to grow with humility.[51]

Notes

1 Skhiwiki.org/index.php/*Seva*
2 *Sri Guru Granth Sahibji* (henceforth SGGS), pp. 1350, 1013
3 Gupta Dipankar, "Sikhs are Different, Routinization of 'Sewa' in Times of India", June 11, 2021
4 Johnson John A, "Selfless Service, Part II, Different Types of Seva" (https://www.psychologytoday.com/us/blog/cui-bono/201306/selfless-service-part-ii-different-types-seva)
5 Ibid.
6 Ibid.
7 Ibid.
8 Grewal J.S. Guru Nanak in History (Chandigarh: Panjab University, 1969), 185.
9 https://www.indiatoday.in/news-analysis/story/history-of-sikh-sewa-and-the-principles-emotions-that-drive-it-1800302-2021-05-08 SGGS, p. 967
10 Ibid.
11 SGGS, pp. 15, 1127–28
12 https://www.indiatoday.in/news-analysis/story/history-of-sikh-sewa-and-the-principles-emotions-that-drive-it-1800302-2021-05-08
13 Bachan Gurbachan Singh, Essentials of Sikhism: Seva, in Journal of Sikh Studies, vol XXXIX, 2015, p. 53
14 https://www.indiatoday.in/news-analysis/story/history-of-sikh-sewa-and-the-principles-emotions-that-drive-it-1800302-2021-05-08
15 https://indianexpress.com/article/research/rajkumari-amrit-kaur-the-princess-who-built-aiims-6570937/
16 Bachan Gurbachan Singh, op. cit., p. 44
17 SGGS, p. 286
18 Ibid., p. 25
19 Ibid., p. 26
20 Ibid., p. 490
21 Ibid., p. 43

22 Ibid., p. 125
23 Bachan Gurbachan Singh, op.cit., p. 43
24 Ibid., p. 44
25 SGGS, p. 214
26 Ibid., p. 164
27 Ibid., p. 292
28 Ibid., p. 337
29 https://www.sikhmissionarysociety.org/sms/smssikhism/institutions/seva
30 Sikhiwiki.org, op.cit.
31 SGGS, p. 1374
32 Sikhiwiki.org, op.cit.
33 Bhai Gurdasji varan, p. 27, 1
34 Sikhiwiki.org, op.cit.
35 Gupta Dipankar, op. cit.
36 Johnson, op. cit.
37 https://www.bbc.co.uk/bitesize/guides/zjcbcj6/revision/5
38 https://curlytales.com/this-is-how-the-sikh-community-have-globally-been-offering
    -services-to-the-needy-amid-the-pandemic/
39 https://curlytales.com/punjab-gurudwara-provides-meals-to-madrasa-students-stuck-in
    -covid-19-lockdown/
40 https://www.ndtv.com/campaigns/live-updates-of-dilsesewa-telethon-an-initiative-to
    -provide-oxygen-support-to-covid-19-patients-2441830
41 https://www.indiatoday.in/magazine/cover-story/story/20210531-sikh-temple-opens
    -hospital-in-the-premises-to-treat-covid-patients-1805340-2021-05-22
42 https://www.facebook.com/ggndnewpanvel/   https://www.newslaundry.com/2021/05
    /05/couldnt-take-it-anymore-amid-oxygen-crisis-this-mumbai-gurudwara-is-a-lifeline
    https://economictimes.indiatimes.com/news/politics-and-nation/covid-19-pandemic
    -social-organisations-provide-food-to   needy/articleshow/74789225.cms?utm_source
    =contentofinterestutm_medium=textutm_campaign=cppst
43 https://barusahib.org/portfolio/covid19,   https://barusahib.org/our-programs/rural-eco-
    nomic-uplift/
44 https://www.nbcnews.com/news/world/mass-cremations-india-faces-tsunami-covid-19
    -deaths-n1265592
        https://www.nbcnews.com/news/world/mass-cremations-india-faces-tsunami-covid
    -19-deaths-n1265592
45 https://www.indiatimes.com/lifestyle/11-times-sikh-community-came-to-peoples-res-
    cue-regardless-of-their-religion-caste-or-country-507283.html
        https://www.indiatimes.com/lifestyle/11-times-sikh-community-came-to-peoples
    -rescue-regardless-of-their-religion-caste-or-country-507283.html;   https://www.bbc
    .com/news/world-asia-india-57817615
46 https://unitedsikhs.org/united-sikhs-provide-humanitarian-aid-in-chamrang-road-fire/
47 https://www.ndtv.com/india-news/coronavirus-delhi-as-covid-ravages-delhi-2-men
    -arrange-funerals-for-those-who-have-none-2423886
48 https://www.dw.com/en/india-covid-sikhs/a-57756219
49 https://www.moneylife.in/article/nanded-gurudwara-to-use-all-gold-collected-over-last
    -50-years-for-construction-of-hospitals-and-medical-colleges/63948.html
50 https://www.bbc.com/news/world-asia-india-57817615 https://www.ndtv.com/campaigns
    /live-updates-of-dilsesewa-telethon-an-initiative-to-provide-oxygen-support-to-covid-19
    -patients-2441830
51 https://www.allaboutsikhs.com/sikh-youth/guru-sakhis/must-read-article-for-us-all/
    http://tuhitu.blogspot.com/

References

Bachan, G. S. "Essentials of Sikhism: Seva". *Journal of Sikh Studies*, vol. XXXIX (2015), pp. 43–56.

Grewal, J. S. *Guru Nanak in History*. Chandigarh: Panjab University (1969).

Gupta, D. "Sikhs are Different, Routinization of 'Sewa'". *Times of India* (June 11, 2021).

Johnson John, A. "Selfless Service, Part II, Different Types of Seva". https://www
.psychologytoday.com/us/blog/cui-bono/201306/selfless-service-part-ii-different-types
-seva.

Sri Guru Granth Sahibji (The Holy Granth of the Sikhs). www.srigranth.org

15 The Role of Indian Railways During COVID-19

An Appraisal

Praveen Kumari Singh and Sagar Chahar

Introduction

On March 11, 2020, WHO (World Health Organization) declared COVID-19 a "pandemic" (WHO, 2020), urging countries to take action in the areas of preparedness and readiness, detection, protection, treatment, reducing transmission, sharing innovation, and learning to control the transmission of the virus in the community.

India sprung into action, and a "Janta Curfew" declared by the Prime Minister of India from 7 a.m. to 9 p.m. on March 22, 2020 (Chandana & Basu, 2020) was followed by the nationwide lockdown from March 25, 2020. The lockdown brought a different level of challenge affecting the daily lives of people and required out-of-the-box solutions. Indian Railways played a very important role during this lockdown and the period that followed by maintaining the supply chain across the country in various lockdowns across India. This chapter is an attempt to document and deliberate on various steps taken by Indian Railways to deal with unprecedented challenges both at the human and national levels for three waves of COVID-19 For better understanding of the larger context, operational issues and challenges associated with structures and functionalities are also detailed and deliberated.

Indian Railways: Brief Background

Indian Railways, one of the largest rail networks in the world (67,956 km route as of March 31, 2020, Railway Board, Ministry of Railways, 2020a) traverses the length and breadth of the country carrying materials, passengers, and goods, and has aptly earned the title of the "Lifeline of the Nation". Historically, railways have played a vital role in the economic growth of the country. It is estimated that Indian Railways carried 22.15 million passengers and 3.32 million tonnes of freight each day during 2019–20 (Railway Board, Ministry of Railways, 2020a). This vast organization is run by a multi-tier administrative structure headed by the Railway Board at the apex level, has 17 different zones with operational administrative sub-categories of divisions (68 in total) headed by a Divisional Railway Manager. Apart from the above, there are production units, training establishments, public sector enterprises, and other offices working under the superintendence of the Railway Board. Main functional operations of Indian Railways includes coaching (movement of Mail Express trains, passenger trains, suburban trains, and parcel special

DOI: 10.4324/9781003304517-19

trains), goods (movement of freight trains carrying bulk commodities) and production units (various production units manufacturing locomotives, coaches etc.).

Coaching

To visualize the scale of operations carried out by Indian Railways, it is pertinent to note that in 2019–20, Indian Railways carried 8,086 million passengers, out of which 56.85% were suburban passengers and 43.15% were non-suburban, with average lead (i.e., average distance traveled by a single passenger) of 29.8 km and 236.7 km respectively, and the earnings being 20.73 paise per passenger km and 52.35 paise per passenger km respectively (Railway Board, Ministry of Railways, 2020a).

Goods

Freight is a major earning source for Indian Railways, and it also ensures supply chain across various industries across the length and breadth of the country. In 2019–20, Indian Railways loaded 1212.22 million tonnes and had a freight output of 708 billion net-tonne kilometers (NTKM) with an average lead of 586 km which led to an earning of INR 111,472.30 crore (Railway Board, Ministry of Railways, 2020a). The Top 5 commodities carried by Indian Railways in fiscal year (FY) 2019–20 were coal (48.57% of total commodity), iron ore (12.69% of total commodity), cement (9.11% of total commodity), iron and steel (4.40% of total commodity) and chemical manure (4.25% of total commodity). As these commodities are raw materials for various sectors which in turn produce output in the form of goods, the importance of Indian Railways in supply chains can be realized.

Production Units

Railways have a lot of production units across different places in the country, equipped with large manpower of good skills. Indian Railways mobilized its resources to manufacture personal protective equipment (PPE) kits, HAZMAT suits and coveralls, sanitizers, sanitizer dispensing machines, sample collection booths, hospital beds and furniture, oxygen concentrators, and even ventilators which was made possible by effective resource management, sheer determination, resilience, and the innovation of the dedicated workforce at railway production units and workshops (Agrawal, 2021). South Eastern Railway (SER) through its Kharagpur workshop, had started manufacturing PPE kits as early as April 2020 (South Eastern Railway, 2020).

Railways at a Glance

To provide a bird's eye view of the whole of Indian Railways, Table 15.1 shows the different assets available with Indian Railways (Railway Board, Ministry of Railways, 2020a):

Table 15.1 Indian Railways at a Glance as of March 31, 2020

S No.	Asset		Count
1.	Locomotive	Steam	39
		Diesel	5,898
		Electric	6,972
2.	Coaches	Electric Multiple Unit (EMU)	11,360
		Conventional Coaches	57,083
		Diesel Multiple Unit (DMU)	1,793
		Other Coaching Vehicle (luggage vans, mail vans, parcel vans)	6,372
3.	Wagons	Total	293,077
		Covered Wagons	67,011
		Open High Sided	169,871
		Open Low Sided	17,473
		Other Types	23,664
		Brake Vans/Dept Wagons	15,058
4.	Regular Employees	Total	1,253,592
5.	Losses in Revenue due to Social Service Obligations	Essential Commodities carried below Cost	Rs. 301.01 Crore
		Revenue foregone due to Concessions in Pas5senger Fares	Rs. 2,058.61 Crores
		Loss on EMU Suburban Services	IRs. 6,937.72 Crore
		Uneconomic Branch Lines	Rs. 2,396.82 Crore
		Pricing of Passenger Fares below Cost	Rs. 45,430.56 Crore

First Wave of COVID-19 and Indian Railways

COVID-19 came as a shock to the world, which was working at a very high pace, and most of the countries were unprepared. It was in this backdrop that India announced a countrywide lockdown from March 25, 2020 for 21 days. The Prime Minister of India, while addressing the nation, stated that this lockdown period would be critical to build up resources essential to fight the virus, like the number of coronavirus testing facilities, personal protective equipment (PPE), isolation beds, ICU beds, ventilators, and other essential equipment. Simultaneously, the training of medical and paramedical manpower will also be undertaken (Roy, 2020).

Indian Railways, apart from having a huge network and running a significant number of trains, had a well-established medical network. There are 125 railway hospitals with 13,963 indoor beds and there are 622 specialist doctors (doctors with at least a Postgraduate degree beyond MBBS/BDS) (Health Directorate, 2021). The breakdown of the healthcare workers is as follows:

It was expected that Indian Railways with its medical infrastructure would have a critical role to play in the fight against COVID. The Health Directorate at Railway Board came out with guidelines regarding COVID-19. Early measures taken up by Railways include setting up a control room, disinfection of platforms and stations, coaches, cleaning of frequently touched surfaces, cleaning of air filters, posters and announcements at stations for COVID-19 awareness in Hindi and English,

Table 15.2 Health Care Workers in Indian Railways (Health Directorate, 2021)

S No.	Type of Health Care Worker	Total Number
1.	Regularly Appointed Medical Officers	2,506
2.	Senior Resident, Junior Resident, House Officers	1,000
3.	Visiting Specialists	575
4.	Group B Officers (Nursing, Physiotherapy, Pharmacy, Dietetics, Health Education)	194
5.	Non Gazetted (Group C)	14,174
6.	Non Gazetted (Group D)	40,163

and directive to separate 20% of beds for suspected COVID-19 patients in railway hospitals (Srivastava, 2020)

Dos and Don'ts issued by the Department of Personnel and Training (DoPT) were reiterated by the Railway Board. With the delegation of Powers under Disaster Management Act, 2005 to contain the spread of the Pandemic, one ADRM (Additional Divisional Railway Manager)/Division was appointed as Nodal Officer to enhance preparedness and containment of COVID-19 (Railway Board, Ministry of Railways, 2020). Zonal Railways and the IRCTC (Indian Railway Catering and Tourism Corporation) gave advice as to how food handlers at various places across the Indian Railways network should take preventive steps including the washing of hands, disinfection of frequently touched surfaces, not to attend stalls in case of any symptom, and frequent washing of clothes, etc. (Railway Board, Indian Railway, 2020c). A letter was issued by Additional Member Mechanical Engineering on March 16, 2020 which reiterated the guidelines to be followed for the disinfection of coaches, curtains, blankets, and bed sheet to be withdrawn from coaches, and air conditioning temperature to be maintained at 24-25 degree Centigrade (Railway Board, Ministry of Railways, 2020e).

There was guidance from the Health Directorate Railway Board to place young, healthy medical professionals preferably, for monitoring potential cases over those medical professionals who were older with comorbidities (Health Directorate, Railway Board, 2020).There were instructions to operate offices with skeletal staff.

Following the nationwide lockdown, mail-express, suburban trains were canceled initially until March 31, 2020 (Coaching Directorate, Railway Board, 2020). However, freight trains continued to run. This cancellation was further extended until April 14, 2020. Moreover, the production units were stopped until March 31, 2020. This was a crisis time during the lockdown, and maintaining supply chains was crucial. Operations of freight and parcel trains were critical during this period to ensure supply chains are maintained. This, therefore, brings to the fore the active role played by Indian Railways during COVID-19.

Operations of Freight Trains during COVID-19

Operating freight trains as a major link in the economy of the country and also for the revenue of Indian Railways became critical as the lockdown stopped the movement of vehicles on the road. The country still required energy, farmers required fertilizers, there were essential requirements of moving medical equipment and food grains, to maintain the supply chain to name a few. In order to appreciate the role played by freight trains in this operation, it is important to have a beginner-level understanding of how freight trains work in Indian Railways.

Working of Freight Trains

Freight trains carry commodities in bulk from a loading point to an unloading point. Therefore, these are the O-D pairs (Origin-Destination) between which the freight trains move. Further, there is a requirement of locomotives to haul the train and train examination staff to ensure the train is fit to move safely. The locomotive is run by a loco pilot and an assistant loco pilot, and overall in charge of the train is a train manager to ensure safe movement. All the trains are planned at the Division and these Divisions host a control which has the staff from all train-running departments at one place collaborating and planning swift and safe running of trains. The train is monitored at all times, and for overall coordination there is a conference among the divisions with their Zonal Headquarters and also with the Railway Board on a daily basis. Along with this, there is a fixed and strict limit in terms of the time duration where running staff can be asked to work on trains, which requires manpower planning. Also, every station, whether the train stops or not, is manned by a station master (if it's a block station), and the role of station master is very critical in terms of allowing trains to move from one station to another based on the system of working.[1] Further, there are many categories of staff who also play an important role in the background such as the track man or shunting staff, who are very critical for the safe running of trains. Also, there is a requirement of security staff to ensure the assets of Railways are protected at all times. It is within this machinery that railways operate and this is just giving a bird's eye view. So, in the situation of a lockdown, all these segments have to be coordinated (which had human resources) to ensure that the trains run. Due to the fear prevalent among society about the virus, it was a challenge to ensure that railway staff attended duty without fail to ensure the wheels of the country were moving.

Movement of Freight Trains during COVID-19

Due to reduction in demand of feul, coal production and coal loading decreased but need for critical supplies in the form of foodgrains and other essential commodities increased. Indian Railway's critical role in the supply chain can be gauged from special trains run by them (Jacob & Jai, 2020).

PM Garib Kalyan Yojana and Movement of Food Grains

During the lockdown period, there was an acute requirement of providing food grains at public distribution system (PDS) shops to ensure no food scarcity occurred at any place in the country. From April 1, 2020 to June 9, 2020 Indian Railways loaded 12.56 million tonnes of food grains as compared to 6.7 million tonnes in the same period last year (Nandi, 2020). Under Prime Minister Garib Kalyan Ann Yojana, 80 crore individuals were covered which is 2/3rds of India's population (Ministry of Finance, 2020). Northern Railways ran "Annaporna Trains" which were long-haul trains and covered states like Assam, Bihar, Goa, Gujarat, Karnataka, Maharashtra, Manipur, Nagaland, Odisha, Tamil Nadu, Uttar Pradesh, West Bengal, and Mizoram. Under normal circumstances, one freight train containing 42 covered wagons loaded with food grains carries around 2600 tonnes, but in the new concept two freight trains means 42 + 42 = 84 covered wagons with 5200 tonnes of food grains will be moved in a single path to reduce the journey time of the freight trains to their respective destinations (Ministry of Railways, 2020a).

Transportation of Milk: Doodh Duronto

To maintain the supply chain of milk, railways ran special trains carrying milk. South Central Railway introduced the concept of Doodh Duronto from Renigunta, State of Andhra Pradesh to Delhi with milk tankers of 40,000 liters each. The first such train had 6 such milk tankers carrying 2.4 lakh liters from Renigunta to Hazrat Nizamuddin on March 26, 2020 and ran without any detention on the way with an average speed of 110 km/hr and reached the destination in a period of 36 hours (Nag, 2020). By August 2021, the transportation via the Doodh Duronto had crossed 10 crore liters of milk (Nag, Milk transportation from Renigunta to Delhi: Indian Railways Doodh Duronto trains cross 10 crore liters mark, 2021).

Parcel Trains and Transportation of Medical Related Equipment

The dominant mode of transporting goods in India, which is through trucks, was stopped in the initial lockdown. As freight trains were running without restrictions, trains became the dominant mode to transport for goods and commodities across the country at almost pre-pandemic levels (Alicke, Dutta, Ganesh, KB, & Yadav, 2021). Railways intervened to transport goods which were not in bulk but in smaller quantities with multiple consignees and consignors for different destinations. Railways ran COVID-19 parcel special trains. Since the start of the nationwide lockdown in March 2020, up to 20 days of running such parcel specials had carried 20,474 tonnes of consignments and earned a revenue of INR 7.54 crore (PTI, 2020b). There were innumerable stories of railways helping those who had run out of medicines and providing them with the medicines at the right time. During the first lockdown, railways transported 1,150 tonnes of medical equipment (PTI, 2020c). A story worth mentioning is that of the transportation of camel milk by railways from Rajasthan to Mumbai. After receiving the request which was highlighted by a senior Indian Police Service officer on Twitter, the railways ensured a non-scheduled stop for a parcel special train running from Ludhiana to Bandra at Falna near Ajmer in Rajasthan, from where the milk was to be supplied and this was transported via this parcel train. This was lauded by the then Minister of Railways, Sh. Piyush Goyal too (Economic Times, 2020).

Kisan Rail Services

To ensure that farmer produce reaches far-flung places in a time-bound manner, railways came up with an innovative approach of running Kisan Trains. Ministry of Railways stated

"Kisan Rails are based on the concept of multi commodity, multi consignor, multi consignee and multi stoppages – to help small farmers with lesser produce to transport their consignment without any middleman". (Railway Board, Ministry of Railways, 2021)

This was due to an all-round effort of Central and State Governments to ensure that inputs reached farmers on time and the produce reached markets without much disruption. The first such train ran on August 7, 2020 between Devlali (Maharashtra) and Danapur (Bihar). The major features of Kisan Rail are (PIB, 2021): No limitation on minimum quantity of produce to be transported so that marginal and small farmers can also avail the services, trains run on a timetabled path to maintain the punctuality, 50% of transportation costs are provided by the Ministry of Food Processing as a subsidy to farmers to further lower the costs under the Operations Green Scheme (Tomato-Onion-Potato), commodities are charged under the P scale of parcel tariff. As of June 2021, 60 routes have been operationalized and up to December 24, 2021, railways ran 1806 Kisan Rail services and carried 5.9 lakh tonnes of agricultural products (Ministry of Railways, 2022).

COVID-19 Isolation Coaches

There was a surplus of coaches across the network of Indian Railways due to the stoppage of Mail Express trains. Due to prevailing uncertainty about COVID and its spread, the concept of COVID isolation coaches came up and the guidelines for the creation of such coaches were issued on March 30, 2020 by the Railway Board to various zones (Railway Board, 2020). The coaches were suitably altered; for example, the first cabin near the bathing room was provided with two hospital/plastic curtains transversely in the aisle so that the entry and exit to the entire eight-berth cabin could be screened off. The cabin was used as a store/paramedic area. Two oxygen cylinders were provided by the Medical Department, for which suitable clamping arrangement on the side berth was provided, and middle berths were removed to make space. In order to insulate the coach from heat, protect the isolation coaches from mosquitoes and to ensure proper disposal of biomedical waste there was bamboo/khus mats provided, mosquito nets were provided, color coded dustbin with garbage bags were provided respectively.

These coaches were to be deputed based on the requests given by the State Government and can accommodate 16–18 patients at the same time. In order to cite the examples of deployment of these coaches, the Table 15.3 gives a concise view (Ministry of Railways, 2021):

Table 15.3 COVID Coaches Deployment as of May 7, 2021

S No.	Place and State of Deployment	No of Coaches Deployed	No. of Beds	No. of Patients Admitted and Discharge
1.	Guwahati, Assam	21	336	Newly requested by the State Govt. on May 2021
2.	Badarpur, Assam	20	320	Newly requested by the State Govt. on May 2021
3.	Sabarmati, Gujarat	10	160	Newly requested by the State Govt. on May 2021
4.	Chandoliya, Gujarat	6	96	Newly requested by the State Govt. on May 2021
5.	Dimapur, Nagaland	10	160	Newly requested by the State Govt. on May 2021
6.	Ajni, Inland Container Depot, Nagpur, Maharashtra	11	176	9 admitted and 6 discharged
7.	Tihi, Indore, Madhya Pradesh	22	320	19 admitted and 1 discharged
8.	Anand Vihar and Shakurbasti, Delhi	75	1200	5 admissions and all discharged
9.	Bhopal, Madhya Pradesh	20	320	28 admissions and 10 discharged

Shramik and Other Special Trains

COVID-induced lockdown during the first wave involved the halting of trains, flights, and buses on roads for public transportation. This led to people getting stuck wherever they were, and authorities also requested that people remained where they wherere and did not venture elsewhere. This created a unique situation as lots of travel and movement of people occurs for various reasons across the country, along with usual migration. People migrate and relocate to different places for studies, job opportunities, and progression of their careers.

As per the Economic Survey 2016–17, the internal work-related migration, using railway data for the period 2011–2016, indicates that an average of 9 million people move between the states (Chief Economic Advisor, 2017). Further, relatively less developed states such as Bihar, Uttar Pradesh, have net outmigration and relatively more developed states have net inmigration like Goa, Maharashtra, Gujarat, Tamil Nadu, Karnataka, and Kerala (Chief Economic Advisor, 2017).

There are many prestigious educational institutes located across the country which includes many Indian Institutes of Technology (IITs), National Institutes of Technology (NITs), All India Institutes of Medical Sciences and Research (AIIMS), medical colleges, and degree colleges across the states. Apart from this, there are a few cities which are known for the student influx like Kota in Rajasthan. During the lockdown, such institutions were closed for physical attendance and such students required transport to their hometowns.

The need to provide special transit services in a manner with minimum risk of spreading the virus required a complete new protocol adhering to COVID-19

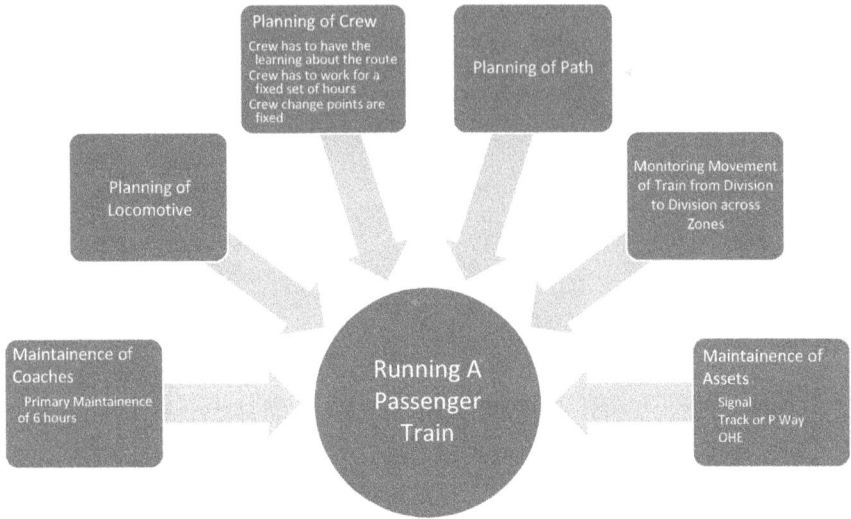

Figure 15.1 Flow Chart of Basic Schematic of Running a Passenger Train

appropriate behavior. Running a train as illustrated before is a complex process with an interplay of multiple departments. The Operating Department is responsible for overall coordination for movement of a train. Apart from moving the train from station to station across the route and monitoring the movement of trains from a centralized place called Divisional Control, the Operating Department is involved in the planning of the train. Further, the Mechanical and Electrical Department are responsible for maintenance of coaches and locomotives. The Commercial Department looks after the passenger conveniences and the fare structure in the train along with taking customer complaints and talking with State Governments. The Railway Protection Force is entrusted with maintaining security of passengers and railway property and also ensuring crowd management at stations. Engineering, Signal and Telecommunication, and Overhead Equipment (OHE) Departments are involved in maintenance of assets.

Passenger trains are run by people in locomotives which are called the Loco Pilot and Assistant Loco Pilot, and in the rear end of the train it is manned by guards called the running staff. The running staff have a set duration of working hours and have knowledge about set routes in order to ensure safety, and hence crew planning comes under a set of planning measures by the Operating Department.

Running of Shramik Special Train

The trains were run with intricate planning as the origin and destination were known only a few hours before the departure. The State Governments were to give the list of passengers and the destination. Railway planning was set in motion after that.

Since its inaugural run on May 1, 2020, the railways ran 4,621 Shramik Express services up to August 8, 2020 (Pib Delhi, 2020). Around 67 lakh passengers were carried in the Shramik special trains. Out of 4,621 trains, around 79% of trains carried passengers to 3 states: Uttar Pradesh, Bihar, and West Bengal. Gujarat, Maharashtra, and Punjab accounted for 49% of outgoing Shramik special trains (Jadhav, 2020). The enormity of performing such operations efficiently and safely was significant for Indian Railways. The challenges faced by Indian Railways were innumerable, unique, and tough. Railway staff also contractedCOVID-19, reducing the staff strength. During this period, approximately 40,000 railway staff tested positive and nearly 700 died (Dastidar, 2021). Along with this, there were issues from private societies that did not allow such frequent movement of railway staff who lived in these societies. Moreover, the demand and supply were mainly from few select states to a few select states, which led to congestion on those routes. Since the movement of trains was frequent, it was a massive task to move all the trains on the same route. This problem was further complicated by the time required for deboarding "since COVID-19 protocol meant phased deboarding. The trains hence got "bunched up" and with the fixed upper limit in line capacity, trains had to move via different routes. This was seen via trains getting rerouted, which made headlines; for example a train bound for Gorakhpur was routed to Rourkela (Desk, 2020).

Moreover, the demand surge for the trains was significant and it started impacting maintenance of rakes. As maintenance happened at designated sites called "pit lines", with rapid demand for cities such as Mumbai, Surat, the capacity of the pit line was stretched to its highest capacity. The staff also lived at different places and it was difficult to call all the staff regularly and hence the staff was also overstretched. In order to solve this problem (availability of pit lines and staff for examining the rakes) which got accentuated by 66% of demand originating from Mumbai itself, so 8–9 rakes were maintained nearby Mumbai region i.e. at Bhusaval, Sholapur, Nagpur division of Central Railway Sutar, 2020). Ensuring the COVID-19 protocol while boarding and deboarding was a very critical thing and theh Railway Protection Force and Station Directors completed a close coordination job with the State Governments. Providing water and food was a mammoth exercise and distribution was managed with close coordination with the Indian Railway Catering and Tourism Corporation (IRCTC). Indian Railways stepped up to the monumental task with no precedence or past experience of this magnitude to refer to or rely on. For Indian Railways, as the most affordable, safe, and mass mode of transport, it was a conscious call of duty.

Other Efforts by Indian Railway

Apart from the previously-mentioned specific steps, Indian Railways also made use of its resources to provide relief to people during the COVID-19 pandemic.

Contribution to PM CARES Fund by Railway Employees

The railway is a massive organization with 1,218,335 employees on its payroll as of July 1, 2020 (Press Trust of India, 2020). The voluntary monetary contribution for assistance for COVID-related expenses like the Prime Minister's Citizen

Assistance and Relief in Emergency Situations Fund (PM CARES) was done by the employees. Indian Railways in a combined manner donated Rs. 151 crore to the PM CARES Fund (PTI, 2020a).

Food Preparation by IRCTC Base Kitchen

IRCTC Base Kitchen has a very strong supply chain ensuring food and catering services onboard trains. Due to the announcement of COVID-induced lockdown and the subsequent closure of mail/express and passenger trains, the infrastructure of the base kitchens could have been used. This was seen from the offer that IRCTC Base Kitchen provided to the State Governments of 2.6 lakh meals/day (Ministry of Railways, 2020b).

Second COVID-19 Wave: Indian Railways

During the first COVID-19 outbreak, the country witnessed a complet nationwide lockdown. Following the first nationwide lockdown, the Government of India came up with the "Unlock Guideline" which was a phased reopening of all the restrictions. With this phased reopening the nationwide confirmed cases increased, with the first peak observed in September 2020. Following this, there was a decline in the number of cases and test-positivity rate. The lowest test-positivity rate following this was on February 15 of 1.5%. However, a new "Variant of Concern" emerged. The Delta variant was designated a "variant of interest" by the World Health Organization (WHO) on April 4, 2021 and a "variant of concern" being designated on May 11, 2021 with earliest samples being seen in October 2020 (WHO, n.d.). This variant drove the second COVID-19 wave in India, where demand for transportation changed from the first wave and the major significant thing that was required now was medical oxygen.

Oxygen requirement increased significantly in India. This was due to the fact that the virus attacked the lower respiratory tract and involved the lungs causing oxygen exchange in the blood to reduce. This fact, along with the highly contagious nature of the virus, and the economy back in a flow, led to many cases and proportionately raised the oxygen requirements. Further, the vaccination rollout was for the healthcare workers, frontline workers, and the elderly who were the most vulnerable. All these factors contributed to a high positivity rate, high case load, and increased oxygen requirement.

Supply Chain of Liquid Medical Oxygen (LMO)

Production of LMO during the peak of the second COVID-19 wave in India was 7000–8000 tonnes per day with significant chunk of around 2000–3000 tonnes in captivity with steel plants which is required to enrich the blast furnace. Further, out of the total gaseous oxygen produced by thee steel plants, only about 5–10% can be converted to LMO that is meant for the health sector (Roy & Nair, 2021). Major steel plants were located in eastern parts of the country whereas the cities where demand of oxygen rose rapidly were in the western, northern and southern parts of

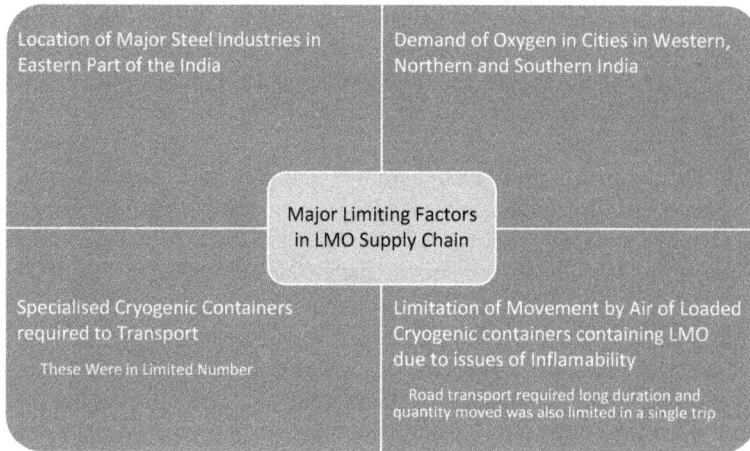

Figure 15.2 Bottle Necks in the Supply Chain of LMO

India. Further, movement of LMO required specialized cryogenic tankers which were limited in quantity at the time.

In order to solve this issue of logistics, Indian Railways came up with Oxygen Express.

Oxygen Express

Railways had experience of running ro-ro (roll on-roll off) service. Konkan Railway had run ro-ro services regularly and Indian Railways, in order to reduce the turnaround time of LMO trucks and also enhance the movement of large number of trucks in a single trip via uninterrupted Green corridor, Railways leveraged the use of Ro-Ro service to transport LMO trucks across the country. The DBKM/BOMN, BRN are different types of wagons that can be used to carry trucks. Further, since the trucks were carrying inflammable material and it was the first time such an experiment was done, it was necessary that speed and other factors were ensured which can unduly affect the balance of trucks while on the move. Another factor to be taken into consideration was OHE (Overhead Equipment) which has a voltage of 25,000 volts. There is a requirement of minimum clearance from this OHE, i.e., contact wire and the OHE height from the rail level is different at different places. Hence, an analysis of the route by maintaining minimum clearance of the truck-wagon combination from the rail level is to be maintained and any such clearance which is not in the safety limits can be the limiting factor. There was also a clearance required for roads over bridges (ROBs).

For example, the truck with the wagon can be a total of 4,500 mm and there is a requirement of maintaining two clearances, i.e., gross clearance (clearance between cconsignment and fixed structure in stationary condition) of 250mm and net clearance (clearance between consignment and fixed structure in moving condition) of 150 mm for Class A Over Dimensional Consignment (ODC).

Along with this, there has to be a facility for loading the trucks and unloading with a ramp facility along the rail from where the trucks can be loaded on the wagon.

Moreover, in order to ensure the stability of trucks, they have to be tied properly on the wagon. Furthermore, the truck drivers need some accommodation during the passage of the train and security for the rake, for which Railway Protection Force (RPF) need to accompany. For this, there was a sleeper coach attached at the end.

The movement was across zones, and there was a need to have intricate coordination for the movement. Also, the BOMN, which is a specialized type of wagon, is not available in the same numbers as the BCN, BOXN types of wagons, and thereby it could also become a limiting factor for ro-ro movement.

With the constant demand rising and the above-mentioned constraints, there were imports of cryogenic tankers. These tankers were placed in a frame which was equal in dimensions to an ISO container and thereby could be transported via flat container wagons, limiting the constraints of ODC and route restrictions. ODC movement has a speed restriction on account of Safety reasons but with the cryogenic containers in form of ISO containers were placed on BCLA wagons with twist lock mechanism which allowed it to be moved on maximum permissible speed.

Guidelines for Oxygen Special

In order to initiate Oxygen Special, a set of guidelines, which covered a lot of things, were brought out by Indian Railways on April 16, 2021 by a special circular referred to Rates circular no 16 of 2021 which has given the rating of transporting LMO with the following details (Railway Board, 2021):

1. Payload weight issued by road weighbridge duly certified by Legal Metrology Department of State Government was used as chargeable weight which, along with tare weight of wagon, could not exceed the permissible carrying capacity (PCC) of the route.
2. Charging of trucks was in Class LR3 which is one of the lowest class rates.
3. Busy Season surcharge, Development charge was not levied.
4. A free time of 5 hours was allowed at loading and unloading points.
5. Securing trucks and lashing were to be done by the customer.
6. Persons accompanying the trucks were to buy a second class ticket (ordinary fare) for the journey.

Further, when the cryogenic tankers were carried on flat container wagons, the charge was on Haulage Charge per TEU basis and there was no Haulage charge on empty flat cryogenic tankers carried on container flat wagons. Moreover, for handling such trains, no terminal charge or terminal access charge was levied.

Route and Statistics of Oxygen Express

Oxygen Express was a major transformation in the thinking process and logistics of oxygen transport. From the first loaded Oxygen Express that ran on April 22,

2021, between Visakhapatnam Steel Siding to Nashik Road via Nagpur until the last Oxygen Special from Rourkela to the CONCOR (Container Corporation of India) Terminal in Visakhapatnam district which ran on September 23, 2021, the railways transported 36,840 tonnes of liquid oxygen and a total of 899 Oxygen Express trains ran (PIB Delhi, 2022). The routes were majorly to oxygen deficient areas based on the wave of COVID-19 experienced. For example,Maharashtra, Delhi, and Lucknow saw a rapid rise in positive cases in April and were initial routes and then it diverted to states like Telangana, Karnataka, and Tamil Nadu gradually.

Based on a monthly analysis of routes for the first two months of movement of the Oxygen Express the findings in Table 15.4 were seen.

Hence, the analysis shows the movement mainly from the eastern part of the country to other parts, with the states that have major metropolitan centers being receivers of LMO.

Apart from this, Indian Railways even sent LMO to Bangladesh via the Petrapole-Benapole route totaling 3911.41 Million Tonnes (MT) (PIB Delhi, 2022).

Indian Railways took extra efforts to ensure that such oxygen services were started. There was construction of ramps in a matter of days; for example, they were created in Vizag, Angul, and Bhilai rapidly.

Table 15.4 Route Analysis of Oxygen Special Trains in April, May 2021

S No.	Month	Total No. of Loaded Oxygen Special	Originating States	Destination States
1.	April 2021	17 trips with 57 loaded tankers	53% from Jharkhand, 11.6% from Odisha, 17.6% from Madhya Pradesh, 5% each from Chattisgarh, Gujarat	41% to Uttar Pradesh, 11.7% to Maharashtra, 17.6% to Delhi NCR, 23.5% to Madhya Pradesh, 5.8% to Gujarat
2.	May 2021	317 trips with 1141 loaded tankers	31.32% originated from Jharkhand, 30% originated from Odisha, 22.7% from Gujarat, 5.9% originated from West Bengal, Rest movements originated from Maharashtra, Tamil Nadu, Madhya Pradesh, Uttar Pradesh which were only for redistribution from state capital to secondary centre.	30% to Delhi NCR, 14.74% trips to Andhra Pradesh, 14.51% Trips to Uttar Pradesh, 11.67% to Tamil Nadu, 7.2% to Karnataka, 6.62% trips to Madhya Pradesh, 6.3% trips to Telangana, less than 5% each to Punjab, Rajasthan, Kerala, Uttarakhand

Source: Ministry of Railways

Govt. of Maharashtra, Madhya Pradesh approached Min. of Railways for Carrying LMO over Rail

↓

Railways carried out feasibility analysis of the route

↓

Model of Road Tanker T 1618 along with wagon had a height of 3320mm + 1290 mm (Truck+Wagon)

↓

On 15.04.2021, a DBKM wagon was placed at Kalamboli Siding in Maharashtra and a joint survey with T 1618 truck was carried out

↓

Necessary Technical and fare guidelines were issued by Railway board on 16.04.2021

↓

Kalamboli Ramp was ready by 19.04.2021

↓

First Oxygen Express with 7 tankers (Empty) ran from Kalamboli to Vishakapatnam on 19.04.2021

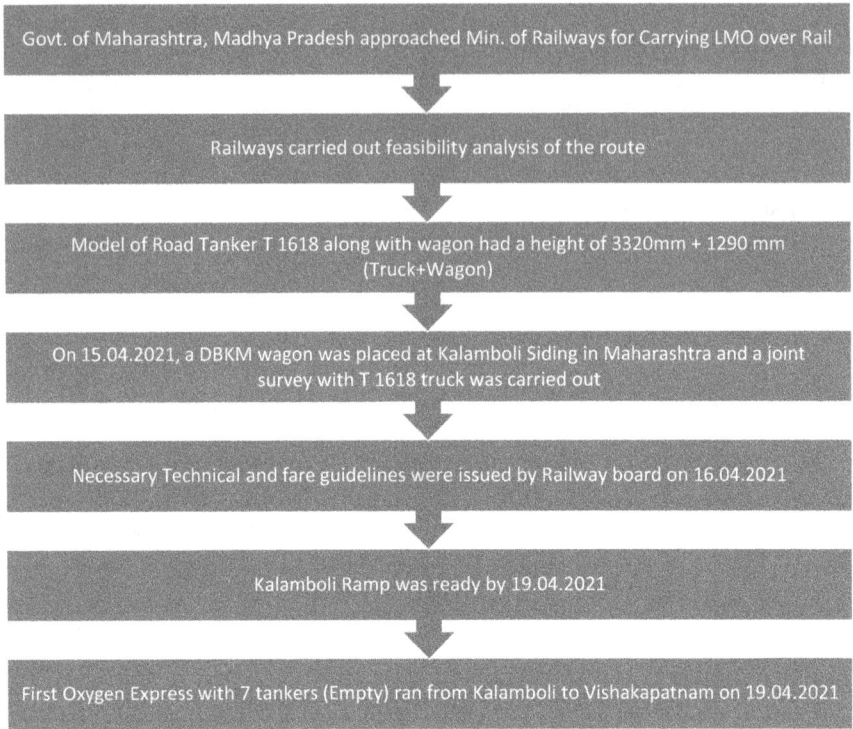

Figure 15.3 Flow Chart Showing the Planning Process of First Oxygen Special.

In order to see the rapid pace with which things moved following examples of planning processes, the first Oxygen Express between Kalamboli, Maharashtra, and Vishakhapatnam is seen (News, 2021) in Figure 15.3.

Conclusion

COVID was an extraordinary event and disrupted the usual way of life across the world. In the transportation sector, it reinforced the indispensability of Indian Railways as it truly acted as a lifeline of the nation. The Prime Minister of India, while inaugurating a section of the Eastern Dedicated Freight Corridor, stated that India will never forget the contribution of Indian Railways during COVID-19. It also led to lateral and innovative ways of thinking and planning for railways especially in terms of how to enhance the railway's share of freight. The National Rail Plan has highlighted that and provided a road map on how to achieve 45% of freight share by railways by 2045. Railways during COVID-19 came up with multiple rail user-friendly schemes to enhance the loading of freight. Recently, the Minister of Railways has given a newer approach for the railways in the form of "Hungry for Cargo" and how the modal share of freight is to increase. The railways, as a result is making records and recently on January 26, 2022 achieved a target of 4.1 million tonnes loaded on a single day. The railway industry, in the future, is looking to enhance capacity, execute projects, ensure safe, efficient, and punctual transportation for freight users and passenger together.

Note

1 System of working: There are a set of rules, procedures by which a train runs between two stations. These set of rules and procedure is called system of working. There are different types of system of working but broadly two system of working are most prevalent:

- Absolute Block System
- Automatic Block System

Bibliography

Agrawal, P. (2021, May 17). *The Role of Indian Railways in COVID-19 crisis management.* Retrieved from Global Railway Review: https://www.globalrailwayreview.com/article /123127/indian-railways-covid19-crisis-management/

Alicke, K., Dutta, S., Ganesh, K., KB, R., & Yadav, H. (2021, December 14). *India's Postpandemic Logistics Sector: The Need for Technological Change.* Retrieved from Mckinsey and Company: https://www.mckinsey.com/industries/travel-logistics -and-infrastructure/our-insights/indias-postpandemic-logistics-sector-the-need-for -technological-change

Chandana, H., & Basu, M. (2020, March 19). *Modi Announces 'Janata Curfew' on 22 March, Urges for Resolve, Restraint to Fight Coronavirus.* Retrieved from ThePrint: https://theprint.in/india/modi-announces-janata-curfew-on-22-march-urges-for-resolve -restraint-to-fight-coronavirus/384138/

Chief Economic Advisor. (2017). *Economic Survey 2016–17.* Delhi: Ministry of Finance .

Coaching Directorate, Railway Board. (2020, March 23). *Cancellation of Train Services in the Wake of COVID-19.* Retrieved from Indian railways: https://indianrailways.gov.in/ railwayboard/uploads/directorate/safety/pdf/Cancellation_Trains_220320.pdf

Dastidar, A. G. (2021, January 1). *Shramik Specials: 'When the Train Left, We Broke into an Applause... It Was Spontaneous'.* Retrieved from Indian Express: https://indianexpress .com/article/india/shramik-trains-covid-19-india-lockdown-7128238/

Desk, E. W. (2020, May 23). *Passengers Left Baffled as UP-Bound Shramik Train Runs on Diverted Route, Railways Responds.* Retrieved from Indian Express: https:// indianexpress.com/article/india/train-ferrying-migrants-from-mumbai-to-up-diverted-to -odisha-6423966/

Economic Times. (2020, April 12). *Indian Railways Delivers Camel Milk for Autistic Child.* Retrieved from Economic Times: https://economictimes.indiatimes.com/industry /transportation/railways/indian-railways-delivers-camel-milk-to-the-mother-for-her -autistic-child/railways-ferries-20-ltr-of-camel-milk/slideshow/75106303.cms

Health Directorate. (2021, May 22). *Facilities.* Retrieved from Indian Railways: https:// indianrailways.gov.in/railwayboard/view_section.jsp?id=0,1,304,366,519,751

Health Directorate, Railway Board. (2020, March 20). *COVID 19 Preparedness.* Retrieved from Indian Railways: https://indianrailways.gov.in/railwayboard/uploads/directorate/ health/pdf/2020/spread_COVID_200320.pdf

Jacob, S., & Jai, S. (2020, June 7). *Rail Freight Traffic Drops 28% in April–May Amid Covid-19 Lockdown.* Retrieved from Business Standard: https://www.business-standard .com/article/economy-policy/rail-freight-traffic-drops-28-in-april-may-amid-covid-19 -lockdown-120060701026_1.html

Jadhav, R. (2020, October 22). *79% of Shramik Trains Were Operated to UP, Bihar, West Bengal Between May and August.* Retrieved from TheHindu Businessline: https://www

.thehindubusinessline.com/data-stories/data-focus/79-of-shramik-trains-were-operated
-to-up-bihar-west-bengal-between-may-and-august/article32921627.ece

Ministry of Finance. (2020, March 26). *Finance Minister Announces Rs 1.70 Lakh Crore Relief Package Under Pradhan Mantri Garib Kalyan Yojana for the Poor to Help Them Fight the Battle Against Corona Virus*. Retrieved from Pib: https://pib.gov.in/ PressReleasePage.aspx?PRID=1608345

Ministry of Railways. (2022, January 01). *Year 2021 Has Been a 'Year of Major Transformation' for Indian Railways*. Retrieved from Press Information Bureau: https:// pib.gov.in/PressReleseDetail.aspx?PRID=1786819

Ministry of Railways. (2020a, April 17). *Indian Railways Introduces Innovative Ideas and Registers Record Landmarks Freight Movement During COVID-19 Lockdown*. Retrieved from Press Information Bureau: https://pib.gov.in/newsite/PrintRelease.aspx ?relid=202336

Ministry of Railways. (2020b, April 22). *Ministry of Railways Offers to Supply 2.6 Lakh Meals Daily from Various Railway Kitchens Across the Country to States*. Retrieved from Public Information Bureau: https://pib.gov.in/PressReleasePage.aspx?PRID=1616985

Ministry of Railways. (2021, May 7). *Railway Provides 21 Isolation Coaches at Guwahati and 20 Isolation Coaches at Badarpur Near Silchar in Assam (N.F. Railway)*. Retrieved from Public Information Bureau: https://pib.gov.in/PressReleasePage.aspx?PRID =1716788

Nag, D. (2020, November 16). *Indian Railways' Doodh Duronto Special Train Ensures Uninterrupted Supply of Milk!* Retrieved from Financial Express: https://www .financialexpress.com/infrastructure/railways/indian-railways-doodh-duronto-special -train-ensures-uninterrupted-supply-of-milk-check-details-here/2129313/

Nag, D. (2021, August 11). *Milk Transportation from Renigunta to Delhi: Indian Railways Doodh Duronto Trains Cross 10 Crore Litres Mark*. Retrieved from Financial Express: https://www.financialexpress.com/infrastructure/railways/milk-transportation-from -renigunta-to-delhi-indian-railways-doodh-duronto-trains-cross-10-crore-litres-mark /2308440/

Nandi, T. (2020, June 11). *Indian Railways Ferried 31.90 Lakh Wagons to Keep Supply Chain Functional*. Retrieved from Mint: https://www.livemint.com/news/india/indian-railways -ferried-31-90-lakh-wagons-to-keep-supply-chain-functional-11591818060377.html

National Health Mission. (2021). *Draft Guidance Note on Liquid Medical Oxygen (LMO) Storage Tanks*. New Delhi: Ministry of Health and Family Welfare.

News, R. (2021, April 19). *Indian Railways to Run Oxygen Express to Transport Liquid Medical Oxygen and Oxygen Cylinders*. Retrieved from Rail Analysis India: https://news .railanalysis.com/indian-railways-to-run-oxygen-express-to-transport-liquid-medical -oxygen-and-oxygen-cylinders/

PIB. (2021). *Kisan Rail Service*. Retrieved from VIKASPEDIA: https://vikaspedia.in/ agriculture/national-schemes-for-farmers/kisan-rail-service

PIB Delhi. (2020, September 16). *Shramik and Special Train Services*. Retrieved from Public Information Bureau: https://www.pib.gov.in/PressReleasePage.aspx?PRID =1655121

PIB Delhi. (2022, January 1). *Year 2021 has been a 'Year of Major Transformation' for Indian Railways*. Retrieved from PIB: https://pib.gov.in/PressReleaseIframePage.aspx ?PRID=1786819

Press Trust of India. (2020, July 04). *No Job Cuts But Profiles of Employees May Change, Says Railways*. Retrieved from Hindustan Times: https://www.hindustantimes.com/ india-news/no-job-cuts-but-profiles-of-employees-may-change-says-railways/story-scT Ogwe2rD7zN4UVBW9SoL.html

PTI. (2020a, March 29). *Railways Donates ₹151 cr to PM-CARES Fund: Piyush Goyal*. Retrieved from Thehindu Businessline: https://www.thehindubusinessline.com/news/ railways-donates-151-cr-to-pm-cares-fund-piyush-goyal/article31197747.ece

PTI. (2020b, April 15). *COVID-19: Parcel Trains Loaded 20,474 Tonnes of Essential Goods During Lockdown.* Retrieved from The New Indian Express: https://www .newindianexpress.com/nation/2020/apr/15/covid-19-parcel-trains-loaded-20474 -tonnes-of-essential-goods-during-lockdown-2130545.html

PTI. (2020c, April 19). *Coronavirus Lockdown | Transported 1,150 Tonnes of Medical Items, Says Railways.* Retrieved from TheHindu: https://www.thehindu.com/news/ national/coronavirus-lockdown-transported-1150-tonnes-of-medical-items-railways/ article31382310.ece

Railway Board. (2020, March 12). *COVID-19 Preparedness.* Retrieved from Indian Railway: https://indianrailways.gov.in/railwayboard/uploads/directorate/health/pdf /2020/Spreading_120320.pdf

Railway Board. (2020, March 30). *COVID-19 - Conversion of Coaches to Serve as Quarantine/isolation Facilities.* Retrieved from Indian Railway: https://indianrailways .gov.in/railwayboard/uploads/directorate/mec_engg/downloads/Coaching/2020/ Conversion%2BCoaches_300320.pdf

Railway Board. (2021, April 16). *Transportation of Liquid Medical Oxygen on Cryogenic Tankers by Railways.* Retrieved from Indianrailways: https://indianrailways.gov.in/ railwayboard/uploads/directorate/traffic_comm/Freight-Rate-Circular-2021/RC%2016 %20of%202021%20covid%20relief.pdf

Railway Board, Indian Railway. (2020, March 17). *COVID-19 Prepardness.* Retrieved from Indian Railways: https://indianrailways.gov.in/railwayboard/uploads/directorate/health/ pdf/2020/Preventive_measures_170320.pdf

Railway Board, Ministry of Railways. (2020a). *Indian Railways Yearbook 2019–20.* New Delhi: Government of India.

Railway Board, Ministry of Railways. (2020b, March 05). *COVID-19 Preparedness.* Retrieved from Indian Railways: https://indianrailways.gov.in/railwayboard/uploads/ directorate/corona/Establishment_050320.pdf

Railway Board, Ministry of Railways. (2020c, March 06). *COVID-19 Preparedness.* Retrieved from Indian Railways: https://indianrailways.gov.in/railwayboard/uploads/ directorate/Environment_Management/2020/Corona_Virus_Alert_060320.pdf

Railway Board, Ministry of Railways. (2020d, March 17). *COVID-19 Prepardness.* Retrieved from Indian Railway: https://indianrailways.gov.in/railwayboard/uploads/ directorate/health/pdf/2020/Delegation_Powers_170320.pdf

Railway Board, Ministry of Railways. (2020e, March 16). *COVID-19 Prepardness.* Retrieved from Indian Railways: https://indianrailways.gov.in/railwayboard/uploads/directorate/ mec_engg/downloads/freight/2020/AM%20ME%2016_03_2020%20Corona.pdf

Railway Board, Ministry of Railways. (2021). *Kisan Rail A Boon for Farmers.* Delhi: Ministry of Railways.

Roy, D. (2020, March 24). *"No Other Way": Full Text Of PM Modi's Speech Announcing Lockdown.* Retrieved from NDTV: https://www.ndtv.com/india-news/coronavirus-india -lockdown-full-text-of-pm-narendra-modis-speech-announcing-covid-19-lockdown -2200156

Roy, D., & Nair, A. (2021, June 15). *Managing the Medical Oxygen Supply Chain in India.* Retrieved from TheHindu BusinessLine: https://www.thehindubusinessline.com/opinion /columns/managing-the-medical-oxygen-supply-chain-in-india/article34819519.ece

Srivastava, V. (2020, March 09). *COVID-19 Preparedness.* Retrieved from Indian Railways: https://indianrailways.gov.in/railwayboard/uploads/directorate/health/pdf/ jpg2pdf.pdf

Sutar, S. (2020, June 10). *Shramik Specials – Central Railway Rises to the Need; Gigantic Exercise in Planning, Maintaining and Running Trains During COVID19.* Retrieved from Central Railway: https://cr.indianrailways.gov.in/view_detail.jsp?lang=0&id =0,4,268&dcd=5440&did=15917051887200ECA5C91826D06E24825E208CD37 D4AD

South Eastern Railway. (2020, April 16). *South Eastern Railway Manufactures PPE Kits To Fight Against Covid-19*. Retrieved from South Eastern Railway: https://ser .indianrailways.gov.in/view_detail.jsp?lang=0&dcd=4107&id=0,4,423

WHO. (n.d.). *Tracking SARS-CoV-2 Variants*. Retrieved from World Health Organisation: https://www.who.int/en/activities/tracking-SARS-CoV-2-variants/

WHO. (2020, March 11). *WHO Director-General's Opening Remarks at the Media Briefing on COVID-19 −11 March 2020*. Retrieved from who.int: https://www.who.int/director -general/speeches/detail/who-director-general-s-opening-remarks-at-the-media-briefing -on-covid-19---11-march-2020

Part IV

Indian States' Responses to the COVID-19 Pandemic

16 COVID-19 and the Politics of Lockdowns in Kashmir

Shakhoor Ahmad Wani

Introduction

The first case of COVID-19 was detected in Kashmir in March 2020 and the lockdown ensued as in other places of India where the virus had made inroads. Elsewhere, in India or outside, the lockdown, sometimes violently enforced, was a novel method to curtail public movement and restrict social gatherings. In Kashmir, familiar with lockdowns that could stretch for months together, its novelty rested in its overtly non-political nature. When the Indian Government announced a countrywide lockdown in March 2020 to stymie the spread of COVID-19, Kashmir had barely begun to crawl out of a six-month lockdown. In August 2019, the Government of India voided all clauses of Article 370 of the Indian Constitution—a provision that provided a semblance of autonomy to the region—and days later bifurcated the erstwhile state of Jammu and Kashmir (J&K) into two centrally administered union territories. These changes had been followed by strict restrictions on the movement of people and a strict communication blockade. By March, the government had begun to ease some of the restrictions on movement and provided access to a list of government-approved sites on 2G Internet. In early March, broadband was restored, and some local politicians were released from jail. Then soon after the case was detected, the lockdown was re-imposed with new rules and restrictions.

While the COVID-19 pandemic has affected nearly every society and left a trail of wrecked lives and economies in its wake, the severity of its impact is highly differentiated. It has exposed and exacerbated pre-existing inequalities. Kashmir was already at a serious disadvantage, not only due to its dilapidated infrastructure, but the debilitating circumstances engendered by the August 2019 decision. The attendant stringent restrictions had brought life in the valley to a grinding halt. Educational institutions were closed, communications lines disrupted, and businesses shut. The derailment of economic activity added to the privations of the local population and resulted in losses amounting to several billion dollars. Thus, when COVID-19 restrictions were imposed in March 2020, Kashmiris were already teetering on the precipice. Students had lost an invaluable six months, thousands had lost their jobs, and many families were pushed into penury.

This chapter documents not only the untold suffering wrought by COVID-19 in Kashmir, but also tells us how in conflict situations politics often trumps public health considerations. It focuses mostly on the first wave when Kashmir was

DOI: 10.4324/9781003304517-21

already under a severe clampdown and had to tackle the novel disease in a climate of uncertainty and information darkness. The chapter describes the ways in which Kashmiri experiences during the pandemic were distinct from other communities. The Central Government's misplaced priorities and a warped view of national security meant that the stifling communication blockade was not lifted until several months had passed causing incalculable losses in education, livelihood, and lives. The politics over public health meant that the people were, for a large part of the initial wave, deprived of a seamless internet— the lifeblood of an immobile but hyperconnected world. The chapter begins with an overview of an overstretched public healthcare system, the troubles faced by health officials in dealing with a novel virus in the midst of an information blackout, and importantly it underlines the critical role that community-based organizations played in organizing medical and other forms of aid. The second section focuses on the communication lockdown that preceded the pandemic lockdown and how it impeded Kashmir's fight against the virus. Restrictions on physical mobility and lack of access to the internet affected every sector from health and education to the economy. It argues that the state's response to any emergency situation in Kashmir is invariably militarized. New Delhi's policies towards Kashmir tend to be shaped by a narrow prism of national security, which explains why it often takes measures that are seemingly imprudent and unwarranted. The third section provides brief snapshots into the losses that Kashmir suffered on account of the two successive lockdowns.

COVID-19 and the Health Infrastructure: An Overview

Unlike a seemingly interminable military lockdown that commenced in August 2019, the COVID-19 lockdown enjoyed a broader legitimacy among the populace. It stemmed, firstly, from the basic survival instincts among the people that an enforced quarantine is for their own good, as it minimizes the exposure to infected people; secondly, from an acute awareness of a crumbling medical infrastructure in Kashmir. Conscious of how the virus had wrecked the lives and economies and overwhelmed the world-class healthcare systems in the developed world, people in Kashmir could foresee that COVID-19 portends a grim future for them. A community-level response system was initiated at many places by forming *mohalla* level committees tasked to enforce lockdown and more importantly assist authorities by informing them about people with travel histories in their areas. Mosque loudspeakers were used to exhort people with COVID-19 like symptoms to get tested at hospitals.

Kashmir, like many other places, is beset with similar challenges posed by the rapidly proliferating virus, but a derelict healthcare system makes the problem more challenging. Hospitals even in normal times are overburdened and unable to provide timely and satisfactory treatment to the patients. An official audit of the healthcare system in 2018 revealed that the existing manpower was "barely sufficient to handle the patient flows and that was pre-pandemic" (Radhakrishnan, 2020). The hospitals have an acute shortage of nursing staff. "Against a requirement of 3,193 nurses ... there are only 1,290 sanctioned posts of staff nurses in the [former] Jammu and Kashmir state with a deficit of 1,903 posts which need to be created" (Aljazeera, 2020). No recruitment has been done in more than 20 years (Tramboo, 2020). Similarly, Kashmir lacks the required number of doctors. The audit found that the doctor-to-patient ratio in the Kashmir region is one of the lowest in India. "Compared to the doctor-patient ratio of 1:2,000 in India, Jammu and Kashmir has one allopathic doctor for 3,866 people against the WHO norm of one doctor for 1,000 population" (Aljazeera, 2020). There are scores of unemployed doctors whose services could have been employed by the government to better prepare for the impending health emergency (Tramboo, 2020).

The initial wave was particularly exacting. As the government persisted with the lockdown, the severity with which it was enforced caused enormous hardships to the people, the migrant labourers in particular. The dire threat to the livelihood of the downtrodden and the risk of mass impoverishment impelled the government to ease some of the curbs to revive the economic activity. Meanwhile, the number of new infections began witnessing a sharp upswing. The total figure of detected cases in Kashmir by the end of 2021 had crossed 300,000. The region is behind on diagnostic testing; therefore, the actual number of infected cases may well be much higher than the official numbers.

The rising cases put an enormous strain on the already under-resourced public hospitals. Doctors have complained of shortages of PPEs (personal protection equipment), even for those directly dealing with COVID-19 cases. According to reports, in April 2020 Kashmir valley with a population of around 8 million had less than 100 ventilators and only 85 intensive care unit (ICU) beds (Wani, 2020). While some months later, several hundred ventilators were allocated to J&K, many were left unused for want of skilled manpower. Similarly, there was an acute shortage of oxygen and an inadequate number of ICU beds (Rashid, 2021). Everyday conversations in Kashmir were filled with anxieties about finding a bed in hospitals for those with symptoms (Sharma, 2021, 142). With cases spiraling and the number of people needing critical care increasing, the situation in Kashmir could have become much worse if not for critical interventions by community-based organizations. Kashmir recorded more cases but witnessed fewer deaths than Jammu. One of the reasons was the role that local organisations, and volunteer groups played. The non-governmental organizations (NGOs) like *Athrout* rushed in with concentrators and mini-ventilators to arrange oxygen for those in need despite the hurdles from an unfriendly administration (Rashid, 2021).

COVID-19 not only led to the loss of many lives, it also kept families from mourning the loss of their loved ones. Kashmiris, like many other societies, have an elaborate set of rituals and practices which are performed to honor the deceased person and console the bereaved. Due to the physical distancing measures, grieving became an isolated experience bereft of any emotional support (Hamid and Jahangir, 2020, 3). Here too, NGOs played an important role in assisting with dignified funeral services. The lockdowns have also aggravated the mental health crisis in the valley. Decades of political turmoil have caused nearly 1.8 million Kashmiris, or about half of all adults, to develop some form of mental disorder, according to a study by Doctors Without Borders in 2015. Due to pandemic-induced social isolation and the communication blackout, the number of patients seeking psychiatric care increased manifold. However, the valley has fewer than 60 psychiatrists and is ill-equipped to deal with the looming psychological crisis (Yasir, 2020).

COVID-19 also caused many indirect deaths and much suffering due to many restrictions and protocols. Many out-patient departments (OPDs) and in-patient departments (IPDs) in government hospitals were closed and turned into COVID-19 sanatoriums. The valley's three major government hospitals Jehlem Valley College (JVC) Bemina, Chest Disease (CD), and JawaharLal Nehru Memorial (JLNM) were exclusively dedicated to COVID-19 patients. In a region where decades of neglect and administrative apathy had left the healthcare system ill-equipped and understaffed, closing off the hospitals severely affected general and emergency patient care and increased the burden on remaining hospitals (Hamid and Jahangir, 2020, 7).

Not only did the administration lag in its preparedness, its actions may well have directly contributed to the spread of the virus. At a time when states around the country were restricting gatherings, the administration actively promoted tourism festivals. Kashmir Tulip Festival in April 2021 attracted thousands of visitors. Tourists visiting Kashmir were subjected to minimal testing and many concealed their travel histories to avoid administrative quarantines. Many attributed the steep rise in the number of detected cases to the government's decision to promote tourism in the midst of a raging pandemic. While successive governments at the state and national levels have harped on tourism as a fulcrum for revitalizing the region's economy, it is an unstated fact that tourism in Kashmir is not an economic but a political project. Tourism contributes less than 7% to J&K's gross domestic product (GDP), yet it occupies a central position in the government's developmental discourses (Rashid, 2021). An increase in the tourist footfall is used as an important metric to declare "normalcy" in Kashmir. Thus, the seemingly imprudent exercise of organizing tourism festivals during a pandemic was perhaps meant to carry a political message that Kashmir post-article 370 was moving towards "better times". Public health takes a backseat in Kashmir where concerns over national security and projecting normalcy are paramount.

The Political Lockdown within the Pandemic Lockdown

On 5 August 2019, the day the Indian Government scrapped Article 370, internet and cellular services were snapped along with other restrictions to limit people's movements. The state's political leadership, including three former chief ministers, were put in jails or kept under house arrest to forestall any protests against New Delhi's decision. Several thousand additional troops were flown in to enforce the lockdown. The severe communication blockade, which lasted for six months, brought life in Kashmir to a standstill. It shattered the economy, wrecked livelihoods, and wrought untold miseries on the people. The valley faced shortages of medicines, and access to hospitals and clinics was impeded by barricades and check-posts. Many people died of treatable illnesses because of a lack of timely medical attention (Yasir and Gettleman, 2019).

As some of the restrictions were being relaxed, like the restoration of 2G internet and removal of barricades, and life was limping back to "normal" a new set of restrictions were imposed in March 2021 to prevent the spread of the virus. The new curbs further exacerbated the precarity of daily life in Kashmir. The people in the valley lived under a complete or partial communication blockade for around nine months. Kashmir had a pre-existing mental health problem which has now been exacerbated due to COVID-19. Across the world, people relied on the Internet to connect with friends and family during the times of self-isolation and social distancing. Virtual mediums allowed people to stay in touch and helped mitigate the adverse effects of quarantines and lockdowns. The importance of technology in assuaging the psychological impact of quarantine was also underlined by medical studies. An article in the medical journal *The Lancet* noted that the internet and particularly "social media could play an important part in communication with those far away, allowing people who are quarantined to update their loved ones about their situation and reassure them that they are well". It argued that those under lockdowns and quarantines be provided "with mobile phones, cords and outlets for charging devices, and robust WiFi networks with internet access to allow them to communicate directly with loved ones could reduce feelings of isolation, stress, and panic" (Brooks et al., 2020, 918). In the absence of high-speed internet, Kashmiris had limited means to connect with their loved ones, to reassure them of their well-being, and seek assurances. It also deprived them of an important medium of entertainment which caused an increase in anxieties and distress and thus compounded the mental health problems of Kashmiris.

Needless to say that modern information communication technologies (ICTs), especially the internet, has become the bedrock of our globalized world. It provides us with a medium of instantaneous data exchanges and a repository of information. The need for a seamless internet as well as our reliance on it was amply demonstrated during the pandemic. Initially as a source of information about a disease we knew little about and later as a medium to work from home as the world shut down and businesses, education, and even health services went online. Yet the Internet is the first casualty whenever the local administration senses a slight possibility for eruption of political unrest. From 2012 to 2019, the internet was shut down 206 times by the authorities. In 2016, mobile internet was suspended for more than four months (Maqbool, 2020).

COVID-19 has posed enormous challenges and different societies have fared differently depending on their resources, health infrastructure, and leadership. While the virus infects indiscriminately and moves irreverently across national boundaries, it can be more pernicious to the underprivileged. Kashmir, with a ramshackle health infrastructure and a society torn by decades long political violence, stands as particularly vulnerable. The Internet lockdown accentuated Kashmir's predicament and derailed its fight against COVID-19 from the very outset. Doctors and other healthcare officials on the COVID-19 frontlines struggled to harness ICTs at a time when little was known about the disease and uncertainties loomed large.

The blockade prevented doctors from accessing guidelines updated regularly by the Indian Council of Medical Research and WHO and from keeping themselves abreast of all the latest information and research on COVID-19. It scuppered existing online initiatives that provided emergency care via social media applications. For instance, the "Save Heart Initiative", a WhatsApp group started by valley-based cardiologists in 2016, "which emerged as a saviour for heart patients in Jammu and Kashmir", came to a halt once internet services were ceased (James, 2020). A similar telemedicine initiative by the Doctors Association Kashmir (DAK), after outpatient departments in major hospitals were shut down, to offer consultations on the phone was also thwarted by the lack of 4G Internet. Telemedicine requires doctors to analyze reports and scans of patients online and consult them through video conferencing—a near impossibility due to the lack of high-speed internet (Ali, 2020). Authorities refused to address their grievances and instead cracked down hard on dissent. Doctors protesting against the dearth of protective gears and lack of 4G Internet were threatened with punishment including six months in prison for speaking publicly about the risky working conditions and shortages of equipment (Khan and Perrigo, 2020).

The pandemic lockdown, like all the lockdowns in the region, was enforced in an excessively militarized way. The State's response to COVID-19 seemed to mesh with its counterinsurgency measures. Roads were barricaded with concertina wires and patrolled by gun wielding policemen and paramilitary men. People were assaulted by security personnel and FIRs registered against them for violating lockdown, there were many instances where health workers, including doctors, were beaten or harassed, overriding Prime Minister Narendra Modi's counsel to his countrymen to treat doctors as soldiers without uniforms (Muzamil and Nabi, 2020; Haziq, 2020). In areas where cases were detected and red zones declared, roads were dug and iron bars were erected to restrict inward and outward movement of people. The garrisoning of roads with semi-permanent structures blocked passages for emergency services.

The social and economic costs are especially grave and hard to ignore. As people around the globe switched on to the online world, with the "work from home" model gaining increasing acceptance in response to lockdowns, the same coping mechanism was virtually impossible in Kashmir because 4G Internet remained cut off (Khan and Perrigo, 2020). Many people who had returned home due to the pandemic could not "work from home" and could not retain their jobs. Education has been hit particularly hard due to continuous lockdowns. Following the August decision, some 13,600 public and private educational institutes remained shut for nearly 6 months confining students and teachers to their homes (Nadaf, 2021). Nearly six months later, as some of the restrictions were being gradually lifted, the whole country entered into a nationwide lockdown in March 2020 as the number of COVID-19 cases continued to rise steeply. Between 2019 and March 2020, schools and colleges in Kashmir functioned for barely 100 days, the bulk of which were pre-August 2019.

Educational institutions around the country switched to remote learning alternatives. Many schools in Kashmir began to offer online classes, however, their efforts were derailed from the outset. While Internet was partially restored in January 2020, the speed was restricted to 2G connectivity and internet access limited to only 301 "white listed" websites with no access to any social media platforms (Nadaf, 2021). It was the longest-ever internet shutdown imposed in a democracy, according to Access Now, an advocacy group that tracks internet suspensions worldwide (Maqbool, 2020). With such low-speeds, video-streaming became near impossible and most students could not connect to the online apps (like Zoom, Google Meet etc.) commonly used to host online lectures (Majid and Kouser, 2020). They found it difficult to attend webinars or submit assignments and small videos uploaded on these applications took hours to download. The teachers had a hard time reaching out to their students.

Research scholars too bore the brunt. In the absence of well-staffed libraries and sparse bookshops, they rely heavily on the internet both as a veritable endless repository of knowledge and as a medium to purchase books at discounted rates from e-commerce platforms like Amazon and Flipkart. Lack of access to the internet cost them months of research work (Yousuf et al., 2020). Kashmiris with an urgent need to access the internet began to undertake a 70-mile journey to reach the nearest bordering town of Banihal in the Jammu region where broadband Internet was readily accessible, once the train services resumed in November 2019. Called the Internet Express, hundreds boarded the traun every day to get online and return the same day (Masih et al., 2019). The internet lockdown accentuated inequalities because the privileged were able to escape to different parts of India whereas those stuck in Kashmir lost time as well as opportunities.

COVID-19 has had a differential impact on societies it has spread in, but the lack of high-speed internet has compounded the problems for nearly every resident of the union territory. Civil society members from within and outside Kashmir have employed different legal and non-legal methods to demand restoration of Internet services. A collective of doctors in India wrote to the Prime Minister on 4G Internet access for Jammu and Kashmir but to no avail (The Wire Staff, 2020). More than 170 academics from around the world have written a letter to the World Health Organization and United Nations (UN) special rapporteurs about the restoration of high-speed internet in Kashmir. Amnesty International has also condemned the continuous suspension of high-speed internet in the region and has asked the Indian authorities to fully restore it (Aljazeera, 2020). The Private Schools Association of Jammu and Kashmir (PSAJK) filed a petition in the Supreme Court arguing that lack of high speed Internet is infringing the fundamental right to education and demanded immediate restoration of the 4G connectivity (Ashiq, 2021).

New Delhi has not relented on its stance on 4G in Kashmir despite protests from several quarters, despite the fact that various court judgements have established that human rights cannot be adequately realized without access to the internet. The United Nations also declared access to the internet a human right in 2016. Ironically, the Supreme Court of India, which in its judgement in Anuradha Bhasin vs Union of India (2020) recognized the freedoms of "speech and expression" and "trade and commerce" through the medium of the internet as a fundamental right, refused to lift the restrictions in the interest of national security (Khandelwal,

2021). The high speed internet remained suspended for 18 months and was finally restored in February 2021. Its continued ban was justified, albeit tenuously, on the assumption that high-speed internet helps terrorists. Although there is no tangible evidence to support this line of reasoning, the Supreme Court too invoked the vaguely defined notion of national security to deprive Kashmiris of access to the internet. The Court's judgments recognised the State's right to impose reasonable restrictions but without scrutinizing the government's claims. It is ironic that even the Jammu and Kashmir High Court, irked at the poor internet connectivity, lamented that, "it has been impossible to have even a bare semblance of a hearing" (Ashiq, 2020).

The high-speed Internet remained suspended for 18 months and was finally restored in February 2021. In this age of hyper-connectivity, Kashmir kept cloistered in the semi-dark information curtain, suffered incalculable losses in education, jobs, and lives. The stringent communication blockade compromised Kashmiris' fight against COVID-19 from the very beginning.

Socio-Economic Costs

Kashmiris under continuous lockdown from August 2019 to the middle of 2020 are reeling under severe economic slump. The political lockdown imposed in the aftermath of Article 370 had already taken its toll before the pandemic lockdown could exacerbate Kashmir's economic woes. Every sector of the economy suffered losses, and those on the lower rungs of society are on the brink of mass pauperization. Industries faced major losses due to the restriction on transport and closure of markets. Internet-based companies either shut off permanently or relocated their base to locations outside Kashmir. Other sectors like carpet and garments industries, which depend on online orders, were hit hard (Dagia, 2020).

The public transport system became dysfunctional and suffered nearly 100% loss in business. There are more than 60,000 commercial transport vehicles in Kashmir, a source of livelihood for over 1 lakh families (Qadir, 2021). Many lost their livelihood and found it increasingly difficult to pay off their loans. According to the Kashmir Chamber of Commerce and Industry (KCCI), the transport and communications sector suffered a loss of Rs. 2,267 crores from August to December 2019. The pandemic lockdown badly affected the fruit industry in Kashmir. Horticulture is the second most important sector of Kashmir's economy. It contributes about 10% to Jammu and Kashmir's economy and involves 700,000 families or 3.5 million people directly or indirectly (Qadir, 2021). Within this sector, the apple industry dominates producing 2.2 million metric tonnes every year, i.e., 70% of the country's total production and worth Rs. 80 billion (Wani, 2021). By March 2020, when the whole country was put under a lockdown, more than three million cartons of apples were lying in cold storage as there was no market (Masoodi, 2020).

J&K has a comparatively small manufacturing sector, it provides employment to around 3.5% of the working population. This sector too has faced very considerable losses due to the double lockdown (Ayoub, 2020). The region depends heavily on agriculture, horticulture, and tourism, and all these industries were adversely affected by the lockdowns. Other important sectors like handicrafts, manufacture, real estate, transport, information technology (IT), and small businesses, including start-ups, and financial services were equally hit and saw a massive drop of 50% in revenue. Tourist seasons have passed without any business. Hoteliers, tour operators, and transporters associated with the industry bore huge losses. According to government figures, by the end of 2019, tourist receipts were down 71%, and 86–90% according to industry reports (The Forum for Human Rights in Jammu and Kashmir, 2020). The severe restrictions on movement and lack of internet caused significant losses to the tourism and handicrafts sector. Officials in the tourism department estimate that Kashmir tourism lost about Rs. 1,168 crore from January 4, 2019 to June 30, 2020 (The Kashmir Walla, 2020). Handicrafts alone, were providing an income to more than 3 lakh artisans, i.e., 7% of the workforce (Ayoub, 2020). The lockdowns resulted in the loss of an estimated 144,500 jobs in the tourism and handicrafts sector (The Forum for Human Rights in Jammu and Kashmir, 2020).

Unemployment is already a major issue in Kashmir due to unabating political unrest and the resultant absence of a thriving private sector. The consecutive lockdowns have worsened the unemployment crisis in Kashmir. In October 2021, Jammu and Kashmir had an unemployment rate of 22.2%, the highest in the country (Akmali, 2021). The KCCI estimates that by December 2019, i.e., within 4 months of the initial lockdown, the state suffered a loss of roughly $2.4 billion, while job losses in the valley were slightly under half a million. By June 2020, the losses were estimated at $5.3 billion (Dagia, 2020). To help rejuvenate the economy after 3 months of COVID-19 lockdown, the Government of India announced a $265 billion stimulus package in May 2021. There was, however, no relief measures or economic assistance to the Jammu and Kashmir industries for the preceding eight months of lockdown (Dagia, 2020). Even the seemingly massive economic package was in reality largely based on debt financing and was thus a highly inadequate response to the financial problems of J&K's businesses and households. As one report observed "businesses in J&K were expecting interest remissions, tax holidays and equity infusion, but all they got was an unwanted EMI deferment, extension in tax payment dates and the promise of more debt" (Ayoub, 2020).

Contrary to the demands of local businessmen for Kashmir-specific incentives to ameliorate the devastating impact of lockdowns, the Union Government used the exceptional circumstances engendered by COVID-19 as an opportunity to introduce or amend a flurry of laws that are likely to exacerbate local grievances. The most controversial among these is the legislation of new domicile laws which stipulate that anyone who had lived in the state for 15 years, or had studied there for 7 years, would be eligible for domicile. Earlier, government jobs were reserved for permanent residents of the erstwhile state and non-local residents were prohibited from buying land in J&K due to the protections provided in article 35A. At a time when unemployment in the region is almost twice the national average and a quarter of its educated young are unemployed, the new domicile rules are bound to make the limited employment opportunities even scarcer (The Forum for Human Rights in Jammu and Kashmir, 2020).

256 Shakhoor Ahmad Wani

Kashmiris fiercely oppose the domicile law and suspect it to be a carefully designed ploy to alter the region's demography. An unprecedented health emergency in the immediate aftermath of the tumultuous post August 5 decision could have been leveraged as an opportunity to bring together different sections of the society and relegate political divisions to the background. An empathetic New Delhi should have immediately lifted the communication blockade, released political prisoners, invested in upgrading healthcare, and introduced an economic package to revive the economy. Instead, it slipped in domicile law in the middle of the pandemic thus widening the mistrust between Kashmir and New Delhi. The fact that the Union Government is engineering such radical changes in the region at a time when J&K does not have its own elected government flies in the face of democratic governance.

Conclusion

COVID-19 moved swiftly and indiscriminately across national boundaries. It infected and killed several million people and derailed economies. Pandemics, as COVID-19 has demonstrated, can be a democratizing experience, in that both the privileged and the poor contracted the virus and lose loved ones. Nevertheless, they do not affect everyone in the same way. They expose and amplify pre-existing inequalities. Countries with advanced and affordable health infrastructure and effective leadership are better placed to mitigate the losses. In the developing world, the impact has been particularly harsh. The under-resourced and understaffed public healthcare systems are overwhelmed, costing innumerable human lives. The indirect impact is more enduring and devastating. It has pushed millions into abject poverty and thus widened inequalities within and across countries.

When the virus first hit Kashmir in March 2020, it was at greater risk than most other places. It suffered from double vulnerability. In August 2019, Kashmir's quasi-autonomous status within the Indian Union was revoked, and a stringent lockdown was imposed. Restrictions on physical mobility and lack of cellular and internet services, which extended for several months, took a heavy toll on the economy, education, and health of its residents. Economic losses ran into several billion dollars, and unemployment rates exploded. As some of the curbs were being relaxed and the internet partially restored at the turn of the new year, a country-wide pandemic lockdown was imposed to break the chain of spiraling infections. Faced with a decrepit public healthcare system and doctors struggling to glean information about the novel disease on the 2G internet, Kashmiris stared into a bleak future. The continuous lockdowns exacerbated the mental health crisis in the valley. However, continued political unrest has also turned Kashmir into a resilient society with strong supportive community structures. Many NGOs, volunteer groups, and local *mohalla* committees stepped up and provided critical medical care and essential non-medical supplies.

The COVID-19 pandemic also demonstrated that New Delhi's response to the crises, be they political or public health emergency, is invariably mediated by a parochial national security framework. The government organized tourism festivals in the middle of the pandemic, which attracted thousands of visitors, to show the return of "normalcy" in the valley. At a time when the Central Government could have provided an economic package to compensate for pre-COVID-19 losses, it was more focused on initiating deep structural changes on the ground. It used the cover of the pandemic to hastily alter the domicile and property law that allows non-local Kashmiris to apply for public-sector jobs and buy land in Kashmir. Thus the already limited employment opportunities will become even scarcer.

New Delhi even refused to lift restrictions on the internet in the middle of the pandemic for many crucial months citing "security of the state and maintenance of public order". The communication blackout hindered the health worker's fight against the virus. People died of treatable illnesses as there was no way to reach doctors. Health infrastructure was already inadequate and moreover major hospitals in the summer capital were designated for only COVID-19 cases making many public hospitals largely inaccessible to non-COVID-19 patients. Telemedicine initiatives by local doctors could not take off for want of high-speed Internet. Education became a serious casualty due to continuous lockdowns and institutions remained largely shut from August 2019 to March 2020. While students in other parts of India quickly switched to remote learning, Kashmiris initially had no such option. Later, when 2G internet was available, they found it difficult to connect to online learning platforms. COVID-19 thus accentuated inequalities both between students from the valley and other states, and within the region, between those privileged enough to shift their base outside Kashmir and the less fortunate who were stuck on the other side of the information curtain.

References

Akmali, Mukeet. 2021. "At 22.2%, J&K Has Highest Unemployment Rate in India." *Greater Kashmir*. November 20, 2021. Accessed January 21, 2022. https://www.greaterkashmir.com/kashmir/at-222-jk-has-highest-unemployment-rate-in-india

Ali, Muddasir. 2020. "Slow Internet Is Speeding the Spread of the Coronavirus in Kashmir." *Foreign Policy*, April 13, 2020. Accessed June 15, 2020. https://foreignpolicy.com/2020/04/13/slow-internet-speeding-spread-coronavirus-kashmir-india-lockdown/

Aljazeera. 2020. "'We'll Die Like Cattle': Kashmiris Fear Coronavirus Outbreak." March 23, 2020. Accessed June 20, 2020. https://www.aljazeera.com/news/2020/03/die-cattle-kashmiris-fear-coronavirus-outbreak-200322151405218.html

Ashiq, Peerzada. 2020. "J&K High Court Summons U.T.'s Home Secretary over 'Poor Internet Connectivity'." *The Hindu*, July 15, 2020. Accessed January 13, 2022. https://www.thehindu.com/news/national/other-states/jk-high-court-summons-uts-home-secretary-over-poor-internet-connectivity/article32088598.ece

Ashiq, Peerzada. 2021. "J&K Private Schools' Body Moves SC for 4G Internet." *The Hindu*, Jan 23, 2021. Accessed Jan 13, 2022. https://www.thehindu.com/news/national/other-states/jk-private-schools-body-moves-sc-for-4g-internet/article33639109.ece

Ayoub, Ejaz. 2020. "With One Lockdown After Another, J&K's Economy Is Shuttered and Shattered." *The Wire*, May 27, 2020. Accessed January 15, 2022. https://thewire.in/economy/with-one-lockdown-after-another-jks-economy-is-shuttered-and-shattered

Brooks, Samantha K. et al. 2020. "The Psychological Impact of Quarantine and How to Reduce It: Rapid Review of the Evidence." *Lancet*, 395(10227): 912–920.

Dagia, Niha. 2020. "Perpetual Silence: Kashmir's Economy Slumps Under Lockdown." *The Diplomat*, August 14, 2020. Accessed January 09, 2022. https://thediplomat.com/2020/08/perpetual-silence-kashmirs-economy-slumps-under-lockdown/

Hamid, Wasia, and M. Saleem Jahangir. 2020. "Dying, Death and Mourning amid COVID-19 Pandemic in Kashmir: A Qualitative Study." *OMEGA–Journal of Death and Dying*, 1–26. Accessed May 10, 2021. https://doi.org/10.1177/0030222820953708

Haziq, Mohammad. 2020. "Kashmir's 'COVID Warriors' Are Under Siege." *The Diplomat*, June 15, 2020. Accessed January 25, 2022. https://thediplomat.com/2020/06/kashmirs-covid-warriors-are-under-siege/

James, Nandana. 2020. "In Kashmir, It's a Different Lockdown Amid the Coronavirus Pandemic." *The Hindu BusinessLine*, May 10, 2020. Accessed February 10, 2022. https://www.thehindubusinessline.com/news/variety/in-kashmir-its-a-different-lockdown-amid-the-coronavirus-pandemic/article31552461.ece

Khan, Ahmer and Billy Perrigo. 2020. "What Life Is Like Inside the World's Longest Lockdown." *Time*, May 5, 2020. Accessed June 27, 2020. https://time.com/5832256/kashmir-lockdown-coronavirus/

Khandelwal, Kashish. 2021. "Covid-19 and the Year-long Internet Restrictions in Jammu & Kashmir," *South Asia @ LSE*, May 10, 2021. Accessed January 12, 2022. https://blogs.lse.ac.uk/southasia/2021/05/10/covid-19-and-the-year-long-internet-restrictions-in-jammu-kashmir/

Majid, Ishfaq and Shazia Kouser. 2020. "As Life Moves Online Amid the Pandemic, Kashmiri Education Is Being Left Behind." *The Diplomat*, June 16, 2020. Accessed July 6, 2020. https://thediplomat.com/2020/06/as-life-moves-online-amid-the-pandemic-kashmiri-education-is-being-left-behind/

Maqbool, Majid. 2020. "I'm a Journalist Who Lived Through Kashmir's Traumatic Internet Blackout, which Started One Year Ago." *Business Insider*, Aug 5, 2020. Accessed January 05, 2022. https://www.businessinsider.com/india-kashmir-internet-blackout-anniversary-i-lived-through-it-2020-8?IR=T

Masih, Niha et al. 2019. "India's Internet Shutdown in Kashmir Is the Longest Ever in a Democracy." *The Washington Post*, December 16, 2019. Accessed January 12, 2022. https://www.washingtonpost.com/world/asia_pacific/indias-internet-shutdown-in-kashmir-is-now-the-longest-ever-in-a-democracy/2019/12/15/bb0693ea-1dfc-11ea-977a-15a6710ed6da_story.html

Masoodi, Nazir. 2020. "Amid Lockdown, 3 Million Cartons of Apples Lying In Kashmir Cold Storage." *NDTV*, April 27, 2020. Accessed January 23, 2022. https://www.ndtv.com/india-news/coronavirus-amid-lockdown-3-million-cartons-of-apples-lying-in-kashmir-cold-storage-2219068

Muzamil, Peerzada S. and Wasim Nabi. 2020. "'Third World Region of a Third World Country': How Kashmir Struggles With the Coronavirus." *The Wire*, April 4, 2020. Accessed June 24, 2020. https://thewire.in/rights/kashmir-coronavirus-covid-19-internet

Nadaf, Arif H. 2021. "'Lockdown Within a Lockdown': The 'Digital Redlining' and Paralyzed Online Teaching During COVID-19 in Kashmir, A Conflict Territory." *Communication, Culture and Critique*, 14: 343–346.

Qadir, Gafira. 2021. "'Economy on Deathbed': The Great Depression in Kashmir." *The Kashmir Walla*, May 10, 2021. Accessed January 23, 2022. https://thekashmirwalla.com/economy-on-deathbed-the-great-depression-in-kashmir/

Radhakrishnan, Adi. 2020. "COVID-19: Restricted Internet Impacts on Health in Kashmir." *Health and Human Rights Journal*, April 15, 2020. Accessed Feb 10, 2022. https://www.hhrjournal.org/2020/04/covid-19-restricted-internet-impacts-on-health-in-kashmir/

Rashid, Adil. 2021. "Kashmir's Ill-Equipped Health System and Government's Push for Tourism Led to a COVID Crisis." *The Caravan*, May 31, 2021. Accessed January

21, 2022. https://caravanmagazine.in/health/kashmirs-ill-equipped-health-system-and
-indias-push-for-tourism-led-to-a-covid-crisis

Sharma, Sarbani. 2021. "Redefining Public Health and Life in Occupation? COVID-19
Pandemic in Kashmir." *Society and Culture in South Asia*, 7(1): 141–147.

The Forum for Human Rights in Jammu and Kashmir. 2020. "Jammu and Kashmir: The
Impact of Lockdowns on Human Rights." August 2019 to July 2020 Report. Accessed
January 15, 2022. https://kashmirscholars.files.wordpress.com/2020/07/jammu-and
-kashmir-impact-of-lockdown-on-human-rights-report-july-23-2020.pdf

The Kashmir Walla. 2020. "J-K Tourism Industry lost 1168 Crore Rupees to art-370, COVID-
19 Lockdowns." August 26, 2020. Accessed January 15, 2022. https://thekashmirwalla
.com/j-k-tourism-industry-lost-1168-crore-rupees-to-art-370-covid-19-lockdowns/

The Wire Staff. 2020. "Doctors Write Open Letter to PM Modi on 4G Access for Jammu and
Kashmir." *The Wire*, March 26, 2020. Accessed June 27, 2020. https://thewire.in/rights/
doctors-write-open-letter-to-pm-modi-on-4g-access-for-jammu-and-kashmir

Tramboo, Irfan. 2020. "How Kashmir Is fighting the Covid-19 Pandemic." *Livemint*, April
17, 2020. Accessed July 4, 2020. https://www.livemint.com/mint-lounge/features/how
-kashmir-is-fighting-the-covid-19-pandemic-11587100054912.html

Wani, Ayjaz. 2021. "Perspectives on the 'New Normal' in Kashmir." *ORF*, March 16 2021.
Accessed January 23, 2022. https://www.orfonline.org/research/perspectives-on-the
-new-normal-in-kashmir/#_ednref39

Wani, Riyaz. 2020. "COVID-19 and the Interplay of Disease and Conflict in Kashmir."
Stimson Center, May 3, 2020. Accessed January 7, 2022, https://www.stimson.org/2020
/covid-19-and-the- interplay-of-disease-and-conflict-in-kashmir/

Yasir, Sameer. 2020. "Kashmir, Under Siege and Lockdown, Faces a Mental Health Crisis."
The New York Times, April 26, 2020. Accessed January 11, 2022. https://www.nytimes
.com/2020/04/26/world/asia/kasmir-india-mental-health-coronavirus.html

Yasir, Sameer & Gettleman, Jeffrey. 2019. "In Kashmir, a Race Against Death, With No
Way to Call a Doctor." *The New York Times*, October 7, 2019. Accessed January 13,
2022.https://www.nytimes.com/2019/10/07/world/asia/kashmir-doctors-phone.html

Yousuf et al. 2020. "'I See My Dreams Vanishing': Kashmiri Researchers During the
Internet Blockade." *The Caravan*, April 5, 2020. Accessed January 15, 2022. https://
caravanmagazine.in/education/i-see-my-dreams-vanishing-kashmiri-researchers-about
-the-internet-blockade

17 Conducting Bihar Assembly Elections 2020 during the COVID-19 Pandemic

Jeetendra Kumar

Introduction

Bihar is a state in eastern India with the third highest population among India's states, with over 104 million residents according to the 2011 census. It was the sole Indian state to hold full-fledged elections during the Covid-19 pandemic in 2020, with 243 lawmakers to be elected by 72.9 million registered voters (Economic Times/PTI 2020a). Bihar's assembly elections at the time COVID-19 was a major electoral test for the incumbent and the present Chief Minister Nitish Kumar-led National Democratic Alliance (NDA) and the opposition parties. The NDA comprised of the Bharatiya Janata Party (BJP), Janata Dal (United) (JD(U)), Vikassheel Insaan Party (VIP), and Hindustani Awam Morcha (HAM) (Secular) while the opposition, under the umbrella of Mahagathbandhan (major-coalition), had the Rashtriya Janata Dal (RJD), Indian National Congress (INC), Communist Party of India, Communist Party of India (Marxist), and Communist Party of India (Marxist- Leninist). Rashtriya Lok Samta Party (RLSP). All India Majlis-e-Ittehad-ul-Muslimeen (AIMIM) fought independently. Interestingly, the Lok Janshakti Party (LJP) put up its candidates against the JD(U) but not on the seats contested by the BJP.

More than the political parties, the state assembly elections were a big challenge for the Election Commission (EC) of India that had to conduct the first full-fledged elections with all precautionary measures so that the virus did not spread further. This chapteranalyses the condition of the COVID-19 pandemic at the time of the assembly elections and debates around the conduct of assembly elections among political parties. The significant part of this chapter focuses on the EC and its operationalization of guidelines pertaining to pandemics and management of Bihar's assembly elections. The last section looks into the outcome in terms of its success and various resultant challenges.

COVID-19 and Initial Debates on Bihar Assembly Elections

Like other parts of India, COVID-19 has severely affected Bihar, which does not have good public health infrastructure. The state spends only about 4.1% of its total budget dedicated to health (Gupta 2020). The NITI Ayog health indices saw

DOI: 10.4324/9781003304517-22

decline in Bihar from 22 to 28 out of the total 28 states between the years 2017–18 and 2019–20 (Sen 2020). Fortunately, the weak health infrastructure had to deal with a low number of COVID-19 patients, as the number did not spike as high as in some other big Indian states. The number of virus-affected people in Bihar was 2.19 lakh with 1,113 deaths and 2.11 lakh recovered as of November 4, 2020. There were questions about the number of tests carried out. It is estimated that only about 1.14 crores out of the 12.3 crore residents of the population in Bihar were tested (Jeelani 2020). There was not even an adequate number of testing kits to test the people (Singh 2020). Besides, COVID-19 also caused a loss of jobs and a tough situation in the cities due to a lack of money and inadequate savings. COVID-19 and the lockdown in Bihar have had a significant impact on people's economic activity and employment. According to the Centre for Monitoring Indian Economy (CMIE), Bihar's unemployment rate was 46.6% in April 2020 (or 20 percentage points above the national rate) (Singh 2020, March 31).

To control the spread of COVID-19, the Union government of India imposed a nation-wide lockdown on March 25, 2020. This halted all economic activities except those that come under the category of "essential services". As a result, many of the Bihari migrants working in other states of India lost their jobs and were forced by the pandemic situation to return to their homes. According to an estimate, the number of intra-state and inter-state migrants in Bihar before the outbreak of the pandemic was about one crore. Out of that, more than 30 lakh migrated to other states of India for work (Pushpendra & Singh 2020). The outbreak of COVID-19 and related crisis situations forced somewhere between 25 lakh and 30 lakh of the inter-state migrants to return to Bihar (Mehrotra & Roy 2020). Many migrant workers evaded the screening at the state's border transit camps. It was tough to persuade them to stay in quarantine for 14 days. There have also been numerous reports of missing migrants from the quarantine center (Tewary 2020). Some returnee migrants have encountered social ostracism as a result of COVID-19. Posters with the words "Outsiders are not allowed" welcomed those coming home in some villages and towns, causing tensions among the locals (Agrawal 2020). Due to a lack of testing kits, many of these returnee migrants were not tested for the virus at first. For example, more than 4,000 people returned to the Gulf countries in particular (Singh 2020, March 31).

In such a global health emergency, assembly elections were difficult to even imagine. Most of the state's political parties were not in favor of conducting elections at the time of the pandemic, mainly due to campaign-related limitations. The major opposition party of the state, RJD, and partly a part of the NDA, LJP, were in favour of deferring the elections until the pandemic subsided (Chopra 2020). The RJD's reluctance to defer the election was seen as an endeavor by the party to take the moral high ground, projecting itself as the well-wisher of the common people and demonstrating its concern for the health of the common man amidst the pandemic (Kumar 2020). Such a stance was undertaken by several contesting parties, including LJP. However, on the contrary, the BJP and JD(U) wanted elections to be held on time (Chaurasia 2020). They had started the virtual rallies far before the formal announcement of the election was made by the EC. The incumbent wanted to cash in on political gains by showing the voters how "successfully" they were managing the pandemic. They also thought that any delay in holding assembly elections could anger people (Kumar 2020) further due to what many be seen as "gross mismanagement of COVID-19" situation by the state government, and the outcome may be against the incumbent.

As COVID-19 forces people to maintain social distancing to restrict the virus from spreading, the conventional style of mass rallies, door-to-door canvassing, use of banners, pasting posters, and distributing leaflets had to shift to a digital form of campaigning. In the highly digitally unequal Bihar, virtual campaigning was seen as disadvantageous for many parties such as the Congress, Communist Party of India (CPI) and Communist Party of India (Marxist) who were then in favor of limited door-to-door campaigning. However, the digitally active parties such as the BJP had supported and became highly active in virtual campaigning since it was decided that the assembly elections would be held on time. The BJP also suggested that the expenditure limit for a candidate should be increased to meet added election expenses arising out of COVID-19 guidelines for election. As per prevailing ECI laws, the electoral expense per candidate was limited to 28 lakh in assembly election (Times of India 2020). Even ballot-paper based election rather than through EVMs were favored by the Congress and the RJD as multiples uses of buttons would carry the risk of contamination and perpetuate the spread of the corona infection (The Wire 2020).

Taking into account of the COVID-19 situation in Bihar and to let the new assembly constituted before November 29, 2020, the last day of the then assembly, the EC decided to hold elections with health related precautionary measures. In the past, there had been times when elections had been postponed. One such instance was postponement of the then ongoing parliamentary elections for three weeks in 1991, after the assassination of the then-Prime Minister and leader of the Congress party, Rajiv Gandhi, in Tamil Nadu (Chopra 2020). In normal circumstances, the elections to the assembly or parliament have to be held within six months of their dissolution.

Management of Elections and the Election Commission: Initiatives and Operationalisation

Given the pandemic situation, globally between February 21 and December 27 2020, 79 countries successfully conducted elections and a referendum. On the other hand, in the same period at least 75 countries and territories decided to postpone elections and referendums (IDEA 2020). The challenge in India was to conduct the electoral process that runs into several phases: first, the pre-election period encompasses training, information, and voter registration; second, the electoral period comprises filing nominations, scrutiny, campaigns, voting, and the announcement of results, and third, including review, reform, and strategies (Landman & Splendore 2020: 1062). Majorly, these responsibilities are performed under Article 324 of the Indian Constitution by the EC, who is empowered with the power of "superintendence, direction, and control of the entire process for conduct of elections to Parliament and Legislature (state legislative assembly & state legislative council) of every State…" (Government of India 2007, 197).

Discussion to conduct the assembly election in Bihar began in May 2020, incorporating the global experience of conducting elections successfully at the time of COVID-19 (Phadnis 2020). The EC had to conduct safe and inclusive elections. "No Voter is left behind" was the hallmark of the election in Bihar.

After internal discussions, the Chief Election Commissioner (CEC) started the consultation process with the political parties on July 17, 2020. The CEC asked for suggestions from the political parties on the elections. Before the Bihar assembly elections, elections for some of the seats for the upper house of the Indian parliament Rajya Sabha and the state legislative council were conducted by the EC. Unlike the Rajya Sabha and legislative assembly, the Bihar assembly elections were a full-fledged election to be conducted across the state during the COVID-19 pandemic.

The EC, after deliberations and suggestions from the political parties, with many political parties still making a case to postpone assembly elections, announced on September 25, 2020 that elections for all 243 seats in Bihar would be held in October–November. The 2020, assembly elections were to be held in three phases, unlike the 2015 assembly elections that were carried out in five phases. In the first phase, nomination was to begin with the date of issue of notification on October 1, 2020, and voting was to be held on October 28, 2020, for 71 assembly constituencies. In the second phase, nomination was to commence with the date of notification on October 9, 2020, and voting for this phase was fixed on November 3, 2020, for 94 assembly constituencies. The last phase had 78 assembly seats for polling, nomination for which began on October 13, 2020, and the electorate exercised their franchise on November 7, 2020. The counting of votes was fixed on November 10, 2020 (Election Commission of India 2020a). Shaping the way for the smooth conduct of elections required proper and effective implementation of the general guidelines issued by the Election Commission on August 21, 2020, and subsequent guidelines encompassing each stage of the election covering every personnel involved in the electoral process (Election Commission of India 2020b). The conduct of the electoral process amid pandemics needs greater analysis reflecting its efficacy and challenges.

Nominations for Assembly Elections

To avoid physical contact, there was an option of an online platform for the Chief Electoral Officer (CEO) or District Election Officers (DEO) to file the nomination by the candidate and submit security deposits as well as an affidavit and its printed form for submission to the returning officer for scrutiny of nominations along with other guidelines (Election Commission of India 2020b, 2–3). Unlike past assembly elections marked by a large number of supporters and slogan shouting during the filing of nomination, the limit of only two persons to accompany the candidate during the filing of nomination was allowed and only two vehicles to avoid large crowds were under the guidelines. Arrangements of spacious places for such a nomination as well as the allocation of staggered time slots by the returning officer for prospective candidates were provided under the guidelines (Election

Commission of India 2020b, 2–3). The online option of filing the nomination, security deposits, and affidavits was in place to minimize direct contact but were not mandatory in nature (Election Commission of India 2020b, 2–3). This was the first time that a candidate had the option to submit their security deposits online. However, the online alternate for the candidates was "scantly used because of lack of the candidate's proficiency to avail this option as well nomination and its submission offline crates mobilization as well connect with people to win an election" (a Block Development Officer (BDO) involved in the election process told Jeetendra). Another official engaged in the election process, on condition of anonymity, said that "the candidates had come with both filled online nomination form as well as offline nomination forms ready and some of them also used the online mode for security deposit".

On implementation of the COVID-19 rules, a Sub-Divisional Magistrate (SDM) on the condition of anonymity, said "the Standard operating procedure (SOPs) of nomination were largely followed by majority of the candidates contesting elections, as during election process, the electoral body, with local bureaucrats on the ground was powerful in implementation of COVID-19 related guidelines". Several arrangements were in place for ensuring a safe nomination process, i.e., installing barricades, adequate security to disallow more than the stipulated number of two persons for the submission of the nomination form, following sanitization norms, and wearing masks, were followed in the initial phase of filing nominations, were seen as unusual in comparison to elections in normal times. From the perspective of the personnel involved in the electoral process, "they confirmed that basic sanitization and wearing mask norms were on the ground much before the actual rolling of electoral process, thus, it continued during the elections also" (confirmed by the SDM).

Campaign for Assembly Elections

The pandemic would test-whether prominence of digital platforms and social media platforms would prevail in the election or if physical rallies to connect directly to people would be the reality, or if both would co-exist. Milan Vaishanav (2020) says that political campaigns since 2014 have marked a shift, making way for digital campaigning, micro-targeting, and online mobilization with use of a range of platforms like Facebook, Twitter/X, and WhatsApp. Vaishanav opines that the use of these would be further reinforced with the advent of the pandemic, but simultaneously signifies the vitality of physical connection with people (Vaishanav 2020). Campaigns began after the EC cleared up any uncertainty about the possibility of holding assembly elections in Bihar. However, the NDA alliance prominently comprised of BJP and JD(U) began a virtual campaign six months before the dates were decided. The BJP hired 10,000 people working as office bearers in the IT department of the party and dedicated5 people at each polling booth having to have smartphones amounting to a total 4 lakh working directly with the national IT team of the party (Ananthanarayanan 2020). Spreading its virtual wings, the BJP appointed head cells at each *Shakti Kendra*[1] and created more than 50,000 WhatsApp groups aimed to cover all booths in Bihar. Shah's virtual rally was also televised through live-streaming on LED television sets in 72,000 booths across the state (Shanker 2020). Addressing the first virtual rally in Bihar on June 7, 2020, the Union Home Minister and BJP leader, Amit Shah, highlighted the achievements of the Nitish Kumar-led government in the last 15 years (Businesstoday.in, 2020). Praising Nitish Kumar's administration, Shah said, "Bihar has moved from *jungle raj* (anarchy) to *janta raj* (democracy) under the NDA" (Katiyar 2020). The major opposition party led by the RJD, hit the ground with its physical rallies, and the same day organized a state-wide protest against the Nitish Kumar government and declared it "*Garib Adhikar Divas*" (Poor Rights Day)(Katiyar 2020).

Like the BJP, its partner, JD(U) had also started organizing virtual rallies. In the month of May 2020, it plunged into strengthening its social media platform with the assistance of some students from the prestigious Indian Institute of Technology (IIT), who returned to the state in the midst of the pandemic (Ananthanarayanan 2020).

On the other hand, opposition parties lacked both resources and manpower to hold virtual rallies and demanded the postponement of elections until the pandemic subsided (Mishra 2020). An RJD Member of the Legislative Assembly, who wished to remain anonymous, said, "We do not have the resources and even workers to enable Tejashwi Yadav to address a large number of party workers. It is an uneven battle" (Mishra 2020). Some of the opposition leaders including Tejashwi Yadav were active on Twitter/X and shared videos on the social media platform, Largely lacking the resource in virtual campaigns, Professor Sanjay Kumar of the Centre for the Study of Developing Societies (CSDS) regarded the burgeoning role of social media to significantly benefit national parties— especially both the BJP and Congress compared to the regional parties (Prakash 2020). On the other side, Vaishanav (2020) regards that few Indian politicians gain their significance from the "street power". For instance, RJD in Bihar, AAP in Delhi and Shiv Sena in Maharashtra.

Among these contestations around advantage and limitations of digital platforms in the state and for parties, the EC guidelines called for limited door-to-door campaigns with five persons, and the performance of road-shows with a convoy of five vehicles followed by the next convoy. Besides, the public meetings in large grounds maintaining social distancing were to be observed and Chief Election Officers in states were to supervise these meetins in every constituency. Sanitizers, soap, and water needed to be available at every gate leading to the grounds (Phadnis 2020).

What was seen regarding the campaign, it began in the state, largely began with a virtual platform, but soon it saw an increase in physical rallies. Contrary to the guidelines, the campaigns saw a contravention of the SOPs, with rallies of top leaders including Nitish Kumar and the grand alliance's chief ministerial candidate Tejashwi Yadav without face masks (Supraja 2020). According to the Chief Electoral Officer (CEO) of Bihar, 156 cases were registered against the "organisers" of rallies and meetings of various leaders and candidates for violating COVID-19 guidelines (PTI 2020).

People pushing during massive election rallies crowded with people, mostly unmasked, could be seen in many cases. Social distancing protocols in electoral rallies were impractical and hard to follow. Besides campaigns by major leaders, interactions with officials who wished to remain anonymous revealed that "several constituencies saw limited number of rallies and grounds identified for rallies were scarcely used by the candidates because of the fear of the virus".

The Election Day

Before the elections dates were announced, Bihar's Chief Electoral Officer (CEO), H.R. Srinivas, said, "Our job is to prepare for elections assuming they would be held in time. The final decision rests with the ECI" (Singh 2020 13 July). Besides, the CEO also confirmed that the electronic voting machines and voter-verified paper audit trail (VVPAT) had reached all the districts and the training of returning officers was conducted several rounds in advance. Around 5.3 lakh election officials were given special training in the wake of the pandemic. Coordination among the state machinery, police forces, and all poll personnel was vital to implement and conduct the election while maintaining COVID-19 protocols (Rajesh Kumar 2020).

To manage polling stations, the Election Commission's (EC) circular had directed to limit the number of electors to 1,000 voters in each polling station, reduced from 1,500, and therefore created additional auxiliary polling stations. There was a jump in the numbers of the polling stations from 72,723 to 106, 515, a quantum jump of 46.48% (CEO Bihar 2020). The voting timing was extended by an hour. Nevertheless, most of the polling stations, mostly located in schools, lacked the capacity to accommodate even 1,000 people with satisfactory social distancing.

Inclusivity of the electorate in pandemics was ensured through EC's SVEEP (Systematic Voter Education for Electoral Participation) program. In Bihar, SVEEP was employed to create COVID-19 related awareness for the safe conduct of the election, use of EVMs, and to increase voter's registration and participation. Posters, songs, audio messages, and dozens of video messages were used to create awareness of both voting and the pandemic. The EC machinery undertook electoral rolls revision and special initiative to enrolll returnee migrants during the pandemic in the state. Thus, more than 2.3 lakh such eligible citizens got enrolled through this effort (Election Commission of India 2020b, 3–4). The EC also extended the scope of postal ballot for vulnerable sections of the population, including senior citizens over the age of 80, COVID-19-positive patients, persons with disabilities, and voters employed in essential services (Indian Express 2020a).

The EC guidelines also catered to the requirements of all personnel involved in election-related activity. Mandatory use of masks, thermal scanning of all persons, provision of sanitizer and soap, use of large halls for social distancing, and periodic sanitization of EVMs as well as voting premises were essential. The EC ordered that polling materials, banners, posters, etc., needed to be stored in large well-ventilated halls. Para-health or Accredited Social Health Activist (ASHA) workers were to be employed to carry out thermal scanning of voters, and sanitization was to be done regularly throughout the polling exercise (Election Commission of India 2020b, 4–5).

For safety of polling staff and security personnel, 18 lakh face shields, 70 lakh face masks, and 5.4 lakh single-use rubber gloves were procured (PTI 2020). To use EVMs safely, 7.21 crore "one hand" single use polythene gloves were made available. The EC ensured that this waste reached public health centers to be recycled (PTI 2020). Ensuring these requirements are in place, the Bihar administration, especially the Health Departmen,t played a significant role in ensuring health and safety protocols remained in place in the conduct of the election. The training of approximately 10 lakh ASHA workers and *Jeevika didis* (members of self-help groups (SHGs)) was provided. They assisted in packaging the procured items into kits (masks, face shields, etc.) at the nodal centers in Patna, Muzaffarpur, and Purnia. Further, these kits were delivered to district magistrates and superintendents of police for booth-wise distribution. Auxiliary nurse midwives (ANMs), paramedics, and ASHA workers were trained to conduct thermal scanning at polling stations. Bags and bins were provided at each polling station for collection of waste to be delivered to the nearest health facility center (PTI 2021).

Counting of Votes

After the elections were held, to count the votes only seven tables in each hall were allowed to be used to avoid overcrowding. Proper sanitization of the strong room as well as cases of control units (CUs) or voter-verified paper audit trail (VVPAT) were done to contain the spread of Corona virus. The counting center was to be disinfected at regular intervals (Election Commission of India 2020b, 7–8). An official, who wished to remain anonymous, revealed that these norms of sanitization were indeed taking place.

The counting for the assembly elections saw a delay compared to past elections, as the number of polling stations was increased by 46% percent, there was an increased number of EVMs at these polling stations, as well as a reduced number of counting tables for each constituency. Even the number of postal ballots increased due to the inclusion of a section of electorate taking into account that a pandemic may lead to delay in the whole counting process, unusual of the previous elections. To counter the fear of the electorate as well as contesting candidates, the EC held four press conferences to clarify several issues of delay in counting, complaints of the irregularities in counting, as well as rejection of postal ballots in cases of a close margin of winnability of the candidates.

Outcome and Challenges

With all the above-mentioned arrangements, the EC eventually managed to conduct safe and fair assembly elections in Bihar. Mr. Sunil Arora, Chief Election Commissioner, at the conclusion of the poll said,

> We were able to conduct a Covid-safe election, with a voter turnout of 57.34 per cent, which was higher than in 2015…The Bihar election was not only a priority for us but a necessity of our electoral democracy. We had to build

confidence among the voters that the polling station would be a place safe for them to come and vote.

(National Herald/PTI December 2020).

Dr. S. Y. Quraishi, a former Chief Election Commissioner, admired the work of the ECI and said, "At a time when all countries of the world are looking at each other for lessons, Bihar could provide a leading example of successful election manage-ment, and the ECI a leading electoral management body" (Quraishi 2020).

The results saw the NDA returning to power with 125 seats while the Mahagathbandhan won 110 seats. According to the Lokniti-CSDS post- poll sur-vey 2020, the Bihar elections were closely contested in recent times where the NDA had a slim majority of 37.3% votes while the Mahagathbandhan captured 37.2% of total polled votes (Sardesai 2020). Individually, the BJP had 74 Assembly seats in its account and its ally JD(U) won just 43 seats. Other allies of the NDA, Vikassheel Insaan Party (VIP), and Hindustani Awam Morcha (Secular), won 4 seats each. The RJD won 75 seats, the Congress won 19 seats, CPI-ML won 12 seats, and CPI-M and CPI won 2 seats each.

Largely, the verdict was reflective of issues raised during elections campaign, among them, development had been a consistent issue for voters in the 2015 assembly election where 31% regarded it as important, whereas the CSDS post-poll survey 2020 reports that 36% of the voters had it in the mind while voting. The issue of unemployment had created a lot of heat during the campaign with the promise of 10 lakh jobs for voters by Tejaswi Yadav and similar proposals made by the BJP that promised to create 19 lakh jobs. The issue of unemployment remained a significant issue for 20% of the electorate as per CSDS post-poll survey 2020. This shows a considerable jump when compared with 2015 post-poll findings that pegged it at just 9% of voters. Political leaders also raised the issue of management of COVID-19 in the state. Tejashwi Yadav, during the early phases of campaign-ing, raised the mismanagement of the pandemic by the state government. He also accused the state government of being insensitive towards the migrant workers that returned to Bihar. The BJP promised free coronavirus vaccines to people of Bihar if voted to power. Contrary to the leaders, the CSDS post-poll survey shows that largely coronavirus/lockdown/migrant crisis did not have substantial impact on the voting behavior of people as only 0.1% of voters considered it an important issue (Lokniti 2020: 2–3; Lokniti 2020a, 3). Thus, development and unemploy-ment remained primary issues of concern in the election with scant attention to issue of coronavirus as well as the migrant crisis.

The end of the election process required introspection on the part of the EC machinery. Global experiences of elections during COVID-19 put forth challenges, as James and Alihodzic (2020) identify that threats to deliberation marked with limited political meetings deny electorate engagement with candidates and vice versa in such elections. These elections also offered the incumbent advantage over newcomer candidates, as evident from elections in South Korea, New Zealand, and Poland, thus flouting the principle of equality for the contesting candidates. The pandemic requires additional funding to run safe and accessible elections, for instances, provision of appropriate personal protective equipment (PPE) and hand sanitizer for voters and election workers. Therefore, it runs the risk of overburdening the elections, as a study on the cost of running 8 elections during COVID-19, based on publicly stated estimates, found increased costs of between $0.37 and $7.84 per voter (Cousins 2020, 2–3). These challenges are also reflect in some of the apprehensions in the Bihar case.

In Bihar, in many cases, the shift to virtual rallies and massive election rallies was held by both sides, NDA and Mahagathbandhan, packed with crowds, mostly unmasked. These crowds were a reflection of the prevailing overall attitude towards COVID-19 in the state. The EC seems to be partly complicit with the impracticality of social distancing in electoral rallies (Hasin 2020). In the pandemic, the campaign was characterized by the use of social media and electronic means by the political parties. However, as reflected in Jeetendra Kumar's survey, a sizeable population, approximately 25% of the state, was unaware of these platforms. Kantar Indian Market Research Bureau (IMRB), a marketing agency, in its ICUBE report 2018, earmarked the state for showing the highest growth in new internet users both in urban as well as rural areas. At the same time, the Internet and Mobile Association of India (IAMAI)-Nielsen report on "Digital in India 2019" pegs the state's Internet use at 37% (IAMAI-Nielsen 2019). These data reveal that the state lacks digital infrastructure as well as capacity compared with several other Indian states, posing challenge in connecting the electorate and the politicians on a large scale virtually while the pandemic persists.

Moreover, the insurmountable task for the EC to micromanage the use or misuse of platforms including WhatsApp, Facebook, YouTube, Zoom, and Google for campaigning (Ranjan and Kumar, 2020) continued to remain a challenge for future elections, giving advantage to the resourceful party with a large organisation to maintain an IT cell and depriving smaller, as well as regional, parties, of the opportunity to compete fairly in the electoral process. A step in this direction undertaken by the EC, moved to increase the expenditure limit to cover expenditure on the digital platform and other COVID-19-related health requirements, besides traditional expenses in a usual election, i.e., expense of public meetings, rallies, and advertisements by the candidate. For the pandemic, the EC enhanced the election expenditure for each candidate in the assembly election in Bihar from 28 lakh to 30.8 lakh (The Economic Times, 2020). This was some relief for the candidates.

Landman and Splendore (2020) in their work, *Pandemic Democracy: Elections and COVID-19*, argued that pandemics could prove to be a disincentive for the electorate to cast their votes, affecting overall turnout. This turnout remains vital to provide "the legitimacy of an election providing electoral mandates to leaders, and as a barometer for the health of democracy in general" (Landman & Splendore 2020, 1062). In the state, apprehension hovered in the early days of elections as people felt uneasy about going to polling booths given the upsurge of COVID-19 infections in the state (Ranjan & Kumar 2020, 8). This implied that it might affect the voting percentage and inclusivity of the election. Such apprehension was put aside as the election process got underway. The EC data mirrors that despite the pandemic, voter turnout was remarkable at 57.05% in the 2020 assembly elections, marginally higher by 0.39% than 56.66% in the 2015 assembly election (CEO Bihar 2020). However the female turnout in the assembly election 2020 saw a minuscule dip compared to the previous 2015 assembly election in the state as well as the 2019 general election, still, it was 59.69%, higher than the male turnout at 54.68% (CEO Bihar 2020). Thus, the assembly did not see any substantial drop in the percentage of the electoral turnout despite the pandemic. On the other side, the Lokniti-CSDS Bihar post-poll survey 2020 attributes electorate staying out of the station and feeling unwell as a major reason for not casting a vote. Fear of coronavirus was also a valid reason for 7% of the respondents; this is the third important rationale behind not turning up for voting. Thus, the normal election could have seen a further surge in electoral turnout.

The counting process in the elections raised concern over the discrepancies in the winners' lists. There was doubt and rumor in ten constituencies in which results were delayed, though assurance of its investigation came from the EC. The delay was caused due to recounting of the postal ballots and retabulation of the totals shown by each EVM as the margin of victory was very close. The rejection of postal ballots gives much scope for suspicion (Quraishi 2020). Politically, such suspicions were raised by Tejashwi Yadav, who addressed his first conference after the announcement of results and raised suspicion over 20 Mahagathbandhan candidates that lost by a slim margin and threatened to move to court if their concerns were not addressed. He called for recounting of postal ballots in these constituencies and provided details of valid and invalid votes. Tejashwi said:

> We firmly believe that we [the Mahagathbandhan] won not 110 but 130 seats. The ECI did not abide by its own rule on counting the postal ballots first … We also wonder how 500 to 700 to 900 postal ballots were declared invalid. The ECI has to satisfy queries of our candidates or else we will move court.
>
> (Venkitesh 2020)

Another major challenge was the cleaning of nearly 160 tonnes of biomedical waste in the form of gloves, face masks, and empty sanitizer bottles used by polling personnel and voters that was generated during the Bihar assembly polls held amid the COVID-19 pandemic (PTI 2020). Such accumulations are a threat to bio waste that needs effective recycling for public health. Thus, pandemics with their outcomes present several challenges to electoral democracy.

Conclusion

The conduct of assembly elections 2020 in the wake of the pandemic was thought unfeasible by many at the outset in Bihar. Certain political parties were averse to conducting the election given Bihar's electorate size and the intensity of the COVID-19 spread in the first wave of the pandemic. The consultations of the EC with multiple stakeholders on the experiences of several countries to conduct elections amidst the pandemic led to the decision to conduct the election. The conduct of successful election was encountered with several challenges due to holding the assembly election in Bihar at the time of the COVID-19 pandemic. The political parties were divided over the timing of the elections but finally all of them participated. To control the spread of the coronavirus, various guidelines were issued but almost all political parties violated them during their campaign. Earlier, the parties such as BJP and JD(U) held virtual rallies but later they too, like others, relied more on traditional modes of campaigning.

More than the political parties, holding a three-phase assembly election in Bihar was a litmus test for the EC. The guidelines set up by the EC and the use of limited resources to conduct free and fair assembly elections have been explained in this chapter. The success of the Bihar elections can be largely attributed to the way it was managed by the EC, albeit with some limitations on certain polling booths. Its model of conduct of elections guided the Election Commission to undertake assembly elections in 2021 in West Bengal, Tamil Nadu, Kerala, Assam, and Puducherry amidst the pandemic, and several elections thereafter in India.

Note

1 The BJP has divided the state into 5,500 mandals and 9,500 *Shakti Kendras*. Each *Shakti Kendra* will monitor the functioning of six to seven booths.

References

Ananthanarayanan, Aditi (2020, October 20). Digital elections: The new normal in Covid-hit Bihar. *Timesnownews.com*. Retrieved from https://www.timesnownews.com/india/bihar/article/digital-elections-the-new-normal-in-covid-hit-bihar/670034

Agrawal, Parul (2020, April 3). Covid-19 lockdown: Bihar migrants who fled cities face ostracism at home. *Scroll.in*. https://scroll.in/article/958010/covid-19-lockdown-bihar-migrants-who-fled-cities-face-ostracism-at-home. Accessed on 10 July 2020.

Bihar Health Dept (2020, July 29). twitter handle @BiharHealthDept #BiharFightsCorona. https://twitter.com/BiharHealthDept/status/1288086432402141186/photo/1. Accessed on 29 July 2020.

Businesstoday.in (2020, June 7). Amit Shah holds first of its kind virtual rally in Bihar; here are key highlights. *Businesstoday.in*. Retrieved from https://www.businesstoday.in/current/economy-politics/amit-shah-holds-first-of-its-kind-virtual-rally-in-bihar-here-are-key-highlights/story/406222.html

CEO Bihar (2020). Retrieved from https://twitter.com/CEOBihar/status/1325773640424542210/photo/1.

Chaurasia, Manoj (2020, July 12). Only BJP and JD-U want elections in Bihar at time of Corona pandemic. *The Statesman*. Retrieved from https://www.thestatesman.com/india/bjp-jd-u-want-elections-bihar-time-corona-pandemic-1502908220.html.

Chopra, Ritika (2020, July 12). Explained: Is EC empowered to delay Bihar elections due to Covid-19?. *The Indian Express*.

Cousins, Charlotte (2020, December 15). Holding elections during the COVID-19 pandemic. Retrieved from https://www.cfr.org/backgrounder/how-countries-are-holding-elections-during-covid-19-pandemic

Economic Times (2020a, August 23). The/PTI, 'Bihar Assembly polls on time, despite demands to postpone, say election commission sources. https:// economictimes.indiatimes.com/news/politics-and-nation/bihar-assembly-polls-on-time-despite-demands-to-postpo ne-say-election-commission-sources/articleshow/77702712.cms. Accessed 25 September 2021.

Election commission of India (2020a). *Schedule for General Election to the Legislative Assembly of Bihar-2020*. New Delhi: Election commission of India.

Election commission of India (2020b). *Broad Guidelines for Conduct of General Elections/ Bye-Elections During Covid-19, Document No- 324.6.EPS.OT.001.2020*. New Delhi: Election commission of India.

Government of India (2007). *Elections in the Constitution of India*. Government of India. Ministry of Law and Justice.

Gupta, Shaibal (2020, May 12). Why Covid-19 poses a sharp challenge for Bihar. *The Hindustan Times*.

Hasin, Fahad (2020, October 23). Bihar Elections: EC has a responsibility to hold free and fair polls but it can't lose sight of COVID-19 either. *First Post*.

IAMAI-Nielsen (2019). Digital in India 2019-Round 2 Report, IAMAI-Nielsen. Retrieved from   https://cms.iamai.in/Content/ResearchPapers/%22286f4d7-424f-4bde-be88-6415fe5021d5.pdf

IDEA (2020).Global overview of Covid-19 impact on elections. Retrieved from https://www.idea.int/news-media/multimedia-reports/global-overview-covid-19-impact-elections

James, Toby S. &Alihodzic, Anglia Sead (2019, August 20). When is it democratic to postpone an election? Elections during natural disasters, COVID-19, and emergency situations. *Election Law Journal Rules Politics and Policy*, 19(3).

Jeelani, Gulam (2020, November 05). Encouraging' voter turnout amid COVID-19: What it means. Retrieved from https://www.moneycontrol.com/news/coronavirus/bihar-election-2020-encouraging-voter-turnout-amid-covid-19-what-it-means-6070381.html

Katiyar, Prerna (2020, June14). With Amit Shah's virtual rally, the BJP has already sounded the poll bugle in Bihar. *The Economic Times*.

Kumar, Manoj (2020, July 12). Bihar NDA partners in a pickle as parties urge EC to defer Assembly polls. *Hindustan Times*.

Landman, Todd & Splendore, Luca Di Gennaro (2020). Pandemic democracy: Elections and COVID-19. *Journal of Risk Research*, 23(7–8), 1060–1066.

LokNiti (2020). State election studies pre poll (mid-October). Retrieved from https://www.lokniti.org/media/PDF-upload/1606577835_22658400_download_report.pdf

Mehrotra, Santosh & Roy, Baikunth (2020, June 23). Will Bihar's economy rise to the reverse migration challenge?. *The Wire*. Retrieved from https://thewire.in/labour/bihar-economy-reverse-migration-challenge.

Mishra, Dipak (2020, June 27). Can't match BJP's e-rallies, so Bihar opposition now wants EC to allow traditionalrallies. *The Print*. https://theprint.in/politics/cant-match-bjps-e-rallies-so-bihar-opposition-now-wants-ec-to-allow-traditional-rallies/449835/. Accessed on 15 July 2020.

National Herald/PTI (2020 December 28). *EC Held Covid-Safe Elections in Bihar; Now Preparing for Polls Next Year: Sunil Arora on EC's 2020*. New Delhi: National Herald/ PTI.

Phadnis, Aditi (2020, October 19).Voting in the shadow of Covid-19: How the EC prepared for Bihar polls. *Business Standard*.

Prakash, Om (2020, June 4). Bihar Vidhansabha Chunav 2020: Carona Ke Baad Kaise Chala Jayega Siyasi Daav, Kitna Alag Hoga. *NEWS18 Hindi*. Retrieved from https://hindi.news18.com/news/nation/bihar-assembly-elections-2020-how-much-will-election-campaign-change-after-corona-migrant-workers-voting-behavior-csds-bjp-jdu-rjd-dlop-3142042.html

PTI. (2020, December 28). EC held COVID-safe elections in Bihar; now preparing for polls next year: CEC Arora. *The Hindu*.

PTI. (2021, January 27). Bihar to guide poll-bound states on conducting elections amid COVID pandemic. Retrieved from https://www.thehindu.com/news/national/other -states/bihar-to-guide-poll-bound-states-on-conducting-elections-amid-covid-pandemic /article33676338.ece

Pushpendra, Singh, Dilip. (2020, April 20). A change in migrant policy. *The Hindu.*

Quraishi, S Y (2020, November 12). Bihar can be a leading example of how to successfully conduct a poll in difficult times. *The Indian Express.*

Ranjan, Amit & Kumar, Jeetendra (2020). Bihar assembly elections: Politics in the times of COVID-19, ISAS Working Paper, No. 332,1–8, 07August.

Sardesai, Shreyas (2020, November 12). Decoding the close Bihar verdict. *Indian Express.*

Sen, Pia (2020, November 24), A health plan for Bihar. *Indian Express.*

Shanker, Arnimesh (2020, July 1). 9,500 IT cell heads, 72,000 WhatsApp groups-how BJP is preparing for Bihar poll battle. *The Print.* Retrieved from https://theprint.in/politics /9500-it-cell-heads-72000-whatsapp-groups-how-bjp-is-preparing-for-bihar-poll-battle /451740/

Singh, Santosh (2020, March 31). Bihar: Over 4000 returned from Gulf, only 500 tested for Covid-19', *The Indian Express.*

Singh, Santosh (2020, July13). Preparing on assumption that Bihar polls will be held as per schedule: CEO. *The Indian Express.*

Supraja, Mahesh (2020, October27). How Bihar is ensuring a 'safe and secure' election during COVID-19 pandemic. *The New Indian Express.*

Tewary, Amarnath (2020, April 8). Migrant workers slip out of Bihar quarantine centres at night, return by day. *The Hindu.*

Thakur, Rajesh Kumar (2020, November 7). Conducting elections amid pandemic wasn't easy, says Bihar chief electoral officer. *The New Indian Express.*

The Economic Times. (2020, October 19). 10% hike in expenditure cap for election candidates ahead of polls.

The Indian Express. (2020, August 27). Explainer: How the election commission plans to conduct polls during the pandemic. *The Wire.* https://thewire.in/government/explainer -bihar-assembly-election-guidelines- pandemic-covid-19-coronavirus

The Indian Express. (2020, November 15). Explained ideas: How India's election commission passed the Covid-19 test. *The Indian Express.*

Times of India. (2020, August 8). Bihar polls: Increase limit on election expenditure, BJP. *Times of India.*

Vaishanav, Milan (2020, June 07). Covid-19 is reshaping political campaigns in India. *Business standard.* Retrieved from https://carnegieendowment.org/2020/06/07/covid-19 -is-reshaping-political-campaigns-in-india-pub-82006

Venkitesh, Ramakrishnan (2020, December 04). Lessons from the Bihar assembly election. Retrieved from https://frontline.thehindu.com/cover-story/lessons-from-bihar/ article33101834.ece

18 Public Education in Times of COVID-19

Praveen Kumari Singh and Vasundhra Singh

Introduction

COVID-19 jolted the world with its sudden appearance and complete take over within a matter of days. Given that the global health index is the one segment that took the hardest hit, the economy and education sector weren't that far behind in getting the brunt of it. This chapter argues that there has been an insurmountable learning loss that had only two years in the aftermath of the pandemic, come to the surface, and is still prevalent. The repercussions of which can still be seen till today's date. More so, it also argues that while the immediate focus in the public school education system was put on senior secondary students, the primary school students have gotten lost in the midst of larger executive interventions. The chapter presents National Assessment Survey (NAS) data for the building block classes of the three parts of the public schools, and discusses the interventions put in place to overcome the learning challenges.

Public School Education in India

Beginning in the early 1990s, India saw a major push for the universalization of primary education. This development began right after the Indian Government's Sarva Shiksha Abhiyaan, which was further solidified by the Right to Education Act 2009, guaranteeing free and compulsory education to all children between the ages of 6 to 14, alongside guarantees relating to access and quality of education. In India, public schools are notable among institutional places where marginal or oppressed students are the majority. Given the composition of the student bodies, it becomes pertinent to look into the state of public school education in India, through the lens of systematic factors and trends in the public education sector, with their influences on the same.

The issue of a stagnant, instead of a much declining, rate of enrollment in public schools, despite well-intentioned legislations, fails to produce on-ground impact. This is because child labor continues to be a challenge that has not yet been fully tackled. The 2014 Human Rights Watch report estimated that out of the 13 million children were not attending school, but instead were working, the majority of this number belonged to dalit, adivasi, and minority communities. Often, in such cases, schools functioning with 40% or less capacity are merged or consolidated with others, however, it has been noticed that factors of physical distance from schools to

DOI: 10.4324/9781003304517-23

the students' residences are rarely taken into account. In such circumstances, even the government incentives of free meals and bicycles, in certain instances, have not been able to attract students to enroll.

On top of that, adding a pandemic that has essentially stopped mobilization furthers this decline in school enrollments and spikes the dropout rates to another extent.

Impact of COVID-19

Following the COVID-19 induced lockdown in March 2020, educational institutes were shut down for months. This closure came at a critical point in the education calendar of India, marked by final assessments and leaving examinations for board classes. This disruption, and continued lockdowns have had different implications for students across the socio-economic spectrum, especially in terms of learning outcomes, food and nutrition, and economic security.

Impact on Dropout Rates

According to UNESCO, approximately 0.32 billion students in India have been affected by school closures due to the COVID-19 pandemic. Of these, almost 84% reside in rural areas, while 70% attend government schools. Short-term disruptions in schooling have been shown to lead to permanent dropouts among the poor in the past. In 2015, India's average secondary school dropout rate was 17.06%, with significantly higher rates in rural areas. One observation for this is the loss of parental employment, which is then supplanted with child labor. The lockdown's unavoidable economic consequences are likely to lower many impoverished households' earning ability and raise the possible cost of sending children to school, particularly in rural India. As a result, children may be pushed into the labor market.

Girls, who are frequently excluded from home resource allocation decisions, are likely to have higher dropout rates, given that they may be required to undertake additional household duties as parents undertake increased labor hours to cope with the economic distress. Likewise, these economic difficulties are more capable of affecting children from marginalized communities, such as those who are already enduring higher dropout rates due to caste, tribe, or religion. Dropping out might significantly contribute to more child marriages, domestic abuse, early pregnancies, and a variety of other developmental concerns. In the meantimr, without school tuition waivers, dropout rates are likely to worsen as educational costs become unattainable for many. However, during the lockdown, certain state governments, including those of Haryana, Punjab, Uttar Pradesh, Himachal Pradesh, and Jharkhand attempted to implement tuition and other school expense waivers.

Impact on Disparity

Some educational institutions have taken a significant step to assure curriculum continuity by moving lectures online, requiring both students and teachers to also have personal computers and stable internet. If school and university examinations are held as scheduled with no compensatory classes, students who do not have access to these computer and network facilities are likely to be disadvantaged. Exam postponement, on the other hand, may cause students to miss out on job opportunities. During the lockdown, the dialogue about education was mostly focused on online or televised learning. In fact, education itself is described as part of online and digital learning platforms in India's USD 260 billion fiscal stimulus plan. Mizoram, West Bengal, and Haryana are among the Indian states that have implemented daily televised lectures, a collaborative effort between the Ministry of Education and television service providers to provide specific channels for this purpose. These efforts, however, are inaccessible to the rural and urban poor who have limited or no access to electricity and network resources. According to the Annual Status of Education Report of 2018, students who attend urban private schools benefit most from online programs, and they already exceed government school students on major learning measures.

Impact on Food Security and Nutrition

According to the World Food Program, India's Mid-day Meal (MDM) program is the world's largest school feeding program, serving around 144 million children and covering approximately 80% of primary school students. The temporary suspension of mid-day meals and supplementary nutrition programs, which has widespread and significant ramifications for children's nutrition and food security across the country, is one of the most significant effects of the lockdown and subsequent school closures. MDMs have been found to dramatically enhance enrollment, attendance, retention, learning results, gender and socioeconomic equity, and most critically nutrition, despite regional inequalities in outreach and food quality. MDM's school meals serve as a substitute rather than a complimentary meal for economically disadvantaged families, preventing endemic hunger for the entire family. The months of lockdown in India have already disrupted the agricultural supply chain, resulting in food shortages. As a result, disruptions in school feeding programs are likely to worsen food insecurity, especially among those who are already malnourished, notably girls, who, like older women, eat last and eat less at home than boys and men.

Gravity of Learning Loss

To assess the impact of COVID-19 on learning, it is important to first identify the meaning of learning loss. In this chapter, as in the general term, any loss of knowledge or skills, and/or deceleration of or interruption to academic progress, most commonly due to extended gaps or discontinuities in a student's education is identified as learning loss. In the pre-pandemic times, these losses and gaps could be driven by summer breaks, interruptions to formal education, dropouts, school absences, and teaching ineffectiveness. Two main types of learning losses, categorized as "forgetting" and "forgoing", are the ones that the chapter will be focusing on. The former refers to the loss of previously acquired earnings, and latter means expected learning that does not take place as schools are closed to in-person learning. It has been realized that on top of forgetting and forgoing, additional learning losses could accumulate even after students return to school. Learning is a process in which new skills are built on top of old ones. Evidence from previous disasters shows that school closures often have long-term consequences: affected children have lower educational attainment, lower wages, and increased unemployment as adults. There has been evidence that part of the long-term losses are attributable to slower learning once children return to school, consequently, learning losses associated with the pandemic may result in compounded negative consequences for this generation of students by harming children's future learning trajectories. If children lose essential building blocks for future learning during school closures and are not helped to recover them, learning will continue at a slower pace than before. The current crisis presents an opportunity, since to recover learning losses, students must be put on an accelerated learning recovery trajectory.

According to a collaborative report recently published by the World Bank, UNESCO, and UNICEF, titled "State of the Global Education Crisis: A Path to Recovery Report", the share of children living in countries with low and middle income already displayed 53% learning poverty since before the pandemic even began. Factoring in the damage that COVID-19 has caused, this percentage could reach 70% given the long-term closure of schools and the ineffectiveness of remote learning.

The global education disruption created by the COVID-19 pandemic is unprecedented, and its impacts on learning have been devastating. The crisis brought education systems all across the world to a standstill, with more than 1.6 billion students affected by school closures. While nearly every country in the world provided students with remote learning possibilities, the quality and scope of these programs varied widely, and they were only partial alternatives for in-person schooling. Schools are still suspended for millions of children and young people now nearly 2 years later, and millions more are at risk of never returning to school. As of 2024, the number of students enrolling back into schools has slightly increased as the schools have reopened, but it is still nowhere close to what it should have been. The growing volume of research on the effects of school closures on children's learning paints a bleak picture. Recent learning assessments suggest that children in many countries have missed out on most or all of the academic learning they would have gained in school, with younger and more marginalized children typically missing out the most. In rural Karnataka (India), the share of grade three students in government schools able to perform simple subtraction fell from 24% in 2018 to only 16% in 2020. The worldwide learning problem has worsened far more than originally anticipated: this generation of students now faces a loss of $17 trillion in lifetime earnings in present value as a result of school closures, or 14% of global gross domstic product (GDP) today, far more than the $10 trillion projected in 2020.

Extensive Inequality in Education

Full and partial school closures lasted an average of 224 days around the world. School closures in low- and middle-income nations, on the other hand, often lasted longer and were less productive than in high-income countries. Many teachers in low- and middle-income countries received little professional development support when they transitioned to remote learning, leaving them unprepared to interact with students and guardians. The capability of families to respond to the shock at home varies depending on their income level. Children from low-income families were less likely than other students to benefit from remote learning, owing to a lack of energy, internet access, equipment, and parental assistance. Remote learning is seldom designed in a manner that matches the developmental requirements of young students with disabilities, who have been frequently left out of governments' legislative responses. During school closures, girls faced far more impediments in education, since social norms, restricted digital proficiency, and a lack of access to gadgets impeded their capacity to continue learning.

The Image name/source "Students affected by school closures. State of the Global Education Crisis: A Path to Recovery Report 2021" represents Hundreds of millions of students in low- and middle-income countries that have been affected by full and partial school closures since the start of the pandemic.

Stagnant Progress in Other Domains for Children

Schools typically provide important services that go beyond education and provide safe havens for students. Children's health and safety were compromised during school closures, with domestic abuse and child labor on the rise. During school closures around the world, more than 370 million children lost out on school meals, losing what, for some of them is their only reliable supply of food and daily nutrition. The mental health crisis among youngsters has reached epidemic proportions. Advances in gender equality are jeopardized, with school closures putting an estimated 10 million additional girls at danger of early marriage and dropping out over the next decade.

Measures Taken by the Government

As the pandemic raged on, all state governments instructed for the classes to be shifted to the online module of learning. In a manner, the lockdown accelerated the adoption of digital technology. Looking at this challenge of colleges and schools being shut, the Government of India, as well as state governments and private players have undertaken multiple initiatives. The Ministry of Education has made several arrangements, including online portals and educational channels through Direct-to-Home (DTH) TV and radios for students to continue learning. During lockdown, teachers and students are shifted to popular social media tools like WhatsApp, Zoom, Google Meet, Telegram, YouTube Live, Facebook Live, etc. for online teaching-learning systems. Alongside that, the Ministry of Education launched digital initiatives for both secondary and higher education such as:

Diksha portal—Containing e-Learning content for students, teachers, and parents aligned to the curriculum, including video lessons, worksheets, textbooks and assessments.

E-Pathshala— An e-learning app by National Council of Educational Research and Training (NCERT) for classes 1 to 12 in multiple languages. The app houses books, videos, audio, etc. aimed at students, educators, and parents in multiple languages.

The NROER (National Repository of Open Educational Resources) portal provides a host of resources for students and teachers in multiple languages including books, interactive modules, and videos including a host of STEM-based games.

Swayam is the national online education platform hosting 1,900 courses covering both school (classes 9 to 12) and higher education (undergraduate, postgraduate programs) in all subjects including engineering, humanities and social sciences, law, and management courses.

Swayam Prabha has 32 DTH TV channels transmitting educational contents on a 24/7 basis. These channels are available for viewing all across the country using DD Free Dish Set Top Box and Antenna. The channels cover both school education (classes 9 to 12) and higher education (undergraduate, postgraduate, engineering, out-of-school children, vocational courses, and teacher training) in arts, science, commerce, performing arts, social sciences and humanities subjects, engineering, technology, law, medicine, and agriculture.

On a state level, Haryana took some of its own initiatives and introduced Avsar and Saksham Samiksha apps. The Avsar app was launched in October 2020 to supplement home learning amidst school closures due to COVID-19. It has three main components: 1) Daily surveys—short survey post each EDUSAT telecast to mark attendance, 2) Weekly assessments—for students of all grades based on a weekly EDUSAT syllabus, and 3) Content library—additional learning resources such as PDFs, videos, and HOTS questions.

The Haryana government introduced the Saksham Samiksha open-source mobile app to maintain accountability in the governance ecosystem through streamlined data collection. Samiksha, in that manner, is presented as a modular, interoperable, scalable, and a configurable product. The app is designed primarily for four users—teachers, school heads, mentors, and monitors. In the app, they mark student and teacher attendance and temperature, record academic observations from school visits, and collect from monitoring school visits. The app has three functional screens—the login screen, profile screen, and the home page. Among the guidelines issued by the Department of School Education and Literacy are PRAGYATA guidelines on digital education that focus on the methodology of online/blended/digital education for students who are presently at home due to the closure of schools. It recommends screen times for different categories of students and also shares the dos and Don'ts of cybersecurity. The department also launched the Learning Enhancement Guidelines for Continuous Learning that specifically focused on students with limited or no access to digital devices during the COVID-19 pandemic. In order to mitigate the loss of learning, a COVID Action Plan was put in place as a roadmap for various focus areas, and interventions for implementation include developing efficient home learning modules, building teacher capacity, and systemic involvement of parents, community, and local self-governments volunteers, etc.

The Case of Haryana

The chapter used snowball sampling as the methodology on a sample size of ten administrators and ten teachers, across five blocks each, in the districts of Rohtak and Jhajjar in Haryana. And structured telephonic interviews were conducted for all participants of the survey. The administrator sample was divided amongst Principals, Headmasters, Block Elementary Education Officer (BEEO), and Block Education Officer (BEO), and the teacher sample was divided between PGT, TGT, and PRT teachers.

While conducting the interviews, with both the teachers and the administrators, we learn that since the inception of COVID-19, classroom learning had taken a shift towards online learning. In doing so, applications like WhatsApp, Youtube, and Zoom, became the primary source of distributing information and teaching, keeping up to date with the syllabus structures. However, it was soon realized that only 50% of students had access to smartphones, tablets, and/or computer systems, which pointed out the technical constraints and the immediate ineffectiveness of e-learning. Out of that 50%, the response rate on these apps was recorded for just half of the students. In order to rectify this situation, the education department introduced the concept of "Friend Access", which allowed students to login into these apps from devices belonging to either their teacher, any relative, neighbor, or their friend, and simultaneously launched a DTH channel that played public school curriculums on TV at all times. However, according to a government survey dated June 30, 2021, around 1,034,000 students still found themselves without any access to digital devices. Correspondingly, a private survey also found that 20% of teachers were also unable to participate in the online learning model due to technical constraints, among other reasons. Another problem that was widely highlighted was the issue of security and privacy for students attempting tests and quizzes on the Avsar app. The app requires a student registration number and the date of birth for logging in, however, given that the registration numbers are basically just roll numbers often known to everyone in the class, it has come to light that several student's quizzes are getting tampered with. There have also been issues of glitches in the app that have sometimes failed to record the progress of the students.

The concern of digital depravity has left the students, their parents, and teachers in a hassled conundrum. In many cases, school teachers have been approached by students and parents, and they had to take the tests and quizzes after logging in from the teacher's phone. Nearly all such cases involved students from the economically marginalized communities. This involves traveling in an already dangerous time, putting a lot of people at risk of contracting COVID-19.

Another concern is about the actual consumption of the materials put out on the app. The app offers modules, after completing which it takes you to the quizzes. However, there is no time constraint that allows for the material to be actually processed before it takes you to the quiz, meaning that the students may as well be flipping through the module quickly and going directly to the quiz.

Given these concerns and in the attempt to create a more holistic learning environment, schools reached out to the parents to devise a network that benefits the students by method of calls and in-person meetings. When schools started reopening, however, 30% of parents were still out of contact.

Currently in Haryana, energized textbooks on DIKSHA are available in two mediums. There are 197 total prescribed textbooks; number of energized textbooks is also the same.

NISTHA, training module for teachers, records only 63,239 teachers who have completed their online training as opposed to the 88,716 teachers who did it in the offline mode.

State interventions for students without any digital devices include home visits by teachers and volunteers, but there is no data available on them yet.

Regarding device distribution, so far no devices have been distributed among students, but 1,487 laptops have been given to the teachers, and a plan has been approved to distribute 1 tablet per school for 14,355 schools so far. In terms of other digital interventions, Haryana has invested in smart classrooms, Information and Communications Technology (ICT) labs, e-repositories, interactive resource courses, e-books, educational TV and radio channels, orientation programs for parents as well as teachers, among others.

The Haryana government pivoted an effort to mainstream out-of-school students during the first phase by establishing Special Training Centers, focusing on 8–12 children in one group based on regional locality, and continued this project throughout. There is a constant survey of digital devices by the network created between district officials, Assistant Block Resource Coordinators (ABRCs), BEOs, school administrators, teachers, and parents. The government also indulged in a textbook and workbook exchange program to facilitate constant learnings and linked the EDUSAT program to televisions. Moreover, there has been a continuous effort by volunteers associated with National Cadet Corps (NCC) Students, Scout and Guide Students, and Students of higher classes for teaching and checking homework of the student. The launch of "Ghar se padhao WhatsApp Campaign" created as part of the Saksham Haryana Program focuses on academic videos and worksheets for core subjects—Hindi, Math, Science, and environmental science (EVS) as per State Council of Educational Research and Training's (SCERT) month-wise distribution of syllabus. And there has been active participation in home learning due to the weekly short online quizzes held for classes 5–12 on topics shared via WhatsApp in that week. Quizzes for classes 5–8 focus on core subjects: Math, Hindi, Science, and EVS, and quizzes for classes 9–12 focus on Math and Science.

What has been seen to be missing so far from this discussion is the impact the pandemic has had on the primary school students (classes 1–5). It should come as no surprise that children in that age group, especially the ones coming from economically marginalized groups, suffer the most. They miss out on nutrition, education, cognitive and social development, and generally are not considered as an immediate priority. Learning for them in an online setup creates a disadvantage that sets them further back than their peers who come from slightly better-off backgrounds.

Certain steps that could be taken to advance school and student performance in this pandemic lie in the systematic utilization of the already allocated COVID-19 budgets. Creating a roadmap to opening the schools, setting up sanitation points, and investing in protective gear so that students may come back to their institutions in a phased manner would do wonders for the wholesome development of the students. Alongside that, it has become pertinent to engage with the rural digital infrastructure interventions that may speed up the process of providing digital devices, especially to those families/students under below poverty line (BPL) that are currently not covered under any other education-related benefits. The times are tough, and huge efforts have been made by various stakeholders yet there are multitudes of challenges that need to be overcome in order to bridge the gap of learning deficit caused due to this pandemic.

According to the National Assessment Survey (NAS) and the student assessment tests that are conducted half-yearly and annually, students are showing a learning gap of about 2 years on average. It becomes a problem for students, especially those who are currently enrolled in classes 3, 5, and 8, but their learning levels are at classes 1, 3, and 6 respectively. Given that the formerly mentioned grades are the building block levels for the transition into secondary, senior secondary schools, and undergraduate levels, it becomes essential to ensure that the education and the learning that is being imparted is actually being registered and sustained by the students.

Based on the latest NAS report, the average of a class 3 student pre COVID-19 in subjects like EVS, Hindi and Math has dropped from 70%, 82%, and 66% to 49%, 62%, and 45% respectively (additional data is mentioned in the annexure). Following this, the Government of Haryana has launched a Foundational Literacy and Numeracy program. This programme launches in April 2022, and places students of classes 1–3 as the first priority. Formulated under the NIPUN Haryana Mission, that was created for actualization of the New Education Policy of India, the program looks to provide initially a three-day training to primary (PRT) teachers across all blocks in Haryana, and then moves to establish a month long "entry level knowledge" program for class 1 students at the beginning of the academic year.

Conclusions

Reopening schools should be a top priority for all governments. The cost of keeping schools closed is high, and it threatens to stifle a generation of children and youth while deepening pre-pandemic inequalities. Reopening and maintaining schools should therefore be a major priority for states, as mounting data suggests that with the right safeguards in place, health hazards to children and educators may be reduced. Reopening is the single most effective way for countries to start reversing learning deficits. While substantial losses in reading and math have now been documented and show variations across states, grades, subjects, and students' characteristics, evidence on learning loss generally remains scarce. It is critical for policymakers, school administrators, and teachers to have access to learning data that reflect their context, and for learning data to be disaggregated by various sub-groups of students so that they can target instruction and accelerate students' learning recovery. To prevent learning losses from accumulating once children are back in school, the country should adopt learning recovery programs consisting of evidence-based strategies, as has been done in Haryana. Learning recovery programs can compensate for the losses by combining a contextually appropriate mix of proven techniques for promoting foundational learning: curriculum consolidation, instructional time extension, and learning efficiency through targeted instruction, structured pedagogy, small-group tutoring, and self-guided learning programs. School closures disrupted not just learning but also the supply of key services such as school meals, security, and psychological support, affecting children's general well-being and mental health. Reopening schools and supporting them to provide comprehensive services promoting well-being and psychosocial support, addressing children's socioemotional losses, is a priority. Improving mechanisms to generate fast and accurate data is crucial for evaluating policy responses and generating lessons learned for the next educational disruption. More inquiry is needed to understand what works and how to scale what works to the system level to close the implementation gap between policy and improved student learning. Now is the opportunity to go from disaster to restoration, then to resilient and transformational education systems that actually provide learning and well-being for all children and youth.

Bibliography

Afridi, F. (2011). The Impact of School Meals on School Participation: Evidence from Rural India. *Journal of Development Studies*, 47(11), 1636–1656.

Alvi, M., & Gupta, M. (2020). Learning in Times of Lockdown: How Covid-19 Is Affecting Education and Food Security in India. *Food Security*, 12, 793–796.

Ambast, S. (2019). The Public School Education System and Subalternity in India. *Journal Perferias*.

Annual Status of Education Report. (2018). ASER 2018 - ASER Centre. Retrieved May 8, 2020.

Arbaugh, J. B. (2000). How Classroom Environment and Student Engagement Affect Learning in Internet-Based MBA Courses. *Business Communication Quarterly*, 63(4), 9–26.

Bandura, A. (1986). *Social Foundations of Thought and Action: A Social Cognitive Theory.* Englewood Cliffs, NJ: Prentice-Hall.

Belot, M., & Webbink, D. (2010). *Do Teachers Strike Harm Educational Attainment of Students.* CEIS.

Chowdhury, S. R. (2019). The Correlation Between Midday Meals and Learning Outcomes | India Development Review. Retrieved May 8, 2020.

COVID- Campaign, Department of School Education, Government of Haryana.

COVID- Campaign, Ministry of Education, Government of India.

David, J., & Willén, A. (2019). The Long-Run Effects of Teacher Strikes: Evidence from Argentina. *Journal of Labor Economics, University of Chicago Press*, 37(4), 1097–1139.

Department of Elementary Education, Government of Haryana.

Gilbert, B. (2015). Online learning Revealing the Benefits and Challenges Education Masters Paper 303.

Initiatives by School Education Sector in 2020-21 for Continuing Teaching and Learning in 2022, Ministry of Education, Government of India (2021).

International Institute for Population Sciences (IIPS) and ICF. (2017). *National Family Health Survey (NFHS-4), 2015–16: India.* Mumbai: IIPS.

Jena, P. K. (2020). Impact of Pandemic COVID-19 on Education in India. *International Journal of Current Research (IJCR)*, 12(7), 12582–12586.

Kamila, C.-R. (2018). Estimating the Effect of Early-Childhood Citizenship on Education Using Policy Changes as Instruments. *Applied Economics Letters*, 25(20), 1426–1431.

Malik. (2015). RTE and Marginal Communities: A Perspective from the Field. *Economic and Political Weekly*, l(5), 25–27.

Muthuprasad, T., Aiswarya, S., Aditya, K. S., & Jha, G. K. (2021). Students' Perception and Preference for Online Education in India During COVID -19 Pandemic. *Social Sciences & Humanities Open*, 3(1).

Pragyata Guidelines for Digital Education Department of School Education & Literacy Ministry of Human Resource Development, Government of India.

Ramachandran, V., & Naorem, T. (2013). What It Means To Be a Dalit or Tribal Child in Our Schools: A Synthesis of a Six-State Qualitative Study. *Economic and Political Weekly*, XLVIII(43–44), 43–52.

The State of the Global Education Crisis: A Path to Recovery. A joint UNESCO, UNICEF, and World Bank Report, 2021.

UNESCO, Global Education Monitoring Report. 2018, 2020, 2021.

UNESCO, UNICEF, World Bank, and OECD, Annual Report. 2020, 2021.

UNESCO School closure calendar, as of the end of October/2021.

UNICEF, Annual Report. 2021a, 2020b.

Annexure

Data provided by DIET Haryana

Remedial Data for Class 3

Index	Learning Loss Observed	Learning Loss Not Observed

District Level Performance

Public Education in Times of COVID-19   285

	Grade 3														
	EVS					Hindi					Maths				
Pre-COVID Level	70%	83%	83%	54%	53%	69%	82%	90%	82%	59%	66%	67%	66%	82%	67%
Difficulty level	Medium	Difficult	Difficult	Medium	Easy	Medium	Difficult	Easy	Difficult	Medium	Easy	Medium	Easy	Difficult	Medium
LOs	E302	E310	E310	E303	E305	L304	L304	L304	L304	L304	M312	M305	M312	M317	M305
Ambala	49%	57%	51%	52%	46%	74%	62%	59%	63%	56%	45%	37%	47%	45%	35%
Bhiwani	50%	57%	53%	53%	49%	73%	64%	61%	59%	57%	49%	40%	53%	48%	39%
Charkhi Dadri	58%	64%	59%	60%	52%	76%	66%	63%	66%	58%	51%	41%	53%	51%	45%
Faridabad	61%	70%	67%	66%	54%	81%	71%	71%	73%	66%	62%	53%	63%	59%	52%
Fatehabad	44%	49%	46%	46%	41%	69%	56%	55%	57%	50%	40%	33%	43%	41%	33%
Gurugram	57%	64%	60%	59%	57%	79%	68%	68%	68%	65%	53%	44%	56%	54%	43%
Hisar	50%	57%	52%	53%	48%	71%	57%	59%	61%	54%	46%	37%	49%	46%	40%
Jhajjar	53%	59%	55%	59%	50%	75%	63%	64%	65%	57%	47%	42%	53%	52%	44%
Jind	46%	53%	50%	53%	46%	73%	59%	57%	59%	50%	46%	32%	46%	39%	34%
Kaithal	51%	60%	52%	53%	53%	71%	60%	57%	61%	54%	48%	41%	51%	48%	44%
Karnal	54%	60%	56%	56%	55%	73%	63%	62%	64%	57%	51%	42%	53%	50%	45%
Kurukshetra	51%	63%	58%	59%	53%	76%	63%	61%	66%	59%	52%	38%	50%	47%	40%
Mahendragarh	57%	64%	58%	60%	55%	77%	64%	66%	66%	62%	53%	41%	56%	52%	46%
Panchkula	49%	58%	53%	52%	52%	69%	60%	63%	63%	57%	50%	41%	50%	48%	38%
Palwal	53%	63%	60%	57%	57%	72%	65%	66%	64%	62%	53%	45%	54%	52%	48%
Panipat	54%	62%	58%	58%	56%	75%	65%	64%	65%	59%	53%	46%	55%	50%	45%
Rewari	60%	67%	64%	64%	59%	80%	71%	72%	72%	68%	56%	50%	60%	59%	49%
Rohtak	57%	63%	58%	60%	53%	77%	66%	66%	69%	61%	51%	39%	52%	53%	41%
Sonipat	56%	64%	57%	58%	55%	77%	70%	67%	68%	61%	52%	42%	56%	51%	46%
Yamunanagar	47%	56%	53%	50%	49%	73%	59%	58%	61%	54%	47%	34%	46%	43%	37%
Nuh Mewat	46%	56%	52%	48%	50%	60%	54%	56%	52%	52%	43%	40%	53%	41%	42%
Sirsa	47%	55%	51%	50%	44%	68%	58%	55%	58%	50%	48%	37%	45%	46%	38%

Block Level Performance

District	LOs	EVS					Hindi					Maths				
Pre-COVID Level		70%	83%	83%	54%	53%	69%	82%	90%	82%	59%	66%	67%	66%	82%	67%
Difficulty Level		Medium	Difficult	Difficult	Medium	Easy	Medium	Difficult	Easy	Difficult	Medium	Easy	Medium	Easy	Difficult	Medium
LOs		E302	E310	E310	E303	E305	L304	L304	L304	L304	L304	M312	M305	M312	M317	M305
Jhajjar	Bahadurgarh	52%	57%	57%	61%	48%	72%	59%	65%	65%	56%	46%	43%	53%	53%	46%
Jhajjar	Beri	51%	60%	55%	55%	50%	79%	72%	67%	67%	62%	50%	44%	56%	53%	48%
Jhajjar	Jhajjar	49%	55%	50%	52%	48%	71%	61%	58%	56%	52%	40%	39%	48%	48%	37%
Jhajjar	Matan Hail	63%	67%	60%	64%	56%	78%	66%	67%	73%	62%	51%	42%	61%	57%	47%
Jhajjar	Salhawas	54%	65%	52%	58%	57%	87%	67%	67%	72%	58%	52%	38%	50%	49%	40%
Rohtak	Kalanaur	57%	63%	53%	57%	48%	76%	66%	64%	69%	63%	46%	41%	44%	49%	40%
Rohtak	Lakhan Majra	59%	67%	55%	69%	48%	84%	65%	76%	72%	53%	59%	39%	48%	54%	40%
Rohtak	Meham	55%	54%	50%	49%	50%	73%	65%	62%	69%	61%	47%	35%	50%	47%	46%
Rohtak	Rohtak	58%	65%	63%	64%	58%	78%	68%	66%	69%	63%	53%	43%	55%	55%	40%
Rohtak	Sampla	58%	64%	64%	55%	52%	74%	61%	64%	64%	60%	51%	29%	56%	55%	37%

Competency Codes: Legend

Code	Description
E302	Identifies simple observable features (e.g., shape, colour, texture, aroma) of leaves, trunk, and bark of plants in immediate surroundings
E303	Identifies relationships with and among family members
E305	Describes need of food for people of different age groups, animals/birds, availability of food and water, and use of water at home and surroundings
E310	Guesses properties, estimates quantities of materials/activities in daily life, and verifies using symbols/non-standard units (hand spans, spoon/mugs, etc.)
L304	Reads small texts with comprehension i.e., identifies main ideas, details, sequence, and draws conclusions
M305	Analyses and applies an appropriate number operation in the situation context
M312	Estimates and measures length and distance using standard units like centimeters or meters and identifies relationships
M317	Reads the time correctly to the hour using a clock/watch

Remedial Data for class 5

District Level Performance

	Grade 5																	
	Hindi					Maths				SST					Science			
Pre-COVID Level	68%	68%	68%	93%	68%	60%	79%	69%	79%	67%	79%	59%	55%	67%	61%	64%	60%	75%
Difficulty level	Difficult	Medium	Difficult	Easy	Medium	Medium	Easy	Medium	Easy	Medium	Medium	Medium	Difficult	Medium	Medium	Difficult	Easy	Difficult
LOs	L813	L813	L813	L813	L813	M804	M812	M717	M818	SST726	SST807	SST605	SST625	SST811	SCI804	SCI801	SCI801	SCI811
Ambala	40%	77%	48%	74%	57%	45%	46%	53%	57%	68%	61%	39%	51%	48%	46%	37%	38%	65%
Bhiwani	53%	76%	51%	82%	63%	51%	47%	57%	54%	71%	64%	57%	62%	57%	53%	47%	42%	65%
Charkhi Dadri	61%	82%	55%	89%	68%	51%	50%	54%	67%	70%	65%	39%	60%	59%	60%	52%	50%	72%
Faridabad	59%	78%	61%	81%	64%	59%	62%	65%	64%	75%	71%	67%	70%	67%	71%	61%	60%	71%
Fatehabad	32%	66%	38%	69%	45%	37%	36%	41%	49%	54%	56%	35%	46%	39%	35%	33%	30%	57%
Gurugram	55%	78%	56%	82%	66%	54%	57%	59%	65%	74%	66%	55%	64%	58%	55%	50%	48%	71%
Hisar	43%	75%	45%	78%	57%	44%	43%	50%	56%	65%	62%	41%	56%	50%	46%	43%	41%	65%
Jhajjar	50%	74%	53%	78%	61%	52%	57%	60%	63%	73%	63%	62%	61%	56%	56%	54%	48%	68%
Jind	45%	74%	47%	77%	59%	47%	49%	54%	59%	67%	61%	48%	57%	50%	50%	43%	39%	61%
Kaithal	51%	80%	54%	82%	63%	49%	53%	55%	60%	66%	63%	45%	60%	47%	53%	48%	45%	67%
Karnal	49%	73%	53%	80%	59%	47%	50%	52%	56%	68%	62%	46%	53%	54%	53%	42%	42%	62%
Kurukshetra	51%	79%	54%	82%	61%	51%	56%	59%	59%	71%	66%	48%	60%	58%	57%	47%	47%	74%
Mahendragarh	53%	77%	53%	80%	59%	51%	52%	55%	63%	70%	61%	39%	54%	57%	56%	44%	44%	71%
Nuh Mewat	56%	73%	54%	82%	53%	51%	53%	52%	59%	72%	59%	44%	57%	54%	53%	43%	46%	62%
Palwal	52%	70%	54%	80%	55%	52%	51%	55%	59%	70%	61%	46%	55%	53%	56%	43%	47%	65%
Panchkula	46%	66%	46%	67%	53%	51%	57%	61%	61%	69%	64%	54%	65%	53%	54%	46%	44%	70%
Panipat	56%	78%	57%	82%	62%	54%	57%	58%	65%	71%	62%	52%	60%	58%	56%	48%	47%	63%
Rewari	59%	82%	61%	85%	66%	55%	57%	61%	69%	75%	67%	52%	58%	58%	62%	52%	48%	72%
Rohtak	50%	78%	47%	79%	64%	53%	50%	55%	65%	73%	64%	50%	64%	54%	54%	47%	45%	70%
Sirsa	42%	78%	43%	79%	55%	42%	44%	47%	52%	62%	58%	47%	57%	44%	43%	44%	38%	63%
Sonipat	59%	81%	62%	82%	64%	62%	60%	67%	72%	81%	68%	56%	65%	64%	66%	54%	57%	73%
Yamunanagar	48%	75%	52%	80%	58%	48%	51%	51%	58%	67%	62%	44%	55%	51%	52%	43%	42%	67%

Block Level Performance

		EVS					Hindi					Maths				
Pre-COVID Level		47%	75%	70%	78%	78%	63%	69%	71%	71%	69%	65%	45%	65%	89%	85%
Difficulty Level		Difficult	Easy	Difficult	Medium	Medium	Difficult	Medium	Easy	Easy	Medium	Easy	Medium	Easy	Difficult	Easy
LOs		E509	E508	E513	E503	E503	L508	L508	L508	L508	L508	M412	M514	M412	M505	M514
Jhajjar	Bahadurgarh	63%	77%	65%	48%	65%	59%	65%	73%	73%	62%	56%	61%	45%	51%	53%
Jhajjar	Beri	64%	76%	60%	46%	58%	60%	65%	73%	59%	65%	53%	57%	49%	48%	51%
Jhajjar	Jhajjar	53%	71%	52%	43%	66%	49%	59%	64%	54%	52%	49%	51%	42%	45%	51%
Jhajjar	Matan Hail	63%	71%	63%	46%	69%	63%	68%	74%	71%	67%	58%	60%	55%	52%	60%
Jhajjar	Salhawas	67%	73%	56%	51%	68%	55%	74%	70%	63%	66%	57%	66%	48%	46%	54%
Rohtak	Kalanaur	52%	73%	50%	42%	61%	53%	66%	68%	61%	54%	41%	63%	43%	49%	43%
Rohtak	Lakhan Majra	64%	73%	53%	43%	64%	60%	65%	75%	60%	66%	48%	64%	37%	52%	58%
Rohtak	Meham	50%	72%	55%	36%	69%	50%	64%	71%	58%	61%	47%	67%	38%	45%	49%
Rohtak	Rohtak	60%	74%	64%	44%	67%	59%	65%	75%	64%	65%	51%	60%	49%	51%	57%
Rohtak	Sampla	66%	80%	65%	44%	80%	69%	70%	76%	70%	63%	39%	68%	50%	53%	52%

Competency Codes: Legend

Code	Description
E509	Records observations and experiences; information in an organised manner (e.g., in tables/ sketches/bar graphs/pie charts) and predicts patterns in activities/phenomena (e.g., floating, sinking, mixing, evaporation, germination, spoilage) to establish relation between cause and effect
E508	Guesses (properties, conditions of phenomena), estimates spatial quantities (distance, area, volume, weight etc.), and time in simple standard units and verifies using simple tools/set ups (e.g., floating/sinking/mixing/evaporation/germination/spoilage/breathing/taste)
E513	Suggests ways for hygiene, health, managing waste, disaster/emergency situations and protecting/saving resources
E503	Describes the interdependence among animals, plants, and humans (e.g., communities earning livelihood from animals, dispersal of seeds etc.)
L508	Reads text with comprehension, locates details and sequence of events
M412	Explores the area and perimeter of simple geometrical shapes (triangle, rectangle, square) in terms of given shape as a unit
M514	Applies the four fundamental arithmetic operations in solving problems involving money, length, mass, capacity, and time intervals
M412	Explores the area and perimeter of simple geometrical shapes (triangle, rectangle, square) in terms of given shape as a unit
M505	Finds the number corresponding to part of a collection

Remedial Data for Class 8

District Level Performance

Grade 8

LOs	Hindi					Maths				SST				Science				
Pre-COVID Level	68%	68%	68%	93%	68%	60%	79%	69%	79%	67%	79%	59%	55%	67%	61%	64%	60%	75%
Difficulty level	Difficult	Medium	Difficult	Easy	Medium	Medium	Easy	Medium	Easy	Medium	Medium	Medium	Difficult	Medium	Medium	Difficult	Easy	Difficult
LOs	L813	L813	L813	L813	L813	M804	M812	M717	M818	SST726	SST807	SST605	SST625	SCI811	SCI804	SCI801	SCI801	SCI811
Ambala	40%	77%	48%	74%	57%	45%	46%	53%	57%	68%	61%	39%	51%	48%	46%	37%	38%	65%
Bhiwani	53%	76%	51%	82%	63%	51%	47%	57%	54%	71%	64%	57%	62%	57%	53%	47%	42%	65%
Charkhi Dadri	61%	82%	55%	89%	68%	51%	50%	54%	67%	70%	65%	39%	60%	59%	60%	52%	50%	72%
Faridabad	59%	78%	61%	81%	64%	59%	62%	65%	64%	75%	71%	67%	70%	67%	71%	61%	60%	71%
Fatehabad	32%	66%	38%	69%	45%	37%	36%	41%	49%	54%	56%	35%	46%	39%	35%	33%	30%	57%
Gurugram	55%	78%	56%	82%	66%	54%	57%	59%	65%	74%	66%	55%	64%	58%	55%	50%	48%	71%
Hisar	43%	75%	45%	78%	57%	44%	43%	50%	56%	65%	62%	41%	56%	50%	46%	43%	41%	65%
Jhajjar	50%	74%	53%	78%	61%	52%	57%	60%	63%	73%	63%	62%	61%	56%	56%	54%	48%	68%
Jind	45%	74%	47%	77%	59%	47%	49%	54%	59%	67%	61%	48%	57%	50%	50%	43%	39%	61%
Kaithal	51%	80%	54%	82%	63%	49%	53%	55%	60%	66%	63%	45%	60%	47%	53%	48%	45%	67%
Karnal	49%	73%	53%	80%	59%	47%	50%	52%	56%	68%	62%	46%	53%	54%	53%	42%	42%	62%
Kurukshetra	51%	79%	54%	82%	61%	51%	56%	59%	59%	71%	66%	48%	60%	58%	57%	47%	47%	74%
Mahendragarh	53%	77%	53%	80%	59%	51%	53%	55%	63%	70%	61%	39%	54%	57%	56%	44%	44%	71%
Nuh Mewat	56%	73%	54%	82%	53%	51%	53%	52%	59%	72%	59%	44%	57%	54%	53%	43%	46%	62%
Palwal	52%	70%	54%	80%	55%	52%	51%	55%	59%	70%	61%	46%	55%	53%	56%	43%	47%	65%
Panchkula	46%	66%	46%	67%	53%	51%	57%	61%	61%	69%	64%	54%	65%	53%	54%	46%	44%	70%
Panipat	56%	78%	57%	82%	62%	54%	57%	58%	65%	71%	62%	52%	60%	58%	56%	48%	47%	63%
Rewari	59%	82%	61%	85%	66%	55%	57%	61%	69%	75%	67%	52%	58%	58%	62%	52%	48%	72%
Rohtak	50%	78%	47%	79%	64%	53%	50%	55%	65%	73%	64%	50%	64%	54%	54%	47%	45%	70%
Sirsa	42%	78%	43%	79%	55%	42%	44%	47%	52%	62%	58%	47%	57%	44%	43%	44%	38%	63%
Sonipat	59%	81%	62%	82%	64%	62%	60%	67%	72%	81%	68%	56%	65%	64%	66%	54%	57%	73%
Yamunanagar	48%	75%	52%	80%	58%	48%	51%	51%	58%	67%	62%	44%	55%	51%	52%	43%	42%	67%

Block Level Performance

Grade 8

	Hindi				Maths				SST				Science				
Pre-COVID Level	68%	68%	68%	93%	60%	79%	69%	79%	67%	79%	59%	55%	67%	61%	64%	60%	75%
Difficulty level	Difficult	Medium	Difficult	Easy	Medium	Easy	Medium	Easy	Medium	Medium	Medium	Difficult	Medium	Medium	Difficult	Easy	Difficult
LOs	L813	L813	L813	L813	M804	M812	M717	M818	SST726	SST807	SST605	SST625	SCI811	SCI804	SCI801	SCI801	SCI811
Jhajjar Bahadurgarh	42%	68%	48%	75%	48%	51%	51%	58%	68%	57%	65%	60%	50%	52%	46%	41%	65%
Jhajjar Beri	56%	74%	59%	73%	50%	64%	66%	69%	78%	65%	68%	64%	62%	53%	52%	49%	68%
Jhajjar Jhajjar	48%	74%	49%	77%	52%	62%	63%	64%	68%	60%	53%	57%	65%	63%	66%	58%	70%
Jhajjar Matan Hail	57%	83%	57%	87%	60%	63%	66%	67%	81%	74%	70%	65%	58%	63%	65%	53%	74%
Jhajjar Salhawas	67%	84%	66%	87%	61%	59%	68%	68%	80%	73%	56%	62%	47%	55%	47%	47%	68%
Rohtak Kalanaur	54%	80%	43%	67%	50%	49%	52%	57%	66%	54%	40%	53%	52%	54%	37%	36%	69%
Rohtak Lakhan Majra	38%	65%	46%	71%	42%	55%	55%	67%	70%	66%	58%	64%	49%	52%	42%	35%	68%
Rohtak Meham	46%	81%	44%	80%	47%	37%	46%	59%	76%	74%	46%	65%	47%	52%	38%	35%	59%
Rohtak Rohtak	53%	79%	49%	85%	59%	54%	61%	70%	73%	64%	50%	65%	56%	52%	53%	51%	73%
Rohtak Sampla	52%	81%	55%	83%	56%	57%	59%	70%	76%	63%	59%	72%	65%	62%	57%	56%	77%

Competency Codes: Legend

Code	Description
L813	Reads textual/non-textual materials with comprehension and identifies the details, characters, main idea, and sequence of ideas and events while reading
M804	Finds squares, cubes, square roots, and cube roots of numbers using different methods
M812	Verifies properties of parallelogram and establishes the relationship between them through reasoning
M717	Finds out approximate area of closed shapes by using unit square grid/graph sheet
M818	Finds surface area and volume of cuboidal and cylindrical objects
SST726	Describes the process of election to the legislative assembly
SST807	Justifies judicious use of natural resources
SST818	Analyses the issues related to caste, women, widow remarriage, child marriage, social reforms, and the laws and policies of colonial administration towards these issues
SST605	Identifies latitudes and longitudes, e.g., poles, equator, tropics, States/UTs of India and other neighbouring countries on the globe and the world map
SST625	Describes the functioning of rural and urban local government bodies in sectors like health and education
SCI811	Applies learning of scientific concepts in day-to-day life
SCI804	Relates processes and phenomenon with causes
SCI801	Differentiates materials, organism, and process

19 COVID-19 in Arunachal Pradesh

An Overview

Chaphiak Lowang

Introduction

Arunachal Pradesh, popularly known as the Land of Dawnlit Mountains, is situated in the northeastern states of India. It has a population of 1,382,611 according to the 2011 census and an area of 83,743 square kilometers. It is one of the least populous states of India. It has 27 districts and around 50 different local dialects, although Hindi is spoken as the main connecting and communicating language. Being a relatively underdeveloped state due to continued economic and political neglect by New Delhi and its hostile terrain, it suffers from dilapidated health infrastructure which was one of the main concerns for the people during the COVID-19 pandemic. The first case of coronavirus was reported in March 2020 in the Lohit district of the state when a 31-year-old man, who attended a congregation at Nizamuddin, Delhi tested positive (firstpost, 2020). As the state does not have adequate research facilities, his swab sample had to be sent to Regional Medical Research Centre at Dibrugarh, Assam. Despite inadequate infrastructure, Arunachal Pradesh has had relatively fewer cases of 66,753 and lower fatality rates with 296 deaths according to the recent data of 2024 (Ministry of Health and Family Welfare, GoI, May, 2024), https://www.mohfw.gov.in/. However, as compared to other larger states, Arunachal's response to COVID-19 was more proactive. It was among the 14 Indian states and Union Territories to have responded better than other states with higher tests per million and a commensurate positivity rate lower than the national average (Kalita, 2020). Community organization played an instrumental role in containing the transmission. Historically, community leaders have been at the center of public health crises. Tribalism continues to be the basis of social structure in the state. Each tribal grouping is headed by a chief who wields considerable influence over his tribe. Tribal structure has traditionally dominated the political, social, and economic life in the region. Every tribal community has their own village council which is informal in nature and free of legal and structural formalities. These kinds of self governing informal institutions have catered to fulfilling local needs, providing welfare, and delivering justice to its people. They operate through traditional laws and customs which are considered to be an expression of the will of the people. The existence of these age-old institutions provides a sense of security, stability, and social cohesion which further help in maintaining and preserving age-old traditional values and culture. During the health emergencies, as was

DOI: 10.4324/9781003304517-24

witnessed during the COVID-19 pandemic, these community-based organizations played a critical role from establishing quarantine centers to imposing restrictions on movement.

This chapter provides an overview of COVID-19 in Arunachal Pradesh and its impact on different sectors of the economy and education. It analyses the factors that resulted in the relatively lesser number of infections. The chapter foregrounds the role that community organizations in tribal settings like Arunachal play during public health crises.

The chapter is divided into four sections. The first section deals with the factors responsible for lower infection rates in Arunachal Pradesh. It highlights the inhospitable geographical terrain which makes the state inaccessible and isolated from the rest of the mainland. Lack of transportation and communication systems make it harder to access this place. The second section analyses the multi-dimensional impact of the pandemic ranging from trade to education and tourism. The prolonged lockdown affected every individual in one way or the other. The third section discusses the government initiatives in tackling COVID-19. It argues that the state government took proactive measures like regulating entry points to restrict movement and contain the transmission of viruses. Widespread awareness campaigns were organized and assistance was provided to its people in the form of essential items and cash. The final part of this chapter underlines the centrality of tribal institutions in dealing with the pandemic. It also focuses on many community-based organizations that took the lead in providing relief and aid at the local level much before the government intervened.

Factors Responsible for Lower COVID-19 Infection Rates

Arunachal Pradesh's topographic problems isolate it from the rest of the country, which most likely contributed to the region's delayed transmission of the COVID-19 virus. While the mainland India was grappling with the virus's spread, social media had already played an important role in distributing information and basic precautionary measures such as social separation, mask wearing, and the use of sanitizer. This early awareness allowed the state to prepare more effectively.

Furthermore, the sudden declaration of a countrywide lockdown stranded many people outside the state, aiding in the early prevention of viral transmission. Only later, when lockdown limits were temporarily lifted to allow stranded individuals to return, did the state see a dramatic increase in cases. Arunachal Pradesh has a porous border with Assam, a state with a high number of COVID-19 cases, rendering it especially vulnerable to the virus's spread due to constant movement of people and products.

In response, the state government implemented immediate and stringent measures, such as suspending the issuance of Inner Line Permits (ILP) for non-natives and enforcing a 21-day lockdown, which was subsequently extended. These actions significantly helped control the virus's spread. The government also ceased issuing Protected Area Permits (PAPs) to foreigners, and all movement across the porous international borders was temporarily halted (Choudhury and Achom, 2020). Regular RAT[1] testing at every district entry point was carried out to isolate the infected. At the local level, all the local community institutions and civil society organizations played an important role in strict surveillance of their villages and in implementing the COVID-19 guidelines. The voluntary cooperation with the administration in implementing and executing the policies, programs, and protocols of the lockdown period was made possible due to strong ethnic solidarity, and mutual trust and reciprocity in times of crises.

Traditional values of self-regulated isolation during epidemics, the system of self-governance in tribal communities, and ownership at the village level were some of the reasons for lower infection rates in Arunachal Pradesh. The state is ill-equipped with having only 1 medical college, 6 general hospitals, and 12 district hospitals between 27 districts (Government of Arunachal Pradesh, 2022). Out of these hospitals, only the sole medical college, Tomo Riba Institute of Health and Medical Sciences (TRIHMS) was designated as a treatment center for COVID-19 patients. The hospital has a capacity of 500 beds and has a 4-bed intensice care unit (ICU) with ventilator facilities (Business Standard, 2020). Hence, given the poor condition of health infrastructure, local institutions, without waiting for state machinery to interfere, resorted to self-regulated governance to ensure the social norms were maintained. They made sure that COVID-19 guidelines were strictly adhered to. As a result, villagers were seen erecting temporary barricades, check-ing gates, and fences out of local materials such as bamboo, tree logs, palm leaves, and branches, etc., to ensure no outsiders enter their village premises. Furthermore, the village authorities formed committees and voluntarily engaged themselves in constructing quarantine centers and living huts on a self-help basis for isolation purposes (Arunachal Times, 2020). Awareness programs were organized at the local levels in local languages sensitizing the people on the threat of the virus and on the importance of maintaining physical distancing, home quarantine for 14 days, the use of mask and sanitizers, and the dos and don'ts during the lockdown. They were also seen rendering essential services such as providing and supplying emergency rations to those in need and also distributing hand-made masks, soaps, and disinfectant liquids.

One important factor in the lower infection rates can be attributed to the poor healthcare system in the region. COVID-19 testing facilities were inadequate which led to lower numbers of people being tested and thus fewer reported cases. The nearest testing center is located in Dibrugarh district of Assam which is 370 km away from the nearest district of Arunachal Pradesh, located at Dibang Valley (Sinha, 2020). People are aware of the fact that the state lacks good healthcare system delivery and is a resource-constrained state. TRIHMS in Naharlagun, as mentioned above, the only hospital, was overcrowded and bur-dened with both COVID-19 and non-COVID-19 patients. Having limited capac-ity of COVID-19 wards, limited supply of personal protective equipment (PPE) kits, inadequate beds and ventilators, drugs and other consumables, and most importantly shortage of manpower and skilled staff made the state's task more challenging (Jini, 2020).

Under-preparedness and ill-equipped infrastructure would have resulted in more human losses if it were not for critical interventions made by local tribal institutions and community organizations. Those stranded outside the state were discouraged to return to their home state and moreover, without any testing lab available in the state, it would have been difficult to carry out contact tracing and testing for every individual followed by enforcing quarantine rules.

Impact of COVID-19

The government of Arunachal Pradesh declared a total lockdown on March 23 2020 initially for 21 days which was later extended until April 14 2020. As the end of the 2nd phase of lockdown approached, the government declared the 3rd phase of Lockdown on May, 1 2020 until May 13, 2020 (Government of Arunachal Pradesh, 2020). The prolonged restrictions on movements caused multiple sufferings and challenges for nearly every sector including education, tourism, agriculture, and construction projects (Deori and Konwar, 2020). Among the worst hit were the small traders or business owners, the entrepreneurs, the skilled and the unskilled laborers, migrants, and vendors. The lockdown created a sense of panic, anxiety, and insecurity among the masses which initially led to chaos, hoarding, and shortages of food items and the prices of those essential items available increased sharply (Deccan Herald, 2020). This fear among the masses emanated from the fact that the state is largely dependent on its neighboring state, Assam, for all the necessities such as food items, fuels, industrial or agricultural products, transportation, and even healthcare.

   Despite the fact that Arunachal Pradesh is an agrarian economy dependent largely on agriculture as its major provider of livelihood, most of the essential fruits, vegetables, and daily supplies are sourced from other states, especially Assam (Nair, 2020). The lockdown halted these daily supplies due to a lack of transportation leading to shortages of vegetables in most of the districts (Deccan Herald, 2020). One of the eastern districts, namely, Lohit, is a tea hub of the state solely dependent on tea cultivation as their source of income. The lockdown affected them the most due to restrictions on the movement of people and transportation as they depend on Assam to sell its produce for want of tea factories in the area (Kumar, 2020). In addition, being declared a containment zone after the first COVID-19 case was detected in the Lohit district, plucking and harvesting could not be done on time which affected the quality and resulted in huge losses (Kumar, 2020).

   Arunachal Pradesh has immense tourism potential owing to its rich cultural heritage, landscapes, and varied biodiversity. The tourism sector had just begun to bloom in recent years which came to a standstill during the pandemic. The temporary suspension of Inner Line Permits to tourists due to the pandemic affected the tourism sector since the lockdown imposed coincided with the peak tourist season from March to May. In recent years, the tourism sector had shown remarkable growth and emerged as a major source of employment and income to the youth. During the years 2010–2018, the state witnessed an annual growth rate of 9.42% which is higher than the northeastern regional average of 5.4%. There was an increase in the tourists arrivals from 50,873 (50,560 domestic and 313 foreign tourists) in 2005 to 520,089 (512,436 domestic and 7,653 foreign tourists) in 2018 (Bage and Lama, 2020).

Using time-series data on tourist arrivals from 2005 to 2018, it is estimated that the total tourist arrivals in the state in 2020 would be 6.005 lakhs, had there been no pandemic (Lama, 2020). Due to the lockdown, the state has lost an estimated 33.70% of total tourist arrivals from mid-March to June, which is 2.02 lakh tourists. With the average spending of tourists per person estimated at Rs. 7,585, the total loss in direct sales from tourism was estimated at Rs. 153.27 crore until June, owing to the pandemic. The total loss of income from tourism to the state was estimated at Rs. 142.43 crore, which is 0.91% of the gross state value added (Lama, 2020).

Furthermore, the three-month complete lockdown period starting from April and lasting until June ravaged the entire education system across the nation. The northeast region, compared to the mainland India, already lags behind when it comes to quality education and infrastructure. Arunachal Pradesh is said to have one of the lowest literacy rates (60%) when compared with all other northeastern regions (Chaudhary, 2020). The state already grapples with a lot of issues, such as school and college dropouts, quality of education, shortage and absenteeism of teachers, and inadequate infrastructure, and the pandemic exacerbated these precarities. With the uncertainty and anxiety regarding the COVID-19 surge, reopening of schools and colleges was out of the question. Hence, the authorities, like elsewhere in India, switched to an online teaching mode. To introduce an effective online class system in educational institutions, one must have proper internet network connectivity, good infrastructure, accessories such as functional computers, tablets, or smartphones, and earphones, as well as a proper work or study space. Most importantly, proper training and preparedness need to be imparted to both the teachers and the students for the smooth and effective functioning of online classes.

The experience with remote learning has been below par so far. Almost 60% of the schools and colleges are located in the rural areas with poor access to internet connectivity. Moreover, many poor families could not afford to give their wards a smartphone which is a basic need for a virtual learning system. In such cases, online class remained an unrealized alternative. The pandemic exposed the deep digital divide in our societies between those with access to modern technology and knowledge and those unable to even afford a smartphone to access online class, which goes against the very ethos of India's education policy of providing basic and equal education to all. Although numerous training workshops were organized for equipping teachers to conduct virtual classes, it was nearly impossible to utilize all the virtual tools and technologies. Since only those living in network zones could access the classes, attendance was low in number. Teachers teaching at different colleges and universities, like the author herself, had to dispense with online classes and instead rely on WhatsApp and Google Classroom. Readings and lecture recordings were uploaded on these applications for students to access them later. This deprived students of interactions and class discussions.

Moreover, often they would get distracted with smartphones in their hands and the long recording of lectures without any scope for reciprocation, communication, and interaction made it a difficult task for them to focus as it got very monotonous. Being one of the least literate states, getting students to register for online learning apps such as Google Classroom was itself a challenging task. To access these online learning apps, one needs to have an email ID to be able to register. It was learned that most of the students did not have any email account so this posed another hurdle when it came to submitting assignments or conducting tests. In such cases, simple messaging apps like WhatsApp were used. In general, the pandemic has shattered the entire education system where the weaker sections were affected the most and virtual classes proved ineffective.

COVID-19 does not affect everyone in the same way. Its impact across and within societies remains variegated, as it lays bare existing inequalities and further accentuates them. Studies have revealed that women in northeast India generally, and in Arunachal Pradesh particularly, were among the most affected group. Their predominant roles as caregivers and frontline health workers made them vulnerable and prone to infection. They also faced difficulty in assessing reproductive health services (IWGIA, ILO, 2020). The lockdowns caused an increased burnout for many women and adversely affected their mental/emotional health (Goswami and Narah, 2021). The policy of isolation and confinement due to lockdown also led to increased levels of domestic and gender-based violence (Ngurang, 2021).

Government Initiatives

Arunachal Pradesh was among those few states which performed better than other states in tackling the pandemic. Although the pandemic created fear and uncertainty among the masses, the state government took some proactive steps to contain the spread. It combined efforts with other stakeholders such as health workers, police, community-based organizations, and local self-help groups etc. (Business Standard, 2021). The state government declared a lockdown on March 17, a week before the national lockdown, to ensure that virus did not spread to the already ill-equipped state. Some of the policy initiatives taken by the state government included an immediate halt on issuing permit passes to non-native people. It was also one of the very few states to provide free testing at all the checkpoints to prevent the transmission of the virus (WHO, 2021).

Various contributions and donation forums for effective COVID-19 management were initiated by the government and other community-based organizations to provide aid to its people. The most prominent donation forum was the Chief Minister's Relief Fund. All the government servants supported the cause by forgoing 5% of their salary and 35% from MLAs. Forty-five MLAs contributed 25 lakhs each besides other individuals contributing to the total amount of Rs. 23 crore (Business Standard, 2021). Under the Chief Minister's Relief Fund (CMRF), Rs. 3,500 were provided to those students who were stranded outside due to the lockdown (Utpal, 2020). On similar grounds of providing relief and assistance to the vulnerable sections of the society during emergencies such as pandemic, government under various schemes extended assistance to the economically weaker sections of the state as they were the ones worst affected in pandemic. For instance, under Pradhan Mantri Garib Kalyan Anna Yojana that aims to promote welfare and provide assistance to marginalised people,free rations were provided to 90,000 BPL families including migrant labours as they were among the worst affected. The government also provided three months of free LPG connections to several thousand families under the Ujala scheme, a program launched under Pradhan Mantri Awas Yojana that provides financial support/subsidised rate for LPG gas cylinder connection to the BPL households. Lastly, Farmers registered under the PM Kisan scheme were given Rs. 1000.

There were many awareness campaigns organized by the Indian Medical Association Arunachal Pradesh such as Mask4Arunachal and Mask4all to promote and encourage the use of masks and also to provide free handmade masks. A campaign by the States Doctors Association called Mission Sahayog was organized to provide medical essentials and facilities such as masks, sanitizers, and vitamins etc. (Government of Arunachal Pradesh, 2021). Arunachal Pradesh Women Welfare Society distributed stitched handmade masks along with some cash, food, and other essentials. All these donations and distributions were aimed at helping the needy and underprivileged sections of the districts (Ministry of Rural Development, 2020). The state government had also approved an amount of Rs. 50,000 as ex-gratia to the next of kin of those who died due to COVID-19 from the State Disaster Response Fund (Government of Arunachal Pradesh, East Siang, 2021). The Arunachal Pradesh government actively used digital modes to enhance COVID-19 awareness, distribute standard operating procedures (SOPs), debunk fake news and disinformation. Several social networking sites, including MyGOV Arunachal, Arunachal against Corona, Arunachal IPR, and the Department of Health Arunachal Pradesh, were developed to provide daily updates on the pandemic condition. Additionally, the government released the COVIDcare app for those in quarantine, allowing them to self-report their health status and obtain critical COVID-19 information. Telemedicine services were also implemented in partnership with the State Government and the Indian Medical Association, with phone consultations (Government of Arunachal Pradesh, 2021).

Community Response

One of the reasons for the state to be able to fight the Pandemic despite having poor health facilities and inadequate resources was the teamwork and solidarity shown by every community with their district administration. It was the extraordinary work of the ordinary people that made the state more resilient against the Covid and consequently lower infection and lower fatality rates (Kalita, 2020). The government was able to gain their trust and cooperation in communicating important information to the public regarding the virus. The strong social mobilization included diverse civil society actors/local institutions and provided social safety nets to the most vulnerable sections. The village councils' headmen were helping to enforce the preventive care measures in their respective villages (Katiyar, 2020).

However, the most important factor worth mentioning is the community values, beliefs, and rituals that helped the state in its fight against the virus. Arunachal

Pradesh practices a tradition of isolation and segregation whenever there is a threat from any epidemic or unknown disease. Villages are shut down along with shops and all other activities are shut down, thereby maintaining a strict lockdown. Meanwhile, the local village councils ensure the supply of daily needs and essential services (Banerjee, 2020). The pandemic, in a way revived such age-old rituals and traditions of the tribal land which were followed since time immemorial in cases of epidemic outbreaks. Much before the countrywide lockdown and the state lockdown were announced, the tribal communities of every district imposed self-lockdown in their respective villages to contain the transmission of the virus.

The indigenous rituals were performed in order to prevent the epidemic outbreak in the villages and to ward off the evil spirits that were believed to be responsible for the outbreak of epidemics (Doye and Basar, 2020). The most important component of these rituals used to be village lockdown, self-quarantine, and the setting of rules and restrictions that were to be followed mandatorily by every family in order to ensure no entry and exit is allowed to anyone until the epidemic ceased (Doye and Basar, 2021). Prior to the announcement of lockdown and self-quarantine, it is made sure that an adequate supply of essential items such as food, basic medicines, etc., is stored in every individual house to meet their daily needs. The lockdown would continue for days and weeks and at times for months until the deadly disease ceased. These indigenous rituals are known by different names in different communities. For instance, it is known as "Ali-Ternam" in the Galo community, "Motor" in the Adi community, and "Arrue" in the Nyishi community (Acharya, 2020).

With the advent of COVID-19, these age-old traditional practices were performed by many tribal communities. Self-imposed village lockdowns and self-quarantines were strictly followed after the rituals were performed by the local priests. Temporary gates or barricades were constructed out of bamboo and tree logs at the entrance point to prevent any kind of entry/exit of people and also to ward off the evil spirits or bad omens. The peoplecoming from different parts of the country were not allowed to enter the village premises until quarantined properly (Lepcha, 2020a). Strict patrolling was done at the entrance gates by the villagers on a rotation basis. The villagers of Tirap and Longding districts that share an open border with Myanmar were seen erecting barricades shutting all border roads that link to Myanmar to prevent any kind of cross-border movements (Arunachal Times, 2020).

From the very beginning, as mentioned earlier, individuals at the community level, instead of waiting for government assistance, took a very proactive role in providing aid and services to the needy people. For instance, Mr. John Panyang, a secondary school teacher in the East Siang district, voluntarily took up the responsibility of rendering service to the villagers by setting up a temporary screening center at the Assam-Arunachal Pradesh boundary. In his own capacity, he purchased the required equipment for the screening tests such as masks, gloves, sanitizers, and thermal scanner machines (Tribune, 2020). Likewise, in smaller remote districts of Arunachal Pradesh, local communities are often seen solving problems by themselves rather than waiting for government action. One such incident was witnessed in the Upper Subansiri district where, amidst lockdown, local people were seen constructing a hanging bridge that was washed away by the floods, due to which the movement of people, essential commodities, and medical supplies were affected (Agrawal, 2020). Many such community acts were witnessed where local people came forward to donate or procure essential items as part of the relief camp. The author herself volunteered as a member of one of the donation drive camps—"Masks for Tirap" (Tirap district)—which collected around five lakh rupees in cash which was used to provide essential rations to daily-wage earners. Handmade masks, soaps, sanitizers, and disinfectant sprays were distributed to the villages of the Tirap district and because hospitals in Arunachal lacked the resources, PPE kits and testing kits were procured and supplied to the district hospitals. Awareness campaigns were also organized in local languages.

Women Self Help Group (SHG) provided breakfast, lunch, tea, and refreshments to police personnel engaged in duty for COVID-19 (Ministry of Rural Development, 2020). The Vulnerability Reduction Fund was used by the community institutions for preparing kits comprising of staple foods, cooking oil, and personal hygiene products like washing soaps for the most vulnerable households in the village. AAMYA NGO was instrumental in providing oxygen concentrators in three Eastern districts—Anjaw, Changlang and Lower Dibang Valley—to be installed in their district hospitals (Singh, 2021). Their initiative was largely targeted at migrant workers from Bihar, West Bengal, Uttar Pradesh, Assam and other poor families of the eastern districts. Around 14,000 of these poor vulnerable families were provided with dry rations and medical kits (Singh, 2021).

Mass awareness campaigns and the aids were provided for the native and non-native residents of Eastern Arunachal Pradesh especially Dibang Valley supporting 3,600 adolescent girls, boys, young women, and minors were organized to raise awareness on how to prevent the spread of COVID-19, including tackling stigma and myths surrounding vaccinations. ASHA and Aganwadi Workers were provided with 10,000 face masks, 900 Oximeters, 600 medical kits, and 1,200 dry ration kits to enable them to continue delivering services to COVID-19 patients (Singh, 2021). Other group initiatives included farmers' collectives, such as FPOs in the state, such as Diyun Farmer Producer Organization, promoted by the National Bank for Agriculture and Rural Development (NABARD) in the Changlang district, and the Arunachal Farmer Producer Cooperative Society in Sagalee, Papum Pare, and many others, helped the public by way of supply of fresh homegrown vegetables by engaging themselves in door-to-door delivery (Nair, 2020).

Conclusion

Arunachal Pradesh is a relatively under-developed state among all the other northeastern states due to its unattainable terrain, inadequate transportation and communication infrastructure, lower literacy rates, and under-resourced public healthcare system. Nonetheless, the state performed efficiently in its fight against the COVID-19 pandemic. It had a low fatality rate and better recovery rates. The early response of imposing a lockdown in the state much before the countrywide lockdown was one of the key factors responsible for preventing community transmission. The non-issuance of Inner Line Permits and Protected Area Permits to the outsiders was the first major step taken by the state government. Strict surveillance at the entry and exit checkpoints, regular testing, adherence to SOP guidelines made it possible to contain the virus.

The first case was only reported from the Lohit district after one man returned from the Delhi congregation. The first case led to paranoia, insecurity, and stigmatization after which the government made sure to implement rigorous contact tracing, strict monitoring, and repeated testing for those who came in contact with the infected person and were sent to the quarantine centers thus further preventing the spread of the virus. The government extended the lockdown period for almost three months, from March to May. The prolonged lockdown caused many hardships and challenges, especially for daily-wage earners and migrants, but with the support of the government and many other individuals, community-based organizations, NGOs and self-help groups, relief was provided to the most vulnerable members of the community.

Every tribal community in the state played an engaging and proactive role during the pandemic. Various donation drives and awareness camps were organized to provide relief and educate masses on the importance of following SOPs, and also debunk the fake news, disinformation, and stigmatization related to COVID-19.

Much before the government could provide any kind of assistance, especially in the far-flung areas, people at the local level took initiatives and tried to solve problems in their own capacity. The state machinery did its institutional role of regulating checkpoints/trade points, restricting the movement of men and materials, and initiating vaccination drives. But in a state like Arunachal Pradesh, populated by indigenous peoples, quotidian life is largely organized around traditional community structures and practices. Community structures like village councils made timely interventions and took measures from establishing quarantines to delivering aid to the vulnerable. During the pandemic, every community adopted some form of self-resilience strategies to curb the spread of the virus. Tribal groups harnessed age-old practices and adopted self-isolation; they imposed a complete lockdown of their villages by constructing temporary barricades/gates made out of local materials, restricting entry/exit of outsiders.

Lastly, this pandemic one again exposed the chronic deficiencies in the health infrastructure of the region, hence it taught a lesson that the state needs to invest and upgrade its basic health infrastructure to be better prepared against any future challenges. It has also reinforced the need to minimize the state's over-dependence on neighboring Assam for all its essential needs and build a more self-reliant economy. The lockdown in Assam led to a sharp spike in prices as supply routes were shut. These shortages were more acute in urban areas which are home to migrants, daily-wage earners, businesses etc. than in rural areas which tend to be more self-sufficient. Therefore, the pandemic, by exposing the over-dependence on Assam, can be seen as an opportunity to promote and encourage locally grown products and also create a market for them so that dependency on the outside market is reduced and food crises can be avoided during emergencies.

Note

1 Rapid Antigen Test of a sample of the respiratory tract of a person is a detection test for presence or absence of antigen related to the COVID-19 virus.

References

Acharya, Kankan (2020), "Community values in Arunachal Pradesh high literacy rate in Mizoram ensure strict adherence to coronavirus lockdown", *Firstpost*, Mumbai, 8 April 2020. https://www.firstpost.com/health/community-values-in-arunachal-pradesh-high-literacy-in-mizoram-ensure-strict-adherence-to-coronavirus-lockdown-8240291.html

Agrawal, Palak (2020), "Arunachal Pradesh villagers build hanging bridge for transportation of essential commodities", *The Logical Indian*, Arunachal Pradesh, 13 July 2020. https://thelogicalindian.com/news/locals-in-arunachal-pradesh-constructs-hanging-bridge-22272

Arunachal Times. (2020), "Road links to Myanmar sealed amid covid-19 scare", *Arunachal Times*, Itanagar, 28 March 2020. https://arunachaltimes.in/index.php/2020/03/28/road-links-to-myanmar-sealed-amid-covid-19-scare/

Bage, Bikash and Maila Lama (2020), "Covid-19 Cases and preparedness of a Himalayan state to fight against the pandemic: A study of Arunachal Pradesh", *Journal of the Social Sciences*, 48(3): 3279. https://www.researchgate.net/publication/345241118_Covid-19_Cases_and_Preparedness_of_a_Himalayan_State_to_Fight_Against_the_Pandemic_A_Study_of_Arunachal_Pradesh

Banerjee, Rabi (2020), "Frontier resistance", *The Week*, 26 April 2020. https://www.theweek.in/theweek/current/2020/04/17/frontier-resistance.html

Business Strandard. (2020), "Arunachal designates state run TRIHMS as covid-19 treatment", *Business* Standard, Itanagar, 28 March 2020 https://www.business-standard.com/article/pti-stories/arunachal-designates-state-run-trihms-as-covid-19-treatment-120032800900_1.html

Chaudhary, Ishika (2020), "Rural realities North East", Impact Policy Research Institute [Online:Web]. 25 January 2022. https://www.impriindia.com/insights/event-rural-realities-north-east/

Choudhury, Ratnadip and Debanish Achom (2020), "Manipur shuts border with Myanmar, ban foreigners over virus", *Ndtv*, Guwahati, 10 March 2020. https://www.ndtv.com/india-news/manipur-shuts-border-with-myanmar-to-prevent-coronavirus-spread-2192588

Deccan Herald. (2020), "Arunachal Pradesh faces shortage of vegetables amid coronavirus lockdown", *Deccan Herald*, Itanagar, 18 April 2020. https://www.deccanherald.com/india/arunachal-pradesh-faces-shortage-of-vegetables-amid-coronavirus-lockdown-826915.html

Deori, Umrijyoti and Gitumoni konwar (2020), "Impact of COVID-19 in North Eastern States of India International", *Journal of Health Sciences and Research*, 10(6): 214–215 https://www.ijhsr.org/IJHSR_Vol.10_Issue.6_June2020/33.pdf

Doye, Eli and Gomar Basar (2021), "The tribal response to covid 19 pandemic: A case study of galo tribe of Arunachal Pradesh", *Ensemble*, 1: 24–26 http://www.ensembledrms.in/wp-content/uploads/2021/04/ensemble-2021-sp1-a003-1.pdf

Goswami, Kakali and Yuma Narah (2021), "The effect of Covid-19 on women in northeast India: An inter-sectionalism perspective", *The International Journal of Indian Psychology*, 9(1): 2349–3429. https://ijip.in/pdf-viewer/?id=34119

Government of Arunachal Pradesh. (2020), "Tackling the corona pandemic-Arunachal Pradesh" [Online:Web]. 23 January 2022. https://blog.mygov.in/tackling-the-corona-pandemic-arunachal-pradesh/

Government of Arunachal Pradesh. (2021), "East Siang district Covid 19", *Pasighat*, https://eastsiang.nic.in/notice_category/covid-19/

Government of Arunachal Pradesh. (2022), "Department of health and family welfare, Itanagar", http://health.arunachal.gov.in/?page_id=1154

Government of India. (2020), "Community and institutional response to COVID-19 in India: Role of women's self-help groups and national rural livelihoods mission", *Ministry of Rural Development*, New Delhi, 3 June 2021. https://iwwage.org/wp-content/uploads /2020/12/Swayam-Report.pdf

https://iwwage.org/wp-content/uploads/2020/12/Swayam-Report.pdf

India Spend Team. (2021), "More than half of districts with high covid 19 positivity are Himalayan", *India Spend Team*, 3 July 2021, Mumbai https://www.indiaspend.com/ covid-19/himalaya-district-positivity-rate-infections-testing-759064

International Work Group for Indigenous Affairs and International Labour Organization. (2020), "The impact of Covid-19 on indigenous communities: Insights from indigenous navigators", October 2020. https://www.ilo.org/gender/Informationresources/ Publications/WCMS_757475/lang--en/index.htm

Jini, Moji (2020), "TRIHMS and Covid-19 pandemic in Arunachal Pradesh", *Arunachal Times*, Itanagar, 24 September 2020. https://arunachaltimes.in/index.php/2020/09/24/ trihms-and-covid_19-pandemic-in-arunachalpradesh/

Kalita, Prabin (2020), "five northeast states among 14 with good covid response", *Times of India*, 24 September 2020. https://timesofindia.indiatimes.com/city/guwahati/five -northeast-states-among-14-with-good-covid-response-centre/articleshow/78291341 .cms

Katiyar, Prerna (2020), "How local communities in northeast are at the forefront of fight against coronavirus", *The Economic Times*, 18 July 2020 https://economictimes .indiatimes.com/news/politics-and-nation/how-local-communities-in-northeast-are-at -the-forefront-of-fight-against-coronavirus/articleshow/77038858.cms

Kumar, Pradeep (2020), "Lockdown impact on Arunachal Pradesh tea hubs", *The Telegraph*, Itanagar, 29 April 2020. https://www.telegraphindia.com/north-east/lockdown-impact -on-arunachal-pradesh-tea-hubs/cid/1769091

Lepcha, Damien (2020a), "Arunachal tribes perform age old rituals to stop Covid 19 spread", *Eastmojo*, Arunachal Pradesh, 26 March 2020 https://www.eastmojo.com/news/2020/03 /26/arunachal-tribes-perform-age-old-rituals-to-stop-covid-19-spread/

Lepcha, Irani Sonowal (2020b), "Arunachal government constitutes panel for economic revival", *Eastmojo*, Itanagar, 28 May 2020. https://www.eastmojo.com/news/2020/05 /28/covid-19-arunachal-govt-constitutes-panel-for-economic-revival/

Nair, Gopa Kumaran (2020), "Covid-19 shutdown and pointers for agricultural sector in Arunachal Pradesh", *Arunachal Times*, Itanagar, 23 April 2020 https://arunachaltimes .in/index.php/2020/04/23/covid-19-shut-down-and-pointers-for-agriculture-sector-in -arunachal-pradesh/

Ngurang, Reena (2021), "Mrs Yaji and the lockdown: The plight of a Nyishi woman in a patriarchal society", *The Wire*, 9 April 2021. https://thewire.in/women/mrs-yaji-and-the -lockdown-the-plight-of-a-nyishi-woman-in-a-patriarchal-society

Parashar, Utpal (2020), "Covid-19 lockdown: Stranded people to get financial aid from CM relief fund, announces Arunachal government", *Hindustan Times*, 17 April 2020. https://www.hindustantimes.com/india-news/covid-19-lockdown-stranded-people-to -get-financial-aid-from-cm-relief-fund-announces-arunachal-govt/story-GObw8tgFtaG 6reNncxQZZP.html

PTI. (2020), "Arunachal may reopen for tourists", *Deccan Herald*, Itanagar, 28 September 2020. https://www.deccanherald.com/national/north-and-central/coronavirus-lockdown -arunachal-may-reopen-for-tourists-after-october-says-cm-894388.html

PTI. (2020), "Arunachal Pradesh faces shortage of vegetables amid coronavirus lockdown", *Deccan Herald*, Itanagar, 18 April 2020 https://www.deccanherald.com/national/east -and-northeast/arunachal-pradesh-faces-shortage-of-vegetables

PTI. (2020), "Coronavirus outbreak: Arunachal Pradesh registers first covid-19 case after 31 year old tablighi jamaat attendee tests positive", *Firstpost*, Itanagar, 2 April 2020. https:// www.firstpost.com/health/coronavirus-outbreak-arunachal-pradesh-registers-first-covid -19-case-after-31-year-old-tablighi-jamaat-attendee-tests-positive-8219381.html

PTI. (2020), "Lockdown: Arunachal government to provide financial help to stranded people", *Economic Times*, Itanagar, 16 April 2020. https://economictimes.indiatimes .com/news/politics-and-nation/lockdown-arunachal-government-to-provide-financial -assistance-to-stranded-people/articleshow/75182500.cms

PTI. (2021), "Arunachal could contain spread of covid 19 thanks to teamwork", *Business Standard*, Itanagar, 2 March 2021. https://www.business-standard.com/article/ current-affairs/arunachal-could-contain-spread-of-covid-19-thanks-to-teamwork-cm -121030201171_1.html

PTI. (2021), "Arunachal Pradesh people impose self lockdown as covid cases rise", *Economic Times*, Itanagar, 16 July 2021. https://economictimes.indiatimes.com/news /india/remote-arunachal-circle-people-impose-self-lockdown-as-covid-cases-rise/ articleshow/84475264.cms

Sinha, Biswanath (2020), "Controlling Covid-19: Learnings from the Northeast", *India Development Review*, Mumbai, 22 April 2020. https://idronline.org/controlling-covid -19-learnings-from-the-northeast/

Singh, Shriya (2020), "Covid response in North East Border States-a socio anthropological perspective" [Online:web]. 25 January 2022. https://www.researchgate.net/publication /341435451_Covid_response_in_Northeast_India

The Tribune. (2020), "Arunachal teacher turns into Covid-19 warrior", *The Tribune*, Arunachal, 8 June 2020. https://www.tribuneindia.com/news/schools/arunachal-teacher -willingly-turns-into-covid-19-warrior-96233

WHO. (2021), "WHO's all women team in Arunachal Pradesh brave rough terrain and poor connectivity to provide healthcare in a pandemic", *WHO*, 8 March 2021. https://www .who.int/india/news/feature-stories/detail/who-s-all-women-team-in-arunachal-pradesh -brave-rough-terrain-and-poor-connectivity-to-provide-healthcare-in-a-pa

20 Sikkim's Response to COVID-19

The Fight Continues

Chunku Bhutia

Introduction

The world had its first interface with the new virus which was known as "Coronavirus/COVID-19" when the Wuhan Municipal Health Commission, China, furnished reports on December 31, 2019 about several cases of pneumonia in the Wuhan city of China. The same was confirmed by the World Health Organization (WHO) on January 4, 2020 and it was on January 5, 2020 the World Health Organization published its first technical report on the virus. Thereafter, on January 10, 2020 WHO released important guidelines worldwide pertaining to the virus. It was on January 13, 2020 that COVID-19 was first detected outside Wuhan (China), i.e., in Thailand (WHO, 2020).[1]

Alarming State of COVID-19 in India and Sikkim's Response: Zero COVID-19 Cases in Sikkim

In India, the first COVID-19 case was reported in Kerala on January 30, 2020 and gradually an increase in the number of cases was noticed. Within five months, three states, namely Maharashtra, Delhi, and Gujarat, were identified as hotspots for COVID-19 due to the high rate in these states (Kumar et al. 2020).[2]

It was on March 22, 2020 that the Government of India announced the "Janata Curfew" with a 14-hour lockdown which was later then increased to 21 days lockdown from March 25, 2020 to May 3, 2020. Due to the increasing cases, lockdown was further extended to May 17, 2020 and the identified hotspots across India were put under complete lockdown to prevent community transmission of the virus (Ibid.).

While the rest of the country was grappling with the outbreak and spread of the virus, a small northeastern state, Sikkim, was making headlines as the state with zero COVID-19 cases. So, the initial phases of COVID-19 did not affect Sikkim despite the fact that Sikkim survives majorly on the tourism sector and it shares a border with Tibet (China). Such close geographical proximity of Sikkim to China could have caused havoc for the state, but, on the contrary, the state in the initial phases had its success story to share with the world.

Such a triumph was seen as a result of the several timely precautionary measures taken by the state government (which will be discussed later in this chapter).

DOI: 10.4324/9781003304517-25

However, this triumph was short-lived with the state recording its first COVID-19 case in the month of May. One of the students who returned from Delhi was detected as being COVID-19 positive (The Hindu, May 23, 2020).

Gradually, the number of cases in the state increased from 1 on May 23, 2020, to 300+ cases in 22 July 2020, and 4000+ cases towards the end of the year. Infact, the state suddenly went from being the state with zero COVID-19 cases to being listed as the third state, after Delhi and Punjab, with the highest case-fatality rate (CFR).[3] The state by the end of 2020 had recorded 95 COVID-19 deaths out of 300 active cases. Sikkim's CFR has increased from 1.79% at the end of October 2020 to of 2.07% by mid of November. This was definitely an alarming situation for a small state like Sikkim with a population of approximately only 6 lakh (Taskin, 2020).

As informed by the state health bulletin through their official social media page, in November 2020 the number of tests done was 60,875. The total cases recorded was 4,691 out of which active cases were 289. The total recoveries recorded was 4,218. The maximum positive cases were found in East India. Such data reveals that the health situation in Sikkim seems to be worrisome; however, the efficiency and effort of the health workers in handling it is well reflected in the number of recoveries in the state.

Even in the following year, the state witnessed an increase in the number of cases, but the state began its vaccination drive in the month of January (2021). The first priority was given to the health workers of the state, and initially 120 health workers were vaccinated. By the second week of January, around 16,042 health workers were vaccinated with the first dose. Along with the health workers, even the waste management workers were prioritized for the first dose of the vaccine. The Chief Minister, in an interview with the local daily newspaper, mentioned that

> Vaccination has begun in Sikkim after the arrival of the first lot of 12,500 Covid doses. It will be free of cost for the frontliners. For the second phase, we will act as per the Centre's decision. If they say that the State government must purchase the vaccine then we will buy it and do vaccination of the people here.
>
> (Ongmu, January 17, 2021)

Such statements from the head of the government reflect the preparedness of the state government in tackling such a health emergency.

The state government later declared that for the second phase of the COVID-19 vaccination, those above the age of 50 years along with people who have comorbidities were to be prioritized. In fact, by the end of the year 2021, the state was recorded as 100% vaccinated with the first dose and around 74% of the population had received the second dose as well, thereby making Sikkim the first state in India to be 100% vaccinated. Such an achievement by a small northeastern state deserves attention and highlight, since the most advanced nations and states were grappling with the disease and Sikkim, with its limited infrastructure, health workers, and other frontline workers could achieve such a goal. This definitely boosted the enthusiasm and ethos of every Sikkimese and also restored faith in the government and the health workers which undoubtedly was direly needed given the situation at the time.

However, despite such achievements, the state recorded COVID-19 cases in the year 2021 and also in the following year, though the number of active cases kept decreasing. In December 2021, as reported by the *Business Standard* newspaper on December 2, 2020, 127 active cases, around 31,382 recovered cases, and around 403 deaths were recorded.

Despite the increase in cases, Sikkim once again was in the limelight for being the first state in India to have administered the second dose of vaccine to the eligible population. Such achievements are also reflective of the efficiency and efforts of the frontline workers as well as the people of Sikkim who cooperated with the authorities, guidelines, and the instructions provided.

State Initiative Towards Combating COVID-19: Programmes and Policies

The Government of Sikkim on March 5, 2020, issued a notification stating "in view of the rapid spread of Corona Virus, no Inner Line Permit may be issued w.e.f March 5, 2020, to all foreign nationals" (Government of Sikkim 2020). Further, a few days later (March 17, 2020), the state government announced a complete ban on domestic tourists entering the state (Sikkim Herald 2020, April 17).[4] So, Sikkim closed its borders with West Bengal, Nepal, and China (Nathula Pass). In fact, immediately after the outbreak of the news from Wuhan, China, the state government issued orders to the health officials at the main border Rangpo (Sikkim-West Bengal border) to screen people entering the state from January 28, 2020 onward. In addition, the concerned officials at the borders (both Rangpo and Melli) were directed to maintain proper documentation of every individual entering the state. Such preparedness on the part of the state government proved immensely positive, thereby leading to the state being the only state with zero COVID-19 cases.

Interestingly, even before other states could completely grasp the concept of community transmission, the state government through the Education Department issued a notification on March 18, 2020, for the closure of all government and private universities, colleges, schools, Teacher Education Institutes, training institutes, tutorials, coaching centers, and educational institutions within the state of Sikkim from March 17, 2020 to April 15, 2020, or until further orders. It was also further instructed that the use of the biometric device for attendance was to be replaced with manual attendance and frequent sanitization of the workplace was also to be ensured. Such meticulous preparedness on the part of the state government ensured the safety of every individual within the state.

Furthermore, the Chief Minister of the state Shri P.S. Tamang (Golay) informed that the state has well-equipped medical infrastructure. He mentioned in an interview that the state has

> 166 beds ready to take up coronavirus cases at STNM (Sochaykhang) hospital, 20 beds at CRH (Central Referral Hospital), Tadong and 41 beds at the Army hospital in Libing. STNM hospital has 55 ventilators, CRH and

the Military Hospital have two ventilators each. He also informed about the quarantine centres established by the Centre at SIRD Karfectar, Mining Ground near Rangpo, Power Guest House at Nayabazaar, and SICUN training centre, Assam Lingzey.[5]

Some of the preventive measures adopted in Sikkim were notified through various notifications:

1. A State Task Force and a Sub-divisional Task Force were constituted to tackle the COVID-19 situation.
2. The entry of all domestic and foreign tourists into the state was banned.
3. All educational institutes and anganwadis were closed.
4. The use of recreational facilities such as casinos, gyms, and cinemas were prohibited.
5. The private industries were prohibited from employing migrant workers from outside the state and were ordered to avoid large concentration of workers in one place.
6. The government ordered the suspension of all non-essential work.
7. The supply of all essential commodities such as food grains, vegetables, sanitizers, and masks was allowed.
8. Strict regulation of intra-state movement of private vehicles, two-wheelers, and taxis on an odd-even basis (allowing plying of vehicles on alternate days as per the number plate) was put in place until April 15, 2020. After the announcement of nation wide lockdown, the inter-state movement of vehicles was restricted to vehicles transporting essential goods. These vehicles were to have a permanent pass for such movement. On April 5, intra-state movement of vehicles was restricted to government officials, transportation of essential commodities, banks and PSUs, and media and cable networks. Their passes were made valid only from 8 a.m. to 5 p.m.
9. The state government did not hold several days of budget session instead the session was limited to only two days in order to evade any chances of prolong human contact in such gathering which could lead to spread of the virus.
10. Establishments which were permitted to remain functional included law enforcement agencies, health services, electricity and water services, petrol pumps, and media. Shops for Public Distribution System (PDS), groceries, vegetables, milk, and medicines were only allowed to remain open from 9 a.m. to 4 p.m.
11. The state prohibited the sale of hand sanitizers without a drug manufacturing license label. It also prohibited the sale of N95 masks to the general public without a valid prescription.
12. The state government notified that transit camps (temporary accommodation) were set up for drivers and helpers of vehicles carrying essential goods.
13. Online yoga classes were being conducted to help people stay physically and mentally healthy during COVID-19.
14. Through the Information and Public Relations Department, the Government of Sikkim's awareness program on healthy food and other essential home remedy was being telecasted.

The state's authorities took timely preventive measures to fight the virus rather than taking steps to tackle the situation after its outburst. This anticipative and long-term vision of the state authorities did work in favor of the people of the state; however, absolute containment of the virus could not be guaranteed since the officers were accountable to people of Sikkim residing outside the state, including the students pursuing studies outside the state. So with people returning to the state, the gates were opened for those who were stranded, and inadvertently the virus entered the state. Initially, however, the state was the only onewith zero cases of COVID-19. The Chief Minister informed in an interview with *Times of India* on April 27, 2020, that the Prime Minister lauded the efforts of the state authorities in combating the outbreak of the virus in the state.

Dilemma For Sikkim: Challenges Faced

Besides taking various breakthrough precautionary steps, the state government was challenged with the issue of people stranded outside the state due to the nation-wide lockdown, which included students, patients, and others working in various private firms outside the state. The state government had tough decisions to make since opening the borders for the people stranded could lead to the outbreak of the virus within the state, but on the other hand, the stranded people of Sikkim were appealing to the state government for help and support to enable them to return to the state.

The state government initiated a few immediate measures to reach out to the stranded people:

1. The state government announced that they would provide Rs. 5,000 to each student stranded outside Sikkim during the nationwide lockdown.
2. The state government announced that they woud be providing financial relief of Rs. 30,000 to each patient undergoing treatment and stranded outside Sikkim from the Chief Minister's Relief Fund (The Economic Times, April 16 2020).[6]
3. The state government benignly directed all contractors/employers to pay migrant and casual labourers on the due date without any deductions due to the lockdown. The state government also provided grants worth Rs. 2,000 to the 7,836 registered building and other construction workers.

In addition to such welfare measures adopted for the stranded people, the state government initiated other economic welfare measures to ease the financial losses. One major challenge the state faced was the losses encountered in the tourism sector. For Sikkim, tourism is one of the major economic sectors, and this brutal hit due to COVID-19 meant a considerable loss for the state's economy. The state government, as such, was expected to brainstorm strategies to provide whatever possible help and support to the stakeholders of the tourism sector.

On the other hand, the policymakers gradually began to discuss the possibilities and strategies needed to bring the stranded people back to the state. Such discussion had to be fast-tracked considering the increase in racial attacks on the people of the northeast after the virus outbreak. The northeastern people were being called "corona", and slogans like "Go Corona Go" were also being shouted against the northeastern people (The Print, March 25, 2020). From verbal slurs to being physically attacked in major cities against the northeastern people, the state government had the additional challenge of protecting its people from such racial attacks during COVID 19.

Furthermore, the state government of Sikkim, in May 2020, launched a new online registration system (www.covid19sikkim.org) to facilitate the return of stranded people to Sikkim across different parts of the country. The people wanting to return to the state were to register themselves in the online portal.[7] In May, more than 1,000 people were returned to the state in Sikkim Nationalised Transport (SNT—state-run buses) from Siliguri (West Bengal) through two main checkposts—Rangpo and Melli. All the returnees must stay in designated quarantine centers, and the health officials screen their health at the checkpost (The Hindu, May 13 2020).[8]

The process of bringing back the stranded people began in May, and in the same month, the state recorded the first case of COVID-19. The first COVID-19 positive patient was a 25-year-old youth who had traveled from New Delhi on May 17, 2020, and reached the Melli checkpost on May 19, 2020, through an SNT bus. He was put into a designated quarantine center as per the norms, but later on May 21, 2020, he showed some symptoms and tested positive. Sikkim had recorded its first COVID-19 case; however, the number of cases in the country by then had crossed 1 lakh.[9] Sikkim, through its timely decisions and mechanisms, could contain the widespread disease.

Gradually the cases increased in the state, and the state government had to continue issuing guidelines across the state. The state government continued closing all the educational institutions, and the offices were to run at 50% capacity. Even the odd-even rule for vehicles was continued in the state. There were multiple opinions on the government's decision to allow Sikkim people residing outside to enter the state. As expected, people who were within the state's borders began to express critical remarks on the authorities' decision. The state government, as such, was bounded by the safety of the people within the state since, until the time the stranded Sikkimese people were brought into the state, the number of cases in the state was zero. But with the entry of the stranded people into the state, the virus too found its entry and in no time, Sikkim shifted from being the Green Zone state to that of the state with the third highest case fatality rate (CFR) (as mentioned earlier).

On the other hand, the state government also had to ensure the safety of the people of Sikkim stranded outside and especially with the increase in the racial attacks on people with Mongolian features (mostly northeastern people from India). In some major cities, the authorities had no other choice but to formulate strategies to bring back the students and other people from the state who had been residing outside the state. However, the authorities ensured absolute containment of the disease by setting up reverse transcription polymerase chain reaction (RT-PCR) tests at the border (Rangpo) itself, and even quarantine centers were set up at the border. Despite such meticulous efforts, gradually, the state recorded an increasing number of cases.

The challenge continued, but Sikkim, under visionary leadership, administrative support, and cooperation from the people of Sikkim, could well manage the COVID-19 cases in the state.

Role of Civil Society in Sikkim: Communitarian and Compassionate Approach

In India, civil society is understood as the "voluntary sector, voluntary organisations, non-government organisations, non-profit organisations". The various types of civil society organizations in India are non-government organizations (NGOs), Community-based organizations (CBOs), religious and faith-based organizations, and membership associations (Asian Development Bank 2023).

In Sikkim, the civil society has been very proactive. During the COVID-19 pandemic, several local civil society organizations undertook and initiated various mechanisms to help and support the state in combating the health emergency. Such proactiveness of the civil society organizations was supported and encouraged by the authorities. In March 2020, the state's Chief Minister announced that "whosoever desired to feed stray animals would be allowed to twice a day during the lockdown". In the words of the Chief Minister, "Let us be the voice for the voiceless". This announcement, integrated with the efforts of NGOs like Animals and US, Puppy Paw Rescue, The Guardians of Sikkim, and People of Animals, proved to be of immense help to street animals, specifically street dogs. In addition to these NGOs, the Sikkim Anti-Rabies and Animal Health (SARAH)[10] program also provided additional support to street animals by providing food, shelter, and treatment (IPR March 29 2020).

The state government on April 1, 2020, issued a press release[11] in which they mentioned that "...take stock of preparations on ground at Gram Panchayat Unit (GPU) level for successful implementation of protocols given by the Centre with respect to migrant labours and daily wagers, coordination with NGOs to strengthen awareness on COVID-19, strengthen our present health care system, and assure law and order during the lockdown" and the Director of Sikkim State Disaster Management Authority (SSDMA), Mr. G.C. Khanal called in for a meeting of various stakeholders of the state including the NGO named "The Helping Hand" and he said, "...involvement of NGOs for the cause of defeating entry of Covid-19 in Sikkim". These words of the authorities reflect upon the significant and catalytic role the state expected the NGOs to undertake during the health emergency. The NGO "Helping Hands" Chairman defined the NGO's role in creating awareness among people on the Dos and Don'ts guidelines provided by the National Disaster Management Authority (NDMA). The NGOs were to coordinate with the District Collector to distribute the relief materials. Since the health emergency was not just hazardous for the physical health, but it had an immense impact on the psychological well-being of the people, the state authorities relied on the NGOs to provide counselling and disseminate government information.

Another NGO in Jorethang, South Sikkim, named "Great Mates", carried out a sanitization drive in Jorethang Bazaar in coordination with the municipal corporation. In the bazaar, the NGO sanitized prime public areas like ATMs, public playgrounds, police stations, offices, taxi parking plazas, and a few residential complexes. Furthermore, another NGO known as the "Blood Army of Sikkim" provided hearse vehicles named "Swaargyaan" to people facing difficulties in organizing for the last journey of their loved ones.

Another NGO named "Smile Foundation" initiated the "Health for All" program, which aimed to provide healthcare services to marginalized sections of society in Gangtok, Sikkim.[12]

Besides these several civil society organizations, people at the individual level were also rendering support of every nature during the crisis. One such individual in Sikkim was an entrepreneur Rewaj Chettri (founder of North-East Taxi services) who collected around 1,700 nos. of oximeters for the state from various donors within the country (Dhungel 2021).

Thus, the civil society organizations in Sikkim provided relief materials, setting up quarantine centers during the COVID-19 crisis. The NGOs in the state are involved in multiple sectors like education, healthcare, environment, and social development.

Impact of COVID-19 in Sikkim

Economic Impact

In India, the first state to initiate preventive measures against COVID-19 was Sikkim. But despite such preventative measures, COVID-19 immensely impacted the state's economy. It is known that the economic activity of any state/nation is divided into three categories: primary, secondary, and tertiary sectors. The primary sector includes agriculture, the secondary provides industry, and the tertiary includes the service sector. According to the State Finance Audit Report of 2021, the three industries contributed to the GSDP[13] of Sikkim in the year 2016–2021 in the following manner: the state recorded a marginal increase in the agriculture sector from 9.29% in 2016–2017 to 10.12% in 2020–2021. The secondary sector decreased from 58.67% in 2016–2017 to 52.50% in 2020–2021. There was an increase in the tertiary sector from 26.77% in 2016–2017 to 32.50% in 2020–2021. The same has been depicted in the Figure 20.1 (State Finance Audit Report 2021) (Figure 20.1).

Furthermore, the fluctuations in the three sectors can be understood through the chart below:

Figure 20.2 shows the yearly sectoral growth in gross state domestic product from 22.12% in the year 2016–2017 to 25.39% in the year 2017–2018, after that the industry experienced a dip in the year 2018–2019 showing the income in the agricultural sector as 16.31% and then 8.39% and 8.56% in the years 2019–2020 and 2020–2021 respectively.

Figure 20.3 depicts the fluctuations in the secondary sector of Sikkim. 2016–2017 and 2017–2018 witnessed an increase in income from 16.06% to 27.43%.

SECTORAL CONTRIBUTION T(
STATE DOMESTIC PRODUCT OF TH

70.00%

60.00%

50.00%

40.00%

30.00%

20.00%

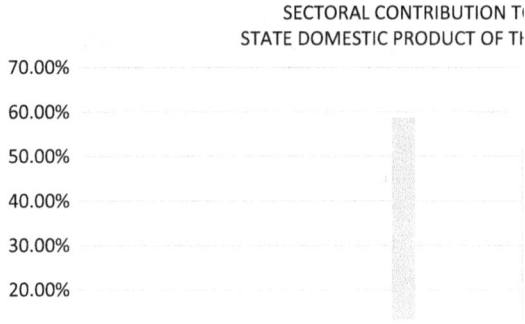

Figure 20.1 Sectoral Contribution to GSDP of Sikkim

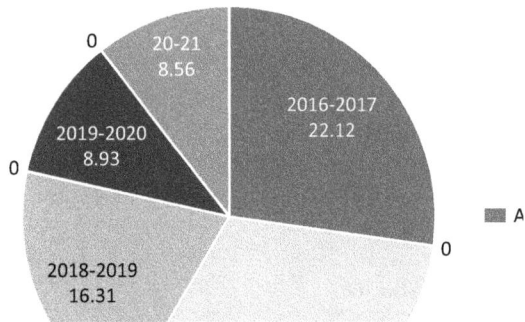

0 — 20-21 8.56 — 2016-2017 22.12 — 2019-2020 8.93 — 0 — 2018-2019 16.31 — A — 0

Figure 20.2 Primary Sector Increases Source: State Finance Audit Report of 2021

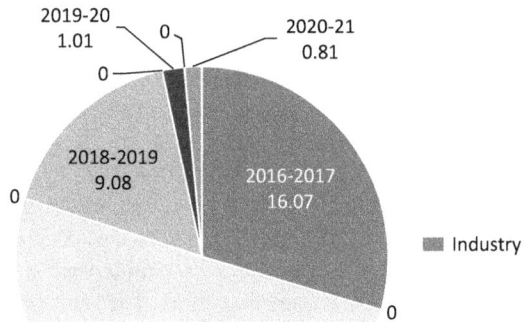

2019-20 1.01 — 0 — 2020-21 0.81 — 0 — 2018-2019 9.08 — 2016-2017 16.07 — 0 — Industry — 0

Figure 20.3 Fluctuations in the Secondary Sector of Sikkim Source: State Finance Audit
        Report of 2021

After that, there was an immense decrease in the sector from 2018 to 2021 (9.08%
to 0.81%).

Figure 20.4 depicts that in the tertiary sector in 2016–17, the percentage of
income was 6.23%. After that, it increased to 10.44% in the following year. In
2018–19, it went up to 19.06%, and then 26.5% in 2019–2020. Yet again, in 2020–
2021, the sector witnessed a dip from 26.5% to 15.44%.

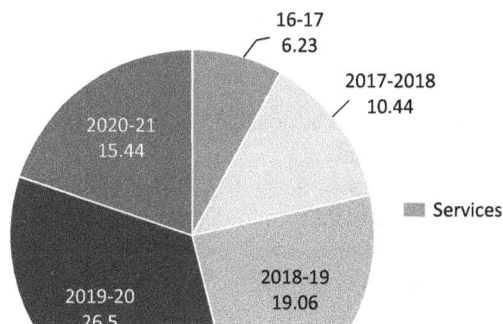

Figure 20.4 Tertiary Sector Source:State Finance Audit Report of 2021

The above data and charts reveal that all three economic sectors were adversely affected during COVID-19, and the tourism sector (tertiary sector) was the most affected. The state closed its borders in the year 2020 until October 2020. The state government also informed that the migrant laborers are also being retained in the form and provided with money, food, and shelter for survival. After that, the state government opened its borders to tourists on October 1, 2020, due to the guidelines of the Central Government. The hotels, homestays and all tourism-related services were also permitted to resume operations. The state authorities issued standard operating procedures (SOPs) for the hotels and the tourism sector.

However, the ill effects of COVID-19 on the tourism industry can be understood from the words of a director of a hotel organization:

> Over 80% of these inns are run on rent. The rent sum for the holder depends on the property's limit, quality, or area. The robust rent sum running Rs 1.5 lakh to 2.5 lakhs for every room every year should be paid ahead of time or in portions.

So, closing the borders would have imposed immense financial pressure on the hoteliers and other stakeholders of the tourism industry. Furthermore, one of the cab drivers in Gangtok mentioned that he is the sole breadwinner in his family and repaying the car loan is a big problem due to the lockdown. The non-payment of the monthly installments of the car loan would leave him jobless. Many such people drive cabs in Sikkim for their livelihood and are likely to lose their jobs due to the COVID-19 lockdown (Bhutia 2020).

As per the Central Government's directives, the state government decided to open its borders to tourists. Such a decision had to be made considering that almost 75% of the state's population is directly or indirectly dependent on the tourism industry. However, it was made clear that the tourism sector should be well managed and the people's health was not to be compromised. Furthermore, the government appointed a state-level Tourism Taskforce to supervise the safe operation of the tourism sector as per the SOP.

The SOPs formulated for the tourists and tourism sector as a whole during Unlock 1.0 were as follows:

1. The first re-opening phase will be considered for domestic tourists and foreign nationals residing in India only.
2. A tourist is advised to possess a valid COVID-negative certificate, (preferably RT-PCR/Truenat test, the real time reverse transcriptase-polymerase chain reaction test used to help detect Covid-19 virus. Truenat is a chip-based rapid molecular test for diagnosis of infectious disease) issued within 72 hours before the date of arrival.
3. A tourist must compulsorily register on the Sikkim Tourism Web Portal before traveling to Sikkim, and a copy of the "Travel Card" issued based on tourist registration should be carried at all times during travel in Sikkim.
4. All tourists traveling in Sikkim must be pre-booked with health and safety compliant accommodation units and travel agents/tour operators.
5. Tourists should ensure that their travel card is updated on the web portal as and when required.
6. All tourists traveling to Sikkim must carry a valid proof of identification.
7. Persons above 65 years of age, persons with comorbidities, pregnant women, and children below 10 years of age are advised to either avoid entirely or limit their travel. While traveling, they are advised to take extra precautions.
8. All Tourists traveling to Sikkim should carry their own set of protective gear, such as face masks/face shields, gloves, hand sanitisers, and thermometers.

In addition to the abovementioned guidelines, the state authorities also laid down similar guidelines for hotel operators and travel agents. The state government has sorted out a middle-path strategy wherein the resuming of the tourism industry considered that a significant munber of the population of the state depended on this sector (as mentioned earlier). Still, safety measures had to be taken to ensure that the escalation of the number of infected people did not happen in the state. But of course, the people understood that these measures were not foolproof. The people followed the guidelines provided religiously, especially since now the tourists were also allowed to enter the state. As a result of such consciousness, the state witnessed a decrease in the number of cases gradually even though the borders were open for tourists; for instance, as per the health bulletin of Sikkim (through social media, the health bulletin updated the public on the number of cases in the state), in September 2020 the active cases recorded ranged from 538 to 672. In October 2020, this ranged from 251 to 642.

The Chairman of the Sikkim Tourism Development Corporation (STDC), Shri Lukendra Rasaily, mentioned that the tourism sector in Sikkim suffered an immense loss of around Rs. 600 crore due to the pandemic. He adds, "The COVID-19 pandemic has had a debilitating impact on the tourism industry, which is the backbone of the state's economy" (Business Standard, December 27 2020).

The state government established an Economic Revival Committee in 2020 under the Chairmanship of Hon'ble MLA Shri Sonam Tshering Venchungpa.

The committee's main objective, as quoted by the Chairman, "is to bring back the economy to its normalcy and to consult with the stakeholders and to support a long-term economic pathway". The committee was to conduct discussions in two phases: one with the state government, and the second phase with the various stakeholders of the economy in the state. The committee was to conduct meetings with Sikkim Hotels and Restaurant Association (SHRA), All Sikkim Travels and Hospitality Association (ASTHA), Sikkim United Tourism Organisation (SUTO), Travel Agents Association of Sikkim (TAAS), Sikkim Association of Adventure Tour Operators (SAATO), Sikkim Amateur Mountaineering Association (SAMA), Sikkim Paragliding Association (SPA), Chamber of Commerce, and Hotel Owners Association. In addition to these, the committee was also to hold meetings with entrepreneurs, the online business Chalak Morcha, Luxury Tourist Vehicle Association, Local Taxi Drivers Association, Main Line Taxi Driver Association, Sikkim Taxi Driver cum Taxi Owners Association, Truck Drivers Association, and Truck Owners Association (Government of Sikkim 2020).[14]

Besides, the authorities initially issued notice for an odd-even rule on all vehicles plying within the state. The notification issued by the state Home Department read as follows:

> Inter-district movement of vehicles, including two-wheelers, shall be allowed on an odd-even basis. The odd-even arrangement shall be as given below: Vehicles with registration numbers ending with odd digit shall be allowed to ply on days with odd dates. Vehicles with registration numbers ending with even digit shall be allowed to ply on days with even dates.

Later, the odd-even rule was applied only to private vehicles, and the government and taxi vehicles were exempted. The state government notified the same in June 2022. This state government's decision can be understood as a step taken to recuperate the losses entailed in the tourism industry and the various stakeholders of the industry. The people possessing private vehicles were compelled to commute through public transport like taxis and buses. This did help, to some extent, support the taxi drivers to recuperate the losses suffered during COVID-19. This decision was criticized since people questioned the exemption of taxis and government vehicles. However, the authorities justified the decision to streamline the intense traffic jam in the state (Dhungel 2022). Besides these, the state government also provided Rs. 6,000 as relief money to all taxi drivers during the lockdown (Shiraz 2022).

Such pertinent steps were taken by the state authorities to help the tourism industry to reboot itself during COVID-19, and post-COVID-19, the tourism industry witnessed immense growth. The State Tourism Department officials said, "We have seen a massive growth of the tourism industry with the arrival of a large number of visitors from across the country since late last year after the state government lifted the lockdown". The tourism department recorded that around 3.08 lakh domestic tourists and around 6,055 foreigners visited the state from October 2021 to March 2022 (Ibid.).

To a great extent, the ill effects of COVID-19 in the economic sector could be subdued with preventive measures, prompt decisions of the state authority, and compliance with the guidelines by the state's people.

Socio-cultural Impact

In India, usually, gender roles are particular. For instance, men are the head of the family who go out in the public space to earn their livelihood and women, on the other hand, are confined to household chores. With such a setup in the family, almost every middle-class family has an employed helping hand to do the household chores under the supervision of the females of the house. However, this system was disrupted by the lockdown imposed during COVID-19. As mentioned, the state declared a lockdown on March 22, 2020. After that, the Central Government announced a pan-India lockdown from March 24, 2020. This led to people being restricted to their respective homes since all offices and institutions were to be shut, and the households were deprived indirectly of house help due to the lockdown. It brought about specific changes in the work dynamics at home since the child caring and house chores were shared between the family members, regardless of gender (Ruppanner et al. 2018).

Furthermore, the cremating rituals of different communities within the state were kept aside, and the government issued guidelines for carrying out death rituals. The state government provided "makeshift crematoriums", i.e., temporary crematoriums, to carry out the final rites of the deceased. In most cases, the families being the primary contact are bound to quarantine themselves. In such a case, the family members pay the last respect and prayers to the COVID-19-infected deceased virtually. In contrast, the last rites are carried out by designated people; like in the case of Sikkim, some Gangtok Municipal workers were responsible for carrying out the funeral rites of the COVID-19-positive deceased.

The state government is compelled to issue several notifications restricting any gathering on any social occasion, including funeral rites. Sikkim witnessed its first COVID-19-related death on July 27, 2020, and as per the Central Government norms, the body of the deceased was not allowed to be taken home to the family; instead, the body was handed over to the Gangtok Municipal Corporation (GMC) for the final rites. It was informed by the Municipal Commissioner that "A GMC team dedicated to collection and disposal of bio-medical wastes from the containment areas was engaged for transportation and funeral of the deceased. They have been doing their duties wearing PPE kits, which was followed for the funeral".[15] The final rites in Sikkim are being carried out in Jalipool crematorium by a Hindu pandit under the guidance of Gangtok Municipal Corporation.

As per the National Directives for COVID-19 management, it was spelled out that the funeral/last rites-related gatherings shall heed social distancing guidelines and the maximum numbers allowed shall be no more than 20. Furthermore, even in marriages, the number of guests was limited to only 50. Such were the changes that were adopted to contain the spread of COVID-19, and these changes affected every individual since marriage and last rites are two significant events out of many where families, friends, and well-wishers come together to celebrate, rejoice, or share sorrow. But with COVID-19, families were seen mourning in seclusion since the COVID-19 restrictions specify that the primary contacts are to be isolated. In most cases, the family members are identified as the direct contacts of the deceased. Similarly, even in marriages, the number of guests has been limited as per the orders of the Government of India. So marriages are being celebrated as a mere family affair, in the presence of only the core family, rather than a social affair.

Even in Sikkim, irrespective of caste, color, or religion, all the funeral rites were carried out in the Jalipool crematorium. Hence, despite the significance of religious rituals and social affairs, COVID-19 triggers a realization that anything that truly matters is the culture and religion of humanity. In addition to these, it needs to be mentioned here that in Sikkim, it is with the outbreak of COVID-19 that the Buddhist monasteries in the year 2020, for the first time since the 1800s, did not organize the annual mask dance known as Khagyad Chaam during Losoong (Bhutia New year) (The Indian Express, December 14, 2020).[16]

As Aristotle says, "Man is by nature a social animal", so lockdown's negative impacts on the people are self-explanatory. The confinement of people in their respective homes did have an effect not just on the physical health but also on the psychological health of the people. Through various social media platforms, the state government showcased talks by doctors on mental health issues, and even yoga instructors were teaching yoga virtually, which was being telecasted through the government's social media page. The state government initiated such steps to curb the harmful impact of COVID-19 on people's daily lives.

Conclusion

Sikkim continued to fight the virus like the rest of the world; however, while the virus and its consequences continued to thrive, the state witnessed responsible community participation, with several NGOs coming forward to provide financial help, food, and shelter to people in need. Considering the economic crunch, several house owners relaxed the house rent charged to their tenants. Such initiatives at the individual level exemplified the community support and humanitarian values that the world needed. The collaborative efforts of the people and the state authorities helped the state to put up a tough fight against COVID-19.

Notes

1 "WHO Timeline—COVID 19" Retrieved from https://www.who.int/news/item/27-04 -2020-who-timeline---covid-19. Accessed on 20 August 2020.
2 Kumar et al. (2020), "The Rise and Impact of Covid-19 in India", *Frontiers of Medicine*, Vol. 7 No. 250.
3 CFR means the ratio of COVID-19 deaths to the total number of deaths recorded.
4 Sikkim Herald (2020, 17 April) "Government Will Ensure that the Lockdown Is More Severe this Time—Chief Minister" *Sikkim Herald.* Retrieved from https://sikkim .gov.in/uploads/SikkimHerald/April_17_0_20200417.pdf?fbclid=IwAR0NwNEMu

Y5UZqSL1SFaLKsd7M1Y0SUT0Tzpl-VIp7qIxxZ-msoFzTtLMk4. Accessed on *25 December 2021.*

5 Dhungel, Pankaj (2020, 30 March) "Sikkim Govt Fully Prepared to Tackle COVID-19 Crisis: CM PS Golay" East Mojo. Retrieved from https://www.eastmojo.com/sik-kim/2020/03/30/sikkim-govt-fully-prepared-to-tackle-covid-19-crisis-cm-ps-golay/. Accessed on 5 April 2020.

6 The Economic Times (2020,16 April) "Sikkim Patients Stranded Outside State to Get Rs 30,000 from Government" *Sikkim Herald.* Retrieved from https://economictimes .indiatimes.com/news/politics-and-nation/sikkim-patients-stranded-outside-state-to-get -rs-30000-from-government/articleshow/75184632.c,ms. Accessed on 27 April 2021.

7 "Online Registration System to Facilitate Return of People of Sikkim Stranded" Retrieved from https://sikkim.gov.in/media/news-announcement/news-info?name =Online+registration+system+to+facilitate+return+of+people+of+Sikkim+stranded. Accessed on 16 March 2021.

8 The Hindu (2020, 13 May) "169 Stranded Sikkim Residents Return to State: Official" *The Hindu.*

9 ET Healthworld (2020, 24 May) 'Sikkim Reports its First COVID-19 Positive Case' *The Economic Times.* Retrieved from https://health.economictimes.indiatimes.com/ news/industry/sikkim-reports-its-first-covid-19-positive-case/75933614. Accessed on 17 March 2021.

10 A collaborative project between the Animal Husbandry Department.

11 Sikkim.gov.in accessed 19 June 2022. of Sikkim, Foundation Brigitte Bardot (France), and the Australian based NGO Vets Beyond Borders.

12 https://www.learnknowmore.com/ngos-in-gangtok-sikkim/ accessed 20 June 2023.

13 Gross State Domestic Product (GSDP) is the value of all the goods and services pro-duced within the boundaries of the state in a given period of time. Growth of GSDP is an important indicator of the state's economy, as it denotes the extent of changes in the level of economic development of the state over a period of time.

14 https://sikkim.gov.in/media/notification-circular accessed 13 June 2022

15 http://www.sikkimexpress.com/news-details/first-covid-death-in-sikkim-last-rites-per-formed-as-per-norms accessed on 25th July, 2020.

16 https://www.newindianexpress.com/nation/2020/dec/14/for-first-time-since-1800s-no -khagyad-chaam-in-sikkim-monasteries-due-to-covid-19-2236102.html accessed on 5th January, 2020.

References

(2020, 24 May) 'Sikkim Reports Its First COVID-19 Positive Case'. *The Economic Times.* Retrieved from https://health.economictimes.indiatimes.com/news/industry/sikkim -reports-its-first-covid-19-positive-case/75933614. Accessed on March 17, 2021.

Asian Development Bank. (2023) Civil Society Brief India, ADB.

Business Standard. (2020, December 27) '2020: Sikkim Suffers Rs 600-Crore Blow as COVID Cripples Tourism Industry'. *Business Standard.*

Dhawan, Bulbul (2020, October 11) 'COVID-19 in India: Sikkim Opens Doors to Domestic Tourists; Issues Travel Guidelines'. *The Financial Express.*

Dhungel, Pankaj (2020, March 30) 'Sikkim Govt Fully Prepared to Tackle COVID-19 Crisis: CM PS Golay'. *East Mojo.*

Dhungel, Pankaj (2021, June 7) 'How Serial Entrepreneur Rewaj Chettri Procured 1,700 Oximeters for Sikkim', *East Mojo.*

Dhungel, Pankaj (2022, June 4) 'Gangtok Odd-Even Rule: Netizens Ask Why Only Private Vehicles?' *East Mojo.*

Government of Sikkim. (2020) 'Corona Virus Infection', dated 05/03/2020, No.Home/ Confdl./119/2020/1274.

Government of Sikkim. (2020) 'The Economic Revival Committee 2020 Constituted'. Retrieved from https://sikkim.gov.in/media/news-announcement/news-info?name=The +Economic+Revival+Committee+2020+constituted.

Government of Sikkim. (2022), "State finances audit report of the comptroller and auditor general of India for the year ended 31 March 2021", Report 1 of 2022.

https://www.learnknowmore.com/ngos-in-gangtok-sikkim/. Accessed on June 20, 2023.

https://www.newindianexpress.com/nation/2020/dec/14/for-first-time-since-1800s-no -khagyad-chaam-in-sikkim-monasteries-due-to-covid-19-2236102.html. Accessed on January 5, 2020.

http://www.sikkimexpress.com/news-details/first-covid-death-in-sikkim-last-rites -performed-as-per-norms. Accessed on July 25, 2020.

IPR. (2020, March 29) 'Compassion in the Time of Corona (COVID-19)'. *Government of Sikkim.*

Kumar et al. (2020) 'The Rise and Impact of Covid-19 in India'. *Frontiers in Medicine*, 7(250).

Ongmu, Dechen (2021, January 17) '120 Gets First Dose As Covid Vaccination Drive Begins In Sikkim'. *Sikkim Express.*

'Online Registration System to Facilitate Return of People of Sikkim Stranded'. Retrieved from https://sikkim.gov.in/media/news-announcement/news-info?name=Online+registration +system+to+facilitate+return+of+people+of+Sikkim+stranded. Accessed on March 16, 2021.

Ruppanner, Leah, Branden Maria, & Turunen Jani. (2018) 'Does Unequal Housework Lead to Divorce? Evidence from Sweden'. *Sociology*, 52(1), 75–94.

Shiraz, Z. (2022, July 24) 'Sikkim Sees Massive Growth of the Tourism Industry Post Covid-19'. *Hindustan Times.*

Siirur, Simrin (2020, March 25) 'Beaten, Abused, Spat On: People From Northeast Endure Racist Slurs Amid Coronavirus Panic'. *The Print.*

Sikkim Herald. (2020, April 17) 'Government Will Ensure the Lockdown Is More Severe This Time-Chief Minister'. *Sikkim Herald.*

Sikkim.gov.in. Accessed on June 19, 2022.

Taskin, Bismee (2020, November 19) 'Why Sikkim Which Had No Covid Cases Till May, Now Has Third Highest Case Fatality Rate'. *The Print.*

The Economic Times. (2020,16 April) 'Sikkim Patients Stranded Outside State to Get Rs 30,000 from Government'. *Sikkim Herald.*

The Hindu. (2020, May 13) '169 Stranded Sikkim Residents Return to State: Official'. *The Hindu.*

The Hindu. (2020, May 23) 'Coronavirus: Sikkim Reports First Covid-19 Case'. *The Hindu.*

'WHO Timeline- COVID 19'. Retrieved from https://www.who.int/news/item/27-04-2020 -who-timeline---covid-19. Accessed on August 20, 2020.

21 Understanding Kerala's Social Model of COVID-19 Containment

Perspectives from Below

P R Rehnamol

Introduction

The outbreak of COVID-19 has hit all the countries across the globe. The Novel Coronavirus, reportedly originated from the Chinese province of Wuhan, has altered what was perceived to be normalcy until then. The whole world came to a standstill during the pandemic. COVID-19 posed unprecedented challenges. The issues of poverty, malnutrition, poor health, absence of labor protection, irregular incomes, lack of social security, and work under unsafe conditions were exacerbated after the outbreak of the pandemic. A major part of the global workforce lost its livelihoods, and the informal workers became more vulnerable as they lack social protection and access to quality health facilities. Prevention of farmers from accessing markets due to trade restrictions during the pandemic led to the disruption of domestic and international food supply chain, thereby affecting the system of food security. Most marginalized sections, especially from low-income countries, migrant laborers, women, children, waged workers, and self-employed agricultural workers, have become more vulnerable during the pandemic (WHO 2020).

The United Nations (UN) described the COVID-19 pandemic as "a human, economic and social crisis" rather than a health crisis. The United Nations Department of Economic and Social Affairs emphasized the fact that the impact of the pandemic is more detrimental, especially for the social sections that fall under the vulnerable categories including the poor, homeless, persons with disabilities, older people, and indigenous communities. The pandemic has exacerbated the issues such as exclusion, inequalities, and discrimination (United Nations 2021). Regions of underdeveloped countries were also hard hit by COVID-19. The South Asian region with almost 2 billion people, witnessed a collapse of its fragile health system during the pandemic (UNICEF 2021). India, the largest country with a dense population in the South Asian region, exploded into much chaos with an unbridled number of infected patients and deaths.

The first case of coronavirus in India was found in Kerala, the tiny southernmost state of India. India's first case of coronavirus infection was reported in Kerala on January 27, 2020 when a 20-year-old female student who was studying at Wuhan University was admitted to the Emergency Department of General Hospital, Thrissur Kerala. Since then, not only the state, but the whole country witnessed a rapid spread of coronavirus (Andrews 2020). Kerala, at the time of

DOI: 10.4324/9781003304517-26

this writing, is undergoing the third wave of the pandemic. The Omicron variant has hit the state. The latest report says that the total infection count in the state is 5,931,945 and the death toll is 53, 191. Among the districts, Ernakulam reported the highest number of cases followed by Thiruvananthapuram and Kozhikode (Indian Express 2022). Both Omicron and Delta variants are spreading across the state with the positivity rate reaching 40.21%. The major reasons for the explosion of COVID-19 cases in Kerala during the second and third waves include political campaigns and meetings, festivals, reopening of schools, colleges, and universities (Jacob 2022). Despite the surge in the cases, the Kerala model of COVID-19 containment is still perceived as a model to be emulated for several reasons.

Amongst the states, Kerala's performance in containing the virus during the first phase received much appreciation from different corners of the world. The trajectory of the case in the state has largely remained in control throughout. Kerala has been a focus of attention for a long time due to its successful dealing with the pandemic. Kerala's response, strategies, and effective implementation of measures to contain the pandemic have been explained in the following sections with a special emphasis on its societal aspects.

Initial Phase of the Pandemic in Kerala

As soon as the case of a student who returned from Wuhan University was reported in Thrissur, the district was immediately under high alert. There was a close analysis of the student's travel history and monitoring of the person's movement and health in the next few days. She was also given the contact information of the District Surveillance Officer after she reported her travel history at a primary healthcare center in Thrissur. As the girl had not shown any symptoms at the time of her arrival, she was advised to remain in isolation at home for at least 28 days. As soon as the officer was informed about the development of symptoms in the patient, she was moved to the isolation ward by the district team. On the same day, a sample of her body fluid was sent to the National Institute of Virology (NIV) at Pune for a test. The first case of COVID-19 in the country was thus reported in Kerala on January 30, 2020. The Health Department authorities became much more vigilant when the patient was admitted to the isolation ward of the district hospital with novel coronavirus infection. A 24-hour control room was soon established at the district medical office under the supervision of District Collectorate. Meanwhile, the Health Department of Kerala sought to track and identify people who might have come in contact with the infected patient. Special isolation rooms were soon arranged at the district hospital. Twenty pay-ward rooms were vacated to accommodate new patients of novel coronavirus. A special medical team was set up with adequate safety measures and proper medicines. A rapid reaction medical team was also set up to immediately transport the infected patients to the hospital (Perappadan 2020). This detailed narration of Kerala's first response to novel coronavirus indicates the care and seriousness with which Kerala dealt with India's first case of COVID-19.

The attentiveness of the medical authorities has been crucial in halting the further spread of the virus. While Kerala was appreciated for its initial response to the global pandemic, the Central Government received widespread flak for its callousness in disseminating the relevant information to the public and containing the virus across the country. The government at the center was criticised for not having a quick response to the cases reported. The government did not respond properly to the 50 cases that were reported initially in the country despite the dangerous trend. The first response of the Central Government in the form of an announcement of a countrywide lockdown with just five hours prior notice further exacerbated the situation of the most vulnerable groups especially the migrant workers in the country (Prashad 2021). While India faced the worst of its crisis with thousands of migrants, including women and children, walking on highways barefoot without food and water, the state of Kerala drew much appreciation not only for its mature handling in containing COVID-19 cases in the state but also for ensuring social protection for the most vulnerable communities.

Responsiveness of the State Mechanism in Kerala

There are several factors responsible for the success of the Kerala model of COVID-19 containment. One of the factors that explains the success of the Kerala model is the responsiveness of the state mechanism. The government of Kerala diligently issued guidelines regarding the pandemic four days before the confirmation of the first case in the state. The state government has taken several steps to prepare the hospitals, including the creation of exclusive isolation wards in anticipation of positive cases. The guideline issued by the government included local testing labs along with "established case definitions, screening and sampling protocol, hospital preparedness, triage and surveillance" (Sneha et al. 2021). Within five days of the World Health Organization's (WHO's) declaration of a global pandemic, the Government of Kerala began its "Break the Chain Campaign" to disseminate information regarding personal hygiene and physical distancing among the public. It also announced Rs. 20,000 crores as a COVID-19 relief package days before the announcement of the national relief package by the Central Government. When the state reported its first case of COVID-19-related death on March 22, 2020, the government issued "advisories on the creation of First-Line Treatment Centres and Corona Care Centres, and mental health guidelines" (Sneha et al. 2021).

The government kept its surveillance on those who were infected. People were often reminded of quarantine rules and other precautionary measures through state-funded campaigns and advertisements in both electronic and non-electronic media. The government strictly and effectively implemented testing, contact tracing, and quarantine guidelines. It's been argued that "because of the state's measures, the number of those who are getting the disease through contact within the state is minimal, largely due to all those entering the state being placed in-home or institutional quarantine" (Seithikurippu et al. 2020). During the relaxation of the first national lockdown and opening of state borders, many Keralites who were stranded outside the state came back home via trains, ships, and roads. During this period also, the state government was very vigilant in keeping records of the returnees. All the returnees had to register their details in the Kerala government's portal. Thus, the government was equipped with complete information of those who were coming from outside. The people with COVID-19 symptoms at the entry point were taken to hospitals under the state's supervision. People with home facilities were asked to follow 14-day-quarantine rules at home. Those who were short of such facilities were also given hospital facilities by the government. Kerala's experience has proven that "home quarantine is as effective as institutional quarantine" (Seithikurippu et al. 2020). The role of the government to disseminate the information of quarantine rules and the monitoring of those returnees by state Accredited Social Health Activist (ASHA) workers played an important role in containing the infection rate to a larger extent.

The government and the local self-governance institutions played a significant role in reducing the burden on hospitals. This, to a large extent, helped the state to avoid a collapse of its health system. The promptness of the Kerala government to respond to the emergency situation with utmost care and responsibility is one of the significant reasons for the successful containment of the pandemic. It is important to note that the success of the performance of the present government is complemented by a robust health and education system that is rooted in the social awakening in the state. Before a detailed analysis of the social factor as a foundational force behind the success of Kerala's COVID-19 containment, the following section gives an overview of special features of Kerala, including an effective education, health, and decentralized system of governance that catalyzed the success of the Kerala model of COVID-19 containment.

Kerala's Healthcare and Education Systems

Effective education and a robust health system have been peculiar features of Kerala that are instrumental in helping the state to make its model a successful one. Kerala's development experience is based on the primacy of social sectors. The greatest share of the expenditure of the government has traditionally been vested in education and health. The growth of the health sector in the state continued even after 1980. The expansion of education, the rise of literacy, and the increase in households' income have fueled the demands for more healthcare facilities in the state. Private facilities in the health sector also expanded exponentially. Kerala's development experience proved that the low level of agricultural production, industrialization, and per capita income could not hinder the expansion and growth of social sectors (Kutty 2000).

Kerala's healthcare delivery is better in comparison to other states (Varghese 2020). Despite the low per-capita income, Kerala shows excellent health indicators including life expectancy and mortality rates that are at par with countries of the first world. Medical care in the private sector and the number of healthcare providers increased in Kerala with a high health awareness of the population (Chacko 1989). The radical decentralization policies in 1996 were instrumental in making the health system responsive to local people in the state (Nabae 2003). The already existing robust health system in Kerala made it easier for the state to deal with the pandemic. Kerala's literacy rate is highest among all states and the primary and secondary education in the state have a 100% enrollment rate. The student-school ratio and the student-teacher ratio in Kerala are highly desirable. Heavy public expenditure in education is particular to Kerala. The investment in education for decades has helped the state to contain the pandemic to a larger extent. It is opined that "with the highest literacy rate, it became easy for the state government to generate awareness for COVID-19" (Kumar et al. 2020).

Decentralized Democratic Governance and COVID-19 in Kerala

Kerala is known for its efficient Panchayat Raj Institutions and a robust decentralized governance system. M. P. Singh and Rekha Saxena have also opined that the major success of Panchayat Raj Institutions was evident in states like Kerala. It's been stated that:

In Kerala, a powerful movement for decentralised development through local level participatory planning was launched. The initiatives of the communist parties presented a more consensual picture of local democracy and development in Kerala where the CPM-led Left Democratic Front and the Congress-led United Democratic Front (UDF) have shared power alternatively on regular basis in recent decades.

(Singh et al. 2021)

The robust decentralized democratic governance, that is particular to Kerala, has also helped the state to implement its COVID-19 strategy successfully. The role of ASHA workers in reaching out to people with medicines and with other help at the grassroots level through the medium and under the supervision of local self-governance institutions during the crisis was significant. The coordination between the local authorities and ASHA workers was helpful to control the movement of the returnees within the state, thereby containing the spread of the virus. In a nutshell, the distinctive features of Kerala that have contributed to the success of the Kerala model of COVID-19 containment include "decentralised institutions and provisions for healthcare, welfare and safety nets, and especially the capacity of a democratic state working in synergy with civil society and enjoying a high degree of consensus and public trust" (Chathukulam and Joseph 2020).

Kerala's Past Experience with Epidemics

Kerala's early experiences with the epidemic have also helped the government to effectively deal with the pandemic. The past experience has helped the state to deliver a rigorous action plan to contain the virus, compared to other states in India (Kumar et al. 2020). The experience of the Health Minister of Kerala, K. K. Shailaja, during early epidemics helped the government to adopt a quick plan to contain COVID-19 though many new challenges have been posed by the current pandemic. In 2018, an even deadlier virus called Nipah was found in Kerala. K.

K. Shailaja's handling of the Nipah Virus received wide appreciation. She was also widely admired for her visit to the village which was the centrepoint of the outbreak. Her experience has been instrumental in initiating an early intervention. This has helped in maintaining a low mortality rate and flattened the curve of COVID-19 infection. Her earlier experience with Nipah taught her that a highly contagious disease that has no vaccine or medication needs to be taken seriously (Spinney 2020).

Has the Kerala Model Withered Away during Second Phase?

Kerala's model of COVID-19 containment was brought into scrutiny by many for its alleged failure in containing the virus in the second phase. During the second wave, the cases peaked in every state from the third week of April to mid-May in 2021. Cases in Kerala also peaked around the same time but at a higher rate than the states including Tamil Nadu, Madhya Pradesh, Uttar Pradesh, and Andhra Pradesh. Kerala couldn't flatten the curve like in the first wave and the cases continued rising from June 2021. In July, Kerala's COVID-19-positive cases accounted for 51% of India's fresh cases. More than 10 districts in the state had a positivity rate of more than 10%. In July, Kerala reported an average of between 17,743 to 22,456 new cases daily (Verma 2021).

When the national positivity rate dipped to 3%, Kerala touched 16% (Joseph 2021). Many have analyzed the failure of the Kerala model from different perspectives. Fall of administration, visionless leadership of Kerala Chief Minister Pinarayi Vijayan, government's imprudence in lockdown rules despite the advice from different quarters, unscientific lockdown relaxations, superficial lockdown, appeasement politics, and failed police machinery are some of the factors that led to the alleged collapse of Kerala's containment strategies during the second wave (Joseph 2021). Better reporting of cases in the state is also cited as a reason for the rise of cases in Kerala. This explanation is corroborated by serosurveys. However, it provides only a partial explanation for the continuing positivity rate in India. Even though 45% of the state's population got at least one dose of vaccination, the positivity rate continued to rise. As of 2024, a total of 2,89,26,947 people got vaccinated, constituting 81.51% of the total population in Kerala (Government of Kerala, 2024). It is also argued that Kerala's "relatively low case fatality ratio of 0.47, against the country average of 1.32, can partly be attributed to a large number of cases" (Sinha 2021). Criticisms were thus largely directed toward the political leadership and government machinery.

Even though there are widespread criticisms against the Kerala model, especially from the political quarters, many experts are still in favor of the Kerala model as an effective way to contain COVID-19. For instance, Dr. Shahid Jameel, a famous virologist and the former head of the Indian SARS-COV-2 Genomics Consortia (INSACOG), opined that Kerala should continue with its strategy with more emphasis on more vaccinations (Nair 2021). The seroprevalence survey of the Indian Council of Medical Research (ICMR) showed that only 44% of the population in Kerala has been infected, which is the lowest in the country. When the average seropositivity at the national level was 67%, other states showed 75%, which was clearly higher than Kerala. The seroprevalence survey estimates the percentage of people who have antibodies against SARS-Cov-2 and shows the number of people in a given population who were previously infected with SARS-COV-2. Kerala has been testing, tracing, and reporting the cases honestly in comparison to other states. The low seropositivity of Kerala indicates that the state was successful in protecting its people. Other states couldn't protect the people and they have been exposed. Kerala's positivity rate during the first and second waves hasn't changed much in comparison to the national percentage. In the first wave, Kerala had 8.5% to 9% of India's cases and it was 9.5% during the second wave. In other words, the relative infection output during the first and second waves has remained almost the same in comparison to the rest of the country (Nair 2021).

Even if the cases were high in Kerala, the state hasn't witnessed a shortage of oxygen, hospital beds, and medicines due to its robust health system. States like Delhi saw an acute shortage of oxygen and hospital beds during the peak of the second wave. During the outbreak of COVID19 in April 2021, Kerala was one state which did not face an oxygen crisis in the second wave, whereas the rest of India saw innumerable deaths and thousands of sad stories of patients dying for the want of oxygen (Thadhani 2021). As per the report of the *Observer Research Foundation* issued in June 2021, it was found that several states in India could not sustain the surge in the increase of the COVID-19 cases and the high demand for oxygen. The availability of cryogenic oxygen tankers in India was about 1,200, which was grossly below the required number (Mukherjee 2021). The crisis was so severe that the government had to airlift oxygen tankers from other countries and from other locations in India. For the rapid transportation of liquid medical oxygen, special trains were run, and the state government of Delhi was looking at importing cryogenic tankers from Thailand and plants from France (Joshi 2021). Even though the government could increase the number from 1,200 to 2,000, this number would be grossly insufficient if a similar wave of COVID-19 occurs again. The government allocated 162 oxygen plants by January 2021 by the time when the first wave of COVID-19 subsuded. The majority of the states did not immediately move and work on establishing the oxygen plants as the Indian states were not anticipating a similar crisis in April 2021.

Kerala was the only state which was self-sufficient in oxygen availability. Even though it was one of the states most affected by COVID-19, ithad augmented 23 oxygen plants since the onset of COVID-19 to supply liquid medical oxygen as per requirement. Kerala, by April 2021, based on its caseload of COVID-19, needed less than 100 tonnes of medical oxygen in hospitals whereas it had a capacity of production for more than 200 tonnes. Since the first case of COVID-19 was observed in January 2020 in Kerala, the state was on alert and was able to augment its supplies by utilizing the existing capacities and expanding the existing oxygen capacities in several manufacturing plants (Dutta 2021). Similarly, the second lesson Kerala learned from its first wave of COVID-19 was to increase the intensive care unit (ICU) beds and thereby estimate and plan for the required oxygen supply. Kerala by April 2021 was enabled to not only take care of its oxygen needs but also to supply to Karnataka, Tamil Nadu, Goa, and Delhi (Rajagopal 2021).

Moreover, Kerala's hospitalization rate for COVID-19 was 3% as compared to the nationwide rate of 5%. The fatality rate of Kerala remained low at 0.5% in comparison to the national average of 1.4% (Peterson 2021). Kerala managed to reduce the mortality rate through proper hospital care and attention. Even if there was a high positivity rate, Kerala was prepared to address the high caseloads through its robust public health system (Jacob 2021). Kerala performed well to contain the pandemic in its entirety. The fatality rate in Kerala, the proportion of people who die among those tested positive, remained low as compared to other states. The state has also not witnessed any shortage of oxygen or hospital beds. The hospitals in the state have also not been overwhelmed with patients (Biswas 2020). Though the number of cases rose in the state due to the returning of Keralites from different states and countries, the fatality rate remained low. Kerala could vaccinate 71% of its population with one dose and 26% with two doses by 27 August 2022. Giridhara R. Babu, a professor of epidemiology at the Indian Institute of Public Health, Bengaluru opined that a rise in the number doesn't mean a failed strategy. Early detection, better management, and the expansion of vaccination coverage are some of the lessons that can still be learned from the Kerala model by other states (Babu 2021).

The criticism of the Kerala model is predominantly politically charged. Most of the criticisms seem to be directed at the politics of Pinarayi Vijayan. As this chapter argues, there is not much attention or significance given to the social part of the Kerala model containment strategy as an explanation for its success. In other words, there is complete negligence of the socio-cultural factors to understand the COVID-19 management in Kerala. The societal perspective was absent in both appraisal and criticism of the Kerala model of COVID-19 containment. While the criticisms against the Kerala model largely remained political, the society or the people were immune from the flak as they largely remained prudent during the second wave as they did in the first phase. Though the government couldn't be consistent with the effective strategies, the people and the society in Kerala have largely remained responsive and responsible. However, it must be reiterated that the factor of "social" or societal behavior found no place in the explanation of the success of the Kerala model.

Understanding the "Social"

It is important to understand and analyze the success of the Kerala model of COVID-19 containment from a bottom-up approach or from a societal perspective. To understand the Kerala COVID-19 containment model and the factors behind its successful implementation, one needs to go deeper and analyze the underlying societal structures and behavior in which the nature of the governance mechanisms is fundamentally rooted. None of the analysis, discussions, or debates have highlighted the contribution of the society and social movements to make the model a success. The social movements and reformation in Kerala have shaped and prepared the society to respond to government decisions with rationality and scientific temperament. The historical factors and developments such as the enlightenment movement and social reformation in the 19th and 20th centuries Kerala have already moulded their society into a more pro-science and rational entity. This factor has indirectly helped the state and the government to execute their actions and plans more easily. It would be wrong to assume that the performance of the political party in power or the state governments can single-handedly determine the success of containment of a pandemic such as that of COVID-19. It is very important to have a sensible society and population to respond to the guidelines issued by the government. It must also be noted that the "political" can't be separated from the "social". In other words, the individuals that represent the government are an integral part of society. No political entity or government can operate in isolation. A society that is largely built on modernity and enlightenment ideals is always complementary to modern governmental mechanisms. The contract between the state and society in Kerala has been well established on the basis of enlightenment ideals of science, logic, and rationality. This also explains the scientific temperament among a significant number of people in Kerala that has helped the government to implement its measures without much difficulty.

Even the effective and robust health system that is cited as a factor behind the success of the Kerala model has its historical connection with the "social". The scientific temperament and rationality with which the government and the society successfully dealt with the pandemic and the social awakening that emphasized the significance of an effective health and education system are rooted in the enlightenment movement and social reformation of Kerala. In other words, the social consciousness developed as a result of social movements and reformation has significantly contributed to the growth of the healthcare system in Kerala. For instance, V. Raman Kutty has argued that the health development in the state can be attributed to factors including accessible education, political consciousness, and social movements (Kutty 2000). Even before the formation of present Kerala, a social consciousness to promote education and health was already laid out. Consequently, various governments that assumed power in modern Kerala have emphasized the social sectors in their development discourse as a continuing legacy of the social reformation and movements. It is also argued that;

> a contributing factor to the agitations of the early 20th century was the cultural renaissance taking place in Kerala, spurred in part by the rapid growth of literacy...high literacy levels achieved by Kerala have contributed significantly toward raising awareness for health care issues...Kerala health care consumption is embedded in the socio-political set-up of the society.
> (Varman and Gopal 2008)

Socio-cultural factors were responsible for the high level of education, collective consciousness, and better health care in Kerala. Kerala has a "socially embedded health care model" (Varman and Gopal 2008). It is evident that the robust healthcare system has its roots in the social awakening and the cultural renaissance movements of 19th and 20th century Kerala. Therefore, the success of Kerala's health model and the Kerala model of COVID-19 containment has a direct link with the "social" factor.

The states' guidelines regarding the quarantine rules were very effective for the containment of the virus. Kerala's society and the people have co-operated with the state with utmost responsibility. The maturity of the society as responsible citizens was reflected in their following of the quarantine rules and other government instructions. Social or public awareness was also a crucial factor in defining the success of any government to contain the pandemic. It has been argued that "for pandemics such as COVID-19, public awareness via dissemination of reliable information in real-time plays a significant role in controlling the spread of the disease" (Ulahannan 2020). Kerala's society was very much aware of the ways through which one needs to fight the pandemic. The Health Minister of Kerala during COVID-19, K. K. Shailaja also admitted the fact that one of the factors that contributed to the success of the state to contain the pandemic is literacy and understanding among the people. She stated that "people understand why they must stay at home. You can explain it to them" (Spinney 2020). Most of the factors that are touted as responsible for the success of COVID-19 containment, including literacy and awareness among people, are directly or indirectly connected to the very foundational nature of the society of Kerala. The responsibility of the Kerala society and the interconnectedness between the social and the political gives an insight into the significance of "social" in containing the pandemic. Hence, it is very important to understand the major historical developments and incidents including the social reform movements that were very instrumental in shaping and defining the nature of Kerala's society.

The social reform movement of Kerala was led by leaders like Sree Narayana Guru, Ayyankali, Chattambi Swamikal, Sahodaran Ayyappan, Poykayil Appachan, and Sri Narayana Guru. They fought against the caste system and have been instrumental in presenting a rational social order for Kerala. Sri Narayana Guru taught that equality, education, and cleanliness are important for societal growth (Pandey 2020). Ayyankali fought against the feudal upper caste lords for the education of Dalit girls and boys who were denied an education by the Hindu social order in Kerala. The robust educational system that Kerala is flaunting is rooted in Ayyankali's fight for an egalitarian educational model. The Malayali public conscience of accepting universal access to education irrespective of caste and gender in independent Kerala has been shaped by the struggle of Ayyankali. The value of education was later on included in the development discourse of Kerala by the successive governments. The improvements in the education system in Kerala thus have roots in Ayyankali's advocacy for free and compulsory education for all.

Vaikunda Swami and his organization, named "Samatva Samajam", in Kerala fought against superstitious practices. Vakkam Abdul Khadir Maulavi was instrumental in bringing about progress in the educational and social status of Muslim communities in India. The modernizing spirit brought by the social reformers brought revolutionary changes in the behavioral patterns of people and the society. The leadership of the organizations that formed against the social and economic oppression and around caste, inculcated a progressive spirit for a new society in

Kerala (Lal 2015). The reformers who fought against social and economic injustices created a massive intellectual movement and "these trends put the society on the path of modern thought and education" (Khadeeja 1995).

The social reforms and the Enlightenment ideals that shaped the society are a distinctive feature of Kerala. The superstitions and the social obscurantism that engulfed Kerala's society were banished to a larger extent due to the Renaissance movement of Kerala. Early social practices and rituals of Kerala were quite irrational. Caste, untouchability, witchcraft, serpent worship, and other regressive social practices existed in Kerala. The social order of Kerala was earlier determined largely by Hindu religious laws. More restrictions were imposed upon the people at the lower end of the social hierarchy. Social reformation has helped the state to get away with unscientific and irrational social customs. The western schooling and education spread by the Christian missionaries also helped Kerala to grow more scientific and rational. Additionally, the multifarious Renaissance movement of the late 19th century to the mid-20th century has shaped society and the state into a modern entity.

The social reform movement or Enlightenment ideals promoted by the leaders from the marginalized groups left a deep impact and influence on Kerala's society which helped the state even during a pandemic that is supposed to be contained scientifically. The rationalist and the scientific temper that has grown the state after the reform movement hasn't dissipated. The contrast between Kerala and other states in terms of scientific temper and rationality was more evident when the latter opted for tapping plates and ringing bells to get rid of coronavirus. Kerala's society to a larger extent has stayed away from such irrational acts and adopted the scientific and rational ways of testing, tracing, and isolation to tackle the pandemic and the credit definitely goes to the Enlightenment ideals and social reform movement led by leaders from the margins. Therefore, Kerala's successful containment of a pandemic also lies in the socio-cultural factors that have shaped a robust education and health system for decades along with a rational society that was reciprocal to the government's efforts to control the pandemic.

Conclusion

The understanding of Kerala's model of COVID-19 containment from the perspective of the state may give some insights into the government's efficiency in dealing with the pandemic. However, it would not be comprehensive as it would reflect the limitations of a top-down approach. What has often been ignored in the analysis of Kerala's experience with COVID-19 is the role of the society, the people, and the historical-philosophical foundations within which the state and the society are defined and shaped. Since the relationship between the "social" and the "political" is complimentary, an understanding of the social is important to explain the performance of the political, especially the functioning of government mechanisms. Kerala's society has largely been influenced by the Enlightenment and Renaissance movements led by the leaders of the marginalized. The foundation of the state on Enlightenment ideals has helped the state to nurture the modern ideals of scientific temper, rationalism, and logic. This has helped modern Kerala to perform much better in almost all sectors with much scientific zeal. The foundation and legacy of the Renaissance ideas still hold significance which was evident in the responsible behavior of the society and the people during the crisis.

Kerala's distinctiveness of having a social model based on the ideals of renaissance and enlightenment can be a good model for many other states to imitate. A sensitive, mature, and educated society is very significant, especially in a situation where collective consciousness and responsibility are required. The pandemic has already proven that containment is impossible without any cooperation of the responsible individuals who constitute both society and polity. Even though the governments in other states sought to perform better to contain the pandemic, the response of the society was very dismal. In many states, both the state and the society have behaved with utmost carelessness with no scientific temper, which again shows the complementary relationship between the two. Kerala's social model of Enlightenment and Renaissance cannot only be the best way out for those states that are lagging in imbibing the modern ideals but also to confidently address the unexpected pandemic like COVID-19 with collective responsibility and consciousness.

References

Andrews, M.A. et al. 2020. "First Confirmed Case of COVID-19 Infection in India: A Case Report". *Indian Journal of Medical Research* 151. No. 5: 490–492. Accessed 6 February 2022. https://www.ncbi.nlm.nih.gov/pmc/articles/PMC7530459/#:~:text=We%20present%20here%20the%20first,dry%20cough%20and%20sore%20throat.

Babu, Giridhara R. (2021), "Why Kerala's response to COVID-19 has positive lessons for India", *The Wire*, 31 August 2021. Accessed 15 February 2022. https://thewire.in/health/why-keralas-response-to-covid-19-has-positive-lessons-for-india

Bhuyan, Anoo. 2021. "Experts Criticise India's Complacency Over COVID-19". *World Report 397*: 1611–1612. Accessed February 4, 2022. https://doi.org/10.1016/S0140-6736(21)00993-4.

Biswas, Soutik. (2020), "India coronavirus: How Kerala's Covid 'success story' came undone", *BBC News*, 21 July 2020. Accessed 14 February 2022. https://www.bbc.com/news/world-asia-india-53431672

Chacko, Sunil. 1989. "Health Care in Transition in Kerala". *The Lancet.* September 9, 1989. Accessed February 22, 2022. file:///C:/Users/ADMIN/Downloads/S0140-6736(89)90739-3.pdf.

Chathukulam, Jos and Joseph Tharamangalam. 2020. "The Kerala Model in the Time of COVID19: Rethinking State, Society, and Democracy". *Elsevier Public Health Emergency Collection*, September 23. Accessed February 10, 2022. https://www.ncbi.nlm.nih.gov/pmc/articles/PMC7510531/.

Dutta, Prakash K. 2021. "Why Kerala Is Not Facing Oxygen Crisis in Covid-19 Second Wave". *India Today*, April 27, 2021. Accessed February 17, 2022. https://www.indiatoday.in/coronavirus-outbreak/story/kerala-oxygen-crisis-covid-19-second-wave-1795603-2021-04-27.

Government of Kerala. (2024), "COVID-19 Battle". Accessed 25 May 2024. https://dashboard.kerala.gov.in/covid/

Indian Express. 2022. "Coronavirus Omicron India Highlights: Kerala Reports 50,812 Fresh Infections; Over 3.36 Lakh Active Cases in State". January 30, 2022. Accessed February 22, 2022. https://indianexpress.com/article/india/coronavirus-omicron-india-live-news-third-wave-health-ministry-covid-delhi-mumbai-7743484/

Jacob, Jeemon. 2022. "How Omicron Has Triggered a Massive Third Wave in Kerala". *India Today*, January 20, 2022. Accessed February 22, 2022. https://www.indiatoday.in /india-today-insight/story/how-omicron-has-triggered-a-massive-third-wave-in-kerala -1902475-2022-01-20.

Jacob, Shine. (2021), "Despite higher covid cases, Kerala model still a success; Experts", *Business Standard*, 13 December 2021. Accessed 14 February 2022. https://www .business-standard.com/article/current-affairs/despite-higher-covid-cases-kerala-model -still-a-success-experts-121121300059_1.html

Joseph, Anoop Antony. 2021. "Why Kerala Model of Failed COVID Handling Should Learn From UP". *The Indian Express*, August 18, 2021. Accessed February 18, 2022. https://indianexpress.com/article/opinion/kerala-uttar-pradesh-covid-management -second-wave-7460292/.

Joshi, Mallica. 2021. "Delhi to Import 18 Oxygen Tankers from Bangkok, 21 Oxygen Plants from France: Kejriwal". *The Indian Express*, April 27, 2021. Accessed February 15, 2022. https://indianexpress.com/article/cities/delhi/delhi-import-18-oxygen-tankers-bangkok-21 -oxygen-plants-france-kejriwal-7291237/.

Kerala could vaccinate 81.51% of its total population by 2024 (Government of Kerala, 2024) Reference: Reference: Government of Kerala. (2024), "COVID-19 Battle". Accessed 25 May 2024. https://dashboard.kerala.gov.in/covid/

Khadeeja, P. (1995), "Social reforms movements among the Kerala Muslims (19 th to 20 th century)", *Proceedings of the Indian History Congress*, 56(1): 681–691.

Kumar, Udhaya S. et al. 2020. "Kerala, India's Front Runner in Novel Coronavirus Disease (COVID-19), Frontiers in Medicine". Accessed February 4, 2022. https://www .frontiersin.org/articles/10.3389/fmed.2020.00355/full.

Kutty, V. Raman. 2000. "Historical Analysis of the Development of Health Care Facilities in Kerala State, India". *Health Policy and Planning* 15. No. 1: 103–109.

Lal, Amrith. (2015), "Why the BJP may be misreading the legacy of social reforms in Kerala", *The Indian Express*, 6 October 2015. Accessed 15 February 2022. https:// indianexpress.com/article/explained/in-fact-why-the-bjp-may-be-misreading-the-legacy -of-social-reforms-in-kerala/

Mukherjee, Biman. 2021. "India Has Always Had Enough Oxygen". Accessed February 15, 2022. https://fortune.com/2021/05/18/india-covid-cases-crisis-oxygen-shortage -supply/#:~:text=After%20being%20taken%20aback%20by,of%20now%2C%E2%80 %9D%20said%20Rao.

Nabae, Koji. 2003. "The Health Care System in Kerala-Its Past Accomplishments and New Challenges". *Public Health* 52. No. 2: 140–145. Accessed February 21, 2022. https:// www.niph.go.jp/journal/data/52-2/200352020010.pdf.

Nair, Preeta. (2021), "Interview with Shahid Jameel, criticism against Kerala's covid management unwarranted: Virologist Shahid Jameel", *The Outlook*, 2 August 2021. Accessed 14 February 2022. https://www.outlookindia.com/website/story/india-news -criticism-against-keralas-covid-management-unwarranted-virologist-shahid-jameel /390153

Pandey, Kirti. (2020), "Sree Narayana Guru, the social reformer, educationist, spiritual leader who preached through practice", *Times Now News*, 28 August 2020. Accessed 15 February 2022. https://www.timesnownews.com/india/article/narayana-guru-social -reformer-educationist-spiritual-leader-from-kerala-ezhava-taught-equality-enterprise -sarada-mutt-sivagiri/644009.

Perappadan, Bindu Shajan. 2020. "India's First Coronavirus Infection Confirmed in Kerala". *The Hindu*, January 30, 2020. Accessed January 30, 2022. https://www.thehindu.com /news/national/indias-first-coronavirus-infection-confirmed-in-kerala/article30691004 .ece.

Peterson, Hannah Ellis. (2021), "Why Kerala is still in the grip of India's second wave of covid", *The Guardian*, 15 September 2021. Accessed 13 February 2022. https://www

.theguardian.com/world/2021/sep/15/why-kerala-is-still-in-the-grip-of-indias-second-wave-of-covid

Prashad, Vijay. 2021. "India's Covid Crisis is Mostly Modi's Fault". *Asia Times*, April 24, 2021. Accessed January 30, 2022. https://asiatimes.com/2021/04/the-covid-19-catastrophe-in-india-keeps-growing/.

Rajagopal, Vivek. 2021. "Kerala to Supply oxygen to Delhi After Requests from CM Arvind Kejriwal, Malayali Organisations". *India Today*, April 27, 2021. Accessed February 8, 2022. https://www.indiatoday.in/coronavirus-outbreak/story/kerala-oxygen-supply-delhi-arvind-kejriwal-malayali-organisations-requests-1795309-2021-04-27.

Seithikurippu, R. et al. 2020. "Dealing with a Pandemic: The Kerala Model of Containment Strategy for COVID-19". *Pathogens and Global Health* 114. No. 5: 232–233.

Singh, M.P. and Rekha Saxena. 2021. *Indian Politics. Constitutional Foundations and Institutional Functioning*. New Delhi: PHI Learning.

Sinha, Amitabh. (2021), "Explained: What's behind the stubborn upward covid-19 trend in Kerala?", *Indian Express*, 15 July 2021. Accessed 14 February 2022. https://indianexpress.com/article/explained/covid-19-numbers-explained-what-is-behind-the-stubborn-upward-trend-in-kerala-7395486/

Sneha, P. et al. 2021. "The First Wave of the COVID-19 Pandemic in Kerala- A state Capacity Perspective". March 26, 2021. Accessed February 10, 2022. https://www.idfcinstitute.org/knowledge/publications/working-and-briefing-papers/covid-19-pandemic-in-kerala/.

Spinney, Laura. 2020. "The Coronavirus Slayer: How Kerala's Rock Star Health Minister Helped Save it from COVID-19". *The Guardian*, May 14, 2020. Accessed February 12, 2022. https://www.theguardian.com/world/2020/may/14/the-coronavirus-slayer-how-keralas-rock-star-health-minister-helped-save-it-from-covid-19.

Thadhani, Amit. 2021. "Preventing a Repeat of the COVID-19 Second-Wave Oxygen Crisis in India". Accessed February 15, 2022. https://www.orfonline.org/research/preventing-a-repeat-of-the-covid-19-second-wave-oxygen-crisis-in-india/#:~:text=Oxygen%20tankers%20have%20now%20been,recorded%20on%204%20May%202021.

Ulahannan, Jijo Pulickiyil et al. (2020), "A citizen science initiative for open data and visualisation of COVID-19 outbreak in Kerala, India", *Journal of the American Medical Informatics Association*, 27(12): 1913–1920.

UNICEF. 2021. "Direct and Indirect Effects of COVID-19 Pandemic and Response in South Asia". Accessed January 30, 2022. https://www.unicef.org/rosa/reports/direct-and-indirect-effects-covid-19-pandemic-and-response-south-asia.

United Nations. 2021. "Everyone Included: Social Impact of COVID-19". Accessed 30 January 31, 2022. https://www.un.org/development/desa/dspd/everyone-included-covid-19.html.

Varghese, Bipin T. 2020. "The Kerala Model of Health Care Deliver and Its impact on Oral Cancer Care During the COVID 19 Pandemic". Accessed February 9, 2022. https://www.ncbi.nlm.nih.gov/pmc/articles/PMC7196376/.

Varman, Rohit and Gopal Kappiarath. 2008. "The Political Economy of Markets and Development: A Case Study of Health Care Consumption in the State of Kerala, India". *Critical Sociology* 34. No. 1: 81–98.

Verma, Sanju. 2021. "Covid Pandemic and the Failed Kerala Model". *The Daily Guardian*, July 31, 2021. Accessed February 10, 2022. https://thedailyguardian.com/covid-pandemic-and-the-failed-kerala-model/.

WHO. 2020. "Impact of COVID-19 on People's Livelihoods, Their Health, and Our Food Systems". Accessed January 30, 2022. https://www.who.int/news/item/13-10-2020-impact-of-covid-19-on-people's-livelihoods-their-health-and-our-food-systems#:~:text=The%20economic%20and%20social%20disruption,the%20end%20of%20the%20year

22 Government of India's Policies to Face the COVID-19 Challenges in Education, Economy, and Health Sectors

Arushi Sharma, and Aishe Debnath

To restrict the spread of coronavirus, the Prime Minister of India, Narendra Modi, announced a nationwide lockdown on March 24, 2020, which led to many significant changes in all spheres. COVID-19 brought changes in the normal lifestyles of people and the functioning of various sectors of the economy. According to a British Broadcasting Corporation (BBC) report, India became the third-worst Covid-affected country worldwide by June 2020. The initial spread of COVID-19 in India recorded very few deaths. The fatality rate was less compared to other developing countries of the world primarily due to a stringent lockdown and a demographic dividend. Imposing the lockdown at an appropriate time stopped mobility of people which reduced the spread of the COVID-19 virus during the first of three waves of the pandemic until March 2022.

The nationwide lockdown halted the functioning of industrial and other sectors which came as a blow to the Indian economy. The closure of industrial units, tourist spots, hotels, restrictions on people's movement etc. led to a rise in unemployment and a steep decline in gross domestic product (GDP). The economic constraints of the country pressurised the Government of India to proceed with the unlocking process on May 30, 2021 to balance sustenance. The unlocking process again surged with the second and third waves of COVID-19 in the years 2021 and 2022 respectively. Besides the economy, the health sector came under high stress. The sudden outbreak of COVID-19 raised many questions as the high number of cases created mayhem due to the lack of awareness about the virus, insufficient beds and ventilators, and shortage of medical personnel and other essential health facilities. Private hospitals were also charging huge fees to provide beds to COVID-19-affected people. The burden on the country's poor health infrastructure declined only after vaccines were introduced and people volunteered to be inoculated. Another sector that is still under the shadow of COVID-19 is education. The pandemic has had a considerable impact on the education sector of the whole country. The gap between rural and urban children's education has been further widened due to the pandemic. India has seen the highest illiteracy rate during this period as compared to the past few years. Specifically, female students have suffered the most.

This chapter aims to examine the policy decisions taken by the Central Government of India in the economic, education, and health sectors to tackle the challenges faced due to the COVID-19 pandemic. It highlights the policies which brought some changes in the field of health, education, and the economy. The

DOI: 10.4324/9781003304517-27

authors argue that some of the decisions made by the Indian government helped to control the spread of COVID-19 and provided some relief to people in distress while, at the same time, the government's attitude towards the migrant workers led to deaths on the streets of India. Second, COVID-19 has exposed India's poor health infrastructure. The government talked about improving it, but after the COVID-19 numbers were subsidized little has been done in this sector. Third, staying away from schools for a long period of time and the digital divide have deeply affected children's all-round development and growth.

Economic Policies

2020 and 2021 have been difficult years for economies across the globe owing to the multiple waves of the COVID-19 infection, subsequent lockdowns, disruptions in the supply chain, and a return of inflation. Faced with the rising number of infections across several waves and the economic hardships, the Government of India offered safety nets to its citizens to tide them over during this challenging situation. In addition, it also strived to increase capital expenditure on infrastructure to build back medium-term demand and aggressively implemented supply-side measures in order to ensure a sustained long-term expansion of the economy. In response to the extreme uncertainty that accompanied a "once-in-a-century" pandemic, the government commissioned a careful mix of emergency support along with economic policy actions to provide a cushion against the pandemic-induced shocks while simultaneously adapting to a dynamic situation.

As per the press release by the Government of India in June 2021, Finance Minister Nirmala Sitharaman announced a relief package of Rs. 628,993 crore to support the Indian economy in its fight against the COVID-19 pandemic. Under this scheme, an additional credit of Rs. 1.1 lakh crore was directed towards businesses. This included Rs. 50,000 crore for the health sector and Rs. 60,000 crore for other sectors, including tourism which has received a tremendous blow due to the travel restrictions imposed to curb the spread of the virus. (The Press Information Bureau, Government of India, 2021).

The government decided to expand the Emergency Credit Line Guarantee Scheme (ECLGS), launched as part of the *Aatma Nirbhar Bharat* Package in May 2020, by Rs. 1.5 lakh crore. A completely new scheme, the Credit Guarantee Scheme, aims to facilitate loans to 25 lakh people who are served by the network of Micro Finance Institutions (MFIs). This included the provision to provide financial support to more than 11,000 Registered tourists/guides/travel and tourism stakeholders. The Aatma Nirbhar Bharat Rozgar Yojana, launched on October 1, 2020 to incentivize employers for the creation of new employment, restoration of loss of employment through the Employees' Provident Fund Organization (EPFO), has been extended until March 31, 2022. The Pradhan Mantri Garib Kalyan Anna Yojana (PMGKAY), launched initially for the period from April to June 2020 to ameliorate the hardships faced by the poor due to economic disruption caused by the COVID-19 pandemic, was extended until November 2020. Following the second wave of the pandemic, the scheme was relaunched in May to November 2021 to ensure food security of the poor/vulnerable (The Press Information Bureau, Government of India, 2021). Even with the scheme announced, there was an inexplicable delay in distributing foodgrains from the public distribution system to those in need which caused tremendous damage to a section of the population. Before the lockdown, the Central Government (through the Food Corporation of India or FCI) held around 77 million tonnes of foodgrain, more than 3 times the buffer stock requirement. Yet, there was a very limited free distribution of additional foodgrains to those who were covered by the National Food Security Act, but even a month after the scheme being announced, only 2.2 million tonnes of this had been distributed to states (Ghosh, 2020).

The government also initiated a Rs. 33,000 crore boost for project exports through the National Export Insurance Account (NEIA), Rs. 88,000 crore boost to Export Insurance Cover, Rs. 19,041 crores for broadband to each village through the BharatNet Public Private Partnership (PPP) Model, and has provided an extension of tenure for the Production Linked Incentive (PLI) Scheme for Large Scale Electronics Manufacturing until 2025–26 (The Press Information Bureau, Government of India, 2021).

The Government of India released Rs. 30,944 crore to benefit 20.64 crore women, with Jan Dhan Accounts by transferring Rs. 500 to their accounts per month starting from April 2020. It also released Rs. 2,814 crore covering 2.82 crore beneficiaries from the vulnerable sections of society and Rs. 1.8 lakh crore for more than 10 crore farmer families as of January 1, 2022 under the Pradhan Mantri Kisan Samman Nidhi. The government suspended the initiation of the corporate insolvency process under the Insolvency and Bankruptcy Code for 1 year, increased the minimum threshold from Rs. 1 lakh to 1 crore, approved the Term Liquidity Facility of Rs. 50,000 crore for Emergency Health Services by the Reserve Bank of India (RBI) up to March 31, 2022, and sanctioned Rs. 7,500 crore for the Credit Guarantee Scheme to Micro Finance Institutions (MFIs). Rs. 30,000 crore was allocated for Additional Emergency Working Capital Funding for farmers through the National Bank for Agriculture and Rural Development (NABARD) and a loan guarantee scheme of Rs. 1.1 lakh crore was allocated for COVID-19 affected sectors—health infrastructure, tourism, etc. (Economic Survey 2021–22, MoF, GOI).

Rs. 111,171 crore was released in 2020–21 under the Mahatma Gandhi National Rural Employment Guarantee Scheme (MGNREGS) which provided employment to 11.2 crore people generating 389.2 crore person-days. In 2021–22, under the same scheme, funds of Rs. 68,233 crore were released providing employment to 8.85 crore people generating 240.4 crore person-days. Under this scheme, wage rate was increased by Rs. 20 above that of 2019–20 which benefitted nearly 13.62 crore families (Economic Survey 2021–22, MoF, GOI).

The government also launched Aatmanirbhar Bharat Rojgar Yojana (ABRY) to reduce the financial burden of the employers and encourage them to hire more workers, implemented by the Employees' Provident Fund Organization (EPFO) (Economic Survey 2021–22, MoF, GOI).

In addition, micro, small, and medium enterprises (MSMEs) were granted a 6-month moratorium and deferment of interest for all term loans from March 1 to

August 31, 2020. Along with MSMEs, the government also announced a 100% guarantee for additional funding of up to Rs. 4.5 lakh crore to businesses that were hard hit due to COVID-19. It also provided Rs. 36,899 crore and Rs. 22,959 crore in 2020–21 and 2021–22 respectively to MSMEs under the Credit Guarantee Scheme.

The MSME sector was suffering distress even before the pandemic struck due to demonetization, Goods and Service Tax (GST), and a prolonged economic slowdown in terms of declining demand and revenue (Dubey and Sahu, 2020). While the government offered collateral-free loans, firms are not looking to the future (Purohit, 2020) but are seeking ways of fixing the current demand problem instead. When millions of people are losing their jobs as a result of the lockdown and subsequent shutting of many industries, when purchasing power is declining in the country, firms would not borrow more to increase production without any effective demand. Dubey and Sahu (2020) rightly notes that "supply itself does not create any demand i.e., they would not show any eagerness in taking up more loans".

Former Reserve Bank of India (RBI) governor Raghuram Rajan in an interview with *The Wire* in 2020, commenting on the Atmanirbhar Bharat economic package, said that no measure is adequate in this crisis, especially in India's case. Loans provided to MSMEs in the proposed package take time to work, but, on the other hand, hunger is an immediate problem which needs to be addressed first (Dhasmana, 2020). Similarly, Abhijit Banerjee (2020), Nobel Prize winner in Economics stated that "purchasing power in India is not very high and due to lockdown, the poor people of country, now, do not have much money in their pocket and hardly have any purchasing power today. Currently, there is a huge decline in demand in the market". (Dubey & Sahu, 2020)

International Labour Organization (ILO) released a report entitled, "COVID-19 and the World of Work: Impact and Policy Responses" on March 18, 2020, which explained that the crisis has "already transformed into an economic and labour market shock, impacting not only supply (production of goods and services) but also demand (consumption and investment)". International Monetary Fund Managing Director, Kristalina Georgieva, considers the COVID-19 pandemic the most disastrous economic collapse since the Great Depression. She stated that

> advanced economies are generally in a better position to respond to the crisis, but many emerging markets and low-income countries face significant challenges. They are badly affected by outward capital flows, and domestic activity will be severely impacted as countries respond to the epidemic.
> (International Monetary Fund, 2022)

The pandemic led to a sharp decline in wage incomes and self-employed livelihoods. In spite of the economy being frail, official relief that was announced amounted to being extremely minuscule when looked at the vast population it was meant to address. Ray and Subramaniam (2020) rightly note that, though there was an opportunity to speedily implement feasible policies within the current institutional framework, the central government displayed extreme frugality. The first COVID-19 relief package that was announced by the government comprised of many items which were already committed to public spending. The additional expenditure was only around 0.5% of gross domestic product (GDP). Over the next few weeks, the Prime Minister announced another package which was claimed to be equivalent to 10% of GDP. However, a considerable section of this package was in the form of credit guarantees and other liquidity provisions that did not require any additional fiscal outlay (Ghosh, 2020). The total additional public spending that was announced by the end of May 2020 amounted to only around 1% of the GDP (CBGA, 2020), and a considerable amount of this had not reached people (Ghosh, 2020).

According to the Centre for Monitoring Indian Economy Pvt. Ltd., the unemployment rate in India at the onset of the pandemic between January and April 2020 was as high as 10.40% with higher rates of unemployment prevailing among females (18.5%) than males (9.4%). The numbers saw a rise in the period from May to August 2020 with unemployment rates as high as 11.55%. The Aatma Nirbhar Bharat Rozgar Yojana was launched on October 1, 2020 and during this period, from September to December 2020, there was a noticeable drop in the unemployment rates to 7.08%. There was a further drop to 6.83% between January and April 2021. However, there was a trend of increase in unemployment rates to 8.57% again in May and August 2021. It declined again in the next quarter between September and December 2021 to 7.31%, still reflecting higher unemployment among women (12.8%) than in men (6.7%).

Policies in the Field of Education

As the pandemic started gaining a foothold in the country, the government was forced to temporarily suspend the functioning of all schools, colleges, and universities keeping in line with the lockdown rules. Examinations were postponed, and admission procedures were delayed. It was assumed that as soon as the transmission of the virus was under control, educational institutes in the country would be back on track. However, this temporary suspension lasted for two long years. The educational system in India still follows traditional methods of classroom interaction and teaching. Online teaching-learning was a challenging task for many as India's rural areas are still not digitally connected.

The children in rural areas suffered severely after the government announced an online model of teaching-learning. As per a survey report published in *Trading Economics* in 2020, India has 65.07% of its population living in rural areas. These children endured the maximum hardships as most of them depended on government schools to get a mid-day meal. During the pandemic, the situation became much more complex when the doors to schools were shut. In this scenario, these children could neither learn nor get their daily meal. At the onset of the pandemic, both educators and students were quite confused and did not understand how to cope with this crisis that compelled the closure of educational institutions. The prolonged period of lockdown compelled teachers and students to continue their educational activities online. Educators now assign work to students via the internet and deliver lectures using several video conferencing tools like Zoom, Google Meet, Facebook, Youtube, Skype etc.

In alignment with the government guidelines, the Central Board of Secondary Education (CBSE), in consultation with the National Council of Educational Research and Training (NCERT), issued an order on April 10, 2020, stating that all students in classes 1 to 8 should be promoted to the next class/grade. Schools that have not been able to conduct online exams for classes 9 and 11 should also promote the students of both grades to the next grade based on their assessments on project work, periodic tests, and term exams, etc. that had already been conducted. In instances where students could not clear the aforementioned process, schools were advised to provide remedial interventions and provide the opportunity for appearing in subsequent tests either in an online or offline mode. For 12th board exams in India, the Central Board of Secondary Education (CBSE) put forth the system of conducting examinations only for those subjects that are crucial for admission to higher education institutions.

All schools, colleges, and universities were directed to operate in a work-from-home online mode. By this method, the learning could continue and students could safely learn from their houses, and teachers and other academicians could teach from the safe zones of their homes. All state governments were told to follow this plan. Digital learning turned out to be the biggest savior in this time. Learning would have been next to impossible if not for online learning.

As mentioned in "Indian National Commission for Cooperation With UNESCO Response To COVID-19", The Ministry of Human Resources Development took a great initiative to deal with the challenges of all educational institutions. They started "promoting digital education through online educational platform and through the mediums of Television and RADIO" for urban and rural children. In urban areas, the teachers assigned work to students via the Internet as they delivered lectures through video conferencing using different Apps like Zoom, Google Meets Facebook, YouTube, Skype, etc. Television and radio were the accessible approaches for rural areas. There were WhatsApp groups of guardians, teachers, students, and parents for better understanding and communication. In the case of students from rural areas, challenges were more as they do not possess cell phones or internet connections. In urban areas, this online teaching-learning process was not a new process as the ministry has materialized a number of online platforms from the last few years even before COVID-19, for instance, Swayam, DIKSHA, National Repository of Open Educational Resources (NROER), Swayam Prabha, and the National Digital Library, but the access to these online teaching-learning platforms increased during the pandemic. According to reports of the "Indian National Commission for Cooperation With UNESCO Response To COVID-19" it is declared that "During the lockdown period these contents have been accessed nearly 215 million times" (Pg. 1). These online learning portals have the content available, which is created by teachers of concerned subjects under the national boards of education. The portal has a proper curriculum, textbooks, and video lessons for better understanding, assessments and exercises. This portal has books available for every student from class 1 to class 12, in fact many undergraduate and postgraduate classes too. It has books in multiple languages like Hindi, English, and Urdu. Few portals have conventional methods of teaching with interactions with the students. The "Indian National Commission For Cooperation With UNESCO Response To COVID-19" reports stated that

> in addition to the above there are many other resources deployed by University Grants Commission (UGC), National Institute of Open Schooling (NIOS) and Indira Gandhi National Open University (IGNOU) which are being intensified. The lockdown period has seen a huge upsurge in digital learning. The access to the above digital resources has grown nearly five times.

The Government of India's Ministry of Education issued various guidelines named the Pragyata Guidelines on Digital Education, which discussed

> the methodology, time spent, etc. for online/blended/digital education for students who are presently at home due to the closure of schools. The guidelines recommend screen time for different categories of students. It also provides sufficient Do's and Don'ts regarding ergonomics and cyber safety.
>
> (Pg. 5)

Even after so much effort on digital teaching-learning models, studies show that these online methods have certain limitations attached to them such as unequal distribution of time of teachers, negligence of weak students, no support in learning at home in some cases, and technical glitches. To make a report on these kinds of cases or to study the loss of learning of various students

> during and after the lockdown, the MHRD entrusted NCERT with the task of constituting a committee, comprising of academic and curricular experts drawn from NCERT, NIEPA, CBSE, Kendriya Vidyalaya's (KVS) and Navodaya Vidyalaya's (NVS). The Committee conducted a survey in KVS, NVS and CBSE schools for collecting information about various digital modes being used by students to receive online education and their concerns regarding children not having digital devices. Further, discussions were held with SCERTs (on 22.06.2020) to gather information about the initiatives taken up by them in their state/UT.
>
> (Government of India, Ministry of Education, 2020, Pg. 8)

Though the government is ready to initiate research on the gaps related to education during this pandemic, one cannot ignore the fact that so much damage was caused to education due to the closure of schools and online platforms, as India is not a developed country but a developing one and technology has not reached every part of India.

The government has not ignored the children of migrant laborers and issued guidelines to continue their education as they were displaced due to lockdown in the country. These guidelines focus on providing admission to the in-migrant children in the nearby government schools without the requirement of submitting any document except an identity card. As per these guidelines, the residential school students should also be provided temporary admission in schools nearby their homes, as they may not go back to their residential schools during COVID19.

(Pg. 8)

The reality was different as these children faced different types of challenges to continue education, for instance there were no government schools nearby some areas, and some students had to drop out of the school because of their parents lack of income. According to *India Today*'s news report on November 21, 2021, The Education Minister Dharmendra Pradhan expressed the sad fact "that around 15 crore children are currently out of the education system". In fact *The Unified District Indormation System for Education* reported that the number of drop-out from 2019–20 of primary and upper primary including both the genders is 16.1% (Pg. 99). This data does not include the number of children who were never enrolled in school. These problems were intensified during the lockdown period with the closure of schools.

There have been many positive impacts of digital learning that took place during the course of the pandemic. The digital learning transformation opened up gates for a blended form of teaching where a digital, as well as a human, source is being used to carry on the methods of teaching. Secondly, the importance of soft learning increased. Many books and libraries were made free to use at this time as students couldn't stretch to the cost of their own hard copies. They turned to soft copy for learning of the material. Many national and international faculties across borders collaborated that paved the way for new forms of learning. Education was not limited to the classroom anymore as students gained worldwide exposure at this time. Many prestigious universities like Oxford and Cambridge introduced courses completely free of cost for students. This also increased the demand for open school learning and distance education. These were not given as much importance before.

As much as there have been positive impacts of enclosed and digital learning, there have been many negative impacts too. Many teachers who were acquainted with the traditional methods of teaching found it very difficult to adapt to teaching on digital platforms. Students who couldn't buy a smartphone or a laptop could not longer continue their education. They had to stop going to schools and manage to earn a livelihood along with the other members of their families. The lockdown also put additional pressure on parents. They had to monitor and manage the education of their children much more than simply sending them to school. For junior students, no outdoor activity was allowed. This restricted them from more outdoor learning experiences.

During COVID-19, technology affected the teachers and students differently. It is like a nightmare for teachers and forced them to adopt the digital platforms in the form of online classes to which they were not familiar. Techno stress or stress induced due to technology has physical implications like headaches, eyestrain, anxiety, backaches, irritability, and stomach problems etc. and often leads to burnout. Apart from teachers', students are sharing this burden of technostress, which is leading to low productivity, dropouts, and deviation from academic work. Many researches have shown that technostress directly affects teacher's and student's individual and organizational productivity. In particular, in the absence of situational coping mechanisms, technostress gradually exhausts individuals, leading to burnout. One cannot define technostress as a disease, which causes health issues, rather it is a psychological hindrance of an individual because of technology directly or indirectly. As it affects an individuals' health it results in techno-invasion and techno-insecurity as an outcome of burnout, which is associated with negative outcomes on organizational and individual levels, including lower productivity, low job satisfaction, as well as higher absenteeism (Technostress Creators and Burnout: A Job Demands-Resources Perspective, 2018)

During online teaching, not only were students given training to attend sessions but teachers were enrolled in special training programs for effective online teaching. In 2020, the Government of India, Ministry of Education, Department of School Education & Literacy presented a report on the initiatives/actions taken to mitigate the effect of the COVID-19 pandemic where they mentioned that

> CBSE, KVS and Jawahar Navodaya Vidyalaya (JNV) undertook a massive exercise to build online teaching capacities of their teachers as soon as the lockdown started, to ensure continuity of learning through online means, wherever possible. In the process, CBSE has trained 4,80,000 teachers (during April–September 2020), KVS trained 15855 and JNV trained 9085 teachers all India. Training was also imparted by NVS to teachers regarding online assessment and GeoGebra.
>
> (Pg. 14)

To build teachers' capacity, the government has also launched the National Initiative for School Heads and Teachers for Their Holistic Advancement (NISHTHA) Online, to cover "all 4,200,000 elementary school teachers and school heads of the country" (Pg. 11). There is a total of 18 modules in this program, out of which 12 are reserved for teachers, 5 for the heads of schools, and 1 special module on teaching-learning during the COVID-19 pandemic.

The delayed approach of online teaching in many states and the continuous lockdown impacted the admission procedures in many schools and colleges. Entrance examinations were canceled and postponed, and a lot of confusion and chaos ensued. Competitive exams like the interview round of the Union Public Service Commission were postponed, and board examinations of classes 10 and 12 were canceled. This put a lot of pressure on educational institutes and students as well. Students lost their placement opportunities because of the lockdown.

Health Policies

In the fight against the deadly disease, the government approved the India COVID-19 Emergency Response and Health System preparedness package to prevent, detect, and respond to the threat posed by COVID-19 and strengthen national health systems for preparedness in India. To contain the local spread of COVID, the government laid out a micro containment plan based on geographical dimensions of the state, district, block, and municipality. This categorization aided in identifying containment zones based on the extent of cases/contacts mapped. The containment zones were further divided into sectors with 50 or 30 houses depending on the severity and requirements of specific areas and each sector was assigned District Collectors/District Magistrates as nodal officers in their respective districts (Ministry of Health and Family Welfare, 2020).

Several functionaries like Accredited Social Health Activist (ASHA) workers, auxiliary nurse midwives (ANM), and Anganwadi (AWW) workers were assigned responsibilities like regularly visiting houses to search for clinically suspected cases, identifying contacts of suspected or confirmed cases of COVID-19, maintaining a record of suspected and confirmed cases along with their close contacts, and reporting the same to their supervisory medical officer. Additionally, they were also responsible for creating community awareness about the prevention of transmission of the virus, guidelines for home quarantine, and recognizing the signs and symptoms of the disease. The team was also required to counsel individuals to take precautions to avoid contact with those who showed symptoms suggestive of COVID-19, to ensure the usage and proper disposal of three-layered surgical masks during home quarantine, and to educate the family members about precautions to be taken while taking care of persons under home quarantine. The government also sanctioned an emergency financial package of Rs. 15,000 crores for healthcare towards strengthening of personal protection equipment (PPE) for medical professionals, increasing isolation wards and intensive care unit (ICU) beds, and for the training of medical and paramedical manpower.

While classifying the areas for the containment of the virus aided in slowing down the transmission, assigning functionaries like ASHA workers, ANM, and AWW workers with extensive responsibilities to spread awareness and maintain a record of COVID-19 tests and COVID-19 positive cases while not equipping them with the necessary resources is a major drawback of the plan. While these workers were supposed to be on the frontline, they were denied resources available to other frontline workers like personal protective equipment (PPE) kits. On demanding PPE kits for these workers, a senior Delhi government official in an interview with *Hindustan Times* (April 2020) was of the opinion that,

> They don't require PPE, as they are supposed to maintain a social distance while collecting information from people during the door-to-door survey. They are provided a basic kit comprising masks, gloves and sanitisers. PPE kits are to be used by hospital staff.

Considering the high rates of transmission of the virus, this lax attitude of government officials towards frontline workers who formed the backbone of the fight against COVID-19 at the grassroots level was appalling.

Speaking in the Rajya Sabha, Minister of State (MoS) and Health, Ashwini Choubey, said that 44 ASHA workers in the country had lost their lives as per intimations received from the states until January 22, 2021 (Press Trust of India, 2021).

While the Prime Minister, Narendra Modi, promised Rs. 50 lakh insurance cover for the nation's frontline workers (under the Pradhan Mantri Garib Kalyan Package) in 2020, a report published in *The Leaflet* (2021) suggests that only 0.013% of healthcare workers have received these benefits. Victims and their families face several procedural barriers like states refusing to conduct post-death tests, employers of the victims refusing to issue a certificate showing that they contracted the infection on COVID-19 duty or died as a result of an accident while on COVID-19 duty unless the health care worker came in direct contact with a COVID-19-positive case, and ambiguity over what amounts being "drafted" or "requisitioned" by the government for COVID-19 duty (Anusha & Singh, 2021).

In addition, several officers, municipality, panchayat staff, and civil society volunteers were assigned the task of providing public information and conduct communication campaigns targeting schools, colleges, workplaces, self-help groups, religious leaders, teachers, and postmen etc. Their aim was to create awareness in the community, encourage the community to engage in frequent hand washing, follow respiratory etiquettes and self-monitoring of health, and report to the health workers about persons in their vicinity having a cough, fever, or breathing difficulty. The government also constituted teams for human health surveillance, followed rigorous contact tracing for suspected or confirmed cases, teamed up with private laboratories to support the existing infrastructure of government laboratories, identified and mapped ambulance and health facilities in every zone, provided training on donning and discarding PPE, set up control rooms to provide data about the availability of hospital beds, oxygen, and monitor the caseload continuously.

Until September 2020, the government granted an exemption on basic customs duty and health cess on the import of ventilators, PPEs, masks, test kits, and inputs used to manufacture these.

Police authorities in every state and Union territory (UT) have been directed to provide the necessary security to doctors and medical staff in hospitals and in places where patients diagnosed with COVID-19 are quarantined. The Ministry of Ayush also released Ayurveda's immunity-boosting measures for self-care during COVID-19. While the benefits of Ayurveda remain noteworthy, a public launch of an alleged "cure" for COVID-19 "Coronil", claiming to have been approved by the AYUSH Ministry created a furore in the country. Considering the critical situation of public health, it took considerable time for the ministry to issue an official statement barring Patanjali from selling the drug (Narayanan, 2020).

With respect to mental health, the Ministry of Health and Family Welfare (MoHFW) issued an advisory to citizens titled "How to Mind Our Minds during the COVID-19" which provided a guide to understanding the importance of lockdown, how to handle social isolation effectively, the importance of focussing on facts, being wary of and rejecting rumors and theories, handling emotional problems effectively, understandong and addressing emotional issues after recovery, and recognizing mental health problems in oneself and those around them. The government also proclaimed the provision of a trained counselor and/or community group leader belonging to all faiths to visit the relief camps/shelter homes and deal with any consternation that the migrants might be going through. Several videos, webinars, and guidelines on well-being and mental health of the elderly, children, and migrants, along with resources to spread awareness about discrimination and social stigma associated with COVID-19 were released and made available on the official website of the Ministry of Health and Family Welfare (MoHFW). In addition, there were also resources made available on yoga and meditation to deal with the stress associated with the pandemic.

While the government has made these resources available on the official website of the Ministry of Health and Family Welfare (MoHFW), not much awareness has been spread about it. As important as it was to ensure physical safety and health, mental health, in comparison, remained in the shadows. While there were attempts made to focus on yoga and meditation, awareness and understanding of the importance of mental health, identifying warning signs, and addressing stigma associated with mental health issues received little to no attention from the government. Though the government made available certain online resources for citizens to access, it did not initiate the formulation of any policies or packages to emphasize or even ignite the mental health movement. There was an absence of any regulations or guidelines about how to legally handle mental health issues at the workplace and what concessions could be provided to ensure employees' health and safety, not just physical but also emotional safety and health. Much like with physical health a crucial indicator of India's decline in terms of emotional and mental well-being is evident in its ever-degrading position in the World Happiness Index. In 2018, India ranked 133 out of 156 nations, already a dire situation which further worsened to 136 out of 146 nations in 2022 (Gallup World Poll Data, 2022).

India's national COVID-19 vaccination program focused on strengthening the research and development (R&D) capacity to encourage and enable manufacturing of vaccines in India and vaccinating every suitable candidate as fast as possible. The government founded the "Task Force for Focused Research on Corona Vaccine" (constituted in April 2020), to encourage domestic R&D of drugs, diagnostics, and vaccines, headed by Principal Scientific Advisor to the Government of India. "National Expert Group on Vaccine Administration for COVID-19" (NEGVAC), (constituted in August 2020), formulated a comprehensive action plan for vaccine administration, co-chaired by Member (Health) NITI Aayog and Union Health Secretary.

Under the National COVID-19 Vaccination Program, which spanned from January 16 to April 30, 2021, the Government of India procured 100% of the vaccine doses for the state governments free of cost, who were in turn required to administer vaccination free of cost to defined priority groups. To further boost the pace of vaccination, the government teamed up with private hospitals where individuals could choose to get vaccinated at a prescribed rate. The guidelines for vaccination were revised following the state governments' suggestions to provide them with the autonomy to procure a vaccine directly and administer them as per their own prioritization based on local requirements. Under the revised guidelines which came into effect from May 1, 2021, the government would then procure only 50% of the vaccines produced and distribute them to the state governments free of cost for administering to priority groups. In addition, private hospitals were also given the liberty to directly procure from the remaining 50% vaccine pool. However, owing to the challenges faced by state governments with respect to the funding, procurement, and logistics of vaccines, the guidelines were revised again for the government to procure 75% of the vaccines being produced by the manufacturers in the country. The vaccines were provided free of cost to states/UTs who administered the doses to all citizens as per priority through government vaccination centers. Vaccinations were prioritized for healthcare workers, frontline workers, citizens above 45 years of age, citizens whose second dose had become due, followed by citizens who were 18 years of age and above, and recently adolescents in the age group of 15 to 18 years. The vaccination program was digitized using the CoWIN platform which allowed every citizen to pre-book vaccination appointments in addition to the onsite registration facility.

Within the first quarter of the pandemic, April 2021, India had recorded more than 48,000 deaths and more than 6.9 million new cases (covid19india.org). According to research by Subramanian (2021), this surge, which continued into May 2021, occurred after a decline in the number of cases and fatalities and at the same time, India administered more than 84 million doses of vaccine, averaging 2.8 million doses per day in April 2021.

The report further states that, as of May 19, 2021, an India vaccine tracker recorded that more than 186 million doses had been administered, being preceded by only the USA and China. Unfortunately, in an attempt to vaccinate hundreds of millions of people, cOVID-19-appropriate behavior, social distancing guidelines, and norms were often overlooked as several vaccination centers reported excessive overcrowding which could easily turn out to be a super spreader event. People in several vaccination centers complained of long wait times, overcrowding, and even centers running out of vaccine supply (Times Of India, 2021).

According to the Economic Survey, Ministry of Finance (2015–20), India's public health expenditure (sum of central and state spending) has remained between 1.2% to 1.6% of GDP between 2008–09 and 2019–20. This expenditure is comparatively lower when looked at in comparison to other countries such as China (3.2%), USA (8.5%), and Germany (9.4%). While the Health Ministry was allocated Rs. 64,609 crores in 2019–20, there was an increase of 3.9% to Rs. 67,112 crore in 2020–21 while battling the onset and spread of COVID-19 in the country. Under the Ministry, the Department of Health and Family Welfare accounts for 97% of the Ministry's allocation, at Rs. 65,012 crore. Whereas, the Department of Health Research is allocated Rs. 2,100 crore (3% of the allocation). In the last 15 years, the allocation to the Department of Health and Family Welfare has increased from Rs. 11,366 crore in 2006–07 to Rs. 65,012 crore in 2020–21 (Economic Survey, 2015–16) (Economic Survey, 2016–17) (Economic Survey, 2019–20).

The National Health Mission (NHM), which focuses on strengthening public health systems and healthcare delivery in India, consists of two sub-missions, the National Rural Health Mission (focused on rural areas) and the National Urban Health Mission (focused on urban areas). The various components under NHM include reproductive, maternal, newborn, and child health services, the National Rural Health Mission (NRHM) Flexi Pool for strengthening health resource systems, innovations, and information, immunization including the Pulse Polio Programme, infrastructure maintenance, and National Disease Control Programme. The allocation for NHM in 2020–21 saw a decline of 1% to Rs. 33,400 crore over the revised estimates of 2019–20. The NHM's percentage share in the total budget has decreased from 73% in 2006–07 to 50% in 2020–21 (Mann, 2020).

The NHM aims to ensure universal access to equitable, affordable, and quality healthcare services by improving the health infrastructure and enhancing service delivery by training human resources in healthcare. Healthcare infrastructure in India can be categorized into *physical infrastructure* and the *human resources* that provide medical services. In terms of the physical infrastructure, depending on the level of care required, healthcare in India is broadly classified into three types, primary care (provided at primary health centers), secondary care (provided at district hospitals), and tertiary care institutions (provided at specialized hospitals like AIIMS). According to a report published in Chapter VIII of the Public Health Care System, Planning Commission of India, the primary health care infrastructure, which provides the first level of contact between health professionals and the population, consists of a three-tier system of sub-centers (SCs), primary health centers (PHCs), and community health centers (CHCs).

According to the Rural Health Statistics 2018, there has been a significant shortfall at different levels of the healthcare delivery system from 2005 to 2018. As of 2018, one year before the pandemic hit the world, there was a shortage of 2,188 CHCs, 6,430 PHCs, and 32,900 SCs. The Ministry of Health and Family Welfare has noted that the existing ones are also poorly equipped and have inadequate infrastructure, with many PHCs functioning in erstwhile single room SCs and many SCs in thatched accommodation. Though states were permitted to establish these facilities as per their needs under the National Rural Health Mission (NRHM), many did not do so due to a lack of funds and the inability to close down even existing facilities (not in use) due to administrative bottlenecks.

The National Health Mission (NHM) provides support to states to strengthen existing public health facilities. According to the Health and Family Welfare Statistics (2017) there were 25,778 government hospitals (including community health centers) in India, just before the onset of the deadly pandemic. Further, states have constructed 268 new district hospitals and upgraded 3,288 hospitals (Economic Survey, 2019–20). With regard to secondary and tertiary care, the High-Level Expert Group (HLEG) (2011) recommended that in order to guarantee secondary and tertiary care, equitable access to functional beds must also be provided. According to the World Health Statistics (2020), India ranks among the lowest in this regard, with 0.7 beds per 1,000 people, far below the global average of 3.4 beds. It recommended functional bed capacity should be expanded to 2 beds per 1,000 of the population by 2022.

Between 2014 and 2018, the number of registered doctors increased by 24% from 747,109 to 923,749 (Rural Health Statistics, 2018). However, according to a report published by *Policy Research Studies* (PRS) in India, despite the increase in the number of registered doctors, there has also been a steady increase in the shortfall of doctors, specialists, and surgeons. For example, as of 2018, there was a shortfall of 46% of doctors and 82% of specialists, including surgeons, obstetricians, gynecologists, physicians, and pediatricians in primary health centers across India.

The Pradhan Mantri Jan Arogya Yojana (PMJAY) was launched in September 2018 under the Ayushman Bharat program, to provide a cover of Rs. 5 lakh per family per year to 10.7 crore families belonging to the poor and vulnerable population (MoHFW, 2018). The scheme provides insurance coverage for secondary and tertiary healthcare and pre- and post-hospitalization expenses. In 2020–21, PMJAY was allocated Rs. 6,400 crore, an increase of 100% over the revised estimates of Rs. 3,200 crore in 2019–20. However, an article published in *The New Indian Express* in July 2021 reports that only 6.05 lakh people out of 50 crore eligible people covered under Pradhan Mantri Jan Arogya Yojana, availed of the benefit of the Ayushamn Bharat health insurance scheme for COVID-19 until June 30, 2021. This goes on to reflect that out of an estimated 4,550,000 people who were hospitalized for COVID-19 treatment in public or private hospitals, only 13% got the insurance, indicating poor execution of the program by the government. The report further states that while some states did benefit marginally from PMJAY, some saw effective implementation of the program, there were some states like Punjab and Gujarat, where not even a single person reaped the benefit of the scheme. There was no trace of effective implementation in northeastern states and Union Territories as well (Madhavan, 2021).

Several expert bodies including the High-Level Expert Group (HLEG) set up by the Planning Commission (2011) and the High-Level Group of Health Sector have observed that focusing on prevention and early management of health problems can reduce the need for complicated specialist care provided at the tertiary level. Hence, it recommended that the focus of healthcare provision in the country should be towards providing primary healthcare. In this context, as part of the Ayushman Bharat program, 150,000 existing sub health centers (first contact between health system and population) and primary health centers (referral unit for sub centers) are to be upgraded to health and wellness centers by December 2022. These centers will seek to provide comprehensive primary healthcare, free essential drugs, and diagnostic services.

According to a report by Edwin (2021), as the first wave of the COVID-19 pandemic was declining towards the end of 2020, India had a little more than 1.5 million isolation beds across 15,375 dedicated treatment facilities for a population of 1.38 billion. These figures translate to a skosh over 1 bed per 1,000 people. To add to it, only 18% of these were oxygen-supported beds, according to the 2020–21 annual report of the Ministry of Health and Family Welfare. Each of these dedicated facilities had about 5.2 intensive care unit (ICU) beds on average. In all, there were a total of 80,583 ICU beds for COVID-19 patients and about half of these were ventilator beds (Edwin, 2021).

While the second wave ravaged the country in March–April 2021, there were fewer beds for COVID-19 patients in many parts of the country, especially since the virus made its way into the rural areas where healthcare infrastructure is mostly rudimentary, hospital beds are in short supply, and the nearest ICU bed at least a few hours away. A shortage of oxygen, oxygen cylinders, and concentrators persisted. Although the acute crisis was eventually addressed, it claimed more than 4 lakh lives by the end of June 2021 (Mordani, 2021). Hospitals were crippled by a shortage of doctors, nurses, and other healthcare workers, beds in some prestigious public hospitals such as the All India Institute of Medical Sciences (AIIMS) and Ram Manohar Lohia continued to be inaccessible to the masses as they were said to be reserved for politicians, bureaucrats, members of the judiciary, and other well-connected people and their families. The second wave of the pandemic brutally exposed the inadequacy and unpreparedness of India's healthcare infrastructure to deal with pandemics (Edwin, 2021).

According to a report published by Tina Edwin (2021) in moneycontrol, the Ministry of Health and Family Welfare estimated that India had just about 713,986 hospital beds across 25,778 hospitals in the government sector before the pandemic began. This, however, did not include beds in the primary healthcare centers, most of which are in rural areas and are used to address more routine health problems. In addition, the data on hospitals and hospital beds has not been updated since December 2018 for several states. To add to the already dire scenario, Edwin (2021) reports that there are no accurate estimates of the number of hospital beds available in the private sector. The Center for Disease Dynamics, Economics & Policy (CDDEP), an independent think tank, and Princeton University had estimated that number at 43,487 hospitals and 1,185,242 beds in a study in April 2020.

Assuming the estimates of the health ministry and CDDEP-Princeton University to be accurate, it would appear that India had just about 13.76 beds per 10,000 people when the country was hit by the first wave of the COVID-19 infection in March 2020. In the government sector, it was just about 5.2 beds per 10,000 people. The study has estimated the total number of hospitals at 69,265 with 1,899,228 beds across the country. Not all of these hospitals were available to COVID-19 patients during the first wave or currently(The Center For Disease Dynamics Economics & Policy, 2020).

The same report also notes that critical care beds are scarce. Of the estimated hospital beds in the country, just about 5% were placed in the intensive care units, and only about half of the ICU beds were attached to ventilators. The health ministry estimated that there were about 35,700 ICU beds in the government hospitals of which 17,850 were ventilator beds. These numbers when compared against the sizable population of India amount to about 25.87 ICU beds per one million people in the government sector. That's a frightening scenario for a growing economy even in the best of times, let alone when grappling with a pandemic. The harsh reality of these numbers is that most ICU beds in the private sector are beyond the means of a sizeable proportion of the population. The CDDEP-Princeton University estimated the number of ICU beds in the private sector at about 59,260. Thus, the public and the private sector together have about 68.8 ICU beds per 1 million people. Adding to the shortage and unavailability, the citizens also had to navigate their way through the uneven spread of hospitals and beds. Though a larger proportion of government hospitals are in rural areas, urban areas have a larger share of beds. The government hospitals in rural areas are small and have 12.4 beds on average compared to 102.6 beds in the hospitals in urban areas (Edwin, 2021).

Conclusion

The analysis of the policies framed by the Government of India in the sectors of economy, health, and education during COVID-19 reflects that, as a developing country, the implementation of these policies was not a complete success. During COVID-19, India faced many challenges in various sectors to run the departments and to curb the spread of the virus. It was a struggle to keep India's citizens at a normal pace with the world and to keep them safe. Policies that were developed by the Indian Government in the health sector included the provision of a better health-care structure, a better supply of medicine, more trained staff, better logistics, and more organized human resources helped not only urban but rural people of India. In the rural areas, the government ensured proper surveillance of the COVID-19 patients, arrangements for their isolation and medication, and the setting up sur-veillance in every village for anybody who showed influenza-like symptoms to keep the situation under control. In urban areas, COVID-19 wards were made to keep the patients in isolation and to provide them with good food. The policies for vaccination drives and to offer it in phases by age group made it successful.

In the education sector, the government has taken a giant step by making vari-ous policies for digital education and online platforms to lessen the loss of students incurred as a result of the physical closure of schools, colleges, and universities. Online education made development in this sector possible, but it comes with its pros and cons. As the rural space of India couldn't get access to deal with illit-eracy in the COVID-19 period, the percentage of illiteracy increased and there was a substantial rise in school dropouts. In urban spaces, online education created tech-nological stress on students and teachers equally. One renowned pphthalmologist confirmed that the number of children with eyesight issues of increased during the pandemic and no policies were framed or implemented to check the mental health and physical health of students and teachers due to the high rate of technology usage.

Bibliography

Anusha, R., & Singh, T. (2021, May 24). *Why Have Only 0.013% Healthcare Workers Received Benefits under the PM Garib Kalyan Insurance Scheme?* TheLeaflet, https://theleaflet.in/why-have-only-0-013-healthcare-workers-received-benefits-under-the-pm-garib-kalyan-insurance-scheme/

A Report of the High Level Group of Heath Sector, 15th Finance Commission, https://fincomindia.nic.in/ShowContentOne.aspx?id=27&Section=1

Ayushman Bharat: Costs and Finances of the Prime Minister Jan Arogya Yojana. Institute of Economic Growth, Study Report for the 15th Finance Commission, https://fincomindia.nic.in/ShowContentOne.aspx?id=27&Section=1

Ayushman Bharat –Pradhan Mantri Jan AarogyaYojana (AB-PMJAY) to be launched by Prime Minister Shri Narendra Modi in Ranchi, Jharkahnd on September 23, 2018. Press Information Bureau, Ministry of Health and Family Welfare, September 22, 2018, https://pib.gov.in/Pressreleaseshare.aspx?PRID=1546948

Centre for Budget Governance and Accountability (CBGA). (2020). *Numbers on the Edge: Assessing India's Fiscal Response to Covid-19.* New Delhi: CBGA.

Centre for Monitoring Indian Economy Pvt. Ltd. (2020). *Unemployment in India: A Statistical Profile,* https://unemploymentinindia.cmie.com/

Centre for Monitoring Indian Economy Pvt. Ltd. (2021). *Unemployment in India: A Statistical Profile,* https://unemploymentinindia.cmie.com/

Chapter VIII: Public Health Care System, Planning Commission of India, http://planningcommission.nic.in/aboutus/committee/strgrp/stgp_fmlywel/sgfw_ch8.pdf

Chitlangia, R. (2020, April 20). ASHA Workers' Body Demands PPE Kits After One of Them Contracts Covid-19. *Hindustan Times,* https://www.hindustantimes.com/delhi-news/asha-workers-body-demands-ppe-kits-after-one-of-them-contracts-covid-19/story-ArE1YUPX5lWEpKIQD7Gh1N.html

COVID19-India Ops. (2021), https://www.covid19india.org/

COVID-19 Inter-Ministerial Notifications. (2020, May). Indian National Commission for Cooperation with UNESCO Responding to COVID-19. Accessed on 5 March 2022, https://covid19.india.gov.in/document/indian-national-commission-for-cooperation-with-unesco-responding-to-covid-19/

Demand Nos. 42 & 43, Ministry of Health and Family Welfare, Union Budget 2020–21, https://www.indiabudget.gov.in/doc/eb/sbe42.pdf; https://www.indiabudget.gov.in/doc/eb/sbe43.pdf.

Dhasmana, I. (2020, May 22). India Faces Economic Catastrophe, PMO Can't Handle it by Itself: Rajan. Accessed on 16 June 2020, https://thewire.in/political-economy/india-faces-a-major-economic-catastrophe-pmo-cant-handle-by-itself-says-raghuram-rajan

Dubey, P., & Sahu, K. K. (2020). MSMEs in COVID-19 Crisis and India's Economic Relief Package: A Critical Review. *The International Journal of Indian Psychology, 8*(4), 1651–1656, https://doi.org/10.25215/0804.179

Economic Survey, 2015–16, Ministry of Finance, http://indiabudget.nic.in/budget2016-2017/es2014-15/echapter-vol1.pdf

Economic Survey, 2016–17, Ministry of Finance, http://indiabudget.nic.in/es2016-17/echapter.pdf

Economic Survey, 2019–20, Ministry of Finance, https://www.indiabudget.gov.in/economicsurvey/doc/vol2chapter/echap10_vol2.pdf

Edwin, T. (2021, April 30). *Analysis: India Has Long Been Short of Hospital Beds: The Pandemic Intensified the Shortage.* Moneycontrol, https://www.moneycontrol.com/news/trends/health-trends/analysis-india-has-long-been-short-of-hospital-beds-the-pandemic-intensified-the-shortage-6836021.html

Framework for Implementation, National Urban Health Mission, May, 2013, http://nrhm.gov.in/images/pdf/NUHM/Implementation_Framework_NUHM.pdf

Gallup World Poll Data. (2022, March 18). *Home | The World Happiness Report,* https://worldhappiness.report/

Ghosh, J. (2020). A Critique of the INDIAN Government's Response to the COVID-19 Pandemic. *Journal of Industrial and Business Economics, 47*(3), 519–530, https://doi.org/10.1007/s40812-020-00170-x

Government of India, Ministry of Finance. (2021–22). *Economic Survey: State of the Economy*. Ministry of Finance, Governmnet of India, https://www.indiabudget.gov.in/economicsurvey/

Health and Family Welfare Statistics 2017, Ministry of Health and Family Welfare.

High Level Expert Group Report on Universal Health Coverage for India. Planning Commission of India, November 2011.

Hospital Beds (Per 1,00 People), Work Bank Database, Accessed on 31January 2020, https://data.worldbank.org/indicator/SH.MED.BEDS.ZS

https://pib.gov.in/PressReleasePage.aspx?PRID=1730963

International Labour Organization. (2022, March 18). *COVID-19 and the World of Work: Impact and Policy Responses*. Ilo.Org/Global/Topics/Coronavirus, https://www.ilo.org/wcmsp5/groups/public/---dgreports/---dcomm/documents/briefingnote/wcms_738753.pdf

International Monetary Fund. (2021). *Policy Responses to COVID19*. IMF, https://www.imf.org/en/Topics/imf-and-covid19/Policy-Responses-to-COVID-19

Madhavan, R. (2021, July 22). Only 13 Per Cent of Hospitalized Patients Got PM-JAY: Analysis. *The New Indian Express*, https://www.newindianexpress.com/nation/2021/jul/22/only-13-per-cent-of-hospitalized-patients-got-pm-jay-analysis-2333728.html

Mahapatra, M., & Pati, S. P. (2018, June). Technostress Creators and Burnout: A Job Demands-Resources Perspective. In *Proceedings of the 2018 ACM SIGMIS Conference on Computers and People Research* (pp. 70–77). Accessed on 10 January 2022.

Mann, G. (2020, February 12). *Demand for Grants 2020–21 Analysis: Health and Family Welfare*. PRS Legislative Research, https://prsindia.org/budgets/parliament/demand-for-grants-2020-21-analysis-health-and-family-welfare#:%7E:text=The%20National%20Health%20Mission%20(NHM,revised%20estimates%20of%202019%2D20

Ministry of Health and Family Welfare (MoHFW). (2020). *Micro Plan for Containing Local Transmission of Coronavirus Disease (COVID-19)*. Government of India, https://www.mohfw.gov.in/pdf/ModelMicroplanforcontainmentoflocaltransmissionofCOVID19.pdf

Ministry of Health and Family Welfare (MoHFW). (2020). *Model Micro Plan for Containment of Local Transmission of COVID 19*, https://www.mohfw.gov.in/pdf/ModelMicroplanforcontainmentoflocaltransmissionofCOVID19.pdf

Ministry of Health and Family Welfare (MoHFW). (2021). *Revised Guidelines for implementation of National COVID Vaccination Program*, https://www.mohfw.gov.in/pdf/RevisedVaccinationGuidelines.pdf

Mordani, S. (2021, July 21). 2nd Covid Wave was India's Worst Tragedy Since Partition, Saw up to 49 Lakh Excess Deaths: Report. *India Today*, https://www.indiatoday.in/coronavirus-outbreak/story/2nd-covid-wave-was-india-worst-tragedy-since-partition-saw-up-to-49-lakh-excess-deaths-1830894-2021-07-21

Murali, V. S., & Mariorano, D. (2021, October). *Education During the COVID-19 Pandemic in India*. Accessed on 20 February 2022,https://www.isas.nus.edu.sg/papers/education-during-the-covid-19-pandemic-in-india

Narayanan, K. (2020, July 1). AYUSH Ministry Is Endangering People, Jeopardising A Ponse to Patanjalis Coronil and COVID-19, Warn Experts. *Firstpost*, https://www.firstpost.com/india/patanajali-covid-19-ayush-ministry-weak-response-ramdevs-coronil-stunt-endangers-people-jeopardises-ayurveda-homeopathy-8529151.html

Part I, Rural Health Care System in India, Rural Health Statistics 2018, https://nrhm-mis.nic.in/RURAL%20HEALTH%20STATISTICS/(A)%20RHS%20-%202014/Rural%20Health%20Care%20System%20in%20India.pdf

Press Trust Of India. (2021, February 3). 162 doctors, 107 nurses, 44 ASHA workers died due to Covid in India till 22 January — Govt. ThePrint, https://theprint.in/health/162-doctors-107-nurses-44-asha-workers-died-due-to-covid-in-india-till-22-january-govt/597733/

PTI. (2020, May 12).Not Sure Whether India Will Gain if Businesses Shift from China Due to COVID-19: Abhijit Banerjee. Accessed on 10 June 2020, from https://economictimes .indiatimes.com/news/economy/policy/not-sure-whether-india-will-gain-if-businesses -shift-from-china-due-to-covid-19-abhijit-banerjee/articleshow/75692643.cms?from =mdr

Purohit, D. (2020, May 14)."Demand First, Please, and Then Loans. Accessed on 14 June 2020, from https://www.telegraphindia.com/business/coronavirus-lockdown-what -factories-think-of-economic-package/cid/1772781

Ray, D., & Subramaniam, S. (2020). India's Lockdown: An Interim Report. 20 May Supplement 1, https://debrajray.com/ wp-content/uploads/2020/05/RaySubramanian.pdf

Rural Health Statistics 2018, Health Management Information Systems, Ministry of Health and Family Welfare.

Subramanian, S. V. (2021). India faces a Challenge with Its Mass Vaccination Efforts. *The Lancet Global Health*, *9*(9), e1201–e1202, https://doi.org/10.1016/s2214 -109x(21)00260-6

"Survey Report & Recommendations of Clinical Establishments, Ministry of Health and Family Welfare, 2013, http://clinicalestablishments.nic.in/WriteReadData/788.pdf

Thapar, K. (2020, May 21). India Faces a Major Economic Catastrophe, PMO Can't Handle By Itself, Says Raghuram Rajan. *The Wire*, https://thewire.in/political-economy/india -faces-a-major-economic-catastrophe-pmo-cant-handle-by-itself-says-raghuram-rajan

The Center For Disease Dynamics Economics & Policy. (2020, August 6). *COVID-19 in India: State-Wise Estimates of Current Hospital Beds, ICU Beds, and Ventilators.* Center for Disease Dynamics, Economics & Policy (CDDEP), https://cddep.org/ publications/covid-19-in-india-state-wise-estimates-of-current-hospital-beds-icu-beds -and-ventilators/

The Press Information Bureau. (2021). *Ministry of Finance Relief Package.* Ministry of Finance.

Times of India, TOI. (2021, May 7). Mumbai: Long Waiting Time, Overcrowding Trigger Chaos at Some Vaccine Centres. *The Times of India*, https://timesofindia.indiatimes.com /videos/city/mumbai/mumbai-long-waiting-time-overcrowding-trigger-chaos-at-some -vaccine-centres/videoshow/82449370.cms

Index

communitarian and compassionate
approach 310–311
community-based organizations (CBOs) 55,
57, 248, 292, 310; LGBTIQ community,
role of 55–57
community response, Arunachal Pradesh
297–299
compliance, digitization of 200–201, *201*
constructive beliefs 100
Corona Care Centres 322
"COVID" (Shyam) 158
COVID-19; assistance and reforms 20–22;
and health infrastructure 248–250; in
Kashmir. *see* Kashmir: operations of
freight trains during 229–232; outbreak
of 1–2; second wave of 16–18, 38; as
social stigma 40–41
COVID Action Plan 279
COVID-19 isolation coaches 232, **233**
COVID-19 Mumbai Model 39
COVID-19 pandemic 82; global education
disruption 277; infodemic, rumor, and
vaccine hesitancy 115–118; in Kerala
324; narrative ideas and practices
127–128; and psychology 112; rational
self-management in 99–109, *100, 104*;
rumor 112–*115*; *Seva*, in Sikhism during
216–219; social security 196–197
COVID positive patients, seperate
collection of waste of 71
Credit Guarantee Scheme 336
crew, Air India: experience, evacuation
flights 171; lived experiences of
171–174
culture, of authentic hospitality 175

Dai 31
DAK. *see* Doctors Association
Kashmir (DAK)
Dalits 50, 52
Dance of Death (Wolgemut) 155, 162–163
Danse Macabre. *see* Dance of Death
(Wolgemut)
dasvandh 215
data: Lesbian, Gay, Bisexual, Transgender,
Intersex, and Queer (LGBTIQ)
community 46–47; for transgender
persons in Maharashtra 47
dating apps 55
decentralized democratic governance, in
Kerala 324
"decent work" 195

Delhi Sikh Gurdwara Management
Committee (DSGMC) 217
Delta variant 236
dependency, LGBTIQ community 50–52
depression 140; mean and t-value for urban
and rural students on 142, **143**
Depression, Anxiety and Stress Scale
(DASS-21) 140
Derrida, Jacques 190, 191n10, 191n11;
notion of autoimmunity and hospitality
184–190; notion of deconstruction 186;
"On Hospitality" 185; philosophy of
decentering 187–188; philosophy of
deconstruction 184; *Rogues* 185
destructive beliefs 100
Detrended Fluctuation Analysis 118
developmental disabilities: caregivers of
children with 129–130; working with
children and families with 126
Devender and Pritam 221
Devi, Ambika 160
DiFonzo, N. 112, *113*
DigiLocker 199
digital depravity 280
digital learning, positive impacts of 341
digital literacy 55
digital platforms 89, 197
digitization: of compliance 200–201, *201*;
of pension benefits 198–199, *199*
Diksha portal 278, 281, 339
disability: understanding in Indian context
125–126; working with children
and families with developmental
disabilities 126
disabled young people 124; and
caregivers 130
Disaster Management Act (2005) 14, 229
disaster proofing, of organization 204
discrimination, LGBTIQ community 51–52
Doctors Association Kashmir (DAK) 252
doli-badhai program 47, 58n5
Donovan, Andrew 141
Doodh Duronto 231
Down to Earth (Roy) 162
dread rumors 112
dropout rates, public school education
275–276
Dubey, P. 337

ECLGS. *see* Emergency Credit Line
Guarantee Scheme (ECLGS)
economic policies 335–338, 350